LABOR IN THE AMERICAN ECONOMY

Labor Problems and Union-Management Relations

Richard Scheuch

G. FOX AND COMPANY PROFESSOR OF ECONOMICS
TRINITY COLLEGE
Hartford, Connecticut

HARPER & ROW, PUBLISHERS, New York
Cambridge, Hagerstown, Philadelphia, San Francisco,
London, Mexico City, São Paulo, Sydney

1817

For Fay

Sponsoring Editor: John Greenman
Production Manager: William Lane
Compositor: Maryland Linotype Composition Co., Inc.
Printer and Binder: Halliday Lithograph Corporation
Art Studio: Vantage Art, Inc.

Labor in the American Economy: Labor Problems
and Union-Management Relations

Library of Congress Cataloging in Publication Data

Scheuch, Richard   Date-
   Labor in the American economy.

   Includes bibliographies and index.
   1.   Labor and laboring classes—United States.
2.   Labor economics.   3.   Industrial relations—
United States.   I.   Title.
HD8072.5.S33   331'.0973   81-1036
ISBN 0-06-045774-0   AACR2

Contents

Part II:
THE LABOR MARKET: ANALYSIS AND PROBLEMS

Chapter 4 / THE SUPPLY AND THE DEMAND FOR WORKERS IN THE UNITED STATES

Chapter 5 / WAGE DETERMINATION: BASIC CONCEPTS AND EARLY THEORIES

Part V:
UNION-MANAGEMENT RELATIONS   **447**

Chapter 19 / THE COLLECTIVE BARGAINING PROCESS   **449**

Chapter 20 / COLLECTIVE AGREEMENTS I: EMPLOYEE COMPENSATION
AND HOURS OF WORK   **479**

Preface

The employer-employee relationship is fundamental in industrial societies. Many of the increasingly complex socioeconomic problems of our world either develop from or are affected by it. Consequently, in writing *Labor in the American Economy* I have assumed that an introductory labor course is an important element of modern economics and business administration curricula, and that such courses will continue to be offered to undergraduates. I have found, through teaching many undergraduate students at several institutions, that if the instructor in a *first course* in labor uses a general text as an organizing framework within which to fit his or her particular topic interests, students gain a greater understanding of problems affecting labor and of the ongoing relationship between organized labor and management. Such a text should provide students with a sense of historical perpective, with relevant quantitative information, and with theoretical constructs that will help them to comprehend the past, to identify and analyze the problems of the present, and to predict—or anticipate—future developments. *Labor in the American Economy* has been designed to meet these objectives.

This text's analysis is not limited to those characteristics of the employment relationship that have traditionally concerned the labor economist. It emphasizes applied rather than abstract analysis and stresses historical and institutional materials more than most contemporary labor economics texts. Although it does not ignore the relationship between labor economics in a broad context and union-management relations, this book explores more thoroughly than most such human dimensions of the employment relationship as the extraeconomic needs of present and potential labor force members. The book does not assume reader familiarity with either intermediate-level price theory or national income theory. Indeed, substantial portions should be comprehensible to students not majoring in either economics or business administration.

STRUCTURE AND COVERAGE

Labor in the American Economy consists of five units that examine the development of unions as a response to the work-related human problems of our industrial civilization. Part I provides a historical perspective and contemporary frame of reference for Parts II through V. It includes a unique chapter, "The American Economy Today," which offers an introductory look at United States' economic growth, unemployment, and income distribution. Part II lays a theoretical foundation for the study of labor problems and union-management relations that examines both the operation of labor markets in the absence of unions and how our society has responded to these problems. Although the text acknowledges the validity of certain radical economists' criticisms of our institutional arrangements, it assumes that appropriate corrective action can be taken without radically modifying our mixed enterprise system. Thus, *Labor in the American Economy* views the development of unions and collective bargaining as a significant and politically stabilizing response to American labor problems.

The major portion of the book, Parts III through IV, analyzes union-management relations in the private and public sectors. The topics covered include (1) the history of organized labor in the United States, (2) union and management approaches to collective bargaining, (3) the private institutional and the public regulatory frameworks within which union-management relations are conducted. (4) the bargaining process, (5) the matters subject to bargaining (the content of collective agreements), (6) the economic and extra-economic impact of unions and collective bargaining, and (7) possible developments in the American union movement and in union-management relations in the remaining years of the twentieth century.

FLEXIBILITY OF TOPIC SEQUENCE

I realize that there is disagreement within the profession about the preferred sequence of topics in courses of this kind. Some believe that it is necessary to have a basic understanding of the institutions of unionism and collective bargaining before attempting to apply economic analysis to union-management relations. Others would argue that once the basics of labor market analysis are understood, it is easier to fit imperfections in the system (including the presence of unions) into an established frame of reference.

I have deliberately made each of the five Parts of *Labor in the American Economy* as self-contained as possible so that their order of introduction can be flexible. My own preference regarding topic sequence is reflected in the table of contents, but it is possible for instructors who prefer another sequence to use Parts III, IV, or V (perhaps omitting Chapter 24's concluding observations) before Part II. I feel that Part I, which contains some unusual, and I hope helpful, features should probably come first in all cases. It is also quite possible to resequence the order of individual chapters. But since there are four groups of chapters that have either a chronological development (Chapters 5 and 6, 11 to 13, 16 to 18) or a common focus (20 to 22), I would recommend clustering the chapters in each of these groups.

PEDAGOGICAL FEATURES

The generous use of quotations from, and references to, relevant primary and secondary sources in text footnotes and end-of-chapter annotated bibliographies will direct the interested student to additional readings on specific topics.

Ongoing developments in our dynamic industrial (post-industrial?) society, together with the substantial volume of research currently underway, make any text outdated to some extent by the time it reaches the reader. Essential historical and statistical updating should be provided or initiated by the instructor, either in class or as a part of outside assignments. A number of tables in this book have been left "open-ended" to facilitate this process, since a student's inserting current data often provides a valuable learning experience.

There are questions at the end of each chapter that may be used to stimulate class discussion or for outside assignments.

USE OF SUPPLEMENTARY MATERIALS

Supplementary materials may either be integrated with assignments in the text or used to study selected topics in depth. One of several books of readings and/or case studies presently available may be used as a basic supplement, and bulletins and reports of the Bureau of Labor Statistics of the U.S. Department of Labor, the AFL-CIO, the National Association of Manufacturers, The Conference Board, the Chamber of Commerce of the United States, and national unions and trade organizations will be helpful in the analysis of specific problems.

Articles in journals may be used in upper-division courses. Leading journals in the labor field include *The Industrial and Labor Relations Review*, published at Cornell University by the New York State School of Industrial and Labor Relations; *Industrial Relations, A Journal of Economy and Society*, published at Berkeley by the Institute of Industrial Relations of the University of California; *The International Labour Review*, published by the International Labour Office; *Labor History*, published by the Tamiment Institute in New York; and *The Monthly Labor Review* of the Bureau of Labor Statistics of the U.S. Department of Labor, which includes a number of basic statistical series. In addition, the principal economic journals (e.g., the *American Economic Review*, the *Journal of Political Economy*, and the *Quarterly Journal of Economics*) often include articles of interest to students of labor.

The New York Times and *The Wall Street Journal* have excellent labor coverage. Most newspapers report the more important national and local developments in labor markets and collective bargaining, and local firms and unions will usually respond to requests for information on current labor-management negotiations. Industrial relations executives, local union officials, labor lawyers, and local, state, and federal officials charged with the administration of labor laws may be asked to talk informally to classes; such outside speakers bring a touch of realism into the classroom and are well received by students.

ACKNOWLEDGMENTS

A number of instructors of labor economics and labor relations courses read parts or all of earlier drafts of this text and provided useful comments and suggestions for improvement. I would like to thank the following people for their contributions: Arnold Abo, Northern Michigan University; Solomon Barkin, University of Massachusetts, Amherst; Jesse Benjamin, Rego Park, N.Y.; Roger Bowlby, University of Tennessee, Knoxville; Dennis M. Byrne, University of Akron; William Collier, Kutztown State College; J. B. Dworkin, Purdue University; Blanche Fitzpatrick, Boston University; David A. Gray, University of Texas at Arlington; L. G. Harter, Oregon State University; Barbara Haskew, Middle Tennessee State University; Hirschel Kasper, Oberlin College; John Kennan, Brown University; Charles Krider, University of Kansas; Phillip Lowry, Northern Arizona University; Dave O'Neill, Washington, D.C.; Ed Reiner, University of Southern Colorado; Philip L. Ryan, Iowa State University; Harvey Shore, University of Connecticut; David E. Schulenberger, University of Kansas; Charles Stone, Radford College; and Thomas T. Vernon, Clarion State College. I also appreciate the helpful comments of my colleagues at Trinity College. None of these persons is, of course, responsible for any errors of omission or commission. I am particularly indebted to the many students whose enthusiasm, concern, and questions helped structure the book.

The cooperation of Mrs. Gwendolyn Reynolds and Mrs. Patricia Gatzen, who typed successive drafts of the manuscript, and of Ms. Cheryl Martin, Trinity College documents librarian, helped me avoid the trauma so often associated with such projects.

Above all, I am grateful for the understanding and forbearance of my family during the prolonged period of work on the manuscript. The product of that effort is suggestive rather than exhaustive; a survey rather than a specialized tract; a point of departure rather than a terminus. It is first and foremost a teaching vehicle. It is my hope that, either used alone or with supplementary materials, the text will serve as an exciting and rewarding keystone for a variety of first courses in labor.

Richard Scheuch

Part I
THE DEVELOPMENT OF AMERICAN INDUSTRIAL SOCIETY

Chapter 1
INTRODUCTION

In 1964, former Secretary of Labor George Shultz (then dean of the Graduate School of Business at the University of Chicago) noted that "students who once flocked into courses in 'labor' because labor was a cause, now find other fields more compelling."[1] Since then, students interested in "liberal" causes have become increasingly disenchanted with unions, and especially with union leaders, whom they now identify with the nonradical "establishment." Yet enrollment in labor courses remains high: many students are still very interested in the collective bargaining process and the impact of unions on the economy. They are also concerned about a variety of domestic issues that are related to work and to the employment relationship. They are troubled by the inflationary effects of negotiated wage increases, the impact of strikes in essential industries or in the public sector on the economy, reports of graft and corruption within the union movement, union attempts to obstruct or control changes in technology, the desirability of "right to work" laws, and other similar problems that are often the source of headlines in the popular press.

Students today are also interested in the labor market aspects of such critical social issues as the alleviation of poverty, the elimination of discrimination in employment, the provision of comprehensive health care, and the trade-offs between economic growth and the quality of life. These issues, which have become more prominent as we have resolved, or partially resolved, many of the work-related problems of an earlier day, are related directly to the study of labor as a factor of production and transcend the narrower field of union-management relations.

LABOR PROBLEMS IN INDUSTRIAL SOCIETIES

Most labor problems have a common denominator. They reflect the economic and psychological insecurity of wage earners in industrial and industrializing societies. Generally this insecurity is created by a conflict between two goals: increasing the efficiency of production and improving the "quality" of life. In unionized firms, this conflict between the workers' quest for security and management's quest for more efficient production assumes the form of an institutionalized adversary relationship. The formation of unions and the development of collective bargaining procedures are institutional responses to the labor problems of an industrial civilization.

From the workers' point of view these problems include:

1. the need for employment commensurate with ability for all members of the labor force able and willing to work;
2. the need for general, vocational, or professional training to prepare potential or present members of the labor force for existing or prospective jobs;
3. the need for protection from or compensation for unemployment due to the introduction of new technology;
4. the need for protection against being arbitrarily discharged from a job;
5. the need for wages or salaries that provide an adequate (and hopefully, an ever-rising) standard of living;
6. the need for protection against the erosion of real incomes by inflation;
7. the need for safeguards against on-the-job accidents and occupational diseases;
8. the need for comprehensive health services;
9. the need for income during periods of involuntary unemployment;
10. the need for protection from discrimination in hiring, promoting, and laying off employees; and
11. the need for a satisfying working environment.

Labor problems are a product of their time. As the more critical problems of a period are solved, interest and concern shift to less critical problems, or "new" problems are identified. Thus the problems of a highly industrialized nation differ from those of a less developed nation. In the United States, for example, the employment opportunities available to minority groups and women, the effectiveness of the educational system in preparing people for jobs, and the quality of life in a "postindustrial" society have received greater emphasis in recent years. These new concerns are in part a measure of our affluence. Only in an economy with a high real income per capita do further increases in material wealth and improvements in the quality of life become viable alternatives.

THE RESOLUTION OF LABOR PROBLEMS

The methods used to resolve labor problems reflect the political and social structure of a nation. In a democratic socialist state, basic industries may be nationalized and economic plans developed to achieve social goals set with the consent of the electorate. In a totalitarian system, controls may be imposed on the economy to achieve goals dictated by the central government. In a democratic, capitalist society, solutions may be left to the impersonal mechanisms of the marketplace, legislation may be enacted to prevent or remedy specific problems, or workers may organize unions and seek to negotiate solutions collectively rather than individually. Sometimes, all three approaches may be used in combination, and in many cases their effects may be hard to separate out.[2] Consider, for example, the interplay of forces involved in setting a minimum wage. The level of this wage will be affected by the existing wage structure, which reflects both union and nonunion wage determinations. Moreover, wages must still be set by the market or through collective bargaining for (1) workers earning more than the minimums in covered industries and (2) workers in jobs not covered by the law. What these people earn will be related to the statutory minimum wage and will also influence it.

THE UNION MOVEMENT IN THE UNITED STATES

The majority of workers in the United States are not union members. In 1978, for example, there were 102.5 million persons in the labor force. Of these 102.5 million persons, only 22.7 million, or slightly over 22 percent, belonged to unions, to state and municipal employee associations, or to a professional association of some kind.[3] If these figures seem small, bear in mind that the extent to which unions have succeeded in organizing their potential membership is a better measure of their strength. According to the Bureau of Labor Statistics, in 1978 national unions and associations had organized 26.6 percent of all employees in nonagricultural establishments.[4] Although the government excluded agricultural workers and self-employed individuals in calculating the unions' potential membership base, it included executives, managers, professionals, and foremen, many of whom were unlikely targets for union organizing campaigns. Had these people been excluded, we would have a truer measure of the unions' appeal to nonmanagement workers. Union membership figures also underestimate the number of workers affected by union-management negotiations. Collective bargaining contracts cover nonunion employees in a firm,[5] and the results of negotiations with union firms often have an impact on terms of employment in nonunion firms.

An issue that will concern us later in the book is the extent to which the American union movement will be able to respond to the organizational challenge posed by various categories of unorganized workers, particularly professional and technical workers; other white-collar workers; unskilled or semiskilled service workers, such as laundry and restaurant workers; domestic servants; and agricultural workers. "Labor" problems today do not involve only the stereotyped blue-collar worker employed in manufacturing. Service industries employ an even greater number of workers, and the hourly rated employees in manufacturing plants include a growing number of "white-coverall" technicians. In studying the problems of labor, therefore, we may need to distinguish between problems and issues that concern all members of the labor force and those that are part of the continuing relationship between organized labor and management. An analysis of the problems of unorganized as well as organized workers is an important preliminary to the analysis of union-management relations, not only because of the broader dimensions of the first type of analysis but also because it provides a more meaningful frame of reference for an examination of contemporary collective bargaining.

THE OBJECTIVES OF THE TEXT

This text is designed to help students in an introductory course to (1) comprehend the various facets of "the labor problem" as it has developed and will evolve in the United States; (2) evaluate various proposals to prevent, solve, or lessen the severity of specific labor problems; and (3) develop a sound conceptual framework for analyzing contemporary union-management relations.

A general survey of the problems of labor in our industrial civilization precedes the study of union-management relations, and a description of management's labor relations function precedes the analysis of management's approach to collective bargaining.

Although our analysis of contemporary problems is confined to the American experience, it provides a starting point for analyzing problems elsewhere. Research indicates that it is the *process* of industrialization, rather than the existence of capitalism as such, that gives rise to labor problems.[6] Although the effects of industrialization may vary from one culture to another, the probability that certain problems are universal makes it easier to understand some of the economic, social, and political pressures building up around the globe. By studying American responses to American problems we can also learn something about the needs and options of any labor force in industrial or industrializing nations.*

---

* In fact, studies of the economic development of the Third World have occasioned a reexamination of the conclusions of much of the theoretical literature on the evolution of labor and union movements. Until relatively recently, this literature was usually based on experiences in Great Britain and the United States; experts now recognize that theoretical constructs with such a limited base may lack universality.

THE DISCIPLINARY BASE OF THE BOOK

Many students are aware of the variety of the literature on the subject of labor. Those who attend a large university may have been able to select a first course in labor from a number of disciplines—economics, business administration, sociology, psychology, or industrial engineering. It seems wise, therefore, to say a word about the disciplinary framework of this book. It was written by an economist whose special areas of interest are the human factor in production (labor) and union-management relations. Thus, although the book is not concerned with labor economics in a narrow sense, it does emphasize the economic dimensions of labor problems and union-management relations. More specifically, it applies the more general techniques of economic analysis to a single factor of production, labor.

Readers will find, however, that conventional economic analysis (of the production function, of the allocation of resources, and of the distribution of income to owners of resources) has limited applicability to many of the problems discussed. This is because theoretical formulations of a problem often ignore the human and institutional factors that are of particular concern to students of labor. The most logically consistent theorems or the most internally consistent models may work only in a vacuum. In many cases where they are relevant, they may have to be considerably modified if they are to be of practical value.

Economics is often defined as a discipline concerned with the allocation of scarce resources to alternate ends and the distribution of the resulting output. As such, it is a *social* science; it deals with the economizing aspects of human activity within a dynamic social, political, cultural, and moral (or spiritual) framework. As a discipline, economics has certain methodological limitations. The laboratory controls and the precision of results associated with experiments in the natural sciences are seldom possible in the social sciences. This fact is of special importance in the study of labor problems and union-management relations, which centers on the human factor in economic arrangements. Because neither individuals nor socioeconomic institutions such as unions and corporations can be counted on to behave logically in every situation, the applicability of many of the generalizations we will make is limited. We cannot expect our analysis of labor problems in general to provide precise answers to the problems of *particular* individuals, groups of workers, unions, or firms. This does not mean that our conclusions will be of little practical value, simply that actual decisions about such problems must take unique circumstances into account.

To fully understand contemporary labor market developments, we must analyze the institutional arrangements that affect the employment relationship, including, in a pluralistic society, those developed by unions, by managements, and by the state. The perspectives of other social sciences will aid us in this analysis: a historical perspective will help us to comprehend the present and to anticipate the future; industrial psychology, industrial sociology, and the rapidly growing interdisciplinary field of behavioral science will help us to identify relevant institutional parameters. Emphases on historical perspectives and institutional imperatives are, in fact, distinguishing features of the text.

THE ROLE OF VALUE JUDGMENTS IN ECONOMIC ANALYSES

Another aspect of the study of economics—an aspect of particular importance in the study of labor due to the omnipresent human element—is the need to make normative judgments about controversial issues, especially when government policy must be determined. For example, should minority workers previously excluded from employment be given seniority credits to compensate for past discrimination? Should workers be compelled to join a union as a condition of employment? It may be impossible to answer such questions on the basis of objective evidence, so operational decisions must be based in part on opinions about what seems to be an appropriate course of action. These opinions will reflect people's *values*, their personal conceptions of what is right or wrong. *Value judgments* may be legitimate, but they must still be recognized for what they are. You may already have rather firm opinions on such issues as discrimination in employment, compulsory union membership, the right of public employees to strike, and the inflationary impact of unions. Stop for a moment and consider your reasons for these opinions: are they based on an objective review of available facts, or do they primarily reflect your economic status, your social class, the opinions of your friends, your political sympathies, or the cultural mores of the area where you live? Some attitudes and policies seem so appropriate, so "right" to people that they fail to realize they are not based on objective evidence. Such unconscious value judgments must be avoided. On the other hand, if objective analysis shows that there are several solutions to a problem, it is only reasonable to select the one that conforms most closely to your own set of values, *recognizing that such a choice represents a value judgment*. It is unlikely that a complete consensus could ever be reached on matters involving normative judgments; this is one reason we conventionally identify consensus with majority rule. However, decisions made by the electorate are not immutable. Values change over time, and social consensus is a variable, not a constant.

THE ATTACK FROM THE RADICAL LEFT

During the past decade, so-called "radical," or "New Left," economists have challenged the ability of conventional non-Marxist social science (and to a lesser degree, dogmatic Marxism) to cope with the problems of industrialization. In particular, the members of the New Left reject the assumptions of neoclassical economics, which we will use in our analysis of the operation of the labor and product markets. According to one of their leading spokesmen, Professor Paul M. Sweezey, "We [of the New Left] see the present as the frightful outcome of some four centuries of the history of capitalism, a system the very heart of which is exploitation and inequality and which is now careening out of control toward its final crises and catastrophes."[7]

The views of the New Left are presented most prominently in the *Review of Radical Political Economics*, the journal of the Union for Radical Political

Economics. It is not possible to do justice to these views in a brief commentary, but the thrust of the argument is clear: because of the institutional arrangements of our capitalistic (exploitive) society, we cannot achieve what the radicals identify as necessary economic, political, and social reforms—in essence, the creation of a humane society, based upon neo-Marxist principles, from which exploitive productive relationships have been eliminated and in which income is distributed "equitably." Institutional reform within our capitalist framework is not feasible, since "the technical possibilities apparently open to government [intervention] are . . . drastically limited by the political and economic self-interest of the ruling capitalist class (both domestically and in the network of imperialist relationships abroad)."[8]

Many of the *specific* criticisms of the New Left have considerable merit. For example, they correctly decry the conventional use of the gross national product (the GNP, the total money value of all final goods and services produced in the economy during the year) as a barometer of national well-being; the alienation of many employees, who no longer see work as a source of pride; the fact that externalities (the divergence between "social" and "private" costs and benefits) are usually ignored by private decision makers. Nevertheless, we reject the assumption that such problems require a radical restructuring of our institutional framework. These human problems of an industrial civilization may be resolved in more constructive ways. (For example, tax and revenue policies can be used to encourage private decision makers to include social costs in their economic calculus.) A number of possible reforms are discussed in subsequent chapters. Analyzing labor problems and union-management relations within the context of our existing enterprise system will help to illuminate both the merits and defects of that system from a human standpoint and the viability of proposals for change.

SUMMARY

The objectives (and limitations) of this book should now be clear. It is a survey of labor problems and union-management relations in the United States. It is neither a general treatise attempting to cover the various aspects of the study of labor in detail nor a specialized analysis of a limited aspect of the field. It assumes that the reader is interested in the work-related problems of wage and salary earners in the United States and is prepared to analyze these problems in what is basically an economic frame of reference. It also assumes that students today are interested in analyzing alternative approaches to these problems within the framework of our existing institutional arrangements, approaches that take into account the emergence of the union movement and the development of collective bargaining.

Parts One and Two of the book discuss the chief problems facing wage and salary earners in our economy and various proposals to resolve these problems without recourse to collective bargaining. Part Three reviews the development of unions and collective bargaining in the United States. Part Four discusses government regulation of collective bargaining. Part Five analyzes issues in collective bargaining and the "impact" of unions on union members, firms, and the economy; it also considers possible developments in the American union movement and union-management relations during the remaining years of the twentieth century.

This book's necessarily general analysis and conclusions will have to be qualified or modified in the light of particular circumstances. Also, what may be a socially acceptable method of resolving a problem in our society today may not be viewed with similar favor elsewhere or within our own society at a later point in time. There are, nevertheless, elements of universality in the study of labor problems and union-management relations. The balance between material progress and the quality of life is a critical issue in every industrial or industrializing society. Priorities must be identified and hard economic choices made. The problems that will concern us in this book are of vital importance to our nation, and a failure to resolve them satisfactorily may lead to a restructuring of many of its institutions.

Change as such is not necessarily to be resisted. Economic and social progress have always involved a modification of traditional beliefs, concepts, and modes of behavior, and this adaptive process will continue. Each generation will face new problems: one of the most depressing yet challenging aspects of the "higher" development of humankind has been our inability to attain "final solutions" to problems. As for labor problems, the late Professor Sumner H. Slichter of Harvard University pointed out that

> whether regarded from a scientific or from the ethical point of view, the [labor] problem can never be solved. *As rapidly as it is being solved, it is being created,* not only by technological and institutional changes which alter the nature of working conditions and of jobs, but also by changes in our ideas of what is worthwhile. Every modification in our conception of the good life affects our conception of the labor problem.[9]

This volume, by increasing your understanding of contemporary labor problems and union-management relations in the United States, will help you to identify and to evaluate the potential policy trade-offs that are a measure of the progress, the problems, and the promise of an advanced industrial society. This will, hopefully, enable you to meet the obligations of informed citizenship with greater compassion and confidence.

DISCUSSION QUESTIONS

1. Examine your reasons for electing this course. Do they appear consistent with the objectives of the text? If not, how do you explain the differences between your approach and that of the author?
2. Can you identify some human and work-related problems of industrialization in addition to those outlined in this chapter? Do you believe the author was justified in omitting these additional problems?

3. If all industrializing societies have similar labor problems, how do you explain the markedly different character of the attempts to resolve these problems in various industrial nations?
4. Can you identify three or four labor problems in the United States that may be "solved" within the next decade? Can you identify several problems that may become more critical?
5. Why, if unions and employee associations have organized only 27 percent of the employees in nonagricultural establishments in the United States, does our society place so much emphasis upon union-management relations?
6. Can you provide examples of previously held "objective" beliefs that you would now identify as value judgements?

SELECTED READINGS

Bell, Daniel. *The End of Ideology.* Rev. ed. New York: Collier Books, 1962.
Cochrane, James L. *Industrialism and Industrial Man in Retrospect.* Ann Arbor, Mich.: University Microfilms International, for the Ford Foundation, 1979.
Cole, David L. *The Quest for Industrial Peace.* New York: McGraw-Hill, 1963.
Gutman, Herbert G. *Work, Culture and Society in Industrializing America.* New York: Knopf, 1976.
Kerr, Clark. *Labor and Management in Industrial Society.* Garden City, N.Y.: Doubleday (Anchor Books), 1964.
O'Toole, James, ed. *Work and the Quality of Life.* Cambridge, Mass.: MIT Press, 1974.
Wirtz, W. William. *Labor and the Public Interest.* New York: Harper & Row, 1964.

Notes

1. "Labor Courses Are Not Obsolete," in *Industrial Relations* 4, no. 1 (October 1964): p. 25.
2. For a comprehensive discussion of the development of national industrial relations systems, see John T. Dunlop, *Industrial Relations Systems* (New York: Holt, Rinehart and Winston, 1958), particularly pp. 7–16 and chap. 8.
3. U.S. Department of Labor, "Labor Union and Employee Association Membership—1978," *USDL Release 79–605,* August 31, 1979, Table 2, p. 2.
4. Ibid.
5. In 1976, some 26.9 million workers were covered by union contracts. (U.S. Department of Labor, Bureau of Labor Statistics, *Directory of National Unions and Employee Associations, 1977,* Bulletin 2044, p. 78).
6. Clark Kerr, Frederick H. Harbison, John T. Dunlop, and Charles A. Myers, "The Labour Problem in Economic Development: A Framework for a Reappraisal," in *International Labour Review* 71 no. 3 (March 1955): pp. 226–227. See also the same authors' *Industrialism and Industrial Man,* rev. ed. (New York: Oxford University Press, 1964); and *Industrialism and Industrial Man Reconsidered,* Final Report of the Inter-University Study of Labor Problems in Economic Development (Princeton, N.J.: 1975). The various monographs based on the work of the Inter-University Study of Labor Problems in Economic Development (presently known as the Inter-University Study of Human Resources in National Development) support this conclusion.

7. "Comment," in *Quarterly Journal of Economics* 86, no. 4 (November 1972): p. 660.
8. Howard Sherman, *Radical Political Economy* (New York: Basic Books, 1972), p. 47.
9. "What Is the Labor Problem?" in J. B. S. Hardman, ed., *American Labor Dynamics* (New York: Harcourt Brace Jovanovich, 1928), p. 290. Emphasis in original.

Chapter 2
THE EMERGENCE
OF MODERN
INDUSTRIAL SOCIETY

A look at the development of the American economy will provide a perspective on contemporary labor problems and union-management relations. And since many of our economic arrangements and institutions are derived from British ones, a survey of the growth of industry in Great Britain will help us understand the industrialization process on this side of the Atlantic. We shall have no time to linger over past events and periods, but we can look quickly at broad trends and key developments. As we do so, bear in mind that although teachers find it convenient to label certain "periods" of economic development, the modification of economic and social relationships is continuous. Students often assume that events can be compartmentalized, when in fact they are part of the warp and woof of economic evolution.

It is also a mistake to assume that what is considered the distinctive development in a period, or the most important from our point of view, is also *typical* of that period. Prior to the Industrial Revolution, the nonfarm working population did not consist solely of skilled craftsmen; today, the majority of our own labor force does not consist of blue-collar workers in large factories.

THE MANORIAL SYSTEM

Eleventh-century England had a largely agrarian economy. While some overseas trade was developing and a few towns had become centers of commerce, manors were the center of productive activity. They were administered by a local lord or his heirs, or by a corporate authority such as a monastery. Small manors contained a single village; larger estates included several villages.

The manorial system was characterized by traditional economic and social relationships that imposed a pattern of cooperation upon a community. Manors were basically self-sufficient, with individual productive and social roles determined by a person's status. The *Domesday Survey* of 1085–1086 identified five types of villagers: freemen, sokemen, villeins and cottars (serfs), and slaves.[1] However, the compulsory labor provided by the serfs and slaves was the essential element in the manorial economy.

The Labor Force

Freemen constituted a relatively small proportion (about 12 percent) of the British population in the eleventh century. They included (1) the inhabitants of "free villages" with no obligations to overlords and (2) people who lived on a manor but owed no services to the local lord. *Sokemen* were also relatively few. They did not own land and could not leave the manors on which they lived without the lord's permission, but their duties (seasonal plowing and threshing, for example) were less onerous than those required of serfs or slaves.

Most villagers were *villeins* or *cottars* who tilled their own holdings but were obligated to perform a certain amount of work each week for the lord of the manor. They were also subject to a variety of restrictions on their personal freedom. Villeins usually held relatively large farms, while cottars had only small holdings. To survive, the cottars often had to perform extra work for wages on larger farms or on the lord's domain. Slavery virtually disappeared by the year 1200, the nobility having gradually discovered that it was less expensive to have work done by serfs.

Upward Mobility

Upward mobility was not impossible in feudal times, but it was limited by the economic and social systems. Rigid and often repressive, these systems nevertheless afforded those bound by them a life of considerable stability. The natural resources of the manor were available to the villagers according to customary rules, and economic problems—crop failures or wars—were collective, involving the entire community.

After the thirteenth century, the agricultural labor force was gradually released from its customary obligations to the nobility in return for the payment of rents, and serfdom declined. One reason for the change was a shortage of labor;

another was recognition by the lords that leasing part or all of their domains to individual farmers was a more profitable way of operating.

A TRANSFORMATION OF ECONOMIC LIFE

Between 1300 and 1350, the English economy was transformed by a variety of events: an initial decline in the population, followed by sustained growth; the development of overseas trade; a shift of population from the land; the rise of towns; and the breakdown of customary social and economic relationships. Complex interactions between these factors over three centuries culminated in what we now call the Industrial Revolution. Changes were gradual and often mutually reinforcing; but certain events and basic alterations in productive arrangements deserve to be singled out even in a brief review of the period.

The Black Death

Probably the most important factor in breaking down customary manorial relationships was the labor shortage caused by the great plague of 1345. The Black Death, as the plague was called, ultimately reduced the population by some 30 percent. The lack of workers accelerated changes in the organization of production that had begun during the thirteenth century and caused a dramatic increase in wages. Many men previously "tied" to the land fled from the manors and obtained paid employment either as agricultural workers or in nearby towns. The supply of wage earners increased further as persons dispossessed by the enclosure of communal land and small holdings into large estates were forced to seek work.* A significant wage-earning class thus came into existence well in advance of the Industrial Revolution.

The Development of Merchant Capitalism

During the fifteenth century, the population decline resulting from the Black Death was gradually reversed. High birthrates and the growth of overseas trade led to the fencing in of more land for the production of grain and pasturing of sheep. This caused more people to move to the towns, where labor was still in short supply. The growth of the towns provided larger and more concentrated markets and encouraged greater specialization by makers of various products.

Initially, goods were produced in the towns by independent master craftsmen who ran their own small shops. In order to have some control over production methods and raw materials, the craftsmen formed merchant guilds. They regulated both the quality of work and the number of journeymen by establishing apprenticeship systems. The merchant guilds were not lineal ancestors of modern

---

* The enclosure, or fencing in, of previously open fields in the late Middle Ages was motivated by a desire to create more profitable, consolidated farming units.

unions because they emphasized the interests of the master craftsmen as entrepreneurs rather than the interests of ordinary artisans as wage earners.

Industry during the later Middle Ages was on a small scale and there was considerable upward mobility. The normal progression was from apprentice to journeyman to master. With the growth of trade and the increase in the size of manufacturing establishments, opportunities for advancement became more limited and the social and economic differences between masters and wage earners became more pronounced. Improvements in communications and transportation greatly expanded potential markets, and shops were no longer limited to making goods for local customers. It became necessary to secure larger stocks of raw materials (often imported from other localities or from abroad) and to arrange for the sale of finished products outside the town. This required additional capital and a higher level of entrepreneurial ability, both of which were provided by an emerging *merchant capitalist class*.

The Organization of Production

The first merchant capitalists used a *putting-out system* of production. They supplied raw materials to various craftsmen and in return agreed to purchase their finished goods. The craftsmen, although owning their own shops and regulating their own production, began to lose their independence. They now worked upon the merchants' goods, and they depended on the merchants to dispose of the completed products.

Initially, the putting-out system was based in many instances on domestic production. People worked on materials at home rather than in shops. However, in the larger establishments in the towns, production tended to be centralized in a single workplace. Journeymen and apprentices were hired as employees and given little control over the production process. Opportunities to rise through the ranks became fewer, and the interests of workers began to diverge more and more from the interests of employers, who bore the ultimate responsibility for production. In short, *the development of both a merchant capitalist class and a body of wage earners divorced from ownership of the means of production preceded the growth of the factory system in the late eighteenth and early nineteenth century.*

During the eighteenth century, separate interests bred separate organizations for employers and journeymen. The latter were the precursors of modern trade unions.

As colonial expansion continued to create new markets for English products and new sources of raw materials, the more imaginative members of the British business community began improving their production techniques to increase output. A greater division of labor, increased functional specialization, and minor technological changes made these producers more efficient than their competitors. Under the putting-out system, technological innovations tended to further alter the status of wage earners as the merchant capitalists began to provide not only raw materials but, under leasing arrangements, simple mechanical aids to production as well. These developments preceded the more dramatic technological advances identified with the Industrial Revolution and the development of the factory system.

The Industrial Revolution

The Industrial Revolution is often considered to have begun with the invention of the flying shuttle in 1733. This was followed by a series of major inventions in the textile and other industries. The invention and improvement of the steam engine, initially developed to pump water from coal mines, accelerated the transformation of an agricultural economy into an industrial one. Alert entrepreneurs realized that centralizing production in a single place where machines could be operated by steam or some other source of power was a much more efficient way of operating. The concentrations of buildings and equipment needed to do this required correspondingly large amounts of capital, and the division between employees and the owners of the means of production was heightened.

All these changes were part of a long process of growth; the English economy was *not* transformed overnight. However, by the early 1800s it was clear that the industrial era had arrived. As one of the leading historians of the period observed,

> whether or not such a series of changes should be spoken of as "The Industrial Revolution" might be debated at length. The changes were not merely "industrial," but also social and intellectual. The word "revolution" implies a suddenness of change that is not, in fact, characteristic of economic processes. The system of human relationships that is sometimes called capitalism had its origins long before 1760, and attained its full development long after 1830; there is a danger of overlooking the essential fact of continuity. But the phrase "Industrial Revolution" has been used by a long line of historians and has become so firmly embedded in common speech that it would be pedantic to offer a substitute.[2]

The Impact of the Industrial Revolution

The impact of the Industrial Revolution on English life was profound. It was largely responsible for the economic growth that raised the nation's standard of living, and at the same time it created traumatic social and economic problems that were to lead to the development of socialism, communism, and a host of other reform movements.

The Industrial Revolution created a new way of life for the mass of Britons. We cannot describe all its effects upon economic, political, and social conditions, but we can identify certain developments that had the most marked impact on the working population. These developments include:

1. The emergence of a formal wage system. The payment of wages, which began in the larger productive establishments in the early towns and

under the putting-out system, became general during the Industrial Revolution. Workers were hired as employees and worked, as a matter of course, in their employer's establishment, using the materials, tools, and equipment he provided. Although this entailed a loss of independence for individual workers, it led to the creation of a supply of labor free to move from one job to another—to respond over time to geographical changes in the demand for its services.

2. A gradual movement of population from rural areas to nearby cities and towns helped to meet the demand for labor in the new factories. The supply of urban labor was further increased by immigration from Ireland. In fact, the census returns for 1851 indicated that "in almost all the great towns the migrants from elsewhere outnumbered the people in the town."[3] Birthrates were also high, which often made the increase in the urban population spectacular. Sheffield, for example, had 46,000 inhabitants in 1801, 92,000 in 1831, and 135,000 by 1851.[4] Although the factories provided work for both the migrants from the countryside and those from abroad, this urban growth resulted in serious housing, sanitation, and social problems.

3. The use of women and children for factory work. Women and children were primary sources of factory labor. They had worked before, of course, under the putting-out system, and they continued to work on farms, but their hours and methods of work had not been so rigidly prescribed. A disciplined labor force was essential to efficient factory operations, but the impersonal and arbitrary rules governing most work forces dehumanized the employment relationship and offset the benefits of the workers' increased economic "freedom."

4. The substitution of machinery for human labor. This is often considered the essential element of industrialization. It did not result in general unemployment, although many workers suffered temporary unemployment. Total employment increased throughout the period for a variety of reasons. These included the continued growth of demand, thanks to the development of national and overseas markets and the natural increase in population; improvements in transportation and communications; and the development of efficient capital markets able to finance industrial expansion.

5. An ever increasing proportion of production in response to *anticipated demand*. In producing orders, even in advance, for a local market, businesses had been able to gauge the demand for their products with considerable success. As markets expanded, forecasting demand became riskier. The problem was complicated by:

6. The increasing specialization and interdependence of the economy. In the local economies of an earlier day, the geographic isolation of productive units insulated them against unsettled economic conditions elsewhere. In

the more complicated industrial economy, the demand for a product could decrease for reasons beyond the seller's comprehension or control. In time, economists would recognize the existence of business cycles and the interdependence of economic arrangements, but to the nineteenth-century worker, and often to his employer, employment opportunities seemed to reflect the machinations of a complex, mysterious system.

7. The failure of many workers to share in the abundance created by the new industrial arrangements. The average worker was subject to rigid discipline. Men, women, and children operated dangerous equipment. They could be fired for obscure reasons. They worked for wages that made it difficult or impossible to provide for emergencies or put away funds for their old age, and they inhabited the most wretched slums of the growing industrial centers. The communal security their forebears had enjoyed in earlier stages of economic development had disappeared, replaced by a materialistic culture that often appeared to place little value on human life or happiness.

The Reaction to Industrialization

The economic and social problems that accompanied the Industrial Revolution intensified with the passage of time. Matters were not helped by the doctrine of *laisser-faire*, noninterference by government with free and presumably competitive markets, adopted by nineteenth-century English liberals. Time would demonstrate that a policy of nonintervention was not always in the best interests of workers and that the impersonal mechanism of an unregulated, "free" market economy could not resolve many of the problems of economic development.

The failure of the masses to realize a "better" life led ultimately to attempts by workers and reform elements to do something about the pressures of the new industrial civilization. In Chapter 1, we identified two basic worker responses to such problems: wage earners (and less probably, those on salaries) could organize unions and collectively seek to improve their condition within the framework of the existing economy, or improvements could be sought through political action. Three types of political action are possible:

1. The basic institutions of the system may be deemed acceptable, but government intervention may be sought to ensure that they function effectively and democratically. For example, antitrust laws may be passed in an attempt to maintain competitive markets, labor legislation may prohibit discrimination in employment, and social insurance laws may provide basic economic security for workers and their dependents.

2. Through the establishment of a labor party, workers may seek to modify existing institutions to improve the position of wage earners (and perhaps of farmers and small independent business persons as well). Such an

evolutionary process may lead eventually to a new political system. The union movement may become the nucleus of such a party and hence, an important political as well as economic force.

3. Through political action, organized labor (perhaps as the nucleus of a labor party) may seek to alter existing economic and political institutions radically and create a "new" social order. Any potentially effective methods may be employed, including violent revolution.

The first course of action has been followed in the United States, the second in England and a number of continental and Scandinavian countries, and the third in Marxist and neo-Marxist states. More than one approach may be followed —or be "appropriate"—in a particular nation over the years or at a point in time. A crisis may lead to accelerated changes or to a significant alteration in the philosophy of labor; witness the acceptance by U.S. unions in the 1930s of legislation they had opposed before the economic collapse of 1929—for example, social security and minimum wage laws.

In England, the class structure of society, the relatively uniform ethnic and cultural characteristics of the labor force, and the political traditions of the nation combined to produce a working-class consciousness that led not only to the formation of a pragmatic trade union movement but to the direct involvement of unions in political life. At the turn of the century, the Fabian Society succeeded in converting much of British labor to democratic socialism, and the British Labour party was formed in 1906. Since that date, in contrast to the American experience, British unions have played an aggressive and influential role in the politics of their country. Some 50 percent of all wage and salary workers in Great Britain belong to unions, and since the end of World War II the Labour party has either been in power or been the loyal opposition.

AMERICAN ECONOMIC DEVELOPMENT

The Colonial Labor Force

Colonial America, like England in the late Middle Ages, had a basically agricultural economy. However, since most people owned their own farms, there was a continuing shortage of labor, both for agricultural work and in the towns. As a result, wages were perhaps three times those in England for work of equivalent skill. The colonial work force consisted of free laborers, indentured servants, and slaves. The two-thirds or so of the available laborers who were *indentured servants* were immigrants who agreed, in return for their passage, to be bound in service to a master for a certain number of years—typically four. The contracts of indenture they signed were usually the property of the shipmasters who provided their passage to the colonies. The shipmasters sold the contracts upon arriving in America. There were also *redemptioners*, people who took ship to America and indentured themselves after their arrival to pay for their passage. Finally, there were debtors and felons sentenced to terms of servitude by colonial courts.

Indentured servants were treated as private property and their contracts could be sold. However, they had certain rights. They could appeal to the courts to enforce the conditions of their contracts, and they could work for pay with their masters' permission. On completion of their terms of servitude they became free persons, with all the rights and opportunities of citizens. They received clothing, provisions, and, in some cases, tools, seed, and arms as well. The persistently high demand for workers and the availability of land made it relatively easy for them, then, to become economically as well as legally independent. Despite the importance of indentured men and women as a source of labor, the transitory character of their servitude kept them from developing a community of interest as a social or an economic class.

At the time of the Revolution, the supply of *free labor* consisted of immigrants, indentured servants who had obtained their freedom, and the children of these groups. As it was easy to become a landholder or an independent craftsman, there was a considerable turnover within this component of the labor supply also.

Apprenticeship systems were established in various trades, but the supply of journeymen remained inadequate. This led to a variety of efforts to encourage artisans to emigrate to America. Initially, the English government encouraged such emigration, but it ceased to do so when the demand for labor rose in England during the eighteenth century. The colonies nevertheless continued to attract artisans, not only from other parts of Great Britain but from the Continent as well. It was economically advantageous for journeymen to go to America; wages were high, and there was greater opportunity to become a master craftsman or an entrepreneur.

Slaves were the third component of the colonial labor force. Although slavery was never important in New England and gradually declined outside the South following the Revolution, the assumption that it would disappear as the economy developed proved false. Tragically, it became a key element in the economy of the South.

With the exception of slaves, the colonial labor supply was remarkably fluid. The labor market favored employees rather than employers, and workmen generally enjoyed a higher standard of living than they would have elsewhere. This, together with the widespread belief in America as a land of opportunity, inhibited the development of a working-class consciousness and the growth of unions.

The Development of Industry

The transition to an industrial economy required several centuries in England; parallel developments were compressed into a much shorter period in the United States. The American colonists came from nations that "had reached the handicraft and even the 'manufacturing' stage of production. Consequently, industrial evolution in colonial times was not an evolution of tools and processes, but an evolution of markets to utilize the tools and processes already evolved."[5] As in England, goods were initially produced for personal use or to order for a local market. As improvements in transportation gradually broadened markets, merchant employers began to produce goods in anticipation of demand. After the Revolutionary War, merchant (sales) and employer (production) functions became increasingly separate, and with the continued extension of markets, the distinction between the two became general.

By the 1830s, the volume of production was determined in large part by middlemen, who placed orders on the basis of both current and anticipated demands. The rise of this merchant capitalist group accentuated the difference between entrepreneurial and employee functions. As in England, recognition of the distinction between employers and employees preceded massive changes in production techniques, and the majority of journeymen in the early nineteenth century continued to work with their own hand tools.

The Growth of Factories

The introduction of machinery into the colonies and the development of a factory system were impeded by the attempts of the English to prevent models or drawings of machinery from leaving their country. Parliament prohibited the exportation of tools and machinery, and it is reported that the first models of cotton mill machinery were brought to the United States in the head of Samuel Slater in 1789. Cotton mill machinery was reputedly smuggled in marked as hardware.[6] Textile machines were widely used during the first decades of the nineteenth century, but machine production was not introduced generally until the Civil War.

The shortage of labor we have already described delayed the development of the factory system in the United States. However, once the idea of a division of labor was introduced and operations were simplified, producers were able to employ more unskilled workers, including women and children. This, in turn, led to demands for protective legislation, particularly in New England, where one reform group noted that " 'a large proportion of the operatives in our factories are, and must continue to be, a helpless population. It is indispensable that they should be put under the . . . protection of the law of the land.' "[7]

The Expansion of Markets

The construction of turnpikes, canals, and railroads gradually linked the Atlantic seaboard with the Midwest. This provided new markets for the manufactured goods of the East and led to the extension of the factory system. The consequent increase in the demand for labor was met in part through immigration, in part by a geographical movement of workers to factory areas, and in part through the hiring of women and children. Many of the immigrants of the pre-Civil War period were subsidized, either by American employers eager to obtain cheap, unskilled labor or by civil authorities in Europe anxious to export people who were a burden to their communities.

Immediately before and during the Civil War, the expansion of domestic markets was accelerated by the construction of new railroads and the extension of existing lines and by improvements in communications facilities, including the introduction of the telegraph. Cities grew rapidly, the use of machinery in manufacturing increased, and the principle of the division of labor in the production of goods became more generally accepted.

Despite setbacks occasioned by financial and commercial crises and panics, the first great period of industrial growth in America reached fruition in the 1880s. Immigration reached a peak, with over five million persons entering the country from abroad, and "in foundries and machine-shops the total capital invested increased two and a half times."[8] In some industries, technologically advanced plants employed hundreds or thousands of workers, although the nation would have to wait until the twentieth century for the development of what has become the most widely accepted symbol of American industrialization: vast factories using assembly line methods of production.

The Impact of Industrialization

For various reasons, industrialization in the United States did not produce a clearly defined working-class consciousness. The first colonists supported a philosophy of individualism, and this philosophy continued to dominate both the business community and probably a majority of the labor force during the nineteenth century. In contrast to England, many males received the franchise early in the nineteenth century, and free public education was widely available at an early date. Except among the slaves, there was considerable social and economic mobility, and a belief in unlimited economic opportunity became part of the American tradition. Moreover, until the closing of the frontier in the 1880s, it was possible for workers to escape from the industrial centers of the East to public land in the West. Even if relatively few people actually availed themselves of this opportunity, the fact that it was there operated as a safety valve for various pressures.

Large numbers of semiskilled and unskilled immigrants, particularly those from southern and eastern Europe, were cruelly exploited in the sweatshops and mills of the East. As in England, many families led a dismal existence in the slums of large cities. Economic and financial crises also caused widespread unemployment and suffering. However, for most immigrants, the United States continued to represent political freedom and economic opportunity, and the intangible attributes of American civilization provided some compensation for their lot. This is an insufficient explanation for American labor's general disinterest in collective action during the nineteenth century, but other factors, including ethnic, cultural, and language barriers, contributed to the general quiescence of the masses. Even had they wanted to, the majority of workers could not have joined unions, because membership was usually confined to persons in the skilled trades.

Organized Labor and Political Action

Another characteristic of the American response to industrialization was the general refusal of organized labor to engage in partisan political activity. Many early leaders of the American union movement had been trained on the Continent as socialists, but they were convinced that socialism would not flourish in America. They did not attempt to develop a political labor movement, but instead emphasized a pragmatic type of trade unionism that sought to advance the union member's interests through collective bargaining. Organized labor did not seek to replace capitalism with a more equalitarian system, but instead sought its "fair share" of the abundance created by a market economy dominated by the Protestant work ethic.

Although American unions have become more active politically, particularly since the passage of the Taft-Hartley Act in 1947, they continue to be guided by the same "business union" philosophy and to accept the existing political system. This is an unusual posture for a modern union movement; as Professor Maurice Neufeld has pointed out, "American unions constitute the only labor movement in the world which dares to [fully accept] the fundamental beliefs of the society in which it lives and . . . [to] support . . . the growth and perfection of that system."[9]

This conservative attitude is not unexpected; as we have seen, the United States has long been considered a land of opportunity, and its material achievements over almost two centuries, together with the less tangible values associated with American culture, have sustained that belief. The mass of American workers have never seriously challenged the basic institutions of our economic and political systems, although periodically, usually in response to a crisis, they may support proposals to correct defects in the systems. When these proposals achieve widespread popularity, they are usually appropriated by one or both of the major parties as part of their platform. As a result, independent reform movements capable of attracting worker support have been short-lived or stillborn.

Some Negative Aspects of Economic Development

American economic development had, of course, a darker side. It was accompanied by many serious problems: widespread unemployment during periods of depression; abject working and living conditions for many wage earners, particularly in large cities; weaknesses in the banking system; the proliferation of restrictive business practices and monopolies; the pyramiding of control over corporations through holding companies; the overt resistance of employers to unionization; and the obdurate opposition of political reactionaries to government intervention in the economy.

Following World War II, additional problems aroused concern: continued high unemployment despite sustained economic growth, inflation, "poverty amid affluence," covert and overt discrimination against women and various racial and ethnic groups, and an emphasis on material growth at the expense of a more humane society. However, the persistence of such problems has not weakened the commitment of most workers, including unionists, to the present economic system; they apparently continue to believe that most problems can be resolved without radical changes in that system.

This has disappointed many liberal intellectuals, including some New Left economists, who had hoped to see the union movement become a vehicle for radical reforms of our institutional structure. It also poses a dilemma for the New Left: should they conclude that union leaders (and members) are part of the establishment and that it is useless to try to develop union support for radical initiatives? Or should they assume that it is possible to develop a base of support within the union movement, particularly among younger, less skilled workers and workers who belong to various minority groups?

The Decline of Laisser-Faire Economics

Although we have, as a nation, rejected radical political programs, the institutional fabric of our economic system has been significantly modified as we have responded, essentially on an ad hoc basis, to various problems. As a result, our present system cannot be equated with a free enterprise economy in the nineteenth-century sense of the term; it is a *mixed* capitalistic system. It is not socialistic, but the government has assumed broad responsibilities in many areas, and some restrictions have been placed on individual freedom to further the public welfare.

Although the American union movement lacks the highly political orientation of its European counterparts, such an orientation could develop as a result of massive unemployment or widespread discontent with labor's economic and social progress. This poses a dilemma for the advocates of *laisser-faire* economics: a failure to take minimal measures now to avert an economic depression or the alienation of workers from the present system may lead to more comprehensive governmental intervention or to fundamental changes in our institutional arrangements. A modicum of effective intervention may be the price of maximizing freedom in the long run.

Today, government is big business: in 1979, federal, state, and local governments paid $476.1 billion for final goods and services; there were 15.6 million public employees; the federal debt was $833.8 billion at the end of fiscal 1979. The proliferation of government regulations and programs, most notably since 1929, has also created a considerable superstructure of economic controls. Nevertheless, as a nation, we remain committed to the concept of a "free" economy, one in which additional governmental intervention is considered justified only if, and to the extent that, it is deemed appropriate in the light of other national priorities.

SUMMARY

In this chapter, we have reviewed the development of Great Britain and the United States into industrial societies and identified some of the labor problems which accompanied that transformation. Perhaps the most critical feature of industrialization was the separation of workers from ownership of the means of production. In Great Britain, this led to the rise of a class-conscious labor movement actively involved in politics; in the United States, workers did not develop class consciousness, and the union movement was a pragmatic one that rejected direct political action, preferring to operate within the existing two-party system.

Although as a nation we have rejected radical initiatives, the American government has gradually assumed a broader responsibility for the general welfare. Perhaps the greatest challenge we will face during the remaining decades of this century will be to order our national priorities so that future policy trade-offs reflect a clear social consensus. This will require mediation between interest groups and a willingness to modify established policies in response to changes in whatever consensus is achieved. The government's role in the resolution of labor problems and in the establishment and regulation of collective bargaining, which we shall discuss in later chapters, will illuminate a number of the policy trade-offs the nation will have to consider in the future. Meanwhile, we shall turn to a consideration of certain elements of our "mixed" enterprise system that are of particular concern to students of labor.

DISCUSSION QUESTIONS

1. If economic development is essentially evolutionary, why is so much emphasis placed upon the Industrial Revolution in discussions of British and American economic growth?
2. One reason for the decline of serfdom in England was that lords found that leasing land and individual farms was more profitable. Why might this be true?
3. On what grounds does the author argue that modern unions cannot be equated with craft guilds?
4. Compare and contrast the labor problems that accompanied industrialization in England and the United States.
5. Does the failure of the early leaders of the American Federation of Labor to launch an independent labor party seem reasonable in the light of American economic development?
6. The following chapter discusses "The American Economy Today." Can you anticipate several important positive and negative aspects of our current economic situation that will be discussed in that chapter?

SELECTED READINGS

English and European Economic Development

Dietz, Frederick C. *An Economic History of England.* New York: Holt, Rinehart and Winston, 1942.

Flinn, M. W. *An Economic and Social History of Britain, 1066–1939.* London: Macmillan, 1962.

Heaton, Herbert. *Economic History of Europe.* Rev. ed. New York: Harper & Brothers, 1948.

Murphy, Brian. *A History of the British Economy 1086–1970.* London: Longman, 1973.

Postan, M. M. *The Medieval Economy and Society.* Berkeley and Los Angeles: University of California Press, 1972.

The Industrial Revolution

Ashton, T. S. *The Industrial Revolution: 1760–1830.* London: Oxford University Press, 1948.

Bowditch, John, and Ramsland, Clement, eds. *Voices of the Industrial Revolution: Selected Readings from the Liberal Economists and Their Critics.* Ann Arbor, Mich.: University of Michigan Press, 1961. A variety of views on the economic and social issues raised by the Industrial Revolution.

Hammond, J. L., and Hammond, Barbara. *The Rise of Modern Industry.* 7th ed. London: Methuen, 1947.

Hartwell, R. M., ed. *The Causes of the Industrial Revolution in England.* London: Methuen, 1967.

Mantoux, Paul. *The Industrial Revolution in the Eighteenth Century.* London: Jonathan Cape, 1928.

Marshall, Dorothy. *Industrial England 1776–1851.* New York: Scribner, 1973.

American Economic Development

Brownlee, W. Elliot. *The Dynamics of Ascent: A History of the American Economy.* 2nd ed. New York: Knopf, 1979.

Gunderson, Gerald. *A New Economic History of America.* New York: McGraw-Hill, 1976.

Morris, Richard B. *Government and Labor in Early America.* New York: Columbia University Press, 1946.

Pelling, Henry. *American Labor.* Chicago: University of Chicago Press, 1960.

Rayback, Joseph G. *A History of American Labor.* Expanded and updated. New York: Free Press, 1966.

Robertson, Ross N., and Walton, Gary M. *History of the American Economy.* 4th ed. New York: Harcourt Brace Jovanovich, 1979.

Saposs, David J. "Colonial and Federal Beginnings." in John R. Commons et al., *History of Labour in the United States.* New York: Macmillan, 1918, Vol. I.

Notes

1. Frederick C. Dietz, *An Economic History of England* (New York: Holt, Rinehart and Winston, 1942), p. 36.
2. T. S. Ashton, *The Industrial Revolution: 1760–1830* (London: Oxford University Press, 1948), p. 2. By permission of Oxford University Press.
3. J. L. and Barbara Hammond, *The Bleak Age* (Middlesex: Penguin Books, 1947), p. 34.
4. Ibid.
5. David J. Saposs, "Colonial and Federal Beginnings," in John R. Commons et al., *History of Labour in the United States*, Vol. I, p. 28. (Copyright 1918 by Macmillan Publishing Co., Inc., renewed 1946 by John A. Commons—Vols. I & II); (Copyright 1935 by Macmillan Publishing Co., Inc., renewed 1963 by Fannie S. Perlman and Philip Taft—Vol. IV). Quotations from the same source also cited below and on pp. 257–258 and 283–284.
6. Ibid., p. 76.
7. Helen M. Sumner, "Citizenship," in Commons et al., *History of Labour*, vol. 1, p. 320.
8. Selig Perlman, "Upheaval and Reorganization," in Commons et al., *History of Labour*, vol. 2, pp. 358–359.
9. Maurice F. Neufeld, "Structure and Government of the AFL-CIO," in *Industrial and Labor Relations Review* 9, no. 3 (April 1956). p. 373. Cf. Walter Galenson, "Why the American Labor Movement Is Not Socialist," in *American Review* 1, no. 2 (Winter 1961): pp. 31–51.

Chapter 3
THE AMERICAN ECONOMY TODAY

To the Congress of the United States: . . .

It is often said that we must choose between inflation and unemployment, and that the only way to reduce unemployment is to accept chronic inflation or rigid controls. I reject this view. Inflation and unemployment are not opposites but related symptoms of an unhealth economy . . . if we have a new round of inflation it is likely to bring still more unemployment. Chronically high unemployment is an intolerable waste of human resources and entails an unacceptable loss of material production. Clearly, we must attack inflation and unemployment at the same time; our policies must be balanced.[1]

This paragraph is from the *Economic Report of the President* for 1976. This annual report is submitted to the Congress in accordance with the Employment Act of 1946, which stated at the time of its passage that it was the responsibility of the federal government to (1) create and maintain "conditions under which there will be . . . useful employment opportunities, including self-employment, for those able, willing, and seeking to work" and (2) "promote maximum employment, production, and purchasing power."[2]

In October 1978, the Humphrey-Hawkins Full Employment and Balanced Growth Act (Public Law 95-523) amended the Employment Act to establish broader national economic goals and to require rudimentary economic planning by the federal government. According to President Jimmy Carter's Council of Economic Advisers,

> the new law strengthens the Employment Act in three essential respects. It explicitly identifies national economic priorities and objectives; it directs the President to establish, and the Congress to consider, goals based on those priorities and objectives; and it creates new procedures . . . to improve the coordination and development of economic policies.[3]

Like the Employment Act of 1946, the Humphrey-Hawkins Act makes a full range of opportunities for useful employment at fair rates of pay for everyone able, willing, and seeking to work a national goal. It "also specifies reasonable price stability as a national objective and recognizes the need to improve government policies for dealing with inflation."[4]

The Humphrey-Hawkins Act is a response to the basic economic problems that have confronted the nation since World War II. We enjoy one of the highest per capita real incomes in the world, yet we have failed to realize the objectives of the Employment Act of 1946. Our economic progress has been uneven; recurrent periods of recession and prosperity have affected different subsets of the population in different ways. Many citizens, particularly members of minority groups, have benefited very little from economic growth; most recently, unacceptably high levels of unemployment have persisted during a period of inflationary growth. Serious questions have also been raised about our possible overcommitment to economic goals at the expense of social and environmental ones.

All these problems affect the employment relationship and the welfare of wage and salary workers. They also reemphasize the relevance of the study of labor problems and union-management relations to the ultimate resolution of some of the most critical issues facing the nation. This chapter and the first three chapters in Part Two provide an empirical and theoretical framework for the study of labor problems. This chapter presents a selective (and somewhat impressionistic) overview of the American economy and identifies some of the work-related problems that will be the focus of later chapters. Chapters 4–6 in Part Two describe the operation of labor markets and how wages are determined in the absence of unions.

The statistical information in these chapters has some limitations: it is drawn from a variety of sources, and the results of different studies are not always comparable in terms of the periods they cover, their inclusiveness, or the methods used to obtain them. Moreover, since they generally measure quantitative rather than qualitative dimensions of American life, they may fail to reflect the true impact of economic growth and development on human welfare.

A DIGRESSION ON SOCIAL INDICATORS

The understandable emphasis of economists on the quantifiable dimensions of American life has tended to minimize the contribution of intangible factors to a "good society." It would be helpful if some generally acceptable *social indicators* (measures, say, of the *quality* of health services or the *quality* of education) were available to supplement our indicators of economic well-being (the size of the GNP, the unemployment rate, the inflation rate, and so on). During the Johnson administration, a panel of social scientists was appointed to advise the Department of Health, Education, and Welfare on the measurement of social change and the possibility of preparing a social report comparable to the *Economic Report of the President*. This was one of a number of efforts to develop social indicators. The panel noted that

> curiosity about our social condition would by itself justify an attempt to assess the social health of the Nation. . . . We need "social indicators," . . . to get an idea how well off we really are.
>
> A social report with a set of social indicators . . . could . . . improve public policymaking in at least two ways. First, it could give social problems more visibility. . . . Second, . . . it might . . . make possible a better evaluation of what public programs are accomplishing.[5]

The development of such a report will not be easy, since "there is no consensus as to what the quality of life is all about, and how . . . social indicators should be defined."[6] However, there are some sets of statistics that are related to social conditions and the quality of American life—for example, data on the amount of formal education received by members of the labor force, the number of persons below the "poverty threshold," the pretax and aftertax distribution of personal and family income, and the use of a variety of medical services. Publications prepared by the Bureau of the Census contain a variety of such data. In addition, there are several indexes that show in a rudimentary way the impact of economic growth upon individual welfare. These include a *measure of net economic welfare* (MEW), developed by Professors William Nordhaus and James Tobin (both, at one time or another, members of the Council of Economic Advisers), and a *physical quality of life index* (PQLI), developed by the Overseas Development Council (a Washington, D.C., economic research organization).

Nordhaus and Tobin converted a conventional measure of national output, the GNP, into a new measure by taking into account a number of sources of consumer satisfaction and dissatisfaction not reflected in the GNP. They adjusted GNP data upward to reflect such things as increased leisure and educational services and downward to reflect pollution costs and other disagreeable aspects of urbanization.[7]

The PQLI was designed to help economic planners meet the basic human needs of people in underdeveloped nations.[8] It "is a composite measure with equal weights given to three indicators [of social welfare], literacy, life expectancy and infant mortality."[9] According to a 1977 report, the people of Sri Lanka, one of the poorest nations in the world in terms of per capita output, have a relatively high PQLI of 83. They "live longer and have higher literacy rates than the citizens of almost all other developing countries, including Iran . . . and oil-rich Kuwait."[10] Black Americans had a PQLI of 89 in 1977; white Americans had a PQLI of 97.

THE SIZE OF THE ECONOMY

GNP, NI, NNP, and Employment Data

A country's output is measured by the money value of all the final goods and services it produces during a specified period. This is its *gross national product*. Its *national income* (NI) is defined as the total compensation received by the various factors of production that were responsible for the GNP. If an allowance for the consumption of capital goods (depreciation) is subtracted from a country's GNP, the resulting *net national product* (NNP) is conceptually equivalent to its national income. In the United States, however, the NNP exceeds the NI because indirect business taxes included in product prices do not appear as part of the income of people or firms.

During 1979, the 96.9 million employed persons in our civilian labor force helped to produce a gross national product of almost $2.4 trillion.[11] This compares with a GNP of $982 billion a decade earlier, an increase of almost 150 percent. The rise in real output during this period was considerably less, since prices also rose persistently. Measured in 1972 dollars, the GNP rose from $1,075 billion in 1970 to $1,431 billion in 1979, an increase of some 33 percent.*

Although the number of gainfully employed persons in the civilian labor force rose from 78.6 million in 1970 to 96.9 million in 1979, the absolute number of unemployed persons was also greater in 1979, and the unemployment rate for that year, 5.8 percent, was also higher than the 1970 rate of 4.9 percent.

The $2.4 trillion gross national product of 1979 represented the total value in current dollars of all *final* goods and services produced in the economy during that year. Viewed in terms of expenditures, it represented personal consumption spending of $1,509.8 billion; gross private domestic investments of $387.2 billion; a balance of net exports of goods and services $—4.6 billion; and government purchases of goods and services of $476.4 billion.

As real incomes have risen in the United States, an increasing proportion of the GNP has been spent on services. Table 3.1 shows how the focus of consumption has shifted since World War II.

The number of persons employed in goods-related industries (mining, construction, and manufacturing) increased from 18.5 to 26.6 million between 1950 and 1979; but these industries accounted for only 30 percent of the total employment in nonagricultural establishments in 1979 compared to 41 percent in 1950.

---

* The basic method of correcting a value series for changes in the price level is discussed on pp. 91–92.

Table 3.1 MAJOR COMPONENTS OF THE GROSS NATIONAL PRODUCT[a] (In billions and percentages)

	1950		1979		19___[b]	
Goods	$162.4	57.0%	$1,030.5	44.0%	$	%
Services	88.2	31.0	1,085.1	46.0		
Structures	35.6	12.0	253.2	11.0		

[a] Percentages may not total 100 due to rounding.
[b] Space has been provided here and in subsequent tables and charts to enter current data.
SOURCE: *Economic Report of the President, Transmitted to the Congress January 1980, Together with the Annual Report of the Council of Economic Advisers,* Table B-6, p. 210, and *Survey of Current Business,* 60, no. 4 (April 1980), Table 2, p. 13.

The number of employees in manufacturing establishments actually declined between 1969 and 1971, and again between 1973 and 1975, mainly because of layoffs in cyclically sensitive industries. On the other hand, the number of employees in service-related industries increased dramatically between 1950 and 1979. The number of people working for wholesalers and retailers jumped from 9.4 to 20.1 million; the number of government workers went from 6 to 15.6 million; the number of people working for finance, insurance, and real estate companies or offices went from 1.9 to 5 million; the number employed by transportation firms and public utilities increased from 4 to 5.2 million; and the number providing "services" (for example, hotels and motels, amusement, recreation and repair services) went from 5.4 to 17 million.[12]

We have defined the country's national income as the total compensation received by the entities that produce the GNP, basically equivalent to the GNP less money spent to replace tangible capital equipment and pay indirect business taxes. In 1979, the NI was $1,924.8 billion. The division of this income is described in Table 3.2. Not surprisingly, the compensation of employees (wages and salaries and supplements) accounts for over three-quarters of the total NI.

The goods and services that make up our gross national product are produced by a highly industrialized, highly specialized, highly interdependent economy that makes extensive use of nonhuman energy. The bulk of productive activity is carried on by private enterprises responding to market forces. Most of

Table 3.2 MAJOR COMPONENTS OF NATIONAL INCOME

	(in billions)	
	1979	19___
Compensation of employees	$1,459.2	$
Income of proprietors	130.8	
Rental income of persons	26.9	
Corporate profits (adjusted for inventory valuation and capital consumption)	178.2	
Net interest	129.7	
Total National Income	$1,924.8	$

SOURCE: *Survey of Current Business,* 60, no. 4 (April 1980), Table 7, p. 15.

the $154 billion the federal government spent for goods and services in 1978, for example, went to privately owned firms, and the bulk of the year's state and local public works projects was carried out by private contractors. Government purchases in that year provided employment for an estimated 8.2 million workers in private industry, 14.4 million civilian government employees, 2.1 million military personnel, and 1.5 million employees in government-operated enterprises such as the postal service and publicly owned power stations.[13] Federal monetary and fiscal policies designed to achieve such basic national goals as maximum employment, stable prices, and adequate economic growth also have a significant impact upon the economy. Government taxing and spending decisions greatly affect the distribution of personal income among consumers, as do a broad spectrum of social insurance and public assistance programs.

Our *material* progress is reflected in our GNP. The United States has the largest GNP of any nation, and also one of the highest per capita GNPs in the world. United Nations estimates of the per capita *gross domestic product* of selected nations in 1975 are shown in Table 3.3.* A family's *money income* determines its ability to buy goods or services or save, but an increase in money income does not necessarily mean an increase in real spendable income. To measure a family's available "real" income, we must first adjust its money income for taxes and then adjust the resulting "spendable" income for changes in the price level. For example, the gross weekly earnings of production workers in private nonagricultural industries rose from $119.83 in 1970 to $219.91 in 1979, and the average spendable weekly earnings of married workers with three dependents (their gross earnings less social security and income taxes) rose from $104.90 to $194.82. However, since prices during the ten-year period, increased more than wages, the workers' purchasing power fell by 71¢. Spendable earnings

Table 3.3 THE PER CAPITA GROSS DOMESTIC PRODUCT FOR SELECTED COUNTRIES IN 1975 (in U.S. dollars)

Kuwait	$11,307	Portugal	$1,560
Sweden	8,425	Jamaica	1,434
United States	7,148	Brazil	1,158
Denmark	7,009	Turkey	910
Australia	6,920	Ecuador	608
France	6,352	Egypt	334
Japan	4,404	India	146
Saudi Arabia	4,255	Burma	99
Italy	3,083	Ethiopia	95
Argentina	1,920	Burundi	73

SOURCE: Department of International Economic and Social Affairs, Statistical Office of the United Nations, *Yearbook of National Accounts Statistics, 1977,* vol. 2, Table 1A, pp. 3–9.

* Although conceptually similar, GNP includes production attributable to factors of production supplied by a nation's *residents,* whereas gross domestic product includes production by factors of production *located within* a given nation.

of $194.52 in 1979 were equivalent to spendable earnings of only $89.49 in 1967 dollars.[14] Nevertheless, real incomes have risen significantly in the United States since World War II. Between 1947 and 1972, average spendable earnings for married workers with three dependents measured in 1967 dollars rose by some 46 percent, from $66.73 to $97.11. To many observers, this overall growth record indicates that as a nation we have the ability to achieve a "better" life once we have agreed on its definition and managed to reduce the current rate of inflation.

A CLOSER LOOK AT ECONOMIC GROWTH

The exceptional productivity reflected in our gross national product and our high per capita income is due to a complex of factors: we have a small population relative to a rich base of natural resources; we have an unusually sophisticated economic infrastructure, including an excellent system of general education; and we have a very advanced technology that makes extensive use of capital equipment and nonhuman energy.

An elaborate manufacturing, distribution, and service network supplies American consumers with an almost unbelievable variety of goods and services. The satisfaction of existing wants appears to lead irresistibly to the generation of new wants, and new products appear daily.

A majority of the labor force are now white-collar rather than blue-collar workers, and twice as many workers are employed in service industries as in goods-producing industries. This has led some observers to describe our society as a *postindustrial* society, that is, one "with high levels of productivity, income, technology, information, and urbanisation," and in which employment in the services sector and in research, development, and education is greater than employment in industries producing material goods.[15]

In contrast, in most less developed countries (LDCs), rapid population growth combined with low productivity in the agricultural sector has made it difficult to divert resources from the production of food to the development of the infrastructure needed to raise the per capita GNP. In the Organization of Petroleum Exporting Countries (OPEC), some of which have the highest per capita incomes in the world, the situation is different. The tremendous export surpluses they have as a result of the recent increases in the price of petroleum have made them financially capable of rapid economic development. However, the productivity gap between most of the LDCs and the United States has widened in recent years. On the average, a man-hour of labor in other nations yields less than one-tenth of the output obtained in this country.[16]

Population Growth

In 1977, an estimated 216.8 million persons inhabited the 3.6 million square miles of land that make up the United States. We thus had a population density of 60 persons per square mile (considerably less than that of Europe, where the population per square mile in 1977 was 251).[17] The 1977 population included an estimated 187.4 million whites and 29 million members of "other" races, 87 percent of whom were black.[18]

Net population change is the result of a number of variables. During 1977, for example, the population increased by over 1.7 million persons (0.8 percent). There were 3.3 million births and 1.9 million deaths, and there was a net civilian immigration of 0.3 million.[19] Immigration has always been a significant factor in our economic growth. Prior to World War I, immigrants helped meet the mushrooming demand for labor; more recently, a "brain drain" to the United States has provided technical and professional workers in many fields. According to some estimates, 30 percent of the interns and residents in U.S. hospitals are foreign born and 25 percent of our physicians were educated abroad.

Between 1970 and 1977, our population increased at an annual rate of 0.8 percent. During the same period, population grew annually by 3.6 percent in the Bahama Islands, 5.9 percent in Kuwait, 4.1 percent in Libya, 3 percent in Pakistan, and 3 percent in Saudi Arabia.[20]

A recent estimate of population growth in this country, based on the Bureau of the Census's "intermediate" fertility assumptions, projected populations of 222.2 million in 1980 (an increase of 8.4 percent between 1970 and 1980) and 243.5 million in 1990 (an increase of 9.6 percent between 1980 and 1990).[21]

Urban Growth

The United States has become an urban nation. At the turn of the century, 60 percent of the population lived in rural areas; in 1970, 73.5 percent lived in urban areas; by the year 2000 80 percent of the population will probably be in urban areas. Increased urbanization is the result of two factors: the settlement of large numbers of immigrants in cities and extensive migration from rural areas to cities and suburbs.

The concentration of population in urban areas not only provides a supply of labor for industrial and commercial enterprises but it also creates large markets that encourage specialization by producers and the development of supportive services that would be uneconomical in less densely populated areas. A wider variety of private and public goods and services, including cultural activities, can also be provided when population is concentrated geographically.

The Agricultural Revolution

Increased productivity in agriculture is usually a prerequisite to economic development. In the United States, an "agricultural revolution" resulted in a relative—and ultimately, an absolute—decrease in the farm population as the total population expanded. Between 1920 and 1940, the farm population declined by 1.4 million. It continued to decrease during and after World War II as productivity rose dramatically in the agricultural sector. Between 1950 and 1978, the index of farm output per man-hour rose from 34 to 177 (1967 = 100). The farm population decreased from 23 million to 8 million, and the average number of persons employed annually in agriculture decreased from 9.9 million to 3.9 million.[22]

Growth in the Use of Nonhuman Energy

The American economy is characterized by an unusually high rate of use of non-human energy. In 1977, with less than 5 percent of the world's population, we accounted for 29.4 percent of the entire world's consumption of nonhuman energy.[23] Thus far, capital investment per worker in the United States has remained high; however, the rate of growth of capital per worker—and consequently the rate of growth in the per capita GNP—can be expected to decrease as the relative shift from manufacturing to service industries continues. The average capital investment per employee (including nonproduction workers) in manufacturing was $30,000 in 1971; in petroleum refining, one of the most highly automated industries, it was $192,500.[24]

The substitution of capital equipment for human labor has not been limited to manufacturing processes: machines are largely responsible for the great increase in productivity per worker in the agricultural sector, computers have revolutionized almost every sector of the economy, and our intricate and sophisticated communications and transportation networks are capital intensive. Investment in the development of new processes has been a characteristic of our economic growth. In 1979, we spent an estimated $52 billion on research and development (R&D). The federal government, which provided 50 percent of the money, spent some 60 percent of its R&D budget on national defense and space projects.[25] Although the share of R&D expenditures for projects designed to conserve human and natural resources and protect the environment has increased considerably in recent years, a tremendous amount of work remains to be done in those areas. Federal grants for such basic research are essential, since private firms are reluctant to undertake work that, despite its potential social value, may not provide an adequate financial return.

THE DARKER SIDE OF ECONOMIC GROWTH

Not unexpectedly, there have been negative aspects of the nation's economic development and increasing material affluence. Whether these are an inevitable result of industrialization or are due primarily to institutional factors peculiar to "capitalist" societies is a controversial issue. As we noted in Chapter 1, the New Left, a somewhat nebulous category of critics that includes many radical economists, believes that the "failures" of our society are largely the result of our institutional arrangements and cannot be corrected without fundamental changes in our institutions and our power structure.

Unemployment

Although the total value of our gross national product reached $2.4 trillion in 1979, an average of 6 million workers (5.8 percent of those seeking work) were unemployed during that year.[26] An additional 3.3 million workers who wanted full-time employment were on part-time schedules and 750,000 "discouraged" workers were not actively seeking work, although they wanted employment.

The incidence of unemployment varies considerably among various population groups and in various occupations. In June 1980 the unemployment rate was 7.7 percent. It was 6.9 percent for whites and 14.7 percent for blacks and other races. It was 23.3 percent for males 16 and 17 years of age but only 3.4 percent for males 45 to 49. It was 21.2 percent for white males 16 and 17 years of age, 39.2 percent for other males in the same age group. It was 3.9 percent for white collar workers and 10.3 percent for blue-collar workers. The unemployment rate for blacks and other nonwhites, which historically has been about double that of whites, is particularly disturbing.

Unemployment varies significantly between cities, states, and geographical regions. In June 1980, for example, unemployment on a statewide basis varied from 3.4 percent in Nebraska and Wyoming to 14 percent in Michigan with its hard hit automobile industry. You are probably aware of the high unemployment rates in many central cities and in Appalachia. Long-term unemployment creates particularly serious problems. In 1979, 20 percent of those who were unemployed were without work for 15 weeks or more.

An increase in employment, however welcome, does not always mean a reduction in unemployment. The labor force is growing, and increases in productivity reduce the number of workers required to generate a given level of output. In addition, because of changing job requirements and the higher level of education of new entrants into the labor force, the jobs that are available may fail to make maximum use of the capabilities of many workers, producing a widespread *underemployment* of human resources.

The Distribution of Income

The fact that people are employed does not guarantee them an income that will enable them and their families to enjoy even the minimal level of living considered acceptable by current standards. In 1978, 10.0 percent of the people in this country living in families and 22.1 percent of those classified by the Census Bureau as "unrelated individuals" 14 years of age and over had incomes that put them below the official poverty threshold.[27] The wide disparities in income in the United States are evident from the data in Table 3.4.

The share of the nation's real output that goes to specific individuals and families depends on the amount of money they have to spend or save after paying personal *taxes* and receiving *transfer payments*. Taxes *reduce* spendable income; transfer payments (cash, goods, or services received *but not earned* during an

Table 3.4 THE DISTRIBUTION OF INCOME, 1977–19___

FAMILIES AND UNRELATED INDIVIDUALS RANKED BY INCOME	PERCENTAGE OF AGGREGATE INCOME RECEIVED	
	1977	19—
(Top 5 percent)	(17.3)	( )
Highest fifth	45.2	
Fourth fifth	24.8	
Middle fifth	16.4	
Second fifth	9.7	
Lowest fifth	3.8	
Total	100.0	100.0

SOURCE: U.S. Bureau of the Census, *Current Population Reports*, Series P-60, no. 123, "Money Income of Families and Persons in the United States: 1978," Table 13, p. 62.

income period) *increase* spendable income. Most transfer payments in the United States are the result of government action.

Despite the progressive structure of U.S. personal and corporate income taxes, much less income is redistributed than is commonly thought. This is due to deductions and loopholes that reduce the income tax base and to other regressive taxes such as social security and state and local property taxes.* As we will see in Chapter 9, studies that consider not only direct taxes but indirect taxes and transfer payments indicate that our *effective* tax structure is roughly proportional for the majority of wage and salary earners.

Almost everyone agrees that tax reform is essential. Most economists believe that the effective tax structure should be made more progressive, but some doubt that this can be done without lessening work incentives. Radical economists, as we have noted, believe that our present system of distributing income is inherently unfair and should be scrapped. Other economists believe that a simplified personal income tax structure, with the payment of a negative tax (transfer payment) to persons below the poverty threshold, could redistribute income more equitably.

Poverty

The median family income in the United States was $17,640 in 1978, 10 percent more than in 1977. However, the median income for black families was only $10,880, and that for Hispanic families was only $12,570. Altogether, 16.3 million whites, 7.6 million blacks, and 2.6 million persons of Hispanic origin had incomes below the official poverty threshold ($6,662 for a nonfarm family of four persons). Although the absolute number of poor whites was greater than the number of blacks and members of other races, only 8.7 percent of all whites (compared with 30.6 percent of all blacks and 21.6 percent of all persons of Hispanic origin) were

* A *regressive tax* is one that takes a larger proportion of lower incomes; the tax rate does not have to be inversely related to the tax base.

classified as living in poverty.[28] Thus blacks and other nonwhites were much more likely than whites to be below the poverty threshold. American Indians, migrant workers, farm families, and households headed by women also constitute a disproportionately large sector of the poor. The causes of poverty are interrelated. For example, in 1978 over half of the black families headed by women had incomes below the poverty threshold.[29]

There are no universal standards of poverty. A nation's concept of "the poor" is largely culturally determined and changes with changes in mores or as average levels of living rise. Incomes below the "official" poverty line in the United States would be considered affluent in many nations. As Michael Harrington pointed out in his widely read *The Other America,*

> technology has consistently broadened man's potential [so that] in terms of what is technically possible, we have higher aspirations. Those who suffer levels of life well below those that are possible, even though they live better than medieval knights or Asian peasants, are poor.[30]

We must also distinguish between (1) temporary poverty due to temporary unemployment or a temporary disability and (2) persistent or chronic poverty. The Johnson administration's "War on Poverty" sought to attack chronic poverty. A major objective was to help young persons escape from poverty through educational and training programs that would increase their productivity and help them find work at higher wages.

Persons below the official poverty threshold represent one of our most serious domestic problems. It is generally agreed that these people should be guaranteed a "social" minimum income, one that rises as the real level of per capita income increases. However, there is considerable disagreement about the best way to provide such a guarantee.

It is sometimes argued that as *real* per capita income rises, poverty will gradually disappear. Unfortunately, although the *percentage* of people classified as poor will probably decrease, it may also become increasingly difficult to reduce the absolute number of poor persons. This is because more of those remaining below the poverty threshold will be persons whose potential for unsubsidized employment becomes more limited as worker productivity and wage levels rise. Thus the poverty that persists will become more extreme relative to a rising standard of living.

An economic (income-related) definition of poverty fails to reveal many of the specific problems of different population groups. Earlier in the chapter, we mentioned the dramatic reduction in the U.S. farm population in this century. The absorption of displaced farm workers into other types of productive activity has been remarkable. However, the problems these people encounter in adjusting personally to the alien social climate of the larger cities to which many of them migrate have proved more intractable. Many are educationally disadvantaged members of minority groups, and our failure to integrate them into the urban environment has worsened racial tensions in numerous metropolitan areas.

Demand "Creation"

The contribution of certain types of productive activity to the welfare of consumers is open to question. In a competitive economy, the production of goods and services is presumably triggered by the public's desire to have them. In reality, the creation of markets for products is not left to the consumer; advertisers employ a variety of media to carry their often seductive, and at times subliminal, appeals to the public.

Advertising is a major industry. In 1978 (when a total of $50.4 billion was spent on public and private institutions of higher education), an estimated $43.7 billion was spent on advertising. This included, for example, $589 million in net time and program costs for advertising toiletries and toilet goods on network television.[31] Advertising *may* provide objective information that helps consumers to find products they need or want. Frequently however, it has another goal, as observation of a single evening's crop of TV commercials will demonstrate.

Environmental Problems

The deterioration of the natural environment, particularly in urban areas, has become a matter of increasing concern to Americans. Many problems, including the pollution of water and the atmosphere, the indiscriminate use of pesticides, and the failure to protect our wetlands, wildlife, and other natural resources, seem evidence of a callous disregard for the quality of the environment. The deterioration of the environment is frequently associated with population growth as well as economic development. However, an interim report from a National Commission on Population Growth concludes that "rapidly rising levels of per capita consumption, and technological mismanagement, appear to contribute more to environmental pollution than does a gradual rise in total population.[32] The associate director of the U.S. Bureau of the Census has also disputed the view that population growth is the major challenge to the quality of life in America.[33]

Access to and the Cost of Health Care

The inadequacies of our health care and health delivery systems and the rapid rise in costs that has accompanied attempts to improve these systems constitute major social and economic problems. Despite increasing absolute and relative expenditures for health and medical care (9.1 percent of the GNP in 1979), access to such care is uneven, and our overall health record is not as good as that of some other industrial nations. In 1971, for example, 14 industrial countries had lower infant mortality rates than the United States, and 18 had longer life expectancies for 20-year-old men.[34] The cost of health services in this country continues to mount significantly faster than the cost of other services, and the distribution of health services to those who belong to different races, have different incomes, and live in different areas remains uneven.

Demographic data reflect the differences in health care. In 1977, the infant death rate was 12.3 per thousand live births for whites and 21.7 per thousand for blacks and members of other races. The maternal death rate was 7.7 per thousand live births for whites and 26 for blacks and members of other nonwhite races. Life expectancy at birth was 73.8 years for whites and 68.5 years for blacks and other nonwhites.[35] According to one study,

> in 1970 the 15 counties with the highest per capita incomes had seven times as many patient-care physicians per capita as did the 15 counties with the lowest per capita incomes, twenty-six times as many physician specialists per capita, and three times as many hospital beds per capita.[36]

Social Problems

Personal disorientation, social anomie, and various types of antisocial behavior are symptoms of the failure of an advanced industrial society to devote enough energy, skills, and resources to solving its human problems. The number of patients treated in mental health facilities increased more than 140 percent between 1965 and 1975; violent crimes increased, on the average, 6.3 percent a year from 1967 to 1977; and the number of divorces more than doubled between 1965 and 1977.[37]

Many people think that a failure to derive personal satisfaction from work contributes to such problems, and the quality of people's work lives has, in fact, been of increasing interest to social scientists. Two primary concerns are the extent to which workers' needs are satisfied through the employment relationship and the degree to which unions can help to create more dignified, humane, and satisfying work environments.

THE EXPANSION OF THE PUBLIC SECTOR

As the economic development of a nation proceeds, the public sector typically expands, both absolutely and relatively. This may result from a philosophical commitment to increased government control or it may be a pragmatic response to problems associated with economic growth. The expansion of the public sector in the United States has been based on three national imperatives:

1. The need to provide or subsidize necessary or desirable goods and services that cannot be produced profitably or made generally available at a reasonable cost by private firms. Thus we have public education, public fire and police protection, public medical care for retired persons, public housing, public transport systems, and publicly owned utility companies that supply electricity and water.
2. The need to provide funds and a variety of services to persons unable to work, whose income is insufficient for their needs, or to persons whose

income has been temporarily interrupted or reduced. Thus we have permanent public assistance and social insurance programs and "emergency" measures to help us through depressions and recessions.
3. The need to defend the nation and its allies from military threats. Since World War II, military and defense-related expenditures have grown enormously.

By 1979, over one out of every six employees was a government employee, and government purchases of goods and services amounted to $476.1 billion, or 21 percent of the GNP. Government spending accounted for 8 percent of the GNP prior to 1929, 14 percent in 1933 (during the Depression), 46 percent in 1944 (during World War II), and 20 percent in 1960. Despite projected increases in the absolute size of the government sector, the proportion of the GNP generated directly by the government may stabilize in the near future, and a larger proportion of nondefense expenditures may be made by state and local governments. Contrary to popular belief, the federal government is *not* the major purchaser of goods and services in the public sector. In 1979, federal purchases were $166.3 billion of the GNP while state and local governments spent $309.8 billion.

Despite the continuing expansion of government, critics have charged that our public sector is underdeveloped, that we have failed to provide certain necessary or desirable public goods and services. Further selective expansion of the public sector, it is argued, will not only enhance the material well-being of a greater number of citizens but also improve the "quality" of life. In the early 1960s, the Kennedy administration stressed the desirability of providing additional public goods and services, and the concept of the Great Society as articulated by President Johnson incorporated a variety of goals that extended "far beyond mere affluence." These included the improvement of urban life, the development of natural resources, the provision of consumer information, a program of research and demonstration projects to help meet the country's transportation needs, "a massive new attack on diseases which afflict mankind," and an educational program that would "insure an opportunity to every American child to develop to the full" his or her mind and skills.[38]

Unfortunately, decision makers in the private sector often fail to include social costs and benefits in their economic calculus. In its *Annual Report* transmitted to the Congress in January 1972, President Richard Nixon's Council of Economic Advisers referred specifically to

> issues relating to the continuing effectiveness of the economic system that are now of special concern. They are issues of national policy with respect to improvement of the environment, the supply of energy, research and development, surface freight transportation, and the provision of health care. . . . One aspect common to all of them should be emphasized. . . . They all reveal the difficulties that arise in the absence of an adaptive price system, whether that absence results from the natural condition of the private economy or from government regulation.

The basic environmental problem, for example, is that some resources, like air, are common property and consequently the private economic system does not put a price on their use. The result is overuse or misuse—such as the dumping of excess pollutants into the air. Similarly, much of the knowledge that can be created by research and development becomes a free good, so that private people do not have an adequate incentive to produce it.[39]

Although individual judgments about the desirability of government intervention in specific areas may understandably differ, continued expansion of the nondefense-related public sector appears inevitable. In addition, the federal government will undoubtedly give more consideration to encouraging decision makers in the private sector to give social costs and revenues more weight. The growth of the public sector is not necessarily antithetical to the preservation of established private institutions, and the rejection of radical changes in the nation's institutions and power structure does not imply the rejection of a greater role for government in creating a "better" society.

SUMMARY

We began this chapter with a discussion of economic goals. Once our national priorities have been established by an "appropriate" sociopolitical consensus, and once institutional parameters consistent with these priorities have been identified and accepted, the economic well-being of the population will be determined by (1) the resource base of the nation (the quantity and quality of human, natural, and man-made resources available to produce goods and services); (2) the "state of the arts" (the technical or engineering efficiency with which resources can be used);* (3) whether resources are actually used efficiently both technically *and* economically; (4) whether resources are *fully* employed; (5) our real output per capita (and thus our real income); (6) the distribution of spendable personal income among individuals and families; and (7) the costs and benefits associated with the provision of public rather than private goods.

Each of these necessarily interrelated items has dimensions associated with the efficient and humane use of labor in production and with the problems that stem from efforts to achieve this goal. The continued development of modern technology, the rise of new industries and firms, the decline of established enterprises, the concomitant changes in the demand for labor and the occupational structure of the labor force, the current emphasis on the quality of life, and the expansion of the public sector all have human, economic, and financial costs. However, a nation that has reached our stage of economic development can lessen the human costs of progress significantly. We shall examine various ways of doing this in later chapters.

---

* See page 56 for a discussion of the distinction between engineering and economic efficiency.

DISCUSSION QUESTIONS

1. Why did the Congress find it necessary to pass the Humphrey-Hawkins Act when an Employment Act had already been passed in 1946?
2. This chapter includes a section on "Social Indicators." Do you believe that this was peculiarly appropriate and necessary in a text dealing with labor problems and union-management relations?
3. Why do unions attempt to negotiate COLAs (Cost of Living Adjustments)? Can you think of any adverse impacts of such contract provisions?
4. How have we attempted to achieve a redistribution of income to compensate for the wide disparities in individual shares of our national income? Do you believe that such actions are appropriate in a market economy?
5. Do you agree that "poverty is a good example of a labor problem that can never be solved?"
6. Do you believe that it is now possible for the United States Government to place greater emphasis on improving the "quality of our national life"? To what extent will this require a (relative) contraction in private sector economic activity?

SELECTED READINGS

Social Indicators

Andrews, Frank M. and Withey, Stephen B. *Social Indicators of Well-Being.* New York: Plenum, 1976.

Harbison, Frederick H. "Human Resources as the Wealth of Nations." In *Studies in Labor and Industrialization,* Inter-University Study of Labor Problems in Economic Development. Reprinted for private circulation from *Proceedings of the American Philosophical Society* 115, no. 6 (December 1971).

Industrial Relations Research Association. "Measuring the Quality of Life—Social Indicators." In *Proceedings of the Twenty-Fifth Anniversary Meeting, Industrial Relations Research Association, December 28–29, 1972.* Part IV, pp. 99–119. Madison, Wisc.: Industrial Relations Research Association, 1973.

Liu, Ben-Chieh. *Quality of Life in the U. S., 1970.* Kansas City: Midwest Research Institute, 1973.

Liu, Ben-Chieh. *Quality of Life Indicators in U.S. Metropolitan Areas, 1970.* Washington, D.C.: Washington Environmental Research Center, U.S. Environmental Protection Agency, May 7, 1975.

U.S. Department of Commerce, Office of Federal Statistical Policy and Standards, Bureau of the Census. *Social Indicators 1976.*

Labor Force Data

For up-to-date labor force data, see the current issue of *Employment and Earnings,* a monthly publication of the Bureau of Labor Statistics of the U.S. Department of Labor. Other basic sources of data on employment and national income include the *Employment and Training Report of the President* and the *Statistical Abstract of the United States,* both published annually, and the *Federal Reserve Bulletin,* the *Monthly Labor Review,* and the *Survey of Current Business,* which are published monthly.

Productivity

Fabricant, Solomon. *A Primer on Productivity.* New York: Random House, 1969. An excellent introduction to a complex subject.

Poverty and Affluence

Galbraith, John Kenneth. *The Affluent Society.* Boston: Houghton Mifflin, 1958. An articulate early exposition of how money is spent, or misspent, in America.

Harrington, Michael. *The Other America: Poverty in the United States.* New York: Macmillan, 1962. A popular classic, though many more detailed, and more scholarly, articles and monographs on the subject have appeared since 1962. See for example, U.S. Congress, House, Committee on Education and Labor, *Poverty in the United States,* 88th Cong., 2nd sess., 1964, "a handbook of basic information relative to the problem of poverty in the United States" (p. v.).

The Economic Role of Government

Friedman, Milton. *Capitalism and Freedom.* Chicago: University of Chicago Press, 1962. A neoclassical, noninterventionist position on the growth of the public sector.

Notes

1. *Economic Report of the President, Transmitted to the Congress January 1976, together with the Annual Report of the Council of Economic Advisers,* pp. 3–4. The short title of this annual volume is the *Economic Report of the President;* the more extensive and detailed second report is not usually differentiated from the first report.
2. *Employment Act of 1946, as Amended, with Related Laws* (60 stat. 23), sec. 2.
3. *Economic Report of the President, Transmitted to the Congress January 1979,* p. 107.
4. Ibid.
5. U.S. Department of Health, Education, and Welfare, *Toward a Social Report* (Washington, D.C., 1969), pp. xii–xiii.
6. Ben-Chieu Liu, *Quality of Life Indicators in U.S. Metropolitan Areas, 1970* (Washington, D.C.: Washington Environmental Research Center, U.S. Environmental Protection Agency, May 7, 1975), p. 8.
7. A good brief discussion of this measure is included in Paul A. Samuelson, *Economics,* 11th ed. (New York: McGraw-Hill, 1980), pp. 183–185. Samuelson has named the measure one of "net economic welfare," or NEW.
8. The discussion of the PQLI relies upon Ann Crittenden, "A New Index of the Quality of Life," in *The New York Times,* March 13, 1977, p. F-17.
9. Ibid.
10. Ibid.

11. Unless other sources are identified, the data in this section are from various tables in (1) the appendix to the *Economic Report of the President, 1980* or (2) *Survey of Current Business,* 60, no. 4 (April 1980). The labor force data cited are annual averages.

12. U.S. Department of Labor, Bureau of Labor Statistics, *Employment and Earnings* 27, no. 3 (March 1980): Table B–1 p. 57.

13. *Employment and Training Report of the President, Including Reports by the U.S. Department of Labor and the U.S. Department of Health, Education, and Welfare, Transmitted to the Congress 1979,* Table G–5, p. 388.

14. *Monthly Labor Review* 103, no. 5 (May 1980): Table 20, p. 82.

15. Hans Günter, "Social Policy and the Post-Industrial Society," in *International Institute for Labour Studies Bulletin 10* (1972): footnote 2, p. 114.

16. Solomon Fabricant, *A Primer on Productivity* (New York: Random House, 1969), pp. 173 and 166. According to Fabricant (p. 99), real average wages and salaries per hour (including fringe benefits) increased sixfold in the United States between 1889 and 1965.

17. U.S. Bureau of the Census, *Statistical Abstract of the United States: 1979,* Table 1544, p. 885.

18. Ibid., Table 27, p. 28.

19. Ibid., Table 8, p. 11.

20. Ibid., Table 1544, pp. 885–887.

21. *Employment and Training Report of the President, 1979,* Table E–1, p. 353.

22. *Statistical Abstract of the United States: 1979,* Table 1221, p. 704; Table 1171, p. 681.

23. Ibid., Table 1014, p. 603.

24. U.S. Bureau of the Census, *Statistical Abstract of the United States: 1975,* Table 1258, p. 735.

25. *Statistical Abstract of the United States: 1979,* Table 1046, p. 621; Table 1048, p. 622.

26. Unless another source is cited, employment and unemployment data are from *Employment and Earnings* 27, no. 7 (July 1980).

27. U.S. Bureau of the Census, *Current Population Reports,* Series P–60, no. 124, "Characteristics of the Population Below the Poverty Level: 1978," Table 1, p. 16.

28. U.S. Bureau of the Census, *Current Population Reports,* Series P–60, no. 123, "Money Income in 1977 of Families and Persons in the United States: 1978," p. 1; "Characteristics of the Population Below the Poverty Level: 1978," Table A, p. 2.

29. "Characteristics of the Population Below the Poverty Level: 1978," Table 17, p. 81.

30. Michael Harrington, *The Other America: Poverty in the United States* (New York: Macmillan, 1962), p. 178.

31. *Statistical Abstract of the United States: 1979,* Table 215, p. 137; Table 1000, p. 595; Table 1003, p. 596.

32. U.S. Commission on Population Growth and the American Future, *An Interim Report to the President and the Congress* (Washington, D.C., 1971), p. 17.

33. Conrad F. Taeuber, cited in *The New York Times,* January 14, 1971, p. 1.

34. Charles L. Schultze et al., *Setting National Priorities: The 1972 Budget* (Washington, D.C.: Brookings Institution, 1971), p. 215.

35. *Statistical Abstract of the United States: 1979,* Table 108, p. 75; Table 100, p. 70.

36. Charles L. Schultze et al., *Setting National Priorities: The 1973 Budget* (Washington, D.C.: Brookings Institution, 1972), p. 222, citing J. N. Haug, G. A. Roback, and B. C. Martin, *Distribution of Physicians in the United States, 1970: Regional, State, County, Metropolitan Areas* (Chicago: American Medical Association, 1971), pp. 7, 10, 157–309.

37. *Statistical Abstract of the United States: 1978,* Table 176, p. 115; Table 286, p. 177; Table 78, p. 59.

38. *Economic Report of the President, 1965,* pp. 8 and 20.

39. *Economic Report of the President, 1972,* p. 20.

Part II
THE LABOR MARKET: ANALYSIS AND PROBLEMS

Chapter 4
THE SUPPLY AND THE DEMAND FOR WORKERS IN THE UNITED STATES

An examination of the operation of the labor market, of the basic factors determining the level of wages and employment, and of the extent to which wage theory has helped us understand these matters will provide a foundation for our analysis and evaluation of (1) public and private responses to the work-related human problems of our industrial society and (2) the ongoing institutional relationship between organized labor and management. In this chapter we will begin with a look at "the" labor market in the United States.

The employment relationship in an industrial society such as ours has many extraeconomic dimensions. For most primary wage earners (i.e., those who are the principal source of support for a household), economic security depends on steady employment at an adequate wage, preferably for doing a job that makes use of the wage earner's natural abilities, education, and training. Once these basic requirements have been met, workers will place more emphasis on other aspects of the employment relationship, such as the personal satisfaction they derive from their job.

REAL AND THEORETICAL LABOR MARKETS

To economists, the term *market* suggests an area within which the forces of demand and supply interact to determine the price of a commodity or a factor of production. Such a concept is difficult to define in an operational sense. "The" labor market—that is, the market relating to the demand for, and supply of, labor as a production input—may be described in industrial, occupational, or geographic terms. For example, we may analyze the demand for automobile workers (an industrial group) producing cars for a national market (a geographic entity); or we may discuss the demand for bricklayers, pharmacists, stenographers (three occupational groups) in a particular state (another geographic entity); or, on a more theoretical level, we may talk about the demand for labor in the economy as a whole.

Many apparently simple constructs are actually complex. The demand for many occupations is not limited to a single industry. In any given area, firms in a variety of industries may draw workers (clerical employees, for example) from the same labor pool. Also, a firm's labor market may not coincide with its product markets. A steel corporation producing for a national market may hire most of its workers in essentially local labor markets, although some categories of workers—research chemists and executive trainees, for example—may be hired in national markets. The college you are attending may recruit clerical and maintenance personnel locally but compete in national markets for promising young PhDs, outstanding mature scholars, and high-level administrators.

In the next section, we shall develop a simplified model of the operation of "the" labor market. This abstract exercise—there is really no single market in which the buyers and sellers of labor come together—will provide a basis for the discussion of the present and projected supply of, and demand for, labor in the American economy. Unless the text specifies otherwise, the terms *short run* and *long run* are used to describe chronological periods, not periods within which productive factors are considered variable or fixed.*

A SIMPLE MODEL OF THE LABOR MARKET

The analysis of the supply of and demand for labor and other factors of production is similar to the analysis of the supply of and demand for commodities and services. However, the factors of production are usually demanded by the producers of these commodities and services, not those who consume them. The demand for a factor of production is usually a *derived demand*, derived from the demand for a finished product. In some cases of course, labor services are demanded directly—for example, when consumers need a doctor or a lawyer.

---

* Economists distinguish between *variable* factors of production, the employment of which must be increased if output is to expand, and *fixed* factors, the employment of which remains constant in the short run. In the long run, by definition, all factors are variable.

The Supply of Labor

The members of the population who are available to do productive work (who are "in" the labor market) during a particular period constitute the nation's *labor force*. In the short run, the *potential* labor force consists of all those in the age groups from which the labor force is conventionally drawn who meet minimal hiring standards. The lower and upper age limits of a labor force and the current minimum hiring standards are both economically and culturally determined and may be established in part by statute. In less developed nations, people may enter the labor force as children and work until they die; in more highly developed economies, cultural forces may delay entrance into the labor force and encourage exiting from it at an "appropriate" retirement age. In the long run, changes in fertility and mortality rates, changes in cultural parameters, and net migration will determine the size of the potential labor force.

The *aggregate supply of labor* is the number of hours of work that will be supplied during a given period by those in the labor force. This aggregate supply has both quantitative and qualitative dimensions. It is a function of (1) the number of people in the labor force, (2) the number of hours they work, and (3) the efficiency (i.e., the energy and skill) with which they work in combination with the other factors of production.

The percentage of the population in the labor force at a point in time or on an average day during a particular period is termed the *rate of participation in the labor force*. The *overall* participation rate, while conceptually useful, is of limited analytical value because it may conceal significant differences between the participation rates of various subsets of the population. In the long run, changes in participation rates can be expected to alter the aggregate supply of labor.

The *hours* component of the labor supply will reflect (1) the willingness of workers to work at current wage rates and (2) institutional considerations such as legal limits on daily and weekly hours of work and work schedules established by collective bargaining agreements.

The *efficiency* component of the labor supply is determined by (1) the basic quality of work done, which depends on the innate personal characteristics of the work force and the degree to which these characteristics have been developed through education and training; (2) the degree to which the potential of the labor force is realized in actual employment situations, which depends on (a) the "match" between specific jobs and the skills and abilities of workers and (b) the pace at which individuals are willing to work; and (3) the level of technological development or the "state of the arts" in the nation, particularly the extent to which its production processes are capital intensive. Education and training are investments in *human capital* that increase the quality of the supply of labor. In the long run, changes in the state of the arts and in the duration and quality of general, vocational, and professional education should also increase the efficiency of labor.

Given all these variables, it is easy to see the difficulty of developing an accurate measure of "the" supply of labor at a point in time. However, in the long run, the basic trends in the aggregate, sectoral, and occupational labor supply (and demand for labor) are generally clear, and it is these trends that are significant in making economic projections and planning the disposition of human resources.

It is worth noting that *market employment statistics* are not identical to the numbers of workers in the economy during a period, since homemakers, who are not paid for their services, are not counted as part of the labor force, and no estimate of the value of their labor is included in official national income accounts. (Illegal activities are also excluded.)

The Labor Supply Curve

Although most people derive some satisfaction from work, they expect to be paid for doing it. In a market economy, they exchange their labor for the command over commodities and services represented by money income. Potential participants in the labor force also value nonmarketable uses of time, and the typical worker will put in more hours or seek extra work only so long as the value (or utility*) of the extra income he or she receives is greater than, or equal to, the value (or utility) of the time sacrificed by working additional hours or (re)entering the labor market.

The traditional neoclassical assumption in economics is that a labor supply curve represents the number of hours of work that individuals are willing to offer in the labor market during a specified period of time when various wage rates prevail. Such a curve may be thought of as representing workers' decisions to allocate their time between employment and leisure.

If the price (wage or salary) offered for a unit of labor rises while other variables (such as the price of commodities and other sources of income) remain constant, more units of that type of labor will usually be offered. Economists use the term *ceteris paribus* ("other things being equal") to describe a theoretical model in which variables other than the one under study are assumed to remain constant. Here, prices are one of these other variables, and money wages are therefore a measure of real income.

If we show wages per hour for homogeneous units of labor for an occupation on the vertical axis of a two-dimensional diagram and the number of units (hours) of labor that will be offered in the labor market at various wages on the horizontal axis, we will have an *upward-sloping* labor supply curve. At point *a* on the supply curve, line *SS* in Figure 4.1, *L* hours of labor will be offered at a wage of *W*. If the wage per hour rises from *W* to *W'*, the number of hours of labor offered will rise from L to L'.

---

* Economists define the *utility* of an economic good (a commodity or service) as its capacity to satisfy human wants.

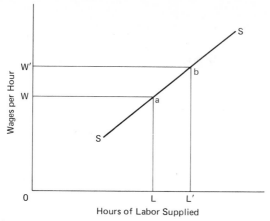

Figure 4.1 A Labor Supply Curve for an Occupation

We will then be at point b on the supply curve. The increase in the supply of labor may be due to workers already in the labor force offering to work more hours at the higher rate or the (re)entry into the labor force of more workers (an increase in the labor force participation rate). If we assume either that all units of labor in the economy are homogeneous or, more realistically, that individual differences in productivity can be converted into different quantities of labor hours of uniform efficiency, the aggregate supply of labor in the economy may be represented by a curve like the one in Figure 4.1.

A Backward-Sloping Curve

The supply curve we have just discussed, sloping upward to the right, is similar to the supply curve for most commodities and for other factors of production. However, economists believe that in the case of labor, the supply curve may bend backward at some point. The argument, briefly, is that in the short run, as wages rise, people will work more because the greater purchasing power of higher wages more than compensates them for the loss of leisure. The substitution of work for leisure is termed a *substitution effect*. However, as the amount of leisure a worker has decreases, the value of additional (marginal) units of leisure rises. At some point, the value of an additional unit of leisure becomes greater than the value of an additional unit of income, and leisure will be chosen instead of further work. This decrease in the relative attraction of work is called an *income effect*. Because of it, at point r in Figure 4.2, at wage level W, the supply curve of labor for an individual, SS, begins to slope backward. The adoption of new lifestyles emphasizing leisure activities may increase the power of the income effect, so that it dominates the substitution effect at a lower wage level. The curve will then bend backward at a lower wage.

A backward-sloping curve may represent the behavior of most *primary* wage

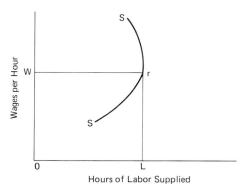

Figure 4.2   A Backward-Sloping Supply Curve for an Individual Worker

earners in the labor market,[1] but even in the short run, the decline in the amount of additional hours such people are willing to work may be more than offset by increases in the labor force participation rates of other demographic subsets, such as married women who work part time. An analysis of the supply of labor must therefore distinguish between individual and aggregate supply curves and also account for differences in labor force participation rates for different groups.

Research has demonstrated that the notion of a direct trade-off between extra income and leisure is overly simplistic, that individuals and families consciously allocate their nonmarket time to both productive and leisure activities. Nonmarket, nonleisure activities include nonpaid household work, commuting, education, and in terms of our measure of GNP, a variety of illegal pursuits. Such activities significantly affect the supply of labor offered by people in a household. For example, the relevant choice for married women, or increasingly for their husbands, may be between (1) labor market activity and (2) some *combination* of productive *nonpaid* household activities and *leisure*.

The Demand for Labor

The demand for labor is based on the *economic efficiency* (cost) of labor relative to other, substitute factors of production. Economic efficiency is different from *technical*, or *engineering*, *efficiency*. A technically less efficient but less costly productive factor will be hired in preference to a more productive but *relatively* more costly factor. The relative cost of each factor of production will depend on the kind of technology available and the interplay of demand and supply in product and factor markets. It will also influence the character and pace of economic development. High labor costs will encourage the development of a capital intensive technology, low labor costs will encourage the substitution of labor for capital.

In a simple model of the economy in which we assume a constant technology and homogeneous units of labor, an employer will hire more workers only as long as it "pays" to do so. Employers typically operate under conditions of diminishing returns; that is, additional inputs of a variable factor of production, in this case labor, used in combination with one or more fixed factors of production, will add proportionately less to an organization's total output. A company will therefore hire more workers until a level of production is reached at which the value of the last worker's output is equal to the cost of employing her or him. During a given period, other things being equal, more units of labor will be hired only if the price of labor is reduced; when wages are lower, it becomes economically more efficient to hire more people. As a result of all this, the demand curve for labor *of a firm* resembles the downward-sloping line *DD* in Figure 4.3. Industry- and economywide demand curves for labor will have similar (but usually steeper) slopes. The extra steepness is due to the decrease in product prices required to sell a larger output. If we assume that line *DD* represents a firm's demand for labor (or the market demand), a reduction in the wage rate from *W* to *W'* will cause an increase in the firm (or all firms)'s work force from *L* to *L'*.

The Interaction of Supply and Demand

In a perfectly competitive economy, the *equilibrium level* of wages and employment would be at the intersection of the supply and demand curves for labor, that is, at point *Eq* in Figure 4.4, where *L* units of labor are employed at a wage rate of *W*. At this point, the wage offered by employers would "clear" the market; all the workers willing to work at this wage would be able to find employment. The equilibrium point represents a stable situation because we have assumed that there are no forces that would cause the wage rate or the number of persons employed to vary. *Eq* is necessarily a *full employment equilibrium*; if it were not, given pure competition, the presence of unemployed workers willing to accept a lower wage would push the wage rate down.

The graphs we have seen show how market forces determine a wage-

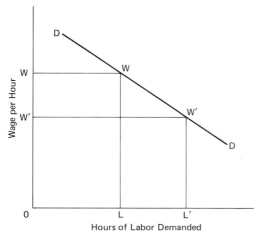

Figure 4.3   A Firm's Demand for Labor

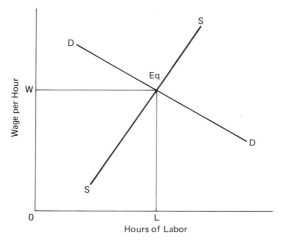

Figure 4.4   An Equilibrium Level of Wages and Employment Under Pure Competition

employment relationship, but they do not accurately depict the operation of actual labor markets. In the real world, the labor supply and the demand for labor depend on such factors as the size and geographic extent of a labor market, the structure of labor and product markets, and the relationship between changes in money wages, the demand for products, and the national output.

The demand for labor and the labor supply are interdependent. Income from employment (which represents a cost of production to employers) enables consumers to purchase commodities and services. The relative strength of consumer demand is a determinant of product prices and consequently of the value of the factors, including labor, employed to produce these products. Nor is the labor force participation rate independent of the demand for labor. In an economy in which wages are above the subsistence level, individual decisions to enter or leave the labor force may be related to the demand for labor as reflected in the market wage rate and the number of job vacancies.

The demand for labor may also respond to changes in the labor supply. In a loose labor market, hiring standards may be raised, and as we have mentioned, the development of capital intensive technology is in part a response to the relative cost of the factors of production.

We have been analyzing the operation of the labor market in general and often abstract terms; in the remainder of the chapter, we will examine the supply of labor and the demand for labor in the United States in greater detail and with a greater degree of realism.

THE U.S. LABOR FORCE

The *labor force* may be defined either as the *total* number of persons in the labor market at a point in time or as the *average* number of persons in the labor market during a given period. A distinction is made between the *total labor force*, including members of the armed forces, and the *civilian labor force*. The size of the civilian labor force is a function of the size of the age groups in the population from which the labor force is drawn; of the degree to which different age groups, sexes, and races participate in the labor market; and of the demands of the military. There is also a difference between the definition of the labor force and the definition of the supply of labor, which involves additional parameters, such as the hours people will work, how hard they work, and their skill.

Basic labor force data for 1970 and 1977, and intermediate growth projections for 1985 and 1990, are shown in Table 4.1. The source of many labor force statistics is the monthly *current population survey (CPS)* conducted by the Bureau of the Census. A scientifically selected sample of some 65,000 households is contacted during the calendar week containing the nineteenth day of each month (the "interview" week). Members of the sample are classified as (1) employed, (2) unemployed, or (3) not in the labor force on the basis of responses to standard questions about their economic activity during the preceding week (the "reference" or "survey" week). A person must be classified as employed or unemployed to be considered part of the labor force. A *discouraged worker* (one who might actively seek employment if he or she believed suitable jobs were available) is not considered part of the labor force. Aggregate estimates of the size of the civilian labor force are developed from the sample data. The employment status of the noninstitutional population 16 years of age and over in 1979 is shown in Table 4.2.

Participation in the Labor Force

Demographic forces (the "natural" forces determining the size and age distribution of the population), modified by cultural variables, are the fundamental determinants of the *potential* supply of labor. In the United States, all members of the noninstitutional population 16 years of age and older are considered potential members in the labor force. The size of this age group can be predicted fairly

Table 4.1 THE CIVILIAN LABOR FORCE

	ACTUAL SIZE		PROJECTED SIZE	
	1970	1977	1985	1990
Civilian noninstitutional population (in thousands)	136,995	156,426	172,935	180,236
Civilian labor force (in thousands)	82,715	97,401	112,953	119,366
Civilian labor force participation rates, annual averages (percentages)	60.4	62.3	65.3	66.2

SOURCE: Data from Paul O. Flaim and Howard N. Fullerton, Jr., "Labor force projections to 1990: three possible paths," in *Monthly Labor Review* 101, no. 12 (December 1978): Table 2, p. 27; Table 3, p. 28; Table 4, p. 29.

Table 4.2 EMPLOYMENT DATA FOR 1979–198_ (in thousands, except percentages)

	1979	19__
Total noninstitutional population 16 years and over	163,120	
Total labor force (incl. armed forces)	104,996	
Percentage of noninstitutional population	64.2	
Civilian labor force	102,908	
Number employed	96,945	
In agriculture	3,297	
In nonagricultural industries	93,648	
Number unemployed	5,963	
Percentage of civilian labor force	5.8	
Persons *not* in labor force	58,623	

SOURCE: *Employment and Earnings* 27, no. 5 (May 1980), Table A-1, p. 19.

accurately for a 16-year period from birth data. It is more difficult to project the actual size of the labor force because the degree to which people participate in the labor market varies over time. Participation rates are calculated for the labor force as a whole and for persons of different ages, sexes, races, marital status, income classes, and levels of education. As a rule, these rates change slowly, although noneconomic factors occasionally have an immediate, dramatic effect. World War II, for example, had a major impact on the participation of women, teenagers, and older persons in the labor force.

A definitive study of participation in the labor force emphasizes that,

like most numbers presented in isolation, [the participation rate] in and of itself is neither provocative or even very interesting. Only when compared with total participation rates in earlier years or in other countries, or when broken down into more readily identifiable components, does it begin to come alive.[2]

Participation in the labor force is a complex phenomenon determined by what people want to do and the income they or their families have or expect to have. For example, if the wages of blue-collar workers rise steadily, a wife who has entered the labor market to help assure a certain level of income for her family may leave the labor force to become a full-time homemaker. On the other hand, an increase in the prospective permanent earnings of professional workers may encourage the college-educated wife of a professional to enter the labor force and hire a housekeeper to do jobs she formerly did herself. The secular increase in the rate at which wives participate in the labor force is explained by the long-run *positive* correlation between their participation in the labor force and their *prospective higher lifetime earnings*, which outweighs the short-run *negative* correlation with their husband's earnings shown in cross-sectional analysis.[3]

Primary workers (the principal wage earners in families, usually defined as men aged 25 to 54) typically exhibit a firm attachment to the labor force, whereas *secondary* workers (many teenagers, older persons, and women with small children at home) tend to be loosely attached to it, entering or leaving it as the number of job opportunities and/or the level of prospective *transitory* (as opposed to *permanent*) earnings fluctuates with the level of business activity.

THE CYCLICAL BEHAVIOR OF PARTICIPATION RATES

Apparently, the participation rate for the labor force as a whole "respond[s] directly to short-run variations in the level of aggregate demand . . . due largely to the behavior of 'secondary' workers."[4] As a corollary, overall participation in the labor force is *inversely related* to the *unemployment rate*. It is higher in areas where the unemployment rate is low and lower in areas where the unemployment rate is higher.[5] As we shall see in Chapter 8, this conclusion has significant implications for public policy.

PAST AND PROJECTED PARTICIPATION RATES

The total labor force participation rate in 1979 was 64.2 percent. Census data indicate that this rate remained remarkably stable in the United States between 1890 and 1940. (See Table 4.3.) Some authorities consider this historical stability "something of a fluke," since in many industrializing countries, there has been a definite tendency for overall participation rates to decline.[6] However, since the end of World War II, the participation rate in the United States has *risen* steadily. Moreover, as we have said before, stability in the overall rate may conceal a significant historical variation in the participation rates of various subsets of the population.

Labor force participation rates for men and women for selected years from 1947 to 1977 are shown in Table 4.4. The high participation rate for men during the primary working years (age 25–54) is expected, but the historical increase in the participation rates for women represents a significant economic and cultural change. The decline in participation rates for young men is due primarily to the longer period of time they spend in school; the decline in the participation rate for men 65 and over is due to the increase in public and private retirement plans and to the availability of health and medical care under social security programs.

Participation rates for both sexes, for different racial groups, and for different

Table 4.3 LABOR FORCE PARTICIPATION RATES, 1890–1970[a]

CENSUS YEAR	PARTICIPATION RATE
1890	52.2%
1900	53.7
1920	54.3
1930	53.2
1940	52.4
1950	55.1
1960	57.3
1970	58.2

[a] Prior to 1950, persons 14 and over were counted as eligible for the labor force.
SOURCE: U.S. Department of Commerce, Bureau of the Census, *Historical Statistics of the United States, Colonial Times to 1970, Bicentennial Edition, Part 1*, Table Series D29–41, p. 132.

Table 4.4 TOTAL LABOR FORCE PARTICIPATION RATES, 1947–19___

AGE GROUP	1947		1957		1967		1977		19___	
	MEN	WOMEN	MEN	WOMEN	MEN	WOMEN	MEN	WOMEN	MEN	WOMEN
16 and over	86.8	31.8	85.5	36.9	81.5	41.2	78.3	48.5		
16 and 17	52.2	29.5	51.1	31.1	47.5	31.0	50.6	42.2		
18 and 19	80.5	52.3	77.7	51.5	70.9	52.3	74.4	60.6		
20 to 24	84.9	44.9	89.8	46.0	87.5	53.4	86.7	66.7		
25 to 34	95.8	32.0	97.3	35.6	97.4	41.9	95.6	59.5		
35 to 44	98.0	36.3	97.9	43.3	97.4	48.1	95.8	59.6		
45 to 54	95.5	32.7	96.4	46.5	95.2	51.8	91.2	55.8		
55 to 64	89.6	24.3	87.5	34.5	84.4	42.4	74.0	41.0		
65 and over	47.8	8.1	37.5	10.5	27.1	9.6	20.1	8.1		

SOURCE: *Employment and Training Report of the President, Including Reports by the U.S. Department of Labor and the U.S. Department of Health, Education, and Welfare, Transmitted to the Congress 1979,* Table A–2, p. 236.

age groups in 1978 are shown in Table 4.5. The relatively low rates for nonwhite males 16–19 and 45–64 suggest a lifetime work pattern significantly different from that of whites, one that is explained by cultural as well as economic forces. For nonwhite women, unlike white women, the participation rate is highest during the primary child-rearing ages (25 to 44).

Table 4.6 shows the participation rates in March 1978 for married and unmarried men and women in various age groups. Note the low participation rates of single (as opposed to married) men and the high participation rates of single women. The participation rate for married women (spouse present) increased dramatically after World War II, going from 20 percent in April of 1947 to 47.6 in March of 1978. The rate of increase has been higher for white wives than for black ones. Between 1965 and 1974, for example, it was 2.6 percent for white wives and 1.2 percent for black wives.[7]

Mechanical household aids and the increase in day care centers, nursery schools, and the like have enabled married women to work outside the home for at least limited periods, and the increase in part-time employment (which is to some extent a response to this fact) has enabled mothers of school age children to work during the school day or when teenagers or male parents are home. Women trained for technical or professional work are likely to reenter the labor force after raising families. Equal Employment Opportunity legislation and the women's rights movement will undoubtedly increase the participation rate of women further, although the rate of increase will probably decrease. According to recent Bureau of Labor Statistics (BLS) intermediate growth projections, the total female labor force participation rate will increase from 48.4 in 1977 to 57.1 by 1990.[8]

In looking at all these statistics, one word of caution is in order. Annual participation rates and employment data conceal the turnover that occurs in the labor force *during* a calendar year. In 1978, for example, when the average number

Table 4.5 CIVILIAN LABOR FORCE PARTICIPATION RATES, 1978

	MEN		WOMEN	
AGE GROUP	WHITES	BLACKS AND OTHER NONWHITES	WHITES	BLACKS AND OTHER NONWHITES
16 and over	78.6	72.1	49.5	53.3
16 and 17 years	55.3	33.2	48.9	27.7
18 and 19 years	75.3	59.5	64.6	48.6
20 to 24 years	87.2	78.0	69.3	62.8
25 to 34 years	96.0	90.9	61.0	68.7
35 to 44 years	96.3	91.0	60.7	67.1
45 to 54 years	92.1	84.5	56.7	59.8
55 to 64 years	73.9	69.1	41.2	43.6
65 and over	20.4	21.3	8.1	10.7

SOURCE: *Employment and Training Report of the President, Including Reports by the U.S. Department of Labor and the U.S. Department of Health, Education, and Welfare, Transmitted to the Congress 1979,* Table A–4, pp. 241–242.

Table 4.6   CIVILIAN LABOR FORCE PARTICIPATION RATES FOR MARRIED AND UNMARRIED PERSONS 16 YEARS OF AGE AND OLDER, MARCH 1978

	SINGLE		MARRIED (SPOUSE PRESENT)		OTHER[a]	
AGE GROUP	MEN	WOMEN	MEN	WOMEN	MEN	WOMEN
Total	69.2	60.5	81.6	47.6	67.1	42.8
Under 20	55.2	48.5	98.4	45.0	b	48.6
20 to 24	78.4	72.2	96.1	58.7	88.2	68.7
25 to 34	87.8	82.3	97.6	55.2	93.0	75.4
35 to 44	84.2	77.7	97.2	57.6	92.2	75.3
45 to 54	79.0	74.0	93.3	52.8	84.9	68.1
55 to 64	58.0	61.4	75.1	36.4	62.5	51.1
65 and over	20.2	17.0	21.0	6.5	14.1	8.7

[a] Includes those widowed, divorced, and separated.
[b] Percentage not shown when base is less than 75,000 persons.
SOURCE: Adapted from *Employment and Training Report of the President, Including Reports by the U.S. Department of Labor and the U.S. Department of Health, Education, and Welfare, Transmitted to the Congress 1979*, Table B–2, pp. 292–293.

of persons employed was 94.4 million, 107 million people were employed at some time.[9]

Aggregate Labor Force Projections

Basic labor force data for 1979 have already been given. According to BLS intermediate growth projections, the civilian labor force will increase to 113 million in 1985 and to 119.4 million in 1990.[10] Although the number of men in the labor force will grow at a slower rate than the number of women, men will compose 55 percent of the labor force in 1990. According to the BLS,

> reflecting, primarily, the sharp decline in the youth population and the anticipated continuation of the decline . . . in labor force participation among older workers, the proportion of the work force accounted for by persons age 25 to 54 should expand from 61 to 70 percent over the 1977–90 period. The growing labor force [participation] rate of persons age 25 to 54, who have had considerable work experience and are generally very productive, should help to sustain the economic growth of the nation.[11]

The Quality of the Labor Supply

According to the late Professor Frederick Harbison,

> the proportion of high-level manpower to the total labor force . . . of a country is a reasonably good measure of that country's stage of economic advancement. And the rate of increase in the stock of high-level manpower is closely associated with a country's rate of economic growth.[12]

The steady improvement in the quality of our labor force is one factor behind the increases in productivity in the United States. The level of education attained by members of the labor force is a convenient proxy for the quality of labor available. The upgrading of our labor force in terms of this criterion is shown in Table 4.7.* The improvement in the level of education of blacks and other nonwhites has been dramatic. In 1957, over 30 percent had no high school education, while in 1977, less than 15 percent were in this position. During the same period, the median number of school years completed by whites rose from 11.6 to 12.6, and the median number completed by blacks and other nonwhites went from 8.4 to 12.2. The relative educational upgrading of nonwhites will undoubtedly continue as older, less educated persons leave the labor force.

Unfortunately, there is no guarantee that the distribution of skills and aptitudes within the labor force will match the demands of employers. The lack of basic reading, mathematical and communications skills, particularly among "disadvantaged" members of the community, is of particular concern. Historically, the educational system has tended to train workers for existing (or even declining) job opportunities rather than those most likely to increase, and it has often neglected the development of transferable general skills.

There are also potential problems at the other end of the educational spectrum. Recent projections suggest that we may be "overeducating" entrants into the labor force by creating a potential supply of college graduates greater than the potential demand for them in jobs they traditionally hold.[13] There is already an oversupply of PhDs in most academic disciplines. Some 323,000 persons are expected to receive the doctorate between 1976 and 1985, but only 192,800 openings in traditional PhD jobs are expected during that period. Thus, 40.3 percent will be forced to find other work if they wish to be employed.[14]

Responsiveness to Changing Occupational Needs

The relation between the labor supply and the demand for labor at the occupational level, which often involves a time lag, also complicates matters. An increase in the wages of a particular occupational group or a projected shortage of qualified workers may attract too many workers to an occupation. In addition, occupational "qualifications" often prove to be flexible; employers may relax hiring standards in tight labor markets, while in loose markets they may insist on educational credentials that are not really needed. Employers may also substitute capital intensive technology for labor intensive processes requiring skills in short supply.

Such occupational imbalances are of particular concern to prospective entrants into the labor force and to unemployed and underemployed workers. If these people were fully aware of existing and prospective job opportunities and were able to make the investment in education and training needed to prepare themselves for these jobs, we would presumably obtain a much better match of workers and jobs. However, much of the "investment" we make in human

---

* Actually, the degree of improvement is understated by the table because older workers tend to fall below the median in the number of school years completed.

Table 4.7 THE PERCENTAGE DISTRIBUTION OF THE CIVILIAN LABOR FORCE 18 YEARS OLD AND OLDER BY YEARS OF SCHOOLING 1957–1977

YEARS OF SCHOOLING COMPLETED	MARCH 1957			MARCH 1967[a]			MARCH 1977[a]		
	TOTAL[a]	WHITES[b]	NON-WHITES[c]	TOTAL	WHITES	NON-WHITES	TOTAL	WHITES	NON-WHITES
Elementary School									
Less than 5 years	6.1	4.3	21.2	3.1	2.2	10.4	1.5	1.2	3.8
5 to 8 years	26.8	25.8	34.9	17.9	16.9	25.5	8.6	8.0	14.0
High school									
1 to 3 years	19.1	19.0	19.3	18.7	18.1	23.7	17.1	16.3	24.4
4 years	29.1	30.8	14.8	36.6	37.7	27.5	39.5	40.1	35.5
College									
1 to 3 years	8.5	9.0	3.9	11.8	12.4	7.2	16.3	16.7	13.4
4 years or more	9.0	9.7	3.4	12.0	12.8	5.8	16.9	17.6	8.9
Median school years completed	11.6	12.1	8.4	12.3	12.3	10.8	12.6	12.6	12.2

[a] 1.4 percent did not report the number of school years completed.
[b] 1.2 percent did not report the number of school years completed.
[c] 2.6 percent did not report the number of school years completed.
[d] Data for persons whose educational attainment was not reported were distributed among the other categories.

SOURCE: *Employment and Training Report of the President, Including Reports by the U.S. Department of Labor and the U.S. Department of Health, Education, and Welfare, Transmitted to the Congress 1978*, Table B–9, p. 247.

capital is not made objectively in accordance with economic projections. Career aspirations and access to higher education are greatly influenced by accidents of birth, personal associations, and location. People employed in secondary labor markets may simply be unable to get the institutional or on-the-job training that would prepare them for jobs in primary labor markets.

Nevertheless, the labor force as a whole appears to have adapted to changing job requirements. *Occupational mobility* is one mechanism by which the supply of labor responds to changes in the demand for specific types of labor. A 1970 study of the status of persons employed in 1965 found the labor force highly responsive to such changes. In fact, "32.3 percent of all [the] workers [studied] in 1965 transferred to a different . . . occupation by 1970."[15] Obviously, the considerable responsiveness of our labor force to changes in the kinds of work available is "an important consideration in developing policies to avoid or alleviate manpower shortages or surpluses."[16]

Geographic Differences in the Labor Supply

Regional variations in the rate of change in the size of the labor force are the result of two factors: differences in natural rates of increase and the *geographic mobility* of workers. Table 4.8 shows percentage changes in population and net migration (net migration from abroad plus net interregional and interdivisional migration) by regions and geographic divisions from 1960 to 1970.

Local and regional imbalances in the labor supply and the demand for labor

Table 4.8 PERCENTAGE CHANGES IN POPULATION AND PERCENT NET MIGRATION, 1960–1970

	PERCENT CHANGES IN POPULATION	NET MIGRATION
United States	13.3	1.7
Regions		
Northeast	9.8	0.7
North Central	9.6	−1.5
South	14.2	1.1
West	24.1	10.2
Divisions		
New England	12.7	3.0
Middle Atlantic	8.9	a
East North Central	11.1	−0.4
West North Central	6.0	−3.9
South Atlantic	18.1	5.1
East South Central	6.3	−5.8
West South Central	14.0	−0.2
Mountain	20.8	4.5
Pacific	25.1	12.0

a Less than 0.05 percent.
SOURCE: *Statistical Abstract of the United States: 1971,* Table 11, p. 13; Table 42, p. 35.

represent a misallocation of resources. Geographic mobility of labor (and/or capital) is essential if such imbalances are to be corrected, particularly in areas where the natural rate of growth of population does not parallel projected changes in the demand for labor.

Geographic movement may result from the positive attraction of a region that is developing well economically or culturally, or from negative pressures such as a lack of job opportunities, relatively poor working conditions, or an adverse social, cultural, or political climate. The growth of the labor force on the Pacific Coast and more recently in the Sun Belt states and the outmigration from certain agricultural areas, notably the South, are examples of such movement.

A small proportion of mobile workers can provide the required degree of geographic mobility in a labor force, and the U.S. population is apparently quite mobile. In 1970, for example, some 26 percent of the population lived in a state other than the one where it was born. Between 1970 and 1975, 46.8 million persons five years old or older moved to a different house in the same county, and 33 million moved to a different county (16.7 million to a different state).[17]

We discussed the increasing urbanization of our population briefly in Chapter 3. Recent urban growth has been mainly in suburban areas and not in central cities. This shift, which is partly a response to (and partly a cause of) the transfer of industrial, commercial, and corporate operations to suburban areas, is further evidence of the reciprocal influence between the demand for labor and the labor supply. However, racial and economic barriers that prevent the migration of disadvantaged central city residents to suburban areas, coupled with inadequate transportation within metropolitan areas, have been a hindrance to the efficient allocation of labor resources.

The Hours Component of the Labor Supply

The number of hours worked each day, week, or year is a key dimension of the supply of labor. We have already noted the rise in part-time employment, which is partly a result of the increased participation of teenagers and women in the labor force and partly the result of more flexible work schedules, particularly in service industries. Flexible workdays and workweeks often represent a pragmatic response to the increased supply of part-time workers. The number of part- and full-time workers in April 1980 is shown in Table 4.9.

Since 1940, a 40-hour workweek has been widely adopted, and in some cities

Table 4.9 PART- AND FULL-TIME WORKERS, APRIL 1980 (in thousands)

Total number of workers	88,242
Workers on part-time schedules for economic reasons	3,542
Workers on voluntary part-time schedules	13,108
Workers on full-time schedules	71,592
40 hours or less	50,957
41 hours or more	20,635

SOURCE: *Employment and Earnings* 27, no. 5 (May 1980): Table A–29, p. 40.

37½- and 35-hour workweeks have become standard for clerical, garment, and construction workers. Additional paid holidays and longer vacations have further reduced the number of hours people work annually. It is estimated that

> for the economy as a whole . . . for the period 1940–60 . . . there was, on the average, an increase of 155 hours of leisure time annually for the full-time employee, thus providing the equivalent of almost 4 weeks of leisure for a person on a standard 40-hour week. This increase in leisure time was almost equally divided between a drop in the average workweek and an increase in paid vacations and holidays.[18]

Between 1948 and 1975, the average number of *hours per week* worked by nonagricultural employees dropped from 40.9 to 38.1. However, women and students average fewer hours of work per week than men who are not students, and this drop appears to reflect changes in the composition of the labor force rather than a general reduction in the number of hours worked.[19] Some firms have also experimented with a four-day workweek, often based on a 9- or 10-hour workday without overtime pay.

A reduction in the standard or scheduled workweek cannot be equated with a corresponding reduction in the total number of hours worked. Within a firm, overtime work at premium pay may be substituted for extra leisure, while in the labor market as a whole, moonlighting may increase. In May 1978, some 4.5 million persons (4.8 percent of the total number employed) held more than one job; there were 3.7 million secondary jobs in nonagricultural industries and 752,000 in agriculture.[20]

Summary

Our analysis of the labor supply indicates that the decrease in the amount of time people are willing to work has been offset by the absolute—and in the case of women, the relative—increase in the number of people in the labor force. This growth in the number of people working, plus a gradual improvement in the quality of labor, has produced an overall increase in the supply of labor in the United States. The provision of job opportunities for our expanding labor force and of educational and vocational programs to train people for them are among the critical challenges facing the nation today.

THE DEMAND FOR LABOR

We have argued that the demand for labor is derived from the demand for products and that it is based on the productivity and cost of labor relative to other factors of production. Changes in the demand for products or in technology will therefore affect the demand for particular occupations or skills. Changes in this demand, represented graphically by *shifts to the left or right in demand curves*, are different from changes in employment stemming from changes in wages, which are represented by *movement along a given labor demand curve*. In analyzing changes in the demand for labor, we will use actual or projected employment as a proxy for demand, recognizing that the level of employment is the result of demand *and* supply forces and that the demand for labor, other things being equal, varies with the price of labor.*

As we move from studying firms or industries to studying the economy as a whole (that is, as we move from microeconomic to macroeconomic analysis), we must recognize that wages and salaries constitute the bulk of personal income and that changes in wages and employment will affect the aggregate level of demand. A level of aggregate demand that provides appropriate employment opportunities at adequate wages for everyone able and willing to work is one of our highest national priorities. Reaching this objective, as we will see in later chapters, will require macroeconomic initiatives as well as microeconomic initiatives designed to improve the functioning of specific product and labor markets. In this connection, it should be noted that "full" employment is not the same as an increase in aggregate demand large enough to reduce the number of persons presently unemployed by some absolute figure. In a dynamic economy, increases in productivity per man-hour and in the supply of labor require continually higher levels of aggregate demand to prevent further increases in the overall unemployment rate.

Employers

The firms that provide the demand for labor vary in size from small shops and farms to such corporate colossi as General Motors, U.S. Steel, and the American Telephone and Telegraph Company; from small-town government units to the federal establishment. In 1975, there were 10.9 million sole proprietorships, 1.1 million partnerships, and slightly over 2 million corporations in the United States.[21] The population of firms changes continually. In 1978 alone, 478,000 new businesses were incorporated, while 24 out of every 10,000 existing commercial and industrial enterprises failed.[22] For the members of the labor force, this turnover means the creation of new job opportunities and the disappearance of old ones. For consumers, it means, hopefully, a continuing response to changing demands.

Employment is concentrated in the nation's larger firms. In mid-March of 1969, for example, establishments reporting under our Federal Old Age, Survivors, Disability and Health Insurance Program were distributed by number of employees as shown in Table 4.10. The data in the table suggest that the "typical" employer is a *small* firm. However, over half the total number of employees in the establishments reporting were employed by firms with 100 or more employees, and over 27 percent worked for firms with 500 or more employees. According to *Fortune*, the 500 largest industrial corporations (ranked by their sales volume) employed 15.3 million persons, or some 18 percent of all nonagricultural workers in 1977.[23] Although generalizations about the size of the typical firm and the

---

* If the number of job vacancies exceeds frictional unemployment at full employment, the demand for labor exceeds the supply of labor.

Table 4.10   U.S. FIRMS DISTRIBUTED BY NUMBER OF EMPLOYEES, 1969

NUMBER OF EMPLOYEES	NUMBER OF FIRMS
1 to 3	1,798,131
4 to 7	720,408
8 to 19	586,055
20 to 49	265,443
50 to 99	86,867
100 to 249	49,529
250 to 499	16,051
500 or more	11,503

SOURCE: *Statistical Abstract of the United States: 1971,* Table 720, p. 463.

"character" of the resulting employment relationship are suspect, it is clear that the vast majority of our labor force consists of *hired employees,* directed and controlled by an increasingly professional managerial class.

Types of Employment

The Department of Labor and the Bureau of the Census identify four basic categories of employment in the United States: wage and salary employment in the private sector, self-employment, unpaid family employment (that is, work without pay for persons to whom one is related by blood or marriage), and wage and salary employment in the public sector. The number of workers in each category in June 1980 is shown in Table 4.11.

Job "opportunities" for the self-employed are often generated by an individual's disposition to be a farmer, a doctor, or her or his "own boss," and the demand for self-employed workers is in part a function of the supply of persons interested in such work. Similarly, the amount of unpaid family employment often reflects the supply of family members available for such work.

There are well-defined trends in employment opportunities within each of the four basic categories. The relative number of wage and salary workers has risen steadily as workers have become increasingly divorced from ownership of the means of production. The number of self-employed persons has decreased absolutely as well as relatively, primarily because of the decrease in the number of

Table 4.11   WORKERS AND TYPES OF EMPLOYMENT

TYPE OF EMPLOYMENT	NUMBER OF WORKERS (IN THOUSANDS)	
	JUNE 1980	_____ 19___
Wage and salary employment, private sector	73,128	
Wage and salary employment, government sector	15,367	
Self-employment	8,426	
Unpaid family employment	855	
Total	97,776	

SOURCE: Data from *Employment and Earnings* 27, no. 7 (July 1980): Table A–23, p. 56.

Table 4.12 ACTUAL AND PROJECTED EMPLOYMENT IN MAJOR INDUSTRIAL SECTORS, SELECTED YEARS, 1959–1990[a]

INDUSTRIAL SECTOR	NUMBER OF EMPLOYEES				
	1959	1968	1973	1977	1980
Total civilian sector[b]	67,563	79,836	88,408	93,715	101,761
Government sector[c]	8,083	11,846	13,738	15,868	15,868
Total private sector	59,480	67,990	74,670	78,526	85,893
Agriculture	5,491	3,663	3,206	2,922	2,974
Nonagriculture	53,989	64,327	71,464	75,604	82,919
Mining	765	634	677	867	1,002
Contract construction	3,680	3,948	4,766	4,672	5,087
Manufacturing	17,001	20,038	20,352	19,844	21,492
Durable goods	9,577	11,792	12,029	11,671	12,929
Nondurable goods	7,424	8,246	8,323	8,173	8,563
Transportation, communication, and public utilities	4,241	4,521	4,867	4,838	5,212
Transportation	2,743	2,840	2,919	2,876	3,098
Communication	874	1,017	1,207	1,203	1,304
Public utilities	624	664	741	759	809
Wholesale and retail trade	13,758	16,329	19,026	20,908	23,351
Wholesale	3,527	4,118	4,688	4,991	5,511
Retail	10,231	12,211	14,338	15,917	17,840
Finance, insurance, and real estate	2,882	3,672	4,433	4,888	5,312
Other services	9,088	12,748	15,254	17,674	19,861
Private households	2,574	2,437	2,089	1,913	1,602

[a] Data for 1980–1990 are projected data.
[b] Includes wage and salary workers, the self-employed, unpaid family workers, and private household workers.
[c] Includes government enterprise employment.
SOURCE: Adapted from Valerie A. Personick, "Industry output and employment: BLS projections to 1990," in *Monthly Labor Review* 102, no. 4 (April 1979): Table 5, p. 10.

family farms, and the number of unpaid family workers has declined for the same reason. The number of government employees, excluding members of the armed forces, has risen substantially in recent years, primarily because of increased hiring by state and local governments.

A second basic breakdown of demand is by the three major producing sectors: the private nonagricultural sector, the private agricultural sector, and the government. Between 1977 and 1990, private nonagricultural employment is expected to increase from 75.6 million to 98.5 million, farm employment is expected to decline from 2.9 to 2.6 million, and government employment is expected to increase from 15.2 to 17.5 million.[24]

Employment in Basic Industrial Sectors

The demand for specific job skills (and changes in job opportunities within geographical areas) is influenced heavily by the relative growth or decline of industrial sectors. The decline in one sector, farming, has already been noted. Table

		AVERAGE ANNUAL RATE OF CHANGE					
1985	1990	1959–68	1968–73	1973–77	1977–80	1980–85	1985–90
111,851	118,615	1.9	2.1	1.5	2.8	1.9	1.2
16,865	17,507	4.3	3.0	2.5	1.5	1.2	.8
94,986	101,108	1.5	1.9	1.3	3.0	2.0	1.3
2,922	2,634	−4.4	−2.6	−2.3	.6	− .4	−2.1
92,064	98,474	2.0	2.1	1.4	3.1	2.1	1.4
1,055	1,072	−2.1	1.3	6.4	5.0	1.0	.3
5,556	5,748	.8	3.8	− .5	2.9	1.8	.7
23,014	23,882	1.8	.3	− .6	2.7	1.4	.7
14,098	14,692	2.3	.4	− .8	3.5	1.7	.8
8,915	9,189	1.2	.2	− .5	1.6	.8	.8
5,516	5,658	.7	1.5	− .1	2.5	1.1	.5
3,270	3,332	.4	.6	− .4	2.5	1.1	.4
1,391	1,473	1.7	3.5	− .1	2.7	1.3	1.2
856	853	.7	2.2	.6	2.2	1.1	− .1
25,907	27,370	1.9	3.1	2.4	3.8	2.1	1.1
5,834	5,888	1.7	2.6	1.6	3.4	1.1	.2
20,073	21,482	2.0	3.3	2.6	3.9	2.4	1.4
6,113	6,695	2.7	3.8	2.5	2.8	2.8	1.8
23,457	26,742	3.8	3.7	3.7	4.0	3.4	2.7
1,447	1,307	− .6	−3.0	−2.2	−5.7	−2.0	−2.0

4.12 shows the actual and projected employment in major sectors reported by the Bureau of Labor Statistics for selected years from 1959 to 1990. According to the BLS, past trends in most major sectors will continue, although the rate of growth of government jobs will be slower than the rate of growth for private jobs.[25]

A relative rise in service industries is generally considered a sign of economic development and affluence. In the United States, employment in these industries has increased steadily relative to employment in goods-producing industries. In 1950, for example, there were 18.5 million nonagricultural workers in goods-producing industries and 26.7 million in service industries. By June of 1980, there were 25.8 million employees on nonagricultural payrolls in goods-producing industries and 65.3 million in service industries.[26]

The relative decline in employment in goods-producing industries should not be equated with an equivalent decline in blue-collar work and an increase in traditional white-collar employment. Many jobs in service industries and in the public sector are unskilled or semiskilled blue-collar jobs, "gray-collar" service jobs, or more highly skilled "white-coverall" jobs.

Table 4.13 PROJECTED CHANGES IN EMPLOYMENT IN SELECTED INDUSTRIES, 1977–1990

		EMPLOYMENT	
INDUSTRY GROUP	INDUSTRY	1977 (ACTUAL)	1990 (PROJECTED)
Transportation	Air transport	380,000	511,000
	Railroads	539,000	450,000
	Trucking	1,290,000	1,587,000
Wholesale and retail trade	Retailing	15,917,000	21,482,000
	Wholesaling	4,991,000	5,888,000
Finance, insurance, and real estate	Banking	1,342,000	2,054,000
	Insurance	1,687,000	2,117,000
Manufacturing— durable goods	Blast furnaces & basic steel	544,000	563,000
	Computers & peripheral equipment	279,000	479,000
	Primary aluminum & alum. products	145,000	171,000
	Radio & television receivers	134,000	137,000

SOURCE: Adapted from Valerie A. Personick, "Industry Output and Employment: BLS Projections to 1990," in *Monthly Labor Review* 102, no. 4 (April 1979): Table 4, pp. 8–9.

Employment in the goods-producing industries, particularly in those producing durable producer and consumer goods, is greatly affected by fluctuations in the overall level of economic activity. During the recession of 1969–1971, for example, although the number of jobs in goods-producing industries dropped by about 800,000, the overall number of jobs grew, primarily because of an increase in employment in the service sector. A continued relative employment decline in the goods-producing sector should produce greater stability in the total demand for labor.

Employment in Specific Industries

Employment may also vary *by industry* within broad industrial categories that include several industries. In the transportation category, for example, increases in employment in air and truck transport will more than offset the absolute decline in railroad employment. Table 4.13 shows projected changes in employment in 11 industries in 4 broad industrial groups. Differences in the growth rate of such industries have obvious implications for manpower development and training programs and for projections of labor force participation rates. The growth of wholesale and retail trade, for example, will produce increased employment opportunities for women, teenagers, and part-time workers.

Changing technology may have a significant impact on employment in a given industry or occupation. In some cases, technological innovation plus an absolute growth in industry output will add to the total number of job opportunities (as in the production of computers, for example). In other cases, as capital is substituted for labor, employment may decline or remain stable despite the growing demand for a product.

The Demand for Workers in Specific Occupations

To the individual worker whose training may vary from the most rudimentary preparation for the world of work to an advanced professional education, to the student making a career decision, or to the public or private official responsible for educational and training programs, the present and projected demands for workers in specific *occupations* are often more significant than *aggregate* data on national or industry employment. The skill and training of workers may not match job opportunities, and even when employment is generally high, workers on layoff or (re)entrants into the labor market may not be able to find jobs commensurate with their capabilities. A lack of worker mobility may contribute to the failure to match workers and jobs, although as we have noted, there appears to be a sufficient core of relatively mobile workers.

Changes in occupational demand are the result of long-run industry and interindustry growth or declines, technological innovation, and the level of business activity, essentially a short-run factor. Although there has been considerable concern about the adverse impact of technology on the demand for specific occupations, a Department of Labor study has concluded that other factors may be more important than technology in determining the occupational composition of our labor force. Apparently,

> the most important of these other factors are: (a) growth in [the] population and its changing age distribution; (b) government policy . . . ; (c) the different rates of . . . growth [in employment] among industries . . . ; (d) institutional factors, such as union-management relationships and practices; (e) the relative supply of persons in different occupations and the substitution effect resulting from a shortage in one occupation and replacement [of one occupational group] by members of another—for example, technicians for engineers.[27]

The study concludes that the different rates of growth in employment in various industries "have been the most important single factor determining the occupational distribution of employment in the United States."[28] Of course there are reciprocal forces at work in occupational labor markets. The demand among employers for various skills and for some types of new technology is in part a response to the types of skills possessed by the labor force. Today, for example, a shortage of doctors and nurses is largely responsible for a growth in the number of paramedical technicians.

In the short run, differential changes in occupational demand are caused by changes in business activity. During a recession, for example, the demand for white-collar workers in manufacturing companies tends to be more stable than the demand for blue-collar production workers. In the long run, job openings are the result of replacement needs plus growth in the demand for various cate-

Table 4.14 PROJECTED EMPLOYMENT AND REASONS FOR JOB OPENINGS IN MAJOR OCCUPATIONAL GROUPS, 1976 TO 1985[a]

OCCUPATIONAL GROUP	EMPLOYMENT (IN THOUSANDS) 1976	(PROJECTED) 1985	PERCENTAGE CHANGES	OPENINGS (IN THOUSANDS), 1976–85 TOTAL	GROWTH	REPLACEMENTS
White-collar workers	43,700	53,500	22.4	24,800	9,800	15,000
Professional and technical workers	13,329	15,800	18.2	6,400	2,400	3,900
Managers and administrators	9,315	11,300	21.0	5,400	2,000	3,400
Sales workers	5,497	6,400	16.6	3,000	900	2,100
Clerical workers	15,558	20,000	28.8	10,000	4,500	5,500
Blue-collar workers	28,958	34,100	17.9	12,800	5,200	7,700
Craft and kindred workers	11,278	13,700	21.6	5,500	2,400	3,100
Operatives	13,356	15,600	16.9	5,800	2,300	3,500
Nonfarm laborers	4,325	4,800	11.3	1,600	500	1,100
Service workers	12,005	14,800	23.4	8,100	2,800	5,300
Private household workers	1,125	900	−18.8	500	−200	700
Other service workers	10,880	13,900	27.7	7,600	3,000	4,600
Farm workers	2,822	1,900	−34.1	200	−1,000	1,200
Total	87,485	104,300	19.2	45,900	16,800	29,100

[a] Details may not add to totals because of rounding.
SOURCE: U.S. Department of Labor, Bureau of Labor Statistics, *Occupational Projections and Training Data*, Bulletin 2020, Table 2, p. 6.

gories of workers. Table 4.14 shows projected changes in employment in major occupational groups between 1976 and 1985 and the reasons for those changes.

Past and projected variations in the demand for the four major categories of workers are shown in Figure 4.5. The relative growth expected in the demand for major occupational groups is also shown in Figure 4.6. If these BLS projections are correct, the *proportion* of white-collar workers in the labor force will remain constant between 1976 and 1985.

There may also be considerable variation in the demand for specific skills within industrial sectors. In the construction industry, for example, the number of machinery operators is expected to increase by about 38 percent between 1976 and 1985, while the number of plasterers is expected to decline by 4.7 percent. During the same period, the number of computer operators is expected to decline by 4 percent, while the number of systems analysts is expected to increase by 32.9 percent.[29]

As Table 4.15 demonstrates, there are significant variations in employment related to sex and race. These variations may reflect discriminatory hiring and promotion policies (basically a demand factor) or social stereotypes of what constitutes "appropriate" work for certain subsets of the population. The underrepresentation of women in the "Managers and administrators" and "Craft and kindred workers" categories, for example, and their overrepresentation in the clerical and service workers categories suggest that we still treat certain types of work as "women's work."

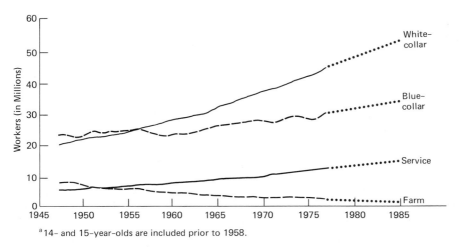

^a14- and 15-year-olds are included prior to 1958.

Figure 4.5   The Changing Demand for Major Types of Workers, 1945–1976 (actual data) and 1977–1985 (projections) (Source: U.S. Department of Labor, Bureau of Labor Statistics, *Occupational Projections and Training Data,* Bulletin 2020, Chart 2, p. 4.)

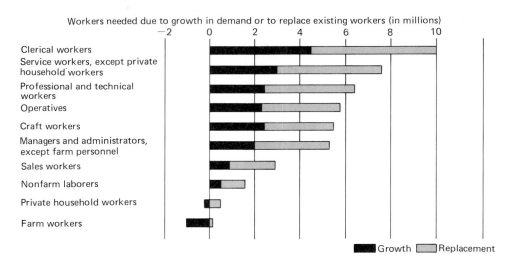

Figure 4.6 Demand Projections for Major Occupational Subsets, 1976–1985 (Source: U.S. Department of Labor, Bureau of Labor Statistics, *Occupational Projections and Training Data*, Bulletin 2020, Chart 3, p. 7.)

SUMMARY

In this chapter, we developed a simple model of the labor market, discussed the basic determinants of the labor supply and the demand for labor, and analyzed the current and projected supply of, and demand for, labor in the United States. The outstanding trends in employment in this country include (1) an absolute decline in employment in the agricultural sector, (2) a relative, and possibly an absolute, decline in blue-collar employment in the manufacturing sector, (3) an absolute and a relative increase in employment in service industries, (4) an absolute and a relative increase in employment in the public sector, and (5) an absolute and a relative increase in the number of white-collar workers, including technical and professional workers.

The projected growth in the labor force is not an accurate measure of the number of additional jobs that must be created to maintain a high level of employment; jobs must also be created to compensate for increases in productivity and to lower an unacceptably high unemployment rate. There is, moreover, no guarantee that new jobs will demand or make optimal use of the specific training and skills of people entering the labor force or workers displaced by changes in the demand for products, the location of industries, or technological innovation. We may, in fact, be "overeducating" many prospective members of the labor force for future jobs, thus laying the groundwork for a widespread underemployment of human resources that may lead, in turn, to frustration and social alienation. Such conditions may create a climate favorable to union growth or to radical political initiatives. On the other hand, if job opportunities continue to

Table 4.15 THE PERCENTAGE DISTRIBUTION OF EMPLOYED PERSONS BY OCCUPATION, SEX, AND RACE, APRIL 1980

	TOTAL	MEN	WOMEN	WHITES	BLACKS AND OTHER NONWHITES
White-collar workers	52.3	42.3	65.8	53.9	39.1
Professional & technical workers	16.3	15.8	17.1	16.8	12.8
Managers & administrators, except farm personnel	10.9	14.0	6.8	11.7	4.8
Sales workers	6.3	6.1	6.4	6.7	2.8
Clerical workers	18.8	6.4	35.4	18.8	18.6
Blue-collar workers	31.6	45.0	13.6	31.2	35.5
Craft and kindred workers	13.0	21.4	1.8	13.4	9.7
Operatives, except transport equipment	10.6	11.1	9.9	10.1	14.1
Transport equipment operatives	3.6	5.8	.7	3.4	5.0
Nonfarm laborers	4.4	6.8	1.3	4.2	6.7
Service workers	13.5	9.0	19.6	12.2	23.6
Private household workers	1.1	a	2.5	.8	3.3
Other service workers	12.4	8.9	17.1	11.4	20.3
Farm workers	2.6	3.8	1.0	2.7	1.8
Farmers & farm managers	1.5	2.3	.4	1.6	.3
Farm laborers & supervisors	1.1	1.5	.7	1.1	1.5
Total (may not equal 100 due to rounding)	100.0	100.0	100.0	100.0	100.0

a Less than 0.05 percent.
SOURCE: *Employment and Earnings* 27, no. 5 (May 1980): Table A–22, p. 36.

decline in industries and occupations that are highly unionized and to expand in areas where unions are weak, unions will find it increasingly difficult to maintain their membership base.

DISCUSSION QUESTIONS

1. It has been argued that American workers are no longer interested primarily in money income; that they are now concerned primarily with the extra-economic dimensions of the employment relationship. Do you agree?
2. Identify the various labor markets in which your college or university hires employees. What problems does this pose for the institution's administration?
3. Would you agree that in terms of labor market participation our economy has recently become more similar to a less developed than to a highly developed nation?
4. Assume that you are employed on an hourly rated summer job. Can you identify a point at which your supply curve of labor hours would become backward bending?
5. What do economists mean when they state that the demand for labor and the supply of labor are interrelated? Does this argue for or against wage reductions during a recessionary period?

6. What factors have affected the labor force participation of members of your family unit during the past decade?
7. Do you believe that the increased educational level of members of the labor force will prove a benefit or detriment in terms of maximizing employment during the next decade?
8. To what extent have you considered prospective labor supply and demand conditions in making career and educational choices? How would you evaluate your decision-making calculus to date?

SELECTED READINGS

Backward-Sloping Supply Curves

Finegan, T. Aldrich. "The Backward-Sloping Supply Curve," and Vatter, Harold G., "Rejoinder." In *Industrial and Labor Relations Review* 15, no. 2 (January 1962): pp. 230–236.
Vatter, Harold G. "On the Folklore of a Backward-Sloping Supply Curve." In *Industrial and Labor Relations Review* 14, no. 4 (July 1961): pp. 578–586.

The American Labor Market

Kreps, Juanita, and Clark, Robert. *Sex, Age, and Work: The Changing Composition of the Labor Force*. Policy Studies in Employment and Welfare, Number 23. Baltimore and London: Johns Hopkins University Press, 1975. See particularly chap. 2.
Lebergott, Stanley. *Manpower in Economic Growth: The American Record Since 1800*. New York: McGraw-Hill, 1964.
Wolfbein, Seymour L. *Employment and Unemployment in the United States: A Study of the American Labor Force*. Chicago: Science Research Associates, 1964.

Labor Force Participation Rates

Bowen, William G., and Finegan, T. Aldrich. *The Economics of Labor Force Participation*. Princeton, N.J.: Princeton University Press, 1969.
Mincer, Jacob. "Labor Force Participation of Married Women." In *Aspects of Labor Economics, a Report of the National Bureau of Economic Research*. Princeton, N.J.: Princeton University Press, 1962, pp. 63–97. A seminal work.
Parnes, Herbert S. "Labor Force Participation and Labor Mobility." In *A Review of Industrial Relations Research*. Vol. 1. Madison, Wisc.: Industrial Relations Research Association, 1970, pp. 1–33.

Hours

Henle, Peter. "Recent Growth of Paid Leisure for U.S. Workers." In *Monthly Labor Review* 85, no. 3 (March 1962): pp. 249–257.
Moore, Geoffrey H., and Hedges, Janice Neipert. "Trends in Labor and Leisure." In *Monthly Labor Review* 94, no. 2 (February 1971): pp. 3–11.
Owen, John D. *Working Hours*. Lexington, Mass.: Heath, 1979.

Sources of Labor Force Data

See the U.S. Department of Labor, Bureau of Labor Statistics' *BLS Handbook of Methods* (Bulletin 1910, pp. 9–12); *Concepts and Methods Used in Labor Force Statistics Derived from the Current Population Survey* (BLS Report No. 463, Series P–23, no. 62, October 1976); and its *Handbook of Labor Statistics, 1975 Reference Edition* (Bulletin 1865), which is updated annually by the current edition of the *Handbook of Labor Statistics*. Other good sources of current data include the *Monthly Labor Review* and the monthly *Employment and Earnings,* both published by the U.S. Department of Labor, Bureau of Labor Statistics, and the current *Employment and Training Report of the President,* which is transmitted to the Congress annually. (First published in 1963, this annual report was entitled the *Manpower and Training Report of the President* until 1976.)

Notes

1. According to T. Aldrich Finegan, "where other things are held constant, adult males with higher hourly earnings work fewer hours per week." ("Hours of Work in the United States: A Cross-sectional Analysis," in *Journal of Political Economy* LXX, no. 5 [October 1962]: p. 466.)
2. William G. Bowen and T. Aldrich Finegan, *The Economics of Labor Force Participation* (Princeton, N.J.: Princeton University Press, 1969), p. 541.
3. Herbert S. Parnes, "Labor Force Participation and Labor Mobility," in *A Review of Industrial Relations Research,* vol. 1 (Madison, Wisc.: Industrial Relations Research Association, 1970), p. 5.
4. Ibid., p. 20.
5. Ibid., pp. 15, 31–32.
6. Bowen and Finegan, *The Economics of Labor Force Participation,* p. 559.
7. Howard Hayghe, "Special Labor Force Report—Marital and Family Characteristics of Workers, March 1974," in *Monthly Labor Review* 98, no. 1 (January 1975): p. 61.
8. Paul O. Flaim and Howard N. Fullerton, Jr., "Labor Force Projections to 1990: Three Possible Paths," in *Monthly Labor Review* 101, no. 12 (December 1978): Table 3, p. 28.
9. *Employment and Training Report of the President, 1979,* Table A–1, p. 233; Table B–14, p. 313.
10. Flaim and Fullerton, "Labor Force Projections to 1990," p. 29.
11. Ibid., p. 30.
12. "High-Level Manpower, Productivity, and Economic Progress," in John T. Dunlop and Vasilii P. Diatchenko, eds., *Labor Productivity* (New York: McGraw-Hill, 1964), p. 330. Original emphasis omitted.
13. Max L. Carey, "Revised Occupational Projections to 1985," in *Monthly Labor Review* 99, no. 1 (November 1976): p. 10.
14. U.S. Department of Labor, Bureau of Labor Statistics, *Occupational Projections and Training Data,* Bulletin 2020, Table 10, p. 22.
15. Dixie Sommers and Alan Eck, "Occupational Mobility in the American Labor Force," in *Monthly Labor Review* 100, no. 1 (January 1977): p. 5.
16. Ibid., p. 3.

17. U.S. Bureau of the Census, *Statistical Abstract of the United States: 1978,* Table 44, p. 38; Table 46, p. 39.

18. Peter Henle, "The Quiet Revolution in Leisure Time," in *Occupational Outlook Quarterly* 9, no. 2 (May 1965).

19. John D. Owen, "Workweeks and Leisure: An Analysis of Trends, 1948–75," in *Monthly Labor Review* 99, no. 8 (August 1976): p. 3.

20. *Employment and Training Report of the President, 1979,* Table B–13, p. 312.

21. *Statistical Abstract of the United States: 1979,* Table 915, p. 555.

22. Ibid., Table 955, p. 573.

23. *Statistical Abstract of the United States: 1978,* Table 939, p. 573.

24. Valerie A. Personick, "Industry Output and Employment: BLS Projections to 1990," in *Monthly Labor Review* 102, no. 4 (April 1979): Table 5, p. 10.

25. Ibid., p. 10. The projections in the table reflect specific assumptions about unemployment, labor productivity, and government taxes and spending—for example, an unemployment rate of 5.5 percent in 1980, 4.7 percent in 1985, and 4.5 percent in 1990. (Ibid., p. 4.)

26. *Employment and Earnings* 27, no. 7 (July 1980): Table B–1, p. 91. Data are preliminary.

27. Ewan Clague, *Effects of Technological Change on Occupational Patterns in the United States* (Washington, D.C.: U.S. Department of Labor, December 8, 1964, mimeo), p. 9.

28. Ibid., p. 7. Original emphasis omitted.

29. U.S. Department of Labor, Bureau of Labor Statistics, *Occupational Projections and Training Data,* Bulletin 2020, Table B–1, pp. 81 and 84.

Chapter 5
WAGE DETERMINATION: BASIC CONCEPTS AND EARLY THEORIES

Psychologists and sociologists have emphasized the variety of needs men and women seek to satisfy in the workplace. Economic, physiological, sociological, and psychological factors determine whether a job is considered good or bad. As we pointed out in Chapter 4, for most workers the basic requirements of a good job are (1) continuity and (2) an adequate wage. Since the wages and salaries that constitute employee *incomes* are production *costs* to employers, the determination of wages is a principal focus of labor economics and one of the most important aspects of collective bargaining.

In this chapter and in Chapter 6, we will review the development of wage theory and see how wages are determined in the absence of unions. In Chapters 19, 20, and 23, we will discuss the determination of wages by collective bargaining and the impact of unions on the wage-employment relationship. First, however, we will examine a number of concepts related to the determination of wages. While many of these concepts, because they have a certain statistical validity, are used as bench marks in establishing company wage policies and in collective bargaining, they are basically analytical devices. "The *reality* of wages is that millions of employees each receive some rate of pay and accumulate certain earnings per hour, per week, and per annum."[1]

The distinction between *wage theories* and *wage criteria* deserves emphasis. Wage criteria, such as changes in the cost of living or a pattern of wage increases in another firm or industry, may be used as bench marks in unilateral employer wage determinations or in collective bargaining, but they do not purport to explain the *process* of wage determination.

BASIC WAGE CONCEPTS

Employers and theoretical economists often view wages simply as a cost of doing business, failing to appreciate that this cost represents the sole or primary source of income for most employees and is a basic determinant of the level of living they enjoy. Labor economists emphasize the distinction between labor and other factors of production. They believe that the theoretical apparatus used to analyze the pricing and employment of other factors of production must be modified considerably when the object of analysis is the contribution of human beings to production.

Wage Rates and Labor Costs

A *wage rate,* the amount paid to a worker per unit of time employed or per unit of output produced, is seldom the same as the total *labor cost* of a unit of output. Under a straight *piecework system,* the wage paid to a worker represents the *direct* wage cost of a unit of output. Under the more common system of paying workers for time worked, the wage cost per unit will depend on the number of units produced and will vary with productivity. Under either system, the total *labor cost* usually exceeds the *wage payment* per worker because the employer also pays for supplementary, or fringe, benefits.

To make theoretical analyses easier, economists often assume (1) that wage costs represent total labor costs and (2) that there is a homogeneous supply of labor. If a work force is homogeneous, the wage cost per unit of output will be the same for workers on piecework or for hourly rated workers who earn the same base rate and use identical equipment.

Hourly Wages and Hourly Earnings

The *straight-time hourly rate* for a job (so many dollars and cents per hour) is termed the *standard,* or *base, rate.* Average hourly *earnings* may exceed the base rate if higher rates are paid for overtime work and for work done during special periods—at night, say, or on holidays.

If overtime work is permitted or encouraged in periods when labor is in short supply, earnings may increase even though base rates of pay remain fixed. The movement of workers to higher pay grades will also produce higher average earnings. Both conditions have contributed to an upward drift in wages in many industrial nations since the 1940s, despite the presumed stability introduced into the wage structure by mandatory controls and government-encouraged "social contracts" between organized labor and employer associations that attempted to limit wage increases to reduce the rate of inflation.

Incentive Systems

Approximately one-quarter of the wage and salary earners in the United States are compensated under some form of *incentive system*. Under a *straight piecework system*, wages are based on the number of units produced; under *bonus systems*, rewards are given for reaching or exceeding a set goal or task; *commissions* are sometimes paid on sales. Incentive systems appeal to employers because they relate wages to output in a precise way. Workers, on the other hand, particularly trade unionists, are suspicious of incentive systems. They believe that the real purpose of such systems is to get workers to produce more without paying them a proportionate increase in wages.*

Supplementary or Fringe Benefits

In addition to direct wages, employers today pay for an increasing number of supplementary benefits received by employees. Some supplementary payments, such as social security contributions, are required by law. Others are benefits provided at the option of the employer or as a result of collective bargaining agreements. Some (such as payments for time called in but not worked or paid lunch hours) may appear in the worker's pay envelope, but many are payments to public and private pension and welfare plans.

Fringe benefits proliferated both during and since World War II, and they constitute an increasing percentage of total labor cost. According to the annual survey of employee benefits published by the U.S. Chamber of Commerce in 1979, the mean benefit payment, including contributions for social security, for 858 firms in 1978 was $2.47 per payroll hour, or 36.9 percent of the firms' total payrolls.[2] The benefit payments included:

1. the employers' share of legally required payments, which equaled 9 percent of the firms' total payroll;
2. the employers' share of pension, insurance, and other agreed upon payments, which equaled 12.2 percent of their total payrolls;
3. paid rest periods, lunch periods, etc., which equaled 3.6 percent of their total payrolls;
4. payments for time not worked (vacations, holidays, sick leave, etc.), which equaled 9.7 percent of their total payrolls; and
5. other items (profit sharing payments, bonuses, etc.), which equaled 2.4 percent of their total payrolls.[3]

* See below, pp. 484–485.

According to the same report, benefit payments for 159 identical companies "increased from 23.4 percent of payroll in 1957 to 29 percent in 1967 and to 40.5 percent in 1978."[4]

WAGE DIFFERENTIALS AND WAGE STRUCTURES

The way wages are determined is generally analyzed on two "levels": (1) on a *microeconomic level,* concentrating on particular occupations, firms, industries, or regions; and (2) on a *macroeconomic level,* studying the wage rate in the economy as a whole and the factors determining labor's share of national income. Labor economists have traditionally been most interested in analyzing (1) how wages are determined within firms and industries and (2) the wages paid to different categories of workers. The concepts of "wage differentials" and "wage structure" have facilitated this type of analysis.

A *wage differential* is an absolute or percentage difference between the base or average wages received by individuals or subsets of workers in specific categories. The concept of a *wage structure* encompasses the relationship between all wage categories. As one study of the subject notes,

> the concept of [a] "wage structure" involves a considerable degree of abstraction. All that one finds in reality is hundreds of thousands of rates for specific jobs in particular establishments. . . .
>
> One is forced by the sheer mass of the material to summarize. It is this process of summarizing which gives rise, in a sense artificially, to the "wage structures" and "wage differentials" which are analyzed by statisticians and economists.[5]

Five basic categories of wage differentials are used in classifying and summarizing wage data: occupational, geographic, interindustry, interplant, and personal differentials.

OCCUPATIONAL DIFFERENCES

There are normally differences in the wage levels of different occupational groups in the same firm or industry in a given geographic area. Table 5.1 illustrates the differences in earnings of people holding various white-collar jobs in Boston banks in December 1976.

GEOGRAPHIC DIFFERENCES

There are often differences in the wages of workers in the same industry and occupation who are in different geographic areas. Table 5.2 shows how the average hourly earnings of general maintenance mechanics in the industrial chemical industry differed in various regions of the country in June of 1976. Sometimes, however, some portion of what appears to be a "geographic" differential is the result of different degrees of union organization in different parts of the country.

Table 5.1 OCCUPATION DIFFERENCES IN EARNINGS IN BOSTON BANKS, DECEMBER 1976

OCCUPATION	AVERAGE HOURLY EARNINGS (STRAIGHT TIME)
Computer systems analysts	$9.34
Consumer loan officers	6.95
Computer operators	4.93
Secretaries	4.86
Stenographers	4.20
Bookkeeping machine operators	3.95
Keypunch operators, full time	3.81
Tellers, full time	3.66
Typists	3.42
File clerks, full time	3.20

SOURCE: U.S. Department of Labor, Bureau of Labor Statistics, *Industry Wage Surveys: Banking and Life Insurance, December 1976,* Bulletin 1988, Table 1, pp. 10–11.

INTERINDUSTRY DIFFERENCES

Often, there are differences in wage levels for workers in the same occupational category and geographic area in different industries. Table 5.3 shows the average hourly earnings of motor vehicle mechanics in industrial sectors in metropolitan areas of the Northeast in 1976.

Comparisons of average hourly rates in different industries are sometimes cited as examples of interindustry differences, but these figures do not necessarily reflect differences in wage rates for workers in the *same occupation.* For example, construction workers, on the average, earn more than workers in wholesale and retail establishments. In 1979, nonsupervisory workers earned an average of $9.26 an hour in contract construction and $5.06 in wholesale and retail trade.[6]

Table 5.2 GEOGRAPHIC DIFFERENCES IN EARNINGS OF GENERAL MAINTENANCE MECHANICS IN THE INDUSTRIAL CHEMICAL INDUSTRY, JUNE 1976

REGION	MEAN HOURLY EARNINGS (STRAIGHT TIME)
United States	$6.61
Southwest	7.28
Pacific	7.08
Mountain	6.74
Great Lakes	6.55
Middle Atlantic	6.49
Border States	6.36
Southeast	6.20
Middle West	6.07
New England	5.36

SOURCE: U.S. Department of Labor, Bureau of Labor Statistics, *Industry Wage Survey: Industrial Chemicals, June 1976,* Bulletin 1978, Table 3, pp. 7–9.

Table 5.3 INTERINDUSTRY DIFFERENCES IN EARNINGS OF MOTOR VEHICLE
MECHANICS IN METROPOLITAN AREAS OF THE NORTHEAST, 1976

INDUSTRIAL SECTOR	AVERAGE HOURLY EARNINGS (STRAIGHT TIME)
Transportation, communications, and other public utilities	$7.13
Nonmanufacturing industries	6.96
Wholesale trade	6.67
Manufacturing	6.31
Retail trade	6.07

SOURCE: U.S. Department of Labor, Bureau of Labor Statistics, *Handbook of Labor Statistics,
1978,* Bulletin 2000, Table 104, pp. 363–367.

However, much of this apparent "interindustry difference" in wages reflects
higher skill requirements and is in fact an *occupational* difference. The greater
degree of unionization in the construction industry and the intermittent nature
of employment in many construction trades also account for part of the difference
in hourly pay rates.

INTERPLANT DIFFERENCES

Even establishments in the same industry and geographic area may pay different
wages for the same type of work. A study of wage variations in cotton textile jobs
in the South, for example, concluded that "[i]nter-firm uniformity of rates in the
same locality for the same grade of labor is rare and exceptional."[7]

PERSONAL DIFFERENCES

Occasionally there are differences in the wages of workers in the same establishment and occupation besides those related to seniority. In firms without systematic rate structures, there may even be a unique rate for almost every worker,
reflecting "the personal efficiency of the individual, the circumstances under
which he [or she] was hired, and the judgment of the foreman or supervisor."[8]
Differences in wages may also reflect discriminatory employment policies. As
Table 5.4 shows, in 1974, women's earnings were lower than men's in every major
occupational group. This would certainly seem to suggest a widespread pattern
of discrimination on the basis of a personal characteristic, sex.

Some General Observations on Wage Differentials

Differences in wages would normally develop in perfectly competitive labor
markets. They would presumably help to allocate resources by *compensating*
workers for differences in the level of education, skill, or effort required by
various jobs and for variations in working conditions in those jobs. Other differences in wages may reflect imperfections in the operation of a labor market, they
may be based on custom, or they may stem from perceived rather than actual
differences in job requirements. Wage differentials that are not required for
efficient resource allocation are termed *real,* or *noncompensating,* differentials.

Table 5.4 THE MEDIAN WEEKLY EARNINGS OF FULL-TIME WAGE AND SALARY WORKERS, BY SEX AND OCCUPATION, MAY 1974

OCCUPATION	MEDIAN WEEKLY EARNINGS		WOMEN'S EARNINGS AS A PERCENTAGE OF MEN'S
	MEN	WOMEN	
Professional and technical workers	$263	$188	71.5
Managers and administrators, except farm employees	274	161	58.8
Sales workers	223	95	42.6
Clerical workers	192	129	67.2
Craft and kindred workers	214	127	59.3
Transport equipment operatives	182	114	62.6
Operatives, except transport	170	107	62.9
Nonfarm laborers	153	106	69.3
Private household workers	a	49	a
Other service workers	152	95	62.5
Farm workers	110	90	81.8

a Less than 0.05 percent of all workers.
SOURCE: Adapted from Thomas F. Bradshaw and John F. Stinson, "Trends in weekly earnings: an analysis," in *Monthly Labor Review* 98, no. 8 (August 1975): Table 4, p. 27.

Unfortunately, the analysis of apparently simple types of wage differentials often proves complex. Job descriptions and job requirements vary from plant to plant and from industry to industry, and one cannot assume that workers of equal training and ability are being compared even within a single job classification. Many apparent interindustry and interpersonal differences in wages are a result of differing skill requirements. The degree of union organization may also account for some portion of such differences.

Through multiple regression analysis, economists today are coming to understand many of the factors contributing to the development of wage differentials, including (1) the North-South differential (which is geographic), (2) the differential between skilled and unskilled labor (which is occupational), and the male-female and black-white differentials, which are based in part on perceived differences often linked to overt or subtle forms of discrimination.

OTHER MEASURES OF ECONOMIC WELL-BEING

Annual Incomes and Take-Home Pay

Workers' annual incomes, which depend on the number of hours worked per week (possibly on more than one job), the continuity of employment throughout the year, and the amount of overtime and other premium pay received, are a better measure of economic well-being than hourly earnings. They are not, however, a completely satisfactory measure of the workers' command over commodities and services in the marketplace. This is because (1) the workers' *take-home pay* in dollars is usually less than they earn and (2) the *real* value of their income may be eroded by inflation or (less frequently) increase when prices fall. As a result, the typical worker is more interested in take-home pay than in gross earnings and is concerned with cost-of-living raises as well as increases in pay based on merit or seniority.

Real and Money Incomes

The emphasis on wage rates and total dollar incomes in labor negotiations and in the media tends to obscure the fundamental concern of workers with their *real* income, that is, with the amount of commodities and services for which the money they earn can be exchanged. When there is inflation, a worker whose after-tax wage or salary increases at a rate greater than the increase in prices will realize an increase in real income, whereas a retired person receiving a fixed income will find that his or her level of living has deteriorated. To measure changes in real incomes, money incomes must be adjusted to compensate for changes in the value of the dollar. Price indexes are used to make such adjustments.

PRICE INDEXES

A *price index* expresses prices in a given year as a percentage of prices in a base year. More precisely, the sum of the prices of *selected* commodities and services in a given year is divided by the sum of the prices of the same commodities and services in an appropriate base year, or perhaps by an average of total prices over a period of years. In essence, this is the procedure followed by the Bureau of Labor Statistics in computing the Consumer Price Index. The CPI is *not*, technically, a general "cost of living" index because it does not measure changes in all living costs.

Since January 1978, the federal government has issued two consumer price indexes: (1) a "new" CPI for all urban consumers, some 80 percent of the population; and (2) a "revised" traditional index based on the prices of a market basket of commodities and services purchased by urban wage and clerical workers and their families, some 35 to 40 percent of the total population.[9] Both indexes presently use 1967 as a base year.

Prices are collected in 85 urban areas for some 400 items. The price of each item in the market basket is "weighted," or multiplied by an appropriate factor, so that the total amount "spent" accurately reflects consumer purchases. The total for each area is weighted according to its population, and data from various areas are combined to get an average index for the United States. This figure is then compared with the base period total of prices for the same items and the fractional result is multiplied by 100 so that the index is expressed relative to a base of 100. The traditional CPI for urban wage earners and clerical workers from 1929 to 1980 is shown in Table 5.5 and that for all urban consumers com-

Table 5.5 THE CONSUMER PRICE INDEX FOR URBAN WAGE EARNERS AND CLERICAL WORKERS, ANNUAL AVERAGES, 1929–198_

				ALL URBAN CONSUMER INDEX	
YEAR	INDEX	YEAR	INDEX	YEAR	INDEX
1929	51.3	1960	88.7		
1933	38.8	1961	89.6		
1939	41.6	1962	90.6		
		1963	91.7		
1940	42.0	1964	92.9		
1941	44.1	1965	94.5		
1942	48.8	1966	97.2		
1943	51.8	1967	100.0		
1944	52.7	1968	104.2		
1945	53.9	1969	109.8		
1946	58.5				
1947	66.9	1970	116.3		
1948	72.1	1971	121.3		
1949	71.4	1972	125.3		
		1973	133.1		
1950	72.1	1974	147.7		
1951	77.8	1975	161.2		
1952	79.5	1976	170.5		
1953	80.1	1977	181.5		
1954	80.5	1978	195.3	1978	195.4
1955	80.2	1979	217.7	1979	217.4
1956	81.4				
1957	84.3	1980	(July) 247.8	1980	(July) 247.6
1958	86.6	1981		1981	
1959	87.3	1982		1982	

SOURCE: *Economic Report of the President, Transmitted to the Congress January 1980, Together with the Annual Report of the Council of Economic Advisers,* Table B–49, p. 259; and *Monthly Labor Review* 103, no. 5 (May 1980): Table 22, p. 85. July 1980 data from U.S. Department of Labor, Bureau of Labor Statistics, *Press Release: USDL-80-52,* August 22, 1980.

mencing in 1978. Space has also been provided in the table for entering new data for both indexes.

WAGE "DEFLATION"

Wages for any year can be "deflated" (expressed in dollars with a constant value) by dividing them by the price index for that year and multiplying by 100. For example, suppose a worker earned $8,000 in 1967, when the CPI was 100. If the worker earned $12,000 in 1970, and if the CPI was 120 in that year, how much did the real income rise? The real wage in 1967 was $\frac{\$8,000}{100} \times (100)$, or $8,000, while in 1970 it was $\frac{\$12,000}{120} \times (100)$, or ten thousand 1967 dollars. Thus, an increase of $4,000, or 50 percent, in the worker's wages between 1967 and 1970 was, as a consequence of a 20 percent rise in prices, equivalent to an increase of only $2,000, or 25 percent, in real wages. (Had the worker earned less than $9,600 in 1970, real income would actually have decreased.)

Conclusion

Our discussion of basic wage and income concepts points up the difficulty of defining "the" wage problem in operationally precise terms. A small business-person, the wage administrator of a large corporation, the union leader in a highly competitive industry with a local product market, the skilled worker in a building trade, and the theoretical economist all have somewhat different perceptions of the process of wage determination.

The wage theories developed to explain (or rationalize?) managerial deci-sions or collective bargaining demands often reflect specific interests or orien-tations, and the assumptions underlying these theories must be identified to determine the contribution they may be able to make to the analysis or resolution of a problem. The following section describes the use, and the limitations, of contemporary wage theories.

THE ROLE OF WAGE THEORIES

Wage theories are attempts by economists to explain, rationally, how wages are determined. Some theorists consider wage theories part of the theory of distribu-tion, which deals with the division of income between several factors of produc-tion. Thus "traditional" wage theories have attempted to explain (1) how the wage rate for a homogeneous group of workers is determined, (2) variations in the wages of different types of labor, and (3) labor's share in the country's national income.

Following World War II, interest shifted to such problems as what deter-mines the general level of real wages and what determines the structure of wage rates among firms, industries, and occupations. Thanks in part to the rapid de-velopment of labor-management relations as a field of study and in part to a growing interest among macroeconomic theorists in the relationships between economic aggregates, these issues became part of the core of wage theory.

Contemporary Wage Analysis

Three examples will show the scope of contemporary wage analysis:

According to *the theory of the firm*, wage decisions are one of a number of operational decisions that must be made on a continuing basis by the manager of a firm. Other decision-making areas include the technical organization of production, product development, market research, pricing policy, sales organiza-tion, accounting, and finance. To a manager, the cost of labor is one determinant of how the various factors of production are combined, of the volume of production, and of the ability of the firm to continue to operate in the short and the long run.

Labor costs are also a key variable in determining the *total* level of employment and output in *all the firms that constitute a given industry*. Analyses of how wages are determined at this level involve the extension to a group of firms of the microanalytical techniques and procedures used in applying the theory to the firm.

A third type of analysis views wage payments as *a component of national income*. As Table 5.6 shows, various types of employee compensation, including wage supplements, are the largest component of national income. These payments are an important determinant of the general level of production, employment, and prices.

A Comment on Wages as a Component of National Income

The data in Table 5.6 appear to contradict a widely held view that the shares of labor and capital in national income have remained relatively constant in the United States. However, the "increase" in labor's share is due largely to a change in the industry mix, particularly a decline in the number of agricultural workers and, more recently, a growth in the number of public employees. The shift of workers from agriculture to other industries decreased the income of unincorporated businesses (a category that included most farm proprietors) and increased employee compensation as the former farm proprietors became wage and salary workers. The growth of the public sector caused a relative increase

Table 5.6 EMPLOYEE COMPENSATION AS A PERCENTAGE OF NATIONAL INCOME, SELECTED YEARS, 1929–198_

YEAR	EMPLOYEE COMPENSATION AS A PERCENTAGE OF NATIONAL INCOME	YEAR	EMPLOYEE COMPENSATION AS A PERCENTAGE OF NATIONAL INCOME
1929	60.2	1970	76.3
1932	73.2	1971	75.8
1937	66.3	1972	75.1
1942	62.8	1973	75.1
1947	66.4	1974	77.1
1952	68.5	1975	76.4
1957	70.8	1976	76.0
1962	71.1	1977	76.0
1967	72.0	1978	75.7
1968	72.8	1979	75.8
1969	74.4	1980	

SOURCE: Data for 1929–1977 are based on the U.S. Department of Labor, Bureau of Labor Statistics, *Handbook of Labor Statistics, 1978,* Bulletin 2000, Table 174, pp. 600–604. Data for 1978 and 1979 are based on *Economic Report of the President, Transmitted to the Congress January 1980, Together with the Annual Report of the Council of Economic Advisers,* Table B–19, p. 224.

in employee compensation because the output of this sector is computed on the basis of labor inputs. When national income data are standardized to take such changes into account, the "share of labor" exhibits greater long-run stability.

THE DEVELOPMENT OF WAGE THEORIES TO 1870

The evolution of wage theory since the Middle Ages has reflected an initial movement from very general theories toward more rigorous microanalytical theories and, more recently, a renewed interest in aggregate theory (macroanalysis) stimulated by the work of John Maynard, Lord Keynes, during the Great Depression.

Economists tend to concentrate on those aspects of economic theory that seem most relevant to the problems of the day, and the history of wage theory represents a series of pragmatic responses to current conditions rather than the conscious refinement of a set of theoretical principles. This does not mean that a review of past theories is useless. On the contrary, as one economist points out, such a review

> is of immediate value to the person who studies the wage question today. . . . [T]he development of wage theory is not so much a progress from doctrines which are less "true" to those which are more so; to a great extent it consists of replacing one theory by another because certain assumptions which may have been reasonably important in one period have become irrelevant or meaningless in the next one.[10]

This section on the development of wage theory is designed to (1) show the assumptions and limitation of past wage theories and (2) provide a framework for analyzing how wages are determined in the American economy.

Early Wage Theories

A "FAIR" WAGE
Ethical, religious, and political beliefs often provide a basis for economic theories. Throughout the medieval period, the discussion of economic questions had strong ethical overtones. According to the "just price" theory of St. Thomas Aquinas, a Christian employer should not exploit any bargaining advantage he might possess but was bound, on moral grounds, to pay his workers a "fair" wage.

MERCANTILISM
The rise of *mercantilism* during the sixteenth and seventeenth centuries brought a shift from ethical to politicoeconomic principles. Wages were to be kept low to enable a nation to compete in world markets and to maintain a "favorable" balance of trade.

THE SUBSISTENCE THEORY
During the eighteenth century and early in the nineteenth century the subsistence theory of wages suggested that economic growth would not raise real

wages. This theory rested on limited assumptions. In the long run, real wages would be determined by the income required for a worker and his family to subsist. If income rose above this amount, earlier marriages would be encouraged, workers would have more children, and the increased supply of labor would exert a downward pressure on wages until income returned to the subsistence level. If wages fell below the minimum needed for subsistence, a rise in the death rate and the postponement of marriages would decrease the supply of labor until a balance was restored. Sophisticated versions of this theory recognized that real wages might, however, increase in the short run.

The trend toward smaller families has produced quite a different scenario in most Western nations; however, the subsistence theory continues to have relevance for many underdeveloped and developing nations, including India, China, and parts of Africa, in which population pressure keeps real incomes at low levels.

The Classical Period

ADAM SMITH

Adam Smith's *Wealth of Nations,* published in 1776, which provided the foundation for classical economic thought, was the first major attempt to synthesize economic theory. However, it is difficult to discern a unified wage theory in Smith's writings; instead, we find bits and pieces that reflect a variety of approaches to the analysis of wage levels. Smith developed a modified subsistence theory to explain the *general* wage level, noting that the demand for labor might temporarily raise wages above the subsistence level. He observed that specific wages depended on the contract made between masters and workmen and held that in ordinary circumstances, "masters must generally have the advantage" in bargaining over the terms of employment. Nevertheless, he was optimistic about the possibility of increasing real wages in the long run. He argued that with an increase in national wealth, the demand for labor would increase and wages would rise; "the liberal reward of labour . . . is the necessary effect, [and] the natural symptom of increasing national wealth."[11]

Smith identified national well-being with individual welfare, and this led him to consider the factors responsible for *individual differences* in wages. He argued that in a competitive labor market wages would tend toward equality, but that differences in wages might arise due to imperfections in a market (a lack of "perfect liberty") and to "certain circumstances in the employments themselves."[12] These circumstances included (1) the ease or hardship, cleanliness or dirtiness, and honorableness or dishonorableness of a job; (2) the easiness and cheapness, or the difficulty and expense, of learning a business; (3) the constancy or inconstancy of employment; (4) the small or great trust that must be reposed in workers; and (5) the probability or improbability of success in different types of employment.[13] Today, wage differentials that compensate people for such differences in occupations are called *compensating* or *equalizing* differentials.

Most members of the classical school of economics assumed that a free market would automatically establish "appropriate" wage differentials and that theoretical analyses could therefore focus on the general wage rate paid to homogeneous units of labor and on labor's share of the national product.

DAVID RICARDO

Other members of the classical school were less hopeful than Smith about the possibility of raising real wages. According to the Malthusian doctrine, increases in population would necessarily outrun increases in the means of subsistence in the long run, and wages would fall to a subsistence level. This subsistence level was not necessarily an *absolute* minimum according to David Ricardo, whose closely reasoned *Principles of Political Economy and Taxation* established him as the foremost classical economist after Smith. It would vary at different times in the same country and differ very materially in different countries. That is, it would essentially depend "on the habits and customs of the people."[14]

Smith had argued that in a primitive economy that did not use capital, the value of a good would reflect the labor time involved in its production. Ricardo used a modified labor theory of value in his model of the operation of the economy. He did *not*, as did Marx at a later date, adopt a *pure* labor theory of value because he recognized that a return must be paid on capital advanced during the production of a good. However, he believed that the quantity of labor embodied in goods was a useful approximation of their value and would explain much about the *relative* structure of prices in an economy.

Variations on the Classical Theme

A number of *early socialist writers,* concerned about the plight of the laboring class in countries experiencing an industrial revolution, used a strict version of the subsistence theory as a basis for their advocacy of political action to improve the workers' condition. In this, they parted company with Smith and Ricardo, who were champions of a *laisser-faire* economy. Ricardo, for example, argued that "like all other contracts, wages should be left to the fair and free competition of the market, and should never be controlled by the interference of the legislature."[15]

KARL MARX

Karl Marx used classical economics, particularly the labor theory of value, as a point of departure for his analysis of the exploitation of the working class. According to Marx, workers in a capitalistic system were exploited because they were not paid in full for the labor they performed. The theoretical reasons advanced to support this thesis were complex, but the essence of the theory may be stated briefly.

Marx believed that labor created all value. The *exchange value* of any commodity was measured by the amount of abstract human labor it contained. This in turn depended on the labor time needed to produce the commodity or, in Marx's terms, on the "socially necessary labor-time" expended in production. In the case of labor itself, this socially necessary labor time was the time required to earn a real income sufficient to sustain life at a subsistence level. The exchange value of labor (the amount the worker had to be paid) was therefore equivalent to a subsistence wage. However, during a workday a worker could produce in total value more than enough to support himself and his dependents. That is, the *use value* of his labor (the exchange value of the total product) was greater than the exchange value of his labor. This difference constituted an *unearned surplus* that was *expropriated* by the employer.

This expropriation was possible because the supply of labor was kept greater than the number of jobs by certain characteristics of the capitalist system, particularly technological progress and recurring economic crises. The competitive threat posed by "the industrial reserve army" of unemployed workers outside the factory gates enabled employers to depress the wages of those at work. Marx concluded that only the overthrow of capitalism would lead to a permanent improvement in the condition of the laboring class. His theory of the exploitation of workers has been incorporated into recent neo-Marxist critiques of capitalist economies.

THE WAGES FUND

Adam Smith, in explaining changes in the level of real wages, argued that wages were paid out of a fund determined by surplus revenue and surplus stock. During the nineteenth century, a more formal theory of a *wages fund* was developed. John Stewart Mill was the leading exponent of the theory, which held that the general wage level was determined by the relationship between the total funds available to pay wages during a given period (demand) and the size of the labor force (supply).

The theory was held to demonstrate the futility of attempts by labor, and by unions in particular, to raise the *general* wage level. However, Mill acknowledged that a group of workers (the members of a union, for example) might raise their wages at the expense of other members of the labor force.

There were several basic errors in this theory, which Mill ultimately abandoned: it failed to explain why labor could not obtain a greater share of a given national product, and it assumed that the amount of capital available to sustain workers was a *fixed* quantity determined by past events and available at the *beginning* of a production period, rather than a *variable* quantity that was the result not just of past accumulations of capital but of *current* production. Despite these limitations, the wages fund theory represented a significant advance because it emphasized the *importance of demand* in determining wages.

In order to explain the determinants of the demand for labor, economists began to examine the relationship between wages and the value of labor. This led to the development and general acceptance of marginal productivity analysis.

MARGINAL PRODUCTIVITY THEORY: THE NEOCLASSICAL PERIOD

Although the rudiments of marginal analysis may be discerned in the writings of earlier economists, the formal theory was developed independently by William Stanley Jevons, Karl Menger, and Leon Walras about 1870. Whereas classical theorists had been interested in explaining the *distribution of national income,* neoclassical theorists used mathematical techniques to analyze *relative prices* in product and resource markets. This approach was first used in analyzing marginal utility in relation to consumer demand and then extended as marginal productivity analysis to the theory of distribution. Phillip H. Wicksteed, Leon Walras, and John Bates Clark were instrumental in this extension of the analysis. Thus, their initial interest was in determining the prices (value) of particular commodities as a function of the demand for them. From these prices, they derived the prices for productive services "and thus moved from the subject of 'value' into that of income-distribution."[16] The neoclassical emphasis on microeconomic analysis led to the neglect of more comprehensive theories dealing with total output and employment and the problems of economic growth.

In its original form, marginal productivity theory assumed that there was perfect competition in both product and factor markets and that this unregulated competition allocated resources in a way that maximized consumer welfare while ensuring full employment. The theory was developed during a period in which nineteenth-century liberalism, exemplified by the doctrine of *laisser-faire,* was under attack from socialists and other groups. Not unexpectedly, the neoclassicists' analysis, with its reassuring political implications, was embraced by nineteenth-century libertarians and in this century by the defenders of private enterprise.

Classical economists had emphasized the supply of labor in explaining how wages were determined. Neoclassical thinkers emphasized the role of demand, explicitly or implicitly assuming the supply of labor to be given. They based their analysis of the demand for labor (and the distribution of income) on a *law of variable proportions* (or *diminishing physical productivity*). Employers, they argued, try to combine the several factors of production so as to maximize profits. In the short run, they are unable to vary the quantity of *every* factor (the amount of capital equipment for example is fixed). If the amount of one or more *variable* inputs used in the production process (that is, one or more factors that are *not fixed* in the short run) is increased, there will be relatively less of the fixed factors to work with, and the use of these additional variable inputs will not bring a proportionate increase in total output. Total output will probably rise, but at a diminishing rate, at least after some level of output is reached. In the terminology of the neoclassicists, the *marginal product* (the *additional* product resulting from the use of another unit of a variable input) *will decrease* as additional units of the variable factor are employed.

This physical law may be understood more easily if we assume that only one

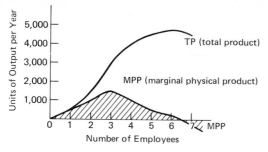

Figure 5.1   Total Output, Marginal Output, and Employment for a Small Firm

factor of production, labor, is variable. Table 5.7 shows what might happen to the yearly production of a small firm if additional workers were employed. Figure 5.1 is a graphical representation of the same situation. Hiring additional workers increases output more than proportionately at first because it permits a more efficient division of labor and more efficient use of capital equipment. After a point however, output per additional worker begins to decline (diminishing physical returns set in.) Thus the *marginal physical product* (MPP) curve first rises and then declines.

The *total area* under the curve represents the firm's total output (in terms of the calculus, the marginal product is the first derivative of the total product).

The Demand for Labor in the Short Run

MPP curves show the marginal *physical* productivity of labor. Employers are not interested in producing a given physical output for its own sake, but in the profit they can make by selling that output. If there is perfect competition in a market, the price of the commodity is not affected by increases in the output of a particular firm and the *value* of the added output will equal the number of units produced times the market price.* An employer, simply by estimating the marginal productivity of labor, can determine whether hiring another worker at a given wage is advantageous. A work force should be expanded so long as the value of the additional physical product produced exceeds or equals the cost of hiring more workers. This will maximize the firm's profits, or minimize its losses, in the short run.**

---

* In perfect competition: (1) many small firms are producing an undifferentiated product; (2) no firm is large enough to affect the prevailing market price by changing its level of output; (3) there is complete freedom of entry into and exit from the industry; and (4) consumers and producers are fully aware of existing market conditions.

** In the short run, fixed costs must be met whether a plant is in operation or shut down. If a firm can cover all its variable costs and some of its fixed costs by continuing to operate, it will minimize its losses.

Table 5.7 TOTAL OUTPUT, MARGINAL OUTPUT, AND EMPLOYMENT FOR A SMALL FIRM

NUMBER OF WORKERS	TOTAL OUTPUT PER YEAR (THOUSANDS OF UNITS)	ADDITION TO TOTAL OUTPUT (MARGINAL PHYSICAL PRODUCT)
1	500	500
2	1,500	1,000
3	3,000	1,500
4	4,000	1,000
5	4,500	500
6	4,750	250
7	4,500	−250

Marginal Productivity Theory as a Theory of Employment

Neoclassical theorists usually assumed that all workers were equally efficient and were paid the same wage. Given the market wage, they argued, employers extended their production until the value of the decreasing marginal product of labor equaled the market wage (the marginal cost of hiring a worker). In Figure 5.2, given a market wage W, which intersects the value of marginal product curve VMP at W', the firm will employ L' workers. Thus the VMP curve is also the firm's demand curve for labor in the short run. Since the demand for labor depends on the demand for the goods it produces, this is termed a *derived demand*.

The supply of labor to the firm, WW, in Figure 5.2 is infinitely elastic because the quantity of labor hired by the firm has no effect on the market price (wage) of labor. The firm can continue to hire additional workers at the same wage for as long as it wishes. If it employs L' workers, its total payroll will equal $W \times L'$, or the area $OL'W'W$.

The aspects of marginal productivity theory we have talked about so far apply to the *employment decisions of a firm*. If we accept the assumption that these employment decisions *do not* affect the market price of labor, the theory may be considered precise but, in an operational sense, superficial. It is precise because, by definition, an employer who succeeds in maximizing profits or minimizing losses necessarily conforms to its assumptions. It is superficial because

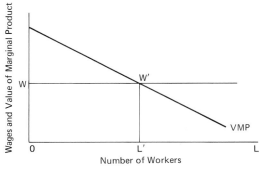

Figure 5.2   An Employment Equilibrium for a Firm, Given Perfect Competition

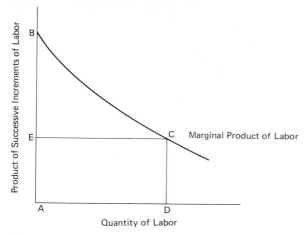

Figure 5.3   The Market Wage Rate (Source: John Bates Clark, *The Distribution of Wealth* [New York: Macmillan, 1899], p. 194.)

it fails to explain the many short-run departures from its assumptions that are made on practical grounds. It is useful in explaining what underlies adjustments in the size of a work force, but it is of limited value in explaining the day-by-day operational decisions of employers.

The Marginal Theory as a Theory of Wages

In addition to explaining the employment decisions of firms, marginal analysis can be used to show how an equilibrium market wage will be determined under static conditions. That is, *assuming a constant supply of labor* (a vertical supply curve), marginal analysis is useful in explaining (1) the general level of wages and (2) the relation between the share of national income going to labor and other factors of production. Used in this way, the marginal theory becomes a *wage theory* rather than an *employment theory*.

Figure 5.3 illustrates the more general applications of marginal analysis. If we assume that competition is perfect, that there are given quantities of all resources, that all workers are equally efficient, and that there is full employment, then (1) all workers will receive a wage equal to the wage of the last worker and (2) the value of the total product less the wage bill will be available for the other factors of production. Given a quantity of labor, *AD*, and a marginal product curve (in real units), *BC*, *AD* laborers will be hired at a wage of *AE*. Since all workers are assumed to be equally efficient, there is no reason to pay any worker a higher wage than that paid to the last worker hired (the marginal worker). The total wage bill is therefore equal to *CD* times *AD*, or the area of the rectangle *ADCE*. The total product, which is the sum of the output of successive individuals, is represented by the area *ADCB* (the integral of the marginal product curve). This total product, less the amount of output used to pay real wages (*ADCE*), will yield the amount of output (*ECB*) available for distribution to the other factors of production.

To summarize: given a supply of homogeneous labor that is fully employed, the marginal productivity of the last person hired determines the general equilibrium level of wages, and the total real wages of the work force equal this wage times the number of persons in the labor force.

Of course, *C* is the long-run equilibrium wage only if *all other things remain constant*. In the short run, if the market wage were to increase, some workers would be unable to find employment. Their willingness to accept lower wages in order to find work would then force wages back to the equilibrium level. In the long run, real wages could be increased by (1) a rise in the productivity of labor (an upward shift of the curve *BC*), (2) a decrease in the supply of labor, or (3) some combination of factors resulting in a rise in productivity relative to the size of the labor force.

Criticisms of Marginal Theory

The more thoughtful proponents of the neoclassical viewpoint have called attention to certain limitations of marginal analysis. John Bates Clark, for example, on whose work Figure 5.3 is based, did not hold that his assumption of a static economy was descriptive of the real world.[17] Moreover, even if there is perfect competition,

> there is no necessity whatsoever for the wage a man receives at a particular moment to equal his marginal product. In so far as the term "marginal product" can be given any sense at all in a changing community, it can only mean the wage a man would ultimately receive if the fundamental conditions of equilibrium . . . were made eternal as they exist at the moment, and the process of settling down followed to its furthest limits. . . . Sometimes the wage must fall below the marginal product, sometimes exceed it.[18]

The fact that businesses may not base operational decisions on marginal analysis does not necessarily mean that it fails to reflect reality. Market behavior may still be in accord with the basic postulates of marginal theory. There are, however, several serious limitations to the theory as an explanation of how wages are determined in *actual labor markets*. These limitations are described briefly below.

THE ASSUMPTION OF PERFECT COMPETITION

The original marginal analysis assumed perfect competition in both product and factor markets. Today we recognize that most markets are imperfect to some degree—that the actions of a particular firm, or union, may influence the price at which the firm's output can be sold or the wage at which an employee can be hired. In Chapter 6, we will see how modern marginal theory has been qualified to accommodate such departures from perfect competition.

THE ASSUMPTION OF A HOMOGENEOUS LABOR SUPPLY

It has been charged that the marginalists, by assuming a homogeneous supply of labor, failed to recognize the existence of wage differentials. However, if we assume that the total supply of labor can be subdivided into categories according to productivity, marginal analysis can explain the demand for different types of labor and the wages prevailing in separate, occupationally defined labor markets within the economy as a whole. The early marginalists did not deal explicitly with the relationship between the wage level and the *supply* of labor within such submarkets. Typically, they took the supply of each type of labor as given, or they assumed, mistakenly, that the problem was not a serious one. J. R. Hicks, for example, himself a leading exponent of marginal analysis, admitted that

> in an opening page of my *Theory of Wages* [published in 1932] I committed myself to the foolish remark that these problems (of the distribution of labour among occupations) are "one of the easiest parts of wage theory." For this I was properly rebuked . . . [and] on this, as on several other matters . . . , I have come to know better.[19]

THE ASSUMPTION OF FULL EMPLOYMENT
AT AN EQUILIBRIUM WAGE

The marginalists assumed that in a perfectly competitive economic system all factors of production would find employment at relevant equilibrium prices. They believed that though temporary, or *frictional*, unemployment would develop in a dynamic economy due to changes in economic variables, the economic system would eventually move toward a new full employment equilibrium. They failed to recognize the possibility of large-scale cyclical or persistent structural unemployment.

A FAILURE TO DEAL WITH THE INCOME
EFFECT OF CHANGES IN WAGES

Marginal analysis is silent on the income effect of wage changes. It states that there will be unemployment if wages are higher than the marginal productivity of labor, thus suggesting that the way to diminish unemployment is to reduce wages. However, wages constitute a significant portion of the country's national income, and a decline in money wages can, by decreasing national income, trigger or accentuate a recession that results in even greater unemployment.

A FAILURE TO DEAL WITH DYNAMIC PHENOMENA

Marginal productivity theory is basically a *demand theory* which assumes that the supply of labor and other factors of production is given. It does not explain why or how the quantity of capital may increase relative to the quantity of labor or how the supply of labor changes over time. The supply of labor and the relative efficiency of labor are each functions of a number of variables. As we saw in Chapter 4, the number of participants in the labor force and the number of people in specific occupations at a particular time (the short-run supply of labor) are functions of the changing level of real and money wages, wage differentials, and of changes in such socioeconomic variables as the age, sex, marital status, and level of education of prospective members of the labor force.

Marginal Productivity Theory Summarized

Marginal productivity theory involves the application of marginal analysis to the pricing of factors of production. This analytical approach does not provide a complete theory of wages. In its original formulation, given perfect competition and a full employment equilibrium, marginal productivity analysis can explain (1) employment decisions (the demand for labor) at the level of the firm, (2) how the general wage level is determined in a static economy, and (3) labor's share of national income.

Marginal analysis has proved less successful in explaining (1) the *structure* of wage rates, (2) *variations* in *wages* and *employment* in a *dynamic* economy, and (3) the failure of the economy to reach and sustain a *full employment* equilibrium. In addition, as originally formulated, it did not address the problem of how wages are determined in *imperfect* product and labor markets.

BARGAINING THEORIES

Before concluding this chapter, we should mention the bargaining theories that were developed during the latter half of the nineteenth century and that recognized that in the real world, even in the absence of unions, a unique equilibrium wage may not be established from the operation of market forces. Sophisticated versions of such theories continue to be used in analyses of how wages are determined in the short run in actual employment situations where there is imperfect information and uncertainty about conditions in labor markets.

Bargaining theory assumes that employers have in mind minimum and maximum wages for the various categories of workers they want to employ. These minimums and maximums are functions of such factors as the wages other employers are paying, the elasticity of demand for the firms' products, and the employers' expectations about changes in prices and wages. The minimums reflect a realistic appraisal of the lowest wages at which firms can attract and hold workers; the maximums reflect the upper limits on what firms can pay and continue to operate profitably.

The firms' present and prospective employees develop similar estimates of their maximum and minimum earnings based on their perception of such factors as the disutility of work, the availability of other job opportunities, and secondary sources of family income. The maximums reflect the wages they would like to get and conceivably could get under existing market conditions, and the minimums are the lowest wages at which they would be willing to work.

If, for a given category of labor, an employer's maximum is above the workers' minimum, a wage can be established that will permit the firm to retain its labor force and operate at a profit. The difference between the employer's maximum offer and the workers' minimum demand constitutes a *bargaining range,* or a *range of indeterminancy.* Short-run considerations will largely determine the wage within this range. In a tight labor market, an employer will be forced to offer a wage closer to the firm's maximum. Although bargaining theory does not necessarily assume the existence of a union, the theory is most useful when applied to a situation in which an employer confronts an organization representing the firms' employees.

DISCUSSION QUESTIONS

1. Distinguish between wage criteria and wage theories. How and to what extent are they interrelated?
2. What new types of fringe benefits do you believe will be introduced or become more general during the coming decade?
3. Why has it proved difficult to measure specific types of wage differentials?
4. Do you believe that changes in the CPI provide an accurate estimate in changes in the "cost of living" of students at your college or university?
5. Assume that the president of your institution has decided to increase faculty salaries on the basis of merit. What factors should be considered in such an evaluation? To what extent do they reflect faculty "productivity"?
6. Why do you think Marxian theory has recently enjoyed a revival among some labor economists in the United States?
7. Why is the demand for labor considered a derived demand? Would this concept apply to the services of the instructor in this course?
8. What might be responsible for the negative section of the MPP curve in Figure 5.1?
9. Do you believe that a wage theory should be able to explain the day-to-day determination of wages in actual labor markets?

SELECTED READINGS

Basic Definitions

Ferguson, Robert H. *Wages, Earnings, and Incomes: Definitions of Terms and Sources of Data.* Ithaca, N.Y.: NYS School of Industrial and Labor Relations, Cornell University, Bulletin 63, July 1971.

Wage Theory

Bellante, Don, and Jackson, Mark. *Labor Economics: Choice in Labor Markets.* New York: McGraw-Hill, 1979.
Cartter, Allan M. *Theory of Wages and Employment.* Homewood, Ill.: Irwin, 1959.
Dobb, Maurice. *Wages.* Rev. ed. New York: Pitman, 1946.
Dunlop, John T., ed. *The Theory of Wage Determination.* New York: St. Martin's Press, 1957.
Hicks, J. R. *The Theory of Wages.* 2nd ed. New York: St. Martin's Press, 1963.

Rees, Albert. *The Economics of Work and Pay.* 2nd ed. New York: Harper & Row, 1979.

Reynolds, Lloyd G., and Taft, Cynthia H. *The Evolution of Wage Structure.* New Haven, Conn.: Yale University Press, 1956.

Robertson, D. J. *The Economics of Wages and the Distribution of Income.* New York: St. Martin's Press, 1961.

Rothschild, K. W. *The Theory of Wages.* New York: Macmillan, 1954.

Taylor, George W., and Pierson, Frank C., eds. *New Concepts in Wage Determination.* New York: McGraw-Hill, 1957.

Classical and Marxist Theories

Original sources include Karl Marx, *Capital: A Critique of Political Economy* (New York: Random House [Modern Library], copyright 1906 by Charles H. Kerr & Co.), which is the first of Marx's famous three-volume work; David Ricardo, *The Principles of Political Economy and Taxation* (Everyman's Library. London: J. M. Dent & Sons, Ltd., and New York: Dutton, 1911); and Adam Smith, *The Wealth of Nations* (New York: Random House [Modern Library], 1937). These works may prove difficult for the noneconomist, and the reader may find it profitable to consult relevant portions of a good text on the history of economic thought. For example, good discussions of Ricardo's labor theory of value are found in M. Blaug, *Economic Theory in Retrospect* (Homewood, Ill.: Irwin, 1962), pp. 85–92, and in Overton H. Taylor, *A History of Economic Thought* (New York: McGraw-Hill, 1960), pp. 187–200. For a good summary of Marx's wage theory, see Erich Roll, *A History of Economic Thought*, 4th ed. (Homewood, Ill.: Irwin, 1974), pp. 260–273.

Notes

1. Arthur M. Ross, "The External Wage Structure," in George W. Taylor and Frank C. Pierson, eds., *New Concepts in Wage Determination* (New York: McGraw-Hill, 1957), p. 174. Emphasis added.

2. U.S. Chamber of Commerce, *Employee Benefits 1978* (Washington, D.C.: U.S. Chamber of Commerce, 1979), p. 5. See also Mitchell Meyer and Harland Fox, *Profile of Employee Benefits: A Research Report from The Conference Board* (New York: The Conference Board, 1974).

3. U.S. Chamber of Commerce, *Employee Benefits 1978*, Table 4, p. 8.

4. Ibid., p. 5.

5. Lloyd G. Reynolds and Cynthia H. Taft, *The Evolution of Wage Structure* (New Haven, Conn.: Yale University Press, 1956), p. 9.

6. *Monthly Labor Review* 103, no. 5 (May 1980): Table 14, p. 77.

7. Richard A. Lester, *Labor and Industrial Relations* (New York: Macmillan, 1951), p. 62.

8. Reynolds and Taft, *The Evolution of Wage Structure,* p. 10.

9. For a description of these indexes, see the Bureau of Labor Statistics' *The Consumer Price Index: Concepts and Content Over the Years,* Report 517.

10. K. W. Rothschild, *The Theory of Wages* (New York: Macmillan, 1954), pp. 2–3.

11. Adam Smith, *The Wealth of Nations* (New York: Random House [Modern Library], 1937), p. 73.
12. Ibid., p. 99.
13. Ibid., pp. 100–107.
14. David Ricardo, *The Principles of Political Economy and Taxation* (Everyman's Library. London: J. M. Dent & Sons, Ltd., and New York: Dutton, 1911), pp. 54–55.
15. Ibid., p. 61.
16. Overton Taylor, *A History of Economic Thought* (New York: McGraw-Hill, 1960), p. 335.
17. Allen M. Cartter, *Theory of Wages and Employment* (Homewood, Ill.: Irwin, 1959), pp. 19–21; 35.
18. J. R. Hicks, *The Theory of Wages,* 2nd ed. (New York: St. Martin's Press, 1963), p. 86.
19. J. R. Hicks, "Economic Foundations of Wage Policy," in *Economic Journal* LXV, no. 259 (September 1955): p. 404. By permission Cambridge University Press.

Chapter 6
WAGE THEORY
AND PRACTICE:
THE MODERN PERIOD

During and after the Depression, wage theory underwent two fundamental changes: (1) marginal analysis was modified to reflect imperfections in product and factor markets; and (2) a new breed of theorists, concerned about the massive, persistent unemployment in Western industrial economies, turned to macroeconomics (aggregative) analysis to explain why these economies had not reached a full-employment equilibrium and to provide a foundation for remedial action. More recent analyses of the labor market have reflected attempts by economists (1) to incorporate institutional factors into what we will term the *New Marginalism*, and (2) to incorporate such imperfections and institutional constraints into a variety of theories that differ from "orthodox" wage theory. In this chapter, we will discuss these developments and evaluate the state of contemporary wage theory without considering unions. We will discuss the application of this theory to the way wages are determined under collective bargaining in Chapter 20.

THE NEW MARGINALISM

At present, most economists who accept the marginal approach to labor market analysis (the New Marginalists) recognize that some of the theory's assumptions require modification in the light of reality. However, they believe that the theory can take imperfections in the market mechanism into account and that it is still a valuable analytical tool. Other microtheorists, particularly labor economists interested in the institutional factors affecting wages, believe that departures from competitive norms are so serious today that a general theory cannot adequately explain how wages are determined.

In discussing marginal analysis in Chapter 5, we assumed that there was perfect competition in both product and factor markets. During the 1930s and 1940s, a number of economists (initially, Edward H. Chamberlin in the United States and Joan Robinson in England) successfully challenged these assumptions. They demonstrated that imperfect competition is actually characteristic of many product and factor markets and developed what is known as *marginal revenue productivity theory* to take this fact into account. This "new" orthodox theory modified the original marginal analysis in two basic respects. It recognized (1) that when there was imperfect competition in a *product market*, the output of an individual firm would affect the market price of the product and (2) that when there was imperfect competition in a *factor market*, such as a labor market, a firm could no longer assume that it would be able to acquire additional units of that factor at a constant price.

Imperfect Product Markets

If there is perfect competition in a product market, an individual producer has no influence over the market price of a commodity, and as Table 6.1 shows, the value of the *marginal physical product* (calculated by multiplying the price by the number of additional units sold) is equal to the *marginal revenue product* (the net addition to total revenue). When there is imperfect competition, the firm cannot increase or decrease its output without affecting the market price of its product. The product has a *downward-sloping demand curve*, either because the firm produces a large enough proportion of the total output of the product to affect its price or because the product is a differentiated one (that is, a product consumers consider unique in some way).

In any event, in order to sell additional units of the product, the price must be lowered, and since all units—not merely the additional ones—must be sold

Table 6.1 THE MARGINAL REVENUE PRODUCT AND THE VALUE OF THE MARGINAL PHYSICAL PRODUCT, GIVEN PERFECT COMPETITION

NUMBER OF UNITS PRODUCED (a)	SELLING PRICE (AVERAGE REVENUE) (b)	TOTAL REVENUE $(a \cdot b)$	MARGINAL PHYSICAL PRODUCT $(a_{x+1} - a_x)$	VALUE OF MARGINAL PHYSICAL PRODUCT $(a_{x+1} - a_x)\,(b)$	MARGINAL REVENUE PRODUCT $(TR_{x+1} - TR_x)$
10	$10	$100	—	—	
11	10	110	1	$10	$10
12	10	120	1	10	10

Table 6.2 THE MARGINAL REVENUE PRODUCT AND THE VALUE OF THE MARGINAL PHYSICAL PRODUCT GIVEN IMPERFECT COMPETITION

NUMBER OF UNITS PRODUCED (a)	SELLING PRICE (AVERAGE REVENUE) (b)	TOTAL REVENUE $(a \cdot b)$	MARGINAL PHYSICAL PRODUCT $(a_{x+1} - a_x)$	VALUE OF MARGINAL PHYSICAL PRODUCT $(a_{x+1} - a_x)$ (b)	MARGINAL REVENUE PRODUCT $(TR_{x+1} - TR_x)$
10	$10.00	$100.00	—	—	—
11	9.50	104.50	1	$9.50	$4.50[a]
12	9.00	108.00	1	9.00	3.50

[a] This figure may also be derived as follows: the eleventh unit added $9.50 to total revenue while 50 cents was lost on each of the ten units that could otherwise have been sold for $10 (.50 × 10 = $5.00). An increase of $9.50 less $5 yields a *net* increase in revenue of $4.50.

at the prevailing market price, the *net* addition to the firm's revenue cannot be measured by multiplying the number of units of its marginal physical product by the price at which they are sold. As Table 6.2 shows, the *marginal revenue product* is less than the value of the marginal physical product times its price (or the marginal *value* product). According to the New Marginalists' general theory, applicable to both perfect and imperfect *product* markets, a firm will employ additional workers until the marginal revenue product of labor equals the price (cost) of labor. At this point, profits will be maximized or, in the short run, losses may be minimized.

The application of the New Marginalism to a firm facing imperfect competition in a product market is illustrated in Figure 6.1. The line *MVP* represents the productivity of labor at different levels of employment in terms of marginal value. The line *MRP* represents its productivity in terms of marginal revenue. *W* is the market wage (the average and marginal cost of hiring an additional worker); *WW* is the supply of labor available to the firm, and *L* is the number of workers employed. Given a wage rate of *W*, the firm should expand its number of employees until *L* workers have been hired; thus, for the firm, marginal revenue productivity analysis provides a theory of employment.

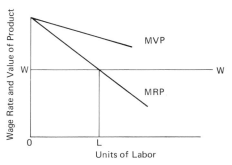

Figure 6.1   Determining Employment Within a Firm in an Imperfect Product Market

Imperfect Labor Markets

Factor markets may also be imperfect. In a perfectly competitive labor market, an employer can hire additional workers at the same wage; the firm's demand for labor does not affect the market price of labor. In real life, however, the decisions of individual employers may affect the market price of labor. A large firm, or a firm employing a large proportion of a given type of labor, will generally affect the going wage rate; and in a tight labor market, it will be forced to offer higher wages to attract additional workers.* Such a firm, which exercises some degree of monopoly power as a *buyer* rather than a seller, is called a *monopsonist*. Its labor supply curve (which is also an average cost curve) is not horizontal but slopes upward to the right.

The marginal cost of labor in such a situation is not equal to the average cost, as was the case under perfect competition, but rises more rapidly. This is because the marginal cost of employing additional workers equals the wages paid to those workers *plus* the wage increases that must be paid to workers already employed, who will presumably demand, at a minimum, the new, higher wage rate. Suppose a corporation has been employing 100 machine tool makers at $3 an hour, or $120 per week per worker, so that its total wage bill has been $12,000 per week. Suppose now that in order to secure ten more workers, it must offer a wage of $4 an hour, or $160 per week. The wages of the ten new workers will total $1,600 a week; but the addition to the total wage bill, or the marginal cost of hiring the new workers, will be $5,600. In addition to paying the new workers, the firm will have to pay another dollar an hour, or $40 a week to each of the 100 workers already employed. This adds another $4,000 to its payroll. (This figure can also be computed by subtracting the old wage bill of $12,000 from the new wage bill of $17,600.)

This impact of new hiring on costs can be incorporated into marginal theory by comparing the marginal revenue product with the marginal cost of taking on more workers rather than with the *wage rate* (the market price or average cost) of the extra workers. In the short run, assuming that a firm is operating above its shutdown point, it will pay an employer to add units of labor (a variable factor) to the production process until the marginal revenue productivity of additional labor (MRPL) equals the marginal cost (MCL) of acquiring that labor. As long as MRPL is greater than MCL, the firm, by adding workers and expanding output, is adding more to its revenues than to its costs. (Either total profits are increasing or total losses are decreasing.) Beyond the point at which MRPL = MCL, the rise in labor costs will outweigh the increase in revenue. (Total profits will decrease or total losses will increase.)

This situation is illustrated in Figure 6.2, in which *MRPL* represents the

---

* Alternatively, the firm might lower its hiring standards, but this would presumably result in a reduced marginal product because of the lower efficiency of the newly hired workers. This too would mean a higher wage bill per unit of output.

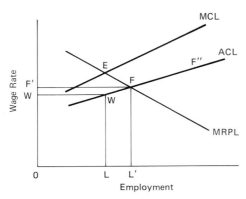

Figure 6.2   Determining the Level of Wages and Employment in a Firm Given Monopsony in the Labor Market

marginal revenue productivity of labor (the derived demand for labor by the firm). *ACL* represents the market wage (the average cost) associated with hiring different quantities of labor (the supply of labor to the firm). *MCL* represents the net addition to total costs that results from hiring additional workers. The *level of employment, L,* is determined by the intersection of the *MRPL* and *MCL* curves at *E.* (*L* is directly below *E* on the *x* axis), and the *wage rate, W,* is equal to *ACL* at the relevant level of employment.

When employers are monopsonists, workers may receive less than the marginal revenue they produce. If, however, through collective action they succeed in getting a wage (*ACL*) equal to the marginal revenue product at *F,* where the supply curve of labor intersects the demand curve for labor, both employment and wages can increase from *L* to *L',* and from *W* to *F*). In effect, this action, which eliminates the so-called "exploitation" of labor, produces a new labor supply curve, *F'FF",* along which, up to point *F,* the average cost of labor equals the marginal cost of labor. The imposition of a statutory minimum wage could have a similar effect.

Summary

In the early marginal theory, which assumed that there was perfect competition in both product and factor markets, the equilibrium level of employment was reached when the value of the marginal product of labor was equal to the market wage. This theory was first modified to take imperfections in product markets into account, and the conclusion was reached that employers would hire additional workers until the marginal revenue product of the last worker hired was equal to the market wage. Modern economists further modified marginal theory to allow for monopsony power in the labor market. According to the final and most general formulation of the theory, additional workers would be hired until the marginal revenue product of the last person employed was equal to the marginal cost of employing that person. This condition holds in both perfectly competitive and imperfectly competitive markets.

The ability to incorporate such modifications into marginal productivity analysis did not satisfy those who charged that this kind of analysis was too abstract and that it failed to explain the actual mechanics of setting wages in the short run. This fact was responsible for the so-called *marginalist controversy* following World War II. The basic issue was whether marginal analysis, taken only as a statement of general tendencies, was so unreal as to be worthless as a working theory, or whether, properly qualified, it was a useful explanation of how wages are determined. We will return to this issue after a short digression into Keynesian economics.

THE IMPACT OF KEYNESIAN ANALYSIS

Keynesian analysis involved a dramatic shift in the orientation of wage theory. Keynes was interested in general (macro) as opposed to specific (micro) analysis, and he developed a theoretical construct that explains how aggregate economic variables determined the equilibrium level of national income.[1] Unlike the more traditional wage theorists, who were interested in determining specific wage rates and the problem of wage structures, the Keynesians were interested in the *general level* of wages, in the impact of changing wage levels on aggregate employment and output, and in labor's absolute and relative share of the national income.

Keynes's theoretical innovations attempted to explain the failure of modern economies to achieve sustained full employment. As we have seen, the classical and neoclassical economists had assumed that a competitive system would automatically reach a full employment equilibrium. True, there would be short-run departures from this equilibrium; but the tendency would be to return to full employment. Faced with the reality of a prolonged depression, Keynes demonstrated that it was also possible to reach a less than full employment equilibrium.*

According to the marginalists, unemployment was the result of a wage in excess of the productivity of labor in terms of marginal revenue, and lowering wages would presumably lead to increased employment. As applied to a single firm, this analysis was logical, but it could not necessarily be extended to the economy as a whole. The Keynesians correctly pointed out that a reduction in wages, by reducing national income, might depress rather than stimulate the economy. Today, orthodox theorists who are not Keynesians have qualified or rejected traditional *equilibrium* analysis. Professor J. R. Hicks, for example, concludes that wages may rise when unemployment is high because of the elasticity of the money supply. He argues that in "the world we now live in . . . [i]nstead of actual wages having to adjust themselves to an equilibrium level, monetary

---

* Keynesian analysis also permits an inflationary equilibrium. In this case, aggregate demand measured in money increases after the economy is producing at capacity.

policy adjusts the equilibrium level of money wages so as to make it conform to the actual level."[2]

Theorists who are quantitatively inclined have developed a variety of economic models that attempt to relate changes in aggregate prices, productivity, employment, and wages. They have focused on the relationship between changes in real and money wages and other, macroeconomic, variables rather than the way specific wage rates are determined.

More recently, theorists have begun to reemphasize microeconomic analysis. Given persistent high unemployment plus sustained inflation, they have become interested in imbalances in product and factor markets and various factors that seem to limit the effectiveness of macroeconomic policies. This has stimulated so-called interest in the microeconomic "foundations" of macroeconomics and in modern "supply side" economics.

CONTEMPORARY WAGE ANALYSIS

We are now ready to discuss the success of orthodox theory in explaining the relationship between wages and employment in the absence of unions. Certainly, the basic assumptions of contemporary wage theory appear to be generally in accord with reality. However, modifications of marginal analysis, the impact of the Keynesian revolution, and advances in statistical and other research techniques have greatly broadened the scope of investigations into the process of wage determination, making it very difficult for any single wage theory to successfully address the variety of wage "questions" that arise. These different questions about wages

> require specialized conceptual tools. One should think, therefore, in terms of an array of "wage theories" oriented toward different kinds of question [sic]. . . . [W]e need a variety of theoretical structures—a theory of collective bargaining relations, a theory of the firm, a theory of the distribution of real national income, a theory of aggregate employment, and so on—each of which will have a wage *aspect* or wage *component*.[3]

Concentrating on such specialized areas has, however, a negative side. Until recently, relatively little effort was directed toward formulating a unified theory of wage determination that not only reflected reality but could be incorporated into the main body of contemporary economic thought. In 1957, Professor John Dunlop, a pioneer in charting new approaches to wage analysis, concluded that empirical and institutional studies of the labor market had led to the development of a "theory of wage-rate determination [that had] involved a retreat to a position largely outside of economic theory."[4] He argued that there was a "need for . . . a body of wage analysis more suitable to *labour market-developments* and to [the] *wage-setting institutions* of the day, drawing upon the central body of economic analysis."[5]

Although such a theory has yet to be developed, interest in manpower economics, in investment in human capital, and in the operation of labor markets has stimulated research that has begun to integrate labor economics into the main corpus of economic theory. The development of sophisticated quantitative models has contributed to this "new thrust."

An introductory text does not need to survey all aspects of contemporary wage analysis, but it should describe the *basic elements* of contemporary wage theory, including recent *radical perspectives,* and help students relate this theory to reality. With these objectives in mind, we shall discuss the application of contemporary labor market theory to

1. the determination of the *general level* of real wages in the economy;
2. the analysis of wage *differentials* between industries, between geographic areas, and between plants or firms in a given industry and locality; and
3. the determination of wages at the *plant level,* which involves a consideration of (a) the general level of wages of the plant's employees and (b) the wage structure within the plant.

These areas of analysis are inevitably related. The determination of wages at the plant or firm level, for example, is affected by the wage and employment decisions of other firms in the same industry or locality. (In this connection, it is important to remember that marginal revenue productivity theory is a theory of the *demand* for labor, *not* a complete theory of wages.)

THE GENERAL LEVEL OF REAL WAGES

The notion of a general wage level is an abstraction; the overall level of money or real wages is not consciously "set." Wage theory should however be able to account for the general level of real wages in the United States relative to levels in other nations and identify the variables responsible for changes in the real wage level in the long run.

Orthodox supply and demand analysis can be used for this purpose, since the general wage level is basically a function of the number of workers in the labor force (the supply of labor) and the absolute and relative productivity of the labor force (reflected in the demand for labor). We have already seen that the supply of labor and the demand for it reflect the interaction of a complex of variables, including the resource base of the nation; the state of its technology; the tendency of people to save or invest earnings; the innovative spirit of businessmen; the character and capabilities of the labor force; and legal, institutional, and cultural factors that may exclude certain groups from, or encourage their participation in, the labor force.

Anything that increases the demand for labor in real terms relative to the supply will increase the level of real wages. In this country, the absolute level of real wages is high because the marginal revenue productivity of labor is high. This is due not only to the quality and quantity of human capital but also to the quality and quantity of other productive resources. Labor has always been relatively scarce in the United States, and this has been a significant factor in the rise in the level of real wages. The marginal productivity of labor is higher when it is used in combination with (more efficient) capital equipment.

Orthodox theory is less successful in explaining variations in the general wage level in the short run. The expectations of consumers and producers and the income effect of changes in wage levels are important determinants of the wage level. Variability, not constancy, characterizes our economy, and marginal analysis is of limited use. For example, it is unrealistic to assume that the supply of labor is fixed in the short run. Changes in labor force participation rates will shift at least segments of the supply curve. Under such conditions, the direction of a wage change resulting from a shift in the aggregate demand for labor may be predicted, but not the new equilibrium wage. Moreover, movement toward a "new" equilibrium may trigger changes in economic variables which alter that equilibrium.

Full Employment

We can no longer assume that the economy automatically moves toward a full-employment equilibrium. Macroanalysis suggests that a reduction in money wages to increase employment in accordance with marginal theory may be self-defeating. The income effect of the wage change may simply initiate a further downward spiral in production and employment. At a minimum, the probable impact of a general wage reduction on such variables as consumer spending, business investment decisions, and anticipated governmental revenues and expenditures must be investigated before the desirability of such a reduction can be assessed.

Macroeconomic theory is useful in analyzing economic trends and in explaining changes in the overall level of employment, production, and money wages; but it does not adequately explain *why* real wages are at a given level. This suggests that rather than considering marginal analysis and macroanalysis as competing theories, we should view them as complementary. Income theory compensates to some extent for the failure of the marginal theory to consider dynamic factors that affect aggregate variables; microeconomic theory helps us to understand the potential impact and limitations of changes in aggregate variables that necessarily function through their impact on *individual* consumers and producers in *particular* product and factor markets.

Wage Patterns

Most economists believe that the general wage level will not be affected by the wage or employment decisions of an individual firm or firms within a particular industry. Others, however, point to the growing conformity to "patterns" set by highly visible collective bargaining agreements. Such patterns may have a considerable impact on particular wage negotiations and on changes in the level of *money* wages in the short run, but they cannot explain why a change in the real wage level is possible, much less determine the magnitude of that change.

Recent studies have failed to find a predictable relationship between increases in money wages in trend-setting firms or industries and increases in the general wage level. Patterns may initiate trends, but this occurs within constraints imposed by macroeconomic variables.

Summary

The general level of wages is not set consciously but is a result of basic economic forces operating over the long run. Orthodox supply and demand analysis is useful in explaining the long-run movement toward an equilibrium real wage level, and marginal revenue productivity theory provides an acceptable explanation of the role of demand in this process. Marginal analysis must be supplemented with modern income analysis (macroanalysis) to explain the relationships between changes in the level of money wages, output, employment, and prices.

WAGE DIFFERENTIALS

Employers are more concerned with problems of wage structure than with movements in the general level of real (and money) wages. Existing wage differentials can be explained to some extent on purely "logical" grounds as a product of supply and demand in relevant labor and product markets. Marginal revenue productivity theory is useful in analyzing these differentials. Qualitative differences (variations in productivity) between workers in two regions help to explain geographic differentials. The labor-capital mix of an industry also affects workers' productivity and the ability of an industry to pay higher wages. Orthodox wage theory assumes that movements of labor or capital in response to wage differentials will reduce *real,* or *noncompensating,* differentials that do not reflect differences in job requirements.

Market imperfections, including a lack of mobility of labor and, to a lesser extent, of capital, will help perpetuate noncompensating wage differentials. Differentials may also reflect past practices in cases where an absence of competition permits employers to continue to conform to such practices. The wage level of a particular industry or area is presumably beyond the control of an individual firm, although pattern setting is of importance in such industries as steel, rubber, and automobiles.

Interindustry Differentials

Interindustry differentials usually *originate* when employers have to pay more than the market wage to attract workers with appropriate training and skills to a particular industry. The persistence of such differentials, and of the resulting industry wage structures, is a function of such factors as the elasticity of the demand for products, the ratio of labor cost to total cost, industry growth patterns, and shifts in the demand of particular industries for particular types of labor.

Geographic Differentials

Geographic differentials result from local or regional imbalances between the supply of labor and the demand for it. Custom and a lack of mobility of labor and capital play significant roles in perpetuating such differentials. Many firms observe a North/South differential on what appear to be traditional grounds. However, the surplus of labor in the South, a result of high rural birthrates and a decreased demand for agricultural labor, has been more significant in maintaining this differential. (The movement of industry to the South and the outmigration of southern workers, on the other hand, has decreased the difference in wages between the North and South to some extent.)

Interplant Differentials

According to orthodox wage theory, wage differentials that do not compensate workers for real differences between jobs should be reduced or disappear in the long run. Wage differentials between workers in similar occupations in plants in the same area, and possibly in the same industry, should persist only if they compensate workers for actual differences between jobs. However, most studies indicate that existing differentials, even those in the same locality, cannot be completely explained in this way. Noncompensating differentials within a locality are a function of a variety of factors, and it is difficult to estimate their magnitude. One study, which compared both the hiring rate for new employees and the average hourly earnings of all employees in a group of "rather homogeneous companies" in the New Haven area, found a surprisingly large dispersion of plant wage levels.[6] The factors accounting for these differences included

> the industry in which the firm [was] engaged, [the] intensity of competition in the industry, and the wage levels of rival producers; the nature of the work and the kind of labor force required; the presence or absence of unionism; the efficiency of plant and equipment; and in some cases the efficiency of management.[7]

DETERMINING WAGES WITHIN A FIRM

In analyzing how wages are determined *within* a plant or firm, we again find variations in earnings that cannot be explained adequately by orthodox wage theory. The immobility of workers and industries, the ties of tradition, a lack of entrepreneurial imagination, and extraeconomic considerations such as a worker's attachment to a given employer or an employer's sense of responsibility toward its labor force may require a modification of the New Marginalism. Apparently, there are noncompensating wage differentials within firms, and there is often little inclination to eliminate them.

Other "practical" problems have made it difficult to develop generally applicable theoretical explanations of how wages are determined within a firm. We are interested in relating the wage structure of a particular firm or plant to labor market variables, but accurate interfirm comparisons are difficult due to the lack of consistency between company wage, fringe benefit, hiring, and promotion policies. It is also difficult to measure the extent to which a firm makes *external comparisons* in developing its *internal* wage structure.

Market imperfections can be incorporated into a properly qualified marginal analysis of how wages are determined within a firm in the short run. For example, the failure of workers to move to firms that pay higher wages or train for higher paying jobs keeps wages at the lower level of marginal revenue productivity resulting from the larger supply of labor. Marginal analysis "explains" this result, but it fails to tell us *why* the "oversupply" of labor in a lower paying firm or occupation persists. If a variety of noneconomic or extraeconomic arguments are brought up to explain such phenomena, the marginal analysis may be so qualified that it becomes little more than a statement of tendencies. In the extreme case in which all departures from marginal revenue productivity theory are explained as rational in terms of economic constraints, the marginal theory becomes tautological.

Although orthodox theory cannot fully explain how wages are determined within firms in the short run, it illuminates the economic constraints that help to set limits on the normal range of wages. The bargaining theory described in the last section of Chapter 5 is useful in this kind of analysis.

In the long run, given either perfect or imperfect competition, employers who are interested in maximizing their profits will tend to conform to, or at least approximate (within the constraints imposed by institutional considerations), the wage and employment levels described by marginal revenue productivity theory. A monopolist or an oligopolist may not choose to maximize profits; but this can be explained as a deviation from, rather than a refutation of, the marginal theory. For example, a firm may be an industry leader in terms of total capacity or sales, even though this involves producing more than its optimum output from a profitability standpoint. Or it may wish to be known as a "good" employer and with this end in view pay wages above the level needed to attract competent workers or assume that it has, in effect, contracted with its workers to maintain existing wage and benefit levels even during recessional periods.*

A firm may rationally pursue policies that are unprofitable in the short run to maximize profits in the long run. For example, assume that a firm employs highly skilled workers on complex operations that require considerable on-the-job training. Faced with a reduction in demand during a recession, it might be

---

* Note that under such *implicit contracts* the level of employment rather than the wage rate can be expected to decline during a recession.

expected to lay off part of its labor force. However, if the firm's management believes that the recession is temporary, it may choose to keep its labor force intact rather than risk being unable to replace furloughed workers at a later date. What might otherwise be considered "unnecessary" short-run losses may become valid outlays when weighed against the cost of training new workers, a result consistent with marginal analysis.

SUMMARY: THE NEW MARGINALISM

Business decisions are not made in the static long run. Reality consists of a succession of short-run responses within a continually changing economic environment that includes as one of its variables the entrepreneur's unique estimate of the future. Indeed,

> the main reason for the cleavage between the theory of the firm and actual business behavior lies in the emphasis of the theory on equilibrium adjustments to known data which are either constant or changing gradually along smooth trend lines. . . . The hypothetical firm lives in a world from which all the really difficult problems have been eliminated. The actual firm, however, lives in a world of uncertainty and of large and sudden shifts in demand. . . .
>
> The cost and revenue curves, as usually defined and explained, do no more than indicate the equilibrium position which would be appropriate to the data existing at a moment in time.[8]

The "validity" of the New Marginalism with respect to wage analysis depends on the level at which wages are being determined and the economic period being considered. Much of the "marginalist controversy" represented a failure to define, or to agree on, the areas in which marginal analyses were applicable.

Marginal revenue productivity analysis correctly emphasizes the interconnections between market wages, the productivity of labor, and the level of employment. This analytical framework is most helpful in explaining the influence of demand on the way the *general* wage level is determined in the *long run;* it becomes increasingly less satisfactory as we approach the problem of the actual structuring of wages *within a firm* in the *short run* under *dynamic conditions.* When a firm's employment decisions have no direct impact on market wages, marginal productivity analysis can provide an adequate explanation of the level of employment within the firm. When a firm's wage and employment decisions do affect the labor market, orthodox theory, properly qualified, can suggest the limits within which operational decisions affecting wages and employment in the short run may be made.

A "properly" qualified marginal productivity theory of the demand for labor cannot by itself explain the relationship between wages and employment. This is a result of the *interaction* of the forces affecting the *demand for* labor *and* the *supply of* labor that were discussed in Chapter 4. The impact of the Keynesian revolution on wage and employment theory must be recognized. Wage theory and the theory of income determination can no longer be considered self-contained constructs.

MOVING TOWARD REALITY: DUNLOP'S MODEL OF WAGE STRUCTURE

Professor John Dunlop, former Secretary of Labor and presently chairman of President Carter's Pay Advisory Committee, one of the nation's outstanding labor economists, in an effort to establish a more realistic analytical framework has developed a model in which he relates decisions determining the wage structure within a firm to external variables. Operationally, two types of interrelated wage decisions are made at the plant or firm level: a decision concerning the *general* level of wages of the plant or firm and decisions that establish the *wage structure within* the plant or firm. A firm may find that it has little effective control over its general wage level, that it is forced to conform to an industry or a geographic pattern. The internal wage structure will probably be consciously determined but related to external variables. According to Dunlop,

> [a] distinction [should] be made between the wage structure within a plant, firm, or other grouping in which wage differentials are set by the same authority and the complex of interfirm or group structures set by a number of different agencies. From the point of view of the individual decision makers, the first wage structure is internal while the second is external.[9]

Dunlop uses three concepts to show the interrelations between the internal and external wage structure: job clusters, wage contours, and key rates.

> A *job cluster* is defined as a stable group of job classifications or work assignments within a firm (wage determining unit) which are so linked together by (a) technology, (b) by the administrative organization of the production process, including policies of transfer and promotion, or (c) by social custom that they have common wage-making characteristics. . . . The internal wage rate structure is to be envisaged as divided into groups of jobs or job clusters. The wage rates for the operations and jobs within a cluster are more closely related in their wage movements than are rates outside the cluster. . . . Ordinarily a job cluster will contain one, or in some cases several, *key rates*.[10]

Managements (and unions) concentrate on *key rates* in considering a plant's internal wage structure. These rates "play a decisive rôle in relating the exterior [rate structure] to the internal rate structure" by serving as a transmission belt for exterior forces affecting specific rates within the plant.[11] This is because the key rates are also evident in "wage contours":

> A *wage contour* is . . . a stable group of firms . . . which are so linked together by (a) similarity of product markets, (b) by resort to similar sources for a labour

force, or (c) by common labour market organization (custom) that they have common wage-making characteristics. . . . A contour for particular occupations [should] be defined both in terms of the product market and the labour market. A contour thus has three dimensions: (a) particular occupations or job clusters, (b) a sector of industry, and (c) a geographical location.[12]

A firm may hire workers from a number of wage contours. Professional engineers, machine tool makers, and accountants, for example, will be in separate contours. Similarly, workers in one trade, truck drivers for example, may be paid different wage rates (be in different wage contours) because the workers are employed by firms producing different products or serving different consumer markets.

A wage contour contains one or more *key bargains* that concentrate on a limited number of *key rates*. These key rates " 'extend' out from the internal structure of the firm to the 'exterior' and constitute the focal points for wage-setting forces among firms within the contour."[13] This analytical apparatus does not constitute a *theory* of wage determination, but it does provide an operational frame of reference that enables theoretical formulations to be more effectively related to the real world of the marketplace.

Internal Wage Structures

Internal wage structures, which are controlled by a common authority, usually offer the greatest scope for independent wage decisions. A firm's freedom to make such decisions depends on a number of variables, including the type of market that exists for its product, the elasticity of the demand for its output, the percentage of its total costs represented by labor costs, whether its industry is expanding or contracting, the stage of the business cycle the economy is in, the tightness of the labor market, the mobility of the firm's workers (whether they are "tied" to the company through pension plans, for example), and the company's hiring practices. (The presence of a union is a major constraint.)

Internal wage decisions may be based on formal procedures, or they may be informal, perhaps intuitive, responses to a particular situation. Most firms attempt to create a simple, consistent wage structure. In small plants, there may be personal reasons for some variation in wage rates for employees performing the same type of work. More generally, and almost invariably in large corporations, wages and wage relationships are standardized.

A firm's management usually tries to ensure that its internal wage structure is in alignment and that it is comprehensible to the labor force. The more consciously these goals are accepted by the management, the more likely it is that some "scientific" method of determining wages will be adopted. This often involves the use of job evaluation procedures. The introduction of a union usually results in more systematic procedures for determining wages and a greater standardization of a firm's wage structure as the union attempts to "take wages out of competition," that is, to ensure that employers competing in the same product market do not gain a competitive advantage as a result of a wage differential.

External Constraints

Attempts to introduce order into an internal wage structure are not independent of external wage structures. Some jobs are considered *key* jobs in terms of an external wage structure, and management consciously pays those holding them current market rates for such work. These rates, or perhaps other key rates tied to them, serve as pegs around which the internal wage structure is organized. However, factors such as unique job descriptions, seniority systems that provide for promotion from within, and elaborate benefit plans that reduce a worker's mobility may insulate internal rate setting from market forces.

In many cases, only the lower paying jobs in a plant (or perhaps certain highly specialized jobs) are filled from the local labor market and have rates tied directly to external factors. The higher priced jobs are filled by promotion from within, and the wage rates or salaries attached to them may reflect a constellation of factors within the plant. In such circumstances, the wage rate for a particular job may do little to explain an employee's willingness to remain in the employ of a given company.

Summary

In the absence of unions, wages are not determined by the free play of market forces in accordance with the postulates of orthodox marginal analysis. On the contrary, employers have considerable latitude in setting wage rates. The actual degree of latitude depends on a complex of factors that varies both over time and within an economic period, as well as from one employer to another. In studying the impact of unions therefore, it is unrealistic to compare the wage structure that develops when there is collective bargaining with a hypothetical wage structure that might exist in a perfectly competitive economy. What is significant is the difference between the wage structure that results from collective bargaining and the wage structure that actually exists in *imperfect, nonunion* labor markets.[14]

RADICAL VIEWS OF THE OPERATION OF LABOR MARKETS

Radical economists, who reject orthodox marginal productivity analysis, have become increasingly critical of the operation of labor markets under "monopoly capitalism." The inability of federal manpower development and training programs to significantly reduce unemployment among certain demographic subsets during the 1960s was one of the factors that encouraged this reassessment of orthodox labor market analysis. Many such programs provided tests of *human capital theory,* which holds that increasing the quality (productivity) of the labor force will create more employment opportunities for people with low incomes and increase their upward mobility. The human capital theory was developed within an orthodox theoretical framework, and the failure of many programs to achieve much in the way of results encouraged some economists to reject marginal productivity "theory."

Four theories that emphasize the failure of labor markets to operate according to the assumptions of marginal productivity theory have provided support for the radical assumption that creative employment and training programs cannot correct basic defects in the operation of labor markets under monopoly capitalism. These theories, which recognize various *institutional* constraints in labor markets, include: (1) a theory based on the distinction between *internal* and *external labor markets*, (2) *a queue theory of hiring*, (3) a *dual labor market* theory, and (4) "the" theory of *labor market segmentation*, which, in a variety of forms, may incorporate aspects of the other theories. The first three theories are conceptually "value free," but may acquire a radical coloration when incorporated into a more comprehensive analysis. Segmented labor market theories are less orthodox in conception and many may be termed radical, that is, they "express a more explicit critique of capitalism, acknowledge their ties to Marxian dialectical analysis, and emphasize class conflicts."[15]

Internal and External Labor Markets

The distinction between *internal* and *external labor markets* is useful in explaining the actual *process* by which wages are set in the short run. It correctly emphasizes that in many employment relationships, the overall wage structure of the firm is the focus of wage policy, not the determination of individual wage rates. According to Peter Doeringer and Michael Piore, the labor market external to the firm corresponds to that "of conventional economic theory where pricing, allocating and training decisions are controlled directly by economic variables."[16] This external labor market is distinguished from the "internal labor market, governed by administrative rules," in which most jobs" "are shielded from the *direct* influences of competitive forces in the external market."[17] These markets "are interconnected . . . and movement between them occurs at certain job classifications which constitute *ports of entry and exit* to and from the internal labor market."[18] These internal labor market relationships "do not support a competitive interpretation of wage determination, except within wide limits [and] . . . the forces which in neoclassical theory yield a determinate wage establish, in the internal market, only a series of constraints."[19]

Rather than contradicting orthodox analysis, this theory may be considered a useful depiction of institutional constraints on how wages are determined in the short run. However, in the radical view, entry into the internal market is consciously restricted to certain categories of workers, and on the job training and access to higher level jobs are available only to present employees. This creates or perpetuates a division within the working class.

The Queue Theory

For radicals a *queue theory* explains the limited job opportunities available to workers whose productivity is low, who are often "disadvantaged," and who may be discriminated against by employers. This theory, which also takes into account certain differences between internal and external labor markets, emphasizes the rigidities in employment relationships in the short run. A firm's decisions about the training of personnel, promotions, and transfers are made in the context of the internal labor market, and most firms enter the external market only when they need more workers. At such times, they typically hire at their first "port of entry."

Hiring decisions are based on employer preferences and perceptions, and potential employees are visualized as arranged in a *queue*, with the most preferred workers at the head. Workers far down the queue may be excluded from employment by arbitrary or discriminatory hiring standards at the port of entry, although they are capable of meeting job performance standards.

An increase in the overall demand for labor may help to lower hiring standards as employers reach farther down the queue, but it may fail to provide (1) employment opportunities for the least preferred workers or (2) improved *permanent* employment opportunities for those immediately ahead of them in the queue. Radicals believe this serves to divide the working class.

The Dual Labor Market Theory

The *dual labor market theory* represents an attempt "to explain the problems of disadvantaged, particularly black, workers in urban areas, [problems] which had previously been attributed to unemployment."[20] Such workers are assumed to be "confined" to a *secondary* labor market because of "residence, inadequate skills, poor work histories, and discrimination."[21] Additional formal education or training may not improve their relative economic status because they will be *denied access* to the *primary* labor market or confined to secondary sector type jobs within the primary sector. According to the dual labor market theory,

> jobs in the primary market possess several of the following characteristics: high wages, good working conditions, employment stability, chances of advancement, equity, and due process in the administration of work rules. Jobs in the secondary market, in contrast, tend to have low wages and fringe benefits, poor working conditions, high labor turnover, little chance of advancement, and often arbitrary and capricious supervision.[22]

The primary labor market consists of stable internal labor markets with ports of entry at which most hiring occurs. Employment in the secondary labor market is less structured, and movement from the secondary to the primary market may be viewed as a queue phenomenon. It is assumed that under existing institutional arrangements, employers in the primary sector may, given a high level of demand, "shift" their demand for additional workers to secondary sector jobs rather than hire disadvantaged workers for primary sector jobs or, alternatively, tailor jobs within the primary sector to the characteristics of secondary workers. Radicals emphasize that this denies such workers access to primary-type jobs.

In a more recent version of this theory, the primary labor market is divided into an upper tier and a lower tier, and the three segments of the labor market are linked "to the sociological distinction between middle-class, working-class, and lower-class subcultures."[23] The provision of traditional education will not provide upward mobility because the increased numbers of working-class students will "swamp the educational environment and impose their own values and norms upon it."[24] If disadvantaged workers gain access to the initial (lowest level) "station" in the primary market, the station will adopt "the characteristics of the secondary jobs from which the new workers had come" and be detached from the upward mobility "chain" within the primary market.[25] Thus, the segmentation of the labor market is perpetuated, and in the absence of significant changes in capitalist institutions, the most disadvantaged workers continue to be relegated to jobs in the secondary sector.

Labor Market Segmentation Theories

The class-oriented version of the dual labor market theory we have just described is representative of a number of theories of *labor market segmentation* or stratification that have radical roots. According to these theories, "barriers to mobility mean that previous work activities rule out certain future possibilities," and once a person has embarked upon a career, "opportunities for future job movement can narrow because of discrimination, limited opportunities for training, certification, [and] promotion, and the differential development of 'affective' personality traits."[26] Segmentation may be associated with an industry or occupation, or it may be based on people's educational background, age, sex, or race. In either case, it may be used as a screening device in making employment decisions. Radical economists believe that segmentation by race, sex, and age has been "actively and consciously fostered . . . in order to 'divide and conquer' the labor force."[27] They call for fundamental changes in our institutional framework to improve the condition of the working class and to end the "increasing social and economic stratification which has eroded and negated the tendency toward a consolidation of a working-class consciousness."[28]

A Concluding Comment

Many segmentation theories are class-oriented. The other theories, while employed by radical economists, can be considered *positive* theories providing "modifications and additions to orthodox theory."[29] This is consistent with our conclusion that marginal analysis provides an adequate description of the impact of demand on the relationship between wages and employment, particularly the general wage-employment equilibrium in the long run. At the firm and industry levels, particularly in the short run, more extensive modifications of the marginal theory are required to account for imperfections in product and labor markets, including a variety of institutional constraints. When these modifications are made, orthodox theory provides a useful framework for analyzing contemporary labor markets.

DISCUSSION QUESTIONS

1. In what ways was it necessary to modify the original marginal productivity analysis to bring it more in accord with reality?
2. Do you believe that the New Marginalism provides a satisfactory response to the critics of the original marginal productivity analysis?
3. Why may marginal analysis and Keynesian analysis be considered complementary?
4. Why does marginal productivity analysis provide an explanation for the role of demand in wage theory rather than a *theory of wage determination?*
5. In what sense does a monopsonist "exploit" labor?
6. What has led to the recent interest in "supply side" economics as contrasted with conventional Keynesian analysis?
7. How does Dunlop relate the wage structure of a firm to external market constraints?
8. How do New Left economists convert a "value free" dual labor market theory into a radical theory of wage determination?

SELECTED READINGS

The New Marginalism

Chamberlin, Edward Hastings. *The Theory of Monopolistic Competition.* Cambridge, Mass.: Harvard University Press, various editions and dates.
Robinson, Joan. *The Economics of Imperfect Competition.* London: Macmillan, 1933.

The Marginalist Controversy

Lester, Richard A. "Shortcomings of Marginal Analysis for Wage-Employment Problems." In *American Economic Review* XXXVI, no. 1 (March 1946): pp. 63–82.
Lester, Richard A.; Machlup, Fritz; and Stigler, G. J. "Communications." In *American Economic Review* XXXVII, no. 1 (March 1947): pp. 135–157.
Machlup, Fritz. "Marginal Analysis and Empirical Research." In *American Economic Review* XXXVI, no. 4, pt. 1 (September 1946): pp. 519–554.
Reynolds, Lloyd G. "Toward a Short-Run Theory of Wages." In *American Economic Review* XXXVIII, no. 3 (June 1948): pp. 289–308.

Contemporary Wage Analysis

Addison, John T. and Siebert, W. Stanley, *The Market for Labor: An Analytical Treatment* (Santa Monica, Cal.: Goodyear, 1979).

Bellante, Don, and Jackson, Mark. *Labor Economics: Choice in Labor Markets.* New York: McGraw-Hill, 1979.

Freedman, Marcia, assisted by Maclachlan, Gretchen. *Labor Markets: Segments and Shelters.* Montclair, N.J.: Allanheld, Osmun & Co., Universe Books, 1976. This and the Addison-Stanley and the Ballante-Jackson textbooks discuss various new developments.

Reder, Melvin W. "Wage Determination in Theory and Practice." In *A Decade of Industrial Relations Research 1946–1956.* Ed. by Neil W. Chamberlain, Frank C. Pierson, and Theresa Wolfson. Industrial Relations Research Association Publication No. 19. New York: Harper & Brothers, 1958. A critical summary of theories of wage structure with an extensive bibliography.

Rees, Albert. *The Economics of Work and Pay.* 2nd ed. New York: Harper & Row, 1979.

Wage Differentials

Lester, Richard A. *Company Wage Policies.* Princeton, N.J.: Industrial Relations Section, Princeton University, 1948.

Reynolds, Lloyd G. *The Structure of Labor Markets.* New York: Harper & Brothers, 1951.

Internal Wage Structures

Hildebrand, George H. "External Influences and the Determination of the Internal Wage Structure." in *Internal Wage Structure.* Ed. by J. L. Meij. Chap. 50, pp. 262–263. Amsterdam: North-Holland Publishing Company, 1963. An excellent reference.

Hugh-Jones, E. M., ed. *Wage-Structure in Theory and Practice.* Amsterdam: North-Holland Publishing Company, 1966. Another excellent reference.

Taylor, George W., and Pierson, Frank C. *New Concepts in Wage Determination.* New York: McGraw-Hill, 1957. Articles by Richard A. Lester, John T. Dunlop, and E. Robert Livernash emphasize the indeterminancy of, and discretion in, wage setting by the firm. The discussion in the text draws heavily from these sources.

Radical Labor Market Theories

Cain, Glen G. "The Challenge of Dual and Radical Theories of the Labor Market to Orthodox Theory." In *American Economic Review* LXV, no. 2 (May 1975): pp. 16–22. An excellent, concise analysis of those theories.

Cain, Glen G. "The Challenge of Segmented Labor Market Theories to Orthodox Theory: A Survey." In *Journal of Economic Literature* XIV, no. 4 (December 1976): pp. 1215–1257. A good critical review of these theories plus an excellent bibliography.

Edwards, Richard C.; Reich, Michael; and Gordon, David M., eds. *Labor Market Segmentation.* Lexington, Mass.: Heath, 1975. A basic reference text that contains articles representative of the radical perspective.

Review of Radical Political Economics. Articles in current issues of the journal of the Union for Radical Political Economics reflect developments in radical theory.

Sherman, Howard. *Radical Political Economy.* New York: Basic Books, 1972.

Notes

1. His *General Theory of Employment, Interest, and Money* appeared in 1936, published in New York by Harcourt Brace & World.
2. J. R. Hicks, "Economic Foundations of Wage Policy," in *Economic Journal* LXV, no. 259 (September 1955): p. 391. By permission Cambridge University Press.
3. Lloyd G. Reynolds, "The State of Wage Theory," in *Proceedings of the Sixth Annual Meeting, Industrial Relations Research Association, 1953* (Madison, Wisc., 1954), p. 235.
4. John T. Dunlop, "The Task of Contemporary Wage Theory," in Dunlop, ed., *The Theory of Wage Determination* (New York: St. Martin's Press, 1957), p. 10.
5. Ibid., p. 13, emphasis added. See also Dunlop's "Policy Decisions and Research in Economics and Industrial Relations," in *Industrial and Labor Relations Review* 30, no. 3 (April 1977): pp. 275–282 and Reynolds's "The State of Wage Theory," p. 234.
6. Lloyd G. Reynolds, *The Structure of Labor Markets,* (New York: Harper & Brothers, 1951), p. 186.
7. Ibid., p. 187.
8. Lloyd G. Reynolds, "Toward a Short-Run Theory of Wages," in *American Economic Review* XXXVIII, no. 3 (June 1948): p. 301.
9. Dunlop, "The Task of Contemporary Wage Theory," p. 15.
10. Ibid., pp. 16–17 (emphasis added).
11. Ibid, p. 17.
12. Ibid. (emphasis added).
13. Ibid., p. 19.
14. See Lloyd G. Reynolds and Cynthia H. Taft, *The Evolution of Wage Structure* (New Haven, Conn.: Yale University Press, 1956), pp. 167–169.
15. Glen G. Cain, "The Challenge of Segmented Labor Market Theories to Orthodox Theory: A Survey," In *Journal of Economic Literature,* XIV, no. 4 (December 1976), p. 1223.
16. Peter B. Doeringer and Michael J. Piore, *Internal Labor Markets and Manpower Analysis* (Lexington, Mass.: Heath, 1971), p. 2.
17. Ibid.
18. Ibid.
19. Ibid., pp. 73, 77.
20. Michael J. Piore, "Notes for a Theory of Labor Market Stratification," in Richard G. Edwards, Michael Reich, and David M. Gordon, eds., *Labor Market Segmentation* (Lexington, Mass.: Heath, 1975), p. 126.
21. Doeringer and Piore, *Internal Labor Markets,* p. 166.
22. Ibid., p. 165.
23. Piore, "Notes for a Theory of Labor Market Stratification," p. 125.
24. Ibid., p. 140.
25. Ibid., p. 139.

26. Howard Birnbaum, "The Economic Effect of Career Origins," in Edwards, Reich, and Gordon, eds., *Labor Market Segmentation*, p. 154.

27. Michael Reich, David M. Gordon, and Richard C. Edwards, "A Theory of Labor Market Segmentation," in *American Economic Review* LXIII, no. 2 (May 1973): p. 361.

28. Howard M. Wachtel, "Class Consciousness and Stratification in the Labor Process," in Edwards, Reich, and Gordon, eds., *Labor Market Segmentation*, p. 99.

29. Glen G. Cain, "The Challenge of Dual and Radical Theories of the Labor Market to Orthodox Theory," in *American Economic Review* LXV, no. 2 (May 1975): p. 21.

Chapter 7
DEFINING, PREVENTING, AND REDUCING UNEMPLOYMENT

The seasonally adjusted unemployment rate may be, "at least in its political implications, the most important single statistic published by the Federal Government."[1]

Unemployment is the most serious continuing threat to the economic security of workers in industrial societies. In individual cases, it can be a source of great suffering. If it is both widespread and persistent, it can create explosive social tensions.

Economists emphasize the *unemployment rate* rather than the *absolute number* of persons *unemployed* because changes in the second variable do not necessarily reflect a worsening or bettering of economic conditions. As the size of the labor force increases, a given unemployment rate will mean a larger absolute number of persons unemployed.

There is no precise measure of *full employment* or, conversely, of an acceptable *minimal rate of unemployment*. The definition of full employment will not remain constant but "can be expected to change with time as demographic, social, and economic factors affect the rates at which workers move in and out of jobs, and in and out of the work force."[2] In the early 1960s, the Council of Economic

Advisers had a "full-employment" target unemployment rate of 4 percent; in 1977, the target rate was closer to 5½ percent.[3]

In this chapter, we will briefly consider basic legislation designed to deal with the unemployment problem, discuss the paradox of persistent high unemployment during sustained inflation, describe how unemployment and employment are measured in the United States, identify the basic types of unemployment, discuss the principal actions that may be taken to reduce or prevent an increase in the unemployment rate, and note the types of income maintenance programs devised to help the unemployed and their families.

FEDERAL "FULL"-EMPLOYMENT LEGISLATION

In earlier chapters, we noted how the classical and neoclassical theorists assumed that a perfectly competitive economy would move automatically toward a full-employment equilibrium. A minimal amount of short-run unemployment was required to accommodate changes in demand and supply in product and factor markets, but any tendency toward large-scale or long-run unemployment would be self-correcting.

The Keynesians, responding to persistent high unemployment during the Depression, argued that advanced industrial economies would not necessarily move toward a full-employment equilibrium and that fiscal and monetary weapons might be required to raise aggregate demand to a level that would provide adequate employment opportunities. Following World War II, Congress passed the Employment Act of 1946, which was designed "to promote maximum employment, production and purchasing power."[4]

During the postwar period, cyclical fluctuations in employment were much reduced, but the level of "prosperity" unemployment increased. In addition, prices increased persistently. In 1978, Congress decided that since the nation's monetary and fiscal policies had failed to produce full employment, higher real incomes, balanced growth, a balanced federal budget, an adequate growth in productivity, proper attention to national priorities, an improved trade balance, and reasonable price stability, other measures were called for to achieve these ends.[5] These "other measures" were incorporated in the Humphrey-Hawkins Full Employment and Balanced Growth Act of 1978, amending the Employment Act of 1946.

The Humphrey-Hawkins Act requires the President to establish "annual numerical goals for employment and unemployment, production, real income, productivity, and prices [to be] designated as short-term goals," as well as annual numerical goals for three successive years, to be designated as medium-term goals. The medium-term goals were to be designed to reduce the unemployment rate to 3 percent among persons aged 20 and over, and 4 percent among persons aged 16 and over. They were also to be designed to achieve a 3 percent inflation rate within five years, provided essential steps taken to reduce inflation did not interfere with the unemployment goals and timetables. Once inflation was reduced to 3 percent, a new goal of zero percent inflation by 1988 was to be established. As we will see, these goals appear unrealistic as we enter the decade of the eighties. However, the act did permit the President to recommend modifications in these timetables. The goals were to be considered desirable objectives, rather than immutable standards.

By 1979, liberals as well as conservatives in Congress had recognized that demand-oriented macroeconomic policies could not ensure full employment without increasing inflation. The Joint Economic Committee noted that such policies would have to be supplemented by microeconomic initiatives designed to develop needed skills among persons seeking entry level jobs and to lessen upward pressures on wages in highly skilled labor markets by increasing the supply of trained workers.[6] The committee also noted that these unemployment programs should be accompanied by measures to increase capital formation.[7] In short, the Joint Economic Committee, in a dramatic shift, recognized that Keynesian policies emphasizing the need for sustained high level aggregate demand, particularly for adequate consumer purchasing power, have not enabled us to attain our basic rational economic objectives and that so-called supply-side economic initiatives are also necessary.

THE TRADE-OFF BETWEEN UNEMPLOYMENT AND INFLATION

Except in 1955, when it decreased slightly, the Consumer Price Index has risen persistently since the end of World War II. It went from 58.5 (1967 = 100) in 1946 to 116.3 in 1970 and to 247.8 in July 1980. Despite all this, the annual unemployment rate in the 1970s never fell below 4.9 percent, and the monthly rate rose to 9.1 percent three times during the recession of 1974–1975. Economists disagree as to the primary causes of the post-World War II inflation. One group lays the blame primarily on *excessive demand,* particularly when bottlenecks (an inability to increase output) develop in specific product markets. A second group emphasizes the role of *cost-push factors,* such as the ability of large firms to raise their prices (possibly in anticipation of general price and wage increases) and the ability of unions to negotiate wage increases in excess of increases in productivity.

In retrospect, most economists believe that increases in aggregate demand were the principal cause of inflation in the 1970s, although cost-push factors assumed more importance for short periods and often helped generate a higher level of demand. Demand is an essential element in both explanations of inflation, since a rise in the general price level due to cost-push factors will not last unless fiscal and monetary authorities permit aggregate demand to reach a level that "validates" the increase.

The Ratchet Effect

The fact that wages and prices tend to be flexible *upward* but inflexible *downward* helps to explain the sometimes hesitant but sustained upward movement in prices in recent years. This has been termed the *ratchet effect.* Collective bargaining agreements covering more than one year, escalator clauses that provide for wage increases pegged to price increases, the spread of wage increases based on patterns established in highly visible collective bargaining relationships, and "implicit contracts" between employers and employees which provide that wages and benefits will not be reduced during economic downturns contribute to the ratchet effect.

The Phillips Curve

The *Phillips curve,* named after Professor A. W. Phillips of the London School of Economics, has been widely used to relate changes in unemployment, prices, and wages and to illustrate the resulting trade-offs. A modified Phillips curve is shown in Figure 7.1.

Assume that productivity per man-hour is rising at a rate of 3 percent per year. The Phillips curve shows that if wages also rise 3 percent a year, prices need not rise because the economy can absorb the increase. Unemployment will average 5½ percent annually under these conditions. To reduce the unemployment rate, prices and wages must rise, the actual increase depending on the target unemployment rate. A target of 3 percent will generate a price rise of about 4½ percent. Although useful for illustrative purposes, the phillips curve does not explain *why* these interrelationships obtain. It was assumed initially that the Phillips curve

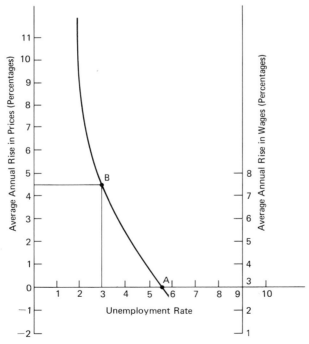

Figure 7.1   Trade-offs Between Wages, Prices, and Employment (Source: Based on Paul A. Samuelson and Robert M. Solow, "Problem of Achieving and Maintaining a Stable Price Level," in *American Economic Review* L, no. 2 [May 1960]: p. 192.)

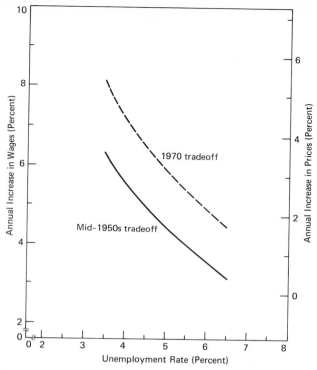

Figure 7.2   A Shift in Trade-offs Between Inflation and Unemployment (Source: Based on George L. Perry, "Changing Labor Markets and Inflation," in *Brookings Paper on Economic Activity* 3 [1970]: Figure 2, p. 432.) Copyright © 1970 by The Brookings Institution, 1775 Massachusetts Avenue, N.W., Washington, D.C., 20036

would fall below the x-axis at high levels of unemployment; that is, that prices would decrease. However, given our recent persistent inflation and the ratchet effect, many economists now believe that a Phillips curve reflecting market realities will lie above the x-axis.

Moreover, despite attempts to improve the inflation-unemployment trade-off, the (short-run) Phillips curve for the United States has apparently shifted upward and to the right. The deterioration in this trade-off is illustrated in Figure 7.2. In 1970, with unemployment at 4 percent, the annual rate of inflation was estimated to have been 1.7 percent higher than it would have been in the economy of the mid-1950s.[8]

Economists have begun to question the validity of the presumed trade-offs between inflation and unemployment represented by the Phillips curve. Some studies have suggested that since 1954, the Phillips curve has not only shifted outward but also become steeper. It is assumed that collective bargaining arrangements now enable "firms and unions to react more rapidly to labor-market conditions."[9] In essence, it is argued that as inflation increases, the public's inflationary expectations will rise, and the rate of inflation will be higher at any given unemployment rate. A long-run Phillips curve incorporating such expectations will therefore be much steeper than a conventional short-run Phillips curve.

In the extreme case in which the wage increases secured by workers correctly anticipate future price increases, the Phillips curve would be a vertical line at what has been termed the *natural rate of unemployment*. It is argued that

> the natural rate of unemployment is a real phenomenon. . . . Purely *nominal* forces . . . cannot change the natural rate. The implication for Phillips curve analysis is most striking—there is no long-run trade-off between inflation and unemployment.[10]

MEASURING UNEMPLOYMENT

The Overall Unemployment Rate

In Chapter 4, we explained how the federal government derives official figures on employment and unemployment from the *Current Population Survey*. Respondents to this sample survey are not asked whether they are "employed" or "unemployed;" their answers to a series of questions determine their status as *employed, unemployed,* or *not in the labor force*. The BLS defines the country's unemployed population as including

> all persons 16 years of age and over who did not work at all during the survey week (except for a temporary illness), and who made at least one specific attempt to find work during the prior 4 weeks. In addition, persons on layoff who may not have searched for work, and those waiting to start a new job within 30 days are included among the unemployed.[11]

Persons enter the ranks of the unemployed by losing a job (or being laid off), leaving a job voluntarily, or failing to find work when they enter or reenter the labor force. The relative importance of each source of unemployment reflects the overall level of economic activity. Figure 7.3 shows the changes in each subgroup of the unemployed during the recession of 1973–1975.

The official unemployment rate underestimates the number of persons who would seek jobs in more prosperous times because it is based on the number of *active* job seekers. It does, however, have "the important quality of representing an actual, effective labor force supply."[12] In response to demands for additional general measures of unemployment, the bureau provides "seven different reasonable definitions of unemployment."[13] These measures are defined, and illustrated for the period 1953–1976, in Figure 7.4. The first measure, U-1, is the most restrictive; U-7 is the broadest measure of unemployment, while U-5 is the conventional unemployment rate.

The Employment-Population Ratio

As a result of the increase in the size of the civilian labor force, due in part to the greater percentage of adult women seeking work, the unemployment rate has

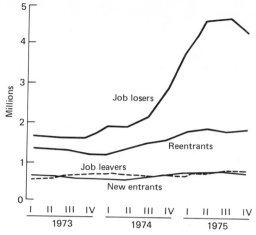

Figure 7.3   Immediate "Causes" of Unemployment, 1973–1975 (Seasonally Adjusted Quarterly Average) (Source: *Employment and Training Report of the President, Including Reports by the U.S. Department of Labor and the U.S. Department of Health, Education, and Welfare, Transmitted to the Congress 1976,* Chart 5, p. 28.)

remained high even when total employment has reached record levels. The use of an *employment-population ratio* (the percentage of the civilian population 16 and over employed) rather than the unemployment rate is designed to "capture" such an "improvement" in the job market. Figure 7.5 shows both measures for the years 1968–1978.

Selected Unemployment Data

The overall unemployment rate conceals the differential impact of unemployment. Table 7.1 illustrates the incidence of unemployment for selected groups in 1969, when unemployment was low, and in 1975, a recession year.

The differential impact of unemployment on workers in major *industries* in 1969 and 1975 is illustrated in Table 7.2. Unemployment rates for experienced workers in different occupations in 1975 are shown in Table 7.3.

The increase in the "severity" of recession unemployment in recent years is suggested by the data in Table 7.4, which show the percentage distribution of the unemployed by duration of unemployment in 1969, when the overall unemployment rate was 3.5 percent, and 1975, when the rate was 8.5 percent.

The queue theory and the dual labor market theory, both of which were discussed in Chapter 6, are consistent with many of the data in the tables. Disadvantaged and inexperienced workers who are at the end of the hiring queue or confined to jobs in the secondary labor market are out of work more frequently and are relatively harder hit by decreases in aggregate demand.

Caveats in Measuring Unemployment

Annual averages conceal the flows into and out of the labor force and employment during a given year and the number of workers experiencing more than a single spell of unemployment. In 1975, a recession year, 101.2 million persons worked at some time during the year, although the average employment figure for the year was 84.8 million. During the same year, unemployment averaged 8.5 percent on an annual basis, but 20.2 percent of the 104.4 million persons who worked or looked for work experienced unemployment.[14]

    An individual becomes an unemployment or employment statistic only if he or she is a participant in the labor force. Consequently, changes in the level of unemployment are not necessarily equal or opposite to changes in the level of

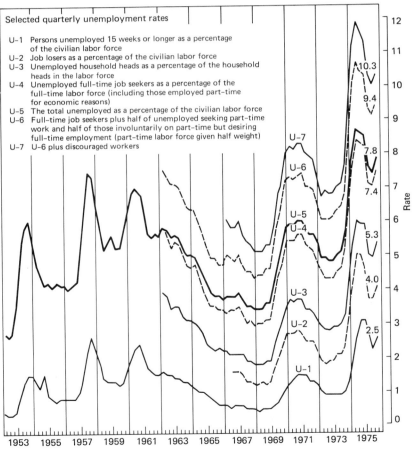

Figure 7.4 BLS Unemployment Indicators (Source: U.S. Department of Labor, Bureau of Labor Statistics, *Labor Force and Unemployment,* Report 486, Chart 2, p. 4.)

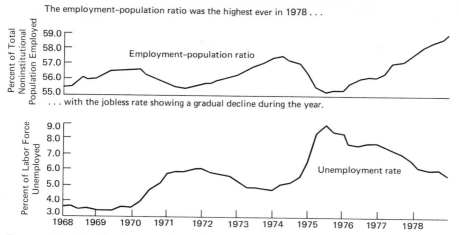

Figure 7.5   The Employment-Population Ratio and the Unemployment Rate, 1968–1978 (Seasonally Adjusted Quarterly Averages) (Source: *Employment and Training Report of the President, Including Reports by the U.S. Department of Labor and the U.S. Department of Health, Education, and Welfare, Transmitted to the Congress 1979,* Chart 1, p. 6.)

employment. Nor can one assume that changes in the level of unemployment will be inversely related in a strict fashion to changes in the level of aggregate demand and output. The substitution of capital for labor or the improvement of technology may result in a greater output from the same or a smaller labor force.

Estimates of the general relationship between changes in the level of output and the unemployment rate are therefore hazardous. One study concluded that "at a given time, each extra 1 percent of real GNP means a decrement, on the average, of about one-third of a percentage point in the unemployment rate."[15] Thus, to

Table 7.1   SELECTED UNEMPLOYMENT RATES, 1969 AND 1975 (percentages)

	1969	1975
All workers	3.5	8.5
Both sexes, ages 16–19	12.2	19.9
Males 20 and over	2.1	6.7
Females 20 and over	3.7	8.0
Whites	3.1	7.8
Blacks and others	6.4	13.9
Experienced workers	3.3	8.2
Heads of households	1.8	5.8
Married men	1.5	5.1
Full-time workers	3.1	8.1
Blue-collar workers	3.9	11.7

SOURCE: *Economic Report of the President, Transmitted to the Congress January 1977, Together with the Annual Report of the Council of Economic Advisers,* Table B–29, p. 221.

Table 7.2 UNEMPLOYMENT RATES IN MAJOR INDUSTRIES, 1969 AND 1975

	1969	1975
Total unemployed*	3.5	8.5
All experienced wage and salary workers	3.3	8.2
Agricultural workers	6.0	10.3
Nonagricultural workers	3.5	9.2
Mining	2.9	4.0
Construction	6.0	18.1
Manufacturing	3.3	10.9
Transportation and public utilities	2.2	5.6
Wholesale and retail trades	4.1	8.7
Finance, insurance, and real estate	2.1	4.9
Service industries	3.5	7.1
Government workers	1.9	4.0

* Also includes the self-employed, unpaid family workers, and those with no previous work experience, data on which are not shown separately.
SOURCE: *Employment and Training Report of the President, Including Reports by the U.S. Department of Labor and the U.S. Department of Health, Education, and Welfare, Transmitted to the Congress 1977*, Table A–22, p. 172.

reduce unemployment from 8.5 to 5.5 percent, the level of aggregate economic activity would have to increase by 9 percent.

TYPES OF UNEMPLOYMENT

At present, most economists recognize three principal types of unemployment: (1) *frictional, or "normal," short-run unemployment*, resulting from changes in demand and supply relationships in a dynamic economy; (2) *demand deficiency*

Table 7.3 UNEMPLOYMENT RATES FOR EXPERIENCED WORKERS IN DIFFERENT OCCUPATIONS, 1975 (percentages)

All workers	8.5	
White-collar workers	4.7	
Professional and technical workers		3.2
Managers and administrators		3.0
Sales workers		5.8
Clerical workers		6.6
Blue-collar workers	11.7	
Craft and kindred workers		8.3
Operatives		13.2
Nonfarm laborers		15.6
Service workers	8.6	
Private household workers		5.4
Other service workers		8.9
Farmers and farm laborers	3.5	

SOURCE: *Employment and Training Report of the President, Including Reports by the U.S. Department of Labor and the U.S. Department of Health, Education, and Welfare, Transmitted to the Congress 1977*, Table A–21, p. 171.

Table 7.4 THE DURATION OF UNEMPLOYMENT, 1969 AND 1975 (percentages)

	1969	1975
Total unemployed	100.0	100.0
Percentage unemployed		
less than 5 weeks	57.5	37.0
5 to 6 weeks	9.3	8.4
7 to 10 weeks	12.9	13.8
11 to 14 weeks	7.1	9.1
15 weeks and over	13.2	31.7
15 to 36 weeks	8.5	16.5
27 weeks and over	4.7	15.2

SOURCE: *Employment and Training Report of the President, Including Reports by the U.S. Department of Labor and the U.S. Department of Health, Education, and Welfare, Transmitted to the Congress 1979*, Table A–26, p. 274.

unemployment, resulting from a level of aggregate demand that is too low to provide jobs for all active and prospective participants in the labor force; and (3) *structural unemployment*, resulting from continuing imbalances (a) between job opportunities and the qualifications (or perceived qualifications) of job applicants or (b) in the geographic distribution of the supply of and demand for labor. There is an additional general category of *unemployables*, persons who cannot join the labor force due to family obligations or who are not considered for employment because of their low productivity.

Frictional, or "Normal," Unemployment

Some unemployment will exist even when there is "full" employment. If the labor market is efficient, the duration of this unemployment will be short. Although the level of unemployment may remain constant, the composition of the unemployed population will vary. This type of *transitional* unemployment is called frictional, or "normal," because it is considered not only inevitable but functional. *Casual* and *seasonal* unemployment are often considered part of normal unemployment.

Casual unemployment is a result of intermittent employment in labor markets characterized by fluctuations in the daily demands for labor and in some cases a permanent surplus of labor. *Seasonal unemployment* "results from the periodic entry of jobseekers into the labor force as well as from the periodic layoff of employed workers."[16] This type of unemployment has a recognizable, often regular, periodicity, and is the result of factors operating within periods of less than a year.

Technological Unemployment

Some economists consider the unemployment resulting from technological change a separate type of unemployment. It is possible to differentiate conceptually between technological innovations that result in a minimal and essentially short-run displacement of labor and innovations that produce more massive and persistent unemployment. Although the distinction is tenuous, the former type of technological unemployment may be construed as frictional, whereas the latter may be considered as structural. From a practical standpoint however, a separate category of technological unemployment is unnecessary and may even mask the variable impact of technological change.

A Note on Automation

Following World War II, economists and government officials became concerned about the increase in unemployment associated with automation. According to one source, "the word 'automation' has more romance than meaning," and as a description of a particular type of technological change it is both complex and vague.[17] In any event, unemployment caused by automation may be considered a variety of technological unemployment. If it is brief, it may be considered frictional; if it is prolonged, it may be explained as structural.

Demand Deficiency Unemployment

Demand deficiency unemployment may be divided into two subcategories: (1) the unemployment associated with downswings in aggregate economic activity and (2) that associated with a continuing failure to generate sufficient aggregate demand to reduce the unemployment rate to the full-employment target rate. Unlike frictional unemployment, which presumably lasts only until a worker has located the best available job, demand deficiency unemployment is the result of too few job opportunities. It is a type of continuing *involuntary unemployment*.

CYCLICAL OR RECESSION UNEMPLOYMENT

The unemployment associated with decreases in overall business activity was considered, until recently, the most significant and costly type of unemployment in industrial market economies. The broad swings in the basic unemployment rate (U-5) from 1953 to 1977 were shown in Figure 7.4.

GROWTH-GAP UNEMPLOYMENT

We have noted the increase in "prosperity unemployment" since World War II and the increase in both the rate of unemployment and the rate of inflation during the recession of 1974–1975. Some economists who reject the structural transformation hypothesis described in the following section and emphasize the need for a higher level of aggregate demand believe that persistent unemployment develops when the economy is unable to grow fast enough. They call this kind of unemployment, which continues at an abnormally high level during the prosperous phase of a business cycle, *growth-gap unemployment*.[18]

Structural Unemployment

During the 1960s, labor market analysts began to emphasize the growth in *structural unemployment,* that is, the long-term (continuing) unemployment resulting from changes in economic variables affecting particular occupations, industries, or geographic areas or from the failure to provide prospective workers with the general education or particular skills required for specific jobs. In 1961, a congressional committee noted that

> distinctions between "frictional" and "structural" unemployment are not sharp. . . . Both commonly are thought of as consequences of impediments to [the] adjustment of labor demand and supply in a dynamic economic system in which there are continuous changes in technology, in consumer tastes, in plant location, and in the composition, distribution, and uses of labor and other resources; since these changes are inherent in our economy, they are considered part of its nature or structure.
>
> The word "structural" frequently implies that the economic changes are massive, extensive, deepseated. . . .[19]

This explanation of long-term unemployment is called the *structural transformation hypothesis.* At a somewhat later date, economists recognized that long-term unemployment could also result from imperfections in the labor market, including discrimination against certain demographic groups.

Structural unemployment and growth-gap unemployment are interrelated. With the growth of aggregate demand, some unemployment identified as structural will disappear; employers will hire farther down the queue, and hiring and job requirements may be modified to absorb workers from the secondary labor market. Structural unemployment that cannot be reduced significantly by increasing the level of aggregate demand without adversely affecting other basic economic goals, including reasonably stable prices, is sometimes termed *hard core unemployment.*

Hidden or Disguised Unemployment

A number of types of unemployment are not included in conventional aggregate unemployment estimates. These include the premature withdrawal of older workers from the labor force; the withdrawal of discouraged workers (frequently women and part-time employees), who would remain in the labor force if enough jobs were available; the underemployment or underutilization of workers, that is, the "employment of persons at jobs that call for less than their highest current level of skill";[20] and the employment on a part-time basis of workers who are available for and want full-time employment.*

---

* However, see Figure 7.4, p. 138. Note that disguised unemployment is not limited to the more highly developed economies; there is also an underemployment of human resources in many agrarian economies in which labor has been overallocated to agriculture.

Unemployables

There will always be some persons who are (1) unable to enter the labor market because their families need their services at home or (2) unable to find work because their marginal revenue productivity is less than the market wage or the statutory minimum wage and they have physical or mental limitations which indicate that their productivity cannot be increased sufficiently to enable them to qualify for available jobs. These *unemployables* must be distinguished from persons excluded from employment by such factors as social legislation (compulsory school attendance), a lack of child care facilities, or discriminatory hiring.

PREVENTING AND LESSENING UNEMPLOYMENT

Keeping the unemployment rate at an acceptably low level requires a variety of preventive and remedial measures. These may be divided into four categories: (1) *general* (macroeconomic) *measures* to keep employment at the highest level consistent with other national priorities (or, conversely, to keep the unemployment rate at the lowest level consistent with this goal); (2) measures to help the labor market to *function more efficiently;* (3) *manpower programs,* both *development and training* and *employment programs;* and (4) public and private programs to provide *income* to unemployed individuals and their families.

The specific components of a balanced attack on unemployment will depend on the level of existing and anticipated unemployment and its distribution. A given program may also have to be modified as its effects are felt.

General Measures

There are two related general objectives of employment policy: the moderation of recurrent fluctuations in employment and the attainment of a "reasonably" non-inflationary full-employment level of national income. This means a reduction in both cyclical (or recession) and growth-gap unemployment. Keynesian analysis provides the foundation for the macroeconomic policies and policy instruments that are presently used for this purpose.

In a Keynesian model of the economy, the level of national income depends on the total level of spending for consumption and investment by the private and public sectors. If the economy is not at a full-employment equilibrium, macroeconomic policies should be used to increase aggregate spending.[21] These policies fall into two broad—and not mutually exclusive—categories: (1) *compensatory* policies designed to moderate fluctuations in the general level of economic activity and employment and (2) policies designed to achieve *sustained full employment.* Compensatory instruments include (1) *automatic,* or "built-in," *stabilizers,* such as the progressive income tax, that are intended to function contracyclically without the need for specific administrative or legislative action; and (2) *discretionary* weapons, such as open market action by the Federal Reserve Board or changes in tax rates made on an ad hoc basis.

As we have noted before, a noninflationary full-employment equilibrium has proved increasingly elusive as the trade-off between unemployment and inflation illustrated by the Phillips curve has worsened. The inflationary expectations now present in the economy make it increasingly difficult to reduce the rate of inflation without an increase in unemployment. It has been pointed out, for example, that "anticipations . . . build a momentum into inflationary movements that takes time to abate and that . . . the distortions and dislocations due to the differential impacts of restraint are serious and protracted."[22] This obviously creates a dilemma for any administration: will the polity that demands a reduction in the rate of inflation accept an antiinflation program that impacts severely upon particular economic sectors and demographic groups?

It should be noted that the attempt by economists to explain certain microeconomic aspects of the modern inflationary process within accepted elements of the postclassical Keynesian analysis has led to interest in what has been termed the microeconomic foundations of macroeconomic analysis.[23]

WAGE-PRICE GUIDEPOSTS

In 1962, President John F. Kennedy's Council of Economic Advisers, recognizing the need to reconcile such goals as noninflationry prices and wages under generally prosperous conditions, formulated certain *wage-price guideposts*. These guideposts were to be used to determine whether wage and price decisions in the private sector were consistent with national economic policy. According to the 1965 *Annual Report* of the council,

1. The general guide for wages is that the percentage increase in total employee compensation per man-hour be equal to the national trend rate of increase in output per man-hour. . . .
2. The general guide for prices calls for stable prices in industries enjoying the same productivity growth as the average for the economy; rising prices in industries with smaller than average productivity gains; and declining prices in industries with greater than average productivity gains.[24]

The administration hoped that a successful guidepost policy would, in effect, shift the Phillips curve for the country to the left and improve the trade-off between wages and inflation at various levels of national income. Unfortunately, the standards established by successive economic councils tended to be viewed by both management and labor as bases from which *upward* adjustments could be made. The surge in inflation that resulted from the escalation of federal expenditures during the Vietnam conflict led to the abandonment of specific guideposts in 1967. The whole experience suggested that in periods of high excess demand, a policy of voluntary adherence to wage-price guideposts would not work. However, the guideposts that were set, by illuminating the connection between wages, prices, and productivity, did focus the attention of labor, management, federal officials, and the public on economic relationships that are often ignored. They also may have served as a modest restraint on inflation.[25]

THE NIXON WAGE-PRICE FREEZE

The country's experience with wage-price controls during the Nixon administration suggests that a wage-price freeze may lower inflationary expectations temporarily but that, except in a national emergency, it is difficult to implement such a policy for more than 6 to 12 months. Moreover, when controls are removed, pent-up pressures on wages and prices are likely to rekindle inflationary expectations.

RECENT EXPERIENCE

Our inability to reduce the unemployment rate despite persistent inflation has been frustrating to economic policy makers. According to George Perry of the Brookings Institution:

> The 1970s differ from previous experience both in the amount of inflation . . . and in the relation between the current inflation and the current unemployment rate. Although recession raised the unemployment rate in 1970 and 1971, the rate of inflation scarcely slackened. . . . [W]ith the end of [wage-price] controls, the private nonfarm [price] deflator rose more than 8 percent in both 1974 and 1975 in the midst of a recession that brought the unemployment rate to a post war record high of 8.5 percent.[26]

Apparently, under current conditions, it may not be possible to lessen inflationary pressures without a degree of monetary and fiscal restraint that would create a politically unacceptable level of unemployment.

THE CARTER WAGE-PRICE "STANDARDS"

Faced with a rising rate of inflation and high unemployment, President Carter, on October 24, 1978, introduced a program of wage-price guidelines, or standards. The objectives were to hold average annual price increases to 5.75 percent and average annual wage gains to 7 percent. The program was backed by limited sanctions, principally the denial of government contracts to firms violating the standards. Although wage increases may have been controlled to some extent by the standard, it was breached in 1979 by a series of major negotiations, and the inflation rate reached 13.9 percent by the end of the year. Price increases for such basic commodities as oil, food, and health care proved particularly troublesome.

RECENT INITIATIVES

In the fall of 1979, the Federal Reserve Board, under its new chairman, Paul Volcker, adopted a policy of monetary restraint that centered on control of the bank reserves used as the base of our money supply. The board hoped that this would reduce the rate of inflation. Unfortunately, the Iranian crisis and periodic increases in the world price of oil have helped to sustain inflationary pressures.

President Carter has disavowed the use of mandatory wage-price controls. He apparently believes that the fight against inflation has priority over attempts to further reduce the unemployment rate. In October 1979, he appointed a new *Pay Advisory Committee,* chaired by Professor John Dunlop of Harvard, to help design the administration's 1980 wage restraint program and monitor wage developments, particularly in highly visible union-management negotiations. This action was part of a "National Accord" reached with organized labor in order to gain its support for the Carter program of *voluntary* price and wage standards. The reader will be able to judge whether this proved feasible during the 1980 election year!

It is clear that there is now a growing consensus among economists that if we are to *simultaneously* reduce the overall unemployment rate and the rate of inflation, less stress should be placed on demand-oriented macroeconomic policies and more on supply-oriented macro- and microeconomic initiatives.

Overcoming Structural Unemployment

A comprehensive attack on structural unemployment will include policies to (1) maintain adequate aggregate demand; (2) provide additional jobs or prevent further decreases in job opportunities in particular industries, occupations, and geographic areas; and (3) increase the employability of workers among whom unemployment is unusually high.

Monetary and fiscal policies and instruments are our first line of defense against structural unemployment. Although hard core unemployment will not be reduced significantly as labor markets tighten during an economic upswing, less stubborn forms of structural unemployment will decline. There will be an increase in the number and quality of jobs available to workers far down the hiring queue or in secondary labor markets.

Monetary and fiscal action to reduce structural unemployment must be supplemented with programs to (1) preserve or create jobs in industries, occupations, or geographic areas with persistent high employment and (2) provide education and training to help the hard core unemployed qualify for jobs.

The recent emphasis on the *kind,* as well as the amount of unemployment, is a by-product of the concern in the 1960s over persistent unemployment, initially the long-term unemployment of white male heads of households. This concern was heightened by worries about the effect of automation. The first programs were designed to match the skills and location of experienced workers with developing job opportunities. The policy thrust gradually shifted however to programs emphasizing the training and placement of the hard core unemployed. In addition, a variety of institutional barriers to employment were attacked under the Civil Rights Act of 1964, the 1963 amendment to the Fair Labor Standards Act that provided "equal pay for equal work," and the Age Discrimination in Employment Act of 1967.

A FURTHER SHIFT IN POLICY EMPHASIS

As time went on, microeconomic employment policy began to stress the provision of jobs—including public employment—for the hard core unemployed and for persons experiencing transitional unemployment during periods of high overall unemployment. This second policy shift was the result of (1) a continuing failure to generate enough employment opportunities in the private sector, (2) the limited success of educational and training programs for the hard core unemployed, and (3) the new job opportunities created by the high rate of growth of the public sector.[27] It was based on two somewhat inconsistent arguments: (1) that hard core structural unemployment could not be reached by fiscal and monetary policies, (2) that a level of aggregate demand high enough to absorb a significant proportion of such unemployment would be unacceptable due to the resulting high rate of inflation.

THE GOVERNMENT AS AN "EMPLOYER OF LAST RESORT"

During the 1970s, there was growing acceptance of the responsibility of government to act as an "employer of last resort" for the long-term unemployed and the "unemployables" excluded from the labor market by their low productivity. In 1977, the Carter administration, as an emergency measure, expanded programs that provided funds for public service employment, public works construction, and countercyclical revenue sharing. In 1978, Title II of the Comprehensive Employment and Training Act was amended to create a special category of public service jobs for disadvantaged workers and the long-term unemployed.

The Humphrey-Hawkins Act established the following *priorities in expanding the number of jobs* with government assistance:

1. the expansion of conventional private sector jobs through the improved use of *general economic and structural policies;*
2. the expansion of private employment with federal assistance;
3. the expansion of public employment; and
4. the provision of jobs by the government as an employer of last resort.[28]

The act also identifies groups that require special help. According to section 104,

> in taking action to reduce unemployment . . . every effort shall be made to reduce . . . differences between the rate of unemployment among youth, women, minorities, handicapped persons, veterans, middle-aged and older persons and other labor force groups and the overall rate of unemployment. . . .

Reducing "Normal" Unemployment

A certain volume of "normal" or *frictional* unemployment is expected and necessary when there is "full" employment (which we define as the maximum level of employment consistent with a "reasonable" level of price inflation). The frictional unemployment that exists when there is full employment is not pathological. Jobs in which the training and skills of those seeking work can be put to good use do exist, and unemployment does not last long. The elimination of imperfections in labor markets—including discriminatory employment practices—will reduce the minimal level of unemployment in prosperous times and make it easier for workers to move from the secondary to the primary labor market.

Both the *casual* and *seasonal* components of normal unemployment can be reduced. Casual labor markets may be organized more efficiently. By limiting the supply of labor attached to a particular local labor market through a work permit system, for example, more regular employment can be provided and annual incomes increased.

Seasonal fluctuations in production and employment can also be reduced. A firm may be able to provide greater continuity of employment by diversifying its products (making both oil burners and air conditioners), producing during an off-season, granting special discounts to off-season purchasers, and improving its forecasting and forward planning. It may also be possible to overcome variations in production resulting from climate or custom. In the automobile industry, for example, the shift in the introduction of new models to the fall from the traditional spring date helped to stabilize job opportunities on an annual basis.

THE U.S. EMPLOYMENT SERVICE (JOB SERVICE)

The U.S. Employment Service (ES) (now known as the Job Service in most states), established by the Wagner-Peyser Act of 1933, represents a continuing effort by the government to increase the efficiency of the labor market by matching workers with jobs. The ES was designed to serve as a national public employment office, providing placement and counseling services as well as information on the labor market. In 1935, with the passage of the Social Security Act, the ES became the agency responsible for administering the *work test* required by the federal-state unemployment insurance system. This had the unfortunate result of categorizing job applicants using the service as marginal workers, so that both employers and workers became reluctant to turn to it for help. Despite such innovations as computerized *job banks* and a computerized *Job Information Service*, most employers do not consider the ES a good source of job applicants, and only 26.3 percent of the unemployed job seekers used public employment agencies in fiscal 1978.[29] During the same period, 15.5 million applicants registered with the ES, employers listed 9.5 million job openings, and the ES placed 4.6 million applicants.[30]

DEVELOPMENT AND TRAINING PROGRAMS

Development and *training programs* are designed to improve the skills and thus the competitive position of people who are presently or potentially part of the *supply* of labor. However, the overall demand for labor must be adequate and discrimination in employment held to a minimum if suitable *continuing* employment is to be provided for program participants.

Finding trainees a job is not enough. Participating in such programs raises people's expectations about the kind of work they can do, and if their expectations are not realized, the result is frustration and alienation. Unfortunately, graduates of training programs may be among the first to be laid off in a recessionary economy because of their lack of seniority.

Measures to maintain or increase the number of job opportunities were discussed earlier in the chapter. Efforts to ensure that every person has equal access to job opportunities will be discussed in Chapters 9 and 18. Our concern here is with programs that represent an investment in human capital, a process that encompasses "activities that influence future monetary and psychic income by increasing the resources in people."[31]

Hopefully, the private and social benefits of such programs will exceed their costs. The productivity of the trainees is raised, their (re)employment reduces the volume of unemployment, transfer payments such as unemployment insurance and welfare benefits are also reduced, and the taxes the new jobholders pay on their income generates new revenues for the government. However, private employers (and frequently community and state officials) are often reluctant to establish training programs that emphasize general rather than specific skills. Given the mobility of labor, they fear that they will not receive an adequate return on their investment before employees leave a firm or a locality or a region for better job opportunities.

The Development of a Federal "Manpower" Policy*

General and vocational education are the oldest and most extensive public programs for preparing people for work. On-the-job training provided by individual firms and apprenticeship programs, often operated under the joint sponsorship of employers and unions, also provide training in specific skills. The GI Bill provided a wide range of educational and training opportunities for veterans of World War II, but there is no comparable program for recent veterans.

During the 1960s, the federal government began to develop a variety of broadly oriented manpower programs. An initial interest in providing *re*training and support services for the growing number of workers (particularly skilled white heads of households) unemployed for long periods as a result of structural changes in the economy was followed by a shift in the focus of public policy to new target groups as a result of the civil rights movement and the War on Poverty.

During the 1970s, federal manpower programs continued to focus on "the problems of minorities and other groups facing competitive disadvantages in central-city labor markets."[32] The Employment and Training (formerly Manpower) Administration in the Department of Labor functions in many respects

---

* The term "manpower" is employed less frequently today.

as an antipoverty agency. A similar focus has been adopted by the National Commission for Employment Policy (formerly the National Commission for Manpower Policy), which was reconstituted in 1978 when the Comprehensive Employment and Training Act of 1973 (CETA) was reauthorized through fiscal 1982.[33]

Federal Manpower Programs

Basic manpower service and training programs have been provided under the Manpower Development and Training Act of 1962 (MDTA); the Economic Opportunity Act of 1964 (EOA); a series of Work Incentive Programs (WIN) for welfare recipients, initially established under a 1967 amendment to the Social Security Act; and the amended Comprehensive Employment and Training Act of 1973 mentioned in the preceding section, which combined programs previously set up under the MDTA and the Public Employment Program.[34] Under the "new Federalism" of the Nixon administration, most of the responsibility for planning and administering manpower programs was transferred to state and local governments.

Several programs have provided funds for acquiring work experience through jobs in the public sector. Improved vocational training is provided under the Vocational Education Act of 1963, as amended, and under CETA; and the U.S. Employment Service provides counseling and job information on a continuing basis. Private employers have also been encouraged by tax offsets and subsidies to hire and train persons who are economically disadvantaged.

Under the Carter administration's economic stimulus program, outlays for various Titles of CETA increased significantly during fiscal 1978, with much of the increase due to the rapid buildup of the Title VI countercyclical public service employment program.[35] During fiscal 1978, there were 3.9 million *first-time* enrollments in the various programs, including CETA, administered by the Department of Labor. There were 965,100 first enrollments under Title I programs, 555,800 under Title VI, almost one million persons participated in the Summer Youth Program, and 561,800 participated in the WIN program for welfare recipients. Almost $7.5 billion in federal funds was committed to these first-time enrollments.[36]

INCOME MAINTENANCE PROGRAMS FOR THE UNEMPLOYED

Unemployment Insurance

People who lose their jobs can turn to a variety of public and private programs for financial help. The joint federal-state *unemployment insurance system* (UI), which is discussed in greater detail in Chapter 8, was established by the Social Security Act of 1935. It provides some income during short periods of *involuntary* unemployment to persons *regularly attached* to the labor force. Benefits are provided for a limited number of weeks to persons who can demonstrate that they have worked during a recent "base" period.

Some 97 percent of all wage and salary employment is covered under the permanent UI program. The basic insurance system is supplemented by special *unemployment compensation programs* covering particular groups of workers, such as service personnel and federal employees, and, on an ad hoc basis during periods of high unemployment, persons who have been receiving regular benefits but are no longer eligible for them because of the length of time they have been out of work.

Other Programs

We have noted that several programs provide jobs rather than insurance benefits to target groups of the unemployed. In addition, allowances related to a state's unemployment benefits are paid to participants in a number of development and training programs and to workers whose unemployment is the result of a national trade policy or a disaster. When unemployment is high, Special Unemployment Assistance (SUA) is provided for individuals not otherwise eligible for unemployment insurance.

Unemployed persons who exhaust their UI benefits or persons whose benefits are insufficient for their needs may apply for general assistance (welfare or relief) from states and localities. General assistance benefits include cash payments, food stamps, and payment for medical and hospital services under the Medicaid program. Unlike UI benefits, to which people have a legal right, welfare payments are dispensed on the basis of a means test.

Private Programs

An increasing number of private firms provide assistance to workers who are permanently laid off and in some cases to those who are *furloughed* (temporarily laid off) as a result of economic factors. Many of these programs have been established under collective bargaining. Their benefits include *termination allowances* based on years of service; *supplemental unemployment benefits* that in combination with UI benefits assure workers on layoff a given percentage of their take-home pay; *relocation allowances* paid when company operations are moved; *early retirement benefits;* and *retraining* for workers displaced as a result of technological change. Unfortunately, workers at the end of the hiring queue and workers whose employment has been limited to jobs in the secondary labor market are unlikely to work for firms providing such benefits.

SUMMARY

Unemployment, which is to some degree inevitable in a dynamic industrial society, is costly in both human and economic terms. The increase in the number of families with more than one wage earner; the short duration of unemployment for most workers; the partial replacement of lost income by UI benefits; and, for some, the benefits provided by various private programs, have made unemployment less traumatic. Nevertheless, the unemployment rate is unnecessarily high, and some who are unemployed do not get enough help from income maintenance programs.

A minimal amount of *frictional* unemployment is both necessary and desirable if the economy is to adjust successfully to continuing changes in economic variables. We must try to ensure that such unemployment is, in fact, minimal by reducing casual and seasonal unemployment and making the labor market function more efficiently. The elimination of discrimination in employment will help us to achieve this last objective.

Other types of unemployment, which are often more costly in terms of lost output and more burdensome personally, have been at unacceptably high levels in recent years. Fiscal and monetary weapons to maintain aggregate demand and offset downward movements in the overall level of economic activity, complemented by appropriate microeconomic employment and training programs, will help to reduce cyclical and recession, growth-gap, and structural unemployment. Recent efforts to reduce the persistently high general unemployment rate have been constrained by the apparently worsening trade-off between unemployment and inflation. Although the Humphrey-Hawkins Act mentions a full-employment target rate of unemployment of 4 percent for 1983, a rate of 5½ percent now seems more consistent with a moderate rate of inflation.

Certain members and potential members of the labor force have unusually high unemployment rates. They are less likely to find stable work in the primary labor market that will qualify them for public or private income maintenance programs should they become unemployed. Other workers whose productivity is low are unable to benefit from general education and training programs and will continue to earn submarginal wages. It appears that the government must subsidize private employment or act as an employer of last resort for such individuals, who are to be distinguished from persons who cannot work because of a personal disability or family responsibilities.

DISCUSSION QUESTIONS

1. What is the current unemployment rate; the employment-population ratio?
2. What does the Council of Economic Advisers currently designate as a high level employment unemployment rate?
3. At the time the manuscript for this book was completed (mid-1980) we were in a recession. Was the recession severe? Which industries and sectors of the economy experienced relatively high unemployment?
4. Does the Phillips curve concept of a trade-off between unemployment and prices appear reasonable?
5. Distinguish between structural and hard-core unemployment.
6. Assuming that certain individuals are "unemployable," how should society provide for them? (This question anticipates the discussion in the following two chapters.)

7. Why have economists begun to (re)emphasize supply-side economics?
8. What problems would be faced in providing unemployment insurance through private carriers?
9. Do you believe that the federal government should provide special assistance to workers laid off as a result of foreign competition?

SELECTED READINGS

Automation and Unemployment

"Automation," an issue of the *Annals of the American Academy of Political and Social Science* 340 (March 1962).

Dunlop, John T., ed. *Automation and Technological Change.* Published for the American Assembly, Columbia University. Englewood Cliffs, N.J.: Prentice-Hall, 1962.

Philipson, Morris, ed. *Automation: Implications for the Future.* New York: Random House (Vintage Books), 1962.

Senate Subcommittee on Employment and Manpower of the Committee on Labor and Public Welfare. *Exploring the Dimensions of the Manpower Revolution.* Vol. I of *Selected Readings in Employment and Manpower,* 88th Cong., 2nd sess.

Shils, Edward B. *Automation and Industrial Relations.* New York: Holt, Rinehart and Winston, 1963.

U.S. Congress, Joint Economic Committee. *New Views on Automation: Papers Submitted to the Subcommittee on Automation and Energy Resources,* 86th Cong., 2nd sess.

Fiscal and Monetary Policy

The annual *Economic Report of the President,* which is published together with the *Annual Report of the Council of Economic Advisers,* the various *Hearings* and other publications of the Joint Economic Committee of the Congress, and the publications of the Brookings Institution and the American Enterprise Institute ("the conservative's Brookings") contain valuable discussions of contemporary policy alternatives and are also rich sources of data.

Wage and Price Controls

Shultz, George P., and Dam, Kenneth W. "Reflections on Wage and Price Controls." In *Industrial and Labor Relations Review* 30, no. 2 (January 1977): pp. 139–151.

U.S. Congress, Congressional Budget Office. *Incomes Policies in the United States: Historical Review and Some Issues.* A summary of our postwar experience with wage-price guideposts and controls through the middle of 1977.

Weber, Arnold R. *In Pursuit of Price Stability, The Wage-Price Freeze of 1971.* Washington, D.C.: Brookings Institution, 1973. See particularly chap. IX.

Development and Training Programs

The most recent *Employment and Training Report of the President* is an excellent source of information on current federal programs. Also useful are the *Annual*

Report and various ongoing studies of the National Commission for Employment Policy (formerly The National Commission for Manpower Policy).

Mangum, Garth L. "Manpower Policies and Worker Status Since the 1930s." Chap. 6 in *Federal Policies and Worker Status Since the Thirties.* Ed. by Joseph P. Goldberg, Eileen Ahern, William Haber, and Rudolph A. Oswald. Madison, Wisc.: Industrial Relations Research Association, 1976.

Mangum, Garth L. "Manpower Research and Manpower Policy." In *A Review of Industrial Relations Research.* Vol. II. Madison, Wisc.: Industrial Relations Research Association, 1971, pp. 61–124. A good summary of research in the field, with extensive bibliographic references.

Income Maintenance Programs

Again, the *Employment and Training Report of the President* is a good source of information. Other references are Raymond Munts, "Policy Development in Unemployment Insurance," in Goldberg et al., eds., *Federal Policies and Worker Status Since the Thirties,* Madison, Wisc.: Industrial Relations Research Association, 1976, pp. 71–106; and John L. Palmer, ed., *Creating Jobs: Public Employment Programs and Wage Subsidies,* Washington, D.C.: Brookings Institution, 1978.

Notes

1. President's Committee to Appraise Employment and Unemployment Statistics, *Measuring Employment and Unemployment,* 1962, p. 9. This committee, chaired by Professor Robert A. Gordon, became known as the Gordon Committee.
2. *Economic Report of the President, Transmitted to the Congress January 1977, Together with the Annual Report of the Council of Economic Advisers,* p. 51.
3. Ibid.
4. *Employment Act of 1946* (60 Stat. 23), sect. 2. See also *supra.,* pp. 29–30.
5. *Full-Employment and Balanced Growth Act of 1978* (92 Stat. 1887), sec. 2(b)(2).
6. 96th Cong. 1st sess., *The Effects of Structural Employment and Training Programs on Inflation and Unemployment.* Report of the Joint Economic Committee. S. Rept. 96–51, pp. 29, 31.
7. Ibid., p. 31.
8. George L. Perry, "Changing Labor Markets and Inflation," in *Brookings Papers on Economic Activity* 3 (1970): p. 433.
9. Michael L. Wachter, "The Changing Cyclical Responsiveness of Wage Inflation," in *Brookings Papers on Economic Activity* 1 (1976): p. 159.
10. Anthony M. Santomero and John J. Seater, "The Inflation-Unemployment Tradeoff: A Critique of the Literature," in *Journal of Economic Literature* XVI, no. 2 (June 1978): p. 515.
11. U.S. Department of Labor, Bureau of Labor Statistics, *Labor Force and Unemployment,* Report 486, p. 3. For a technical analysis of current labor force statistics see: National Commission on Employment and Unemployment Statistics, *Counting the Labor Force* (Washington, D.C.: Government Printing Office, Labor Day 1979). The Commission identified additional labor force data which it believed should be provided on a continuing basis but did not recommend major changes in employment or unemployment definitions.

12. Ibid.
13. Ibid. See also Julius Shiskin, "Employment and Unemployment: the doughnut or the hole," in *Monthly Labor Review* 99, no. 2 (February 1976): pp. 3–10, and Joseph Antos, Wesley Mellow, and Jack E. Triplett, "What is a current equivalent to unemployment rates of the past?" in *Monthly Labor Review*, 102, no. 3 (March 1979): pp. 36–46.
14. *Employment and Training Report of the President, Including Reports by the U.S. Department of Labor and the U.S. Department of Health, Education, and Welfare, Transmitted to the Congress 1977*, Table A–1, p. 135; Table B–14, p. 212; Table B–18, p. 216.
15. Arthur M. Okun, "The Gap Between Actual and Potential Output," in Arthur M. Okun, ed., *The Battle Against Unemployment* (New York: Norton, 1965), p. 17. Another study estimated that "a decline of 2 in unemployment would be associated with a rise of about 3 in employment." (Sophia Cooper and Dennis F. Johnston, *Labor Force Projections for 1970–80, Monthly Labor Review*, 88, no. 2 [February 1965], p. 140). See also Lester T. Thurow, "The Changing Structure of Unemployment," in *Review of Economics and Statistics* XLVII, no. 2 (May 1965): pp. 137–149.
16. U.S. Department of Labor, Bureau of Labor Statistics, *The Extent and Nature of Frictional Unemployment*. Study Paper No. 6, prepared in connection with the Study of Employment, Growth, and Price Levels for the Joint Economic Committee, 86th Cong., 1st. sess., p. 52.
17. George B. Baldwin and George P. Shultz, "Automation: A New Dimension to Old Problems," in *Proceedings of Seventh Annual Meeting, of Industrial Relations Research Association, 1954*, pp. 114–115.
18. 87th Cong., 1st sess., Subcommittee on Economic Statistics of the Joint Economic Committee, *Unemployment: Terminology, Measurement, and Analysis*, Joint Committee Print, p. 9.
19. Ibid., p. 6.
20. President's Committee to Appraise Employment and Unemployment Statistics, *Measuring Employment and Unemployment*, p. 58.
21. This analytical framework is developed in John Maynard Keynes's *General Theory of Employment, Interest and Money* (New York: Harcourt Brace, 1936).
22. Phillip Cagan, *Persistent Inflation: Historical and Policy Essays* (New York: Columbia University Press, 1979), p. 37.
23. See for example Edmund S. Phelps et. al., *Microeconomic Foundations of Employment and Inflation Theory*, (New York: Norton, 1970) and Edmund S. Phelps, *Employment and Inflation: Studies in Macroeconomic Theory I* (New York: Academic Press, 1979).
24. *Economic Report of the President, Transmitted to the Congress January 1965, Together with the Annual Report of the Council of Economic Advisers*, p. 108. Original emphasis omitted.
25. John Sheahan, *The Wage-Price Guideposts* (Washington, D.C.: Brookings Institution, 1967), pp. 90–92.
26. George L. Perry, "Stabilization Policy and Inflation," chap. 7 in Henry Owen and Charles L. Schultze, eds., *Setting National Priorities: The Next Ten Years* (Washington, D.C.: Brookings Institution, 1976), p. 299.
27. Ewan Clague and Leo Kramer, *Manpower Policies and Programs. A Review, 1933–*

75 (Kalamazoo, Mich.: W. E. Upjohn Institute for Employment Research, 1976), p. 84.

28. Humphrey-Hawkins Act, section 102, amending section 2(f) of the Employment Act of 1946.

29. *Employment and Training Report of the President, Including Reports by the U.S. Department of Labor and the U.S. Department of Health, Education, and Welfare, Transmitted to the Congress, 1979,* Table A–29, p. 278.

30. Ibid., p. 63.

31. Gary S. Becker, *Human Capital,* 2nd ed. (New York: National Bureau of Economic Research, 1975), p. 9. Pioneering work in this area has been done by Becker and Professor Theodore W. Schultz of the University of Chicago. See for example, Schultz, "Reflections on Investment in Man," and papers by other authors in "Investment in Human Beings," *Journal of Political Economy,* Supplement, LXX, no. 5 (October 1962), pt. 2.

32. Garth L. Mangum, "Manpower Policies and Worker Status Since the 1930s," in Joseph P. Goldberg, Eileen Ahern, William Haber, and Rudolph A. Oswald, eds., *Federal Policies and Worker Status Since the Thirties* (Madison, Wisc.: Industrial Relations Research Association, 1976), p. 147.

33. Eli Ginzberg, ed., *Jobs for Americans,* published for the American Assembly, Columbia University (Englewood Cliffs, N.J.: Prentice-Hall, 1976), "Introduction."

34. For an analysis of manpower programs during the 1960s see Charles R. Perry, Bernard E. Anderson, Richard L. Rowan, and Herbert R. Northrup, *The Impact of Government Manpower Programs—In General, and on Minorities and Women,* Manpower and Human Resources Studies, No. 4, Industrial Research Unit, The Wharton School (Philadelphia: University of Pennsylvania Press, 1975).

35. *Employment and Training Report of the President, 1979,* p. 32.

36. Ibid., Table F–1, p. 364.

Chapter 8
ECONOMIC INSECURITY—
THE PUBLIC RESPONSE

Economic insecurity is common to all societies, but as we saw in Chapters 2 and 3, it has broader dimensions in modern industrial economies. Serious problems can result from a permanent or temporary loss of income, unavoidable extra expenses, or an inability to earn enough to meet the minimal needs of one's family. The principal *specific* causes of economic insecurity in the United States are retirement from the labor force; the death of a family's primary wage earner; unemployment; work-connected injuries and illnesses; nonwork-connected injuries and illnesses; employment at substandard wages; family responsibilities that make it impossible to work outside the home; and personal factors such as low individual productivity, which may make people unemployable, and discrimination, which may limit people to jobs in the secondary labor market regardless of their qualifications for other work.

People usually focus on their present needs. It is unrealistic to expect every wage earner to provide for the future or for financial emergencies. It is also unrealistic to expect most workers to participate voluntarily in some form of group protection. In the absence of private arrangements to protect people from financial contingencies, the costs associated with their occurrence may be assumed by the government. In this sense, the concept of "social" security is not new. It has however acquired a more specific dimension in that it is used to refer to programs established by *government* "to provide alternative [sources of] income to persons whose normal private incomes have temporarily or permanently disappeared or to remove . . . the burden of some very generally experienced charges on income."[1]

SOCIAL SECURITY PROGRAMS IN THE UNITED STATES

In the United States, where the term originated, *social security* is used to refer to (1) a *family* of public measures to prevent or lessen the impact of economic contingencies; (2) *assistance* and *insurance* programs established in advance by the government to deal with such contingencies; (3) specific programs authorized by the *Social Security Act of 1935*, as amended; and (4) Old Age, Survivors, Disability and Health Insurance (*OASDHI*). The second definition is the one we are most concerned with here.

Workmen's compensation legislation, the several programs established under the amended Social Security Act, and the general assistance (welfare) provided by state and local governments are the core of our present social security arrangements. We do not have a general health insurance program; only five states and Puerto Rico have income maintenance programs for the temporarily disabled, and there is no comprehensive (noncategorical) income maintenance program.

A variety of public and private programs complement or supplement these measures. Our basic defense against unemployment is the fiscal and monetary policies discussed in Chapter 7. The government may also (1) generate income through spending for public works or public employment, (2) "socialize" the costs of certain "necessities" such as housing and education, and (3) use devices such as farm price supports or tariffs to "protect" the income of specific groups.[2]

Personal savings and individual life and health insurance policies provide protection for many families, while employers, often as a result of collective bargaining, have set up a variety of private ("fringe benefit") welfare programs. Individuals who are not steadily employed or who cannot work are not likely to have such personal or group protection.

In this chapter, we will describe the principal provisions of government programs that affect the hours people work, the wages they earn, and their safety on the job. We will also discuss various *social insurance* programs set up by the government to help those who are gainfully employed maintain their incomes after retirement or meet exceptional expenses connected with *specific* contingencies. These programs help to keep people from sinking below the poverty threshold, but they are not designed to combat poverty. Specific antipoverty measures, including various public assistance programs, will be discussed in Chapter 9.

HOURS AND WAGES LEGISLATION

Hours and wages legislation, although excluded from our definition of social security measures, enhances the welfare of workers by helping to prevent their conscious exploitation—insulating "good" employers from competitive pressures that might otherwise compel them to treat workers less generously—and, more generally, by assuring employees of working conditions that are at least minimally acceptable.

The history of hours and wages legislation is complex. For many years, there was no general legislation on the subject. In 1938, the Fair Labor Standards Act (FLSA) established a minimum wage and a basic 40-hour week (effective in 1940) for many workers in firms engaged in interstate commerce. Payment for overtime was set at one and one-half the regular rate. As of January 1, 1981, the minimum wage for some 57 million nonsupervisory employees in the private sector was $3.35 an hour.

Regulating Working Hours: An Introduction

In an agrarian economy in which families are the basic productive unit, individual workers or families have considerable control over their hours of work. Such control is not feasible in most contemporary jobs. For an operation to be efficient, employees must usually work for a uniform period and follow a set production schedule. However, since a work period designed to maximize a firm's profits may be unfair or intolerable from the employees' standpoint, the hours people work have not been left solely to the discretion of employers.

In 1850, the workweek averaged 66 hours in industry and 72 hours in agriculture. Most people worked an 11- or a 12-hour day and a six-day week.[3] Today, an eight-hour day, and a five-day week are generally recognized as standard, although longer workdays and workweeks are common in agriculture and among nonfarm managers, proprietors, and professionals. The long-term decline in average hours has not been continuous, but has reflected social, legislative, and union pressures during particular periods.

Following the Civil War, the workweek was gradually reduced to 60 hours, and unions of skilled workers, which had previously obtained a ten-hour day, attempted to secure an eight-hour day through collective bargaining. In addition, reform groups supported legislation to establish a standard workday of eight hours. Although six states passed eight-hour laws, the laws were not enforced. Following the establishment of the American Federation of Labor (A.F. of L.) in 1886, many of its constituent national unions also launched campaigns to secure an eight-hour workday. Gains were modest; at the turn of the century, the average workweek was 56 hours in nonagricultural employments and 67 hours in agriculture.[4]

During the first two decades of this century, the number of hours worked *daily* was further reduced, generally from ten to eight; and during the 1920s the *standard workweek* was shortened to 5½ days. By 1930, workweeks averaged 55 hours for agricultural workers and 43 hours for other workers. During the Depression, attempts to "spread out" employment led to a further decline in hours. (Most of the codes of fair competition drawn up under the National Industrial Recovery Act [NIRA] for example, established standard workweeks of 40 hours or less.) The workweek was lengthened during World War II, but following the war, most workers returned to a standard (or scheduled) workweek of 40 hours.

Although there has been no further general reduction in the length of the work*day* or work*week*, most people now work fewer hours per *year*. This is the combined result of longer paid vacations and additional paid holidays. Between 1940 and 1960, for example, persons employed full time gained, on the average, almost four weeks of leisure time. They worked 1½ hours less each week, got six days more paid vacation, and had four more paid holidays.[5]

Since 1948, the number of hours worked per week by men not in school has remained fairly constant, averaging about 42.5.[6] However, a few industries have standard workweeks of less than 40 hours. More recently, *flexi-time*—flexible working hours on an individual basis within an expanded workday—has been instituted in some firms while others have adopted a four-day week with a ten-hour workday. The increased interest in the quality of work life suggests that such schedules may become more common during the 1980s. However, these options may not be practical in continuous process industries or in firms organized by unions and in which overtime must be paid after eight hours of work per day.

Diversity will undoubtedly characterize future reductions in work time in the United States. If economic growth continues, there will probably be a greater emphasis on work time that is optimal in the long run. At least one observer has suggested that the standard workweek may disappear in the future, that "it may be more meaningful to talk in terms of the standard workyear; . . . or in terms of a standard work life. . . . [T]hinking in terms of a 40,000-hour work life may seem as natural as today's concept of the 40-hour workweek."[7]

STATE LEGISLATION

Before the twentieth century, most state legislatures were reluctant to pass maximum hours legislation; and the judiciary, reflecting a *laisser-faire* philosophy, tended to hold the laws that were passed unconstitutional. As a rule, the courts held that the right of the individual to freedom of contract must be protected. Protective legislation was considered justified in certain circumstances, however, and the prohibition of child labor as well as the regulation of the hours of labor of female employees, transportation workers, and workers in hazardous occupations were gradually accepted.

Statutes affecting hours of work have (1) set absolute prohibitions on work beyond a specified daily or weekly maximum, (2) established maximums that can be exceeded only under specified (exceptional) conditions, and (3) required the payment of punitive overtime rates for hours worked in excess of a stated maximum. The first type of prohibition commonly applies to work that is potentially hazardous to individual employees or has a direct effect on public health and safety. The second type of maximum once applied to female workers in most states and to workers in public utilities, including transportation in many states. Hours legislation restricted to women was deemed discriminatory under Title VII of the Civil Rights Act, and since 1964, all such laws have been repealed, declared invalid, or changed to permit voluntary overtime or to require premium pay for overtime work.[8] Most general laws regarding working hours establish standard workdays, or workweeks, but permit overtime at a higher rate of pay.

In most states, hours legislation affecting men was limited to hazardous occupations, occupations involving the public safety, and persons doing contract work for the state. The lack of support for more general legislation was due to two factors: (1) the union movement traditionally opposed government intervention, preferring to improve working standards for men through collective bargaining; and (2) when the unions did support such legislation during the Depression, a *federal* statute was passed limiting hours of work on a *general* basis.

FEDERAL LEGISLATION

Except for abortive attempts to prohibit child labor in firms engaged in interstate commerce, no general legislation regulating working hours was passed by the Congress before the Depression. However, the hours of federal employees and transportation workers in firms engaged in interstate commerce were regulated by executive orders or special acts. In the 1930s, mass unemployment triggered support for a drive to reduce the standard workweek in order to create additional jobs. The first broad regulation of hours was included in the *codes of fair competition* established by the *National Industrial Recovery Act,* which was held unconstitutional in May of 1935.[9] In 1936, the *Walsh-Healy Act* established a standard eight-hour day *and* a 40-hour week for workers employed on government contracts worth more than $10,000. Overtime was permitted at one and a half times the prevailing rate for a given type of work.

The federal *Fair Labor Standards Act* of 1938 established general standards for hours and wages.[10] It did *not* establish a *standard workday,* nor did it place a statutory maximum on the number of hours that could be worked *each week.* However, it discouraged long workweeks by providing that after October of 1940 employers would have to pay workers time and a half for every hour worked in excess of 40 hours per week. The act also forbade the employment of children under 16 in covered industries and further limited the employment of minors aged 16 to 18 in hazardous industries.

The Fair Labor Standards Act does not apply to workers in intrastate commerce. Specific exemptions cover supervisory personnel and (in 1978) some 9.6 million private sector nonsupervisory employees, including certain domestic service workers, employees of small retail and service establishments, hired workers on small farms, and state and local government employees. A 1974 amendment extended coverage to six million state and local government employees, but in 1976, the Supreme Court ruled that the act could not be applied to such workers.[11]

During the 1960s, organized labor supported two amendments—neither of which became law—that would ostensibly have provided additional jobs: the first would have lowered the standard workweek to 35 hours; the second would have required the payment of double time for overtime.

Minimum Wage Legislation: An Introduction

State and federal governments have established statutory minimum wage standards in an effort to assure *employed* workers and their dependents an adequate level of living. Such standards may cause some marginal workers to lose their jobs or prevent new employment opportunities from developing in some areas, but this is presumably considered an appropriate social trade-off.

A legal minimum wage (or a minimum standard rate established by collective bargaining) changes the shape of the labor supply curve. In Figure 8.1, for example, demand and supply create a wage rate of W. If a higher legal minimum W' is established, the new labor supply curve becomes W'W'S'S. Under these conditions, L'L workers will be laid off, and L'L'' workers who are available at a wage of W' will not find work. If the minimum wage applies to all jobs, workers who are let go will not find employment anywhere; if the minimum wage is not universally adopted, the newly unemployed workers will increase the supply of labor in other industrial sectors. Other things being equal, this will depress wages in those sectors and create or aggravate the same conditions the minimum wage was designed to correct.

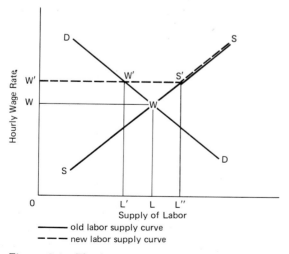

Figure 8.1 The Impact of a Legal Minimum Wage on the Labor Supply Curve

STATE LEGISLATION

Late in the nineteenth century and early in the twentieth century, various reform groups supported minimum wage legislation as a mechanism for improving the standard of living of low-paid workers. There was considerable public support for such legislation and some employer support as well, but the judiciary in a number of states and, prior to 1937, the Supreme Court refused to uphold such laws. In a 1923 decision involving a minimum wage law for women in the District of Columbia, the Supreme Court held that "freedom of contract is . . . the general rule and restraint the exception."[12]

In 1937, the 1923 decision was reversed. Citing an earlier decision, the Court observed that " 'liberty implies the absence of unreasonable regulations and arbitrary restraint, not immunity from reasonable regulations and prohibitions imposed in the interests of the community.' "[13] By 1976, minimum wage laws were in effect in some 40 states, the District of Columbia, and Puerto Rico. Most laws applied to both men and women but in three states they applied only to women.[14]

FEDERAL LEGISLATION

Three types of minimum wage laws have been passed by the federal government. In 1931, the *Davis-Bacon Act* required the payment of "prevailing" wages to persons working on federal construction projects. In 1936, the *Walsh-Healy Act* provided that "prevailing minimum" wages be paid to those working on federal public contracts worth more than $10,000. More general minimum wage standards first appeared under the codes of fair competition established by the *National Industrial Recovery Act* (NIRA).

Although the NIRA was held unconstitutional, traditional arguments in support of minimum wage legislation and the desire to stimulate the economy by increasing consumers' purchasing power led to the passage of the *Fair Labor Standards Act* in 1938. The original wage standards attempted to preserve the basic standards developed under the NIRA codes. Six amendments have mandated a total of 14 changes in the basic minimum through January 1, 1981; the most recent amendment (in 1977) established a basic minimum of $2.65 effective January 1, 1978; $2.90 on January 1, 1979; $3.10 on January 1, 1980; and $3.35 on January 1, 1981.

According to the Equal Pay Amendment of 1963, the same pay standards must apply to both sexes; an employer cannot pay employees of one sex wage rates below those paid to employees of the opposite sex for equal work on jobs requiring similar degrees of skill, effort, and responsibility and performed under similar working conditions.

The Impact of Minimum Wage Legislation

Most economists agree that, other things being equal, the imposition of a statutory minimum wage higher than the market minimum will put some people out of work. However, proponents of minimum wage legislation argue that in a dynamic economy, a rise in the marginal revenue product of labor may enable an employer to pay a higher minimum wage without laying off workers. Such a rise may result from an increase in productivity per man-hour within the firm or an increase in the demand for goods in an expanding economy. In Figure 8.2, for example, given a market wage of W and an initial marginal revenue product curve MRP, the employer will hire E workers. If a minimum wage of W' is established, employment will be reduced to E'. However, if the marginal revenue product curve should shift upward to MRP', E workers will still be hired at the new wage.

Economists who argue that minimum wage legislation has had little impact on employment have relied heavily on a series of studies by the Bureau of Labor Statistics.[15] In general, these studies show (1) that the wages of workers earning less than the minimum have been raised, (2) that unemployment has not increased significantly as a result of raising the statutory minimum or extending the number of jobs covered, and (3) that the unemployment that did develop tended to be in particular firms, industries, or localities. (For example, a high proportion of the typically nonunion workers in nonmetropolitan areas of the South are affected by increases in the federal minimum.)

Changes in the minimum wage have been designed to minimize their impact on employment. According to the Department of Labor, "such changes have always been made with a double awareness—[of] the degree of need, and the extent to which it could be satisfied immediately without harming the people it was intended to help."[16] The wage levels established under the FLSA have been conservative. Increases have followed rather than paralleled or anticipated changes in the general wage level, and amendments have typically established new minimums of about half the average wage in manufacturing. An estimated three million workers were affected by the new $2.65 minimum in 1978, and 5.4 million are expected to be affected by increases mandated through 1981.[17]

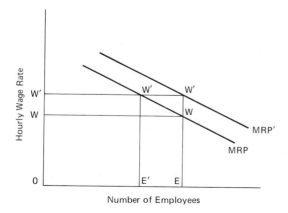

Figure 8.2   The Impact of a Minimum Wage on a Firm's Employment: Two Possibilities

Recent research utilizing more sophisticated techniques suggests (1) that increases in the minimum wage beyond 50 percent of the average wage would be counterproductive and (2) that a separate, lower minimum for teenagers, a proposal opposed by organized labor, is desirable.[18] However, Sar Levitan and Richard Belous, after reviewing relevant research, concluded that

> on balance adult workers appear to be made better off under [minimum wages]. For teenagers the tradeoff is more pronounced. Although the gains from minimum wages are clear, the opportunities to find full-time employment are reduced for young workers. However, . . . even for young workers the income gains are greater than the negative side effects.[19]

Admendments linking the minimum wage to an appropriate index (so that Congress would not have to continually update it through periodic amendments) and providing a lower minimum for teenagers were rejected in 1977.

SOCIAL INSURANCE

Social insurance is provided in the United States by government programs that pay cash benefits to persons whose income from employment has ended or been interrupted by old age, retirement, unemployment, illness, an accident, or death. Benefits are paid under a system set up in advance, and those who receive them have a legal right to them. Most risks covered by social insurance are predictable on an aggregative, if not an individual, basis. However, the term *insurance* is not completely accurate. Private insurance, purchased by individuals or groups, emphasizes *individual equity*; social insurance, which is based on *presumptive social needs*, emphasizes the *adequacy of benefits* rather than equity.[20]

Social insurance is generally compulsory, and participants in a program usually have no choice about the kind or amount of coverage they get or the price they pay for it. Coverage is not based on a contract with individuals, and it is possible to change eligibility requirements, benefit levels, and contribution rates without compromising the integrity of a program. A government program can cover persons who are poor risks, and benefits can be weighted in favor of those whose earnings are low, those who qualify for benefits before establishing much equity in the program, and those with dependents. Such programs need not conform to private actuarial standards. The government has the power to tax, and a social insurance program may be considered financially sound if current and future benefits can be paid out of current and scheduled tax contributions and contingency reserves.

Widespread social insurance is largely a twentieth-century phenomenon. State workmen's compensation programs, which pay medical costs and partially compensate for income loss resulting from on-the-job accidents and job-related illnesses, were introduced in 1908, making them the first type of social insurance to be provided in the United States. No other general programs were established until the Depression, when the often desperate plight of the elderly and the unemployed encouraged action at the federal level. In 1932, the A.F. of L., which had formerly opposed such programs, gave its support to social insurance. In June of 1934, President Franklin D. Roosevelt appointed the Committee on Economic Security to find ways of preventing economic insecurity; and on August 14, 1935, the Social Security Act was passed, "an inevitable consequence of the depression, industrialization, and urbanization."[21] The act established (1) a federal old-age insurance program (OAI), (2) a federal-state unemployment insurance system (UI), and (3) federal-state categorical public assistance (welfare) programs for the needy aged, dependent children, and the blind. The original OAI program has since been expanded to include survivors, disability, and health insurance.

OCCUPATIONAL SAFETY AND HEALTH PROGRAMS

In 1978, there were approximately 5.8 million recorded cases of occupational injury and illness, including 4,590 work-related fatalities. Over 2.4 million of those who were injured and over 50,000 of those with job-related ailments were absent one or more days from work.[22] According to the Department of Health, Education, and Welfare (now the Department of Health and Human Services), as many as 100,000 deaths may result from occupational disease each year.[23]

Occupational injuries and illnesses involve three kinds of costs: outlays to cover medical, hospital, and rehabilitation services; interruptions in the normal flow of income; and the permanent loss of part or all of a worker's income. According to National Safety Council estimates, "the total cost of occupational hazards—in terms of lost wages, medical expenses, insurance claims, production delays, lost time of coworkers, and equipment damage—[was] $9.3 billion during 1971—nearly 1% of the GNP."[24] Serious intangible personal costs are related to these contingencies.

A comprehensive program dealing with these contingencies must be three dimensional. That is, it must include measures to prevent injuries and illnesses, compensation for expenses and loss of income when they occur, and some provision for the physical and mental rehabilitation of victims.

The Occupational Safety and Health Act of 1970

Dissatisfaction with the progress of state and private programs to reduce risks to safety and health in the workplace culminated in the passage of the Occupational Safety and Health Act in 1970. The immediate factor most responsible for the act "was the observed increase in the industrial accident rate, which rose nearly 29% from 1961 to 1970."[25]

The act was designed to encourage "employers and employees . . . to reduce the number of occupational safety and health hazards . . . and to stimulate [them] to institute new [programs] and to perfect existing programs for providing safe and healthful working conditions."[26] It specifies that each employer has a general duty to "furnish . . . employment and a place of employment which are free from recognized hazards." The Occupational Safety and Health Administration (OSHA) in the Department of Labor is responsible for setting mandatory safety and health standards and enforcing the act.

Working environments have been upgraded since the passage of the Occupational Safety and Health Act, but the act has not had the dramatic impact its supporters hoped for.[27] The problem, basically, is a lack of agreement "on the act's goals and on the practical methods of balancing considerations of greater safety and health against considerations of cost."[28]

The National Commission on Workmen's Compensation

Section 27(a)(1) of the Occupational Safety and Health Act established a National Commission on State Workmen's Compensation Laws to conduct "an effective study and objective evaluation" of such legislation. This provision was based on a congressional finding that to be fully protected from job-related injuries or deaths, American workers required "an adequate, prompt, and equitable system of workmen's compensation as well as an effective program of occupational health and safety regulation."[29]

WORKMEN'S COMPENSATION LEGISLATION*

In the nineteenth century, it was generally assumed that employers had an obligation to provide a safe place to work and that workers injured on the job could get compensation for their injuries by suing the employers. Employers however often escaped paying damages by taking advantage of three common law defenses available to them. The first of these defenses was a plea of *contributory negligence*. Workers had to prove not only that their employers were negligent but that they themselves were not negligent in any way. The second defense often used by employers was the *fellow-servant* or *common employment doctrine*. Employers were not to be held responsible for an accident if it was caused by another employee. Finally, employers argued that in accepting employment, workers *assumed the ordinary risks* of a trade. Therefore compensation would be paid only if an unusual (extraordinary) risk had existed.

To help workers recover damages, many states and the federal government passed *employer's liability laws* that made one or more of these defenses invalid. The laws, however, proved ineffectual, and this lead to the passage of workmen's compensation acts, similar to those introduced in Europe in the 1880s. Workmen's compensation legislation is based on the principle of *liability without fault*. The costs of industrial accidents, and to a lesser degree those of occupational disease,

---

* This legislation has begun to be termed *Workers' Compensation* legislation.

are considered social costs that can be allocated to employers, "not because of any presumption that [they are] responsible for every accident which affect[s] . . . employees, but because industrial accidents [are] recognized as one of the inevitable hazards of modern industry."[30]

The first workmen's compensation act was passed by Congress in 1908. The first state law to go into effect and be sustained by the courts was a Wisconsin law passed in 1911. By 1921, workmen's compensation laws were in operation in 44 states and Puerto Rico, and in 1948, Mississippi became the last state to pass such legislation.

General Provisions

In 1976, 47 state laws made it compulsory for most private employers to carry insurance that would pay benefits to victims of job-related injuries, while only three made such coverage elective.[31] Employers who reject coverage where it is elective lose the benefit of common law defenses against employee suits. Most jurisdictions permit employers to buy insurance from commercial carriers or to act as self-insurers (in all but four states). Six jurisdictions require employers to insure through an exclusive state insurance fund and in 12 jurisdictions a state fund competes with private carriers.

Coverage

As of January 1, 1979, some 88 percent of all wage and salary workers were covered by workmen's compensation laws. The most common exemptions covered domestic workers, agricultural workers, and casual laborers. A few statutes limited insurance requirements to specified hazardous occupations or industries, 12 states exempted firms with fewer than a set number of employees, and two states exempted firms with small annual payrolls.

According to the National Commission on Workmen's Compensation,

> the inequities of wide variations [in coverage] among the States in the proportion of labor force covered are compounded by the nature of the exclusions. [Employees in] occupations typically excluded from coverage . . . are disproportionately low-income, less-educated, nonwhite, and female—those least able financially of carrying the burden of disability by themselves.[32]

Types of Benefits and Eligibility

There are four basic types of benefits: periodic cash payment to victims to partially compensate them for lost wages, coverage of medical and hospital bills for victims while they are disabled, funeral benefits and income payments to survivors, and maintenance allowances and appropriate services during a period of rehabilitation.

A worker in a covered job must have his or her ability to work impaired by a work-related injury or disease to quality for benefits. The requirement that an injury or ailment be work related is usually interpreted generously, but in a few states, a problem must result from an accident for compensation to be paid. In 13 states, not all types of occupational illnesses are covered.

MEDICAL BENEFITS
The medical benefits provided by workmen's compensation insurance are generally considered satisfactory. In most jurisdictions, there is no limit on benefits for accidental injuries and full medical benefits are also paid to victims of occupational disease.

INCOME BENEFITS
Income benefits pay some proportion of a worker's weekly earnings at the time of an injury, the onset of an illness, or a death. As of January 1, 1979, the "intended" benefit in all but five states was 66⅔ percent of the weekly wage.[33] Due to dollar maximums however, higher paid workers do not always receive this large a proportion of their previous earnings. To correct this situation, 36 states and the District of Columbia adjust their maximum benefit annually. As of January 1, 1979, the maximum weekly benefit for temporarily disabled workers varied from $45 in Puerto Rico and $87 in Arkansas to $433 in Alaska. Allowances to dependents are paid in only 16 states or under a separate program for federal employees.

REHABILITATION ALLOWANCES
Rehabilitation allowances have not received the same emphasis as payments for medical services and income bentfits. However, some 36 statutes provide rehabilitation benefits and services, and similar services are provided under a federal-state vocational rehabilitation program.

Financing

Workmen's compensation programs are usually financed completely by employers, although in a few states employees pay a minor amount for hospital and medical coverage. Insurance premiums vary according to the industrial classification of the firm and the employer's *experience rating*. The possibility of securing lower rates presumably provides an incentive for employers to try to prevent accidents. In 1977, workmen's compensation costs represented 1.71 percent, and benefits 0.92 percent, of covered firms' payrolls.[34]

Summary

The National Commission on Workmen's Compensation has identified "five major objectives for a modern workmen's compensation program. . . ." These are:

1. broad coverage of employees and of work-related injuries and diseases;
2. substantial protection against an interruption of income;
3. provision of sufficient medical care and rehabilitation services;
4. the encouragement of safety; and
5. an effective system for delivering benefits and services.[35]

The commission concluded that existing state workmen's compensation laws "are in general neither adequate nor equitable." Although it did not recommend the adoption of federal standards when it published its report in 1972, it "was unanimous in its conclusion that congressional intervention may be necessary to bring about [essential] reforms. . . ."[36]

Perhaps the greatest defect in the laws is the lack of complete coverage. In an industrial economy, all workers presumably have the same "ethical claim" to compensation, yet those who need such protection most are often excluded from coverage. Other deficiencies in the laws include the failure of benefit levels to keep pace with increases in average wage levels; a failure to cover continuing medical expenses, particularly in cases of permanent disability; a failure to cover all occupational diseases; a failure to provide adequately for the rehabilitation of injured workers; and inefficient administration. Most states improved their workmen's compensation programs after the national commission submitted its report, though many improvements were apparently made to offset pressure for compulsory federal standards.

TEMPORARY DISABILITY INSURANCE

Only 10 percent of the workdays lost because of accidents or sickness are lost because of work-connected accidents or ailments. Nonoccupational illness and accidents are a much greater problem for members of the labor force and their dependents. *Permanently* and *totally* disabled workers receive partial compensation for lost wages under the Social Security Act as amended, but disability benefits for those incapacitated as a result of nonoccupational accidents or illness are not generally available through public programs. Only five states, Puerto Rico, and the railroad industry provide such income benefits. Typically, coverage parallels that provided by unemployment insurance programs.

Many workers are protected from a loss of income resulting from a nonoccupational disability by *private* group disability and paid sick leave programs. In fact, almost two-thirds of the labor force is eligible for benefits under such programs or the public programs. However, many workers for whom an interruption in income would be particularly burdensome do not have this kind of coverage. In 1963, Professor Margaret Gordon noted that "[o]ne of the most significant gaps in the American social security system is the absence of protection for those who are severely disabled from nonoccupational causes but whose difficulties are not classified as permanent and total."[37] An amendment to the Social Security Act providing such protection is long overdue.

OLD AGE, SURVIVORS, DISABILITY, AND HEALTH INSURANCE

Workmen's compensation legislation was a pragmatic response to a type of economic insecurity that was widely perceived as related to hazards inherent in employment relationships. The Depression emphasized the need to also provide help to those made destitute by unemployment or retirement. Previously, providing for these contingencies had been considered a personal responsibility, but after 1930, it became clear that some kind of minimum protection would have to be provided by government. The Social Security Act of 1935 established separate *old age insurance* (OAI) and *unemployment insurance* (UI) *programs* for this very purpose.

The OAI Program

The economic insecurity of the aged is rooted in compulsory retirement, the difficulty of finding another job if they become unemployed, low income and inadequate resources, relatively high medical and hospital expenses, and social isolation, all underscored by the breakdown of traditional methods of caring for the elderly. The OAI program was designed to provide an income, based on prior work experience, to persons "too old to work and too young to die." The 1935 legislation also authorized federal grants to the states for public assistance (welfare) programs for the needy aged.

OAI is a *compulsory national program* under which *wage-related benefits* based on *prior contributions* are paid as a *matter of right* to eligible workers who retire from the labor force on reaching the age of 65, or on reduced benefits at the age of 62. Basically, the program operates as an intergenerational transfer system, with benefits for retired workers financed by the tax contributions paid on behalf of workers currently in the labor force. These tax moneys are deposited in the Federal Old-Age and Survivors Insurance Trust Fund, administered by a board of trustees composed of the Secretaries of the Treasury, Labor, and Health and Human Services. Initially, the program was financed by payroll taxes on both employers and employees of 1 percent of the first $3,000 of annual earnings. In 1935, some 26 million workers in industrial and commercial establishments, or almost 60 percent of the labor force were covered by the program, and 97 percent of the total wage bill of covered employers was subject to the payroll tax.

The original OAI program involved a number of departures from private insurance principles. The benefit schedule, although related to the employee's wage record, provided relatively higher benefits to low income workers. This "tilt" was designed to establish an adequate "floor" of benefits for all retirees. Moreover, benefits were *not* simple annuities. To receive them, a worker not only had to attain the age of 65, he or she also had to retire from the labor force. Initially, benefits were not paid for any month in which a worker received wages from covered employment.

From the start, it was apparent that the OAI program was not a finished product. It was recognized that (1) benefits would have to be increased if the cost of living rose, (2) the level of real benefits might be increased to allow beneficiaries to share in a general advance in the level of living, (3) coverage might be extended to groups initially excluded, (4) new programs might be introduced, and (5) at some future date it would probably be necessary to fund the program partially from general revenues.

Benefits for Dependents

The Social Security Act was amended on August 10, 1939, before benefit payments were scheduled to begin. The amendments emphasized the *presumptive* need of covered workers *and* their *dependents* or *survivors* and were again a departure from ordinary insurance principles. In short,

> Congress determined that this social insurance system must provide *adequate* benefits regardless of individual contributions—in other words, that the need of the family of the worker who died, perhaps after a limited period of covered employment, is as significant as the need of the worker who lives to old age and can no longer work.[38]

> *Supplemental retirement benefits* were provided for wives and children, and *survivorship benefits* were established for widows, mothers, children, and dependent parents. At this time, the program became known as *Old Age and Survivors Insurance* (OASI). The absolute prohibition on working was abandoned, and retirees were permitted to earn up to $15 a month without losing their benefits for the month. The coverage of the act was also expanded slightly, and the original "full reserve" financing was abandoned in favor of "current cost" financing. Under the new system, the amount of social security taxes collected each year was expected to approximately equal the benefits and the administrative expenses paid during the year, plus a small additional amount needed to maintain the trust funds' contingency reserves at an appropriate level.[39]

Early Postwar Amendments[40]

In 1950, coverage was broadened to include certain farm and domestic workers and self-employed persons, monthly benefits were increased, the payroll tax was increased to 1½ percent for employers and employees, and eligibility requirements were liberalized. As a result, the number of older persons receiving public assistance began to decline, and in February 1951, for the first time, the number of insurance beneficiaries exceeded the number of persons receiving old age assistance.

Benefits were increased again in 1952 and 1954. In 1954, also, coverage was extended to an additional ten million workers, including farm operators and most self-employed professionals.

OASI Becomes OASDI

In 1956, permanently and totally disabled workers were made eligible for retirement benefits after age 50, and the program became known as *Old Age, Survivors, and Disability Insurance* (OASDI). The tax moneys earmarked for disability benefits (some 12 percent of social security payroll tax revenues) are deposited in a separate Federal Disability Insurance Trust Fund. Disability benefits were provided only in cases of *permanent* and *total* disability; the continued exclusion of individuals suffering permanent *partial* disability is a major weakness of the system.

Also in 1956, women became eligible for actuarially reduced retirement benefits at age 62. Coverage was also extended to members of the armed forces and all self-employed professionals, with the exception of doctors. Doctors were excluded because the American Medical Association feared that such coverage might provide an entering wedge for a program of national health insurance.

Amendments from 1958 to 1961

In 1958, the age requirement for disability benefits was dropped, benefits were provided for dependents of disabled workers, and the benefit schedule and retirement "work test" were liberalized. In the same year, a first step was taken toward a medical care program for the aged when the Kerr-Mills Bill provided federal matching grants to the states to help meet the medical expenses of the "medically indigent" aged, that is, persons who were not on relief but could not cope with the costs of necessary medical services.

In 1960, the earnings test, which had required a reduction in benefits equivalent to earnings after a specified level of earnings, was modified so that only one dollar of benefits would be withheld for each two dollars of earnings between specified levels, up to a maximum limit, after which one dollar of benefits would be withheld for each dollar of earnings. In 1961, men were made eligible for actuarially reduced benefits at age 62.

Medicare

In 1965, the Medicare amendments completed the present Old Age, Survivors, Disability, and Health Insurance Program (OASDHI). Part A of the Medicare program is a hospital insurance (HI) program covering not only hospitalization and nursing care but also home health services for persons over 65. There is a deductible provision before payments begin, and a coinsurance feature requires insured persons to pay a portion of their hospital bills. The program is financed by a payroll tax on employers and employees; the money collected is held in a special Federal Hospital Insurance Trust Fund.

Part B of the Medicare program is a supplementary medical insurance program (SMI) that covers 80 percent of "reasonable" charges for a variety of medical services, including those of physicians and surgeons, once a deductible amount has been paid. Persons eligible for HI are automatically enrolled in the SMI program (though they may decline coverage), and they pay a monthly premium ($9.60 as of July 1980) that is matched by a federal subvention *from general revenues.* These contributions are paid into a special Federal Supplementary Medical Insurance Trust Fund.

Developments Since 1965

The basic character of the OASDHI program has not changed since 1965. In 1972, in order to provide automatic increases in benefits related to increases in the cost of living, the benefit level was linked by a formula to both the CPI *and* the level of average earnings in manufacturing. This meant that the benefits of retired workers rose with increases in the CPI and that the benefits of future retirees were based on increases in wages that reflected the rate of inflation *and* increases in the wage level. During the 1970s, this "double indexing" raised prospective benefits for future retirees to levels higher than their preretirement incomes. As a result, Congress "decoupled" the benefit structure in 1977 to eliminate double indexing.*

In 1973, the limit on the earnings of retirees under the age of 72 was eliminated from the retirement test. (There is no limit after age 72). One dollar of benefits is now withheld for every two dollars of earnings above a prescribed amount that is scheduled to increase periodically.

When the Social Security Act was passed, most private pension plans provided for compulsory or voluntary retirement at age 65. Given the high unemployment rate of the thirties, this seemed to most people to be a reasonable retirement age. It was not however based on any objective analysis of the physiology of aging, and during World War II and the immediate postwar period, the increase in average life expectancy, coupled with an increase in the demand for labor, led some experts to urge that older workers be kept in the labor force. More recently, the feeling has grown that compulsory retirement at 65 is unfair to persons who wish to continue to work. Arguments in favor of this position have been reinforced by the changing age composition of the population. Projected increases in the number of persons 65 and over relative to the working population will require proportionately greater outlays to fund retirement benefits as time goes by. In 1978, the Age Discrimination in Employment Act was amended to extend the coverage of the prohibition against discrimination on the basis of age to those 70 or under. In effect, this outlawed mandatory retirement before the age of 70.

---

* In July of 1980 social security benefits were automatically increased 14.3% reflecting the average rate of increase in the CPI from the first quarter of 1979 through the first quarter of 1980.

Current Provisions

The OASDHI program is reviewed on a continuing basis, producing periodic revisions in benefit levels, tax rates, and the tax base. In 1977, declining trust fund balances and huge projected deficits led to major revisions in financing arrangements. The tax rate for employers and employees was increased from 5.85 percent in 1977 to 6.05 percent in 1978, 6.13 percent in 1979, 6.65 percent in 1981, and by steps to 7.65 percent in 1990. A series of increases raised the taxable wage base from $16,500 in 1977 to $29,700 in 1981 and tied further increases to wage inflation. Even so, projections indicate that without additional financing, the disability fund will be depleted by the year 2007 and the retirement fund by 2030.

Limits on earnings were also changed in 1977. Under the new maximums, retirees under 72 would lose one dollar for every two dollars they earned above $4,500 in 1979, $5,000 in 1980, $5,500 in 1981, and $6,000 in 1982, at which time the exemption age would drop to 70.

Eligibility Requirements

Workers must demonstrate a regular attachment to the labor force to qualify for social security benefits. In the usual case, this means they must have worked at least ten years at some type of covered employment. The basic, or *primary*, insurance allowance (PIA) "serves as the base for computing the monthly amounts for all types of benefits payable on the worker's earning record and is related to the worker's average monthly earnings."[41]

Specific benefits are provided on the basis of a wage earner's status as "fully" or "currently" insured. A worker must be *fully insured* to qualify for most types of benefits; that is, he or she must have at least as many quarters of coverage as the number of years elapsing between age 21 and 62 or the date of death or disability, whichever occurs first. However, benefits are paid to survivors if the deceased worker was currently insured. That is, the worker must have had six quarters of coverage within the 13-calendar-quarter period ending with the quarter in which he or she died.

At the end of December 1979, the OASDHI program was paying cash benefits of some $9 billion a month to over 35 million beneficiaries. The average benefit for retired workers was $294.27 per month; for disabled workers it was $322.03. During the same month, payments to hospitals, skilled nursing facilities, and home health agencies totaled $1.7 billion and supplementary medical insurance benefits were $788.8 million.[42]

Current Problems

The payroll tax used to finance social security benefits has been criticized because it is a regressive tax, taking a larger proportion of lower incomes. However, the "tilting" of benefit schedules in favor of those with low incomes, the increase in real benefit levels over time, and the subventions provided out of general revenues to "blanket in" certain newly covered groups and finance supplementary medical insurance mean that the OASDHI system is not regressive in terms of the *total* benefits it generates.[43]

Up to now, the system has been financed on a "pay-as-you-go" basis. However, the projected increase in the number of beneficiaries (from 31 per 100 covered workers in 1977 to between 45 and 50 per 100 workers by 2050), the rapid escalation in hospital and medical costs, and an unexpectedly large number of disability benefits will make it difficult to continue financing the program in this way without dramatic increases in the tax base and/or the payroll tax rate. At the same time, voter resistance to scheduled increases in the payroll tax suggests that even those increases may not materialize. As we have already indicated, the OAI system was never intended to be self-supporting indefinitely. The Committee on Economic Security assumed that the government would eventually contribute to the annual costs of the system out of general revenues. It now appears that a federal subvention to additional segments of the program will be necessary in the near future. Other options include a reduction in the rate of increase of projected benefits, an increase in the age at which a person can retire and receive full benefits, and stricter eligibility requirements for disability benefits.

In December 1979, the seventh Advisory Council on Social Security "urged broad reforms in the Social Security System to assure its solvency for the next 75 years."[44] A number of proposals were advanced by the council, including increasing the age of eligibility for maximum benefits from 65 to 68, shoring up the various trust funds out of general revenues during periods of high unemployment, and using revenues from income taxes to finance the Medicare hospital insurance program. As a result of proposed changes in financing, the current 6.13 percent payroll tax could be reduced to 5.6 percent in 1980, a tax boost would not be required until 2005, and the wage base on which taxes are paid would rise more slowly than under existing legislation.

Less than a month later, however, the National Commission on Social Security, established by Congress in 1977, in an interim report foresaw a potentially serious cash shortage in the social security system and opposed any rollback of the payroll tax increases scheduled for 1981. It suggested that the retirement fund be authorized to borrow from the disability and Medicare trust funds. The final report from this commission on the financing of the system is due in January 1981.[45]

UNEMPLOYMENT INSURANCE

Unemployment is not the same type of actuarial risk as industrial accidents or old age. It is a market phenomenon whose incidence cannot be neatly calculated on the basis of statistical probability, and it is unrealistic, therefore, to expect private carriers to offer broad insurance against it.[46]

The basic provisions of our federal-state unemployment insurance (UI) program were described briefly in the Chapter 7. A product of the Depression, the program was designed to (1) provide benefits to persons regularly attached to the labor force who find themselves involuntarily unemployed for a short period, (2) act as an automatic fiscal stabilizer by paying benefits during periods of unemployment and collecting a greater volume of payroll taxes during periods of prosperity, and (3) encourage employers to maintain a stable labor force through a system of variable tax rates related to the incidence of unemployment among their own employees.

The system was *not* designed to raise the incomes of persons below the official poverty line or to provide benefits during prolonged periods of unemployment. The executive director of President Roosevelt's Committee on Economic Security emphasized that

> unemployment insurance does not eliminate the necessity for relief or emergency employment. It affords limited protection only and it must often be supplemented. But unemployment insurance is for the regularly employed steady industrial workers a valuable first line of defense.[47]

Title III of the Social Security Act, through a tax offset plan, encouraged the states to establish their own unemployment insurance programs. A uniform federal tax is levied on the payrolls of covered employers; but if a state has an unemployment insurance program consistent with the provisions of the national act, employers can in effect use the state tax to offset a large part of their federal tax liability (at present 2.7 of the 3.4 percent tax). By July 1937, all 50 states and the District of Columbia had passed unemployment insurance laws.

Individual states establish their own benefit, eligibility, and coverage standards. Most states have exercised the option of basing an individual employer's payroll tax rate on the extent to which the firm has contributed to unemployment in the past (its *unemployment experience rating*). Understandably, there are wide variations among state plans. They do however have some essential characteristics in common.[48]

Financing

Under the original federal plan, a 3 percent tax was levied on the total payrolls of covered employers. Under a 1939 amendment, the tax was limited to the first $3,000 of earnings (the *wage base*) of each worker. Under the tax offset plan, 0.3 percent was retained by the federal government to cover administrative costs, including the operation of the U.S. Employment Service, and 2.7 percent was, in effect, "returned" to the states. There is no federal tax on employees; only three states levy such taxes. All money collected is held in a federal *Unemployment*

Trust Fund. It is not pooled; each state has a separate account, similar to an individual checking account at a commercial bank.

Employers' experience ratings, which by 1979 were used in all jurisdictions except Puerto Rico, the Virgin Islands, and Washington, are intended to provide an incentive for employers to keep workers on. However, since the conditions creating unemployment are not usually controllable by a firm, the overall impact of experience ratings has not been significant.

Recent increases in benefits, high unemployment rates, and longer periods of unemployment have put a great strain on many states' unemployment insurance reserves. In fiscal 1976, 22 states exhausted their UI funds and were forced to borrow $2.4 billion to pay benefits.[49] In order to put the UI reserves on a sounder financial basis, both the payroll tax and the wage base have been raised. As of January 1980, the taxable wage base was $6,000, the basic payroll tax rate was 3.4 percent, and the net federal tax rate was 0.7 percent.

The benefits paid to federal civilian employees and ex-service personnel, certain extended unemployment benefits, and benefits paid during recent periods of high unemployment to workers normally ineligible have been financed by federal funds rather than payroll taxes. Such benefits are termed unemployment *compensation* (UC) to distinguish them from the benefits paid under the state *insurance* programs (UI). In 1978, an average of 2.4 million persons a week received an average state-insured benefit of $83.67. During fiscal 1978 a total of 7.9 million persons received $10.1 billion in benefits under UI and UC programs.[50]

Coverage

Unemployment insurance originally covered industrial and commercial employers who had eight or more employees in 20 or more weeks in a calendar year. Agricultural workers, domestic servants, family workers, the self-employed, state and local government employees, and employees of nonprofit institutions were exempt. Some two-thirds of the civilian labor force was covered by unemployment insurance in 1938.

Coverage since has been extended on several occasions. Most recently, the Unemployment Compensation Amendments of 1976 extended coverage to state and local government employees and some farm and domestic workers. Over 97 percent of all wage and salary employment is now covered under the permanent federal-state UI system and the permanent programs providing unemployment compensation. Agricultural workers on small farms and domestic workers in small households are the largest categories still excluded from coverage.

Eligibility Requirements

Benefits are designed for workers who are able to demonstrate a *regular* and *recent* attachment to the labor force and who are *involuntarily* unemployed. An unemployed worker must have either a minimum amount of earnings within a specified period or a minimum number of weeks of covered employment to qualify for benefits. He or she must be able to work and be available for work. This *work test* is met initially by registering at a public employment office.

A state cannot deny benefits if a claimant refuses to accept a job that (1) is vacant as a result of a labor dispute; (2) involves substandard wages, hours, or other working conditions; or (3) would require as a condition of employment that the claimant either join a company union or resign from or refrain from joining a bona fide labor organization. Under the Unemployment Compensation Amendments of 1976, states are also prohibited from denying benefits solely on the basis of pregnancy.

A worker does not qualify for benefits if he or she (1) is unable to work or unavailable for work; (2) was discharged for misconduct; (3) left work voluntarily "without good cause"; (4) refuses suitable work; or (5), in all but two states, is involved in a labor dispute.

Disqualification provisions have been tightened in a number of states to reduce the drain on reserves from long-term unemployment at high benefit levels. A 1977 act requires states to disqualify a worker for federally financed extended benefits (beyond 39 weeks) if he or she has refused a job in a line of work different from his or her previous employment or a job that pays less than a previous job but more than the worker's unemployment benefit.

Benefit Schedules

Unemployment benefits are usually based on a worker's wages during a recent base period. For example, the weekly benefit might equal a stated fraction of the worker's wages in that quarter of the base period in which they were highest. Some states use a weighted schedule that gives lower paid workers a higher proportion of their former wages. Under current federal law

> no quantitative State requirements are provided . . . and no common pattern of benefit provisions, comparable to that in coverage and financing has evolved. [Instead] the States have developed diverse and complex formulas for determining worker benefit rights.[51]

Originally, proponents of the unemployment insurance system hoped that it would restore 50 percent of an unemployed worker's after-tax wage loss. However, the establishment of minimum and maximum benefits has "tilted" benefits in favor of less highly paid workers. Benefits have not kept pace with the increase in average wages, although as a result of the extension of the *benefit period,* a greater proportion of total wage losses are recovered when unemployment is prolonged. By 1975, in order to relate benefits to average weekly wages on a continuing basis, 32 states had adopted a sliding formula for calculating maximum benefits.[52]

According to the Bureau of Labor Statistics, the UI program "replaces between one-quarter and one-third of wages lost by beneficiaries during [the] weeks of unemployment for which they receive benefits."[53] Daniel Hamermesh has concluded that "the amount of income, net of taxes, transportation costs, and so forth (including fringe payments) replaced by UI benefits . . . for most individuals . . . is probably close to 50 percent."[54]

In most states, benefits for a given year are related to average weekly earnings in covered employment in the state during the previous year. The estimated average weekly wage in covered employments nationally was $216 in 1977, and the estimated average weekly benefit in 1978 was $85.70, or 39.7 percent of the prior year average weekly earnings. The average weekly benefit ranged from $64.22 in Florida to $103.59 in Iowa and $106.66 in the District of Columbia.[55] It should be noted that these benefits are now subject to the federal income tax after adjusted gross income reaches a certain level ($25,000 for a joint and $20,000 for a single return as of January 1, 1979). In 11 states and the District of Columbia, dependents' allowances are provided in addition to the basic benefits. Many experts believe that the federal government should establish minimum benefit levels, require payment of dependents' allowances, and require that the maximum benefit be related by a formula to the average weekly wages in a state.

The Duration of Benefits

In 1978, only Puerto Rico had a maximum benefit period of less than 26 weeks. However, in 43 jurisdictions, benefit periods were related by formulas to the amount of a worker's earnings or the length of time a job was held. In 1958 and 1961, up to 13 weeks of extended benefits were provided under temporary programs. The Employment Security Amendment of 1970 provided a permanent program of extended benefits for up to 13 weeks, with the extension triggered by specified, high national or state unemployment rates.

In 1975, a temporary Federal Supplemental Benefits Program (FSB) provided benefits for an additional 13 weeks (up to a total of 52), and under separate legislation a further 13 weeks, also on a temporary basis. These programs have expired, and at present up to 39 weeks of benefits are generally available under the regular and extended benefits programs.

A Concluding Comment

Despite the expansion of coverage and increases in the level and duration of benefits, unemployment insurance does not provide enough income for many workers. Those in firms not covered by a state program, those who fail to qualify for benefits, or those who exhaust their benefit eligibility must look elsewhere for help, and the proportion of lost wages restored under many state schedules is too little for many families to meet even their minimal needs. Moreover, due to the absence of uniform federal standards, the system does not always treat people in similar situations in the same way. Obviously, such standards should be established. However, since unemployment benefits for low income workers are not taxed, making them too high may cause people to look for a job only halfheartedly or to take their time searching for work. Hamermesh has recommended that gross benefits for all beneficiaries be raised to two-thirds of weekly earnings during the base period, that benefits be taxed as earnings, and that benefit standards be legislated at the federal level.[56]

Another issue is whether unemployment benefits should be used consciously to combat poverty. The system appears ill suited to such an objective; according to one estimate, in normal years not more than one-fifth of UI payments are to poor households.[57] If the system is to remain an insurance system, the distinction between paying UI benefits to regular members of the labor force and providing income to the poor to raise their standard of living should be sharpened. Unemployment insurance should not be used to achieve an objective that may subvert its primary function. An objective review of these and other issues is forthcoming from the National Commission on Unemployment Compensation, established in 1976 and scheduled to issue its final report by June 30, 1980.

HEALTH INSURANCE

We have seen that workmen's compensation protects employees against the medical expenses and a major part of the income loss associated with occupationally connected accidents and disease; that a significant portion of the labor force is covered by temporary disability laws that provide partial income maintenance during periods of nonoccupationally connected disability; and that the federal Medicare program provides hospital and medical insurance for persons 65 and older. However, there is no general insurance program providing protection against the expenses and income loss associated with off-the-job illness and injury. The lack of a social insurance program covering medical expenses is particularly surprising, since there was an apparent consensus in the 1960s that some type of national health insurance program should be established.

The failure of recent Congresses to establish such a program has been due to (1) disagreement over the objectives and structure of such a program, (2) the fact that the existing Medicare program and Medicaid have met the health care needs of the aged with reasonable success, (3) the fact that most members of the labor force and their dependents are covered by private hospital and medical insurance, and (4) a fear that unless escalating health care costs are first brought under control, a national health insurance program will result in further cost increases without a corresponding increase in the delivery of health care services.

A variety of health insurance proposals have been introduced in Congress. These proposals, which do *not* include insurance against *income lost* while a person is incapacitated, fall into two categories: (1) compulsory insurance programs to be financed by employer and employee contributions and operated by private insurance carriers and (2) compulsory programs to be financed out of · general revenues and/or payroll taxes and operated by the federal government. Both types of proposals must be distinguished from a nationalized system of health care such as that of Great Britain, under which most providers of medical services are government employees and most health care facilities are operated by the government. Nevertheless, the belief that a federal health insurance program represents a first step toward socialized medicine appears to be responsible for much of the opposition to these proposals.

According to a Brookings Institution study, a health insurance program has three primary goals that can be achieved through financial mechanisms: "(1) ensuring that all persons have access to medical care, (2) eliminating the financial hardship of medical bills, and (3) limiting the rise in health care costs."[58] The study suggests that a "plan meeting each of these three goals is unlikely to be acceptable . . . unless it also (1) can be equitably financed, (2) is easy to understand and administer, and (3) is acceptable to providers of medical services and to the public."[59]

An acceptable program will presumably provide greater and more equitable access to medical and hospital care, but it will not necessarily improve health:

> The best estimates are that the medical system . . . affects about 10 per cent of the usual indices for measuring health. . . . The remaining 90 per cent are determined by factors over which doctors have little or no control, . . . individual life style . . . social conditions . . . the physical environment.[60]

The Health Care System

In 1976, almost every citizen 65 and over had health insurance, not only under the Medicare and Supplementary Medical Insurance programs but also under complementary private programs. Some 98.1 percent had hospital insurance under Medicare, 96.8 percent had SMI coverage, and 62.8 percent had some private coverage. Almost four-fifths of the population under 65 had private insurance covering hospital care and physicians' services, three-quarters had insurance covering drugs prescribed out of hospital, and 24 percent had private dental care insurance.[61] Private insurance met 85.8 percent of consumer expenditures for hospital care, 45.9 percent of expenditures for physicians' services, 18.4 percent of expenditures for dental services, and 8.1 percent of the costs of drugs.[62]

Unfortunately, the low income groups most in need of such protection are those least likely to have it. According to the Brookings study mentioned above, six million people below the official poverty threshold are not covered by the federal Medicaid program, "only 41 percent of poor full-time workers have any health insurance, and less than 10 percent have coverage that pays for care in a physician's office." Moreover, "less than 30 percent of the workers who lose their jobs and major source of income retain private health insurance coverage to protect them during this period when they are most vulnerable to the high cost of medical care."[63]

The Cost of Health Care

While the Congress debates the various health insurance proposals, health care costs continue to climb. During fiscal 1965, the year Medicare was passed, the United States spent slightly less than $39 billion ($198 per capita) on health care, or 5.9 percent of the GNP; during fiscal 1977, the country spent $163 billion ($737 per capita) for health services, or 8.8 percent of the GNP.[64] In 1965, the private sector provided three-quarters of these funds; in 1977, the public sector provided over 42 percent. The financing of medical care through Medicare and Medicaid—starting in 1967—has contributed to the steadily increasing public share of such expenditures. In 1977, these programs accounted for $37 billion in benefits, or 26 percent of the $142.6 billion spent for personal health care.[65]

Between 1965 and 1975, the medical care component of the Consumer Price Index (1967 = 100) rose from 89.5 to 168.6 percent, while the CPI as a whole rose from 94.5 to 161.2. The average annual rate of increase in health care expenditures was 8 percent between 1955 and 1965 and 12.2 percent between 1966 and 1975.[66] There is no consensus among economists as to the relative importance of the factors responsible for the rapid escalation of health care expenditures. It is clear however that insurance programs have contributed to this escalation because those covered by such programs tend to consider hospital and medical services free goods. In 1977, 70 percent of all personal health care services were paid for by a third party.[67]

A Concluding Comment

The debate over the specifics of a comprehensive health insurance program continues. There is less certainty about the appropriate trade-off between increased and more costly health care and alternative social choices than there was ten years ago, and this trade-off must be determined before a politically acceptable health insurance program can be developed. Meanwhile, our failure to provide comprehensive protection against the medical costs associated with a nonoccupationally connected disability and the lack of a national program to maintain workers' incomes while such a disability continues constitute serious gaps in our armour against economic insecurity.

SUMMARY

Continuous employment at adequate wages is the basis of economic security in our industrial society. Protection against economic insecurity is provided by a complex of government programs, complemented in the case of most workers by private programs. In addition, hours and wages legislation protect employees by limiting workweeks and setting minimal rates of pay.

Our pluralistic social insurance system is unique. It is composed of state workmen's compensation programs, a limited number of state-sponsored temporary disability programs, a federal-state unemployment insurance program, a comprehensive federal old age, survivors, and disability insurance program, and a comprehensive federal health insurance program for persons 65 and over.

These social insurance programs, which emphasize social adequacy rather than private equity, may prevent destitution and hardship for many workers, but they are not solutions to the "poverty problem." They fail to cover or to adequately help many persons who are chronically unemployed, who are unable to earn a socially adequate minimum wage, or who, due to personal limitations or family responsibilities, are unable to join the labor force. General or categorical income maintenance programs and public assistance programs are essential to help persons below the poverty threshold or those for whom insurance benefits are inadequate.

Although the American social security system lacks the uniformity and the greater degree of equity associated with a comprehensive national program, major modifications in the system appear unlikely. The greatest gaps in the protection currently afforded wage earners are the absence of a general national health insurance program (not to be equated with socialized medicine) and specific national programs covering those who are temporarily or permanently partially disabled. Such programs are essential components of any system that claims to provide comprehensive protection from economic insecurity.

DISCUSSION QUESTIONS

1. Some critics of social security programs argue that workers should be expected to provide protection against the work-related contingencies of an industrial civilization on an individual basis. Evaluate this position.
2. Why are flexible working hours within a longer workday, and a ten-hour day, four-day workweek considered methods of improving the "quality of life"? Do you expect such initiatives to be adopted widely during the next decade?
3. Why do you suppose that unions have not pressed for an amendment to the Fair Labor Standards Act requiring punitive overtime payments after eight hours of work per day (recall that the act requires punitive overtime payments only after forty hours of work per week)
4. Do you believe that we need *federal* workers' compensation legislation?
5. How does our federal old-age insurance program differ from private insurance providing retirement benefits?
6. Why do some economists argue that it will be necessary to fund some (additional) portion of OASDHI from general revenues?
7. Why has it proved particularly difficult to control health care costs?
8. What position did the major political parties adopt on national health insurance during the 1980 campaign? Does it appear that the Congress will adopt some type of national health insurance program during the 1980s?

SELECTED READINGS

Hours and Wages Legislation

American Enterprise Institute for Public Policy Research. *Minimum Wage Legislation, Legislative Analysis.* Washington, D.C.: June 27, 1977.

Levitan, Sar A., and Belous, Richard S. *More than Subsistence: Minimum Wages for the Working Poor.* Baltimore, Md.: Johns Hopkins University Press, 1979. A positive recent assessment.

Millis, Harry A., and Montgomery, Royal E. *Labor's Progress and Some Basic Labor Problems.* New York: McGraw-Hill, 1938. Chap. VI, pp. 278–375. A good overview of the development of hours and wages legislation.

Oswald, Rudolph A. "Fair Labor Standards." Chap. 5 in *Federal Policies and Worker Status Since the Thirties.* Ed. by Joseph P. Goldberg, Eileen Ahern, William Haber, and Rudolph A. Oswald. Madison, Wisc.: Industrial Relations Research Association, 1976.

Peterson, John M., and Stewart, Charles T., Jr. *Employment Effects of Minimum Wage Rates.* Washington, D.C.: American Enterprise Institute for Public Policy Research, August 1969.

U.S. Department of Labor, *Growth of Labor Law in the United States,* 1967, pp. 69–97 and 123–133.

Weiss, Abraham. "A Look at the Minimum Wage and H. R. 100130." In *Labor Law Journal* 27, no. 3 (March 1976): pp. 131–140.

Welch, Finis. *Minimum Wages: Issues and Evidence.* Washington, D.C.: American Enterprise Institute for Public Policy Research, 1978. A recent negative assessment of the impact of minimum wage legislation.

Social Security Legislation

Altmeyer, Arthur J. "The Development and Status of Social Security in America." In *Labor, Management, and Social Policy.* Ed. by Gerald G. Somers. Madison, Wisc.: University of Wisconsin Press, 1963, pp. 123–159.

Derthick, Martha. *Policymaking for Social Security.* Washington, D.C.: Brookings Institution, 1979.

U.S. Department of Health, Education, and Welfare, Social Security Administration. *Social Security Programs in the United States,* 1973.

Workmen's Compensation Laws

Millis, Harry A., and Montgomery, Royal E. *Labor's Risks and Social Insurance.* New York: McGraw-Hill, 1938. Chap. IV, pp. 187–234.

Report of the National Commission on State Workmen's Compensation Laws, Washington, D.C.: July 1972.

Somers, Herman Miles, and Somers, Anne Ramsay. *Workmen's Compensation.* New York: Wiley, 1954, chaps. 1–3.

U.S. Department of Health, Education, and Welfare, Social Security Administration. *Social Security Programs in the United States,* 1973, pp. 72–87.

U.S. Department of Labor. *Growth of Labor Law in the United States, 1967* pp. 137–178.

Weiss, Harry. "Employer's Liability and Workmen's Compensation," in Don D. Lescohier and Elizabeth Brandeis, *History of Labor in the United States, 1896–1932: Working Conditions and Labor Legislation*, Vol. III, pp. 564–610, in John R. Commons et al., *History of Labour in the United States*. New York: Macmillan, 1935.

Temporary Disability Insurance

Price, Daniel N. "Cash Benefits for Short-Term Sickness, 1948–76." In *Social Security Bulletin* 41, no. 10 (October 1978): pp. 3–13. Covers private and public programs.

U.S. Department of Health, Education, and Welfare, Social Security Administration. *Social Security Programs in the United States*, 1973, pp. 87–97.

Old Age Insurance

Boskin, Michael, ed. *The Crisis in Social Security: Problems and Prospects*. San Francisco: Institute for Contemporary Studies, 1978.

Brittain, John A. *The Payroll Tax for Social Security*. Washington, D.C.: Brookings Institution, 1972.

Brown, J. Douglas. *An American Philosophy of Social Security: Evolution and Issues*. Princeton, N.J.: Princeton University Press, 1972.

Brown, J. Douglas. *The Genesis of Social Security in America*. Princeton, N.J.: Industrial Relations Section, Princeton University, 1969. An excellent brief description of the development and passage of the OAI Title of the Social Security Act.

Campbell, Colin D., ed. *Financing Social Security*. Washington, D.C.: American Enterprise Institute for Public Policy Research, 1979.

Cohen, Wilbur J. "The Evolution and Growth of Social Security." Chap. 3 in *Federal Policies and Worker Status Since the Thirties*. Ed. by Joseph P. Goldberg, Eileen Ahern, William Haber, and Rudolph A. Oswald. Madison, Wisc.: Industrial Relations Research Association, 1976.

Munnell, Alicia H. *The Future of Social Security*. Washington, D.C.: Brookings Institution, 1977.

Pechman, Joseph A., Aaron, Henry J., and Taussig, Michael K. *Social Security: Perspectives for Reform*. Washington, D.C.: Brookings Institution, 1968.

Robertson, A. Haeworth. "Financial Status of Social Security Program After the Social Security Amendments of 1977." In *Social Security Bulletin* 41, no. 3 (March 1978): pp. 21–30.

Snee, John, and Ross, Mary. "Social Security Amendments of 1977: Legislative History and Summary of Provisions." In *Social Security Bulletin* 41, no. 3 (March 1978): pp. 3–20.

Van Gorkom, J. W. *Social Security Revisited*. Washington, D.C.: American Enterprise Institute for Public Policy Research, 1979.

U.S. Department of Health, Education, and Welfare, Social Security Administration. *Social Security Handbook*. (See the most recent edition for a detailed analysis of current provisions.) Another source of recent data is the *Social Security Bulletin*, also published by the Social Security Administration.

Unemployment Insurance

Employment and Training Report of the President, Including Reports by the U.S. Department of Labor and the U.S. Department of Health, Education, and Welfare, Transmitted to the Congress 1976. Chap. 2, "The Unemployment Insurance System: Past, Present, and Future."

Hamermesh, Daniel S. *Jobless Pay and the Economy.* Baltimore, Md.: Johns Hopkins University Press, 1977.

Katz, Arnold, ed. "The Economics of Unemployment Insurance: A Symposium." In *Industrial and Labor Relations Review* 30, no. 4, (July 1977).

Munts, Raymond. "Policy Development in Unemployment Insurance," chap. 4 in *Federal Policies and Worker Status Since the Thirties.* Ed. by Joseph P. Goldberg et al. Madison, Wisc.: Industrial Relations Research Association, 1976.

U.S. Department of Health, Education, and Welfare, Social Security Administration. *Social Security Programs in the United States,* 1973, pp. 55–72.

Health Care Costs

Klarman, Herbert E. *The Economics of Health.* New York: Columbia University Press, 1965. A comprehensive analysis.

Klarman, Herbert E., "The Financing of Health Care," in *Daedalus* (Winter 1977), pp. 215–234.

Notes

1. Eveline M. Burns, *Social Security and Public Policy* (New York: McGraw-Hill, 1956), p. 4.
2. Cf. ibid., pp. 2–4.
3. Ewan Clague, *Hours of Work: Background Materials Presented Before the Select Subcommittee on Labor, House Education and Labor Committee, June 11, 1963* (Washington, D.C.: U.S. Department of Labor, mimeo), p. 3 and Table 1.
4. Ibid., p. 3.
5. Peter Henle, "Recent Growth of Paid Leisure for U.S. Workers," in *Monthly Labor Review* 85, no. 3 (March 1962): p. 256.
6. John D. Owen, "Workweeks and leisure: an analysis of trends, 1948–75," in *Monthly Labor Review* 99, no. 8 (August 1976): p. 3.
7. Marcia L. Greenbaum, *The Shorter Workweek,* Bulletin 50 (Ithaca, N.Y.: NYS School of Industrial and Labor Relations, Cornell University, June 1963), p. 50.
8. U.S. Department of Labor, Employment Standards Administration, Women's Bureau, *State Labor Laws in Transition: From Equal Protection to Equal Status for Women,* Pamphlet 15, p. 12.
9. *A. L. A. Schechter Poultry Corp.* v. *United States,* 295 U.S. 495.
10. The constitutionality of the statute was established in *United States* v. *Darby Lumber Co.,* 312 U.S. 100 (1941).
11. *National League of Cities et al.* v. *Usery,* 426 U.S. 833 (1976).
12. *Adkins* v. *Children's Hospital,* 261 U.S. 525 (1923).
13. *West Coast Hotel Co.* v. *Parrish,* 300 U.S. 379 (1937).
14. U.S. Department of Labor, *State Labor Laws in Transition,* p. 3.

15. For ongoing reports of such studies, see the annual *Economic Effects Study, Minimum Wages and Maximum Hours Standards Under the Fair Labor Standards Act,* submitted to the Congress by the Secretary of Labor.
16. U.S. Department of Labor, Wage and Hour and Public Contracts Division, *An Evaluation of the Minimum Wage and Maximum Hours Standards of the Fair Labor Standards Act, Report Submitted to the Congress in Accordance with the Requirements of Section 4(d) of the Fair Labor Standards Act, January, 1965,* p. xi.
17. U.S. Department of Labor, Employment Standards Administration, *Minimum Wages and Maximum Hours Standards Under the Fair Labor Standards Act: An Economic Effects Study Submitted to Congress 1979,* Table 1, p. 19.
18. Cf. Edward M. Gramlich, "Impact of Minimum Wages on Other Wages, Employment, and Family Incomes," in *Brookings Papers on Economic Activity* 2 (1976): pp. 409–451.
19. Sar A. Levitan and Richard D. Belous, *More Than Subsistence: Minimum Wages for the Working Poor* (Baltimore, Md.: Johns Hopkins University Press, 1979), p. 153.
20. Arthur J. Altmeyer, "Some Assumptions and Objectives in Social Security," reprinted from *Survey Graphic,* 1945, in William Haber and Wilbur J. Cohen, eds., *Social Security: Programs, Problems and Policies* (Homewood, Ill.: Irwin, 1960), p. 7.
21. Wilbur J. Cohen, "The Evolution and Growth of Social Security," chap. 3 in Joseph P. Goldberg, Eileen Ahern, William Haber, and Rudolph A. Oswald, eds., *Federal Policies and Worker Status Since the Thirties* (Madison, Wisc.: Industrial Relations Research Association, 1976), p. 53.
22. U.S. Department of Labor, Bureau of Labor Statistics, "Occupational Injuries and Illness for 1978," News Release, USDL–79–788, November 7, 1979, p. 1. and Table 4. Fatality data are for employers with 11 or more employees.
23. Cited in Nicholas Askounes Ashford, *Crisis in the Workplace: Occupational Disease and Injury, A Report to the Ford Foundation* (Cambridge, Mass.: MIT Press, 1976), p. 47.
24. Cited ibid., p. 17.
25. Ibid., p. 46 citing a 1972 Congressional Hearing.
26. 84 *Stat.* 1590, sec 2(b)(1).
27. Cf. Ashford, *Crisis in the Workplace,* particularly chaps. 7 and 13, and Robert Steward Smith, *The Occupational Safety and Health Act: Its goal and its achievements* (Washington, D.C.: American Enterprise Institute for Public Policy Research, January 1976).
28. Smith, *Occupational Safety and Health Act,* p. 1.
29. Sec. 27(a)(1).
30. Herman Miles Somers and Anne Ramsay Somers, *Workmen's Compensation,* (New York: Wiley, 1954), pp. 26–27.
31. These and subsequent 1976 data are from Daniel N. Price, "Workers' Compensation Program in the 1970s," *Social Security Bulletin* 43, no. 5 (May 1979), pp. 3–24.
32. *The Report of the National Commission on Workmen's Compensation,* Washington, D.C.: July 1972, p. 44.
33. 1979 benefit data in this section are based on American Federation of Labor and Congress of Industrial Organizations, "Worker's Compensation and Unemployment Insurance Under State Laws January 1, 1979," Publication No. 36–V.

34. U.S. Bureau of the Census, *Statistical Abstract of the United States: 1979,* Table 564, p. 351.

35. *The Report of the National Commission on Workmen's Compensation,* p. 15. Cf. James Robert Chelius, *Workplace Safety and Health: The Role of Workers' Compensation* (Washington, D.C.: American Enterprise Institute for Public Policy Research, 1977).

36. *The Report of the National Commission on Workmen's Compensation,* pp. 25–26.

37. "U.S. Welfare Policies in Perspective," in *Industrial Relations* 2, no. 2 (February 1963): p. 42.

38. John J. Corson and John W. McConnell, *Economic Needs of Older People* (New York: Twentieth Century Fund, 1956), p. 198.

39. A. Haeworth Robertson, "OASDI: Fiscal Basis and Long-Range Cost Projections," in *Social Security Bulletin* 40, no. 1, (January 1977): p. 22.

40. The discussion of amendments through 1960 draws heavily from Arthur J. Altmeyer, "The Development and Status of Social Security in America," in Gerald G. Somers, ed., *Labor, Management, and Social Policy* (Madison, Wisc.: University of Wisconsin Press, 1963), p. 130 ff.

41. "Effects of OASDI Benefit Increase, June 1976," in *Social Security Bulletin* 39, no. 12 (December 1976): p. 33.

42. *Social Security Bulletin* 43 no. 5 (May 1980): p. 1, Table M–7, p. 37 and Table M–8, p. 38.

43. Cf. Cohen, "The Evolution and Growth of Social Security," p. 66.

44. *The Wall Street Journal,* December 10, 1979, p. 5. The *Executive Summary* and major recommendations of the Advisory Council may be found in *Social Security Bulletin,* 45 no. 2 (February 1980), pp. 3–15.

45. *The New York Times,* January 14, 1980, p. 7.

46. For a contrary view see Harry Malisoff, *The Insurance Character of Unemployment Insurance* (Kalamazoo, Mich.: Upjohn Institute for Employment Research, December 1961), particularly pp. 13–14.

47. Edwin E. Witte, "Job Insurance: Its Limitations and Value," in Robert J. Lampman, ed., *Social Security Perspectives: Essays by Edwin E. Witte* (Madison, Wisc.: University of Wisconsin Press, 1962), p. 229.

48. Unless otherwise indicated, data in the immediately following sections are from the *First Interim Report* (November 1978) and the *Second Report* (July 1979) of the National Commission on Unemployment Compensation.

49. *Employment and Training Report of the President, Including Reports by the U.S. Department of Labor and the U.S. Department of Health, Education, and Welfare, Transmitted to the Congress 1977,* p. 64.

50. *Social Security Bulletin* 43, no. 5 (May 1980): Table M–41, p. 65. *Employment and Training Report of the President, Including Reports by the U.S. Department of Labor and the U.S. Department of Health, Education, and Welfare, Transmitted to the Congress 1979,* p. 59.

51. *First Interim Report of the National Commission on Unemployment Compensation, November 1978,* p. 33.

52. Raymond Munts, "Policy Development in Unemployment Insurance," in Goldberg et al., eds., *Federal Policies and Worker Status Since the Thirties,* p. 83.

53. David L. Edgell and Stephen A. Wandner, "Unemployment insurance: its economic performance," in *Monthly Labor Review* 97, no. 4 (April 1974): p. 33.

54. Daniel S. Hamermesh, *Jobless Pay and the Economy* (Baltimore, Md.: Johns Hopkins University Press, 1977), p. 98.
55. Data exclude Puerto Rico and the Virgin Islands.
56. Op. cit., p. 105.
57. Ben Gillingham, *Cash Transfers: How Much Do They Help the Poor?* Special Report Series (Madison, Wisc.: Institute for Research on Poverty, University of Wisconsin, January 1971), cited in Munts, "Policy Development in Unemployment Insurance," p. 101.
58. Karen Davis, *National Health Insurance: Benefits, Costs, and Consequences* (Washington, D.C.: Brookings Institution, 1975), p. 2.
59. Ibid., p. 5.
60. Aaron Wildavsky, "Doing Better and Feeling Worse: The Political Pathology of Health Policy," in *Daedalus* (Winter 1977): p. 105.
61. Marjorie Smith Carroll, "Private Health Insurance Plans in 1976: An Evaluation," in *Social Security Bulletin* 41, no. 9 (September 1978): pp. 4 and 6.
62. Ibid., p. 14.
63. Davis, *National Health Insurance*, pp. 2, 35. See also Congressional Budget Office, *Profile of Health Care Coverage: The Haves and Have-Nots*, March 1979.
64. Robert M. Gibson and Charles R. Fisher, "National Health Expenditures, Fiscal Year 1977," in *Social Security Bulletin* 41, no. 7 (July 1978): p. 3 and Table 1, p. 5.
65. Ibid.
66. Herbert E. Klarman, "The Financing of Health Care," in *Daedalus* (Winter 1977): Table 1, p. 216.
67. Gibson and Fisher, "National Health Expenditures, 1977," p. 6.

Chapter 9
THREE CONTINUING PROBLEMS: THE DISTRIBUTION OF INCOME, POVERTY, AND DISCRIMINATION

We have already seen that certain groups have a higher incidence of unemployment or are otherwise affected adversely by the operation of our labor markets and other institutional arrangements. For example, in Chapter 3 we observed that members of minority groups often benefit the least from economic growth, partly as a result of overt and institutionalized discrimination, while in Chapter 7 we identified a category of "unemployables," persons who are unable to join the labor force for various reasons or who are not hired because of their low productivity.

An individual or a family may be disadvantaged for several reasons, so that what are conventionally identified as problem groups tend to overlap. For example, the female head of a black family may find it difficult to enter the labor market while her children are young. She may also discover that her race and sex limit the kind of job offers she receives. In this chapter, we will discuss three continuing problems of the labor market: the uneven distribution of income, poverty, and discrimination.

THE DISTRIBUTION OF INCOME

In a perfectly competitive economy, incomes would not be distributed equally. Wages and salaries would vary in accordance with employees' marginal revenue productivities, and other factor payments would also reflect differences in productivity. In reality, many product and factor markets depart from competitive norms. We have discussed a number of ways to improve the functioning of labor markets, from programs to prepare people for jobs to changes in the organization of the labor market. The federal government and many state governments have adopted laws forbidding discrimination in hiring and have regulated certain terms of employment when the terms produced by the labor market have been unsatisfactory. Thus, they have established minimum wage standards and regulated hours of work.

There is an apparent consensus among economists that (1) the extreme variations in income resulting from the operation of our economic system are not essential to the best allocation of resources or the efficient operation of the system and (2) that family or individual incomes below some minimum should be supplemented. More specifically, government taxing and spending power should be used to produce a more equitable distribution of income.

Of course, ideas of what is equitable vary, and radical economists would reject this kind of action as inadequate. In their view, a private enterprise system will never generate fair payments to wage and salary workers nor, when the system is modified by government actions, will it provide an "appropriate" posttax/posttransfer payment distribution of income. We do not agree that achieving greater equity in the distribution of income requires a drastic change in our institutions, but we cannot deny the existence of this alternative paradigm.

The Data Base

Three basic distributions of income can be identified: (1) the *pretax* distribution, including income accrued but not paid; (2) the *posttax* distribution; and (3) the *posttax/posttransfer payment* distribution, including both cash and in-kind payments. Unfortunately, it has proved impossible to measure these distributions exactly. Overall measures of the distribution of income fail to show how much of the inequalities that are found are related to age, race, sex, and other variables, but they do suggest the general character of the distribution of income in the United States.

Data from Internal Revenue Service summaries of *personal income tax returns* are often used to measure inequalities in income. These figures are a rough measure of factor incomes; but they do not include all factor incomes, nor do they include a number of transfer payments—such as social security and welfare benefits—that are important sources of cash income for poorer families.

A commonly cited statistic related to personal income is the *money income estimate* developed annually by the Bureau of the Census and published as part of its *Current Population Reports* (CPR) series.[1] The CPR money income figure includes money wages or salary, net income from both farm and nonfarm employment, dividends and interest but not capital gains, most social security and welfare benefits, unemployment compensation, and government and private employee pensions. It excludes nonmoney transfers such as food stamps, health benefits, and subsidized housing and goods and services produced privately for personal consumption. Table 9.1 shows the percentage shares of CPS money income of families and unrelated individuals from 1947 to 1978. Figure 9.1 relates the percentage distribution of money income to the number of people earning income in families, the amount of education those people have, and the percentage of total family income, nationwide, received by each income group in 1976. It is obvious from both the table and the chart that money income is not distributed equally. Families with the highest incomes have more than their share of income earners, the higher income earners have more education, and the amount of money they earn is disproportionately high.

The Bureau of Economic Analysis (BEA) of the Department of Commerce has developed an expanded measure of *pretax family income* that includes several types of *imputed,* or nonmoney, income—the value of Medicare benefits and the net value of food stamps—but excludes individual contributions for social insurance programs and employer contributions to private health and welfare plans.

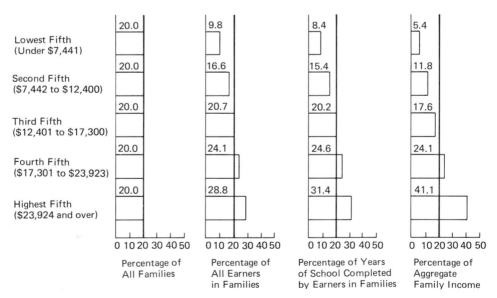

Figure 9.1   The Percentage Distribution of Aggregate Income in 1976 and Selected Characteristics of Families, Ranked by Total Income (Source: Adapted from U.S. Department of Commerce, Bureau of the Census, *Current Population Reports,* Series P-60, no. 114, "Money Income in 1976 of Families and Persons in the United States," cover.)

Table 9.1 THE PERCENTAGE SHARES OF CPS INCOME 1947–1978 OF FAMILIES AND UNRELATED PERSONS

	LOWEST FIFTH	SECOND FIFTH	MIDDLE FIFTH	FOURTH FIFTH	HIGHEST FIFTH	TOP 5 PERCENT
1947	3.5	10.6	16.8	23.6	45.5	18.7
1948	3.5	10.8	17.2	23.9	44.7	18.1
1949	3.2	10.5	17.2	24.2	44.9	17.9
1950	3.1	10.6	17.3	24.1	44.9	18.2
1951	3.5	11.2	17.6	24.1	43.6	17.5
1952	3.5	10.9	17.3	24.1	44.3	18.4
1953	3.2	10.8	17.6	24.5	43.8	17.3
1954	3.1	10.4	17.5	24.7	44.4	17.5
1955	3.3	10.6	17.6	24.6	43.9	17.5
1956	3.4	10.8	17.7	24.5	43.5	17.2
1957[a]	3.4	10.9	18.0	24.7	42.9	16.5
1958	3.5	10.8	17.8	24.6	43.4	16.7
1958	3.3	10.8	17.9	24.8	43.3	16.5
1959	3.2	10.6	17.7	24.7	43.9	17.1
1960	3.2	10.6	17.6	24.7	44.0	17.0
1961	3.1	10.2	17.2	24.6	44.9	17.7
1962	3.4	10.4	17.5	24.8	43.9	16.8
1963	3.4	10.4	17.5	24.8	43.9	16.9
1964	3.4	10.4	17.3	24.8	44.1	17.2
1965	3.6	10.6	17.5	24.8	43.6	16.6
1966	3.8	10.7	17.5	24.7	43.4	16.7
1967	3.6	10.6	17.5	24.8	43.4	16.5
1968	3.8	10.7	17.4	24.7	43.5	16.8
1969	3.7	10.5	17.4	24.7	43.7	16.8
1970	3.6	10.3	17.2	24.7	44.1	16.9
1971	3.7	10.2	17.1	24.7	44.3	17.0
1972	3.7	10.0	16.9	24.7	44.8	17.4
1973	3.8	10.0	16.9	24.8	44.5	17.0
1974	3.8	10.1	16.9	24.8	44.4	16.8
1974[b]	3.9	10.1	16.8	24.7	44.4	16.9
1975	3.9	9.9	16.7	24.9	44.5	17.0
1976	3.8	9.9	16.7	24.9	44.7	17.1
1977	3.8	9.7	16.5	24.9	45.2	17.3
1978	3.8	9.7	16.4	24.8	45.2	17.3
1979						
1980						
1981						

[a] Data for 1947 through 1957 calculated using grouped data. Data for 1959 through 1977 calculated using ungrouped data. Data for 1958 computed both ways.
[b] Based on revised methodology.
SOURCE: U.S. Department of Commerce, Bureau of the Census, *Current Population Reports,* Series P–60, no. 123, "Money Income of Families and Persons in the United States: 1978," Table 13, p. 62.

Table 9.2 illustrates the distribution of family income, based on the BEA's definition of *family personal incomes* (FPIs), from 1929 to 1971. It is obvious that while the inclusion of imputed income does increase the relative share of the lowest fifth somewhat, it does not have a significant leveling effect upon the overall distribution of income.

Any picture of the *after-tax, pretransfer* distribution of income in the United States will reflect the equalizing effect of taxes. It is usually assumed that the federal tax structure is basically progressive. However, the data in column 3 of Table 9.3, which show the combined effect of individual income and payroll taxes on the distribution of income in a sample year, suggest that this effect is modest.

After-tax, posttransfer distribution of income figures are considered a better measure of the actual "welfare" of the population. The *after-tax, postcash transfer* distribution of income in column 5 of Table 9.3 indicates that though cash transfers have had some effect at the lower and upper ends of the income scale, their overall impact, like that of taxes, has been modest.

The Ultimate Effect of Taxes

Economists interested in the welfare implications of income distribution prefer a distribution of income after taxes, cash transfers, and various noncash transfers that also takes into account the *incidence* of various types of taxes—that is, who bears the "final burden" of these taxes. Joseph Pechman and Benjamin Okner, for example, analyzed sample data for 1966 to estimate "the effect of all U.S. taxes on the distribution of income."[2] Their basic definition of income included income earned in the productive process, transfer payments, and capital gains accrued during the year. They attempted to measure the distribution of tax burdens but

Table 9.2 THE PERCENTAGE SHARES OF ALL CONSUMER UNITS IN FAMILY PERSONAL INCOME IN SELECTED YEARS, 1929–1971[a]

	LOWEST FIFTH	SECOND FIFTH	MIDDLE FIFTH	FOURTH FIFTH	HIGHEST FIFTH	TOP 5 PERCENT
1929	3.5	9.0	13.8	19.3	54.4	30.0
1935–36	4.1	9.2	14.1	20.9	51.7	26.5
1941	4.1	9.5	15.3	22.3	48.8	24.0
1944	4.9	10.9	16.2	22.2	45.8	20.7
1947	5.0	11.0	16.0	22.0	46.0	20.9
1950	4.8	10.9	16.1	22.1	46.1	21.4
1956	4.8	11.3	16.3	22.3	45.3	20.2
1961	4.6	10.9	16.3	22.7	45.5	19.6
1964	4.2	10.6	16.4	23.2	45.5	20.0
1970	4.6	10.7	16.4	23.3	44.9	19.2
1971	4.8	10.8	16.4	23.3	44.6	19.1

[a] 1929–1961 estimates from "old series"; 1964–1971 estimates from "new series."
SOURCE: Adapted from Daniel B. Radner and John C. Hinrichs, "Size Distribution of Income in 1964, 1970, and 1971," in *Survey of Current Business* 54, no. 10 (October 1974): Table 10, p. 27.

Table 9.3 THE COMBINED EFFECT OF FEDERAL INDIVIDUAL INCOME AND PAYROLL TAXES AND TRANSFER PAYMENTS ON THE DISTRIBUTION OF INCOME IN 1972

INCOME CATEGORY OF POPULATION	PERCENTAGE OF TOTAL INCOME RECEIVED BEFORE TAXES AND TRANSFERS	PERCENTAGE OF TOTAL INDIVIDUAL INCOME AND PAYROLL TAXES PAID	PERCENTAGE OF TOTAL INCOME RECEIVED AFTER INCOME AND PAYROLL TAXES	PERCENTAGE OF CASH TRANSFERS RECEIVED[a]	PERCENTAGE OF TOTAL INCOME RECEIVED AFTER TAXES AND TRANSFERS
Lowest Fifth	1.7	1.1	1.8	40.2	6.3
Second Fifth	6.6	5.0	7.0	26.8	9.1
Third Fifth	14.5	13.3	14.8	13.1	14.6
Fourth Fifth	24.1	22.8	24.4	10.3	22.8
Highest Fifth	53.1	57.9	51.9	9.6	47.1
Total	100.0	100.0	100.0	100.0	100.0

[a] Includes old age, survivors, and disability insurance, unemployment and workmen's compensation, public and general assistance (welfare), veterans' benefits, and military retirement pay.

SOURCE: Data from Edward R. Fried, Alice M. Rivlin, Charles L. Schultze, and Nancy H. Teeters, *Setting National Priorities: The 1974 Budget,* Tables 3–5, p. 50. Copyright © 1973 by The Brookings Institution, 1775 Massachusetts Avenue, N.W., Washington, D.C. 20036. Based on MERGE file of family units with incomes projected to 1972 levels.

not the distribution of noncash benefits from various governmental activities. Recognizing the disagreement among economists as to just who is affected by different types of taxes and by how much, they developed estimates on the basis of eight sets of assumptions. They found that there was "little difference in effective tax rates" for most adjusted family incomes and that "the tax system has very little effect on the relative distribution of income."[3] Effective total tax rates and rates by type of tax, based on Pechman and Okner's *most progressive* set of assumptions about the incidence of taxes, are shown in Table 9.4.

A Lorenz Curve

The degree of inequality in incomes in a population can be illustrated by a *Lorenz curve* diagram. Such a diagram is constructed by plotting the cumulative percentage of income received by a cumulative percentage of the population or of tax-paying units. A Lorenz curve of the distribution of adjusted family income in the United States before and after taxes, based on Pechman and Okner's most progressive model of the incidence of taxes, is illustrated in Figure 9.2. The line sloping upward at 45° from the origin represents a situation in which income is distributed equally among all family units.

Clearly, after-tax adjusted incomes are somewhat closer to equality than pretax incomes, but the movement toward equality has been relatively slight.

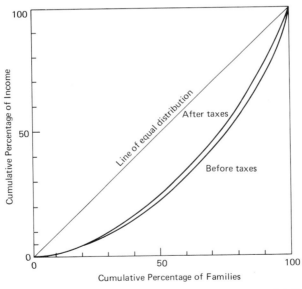

Figure 9.2   Lorenz Curves of the Distribution of Adjusted Family Income Before and After Federal, State, and Local Taxes in 1966, Based on the Most Progressive Assumptions About Their Incidence (Source: Joseph A. Pechman and Benjamin A. Okner, *Who Bears the Tax Burden?* Figure 1–3, p. 7. Copyright © 1974 by The Brookings Institution, 1775 Massachusetts Avenue, N.W., Washington, D.C. 20036.

Table 9.4 EFFECTIVE RATES OF FEDERAL, STATE, AND LOCAL TAXES, BY TYPE, FOR VARIOUS INCOME GROUPS IN 1966

INCOME GROUP[b]	INDIVIDUAL INCOME TAX	CORPORATION INCOME TAX	PROPERTY TAX[a]	SALES AND EXCISE TAXES	PAYROLL TAXES	PERSONAL PROPERTY AND MOTOR VEHICLE TAXES	TOTAL TAXES
Lowest tenth[b]	1.1	1.7	2.1	8.9	2.6	0.4	16.8
Second tenth	2.3	2.1	2.6	7.8	3.8	0.4	18.9
Third tenth	4.0	2.2	2.6	7.1	5.4	0.4	21.7
Fourth tenth	5.4	1.9	2.1	6.7	6.1	0.4	22.6
Fifth tenth	6.3	1.7	1.8	6.4	6.3	0.3	22.8
Sixth tenth	7.0	1.5	1.6	6.1	6.2	0.3	22.7
Seventh tenth	7.5	1.6	1.7	5.7	5.8	0.3	22.7
Eighth tenth	8.3	1.8	1.8	5.5	5.4	0.3	23.1
Ninth tenth	8.8	2.2	2.2	5.0	4.8	0.3	23.3
Highest tenth	11.4	8.1	5.1	3.2	2.2	0.2	30.1
All groups[c]	8.5	3.9	3.0	5.1	4.4	0.3	25.2

[a] The most progressive variant of this tax was used in calculating effective rates.
[b] Includes only family units in the sixth to tenth percentiles.
[c] Includes negative incomes not shown separately.

SOURCE: Adapted from Joseph A. Pechman and Benjamin A. Okner, *Who Bears the Tax Burden?* Table 4-9, p. 61. Copyright © 1974 by The Brookings Institution, 1775 Massachusetts Avenue, N.W., Washington, D.C. 20036. Computed from the 1966 MERGE data file.

According to Pechman and Okner, "[u]nder the most progressive set of assumptions . . . taxes reduce income inequality by less than 5 percent; under the least progressive assumptions [they reduce it] by only about 0.25 percent."[4]

Trends in the Distribution of Income

Have there been any long-run changes in the distribution of income? Table 9.2 (p. 198) suggests that the distribution of *personal income* among families has been stable since the Second World War. According to the study from which the table was taken,

> [w]hen changes in the relative distribution [of family personal income] are examined, three periods can be distinguished: 1929 to 1944, which showed a large shift toward greater equality; 1944 to the early 1960's, which showed little change; and the early 1960's to 1971, which showed a decrease in inequality, although not nearly as large as . . . in the first period.[5]

Although the overall degree of inequality in incomes decreased, the change in the relative distribution was "largely confined" to the bottom and top fifths. The increase in the bottom fifth's share is attributed in part to "an increase in the importance of cash transfer payments and food stamps and of the establishment of the medicare program."[6]

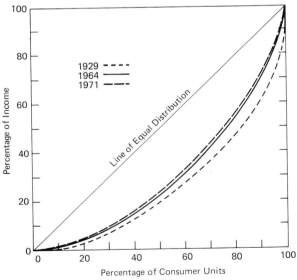

Figure 9.3   Lorenz Curves of Family Personal Income for 1929, 1964, and 1971 (Source: U.S. Department of Commerce, Bureau of Economic Analysis, as presented in Daniel B. Radner and John C. Hinrichs, "Size Distribution of Income in 1964, 1970, and 1971," in *Survey of Current Business* 54, no. 10 [October 1974]: Chart 9, p. 20.)

The Lorenz curves in Figure 9.3, which are based on the BEA's FPI data for 1929, 1964, and 1971, indicate a narrowing of inequalities in income prior to 1964—primarily during the Depression and the Second World War—and an essentially stable distribution of FPI between 1964 and 1971. Other data suggest that the distribution of income may have become more *unequal* in recent years. For example, *earnings* data for 1958 through 1970 for three groups—all wage and salary recipients, all year-round full-time wage earners, and all earners including the self-employed—show "a slow but persistent trend toward inequality."[7]

The increased participation of married women in the labor force for example, has raised the incomes of middle and upper middle groups, while the increased number of elderly people and women raising children alone has added to the number of low income families. Such developments offset the equalizing effects of increases in spending for social welfare. Recent increases in both the social security tax rate and the tax base, which are regressive in terms of the proportion of total wages and salary taxed, also offset the effects of transfer payments.

As we will see in the following section, the impact of recent fiscal policies and transfer programs has been favorable for families below the federal government's official poverty threshold. As a result, some experts feel that finding methods of equalizing the distribution of income may supplant the problem of *poverty* as a subject for public debate.

POVERTY

In 1964, President Lyndon B. Johnson launched a "War on Poverty" to "enable every individual to build his earning power to full capacity" and "to assure all citizens of decent living standards."[8] These objectives were to be achieved through (1) macroeconomic initiatives to create jobs and (2) microeconomic initiatives such as training programs to raise individual productivity.

These initiatives represented a basic shift in public policy simply because they emphasized the *causes* of poverty rather than the symptoms. The administration recognized that a high level of economic activity had to be sustained to reduce the number of poor people but that additional measures were required as well. The strategy of the War on Poverty was to increase the productivity and employability of present and potential workers while continuing public assistance to the aged, the disabled, and poor people unable to work because of their personal limitations or their responsibilities at home.

To some extent, the strategy worked. The various macroeconomic initiatives and antipoverty programs helped reduce the percentage of persons below the official poverty level from 19 percent in 1964 to 11.4 percent in 1978.[9] The tax dollars that funded the programs, in combination with new and existing cash and in-kind transfers, redistributed income to the poorest groups in the population. However, this objective was seen as an end in itself, *not* as a step toward modifying the basic distribution of income in the country in the direction of greater equality.

Different Approaches to the Poverty Problem

Poverty has been described as "probably the most complex and amorphous concept in social science."[10] Persons are poor for different reasons, and an overall attack on poverty requires a variety of strategies. Some families are poor because structural unemployment has put the principal wage earner out of work, because he or she lacks the education or skills required by employers, or because there are few job vacancies in an area. The manpower development and training programs discussed in Chapter 8 help to increase the employability of such people, and improvements in the efficiency of labor markets help match more of them with jobs.

Employment—or training to prepare people for employment—does not always mean an end to poverty. In 1977, 2.6 million heads of some 5.3 million poor families worked. One million of these people worked 50 to 52 weeks, and 912,000 worked full time; 516,000 worked 27 to 49 weeks; and 984,000 worked 1 to 26 weeks.[11] Moreover, as the Census Bureau points out,

> employment . . . is not a feasible alternative for all families. In 1977, there were 2.7 million poor family householders (51 percent of the total) who did not work at all during the year. Of the 2.7 million, almost 800,000 were ill or disabled, and another 400,000 were retired. . . . Additional transfer payments, rather than placement in a job might be more appropriate [for] these householders and their families. . . .[12]

Whether poor people must join the labor force to qualify for transfer payments or whether everyone should be entitled to a minimum income must be decided through the political process. Many Americans fear that a guaranteed income would make people unwilling to work. In the 1960s and 1970s, the Congress rejected proposals by a succession of administrations to substitute some form of income guarantee for the existing welfare system.

The Poverty Population in 1978

Despite the absolute and relative reduction in the number of poor people since the War on Poverty, some 24.5 million persons had incomes below the official poverty level in 1978. The concept of a *money income threshold* (including cash transfers but before taxes) necessary to escape from poverty was developed by the Social Security Administration (SSA) in 1964. A 1955 Department of Agriculture survey had determined that families of three or more spent approximately one-third of their income on food. The SSA therefore set the poverty threshold for these families at three times the cost of the Department of Agriculture's "economy food plan" (Annual adjustments now reflect changes in the CPI rather than changes in the cost of food.)

The basic threshold figure applies to a nonfarm family of four. Thresholds are also computed for rural areas, for families of different sizes, and for individuals living alone in urban or rural areas. As we noted annual revisions are based on changes in the Consumer Price Index. Changes in the average threshold for a four-person family between 1959 and 1978 are shown in Table 9.5. The number of poor people and the poverty rate for the years 1959 to 1978 are shown in Table 9.6.

Poverty is not distributed randomly. According to the Bureau of Census,

> the poverty rate in 1978 for White families (6.9 percent) was much lower than the rates for Black families (27.5 percent) and for families of Spanish origin (20.4 percent). The poverty rates for Black and Spanish-origin [husband-wife] families . . . (11.3 and 11.9 percent, respectively) were higher than the rate for comparable White families (4.7 percent). . . . Families maintained by women with no husband present had a poverty rate of 31.4 percent, far higher than those of husband-wife families or families with a male householder and no wife present (5.2 and 9.2 percent, respectively.)[13]

Moreover, the poverty rate in 1978 was 13.9 percent for persons 65 years of age and over and the poverty rate for families headed by a person 25 years of age or older was, with the exception of high school dropouts, inversely related to the years of school they had completed.[14]

There have been significant changes in the representation of various groups in the poor. For example, the proportion of poor persons living in families with a female head (no husband present) has increased, the proportion of the poor residing in the North has increased relative to the proportion in the South, and the proportion of the poor in metropolitan areas has increased steadily.[15]

The Reduction of Poverty

The decrease in both the absolute number and the proportion of poor people between 1959 and 1978 is clear from Table 9.6. The poverty rate fell from 19 percent in 1964, the year in which the War on Poverty was initiated, to 11.4 percent in 1978. The improvement is more impressive when allowances are made for *non-cash* (in-kind) *transfer payments*. The data in Table 9.7 indicate that in fiscal 1976, after adding these transfers and also netting out federal personal income taxes, employee payroll taxes, and state income taxes, the number of poor families was reduced to 6.6 million, or 8.3 percent. Between 1965 and 1976, the percentage of poor families fell by 56 percent when poverty was measured by income *after taxes and transfers*. It fell by only 28 percent using the Census Bureau's *money income* measure of poverty.[16]

A Relative Measure of Poverty

Both the "official" and "adjusted" measures of poverty define it in terms of absolute income. However, a number of experts believe that a *relative* measure of poverty is more meaningful, particularly if real incomes, in general, are rising. They believe that " 'poverty' in the United States . . . is largely a matter of economic *distance;*" that is, it reflects how far family income falls below "average" incomes.[17] Victor Fuchs has suggested that "we define as poor any family whose

Table 9.5 CHANGES IN THE CONSUMER PRICE INDEX AND THE AVERAGE POVERTY THRESHOLD FOR A NONFARM FAMILY OF FOUR FROM 1959 TO 1978

YEAR	CONSUMER PRICE INDEX (1963 = 100)	AVERAGE THRESHOLD FOR A NONFARM FAMILY OF FOUR
1959	95.2	$2,973
1960	96.7	3,022
1961	97.7	3,054
1962	98.8	3,089
1963	100.0	3,128
1964	101.3	3,169
1965	103.1	3,223
1966	106.0	3,317
1967	109.1	3,410
1968	113.6	3,553
1969	119.7	3,743
1970	126.8	3,968
1971	132.3	4,137
1972	136.6	4,275
1973	145.1	4,540
1974	161.1	5,038
1975	175.8	5,500
1976	185.9	5,815
1977	197.9	6,191
1978	212.9	6,662
1979		
1980		
1981		

SOURCE: U.S. Department of Commerce, Bureau of the Census, *Current Population Reports,* Series P–60, no. 124, "Characteristics of the Population Below the Poverty Level: 1978," Table A–1, p. 206.

income is less than one-half the median family income."[18] According to Fuchs, such a standard

> explicitly recognizes that all so-called "minimum" or "subsistence" budgets are based on contemporary standards and political realities and have no intrinsic or scientific basis [and] focuses attention on what seems to underl[ie] the present concern with poverty, namely, the first tentative gropings toward a national policy with respect to the distribution of income at the lower end of the scale.[19]

Table 9.8, adapted from Fuchs, uses the percentage of families with incomes of less than half the median income to measure the reduction in poverty between 1947 and 1965. His data show that the percentage of poor families was roughly stable during that period. This situation has persisted, which suggests that for the smaller number of persons below the *official* poverty threshold, poverty has become more serious as that threshold has fallen relative to the median level of living. In 1978, for example, when the median family income was $17,640 and the

Table 9.6 PERSONS BELOW THE POVERTY LEVEL AND POVERTY RATES, 1959–1978

(Numbers in thousands, as of March of the following year. Table excludes unrelated individuals under 14 years old, inmates of institutions, and members of the armed forces, except those living off post and those living with families on post.)

YEAR	NUMBER BELOW POVERTY LEVEL TOTAL	IN FAMILIES TOTAL	HEAD	RELATED CHILDREN UNDER 18	OTHER FAMILY MEMBERS	UNRELATED INDIVIDUALS	POVERTY RATE TOTAL	IN FAMILIES TOTAL	HEAD	RELATED CHILDREN UNDER 18	OTHER FAMILY MEMBERS	UNRELATED INDIVIDUALS
1959	39,490	34,562	8,320	17,208	9,034	4,928	22.4	20.8	18.5	26.9	15.9	46.1
1960	39,851	34,925	8,243	17,288	9,394	4,926	22.2	20.7	18.1	26.5	16.2	45.2
1961	39,628	34,509	8,391	16,577	9,541	5,119	21.9	20.3	18.1	25.2	16.5	45.9
1962	38,625	33,623	8,077	16,630	8,916	5,002	21.0	19.4	17.2	24.7	15.1	45.4
1963	36,436	31,498	7,554	15,691	8,253	4,938	19.5	17.9	15.9	22.8	13.8	44.2
1964	36,055	30,912	7,160	15,736	8,016	5,143	19.0	17.4	15.0	22.7	13.3	42.7
1965	33,185	28,358	6,721	14,388	7,249	4,827	17.3	15.8	13.9	20.7	11.8	39.8
1966	30,424	25,614	6,200	12,876	6,538	4,810	15.7	14.2	12.7	18.4	10.5	38.9
1966[a]	28,510	23,809	5,784	12,146	5,879	4,701	14.7	13.1	11.8	17.4	9.5	38.3
1967	27,769	22,771	5,667	11,427	5,677	4,998	14.2	12.5	11.4	16.3	9.1	38.1
1968	25,389	20,695	5,047	10,739	4,909	4,694	12.8	11.3	10.0	15.3	7.8	34.0
1969[b]	24,147	19,175	5,008	9,501	4,667	4,972	12.1	10.4	9.7	13.8	7.2	34.0
1970	25,420	20,330	5,260	10,235	4,835	5,090	12.6	10.9	10.1	14.9	7.4	32.9
1971	25,559	20,405	5,303	10,344	4,757	5,154	12.5	10.8	10.0	15.1	7.2	31.6
1972	24,460	19,577	5,075	10,082	4,420	4,883	11.9	10.3	9.3	14.9	6.6	29.0
1973	22,973	18,299	4,828	9,453	4,018	4,674	11.1	9.7	8.8	14.2	5.9	25.6
1974	24,260	19,440	5,109	10,196	4,135	4,820	11.6	10.2	9.2	15.5	6.0	25.5
1974[a]	23,370	18,817	4,922	9,967	3,928	4,553	11.2	9.9	8.8	15.1	5.7	24.1
1975	25,877	20,789	5,450	10,882	4,457	5,088	12.3	10.9	9.7	16.8	6.4	25.1
1976	24,975	19,632	5,311	10,081	4,240	5,344	11.8	10.3	9.4	15.8	6.0	24.9
1977	24,720	19,505	5,311	10,028	4,165	5,216	11.6	10.2	9.3	16.0	5.9	22.6
1978	24,497	19,062	5,280	9,722	4,059	5,435	11.4	10.0	9.1	19.7	5.7	22.1
1979												
1980												
1981												

[a] Based on revised methodology. Note that money income includes factor incomes plus cash transfer payments.

[b] Beginning with March 1970, CPS data based on 1970 census population controls.

SOURCE: U.S. Department of Commerce, Bureau of the Census, *Current Population Reports*, Series P–60, no. 124, "Characteristics of the Population Below the Poverty Level: 1978," Table 1, p. 16.

Table 9.7 FAMILIES BELOW THE POVERTY LEVEL BEFORE AND AFTER RECEIVING TRANSFER PAYMENTS AND PAYING TAXES IN FISCAL 1976

KINDS OF FAMILIES	BEFORE TAXES AND BEFORE TRANSFERS	FAMILIES BELOW THE POVERTY LEVEL, BASED ON INCOME[a]				
		BEFORE TAXES AND AFTER CASH TRANSFERS[b]	BEFORE TAXES AND AFTER CASH AND IN-KIND TRANSFERS[c]		AFTER TAXES AND AFTER CASH AND IN-KIND TRANSFERS[d]	
			EXCLUDING MEDICAL BENEFITS	INCLUDING MEDICAL BENEFITS	EXCLUDING MEDICAL BENEFITS	INCLUDING MEDICAL BENEFITS
All families:						
Number (millions)	21.4	10.7	9.0	6.4	9.2	6.6
Percentage of all families	27.0	13.5	11.3	8.1	11.5	8.3
Single person families:						
Number (millions)	10.3	5.4	5.0	3.5	5.1	3.7
Percentage of single person families	47.8	25.0	23.2	16.4	23.8	17.0
Multiple person families:						
Number (millions)	11.1	5.3	4.0	2.9	4.0	2.9
Percentage of multiple person families	19.2	9.2	6.9	5.0	7.0	5.1

[a] Data based on 1975 *Current Population Survey,* with adjustments to reflect underreporting of income and changes in the characteristics of the population between the survey year (calendar year 1974) and fiscal year 1976.

[b] Cash transfers include payments under government-financed social insurance and public assistance programs.

[c] In-kind transfers include food stamps, child nutrition assistance, housing assistance, Medicare and Medicaid.

[d] Taxes include federal personal income and employee payroll taxes and state income taxes.

SOURCE: Congressional Budget Office. Data presented in the *Economic Report of the President, Transmitted to the Congress January 1978, Together with the Annual Report of the Council of Economic Advisers,* Table 37, p. 225.

Table 9.8 THE PERCENTAGE OF U.S. FAMILIES CLASSIFIED AS POOR IN RELATION TO THOSE EARNING MEDIAN INCOMES, 1947–1965 (in 1965 dollars)

YEAR	MEDIAN INCOME	PERCENTAGE OF FAMILIES WITH AN INCOME LESS THAN HALF THE MEDIAN[a]
1947	$4,275	18.9
1948	4,178	19.1
1949	4,116	20.2
1950	4,351	20.0
1951	4,507	18.9
1952	4,625	18.9
1953	5,002	19.8
1954	4,889	20.9
1955	5,223	20.0
1956	5,561	19.6
1957	5,554	19.7
1958	5,543	19.8
1959	5,856	20.0
1960	5,991	20.3
1961	6,054	20.3
1962	6,220	19.8
1963	6,444	19.9
1964	6,676	19.9
1965	6,882	20.0

[a] Estimated by interpolation.
SOURCE: Victor Fuchs, "Comment," *Six Papers on the Size Distribution of Wealth and Income*, edited by Lee Soltow (New York: Columbia University Press for the National Bureau of Economic Research, 1969), Table 1, p. 200. Based on U.S. Bureau of the Census, *Current Population Reports*, Series P–60, no. 51.

poverty threshold for an urban family of four was $6,662, 20.8 percent of the families in this country had incomes below $9,000.

The Effect of Government Transfers

The inclusion of government transfer payments in income statistics reduces the number of families and individuals living in poverty. The major *social insurance programs*, which pay benefits to people whose right to them is related to their employment history and current labor force status, were discussed in Chapter 8. These programs, which include (1) Old Age, Survivors, Disability, and Health Insurance; (2) Unemployment Insurance; and (3) Workmen's Compensation, are not restricted to persons with low incomes. In fiscal 1976, for example, "the poorest 20 percent of families received about one-third of the estimated $124 billion spent by federal, state, and local governments for [such] programs."[20]

Public assistance or *welfare* programs are based on a means test. That is, the benefits they pay are based on a demonstrated need for them. These programs, although targeted at people with low incomes, usually limit eligibility for benefits to specific groups such as the indigent aged, the disabled, the blind, and families with dependent children. The amount of benefit payments and the number of beneficiaries under the major government income maintenance programs for fiscal 1977 are shown in Table 9.9.

The Welfare "System"

The various welfare programs based on means tests do not constitute a consciously planned and internally consistent welfare system. They represent a "nonsystem" that addresses—often on a nonuniform basis—the needs of particular population groups.

MEDICAID

Medicaid, currently the largest program,* was established in 1965. It is a federal-state program that provides free medical services to the low income population. Individuals qualify for benefits if they participate in the Aid for Families with Dependent Children or Supplemental Security Income programs, or if they are too poor to afford essential medical care. The states establish eligibility and benefit standards for the "medically indigent." Medicaid costs ballooned from $1.2 billion in 1966 to over $17 billion in 1977.

CATEGORICAL ASSISTANCE PROGRAMS

Under the Social Security Act of 1935, federal funds were provided for public assistance to three low income groups—the *indigent aged,* the *blind,* and *families with dependent children.* In 1950, federal grants were provided to help finance state programs to assist the *permanently and totally disabled.* These "categorical" welfare programs administered by the states are funded out of general federal revenues supplemented by state grants.

SUPPLEMENTAL SECURITY INCOME (SSI)

In 1974, the several adult assistance programs in existence were replaced by a Supplemental Security Income program. The *basic benefits* for individuals and families are uniform and funded out of general federal revenues. States may provide supplementary benefits. In December 1979, some 4.15 million persons received SSI. Almost half these people were elderly, and more than half were disabled.[21]

AID TO FAMILIES WITH DEPENDENT CHILDREN (AFDC)

This program provides financial assistance to a group often identified as "the" welfare problem. Intended originally to help families whose incomes were reduced

---

* The *child nutrition* program aids a greater number of beneficiaries, but total benefit payments are much less.

Table 9.9 GOVERNMENT INCOME MAINTENANCE PROGRAMS IN FISCAL 1977

PROGRAM	DATE ENACTED	FORM OF AID	SOURCE OF FUNDS	BENEFIT PAYMENTS FISCAL 1977 (BILLIONS OF DOLLARS)	BENEFICIARIES IN FISCAL 1977 (MILLIONS)
Social insurance:					
Old age and survivors insurance	1935	Cash	Federal	$71.3	28.5
Medicare	1965	In-kind	Federal	20.8	25.4[a]
Unemployment insurance	1935	Cash	Federal-State	14.3	9.8
Disability insurance	1956	Cash	Federal	11.1	4.7
Workmen's compensation	1908	Cash	Federal-State	6.7	2.6
Veterans' compensation	1917	Cash	Federal	5.7	3.5
Railroad retirement	1937	Cash	Federal	3.8	1.0
Black lung	1969	Cash	Federal	1.0	.5
Public assistance:					
Medicaid	1965	In-kind	Federal-State	16.3	21.6
Aid to families with dependent children	1935	Cash	Federal-State	9.8	11.2
Supplemental security income	1972	Cash	Federal-State	6.2	4.3
Food stamp program	1964	In-kind	Federal	5.0	17.1
Child nutrition	1946	In-kind	Federal	3.5	28.0
Veterans' pensions	1933	Cash	Federal	3.1	3.4
Housing assistance	1937	In-kind	Federal	3.0	7.1
Basic opportunity grants	1972	Cash	Federal	1.4	2.0
General assistance	b	Cash	State	1.3	.9
Earned income tax credit	1975	Cash	Federal	1.3	6.3

[a] Eligible to receive benefits as of July 1, 1977.
[b] Varies by state.

SOURCE: *Economic Report of the President, Transmitted to the Congress January 1978, Together with the Annual Report of the Council of Economic Advisers*, Table 36, p. 222.

by the death, prolonged absence, or incapacity of one or both parents, the program became

> the repository for those welfare cases that involved dependent children whose mothers and fathers or both were neither blind, nor old, nor disabled, nor sick, nor widowed, nor, apparently between jobs, and who, therefore, had, as far as welfare critics were concerned, no obvious excuse to receive public charity in a work-oriented society.[22]

It had been anticipated that the various assistance programs would decline in importance as the number of beneficiaries of social insurance programs increased, but the number of recipients of AFDC assistance continued to expand until 1975. Since then, the number of recipients has declined somewhat (from 11.4 to 10.3 million persons in October 1979).

The original AFDC program did not provide support to families in which both parents were present although the father was unemployed. This was a much criticized deficiency, and in 1962 the Social Security Act was amended to allow states to choose to provide federally funded assistance to such families.

Prior to 1967, the marginal tax rate on the earnings of AFDC families was 100 percent. That is, benefits were reduced one dollar for each dollar of earnings. In 1967, to provide an incentive for beneficiaries to work, the government opted to "disregard" the first $30 per month earned in calculating benefits, and the tax rate on earnings above $30 was reduced to 66⅔ percent. Adult AFDC recipients, including mothers, were required to accept employment and training opportunities. The *Work-Incentive* (WIN) program for mothers also provided grants for day care centers for small children of enrollees.

GENERAL ASSISTANCE

Indigent persons who do not qualify for the categorical programs described above must rely on state or locally financed *general assistance* (welfare) programs, the provisions of which vary widely.

IN-KIND ASSISTANCE

In addition to cash from various assistance programs, the poor may receive several kinds of noncash benefits. *Medicaid* provides medical services. The *food stamp program,* established in 1964, lets low income households purchase food stamps in an amount determined by the family's nutritional needs and income. This program has mushroomed in recent years. In fiscal 1975, a monthly average of some 8.5 million beneficiaries received food stamps costing $4.7 billion. The cost of food stamps may approach $9 billion in fiscal 1980. Other in-kind assistance programs provide food for the elderly (persons 60 and over); scholarships for college students; day care for low income families; public housing; subsidized loans for the purchase of homes; and additional help for homeowners, including subsidies for heating the homes of the poor and near-poor.

A Negative Income Tax

One proposal to reduce poverty without reducing incentives to work is to have a *negative income tax*. Such a tax, in one form or another, appeals to many academics but has failed to generate much popular or legislative support. Some adherents of a negative income tax suggest a guaranteed income to replace some or all of our existing *welfare* programs; others would substitute it for income maintenance programs more generally.

All negative income tax plans involve (1) a guaranteed minimum income from the government, and (2) some kind of tax on additional earnings until a level of income is reached at which the tax equals the guaranteed income. After this point, the tax on income is simply spliced into the existing tax structure. Table 9.10 illustrates the effect of a negative income tax when the basic guaranteed income is $4,000 a year, the tax on additional income is 50 percent, and the break-even point above which income is taxed according to conventional tax schedules is $8,000.

A rudimentary negative income tax does exist under present legislation that allows a tax credit of 10 percent of annual incomes up to $5,000, a credit of $500 for those with incomes between $5,000 and $6,000, and a declining tax credit for higher incomes that reaches zero when incomes reach $10,000.

Welfare Reform?

As we have already pointed out, our present income maintenance programs do not make up an integrated welfare *system*. Comprehensive welfare reform presumably has a high national priority, but it has proved very elusive to date despite the efforts of a succession of administrations. The Nixon *Family Assistance Plan*, basically a negative income tax, was stillborn, and the supposedly liberal 95th Congress showed a singular disinterest in President Carter's welfare reform proposal, his *Program for Better Jobs and Income (PBJI)*.[23] Nevertheless, increasing

Table 9.10   A POSSIBLE NEGATIVE INCOME TAX

GUARANTEED INCOME	ADDITIONAL INCOME	TAX (50% OF ADDITIONAL INCOME)	BENEFIT RETAINED	TOTAL INCOME (NET)
$4,000	$ 0	$ 0	$4,000	$4,000
4,000	1,000	500	3,500	4,500
4,000	2,000	1,000	3,000	5,000
4,000	3,000	1,500	2,500	5,500
4,000	4,000	2,000	2,000	6,000
4,000	5,000	2,500	1,500	6,500
4,000	6,000	3,000	1,000	7,000
4,000	7,000	3,500	500	7,500
4,000	8,000	4,000	0	8,000

recognition is being given to the distinction between (1) the poor who are unable to work (the "unemployables") and (2) those whose earning capacity might be increased as a result of properly designed work and training programs. Eventually, a two-tiered welfare structure may evolve that will distinguish between these two groups.

Poverty: A Concluding Note

Measured by official standards, there is much less poverty today than in 1964. However, the poverty problem now is more serious in two respects: first, a growing proportion of the poor consists of people for whom work at market wages is not possible; and second, as a result of per capita gains in real income, the "official" poor are falling farther behind the median income group in terms of a standard of living.

Our progress in moving people up from poverty has led to increasing interest in reducing inequalities in income. To some, "a focus on inequality, on the gap between high incomes and low, would seem to follow naturally on a decade [1965–1975] in which a minimum level of economic well-being has by and large been assured for all citizens."[24] Such a focus will probably generate proposals to further reduce differences in both income and wealth through government tax and transfer policies. For example, if we believe that inherited wealth perpetuates inequalities in income unrelated to the person's economic contribution, we might make our estate and inheritance taxes more progressive. This would provide greater equality of opportunity for future generations and presumably assure a more equal distribution of earned income.

We must also attempt to ensure that poverty and differences in wages and incomes are not the result of overt or institutionalized discrimination. In the following section we will consider one of our most sensitive domestic problems —discrimination in labor markets.

DISCRIMINATION IN LABOR MARKETS

Discrimination against certain demographic groups is long standing. Moreover, although it can occur at any income level, discrimination always affects economically disadvantaged groups disproportionately. Discrimination may be overt or institutionalized; it may involve direct action against minority groups, or it may be more subtle, as when access to education is limited or degrading stereotypes are perpetuated.

In a perfectly competitive labor market, unequal pay for persons of equivalent ability and training would presumably be eliminated over time. However, where there is discrimination, people are not paid on the basis of their abilities, and the resulting differences in earnings and in the distribution of workers among occupations cannot be ideal. Discrimination will generate a misallocation of human resources and a lower national product, as well as have significant human and social costs.

In this section, we will concentrate on two types of discrimination: (1) against blacks, a minority group, and (2) against women, who constitute a majority of the population and a minority, but a growing proportion, of the labor force.

Types of Discrimination

The principal types of discrimination in the labor market are (1) employment discrimination, (2) occupational discrimination, (3) wage discrimination, and (4) discrimination involving unequal access to educational, training, and promotional opportunities.[25] Wage differentials may involve either unequal pay for equal work, or unequal work—with a difference in earnings—for persons with roughly equivalent abilities and skills.[26]

Today, contrary to popular belief, overt discrimination in hiring and the payment of different wages to members of different demographic groups for similar work in similar establishments are neither the most prevalent nor the most serious forms of labor market discrimination. Discrimination that results in differential access to employment opportunities on an occupational basis or to on-the-job training and promotional opportunities is far more likely to result in differences in earnings. Often, such discrimination occurs before a person even enters the labor market.

STATISTICAL SCREENING AND DISCRIMINATION

Since it can be costly to develop and administer tests that measure an applicant's qualifications for a specific job, employers may set hiring standards that are irrelevant to an applicant's ability to do the job. For example, a high school diploma may be required or a certain score on a standardized test, even though such things have little relationship to the actual job skills needed. Employers may also screen applicants on the basis of their experience with people or their *a priore* beliefs concerning them. Easily recognizable characteristics such as race and sex may be used to predict job performance, and a black or a female whose potential productivity is greater than that of a white or a male may be excluded from employment or given a lower level job.

THE OVERCROWDING HYPOTHESIS

If certain occupations are perceived as particularly "appropriate" for members of a demographic group, social pressures or the educational process may create an oversupply of workers in these occupations and a consequent reduction in relative wage rates. In such cases, employers may not discriminate against applicants overtly but simply function as transmitters for consumer and employee perceptions and preferences.

Measuring Discrimination

It is difficult to develop precise measures of discrimination in labor markets. Simple comparisons of aggregate earnings or of the occupational distribution of demographic groups fail to take into account such variables as age, education, continuity of employment, and whether employment is full time or part time. Moreover, some of these variables may be affected by institutionalized discrimination. In attempting to measure differences in income between whites and blacks, a Congressional Budget Office study concluded that

> many forms of discrimination . . . have a great impact on income disparities [and] the measurement of that influence is elusive. Attempts to measure the effects of discrimination have largely relied on the assumption that discrimination accounts for the difference that remains following adjustment for other factors [i.e., is a residual]. This confounds the effects of many different kinds of racial discrimination —past and present, labor and nonlabor market.[27]

Aggregate data may also fail to reveal significant differences in the extent of discrimination against segments of a demographic group. For example, black high school graduates earn less than white high school dropouts, but the rate of return on a college education may be higher for young black men than for young white ones. Nevertheless, the occupational distribution and earnings of both blacks and women suggest that there is, indeed, discrimination against them.

Discrimination Against Blacks

Black workers tend to be paid less than white workers, to receive less on-the-job training, to have more frequent spells of unemployment, and to be concentrated in certain occupations—frequently dead-end ones—in secondary labor markets. A recent study emphasizes that

> the occupational distributions of blacks and whites differ even among those with the same number of years of schooling completed, though these differences are smaller among the younger age groups. . . . In fact, the income disparities between black and white males are explained in large part by the distributions among the specific occupations.[28]

Table 9.11 illustrates the different *labor force status* of whites, blacks, and persons of Hispanic origin (i.e., whether they are employed or unemployed) and the *major occupational groups* to which they belong. It shows clearly the high representation of minority workers in service jobs and in unskilled and semiskilled occupations, work often associated with secondary labor markets.

Table 9.12, which shows the *median nonwhite income as a percentage of the median white income* over a 25-year span, also suggests that there has been persistent discrimination against nonwhites. There has been a continuing improvement in the income of black women compared with that of white women, which indicates that the low absolute level of black female income is largely the result

Table 9.11 THE STATUS OF WHITES, BLACKS, AND PERSONS OF HISPANIC ORIGIN IN THE LABOR FORCE (annual averages for 1977, numbers in thousands, persons aged 16 and over)

LABOR FORCE STATUS AND OCCUPATIONAL GROUP	WHITES	BLACKS[a]	HISPANICS[b]	
Civilian noninstitutional population	137,595	16,314	7,156	
Civilian labor force	86,107	9,737	4,391	
Employed: Number	80,734	8,384	3,953	
Percent[c]	100.0	100.0	100.0	
White-collar workers	51.7	32.5	31.8	
Professional and technical	15.5	10.1	7.5	
Managers and administrators, except farm	11.4	4.1	5.7	
Sales workers	6.8	2.4	3.7	
Clerical workers	18.0	15.9	15.0	Percentage
Blue-collar workers	32.9	39.4	46.6	Distribution
Craft and kindred workers	13.6	9.1	13.8	Among
Operatives, except transport	11.0	15.6	21.1	Occupations
Transport equipment operatives	3.7	5.8	4.1	
Nonfarm laborers	4.6	9.0	7.7	
Service workers	12.3	26.0	17.1	
Farm workers	3.2	2.2	4.5	
Unemployed	5,373	1,355	438	
Unemployment rate	6.2	13.9	10.0	
Not in labor force	51,488	6,576	2,765	

[a] Data relate to black workers only.
[b] Data on persons of Hispanic origin are tabulated separately, without regard to race, which means that they are also included in the data for white and black workers. According to the 1970 census, 96 percent of the Hispanic population is white.
[c] Detail may not add to totals because of rounding.
SOURCE: *Employment and Training Report of the President, Including Reports by the U.S. Department of Labor and the U.S. Department of Health, Education, and Welfare, Transmitted to the Congress 1978*, Table 6, p. 27.

of discrimination on the basis of *sex* rather than race. This conclusion is supported by the income data for year-round full-time workers in Table 9.13, which show that in 1973, for example, nonwhite women had a median income equal to 88.2 percent of the median income of white women but only 69 percent of the median income of nonwhite men. Nonwhite women earned slightly less than half as much as white men, and white women did little better, earning only 56.3 percent of the median income of white men.

Table 9.14, which compares the total median money income of black and white males in 1977 and which takes into account both their level of education and the number of years of schooling they have had, indicates that whites earn higher incomes than blacks despite equal amounts of education.

A summary of several recent studies of wage differentials based on race and sex concludes that "on average, whites earn . . . 55 percent [more than] blacks"

Table 9.12 THE MEDIAN NONWHITE INCOME AS A PERCENTAGE OF THE MEDIAN WHITE INCOME, AND MEDIAN INCOME RATIOS BY RACE AND SEX FOR SELECTED YEARS, 1948–1974 (adjusted for price changes in 1974 dollars)

| | MEDIAN INCOME RATIO | | |
| | BLACK FAMILIES TO | BLACK WOMEN TO | BLACK MEN TO |
YEAR	WHITE FAMILIES	WHITE WOMEN	WHITE MEN
1948[a]	0.53	0.43	0.54
1953[a]	0.56	0.58	0.55
1959[a]	0.54	0.62	0.47
1964[a]	0.56	0.70	0.57
1969	0.61	0.84	0.58
1974	0.58	0.90	0.61

[a] Data for blacks include persons of "other" races.
SOURCE: U.S. Department of Commerce, Bureau of the Census, "The Social and Economic Status of the Black Population in the United States: An Historical View, 1790–1978," in *Current Population Reports: Special Studies,* Series P–23, no. 80, Table 14, p. 31, and Table 30, p. 46.

and that direct discrimination in labor markets accounts for about 60 percent of this difference.[29] Some segments of the black population, including women, young men, and young male college graduates, have made substantial labor market gains since 1960.[30] Nevertheless, "in 1978, the 25.4 million Blacks in this country remained far behind Whites in almost every social and economic area."[31] Clearly, according to the Department of Commerce, discrimination against nonwhites remains a serious problem.

Discrimination Against Women

Discrimination against women in the labor market stems partly from long-established work practices, partly from popular notions of the role of women, and partly from cultural conditioning. Unlike minority groups, women have probably suffered more from institutional discrimination than from overt discrimination. That is, it has probably been a more important factor in creating the differences in earnings between men and women and the occupational distribution of women workers.

The magnitude of the difference in male and female earnings is suggested by Table 9.15, which shows the median annual earnings of year-round full-time workers 14 and over from 1955 to 1977, and Table 9.16, which shows the median weekly earnings of men and women workers in various occupations and industries in May of 1976. An earlier comparison of the median earnings of men in 423 occupations and women in 391 occupations in 1969 indicated that "[m]en earned more than women in every occupation, except public kindergarten teachers [and that] median earnings [in] the top-ranking occupation for women were about half the earnings [in] the top-ranking occupation for men."[32]

Table 9.13 THE MEDIAN WAGE OR SALARY INCOME OF YEAR-ROUND, FULL-TIME WORKERS,[a] BY SEX AND RACE, IN 1939 AND FROM 1960 TO 1973

YEAR	MEDIAN INCOME				PERCENTAGE OF WHITE MALE MEDIAN INCOME			PERCENTAGE OF NONWHITE MALE MEDIAN INCOME		PERCENTAGE OF WHITE FEMALE MEDIAN INCOME
	WHITE WOMEN	NON-WHITE WOMEN	WHITE MEN	NON-WHITE MEN	WHITE WOMEN	NON-WHITE WOMEN	NON-WHITE MEN	WHITE WOMEN	NON-WHITE WOMEN	NONWHITE WOMEN
1973	$6,544	$5,772	$11,633	$8,363	56.3	49.6	71.9	78.2	69.0	88.2
1972	6,131	5,320	10,786	7,548	56.8	49.3	70.0	81.2	70.5	86.8
1971	5,749	5,181	9,801	6,928	58.7	52.9	70.7	83.0	74.8	90.1
1970	5,490	4,674	9,373	6,598	58.6	49.9	70.4	83.2	70.8	85.1
1969	5,168	4,231	8,876	6,158	58.2	47.7	69.4	83.9	68.7	81.9
1968	4,700	3,677	8,014	5,603	58.6	45.9	69.9	83.9	65.6	78.2
1967	4,394	3,363	7,512	5,069	58.5	44.8	67.5	86.7	66.3	76.5
1966	4,152	2,949	7,164	4,528	58.0	41.2	63.2	91.7	65.1	71.0
1965	3,991	2,816	6,704	4,277	59.5	42.0	63.8	93.3	65.8	70.6
1964	3,859	2,674	6,497	4,285	59.4	41.2	66.0	90.1	62.4	69.3
1963	3,723	2,368	6,277	4,104	59.3	37.7	65.4	90.7	57.7	63.6
1962	3,601	2,278	6,025	3,799	59.8	37.8	63.1	94.8	60.0	63.3
1961	3,480	2,325	5,880	3,883	59.2	39.5	66.0	89.6	59.9	66.8
1960	3,410	2,372	5,662	3,789	60.2	41.9	66.9	90.0	62.6	69.6
1939	863	327	1,419	639	60.8	23.0	45.0	135.1	51.2	37.9

[a] Persons who worked 35 hours or more a week for 50 to 52 weeks.

SOURCE: U.S. Department of Commerce, Bureau of the Census, *Current Population Reports*, Series P-60, nos. 90, 85, 80, 75, 66, 60, 53, 51, 47, 43, 41, 39, 37, 27, and Series P-60, no. 93 (advance report), as cited in U.S. Department of Labor, Employment Standards Administration, Women's Bureau, *1975 Handbook on Women Workers*, Bulletin 297, Table 57, p. 136.

Table 9.14 A COMPARISON OF THE MEDIAN INCOME OF BLACK AND WHITE MALES 18 AND OVER GROUPED BY LEVEL AND YEARS OF SCHOOLING, 1977

LEVEL AND YEARS OF SCHOOLING	MEDIAN INCOME		RATIO OF BLACK INCOME TO WHITE
	BLACKS	WHITES	
Level of schooling			
Elementary	$ 4,554	$ 6,456	0.705
Secondary	7,123	10,861	0.656
College	10,566	14,962	0.706
Years of schooling			
Less than 8	4,209	5,767	0.730
8	5,711	7,201	0.793
9–11	5,608	8,469	0.662
12	8,314	11,879	0.700
13–15	9,230	11,866	0.778
16	11,522	16,570	0.695
17 and over	16,429	19,969	0.823

SOURCE: Based on U.S. Bureau of the Census, *Current Population Reports,* Series P–60, no. 118, "Money Incomes in 1977 of Families and Persons in the United States," Table 47, p. 188.

Women often earn less than men with the *same level of education.* According to Table 9.17, for example, in 1977 women with college degrees earned less than men with one to three years of high school. Such differences are due in part to the more continuous participation of men in the labor force and the greater degree of on-the-job training they received, which is often related to popular stereotypes of women's work. A study cited previously concludes that on the average, men earn 67 percent more than women and that discrimination accounts for 75 percent of this differential.[33]

The disproportionate number of women in certain occupations (for example, the large number of female bank tellers, registered nurses, and elementary and secondary school teachers) is illustrated in Table 9.18. The stereotyping of many jobs as exclusively male creates overcrowding in female occupations, with a consequent relative reduction in women's wages. Moreover, many observers would agree with Victor Fuchs that "neither inherent physical or mental differences nor employer discrimination can explain most of [the male-female] earnings differential" and that "[t]he major explanation . . . is *role differentiation,* which begins in childhood."[34] In other words, differences in the way children perceive the role of men and women in our society affects whether they work, the jobs they seek, where and how long each week they work, the education and training they pursue, and the attitudes of their fellow employees and others toward them as workers.

Women should not only receive equal pay for equal work but also have equal access to employment opportunities and career ladders. Significant progress has been made in changing popular ideas concerning "women's work," particularly with regard to the professions.[35] Most women continue to work in a relatively limited number of occupations, however, and the elimination of occupational

Table 9.15 THE MEDIAN ANNUAL EARNINGS OF YEAR-ROUND FULL-TIME WORKERS 14 AND OVER, BY SEX, 1955–1977

	ANNUAL EARNINGS[a]		
YEAR	WOMEN	MEN	WOMEN'S EARNINGS AS A PERCENTAGE OF MEN'S
1955	$2,719	$4,252	63.9
1956	2,827	4,466	63.3
1957	3,008	4,713	63.8
1958	3,102	4,927	63.0
1959	3,193	5,209	61.3
1960	3,293	5,417	60.8
1961	3,351	5,644	59.4
1962	3,446	5,974	59.5
1963	3,561	5,978	59.6
1964	3,690	6,195	59.6
1965	3,823	6,375	60.0
1966	3,973	6,848	58.0
1967	4,150	7,182	57.8
1968	4,457	7,664	58.2
1969	4,977	8,227	60.5
1970	5,323	8,966	59.4
1971	5,593	9,399	59.5
1972	5,903	10,202	57.9
1973	6,335	11,186	56.6
1974	1,772	11,835	57.2
1975	7,504	12,758	58.8
1976	8,099	13,455	60.2
1977	8,618	14,626	58.9

[a] Data for 1967–1977 include wage and salary income and earnings from self-employment; data for 1955–1966 include wage and salary income only.
SOURCE: U.S. Department of Labor, Women's Bureau, *The Earnings Gap Between Women and Men*, 1979, Table 1, p. 6 from U.S. Department of Commerce, Bureau of the Census, "Money Income of Families and Persons in the United States," Current Population Reports, 1957 to 1977, U.S. Department of Labor, Bureau of Labor Statistics, *Handbook of Labor Statistics*, 1977.

discrimination will require "changing attitudes and dispelling myths about women's capabilities, motivations, and potentialities."[36]

Government Action

The elimination of the patterns of discrimination that have permeated our institutional framework has long been an objective of social reformers. The tight labor markets of World War II helped to break down discrimination in labor markets. However, the conscious national effort that has since been made to assure equal employment opportunities to all Americans through government action was a product of the social and political turbulence of the 1960s. The civil rights and women's liberation movements were the most visible expressions of such action.

Table 9.16 THE MEDIAN USUAL WEEKLY EARNINGS OF FULL-TIME WAGE AND SALARY WORKERS BY SEX AND OCCUPATION, MAY 1976

TYPE OF OCCUPATION AND INDUSTRY	USUAL WEEKLY EARNINGS		WOMEN'S EARNINGS AS A PERCENTAGE OF MEN'S
	WOMEN	MEN	
OCCUPATION			
Professional-technical	$218	$299	73
Managerial-administrative (except on farms)	187	320	58
Sales	111	244	45
Clerical	147	228	64
Craft	149	243	61
Operatives, except transport operatives	121	202	60
Transport equipment operatives	a	216	—
Nonfarm laborers	121	166	73
Service	109	170	64
Farm	107	122	88
INDUSTRY			
Agriculture	$113	$129	88
Construction	167	244	68
Mining	a	280	—
Manufacturing	137	231	59
Durable goods	148	235	63
Nondurable goods	127	222	57
Transport and public utilities	190	270	70
Wholesale trade	148	240	62
Retail trade	113	188	60
Finance, insurance, and real estate	144	270	53
Private household	66	a	—
Miscellaneous services	160	224	71
Public administration	173	269	64

[a] Median not shown where base is less then 75,000.
SOURCE: U.S. Department of Labor, Bureau of Labor Statistics, *U.S. Working Women: A Databook,* Bulletin 1977, Table 36, p. 34.

The most significant *federal initiatives against discrimination* include President Roosevelt's *Executive Order 8802 of June 1941,* which established a Committee on Fair Employment Practices; President Kennedy's *Executive Order 10925 of 1961* and President Johnson's *Executive Order 11246 of 1965,* which required affirmative action programs to increase minority employment in firms working under federal contracts; the *Equal Pay Act amendment of 1963,* which required firms subject to the Fair Labor Standards Act to pay equal compensation to persons performing work of equal skill and with equivalent responsibilities; *Title VII of the Civil Rights Act of 1964,* which makes it unlawful for an employer to fail to hire or to discharge people because of their race, color, religion, sex, or national origin or to discriminate against them in setting compensation, terms,

Table 9.17 THE MEDIAN INCOME OF YEAR-ROUND FULL-TIME WORKERS, GROUPED BY EDUCATION AND SEX, IN 1977 (persons 25 years old and over)

EDUCATION	WOMEN	MEN	WOMEN'S INCOME AS A PERCENTAGE OF MEN'S
Elementary school:			
Less than 8 years	$6,074	$9,419	64.5
8 years	6,564	12,083	54.3
High school:			
1 to 3 years	7,387	13,120	56.3
4 years	8,894	15,434	57.6
College:			
1 to 3 years	10,157	16,235	62.6
4 years	11,609	19,603	59.2
5 years or more	14,338	21,941	65.3

SOURCE: U.S. Department of Labor, Women's Bureau, *The Earnings Gap Between Women and Men*, 1979, Table 8, p. 15, from U.S. Department of Commerce, Bureau of the Census: *Current Population Reports*, P–60, no. 118.

conditions, or privileges of employment; and the amended *Age Discrimination in Employment Act of 1967*, which forbids discrimination in employment on the basis of age against persons between 40 and 70 years old. In addition to the federal government, most states outside the South have laws prohibiting discrimination in employment.* One anomaly in our progress against discrimination has been the failure to pass the *Equal Rights Amendment* (ERA) to the Constitution. The proposed amendment, which passed the Senate in 1972, states that "equality of rights under the law shall not be denied or abridged by the United States or by any State on account of sex."

Affirmative action programs have raised serious questions concerning the balance between (1) the "earned" rights and job equities of present white and male jobholders and (2) the burden placed on nonwhites and women as a result of past discrimination. The threat such programs pose to existing seniority systems and the problems created by "reverse" discrimination are particularly sensitive issues.

Discrimination—A Summary

The economic situation of both blacks and women improved during the 1970s as they achieved more equal access to employment opportunities and to professional training. The labor market successfully absorbed an increasing proportion of women workers, but most of them found jobs in occupations traditionally held by women, and stereotypes of what is "women's work" persist. Both white and non-white women continue to earn less than males in the same occupations, and

* The application of the executive orders and legislation mentioned here to union-management relations is discussed *infra*, pp. 394–395, 429–432, 516–517 and 581.

Table 9.18 THE EMPLOYMENT OF WOMEN IN SELECTED OCCUPATIONS IN 1950, 1970, AND 1976 (numbers in thousands)

TYPE OF OCCUPATION	BOTH SEXES			WOMEN			PERCENTAGE OF ALL WORKERS IN OCCUPATION		
	1950	1970	1976	1950	1970	1976	1950	1970	1976
Professional-technical	4,858	11,452	13,329	1,947	4,576	5,603	40.1	40.0	42.0
Accountants	377	711	866	56	180	233	14.9	25.3	26.9
Engineers	518	1,233	1,190	6	20	21	1.2	1.6	1.8
Lawyers-judges	171	277	413	7	13	38	4.1	4.7	9.2
Physicians-osteopaths	184	280	368	12	25	47	6.5	8.9	12.8
Registered nurses	403	836	999	394	814	965	97.8	97.4	96.6
Teachers, except college and university	1,123	2,750	3,099	837	1,937	2,198	74.5	70.4	70.9
Teachers, college and university[a]	123	492	537	28	139	168	22.8	28.3	31.3
Technicians, excluding medical-dental	102	339	897	21	49	122	20.6	14.5	13.6
Writers, artists, entertainers	124	761	1,099	50	229	381	40.3	30.1	34.7
Managerial-administrative, except on farms	4,894	6,387	9,315	673	1,061	1,942	13.8	16.6	20.8
Bank officials-financial managers	111	313	546	13	55	135	11.7	17.6	24.7
Buyers-purchasing agents	64	361	376	6	75	89	9.4	20.8	23.7
Food service workers	343	323	505	93	109	177	27.1	33.7	35.0
Sales managers-department heads; retail trade	142	212	322	35	51	114	24.6	24.1	35.4
Clerical	6,865	13,783	15,558	4,273	10,150	12,245	62.2	73.6	78.7
Bank tellers	62	251	371	28	216	338	45.2	86.1	91.1
Bookkeepers	716	1,552	1,688	556	1,274	1,519	77.7	82.1	90.0
Cashiers	230	824	1,256	187	692	1,101	81.3	84.0	87.7
Office machine operators	143	563	726	116	414	535	81.1	73.5	73.7
Secretaries-typists	1,580	3,814	4,368	1,494	3,686	4,303	94.6	96.6	98.5
Shipping-receiving clerks	287	413	440	19	59	76	6.6	14.3	17.3

[a] Includes college and university presidents.
SOURCE: U.S. Department of Labor, Bureau of Labor Statistics, *U.S. Working Women: A Databook*, Bulletin 1977, Table 8, p. 9.

statistics show that between 1955 and 1975, the median annual earnings of year-round full-time women workers declined relative to those of men.

The assurance of equality of opportunity provided by government and the maintenance of a high level of aggregate demand will help younger entrants into the labor force, but they may not do much for present members of the labor force who are victims of past discrimination. Workers in secondary labor markets, for example, may already have been denied the general education or specific training that, in the absence of overt discrimination, would enable them to qualify for jobs in primary labor markets.

A CONCLUDING COMMENT

In our overview of the distribution of income, of poverty, and of discrimination in the labor market, there have been several recurrent themes. Adequate aggregate demand and sustained economic growth cannot assure an efficient allocation of our human resources, solve the problem of inadequate incomes, or assure equal access to employment opportunities. Marginal jobs for the poor are not enough. More employment opportunities must be made available in primary labor markets, more effective education and training must be provided present and prospective members of the labor force, and public or subsidized private employment must be provided for workers otherwise unable to earn the socially determined minimum wage. Meanwhile, income maintenance programs must assure persons truly unable to work an appropriate minimal level of living.

To achieve these goals, we must develop coordinated labor market policies and programs consistent with our national priorities. Objective analyses of the need for a further redistribution of income, continuing efforts to reduce the relative and absolute number of the poor, and measures to further reduce discrimination in the labor market are essential components of such a national strategy.

DISCUSSION QUESTIONS

1. Distinguish between the problem of income distribution and the problem of poverty.
2. Do you believe that the distribution of income realized in a perfectly competitive economy would be "fair"?
3. What type of basic distribution of income might a radical economist be expected to emphasize?
4. Do you expect the distribution of income to become more equal during the 1980s?
5. Why did the strategy of the War on Poverty shift during the 1960s?
6. Evaluate the negative income tax as a solution to the poverty problem.
7. Does Fuchs' relative concept of poverty seem reasonable?
8. Distinguish between overt and institutional discrimination. To what extent does each type exist on your campus?
9. Why were labor economists among the first to attack discrimination?

10. Under a seniority system the last hired will be the first laid off during an economic downturn. What implications does this have for affirmative action programs?

SELECTED READINGS

The Distribution of Income

Haveman, Robert H. "Introduction: Poverty and Social Policy in the 1960s and 1970s— An Overview and Some Speculations." In *A Decade of Federal Antipoverty Programs: Achievements, Failures, and Lessons.* New York: Academic Press, 1977.

Pechman, Joseph A., and Okner, Benjamin A. *Who Bears the Tax Burden?* Washington, D.C.: Brookings Institution, 1974.

Taussig, Michael K. "Trends in Inequality of Well-Offness in the United States Since World War II." In *Conference on the Trend in Income Inequality in the U.S., October 29–30, 1976.* Madison, Wisc.: Institute for Research on Poverty, University of Wisconsin.

Poverty

Batchelder, Alan B. *The Economics of Poverty.* New York: Wiley, 1966.

Kershaw, Joseph A. *Government Against Poverty.* Washington, D.C.: Brookings Institution, 1970.

Plotnick, Robert D., and Skidmore, Felicity. *Progress Against Poverty: A Review of the 1964–1974 Decade.* New York: Academic Press, 1975.

The Welfare "System"

Axinn, June, and Levin, Herman. *Social Welfare: A History of the American Response to Need.* New York: Dodd, Mead, 1975.

Chiswick, Barry R. "The Income Transfer System: Impact, Viability, and Proposals for Reform." In *Contemporary Economic Problems, 1977.* Ed. by William Fellner. Washington, D.C.: American Enterprise Institute for Public Policy Research, 1977.

Levitan, Sar A. *Programs in Aid of the Poor.* 3rd ed. Baltimore, Md.: Johns Hopkins University Press, 1976.

Palmer, John L. "Employment and Income Security." In *Setting National Priorities: The 1979 Budget.* Ed. by Joseph A. Pechman. Washington, D.C.: Brookings Institution, 1978, pp. 61–90.

Steiner, Gilbert Y. *The State of Welfare.* Washington, D.C.: Brookings Institution, 1971.

The Negative Income Tax

Marmor, Theodor R., ed. *Poverty Policy: A Compendium of Cash Transfer Proposals.* Chicago: Aldine, 1971.

Moynihan, Daniel P. *The Politics of a Guaranteed Income: The Nixon Administration and the Family Assistance Plan.* New York: Random House (Vintage Books), 1973.

Pechman, Joseph A., and Timpane, R. Michael, eds. *Work Incentives and Income*

Guarantees: The New Jersey Negative Income Tax Experiment. Washington, D.C.: Brookings Institution, 1975.

Rossi, Peter, and Lyall, Katherine C. *Reforming Public Welfare: A Critique of the Negative Income Tax Experiment.* New York: Russell Sage Foundation, 1976.

Welfare Reform

Aaron, Henry J. *Why Is Welfare So Hard to Reform?* Washington, D.C.: Brookings Institution, 1973.

Anderson, Martin. *Welfare: The Political Economy of Welfare Reform in the United States.* Palo Alto, Calif.: Hoover Institution, Stanford University, 1978.

Discrimination in Labor Markets

Ashenfelter, Orley, and Rees, Albert, eds. *Discrimination in Labor Markets.* Princeton, N.J.: Princeton University Press, 1973. See particularly Kenneth Arrow's "The Theory of Discrimination," pp. 3–33.

Becker, Gary S. *The Economics of Discrimination.* 2nd ed. Chicago: University of Chicago Press, 1971.

Madden, Janice Fanning. *The Economics of Sex Discrimination.* Lexington, Mass.: Lexington Books, 1973.

Oaxaca, Ronald L. "Theory and Measurement in the Economics of Discrimination." In *Equal Rights and Industrial Relations.* Ed. by Leonard J. Hausman, et al. Madison, Wisc.: Industrial Relations Research Association, 1977, pp. 1–30.

Thurow, Lester. *Poverty and Discrimination.* Washington, D.C.: Brookings Institution, 1969.

Wallace, Phyllis A., ed. *Equal Employment Opportunity and the AT&T Case.* Cambridge, Mass.: MIT Press, 1976. See particularly Kenneth Boulding's "Towards a Theory of Discrimination," pp. 9–15.

Discrimination Against Blacks

Congressional Budget Office. *Income Disparities Between Black and White Americans.* Washington, D.C.: U.S. Government Printing Office, December 1977.

Ferman, Louis A.; Kornbluh, Joyce L.; and Miller, J. A., eds. *Negroes and Jobs: A Book of Readings.* Ann Arbor, Mich.: University of Michigan Press, 1969.

Freeman, Richard B. "Changes in the Labor Market for Black Americans, 1948–72." In *Brookings Papers on Economic Activity* 1 (1973): pp. 67–131.

Levitan, Sar A.; Johnston, William B.; and Taggart, Robert. *Still a Dream: The Changing Status of Blacks Since 1960.* Cambridge, Mass.: Harvard University Press, 1975.

Marshall, Ray. "The Economics of Racial Discrimination: A Survey." In *Journal of Economic Literature,* XII, no. 3 (September 1974): pp. 849–871.

U.S. Department of Commerce, Bureau of the Census, "The Social and Economic Status of the Black Population in the United States: An Historical View, 1790–1978." In *Current Population Reports: Special Studies,* Series P–23, no. 80.

Discrimination Against Women

Galenson, Marjorie. *Women and Work: An International Comparison.* Ithaca. N.Y.: NYS School of Industrial and Labor Relations, Cornell University, 1973.

Kreps, Juanita M. *Women and the American Economy: A Look to the 1980s.* Published for the American Assembly, Columbia University. Englewood Cliffs, N.J.: Prentice-Hall, 1976.

Lyle, Jerolyn R., and Ross, Jane L. *Women in Industry.* Lexington, Mass.: Lexington Books, 1973.

Stromberg, Ann H., and Harkess, Shirley. *Women Working: Theories and Facts in Perspective.* Palo Alto, Calif.: Mayfield Publishing Co., 1978.

Twentieth Century Fund. *Exploitation from 9 to 5: Report of the Twentieth Century Fund Task Force on Women in Employment.* Lexington, Mass.: Lexington Books, 1975.

Notes

1. Series P–60, available from the U.S. Government Printing Office, Washington, D.C. Data for a given year generally appear in March of the second year following.
2. Joseph A. Pechman and Benjamin A. Okner, *Who Bears the Tax Burden?* (Washington, D.C.: Brookings Institution, 1974), p. 2.
3. Ibid., p. 6.
4. Ibid., p. 64.
5. Daniel B. Radner and John C. Hinrichs, "Size Distribution of Income in 1964, 1970, and 1971," in *Survey of Current Business* 54, no. 10 (October 1974): p. 26.
6. Ibid., p. 27.
7. Peter Henle, "Exploring the Distribution of Earned Income," in *Monthly Labor Review* 95, no. 12 (December 1972): p. 17.
8. *Economic Report of the President, Transmitted to the Congress January 1964, Together with the Annual Report of the Council of Economic Advisers,* p. 15.
9. U.S. Department of Commerce, Bureau of the Census, *Current Population Reports,* Series P–60, no. 124, "Characteristics of the Population Below the Poverty Level: 1978," Table 1, p. 16, and "Money Income and Poverty Status of Families and Persons in the United States: 1978" (advance report), p. 1.
10. J. Douglas Brown, "Social Security in the Years Ahead," in Gerald G. Somers, ed., *The Next Twenty-Five Years of Industrial Relations* (Madison, Wisc.: Industrial Relations Research Association, 1973), p. 126.
11. U.S. Department of Commerce, Bureau of the Census, *Current Population Reports,* Series P–60, 119, "Characteristics of the Population Below the Poverty Level: 1977," Table 5, p. 26.
12. Ibid., p. 7.
13. "Money Income and Poverty Status of Families and Persons in the United States: 1978" (advance report), p. 3.
14. Ibid., Table 20, p. 32; Table 21, p. 34.
15. "Characteristics of the Population Below the Poverty Level: 1977," pp. 3–4.
16. Congressional Budget Office, *Poverty Status of Families Under Alternative Definitions of Income,* Background Paper 17, rev. (June 1977), p. 9.
17. Victor R. Fuchs. "Comment," in Lee Soltow, ed., *Six Papers on the Size Distribution*

of Wealth and Income (New York: Columbia University Press for the National Bureau of Economic Research, 1969), p. 198.

18. Ibid., pp. 198–199.
19. Ibid., p. 199.
20. Congressional Budget Office, *Poverty Status of Families*, p. 3.
21. *Social Security Bulletin* 43, no. 5 (May 1980): Table M–24, p. 51.
22. Laurence E. Lynn, Jr., "A Decade of Policy Developments in the Income-Maintenance System," in Robert H. Haveman, (ed.) *A Decade of Antipoverty Programs: Achievements, Failures, and Lessons* (New York: Academic Press, 1977), p. 73.
23. For a description of this proposal, see the *Economic Report of the President, Transmitted to the Congress January 1978, Together with the Annual Report of the Council of Economic Advisers*, pp. 229–231.
24. Robert H. Haveman, "Introduction: Poverty and Social Policy in the 1960s and 1970s—An Overview and Some Speculations," in Haveman (ed.), *A Decade of Antipoverty Programs*, p. 18.
25. Cf. Gary D. Brown, "Discrimination and pay disparities between white men and women," in *Monthly Labor Review* 101, no. 3 (March 1978): pp. 17–18.
26. Ronald L. Oaxaca, "Theory and Measurement in the Economics of Discrimination," in Leonard J. Hausman, et al., eds., *Equal Rights and Industrial Relations* (Madison, Wisc.: Industrial Relations Research Association, 1977), p. 20.
27. Congressional Budget Office, *Income Disparities Between Black and White Americans* (Washington, D.C.: U.S. Government Printing Office, 1977), pp. xix–xx.
28. Ibid., pp. 26–27.
29. Oaxaca, "Theory and Measurement in the Economics of Discrimination," pp. 25–26.
30. Richard B. Freeman, "Changes in the Labor Market for Black Americans, 1948–72," in *Brookings Papers on Economic Activity* 1 (1973): p. 118.
31. U.S. Department of Commerce, Bureau of the Census, "The Social and Economic Status of the Black Population in the United States: An Historical View, 1790–1978," in *Current Population Reports: Special Studies*, Series P–23, no. 80, p. x.
32. Dixie Sommers, "Occupational rankings for men and women by earnings," in *Monthly Labor Review* 97, no. 8 (August 1974): p. 47.
33. Oaxaca, "Theory and Measurement in the Economics of Discrimination," p. 25.
34. Victor R. Fuchs, "Women's Earnings: Recent Trends and Long-run Prospects," in *Monthly Labor Review* 97, no. 5 (May 1974): p. 23.
35. Victor R. Fuchs, "A Note on Sex Segregation in Professional Occupations," in *Explorations in Economic Research*, National Bureau of Economic Research, 2, no. 1 (Winter 1975): pp. 105 ff.
36. Elizabeth Duncan Koontz, "The Women's Bureau looks to the future," in *Monthly Labor Review* 93, no. 6 (June 1970): p. 9.

Chapter 10
LABOR PROBLEMS IN THE UNITED STATES: AN INTERIM ASSESSMENT

As the title of this chapter suggests, much of our analysis of labor problems has been tentative and incomplete. The term "interim" is justified on two quite different grounds:

1. The labor problems facing our society and the private and public programs advanced to solve them are necessarily infused with a dynamic. We have concentrated on existing problems, and assessments of progress in resolving them must be continually reviewed. Economic security and humane and dignified treatment on the job are the basic demands of our labor force, but the specifics of these demands will vary with circumstances. The fact that labor problems persist despite increasing affluence is not necessarily to be decried. Our very recognition of "new" problems is a mark of economic and social progress and grounds for optimism rather than despair.[1]
2. We have purposely *not* discussed the impact of unions up to this point. We have however laid the groundwork for an analysis of union-management relations, which is an essential component of any overview of labor

problems in the United States. We shall put the frame of reference developed in preceding chapters to good use in the chapters that follow.

SUMMARY: PARTS ONE AND TWO

We shall not review the preceding chapters in detail; our intent is merely to suggest the nature of the labor problems facing our society; to indicate the major types of policies and programs that have been developed to resolve these problems; to suggest the essential components of an agenda for continued action; and, finally, to briefly relate this material to the chapters that follow.[2]

Although the labor problems of highly industrialized and interdependent "mixed" economies are broadly similar, a complex of variables, including the social, political, and ethical values of a society and the institutional framework peculiar to it, will condition the identification of, and responses to, such problems. Economic analysis can countribute to the understanding of these problems in a variety of environments.

In an essentially American frame of reference, we have examined the underlying determinants of the demand for and supply of labor, the factors responsible for changing levels of income and employment, and how wages are determined in the absence of unions. We have seen that in nonunion markets, wages are not determined in the same way as in a competitive model of the economy. This will be important in our assessment of the economic impact of unions. Standards and conditions established as a result of collective bargaining must be compared not only with those in theoretical models but also with the situation in actual labor markets in the absence of unions. The problem of how to deal with imperfections in labor markets has divided professional economists: a minority argue that the economy should be made "more competitive," thereby minimizing the need for government or union intervention. The majority feel that it is unrealistic to expect to achieve—or even closely approximate—a competitive market economy. They assume that market imperfections will persist, and they thereby acknowledge the potential value of a viable union movement. There are however serious differences of opinion as to the appropriate "limits" of union power; these differences will be discussed in the chapters that follow.

We have not argued that it is impossible to improve the operation of labor markets. Public and private measures to provide additional, and more accurate, labor market information; to increase the mobility of labor; to eliminate discrimination; and to train workers in the skills required for existing and developing jobs will help the labor market to function more efficiently. However, we cannot assume that such measures alone will provide all workers with suitable jobs or with objective and humane treatment on the job.

We have considered the economic, social, and human costs of our failure to make the best use of our human resources. We have identified categories of unemployment and underemployment and reviewed proposals to reduce unemployment. We have focused on what is usually referred to as "structural" unemployment and concluded that although it could be significantly reduced by a high enough level of aggregate demand, once the overall unemployment rate reached a fairly low level (possibly between 4 and 5½ percent of the civilian labor force), job vacancies would exist for which many of the unemployed would be unqualified. In addition, unemployment that would not be reduced by conventional manpower training and development programs could develop in certain occupations, industries, or geographic areas. This residual type of unemployment, which is likely to persist, is often referred to as hard core unemployment.

Racial discrimination is probably our most sensitive and potentially explosive domestic problem, and the exceptionally high rates of unemployment of members of minority groups—blacks, American Indians, and those of Hispanic origin—indicate that we must try harder to increase the employability of these groups. Assuring equal employment opportunities to women must also have a very high priority.

We have distinguished between policies to increase the total number of jobs, policies to enhance the employability of individual workers, and policies to match unemployed workers with jobs. We have also stressed the importance of monetary and fiscal policies in achieving a high level of employment. The problem of persistent inflation accompanied by less than full employment has confronted a succession of administrations, and their efforts to reduce the rate of inflation have at best met with only moderate success. We have distinguished between *demand-pull* and *cost-push* inflation and examined the reluctance of private decision makers to conform to a policy of voluntary price and wage restraints or to support price and wage controls. We have seen that reducing unemployment to more "acceptable" levels without increasing inflationary pressures will require a sophisticated combination of public and private measures. In 1966, when unemployment averaged 4 percent, a Department of Labor report correctly observed that

> in meeting the unemployment problems which remain, enlightened fiscal and monetary policies, on the one hand, and manpower, education, anti-poverty, and civil rights programs on the other, will be of [equal] importance.

It went on to say that

> there is little prospect of much further reduction in unemployment without serious inflationary consequences, except as efforts are directed specifically to the persistent concentrations of unemployment and unpreparedness.[3]

Six years later, after experiencing unemployment of nearly 6 percent during a period of general prosperity and persistent inflation, the Council of Economic Advisers observed that even if the administration's efforts to "eradicate the continuing inflationary consequences of the boom that started in mid-1965," were successful, this would still leave questions that have troubled students of the American economy for many years. Are there persistent structural characteristics in the modern American economy that make inflation inevitable, or inevitable in the absence of high unemployment? If so, can these characteristics of the economy be changed?[4]

These questions are equally relevant today.

We have seen that development and training programs have considerable potential for upgrading disadvantaged workers and decreasing underemployment and structural unemployment. Unfortunately, a number of the new—and in some cases highly imaginative—programs that have been developed have failed, and it has been difficult to determine whether this was because they were poorly conceived or poorly implemented. The emphasis on state and local responsibility for such programs during the Nixon administration was unfortunate; in the absence of uniform federal standards and controls, programs were not started in many areas in which they were clearly needed.

Apparently, the private sector will continue to carry the major burden of on-the-job training. However, government subsidies will remain essential wherever the required "investment" in human capital, while clearly desirable in terms of social benefits and costs, will not provide an adequate return to private firms.

The successful development, implementation, and evaluation of employment and training programs require reliable statistical projections of the supply of and demand for labor, not only in the aggregate but also in particular occupations, industries, and geographic areas. The more recent projections of manpower requirements, which are based on input-output tables developed by the U.S. Department of Labor and are updated on a continuing basis to take into account changing patterns of economic development, represent a significant statistical advance. In addition, job vacancy data now enable us to measure labor force utilization more accurately, more effective use is being made of the reorganized federal-state employment service, and a National Computer Job Bank should soon increase the efficiency of that service.

We have discussed several types of protective labor legislation, including hours and wages laws, social security programs, and legislation dealing with the problems of special groups within the labor force. Our analysis of government standards for working hours and wages indicated that if those standards differed from the working conditions that would otherwise result from market forces, the result could be higher costs and prices or some degree of unemployment or both. These "costs" of regulating working conditions are considered acceptable to most members of society.

We have discussed the fact that because minimum wage legislation assumes that covered workers should receive a "social minimum" consistent with our advancing standard of living, persons whose low productivity makes them worth less than this amount to employers may be rendered "unemployable" by such legislation. We have argued that to solve this problem, (1) programs must be developed to improve the skills of those capable of becoming productive members of the labor force and (2) those unable even with training to meet minimal standards of productivity must be given some form of income guarantee or some type of public employment.

We have also analyzed other basic causes of economic insecurity, including old age, on-the-job accidents, occupational disease, and nonoccupationally connected disabilities. We described the development of our pluralistic social security system and identified a number of continuing problems: the need for more adequate coverage under a number of programs; the need to continue to review and revise programs to make sure that benefit standards reflect changes in average income levels and in our concept of what constitutes an appropriate social minimum; the desirability of making welfare benefits available as a matter of right rather than having them depend on a means test; the need for more uniform standards, perhaps nationwide ones, for state programs and for programs operated on a joint federal-state basis; the need to review the present financing of our Old Age, Survivors, Disability, and Health Insurance program; and the desirability of new programs, including temporary disability insurance and some form of compulsory general health insurance.

We have noted that our present system of social security will probably not be modified in any major respect, although some programs may be made more internally consistent by the establishment of more uniform standards, and we have observed how these public security programs have been complemented by an increasingly generous mix of private programs for both groups and individuals. The role of unions in the development of such programs will be discussed in later chapters.

We have reviewed the problems of special groups and of certain subsets of the population and their relationship with "the" problem of poverty. We have discussed the impact of civil rights and equal opportunity legislation on the labor market and concluded that such legislation is a necessary, but not a sufficient, condition for the elimination of discrimination in employment.

We have also noted a common weakness in most of our public programs— the fact that they have not been concerned specifically with the quality of life in the workplace or outside it. We must address these problems if we are to give workers a sense of identification with, and participation in, our increasingly impersonal organizational society. However, we have rejected the conclusion of the New Left that only by a radical restructuring of our institutions can we resolve these problems.

DEALING WITH CONTINUING PROBLEMS

Existing legislation to solve or reduce the severity of the continuing problems of our labor force can and should be improved, and additional legislation passed where necessary. Social security programs and other protective legislation must be continually reviewed to maintain their integrity. In addition, coverage should be extended as soon as possible to workers who are not yet protected by these laws.

Not everyone has benefited from the improvement in living standards and conditions of work made possible by economic development. It will take a broad spectrum of educational and training programs as well as the right monetary and fiscal policies to bring disadvantaged workers into the mainstream of economic life. If we as a nation are to realize our full socioeconomic potential, we will have to make a continued commitment for the foreseeable future in four areas:

1. Monetary and fiscal policies will have to be coordinated to maintain full employment, adequate growth, "reasonable" price stability, and the maximum possible economic freedom. The precise policy mix will depend on the relative weight attached to each objective.
2. More specific policies will have to be designed and implemented to develop the capabilities of each member of the labor force and match workers with jobs on a nondiscriminatory basis.
3. A minimal "socially adequate" level of living will have to be provided for all members of the labor force and their dependents, for those who cannot work because of a personal disability or family responsibilities, and for those who cannot find jobs because their personal productivity is too low.
4. Finally, we will have to decide not only what programs will be needed to achieve the objectives we have mentioned but also what benefits should be sought from future per capita increases in real national income. We will have to decide for example when additional leisure should be preferred to additional goods or services. If goods and services that are desirable from the standpoint of the public welfare are not provided by the private sector because the resulting revenues will not cover projected outlays, we will have to decide whether they should be provided by the government. Right now, we "lack an effective social calculus to give us [a] true valuation of the entire costs and benefits of individual and social purchases,"[5] and it is often impossible to make such decisions objectively. Nevertheless, it is important to weigh such issues consciously, and to reach decisions on a reasonably informed basis, remembering that "the true test of any economic system is whether it betters human life."[6]

The omission of unions from our analysis so far has been, as we have mentioned, deliberate. Most basic labor problems have a potential effect on *all* members of the labor force, and we cannot equate these problems with the problems peculiar to union members. We have seen that even in the absence of unions, labor problems cannot be described purely in terms of an economic calculus. As Professor J. R. Hicks has emphasized, "the labour market is—by nature, and quite independently of Trade Union organisation—a very special kind of market, a market which is likely to develop 'social' as well as purely economic aspects."[7] These extraeconomic dimensions are often neglected in analyses of the operation of labor markets, particularly in theoretical discussions of the role and impact of unions.

PROLOGUE: PARTS THREE, FOUR, AND FIVE

We are now ready to begin our study of unions. We have said that there are two basic reasons for analyzing labor problems before looking at union-management relations, and we will repeat those reasons here:

1. In 1978 only 22 percent of the total labor force (or some 27 percent of the employees in nonagricultural establishments) belonged to national unions, professional associations, or public employee associations. Since most workers are not union members, it is appropriate to study labor problems at least initially in an essentially nonunion frame of reference, while recognizing that unions often influence nonunion employment relationships.
2. There is a methodological advantage in moving from a general subject (the labor force) to a somewhat narrower one (the union sector). Much of the theoretical apparatus relevant to the economic analysis of collective bargaining has already been discussed. The impact of a negotiated wage increase, for example, can be analyzed in much the same way as the impact of a legal minimum wage.

The chapters that follow will deal sequentially with the development of the American union movement; the structure and government of trade unions; management's approach to collective bargaining; the collective bargaining process; government regulation of union-management relations, including collective bargaining in the public sector; the contents of collective agreements; and finally, the impact of unions on the lives of their members, the firms and industries with which they deal, and the national economy. Much of the material in earlier chapters will be applicable to these topics, and it may be helpful to review sections of them occasionally. The discussion of how wages are determined under collective bargaining for example assumes a familiarity with the analysis of wage determination in Chapters 5 and 6.

Many of the economic effects of collective bargaining and of union initiatives relating to the extraeconomic dimensions of the employment relationship cannot be quantified and will be viewed differently by persons of goodwill. As a result, a number of our conclusions about the role and impact of unions will necessarily be tentative and reflect value judgments. What is clear is that American unions have had a significant and generally favorable impact on the extraeconomic dimensions of the employment relationship not only of union members but of many nonunion workers as well. On balance therefore, American unions appear to have been a constructive element in our mixed enterprise economy.

DISCUSSION QUESTIONS

1. How successfully do you believe our society has responded to (a) the economic and (b) the extraeconomic labor problems of the labor force?

2. Can you envision any "new" labor problems which may be "identified" during the next decade?

3. Do you believe macroeconomic or microeconomic analysis has proved most useful in analyzing labor problems?

4. In Parts Three, Four, and Five we will study union-management relations. To what extent do you believe that the labor problems which have been the focus of Parts One and Two will be subject to collective bargaining? (Hint: Think of the orientation of American unions discussed in Part One.)

Notes

1. The changing emphases in successive *Employment and Training* [previously *Manpower*] *Reports of the President* reflect this "recognition" of new problems.

2. Discussions of more recent developments relating to these problems, together with current statistical data, can be found in the most recent *Economic Report of the President* and *Employment and Training Report of the President.*

3. *Manpower Report of the President and a Report on Manpower Requirements, Resources, Utilization, and Training by the U.S. Department of Labor, Transmitted to the Congress March 1966*, p. 2.

4. *Economic Report of the President, Transmitted to the Congress January 1972, Together with the Annual Report of the Council of Economic Advisers*, p. 27.

5. *National Commission on Technology, Automation, and Economic Progress Report: Technology and the American Economy*, vol. 1 (February 1966), p. 76.

6. Arthur F. Burns, *The Management of Prosperity*, 1965 Benjamin F. Fairless Memorial Lectures (New York: Columbia University Press for the Carnegie Institute of Technology, 1966), p. 69.

7. J. R. Hicks, *The Theory of Wages*, 2nd ed. (New York: St. Martin's Press, 1963), p. 317.

Part III

THE DEVELOPMENT OF UNIONS AND COLLECTIVE BARGAINING IN THE UNITED STATES

Chapter 11
HISTORY OF UNIONISM I: THE BEGINNINGS OF UNIONISM UP TO THE FOUNDING OF THE A.F. OF L.

A classic *History of Trade Unionism* defines a *union* as "a continuous association of wage-earners for the purpose of maintaining or improving the conditions of their working lives."[1] As we have mentioned before, forming such organizations is one of several basic responses of wage earners to the pressures and problems of an industrial civilization.

The distinguishing characteristics of a labor union suggested by the definition above are (1) continuity of organization, (2) the limitation of membership to employees (persons earning a wage or salary), and (3) a concern with problems related to the employment relationship. In this chapter and the following two chapters, we will describe the growth of unions in the United States, paying particular attention to the immediate reasons for their growth. First, however, we must make a distinction between *absolute* and *relative* growth. Absolute growth that does not parallel increases in the size of the labor force represents *a relative deterioration* in the membership base of organized labor.

WHY UNIONS GROW

Initially, students of union growth tended to look for single reasons for their popularity, noting for example that fluctuations in membership correlated with cyclical movements in the overall level of economic activity. Now, such simplistic theories have been rejected, and when we stress the importance of one factor at some point or in some period, we do not assume that this factor operated in isolation. We are aware that complex relationships can develop between causal factors, producing a multiplicity of growth patterns. Albert A. Blum, in rejecting various taxonomies of growth variables, has argued that

> [t]here are . . . certain factors in the political, economic, sociological, and industrial relations system at a *given* time of history, which, when joined together, help explain why during that era union membership rose or fell. These same conditions might have a different effect, or no effect at all, at a different period of history.[2]

The principal variables that help to explain the development of unions in this country include:

1. *The stages of the business cycle.* Before the prosperity of the 1920s and the Depression of the 1930s, union membership usually grew during periods of prosperity and shrank or remained the same during recessions and depressions. It is possible that this relationship no longer holds. Some experts believe that unions have reached a membership plateau and will have great difficulty in extending their organizational frontiers any farther, even in periods of sustained prosperity. At the same time, union security arrangements and fringe benefit programs make it less likely that union membership will decline during recessions.

2. *The stages of economic development the nation has passed through.* As industrialization proceeds, unions become more likely. However, in a technologically advanced postindustrial society, this generalization may no longer hold. The introduction of sophisticated automatic technology and computer controls, for example, has cut the relative (and at times the absolute) number of blue-collar workers, and the technicians ("white-coverall" workers) who have supplanted them may be poor prospects for unionization. Economic growth and increasing affluence may also result in the expansion of service industries, which have often proved difficult to organize.

3. *The growth of the labor force.* As a labor force expands, there is a "natural increase" in union membership in occupations, industries, and sectors already organized. This natural increase should be distinguished from increases in membership caused by the unionization of previously unorganized workers. More refined measures of union growth are based on the percentage of organized workers in the civilian labor force and the percentage of employees organized in nonagricultural establishments. The caveats noted in Number 2 apply here also.

4. *The recognition of an identity of interest by workers* in given crafts, plants, industries, or regions or in the nation. However, the social and occupational orientations of technical and professional workers may

encourage them to form associations that do not engage in collective bargaining.

5. *Employer attitudes and policies toward unions and toward the human relations aspects of management.* The character of employer opposition to unions has varied over time and is related to the next variable.

6. *Government* (federal, state, and local) *policies relating to unions and collective bargaining* and the way relevant policies and laws are implemented and interpreted by executives and the judiciary.

7. *The structural types of union organization available.* The membership base of a union should parallel the job structure of that portion of the labor force it hopes to organize. The successful organization of large industrial plants, for example, usually requires an industrial rather than a craft membership base.

8. *The type and adequacy of union leadership.*

9. *The prevailing social, political, and economic philosophy of workers.* Relying primarily on economic action through collective bargaining has apparently favored the growth of a "union" movement rather than a politically oriented "labor" movement.

10. *Public opinion* toward unions. This is generally related to employer and government attitudes toward unions.

Once in existence, a union movement has a reciprocal influence on economic and political institutions. Thus, "as labor organizations grow they become an independent factor affecting the course of their own destiny."[3] However, as we have pointed out before, American unions, unlike unions in many European nations, have generally accepted capitalist institutions and have sought to advance the interests of workers through collective bargaining rather than independent political action.

In this chapter, we will describe the first century of the development of American unions, from their early beginnings as continuous associations in 1794 through the formation of the American Federation of Labor in 1886. Chapter 12 will cover the next sixty years, up to the passage of the Taft-Hartley Act in 1947; and Chapter 13 will cover developments since 1947.

EARLY WORKERS' ORGANIZATIONS

The first *continuing* labor organization in the United States was established by Philadelphia cordwainers (shoemakers working with cordovan leather) in 1794. Before then, "labor" organizations had been formed in a number of cities, particularly by building tradesmen, but these organizations were either temporary or were composed of masters rather than employees.[4] Many of the early organizations of journeymen were basically mutual aid societies concerned with death benefits and other forms of aid rather than wages, and some of the acts under which they were incorporated provided that they would cease to exist as legal entities if they made any attempt to fix wages.[5]

Typically, workers organized in pursuit of a particular goal or to redress a specific grievance. Once the goal was reached or the dispute resolved, the organization lost cohesiveness and expired. Organizations that were intended to be permanent frequently lacked the resources to survive when times were bad. The few that did survive usually emphasized mutual insurance rather than collective bargaining.

Collective bargaining as we know it developed from the practice of submitting a "price list" to individual employers. Initially, the employers simply accepted or rejected the list. Gradually however unions began to request conferences with employers' representatives for the purpose of arriving at a trade agreement. The organizations doing such collective bargaining were usually composed of highly skilled craftsmen who were linked by their common skill and concerned with the problems of a particular trade. The strategic position of such crafts in the production process made employers vulnerable to their demands. However, "there was . . . no 'labour philosophy,' either of cooperation, agrarianism, socialism, or class struggle. The skilled mechanic might expect to become a master, and it did not occur to him to use his organisation as a means of abolishing the wage system."[6]

The expansion of markets early in the nineteenth century accounted for much of the early growth in union membership. The development of turnpikes and canals, by uniting the eastern, midwestern, and southern markets, created competition between localities that put pressure on employers to reduce costs. Wages were slashed, convict labor was used, and apprenticeship systems were disrupted by the employment of migrant workers. In a number of areas, skilled workers responded to these pressures by organizing craft unions to protect established working conditions and rates of pay, and *city centrals* were formed in various urban areas. The latter were composed of unions from a variety of trades interested in mutual action and protection.

The 1820s were a prosperous time in which organized workers generally consolidated their gains and made further advances. It was about this time that the term "union" was first used in a formal sense, appearing in the title of several organizations of factory workers. The growth in the size of employers weakened the identity of interest between masters and journeymen, and the development of the factory system further emphasized the distinction between employers and the employees who worked with the tools and equipment they supplied. According to historian David Saposs, "[l]abour was forced . . . to awaken to its new position . . . the worker, in self-defence, was compelled to fight his former comrade in industry."[7]

The typical workday was from sunup to sundown, and many unions made shortening it a major objective. They stressed the need of workers for additional leisure and for time to perform their duties as citizens. Employers reacted by professing great reluctance to believe that American workers would willingly advocate tampering with the "free" market. When the Boston House Carpenters, for example, asked for a ten-hour day, the master carpenters could only doubt that the idea "originated with any of the faithful and industrious Sons of New England," and hope that this "evil of foreign growth" would "not take root in the favoured soil of Massachusetts," especially not in Boston, "the early rising and industry of whose inhabitants [was] universally proverbial."[8]

Employers attempted to combat unions by having them prosecuted as conspiracies. The early conspiracy cases had challenged the legality of combinations of workers. Now the methods used by unions to achieve their goals came under attack. Unions that employed such weapons as picketing, sympathetic strikes, or a closed shop (one in which union membership was a condition of employment) were declared unlawful. In addition, blacklists of union members and sympathizers were widely circulated.

EARLY POLITICAL ACTION

Also in the 1820s, workers in a number of areas became interested in the possibility of improving their lot through political action. The growth of cities in which large numbers of wage earners worked and lived in close proximity contributed to this heightened political consciousness. Economic conflict was viewed not as a struggle between employers and employees, but as one between the rich and the poor. The political objectives of the workers' organizations were therefore broadly conceived. Their principal demands were for increased leisure and free public education, both goals that transcended the purely economic interests of workers. Political activity was also furthered by a rapid growth in the number and circulation of the workingmen's newspapers.

In Philadelphia, the demand for a ten-hour day led to the formation in 1827 of the Mechanics' Union of Trade Associations, the first city central. In 1828, the association decided to nominate candidates for the next election. The Philadelphia Workingmen's Party was formed and took an interest in a variety of issues, particularly "monopolies, paper money, mechanics' liens, imprisonment for debt, the militia system, lotteries, and public education."[9] As the political activity of the association increased, however, its membership base in the trade unions declined and it became dormant.

Another workingmen's party was formed in New York City. This party came under the influence of Thomas Skidmore, a reformer who advocated a program of equal division of property that became known as *agrarianism*. George Henry Evans, the editor of the *Working Man's Advocate*, was also influential in the movement. A similar political awakening was evident elsewhere, particularly in New England, where numerous local organizations patterned after the New York and Philadelphia parties were established, as well as a politically oriented general labor organization, the New England Association of Farmers, Mechanics and other Workingmen. A significant innovation of this association was the formal extension of the membership base to include factory workers. Although these early workingmen's parties were short lived, they were not without impact; the more popular planks in their platforms were often incorporated into the platform of a major party.

THE GROWTH OF UNIONS

During the 1830s, the evolution of mutual insurance (benevolent) societies into trade unions continued. The number of local trade unions increased, and more city centrals were formed. The period from 1835 to 1837 was one of prosperity, and employer resistance to the demands of organized workers proved low. A number of unions obtained a ten-hour day for their members, as well as wage increases to offset the rising cost of living. The expansion of trade union activity also led to the formation of *employer associations*, which were designed to help their members collectively offset the growing power of unions. These associations differed from earlier employer organizations, which had been concerned primarily with trade matters.

In addition to the growth of local unions and the organization of city centrals, the 1830s witnessed an attempt at organization on a national level. In 1834, the General Trades Union of New York launched a short-lived National Trades' Union, and between 1835 and 1836 five trades—carpenters, combmakers, cordwainers, handloom weavers, and printers—attempted to form permanent national unions to control competition between workers of the same trade in different localities. These embryo national unions, the weaker local unions, and the National Trades' Union disappeared during the economic upheaval of 1837–1842, and the local unions and city centrals that survived did not constitute a unified labor movement. As Table 11.1 shows, there were 300,000 union members in 1836. This was the high-water mark of union membership until 1872 and represented a degree of unionization that would not be reached again for almost 50 years.

Frustrated in their attempts to improve their lot by organizing, workers

Table 11.1 THE ESTIMATED MEMBERSHIP OF LABOR UNIONS IN THE UNITED STATES IN SELECTED YEARS 1836 TO 1897

YEAR	NUMBER OF MEMBERS
1836	300,000
1869	170,000
1872	300,000
1878	50,000
1883	200,000
1885	300,000
1886	1,000,000
1890	400,000
1897	440,000

SOURCE: W. S. Woytinsky, *Employment and Wages in the United States*, Table 67, p. 233. © 1953 by The Twentieth Century Fund, Inc., New York. Reprinted by permission.

tried a variety of alternative solutions, and "for the next dozen years [there was] the most astonishing junction of humanitarianism, bizarre reforms and utopias, protective tariffs and futile labour legislation, known to our history."[10] Labor would not return to pragmatic trade unionism until the 1850s.

1837–1850: INTELLECTUALISM AND THE REVIVAL OF TRADE UNIONISM

Unlike labor movements in many foreign countries, the American union movement has been wary of intellectuals; its leadership has come from the ranks of wage earners, not an educated elite. Segments of American labor were occasionally dominated by intellectuals, but there was no *general* tendency for this to occur except in the period from 1837 to 1850. The problems of early industrialization— the spread of the factory system, the growth of cities, the widespread employment of women and children, periodic unemployment that could not be controlled by individual employees or employers, and unduly long working hours —made workers willing to listen to those who confidently asserted that they had a solution at hand. Actually, most of the proposed solutions were attempts to escape the consequences of fundamental and irreversible changes in our economy. Instead of coming to terms with these consequences, reformers sought to return to a past golden age, one that existed largely in their imaginations. Despite the impracticality of many reform programs, economic and social conditions were conducive to their initial acceptance. Collective action through the medium of unions did not yet appear to be a realistic alternative, and workers did not know where else to turn.

As in earlier cases when workers flirted with political action, the reforms that were proposed lacked a pragmatic wage earner orientation. The problems of factory workers were considered more consciously and given more prominence in publications and debates than in the 1820s, but the objectives of the reform elements were basically humanitarian and transcended the interests of wage earners. The more important reform movements of the period included American "Associationism," which was based on the ideas of Charles Fourier; Horace Greeley's producers' cooperatives; Wilhelm Weitling's bank of exchange, which was to issue paper money to producers according to the value of their products in terms of labor inputs; the "New Agrarianism" of George Henry Evans; and the movement to obtain a ten-hour workday through legislation.[11]

Most of these movements lacked firm foundations; they drew support not from a general belief in their basic principles but from the charisma of strong leaders. These men found fertile soil in which to cultivate their programs, but the programs were often unrelated to the basic qualities of the soil.

Legislation establishing a ten-hour day for factory workers had great popular appeal, but supporters of such laws had only limited success. Many skilled workers had secured a ten-hour day through collective action, but most unorganized factory workers continued to labor 12 to 15 hours a day. The first ten-hour law was passed in New Hampshire in 1847, but it, like laws passed sub-sequently in other states, was ineffective because it did not absolutely prohibit working more than ten hours. With the revival of trade unionism in the 1850s, the movement to achieve a standard ten-hour workday through legislation was re-placed by a union drive to progressively reduce working hours through strikes and trade agreements.

The events of the period from 1837 to 1850 are of more than historical in-terest; they demonstrate the early reluctance of the mass of American labor to give continuing support to reforms that sought to alter established institutions. The short life of the various humanitarian programs proposed in these years helped make the American union movement lastingly wary of both intellectual leaders and political panaceas, and although a labor movement in the broadest sense, dedicated to advancing the interests of all wage earners, failed to material-ize, trade unions did gradually gain acceptance as an appropriate vehicle for the protection and advancement of the interests of wage earners.

The regeneration of a vigorous union movement during this period was favored by the more tolerant attitude of the judiciary in a number of states. This was a result of the decision handed down by Chief Justice Shaw of Massachu-setts in the case of *Commonwealth* v. *Hunt* in 1842. Prior to that decision, combinations of workers were often ruled to be illegal conspiracies; Shaw ruled that unions were legal combinations and held, further, that a strike to obtain a closed shop was lawful. Although the courts continued to curtail union activities on the basis that the ends of those activities or the means used to obtain them were illegal, the Massachusetts decision was widely regarded as establishing the right of workers to organize. However, membership in trade unions continued to be limited in most cases to skilled craftsmen, who saw little benefit in associating with unskilled or semiskilled workers. This attitude continued, with occasional dramatic exceptions, to characterize American unionism until the formation of the CIO during the New Deal.

Unlike earlier trade unions, unions that were formed during the middle of the nineteenth century may be considered lineal forebears of the unions that established the American Federation of Labor. One historian of the period has commented on the

> impressive difference between the "pure and simple" unionism of the middle of the decade and the unionism of the thirties, the forties, and the beginning of this decade. Stripped of universal and glowing ideals, without establishing a single labour paper to carry an appeal to the country, the skilled trades settled down to the cold business of getting more pay for themselves by means of permanent and exclusive organizations.[12]

The rising cost of living was a rallying point for demands for higher pay. Many unions assumed for the first time the function of regulating apprenticeships, with particular emphasis on reducing the number of boys learning a trade. Union security also became an issue, although the importance of closed shops varied locally and from one trade to another. Finally, collective bargaining—then known as *conciliation* or *arbitration*—between a local union and a *group* of employers became more common.[13] Despite these gains, many unions failed to establish a solid organizational base and faded away during the depression of 1854–1855 and the crisis of 1857. However, many of the more firmly established unions survived.

THE RISE OF THE NATIONAL UNION

Six national unions were formed between 1850 and 1859, including the first "true" national to survive, the Typographical Union. This foreshadowed an era of sustained union growth during and after the Civil War, an era that has been called the *period of nationalization* of the American union movement. Improvements in transportation and communications and the destruction of economic localism during the war made national organization more practicable. At the same time, the prosperity of the war and postwar years and the declared friendship of President Abraham Lincoln for labor created an environment conducive to union growth. Finally, there was considerable interest among union leaders in forming national organizations for several reasons:

1. The widening of product markets compelled many unions to enlarge their jurisdictions in order to effectively "control the work." A national union could enforce uniform wage rates, establish uniform standards for apprenticeship and admission to journeyman status, and also protect the work jurisdiction of local unions from encroachment by other unions.
2. In many areas, competition for employment between migratory journeymen and local workers tended to depress wages. National organizations could enforce uniform standards for wages and prevent migrants from undercutting local pay scales. It was not necessary that goods be *produced* for a national market for workers to have a common interest. The objective was to protect *local* wage rates.
3. The organization of employers into trade groups reduced the power of *unaffiliated* local unions and suggested the value of similar cooperative action among union locals.
4. The widespread use of machinery and the increased emphasis on the division of labor split established trades and enabled "green hands" to invade certain industries. National unions would be more able to protect their members from this type of competition.[14]

The impact of national unions varied from industry to industry; in some industries they became a locus of power, while in others they served in an advisory capacity.

Although broader markets generally favored union growth, production for a national market was also responsible for certain retarding influences. The expansion of markets created conditions favorable to the introduction of improved technology that required only semiskilled workers who were ineligible for membership in craft unions. In addition, the growth of multiple plant firms made the organization of unions more difficult.[15]

Aided by a high level of business activity, ten nationals were established between 1863 and 1866. Union growth was checked by the recession of 1866–1868 but resumed immediately thereafter. In all, 26 national unions were formed between 1864 and 1873.

The vicissitudes of union growth are illustrated by events in the shoe industry, which demonstrated "the potential menace of technological change not only to the welfare of the skilled worker but to the trade union established to advance his welfare."[16] Employers in the shoe industry refused to give skilled workers exclusive jurisdiction over machine operations in newly constructed factories. In 1867, to combat the resulting widespread use of "green hands," the journeymen formed a national union, the Order of the Knights of St. Crispin. Membership in the order grew phenomenally; by 1870, it had reached an estimated 50,000 persons, making it the largest labor organization in the nation. Nevertheless, the journeymen shoemakers were unable to protect their jurisdiction, and by 1878 the order had disappeared.

The organization of workers by trades nationally led to a renewed interest in forming a national federation of trade unions, but it was not until 1866 that such a federation materialized. In that year, representatives of a number of eight-hour leagues (groups supporting an eight-hour workday), trade assemblies, and national and local trade unions met in Baltimore as the National Labor Congress. There was considerable interest in getting legislation passed making an eight-hour workday standard, and a number of delegates urged the formation of a labor party to work to that end. Although this was not done, the National Labor Union (NLU) in which both local and national trade unions were represented was established. The National Labor Union supported the Greenback movement as a way of checking the decline in the price level and wages. Greenbacks were inconvertible paper currency (fiat money not convertible into gold) that had been used to help finance the Civil War. The continued use of such currency would presumably result in a rise in the general price level. This interest in monetary matters led to a drift away from pure trade unionism. A circular written by one of its leaders went so far as to declare that "when a just monetary system has been established, there will no longer exist a necessity for trade unions."[17]

The NLU represented a departure from the principles of pragmatic trade unionism and reinforced the opposition of many union leaders to reform movements and independent political action. This opposition was strengthened as a result of labor's unhappy involvement with the Greenback party following the panic of 1873. Unions had lost a great many members, and a number of nationals had gone out of existence. The failure to establish a more permanent organizational base led to attempts to launch a national federation, and when these proved unsuccessful, the Independent party—a farmers' party better known as the Greenback party—secured considerable union support. The party made a dismal showing in the presidential election of 1878, and this was considered further proof of the futility of independent political activity by organized labor. This period in the history of labor is referred to as one of "nationalization" not because of the abortive attempt to launch a national labor party but because of the growth both numerically and in terms of influence of national unions.

UNREST AND VIOLENCE

As we have mentioned, unions lost many of their members in the depression that followed the panic of 1873. Reductions in wages were widespread, unemployment was high, and in some cases unrest among workers led to civil disorders and criminal activity. Violence during the great railroad strike of 1877 resulted in the deployment of federal and state troops; in Pittsburgh, some 20 persons were killed and 29 seriously wounded when units of the state militia attempted to clear the tracks of the Pennsylvania Railroad. The militia was besieged in a roundhouse, and the railroad shop and many cars were fired by the mob. After the troops were ordered out of the city, the mob destroyed railroad property valued at some $5 million.[18]

In the anthracite regions of Pennsylvania, a secret organization known as the Molly Maguires attempted to assert control over miners and mine operations. The order did not hesitate to resort to violence and criminal actions. A Pinkerton operative was instrumental in its final defeat. He infiltrated its governing councils, became the secretary for his district, and when the loss of an anthracite strike resulted in an outburst of violence in 1875, he was able to present evidence on which many members were brought to trial. Twenty-four "Mollies" were convicted of criminal charges, and the order was crushed. Such militant and radical action created widespread antiunion sentiment, and the end of the decade found unions on the defensive.

THE KNIGHTS OF LABOR

The union movement in the 1870s still had no place for semiskilled and unskilled workers, nor was it an effective political force. This created discontent and unrest among many workers, particularly factory operatives, and led to brief flirtations with such radical philosophies as socialism, anarchism, and syndicalism. More significant however was the mushroomlike growth during the early eighties of what had been originally a secret organization, the Noble Order of the Knights of Labor. It was the conflict between the Knights, who had a very broad membership base, and the trade unions, whose jurisdictions were more clearly defined and much more restricted, that led eventually to the establishment of the American Federation of Labor.

The Knights of Labor was organized by nine Philadelphia tailors in 1869. The leader of the original membership, Uriah S. Stephens, had been educated for the ministry. He believed in the essential unity of all workers, and his goal was a single organization that would welcome all wage earners. The Knights developed a broad humanitarian reform program that failed to meet the more specialized interests of craft groups and led ultimately to the defection of most of its trade union membership. The leaders of the Knights were not advocates of direct economic action by workers, although, paradoxically, they were to lead some of the greatest strikes of the century.

Initially, workers in large cities were organized into local *trade assemblies* representing specific trades, but they soon began to be organized on a more general basis as mixed assemblies of workers from a variety of trades. After the panic of 1873, many surviving locals of defunct national unions joined the Knights; previously independent locals were also made welcome. *District assemblies* were formed that consisted of delegates from the local assemblies in a given region or within large cities. By 1878, there were some 9,000 members in 14 such assemblies, and the leadership of the Knights moved to establish a national organization. Early in 1878, a constitution was approved and a permanent central organization established. Local assemblies were to be " 'composed of not less then ten members at least three quarters of whom shall be wage earners.' " Any person over 18 who was " 'working for wages, or who at any time worked for wages' " could become a member, but " 'no person who either [sold], or [made] his living by the sale of, intoxicating drink . . . and no lawyer, doctor or banker' " could be admitted.[19] These provisions, which in effect made the Knights a single union to which almost all workers could belong, were responsible for its characterization as "one big union." The clause opening membership to persons other than wage earners enabled a large number of farmers to join the order, and it was ultimately taken over by agrarian interests.

The Knights emphasized education, mutual aid, and cooperation, and the preamble to its constitution stressed that the battle cry of the order must be "moral worth, not wealth, the true standard of individual and national greatness."[20] At the national level, the order was committed to political action; the local assemblies tended to stress direct economic action and to use strikes as a very effective weapon. In 1879, the secrecy of the order was abolished. In the same year, the national convention provided that district assemblies could be organized to control specific trades. This permitted national trade unions to be organized within the Knights. Membership expanded steadily, reaching a reported 52,000 by 1882.* During this period of early growth, Uriah Stephens was succeeded as Grand Master Workman (executive head of the Knights) by a younger man, Terence V. Powderly, then mayor of Scranton.

The Knights lacked both internal discipline and a sense of responsibility at the local level. The bulk of the membership consisted of unskilled and semi-skilled workers who had no prior history of organization, were unable to prosecute strikes effectively, and were easily replaced by strikebreakers. Thus, one of the

---

* This estimate, like later membership estimates, is suspect because of the considerable turnover in members.

order's greatest strengths—its attraction for the previously unorganized—was also a source of continued weakness. The failure of a telegraphers' strike in 1883 convinced the leaders of the order that continued growth would require a greater willingness to undertake direct economic action. Although the national trade unions had not previously felt menaced by the growth of the Knights, they were concerned over this development and urged the order to return to its "first principles" and leave " 'the management of strikes [and] aught else pertaining to wages and terms of labor' " to the unions.[21]

The unemployment and widespread cuts in wages that accompanied the depression of 1884–1885 created a fertile field for union organization among unskilled and semiskilled operatives who had been excluded from the national craft unions. The Knights were given an opportunity to capitalize on this situation as a result of a dispute on the Wabash Railroad, part of Jay Gould's Southwest System. In 1885, shopmen belonging to the order were discharged by the Wabash, and the Knights threatened to boycott all Wabash rolling stock, an action that would have affected over 20,000 miles of railroad. Gould apparently felt that he could not risk a strike and bowed to the realities of the situation; he "assured the Knights . . . that he believed in labour organisations and in the arbitration of all difficulties, and that he 'would always endeavor to do what was right.' "[22] This widely publicized capitulation resulted in a dramatic increase in the Knights' membership; within half a year, it rose from 150,000 to over 700,000. Unfortunately for the Knights, a second strike against the Gould system in 1886 proved to be the order's Waterloo. Gould was prepared for the strike, and his success encouraged widespread resistance to the order among employers.

The Knights then suffered a series of defeats, one of which, in the Chicago packinghouse dispute of 1886, demonstrated the danger inherent in the great centralization of control within the order. The packinghouse workers had secured an eight-hour day without a strike, after which their employers organized a packers' association. The association informed the workers that the packers would return to a ten-hour day, and when the employees refused to work the additional hours, they were locked out. It was generally believed that the workers were in a relatively strong position, but Powderly ordered the men back to work. The membership was demoralized, not only in Chicago but throughout the nation; it was a blow from which the Knights never recovered.

Other employer groups also took the offensive against organized labor. Previously negotiated trade agreements were ignored, and Pinkerton agents were hired to ferret out union agitators and act as strikebreakers. Lockouts were frequent and union men were blacklisted. By the middle of 1887, membership in the Knights had fallen to slightly over 500,000; "the Great Upheaval of the unskilled and semi-skilled portions of the working class had . . . subsided beneath the strength of the combined employers and the centralisation and unwieldiness of their own organisation."[23]

Meanwhile, the national trade unions, many of which had broken initially with the Knights in 1881 and completely severed relations with the order in 1886, successfully resisted the employers' antiunion campaign and demonstrated their superiority over the "one big union" form of organization. To understand this development, we must look at certain events that began in 1881, when a number of union leaders attempted to launch a permanent federation of national unions.

THE AMERICAN FEDERATION OF LABOR

The New Unionism

Membership in national unions had begun to increase following an upturn in business activity in 1879. New unions were formed, old ones were revived, and by 1886 the nationals had a membership of about 250,000. Most of these organizations were patterned on the "new unionism" of the cigar makers. In 1877, the cigar makers' union, a decentralized and undisciplined organization, had lost a strike against what was called the *tenement house system* of production. Adolph Strasser, president of the international, and Samuel Gompers, president of the New York local, then reorganized the union, using British trade unionism as a model. Control of the organization was centralized in the hands of the international, membership dues were increased, and a benefit system was set up to ensure a stable membership despite fluctuations in business activity.[24] In 1881, Peter J. McGuire organized the United Brotherhood of Carpenters and Joiners along similar lines.

All these men had socialist backgrounds, but as they became involved in the day-to-day problems of unionism, "the socialistic portion of their original philosophy kept receding . . . until they arrived at pure trade unionism."[25] This type of unionism became known as the *new unionism,* and later as *business unionism.* It was a pragmatic type of unionism, using strikes as its principal weapon and emphasizing short-run objectives. As Strasser told a Senate Committee in 1883, "We have no ultimate ends. We are going on from day to day. We are fighting only for immediate objects—objects that can be realised in a few years."[26] In contrast to earlier union movements, business unionism reflected "a philosophy of pure wage-consciousness." It was basically an opportunistic movement, "accepting the existence of capitalism and having for its object the enlarging of the bargaining power of the wage-earner in the sale of his labour."[27] The national unions of the 1880s were not however interested in organizing the unskilled; for such workers, the Knights of Labor was considered a more "appropriate" organization.

The Federation of Organized Trades and Labor Unions

Many union leaders believed that an organization of national unions would be advantageous, particularly from a political standpoint, but the first move in this direction proved premature. In August 1881, a National Federation of Organized Trades and Labor Unions was established at a convention in Pittsburgh. This federation was to be concerned primarily with the passage of labor legislation; when direct economic action was required, its constituent national unions were to act individually. It soon became evident however that the organization was ineffective on the legislative front; little could be accomplished on its annual budget of less than $700.

Meanwhile, as the Knights of Labor expanded its membership base, jurisdictional conflicts developed between the order and the established national unions. The pragmatic objectives of the new unionism also conflicted with the broad reform orientation of the Knights. An attempt by District Assembly 49 of New York City to extend its jurisdiction finally led to an open break between the Knights and the national unions.

The details of the dispute are complex. In 1882, the president of the cigar makers' union, Adolph Strasser, declared that the new president of Local 144, the New York local formerly headed by Samuel Gompers, was ineligible for that office. Socialist elements within the local then established a rival union that they called Progressive Union No. 1. District Assembly 49 of the Knights rallied to the support of this union, which grew rapidly, posing a serious threat to the old national. The Progressive Union ultimately took its 7,000 members into the Knights District Assembly as Local Assembly 2814. National trade union officials, convinced that the Knights were willing to destroy independent unions to expand their own membership, set out to establish a more effective federation of nationals.

The cigar makers sent Gompers as an emissary to other unions to encourage this enterprise, and as a result of his efforts, a group of national trade union leaders issued a call for a general trade union conference in Philadelphia in May of 1886. This conference asserted its conviction that trade unions "'should strictly preserve their distinct and individual autonomy.'"[28] A peace proposal was drawn up, but at a General Assembly in October of 1886, the Knights in effect issued a declaration of war that "furnished the last impetus necessary for the complete unification of the trade unions."[29]

December 1886

Since a conference of trade union officials had been scheduled to meet in Columbus in December 1886, the convention of the Federation of Organized Trades and Labor Unions was shifted to that city. The delegates to the convention attended the conference of trade union officials en masse, and on December 9, 1886, the conference declared itself the first annual convention of the American Federation of Labor (A.F. of L.). A committee then met with a committee chosen by the convention of the older federation, and the two organizations merged. After a further futile attempt to negotiate with the Knights, the convention condemned a number of actions of the order, called on "all workingmen to join the Unions of their respective trades, and [urged] the formation of National and International Unions and the centralisation of all under one head, the American Federation of Labor."[30] A drop in membership soon caused the Knights to adopt a more conciliatory attitude toward the trade unions, but this change came too late; the Knights continued to disintegrate, while the new federation slowly expanded its membership.

THE HAYMARKET SQUARE AFFAIR

An incident in Chicago prior to the formation of the A.F. of L.—the Haymarket Square Affair of 1886—not only added to the difficulties of the Knights but created a general atmosphere of hostility toward unions.[31] Chicago was a center of the eight-hour movement, which was supported locally by the Eight-Hour Association. It was also the home of a group of revolutionary socialists who believed in a mixture of anarchism and socialism known as the *Chicago Idea*. The labor arm of this group, in cooperation with the Eight-Hour Association, organized a strike on May 1, 1886. On May 3, a group of eight-hour strikers went to the McCormick Harvester works, which had been struck for several months, to heckle strikebreakers. Violence ensued, the police fired into the strikers, and at least four persons were killed. August Spies, a socialist leader, called a protest meeting for May 4 at Haymarket Square. Circulars proclaimed that "good speakers [would] be present to denounce the latest atrocious acts of the police, the shooting of our fellow-workmen," and urged the workers to "arm [them]-selves and appear in full force!"[32]

The protest meeting was attended by the mayor, who apparently found it peaceful. After he left, a detachment of 180 policemen marched to the square to break up the meeting. A bomb exploded in the middle of the policemen, wounding 66—seven of whom died—and the police opened fire, wounding or killing a number of workers. The incident was given wide publicity. Although anarchists were apparently to blame, the reputation of the union movement was blackened. The Knights had been one of the principal participants in the Chicago Eight-Hour Association, and this guilt by association contributed to the order's rapid decline.

THE EMERGING UNION MOVEMENT

The first century of trade unionism in the United States was characterized by a tentative acceptance and subsequent rejection of a variety of forms of economic and political action. The decline of the Knights of Labor and the success of the national unions in forging a permanent federation determined the character of the emerging union movement. The autonomous national union, adhering to the precepts of pragmatic business unionism, exercising exclusive jurisdiction in accordance with its federation charter, rejecting independent political action, and operating within the established institutional framework, became the vehicle by which organized labor in the United States would attempt to advance the job-related interests of workers.

The American Federation of Labor was at its founding—and the AFL-CIO continues to be—a loose confederation of autonomous unions jealously guarding their respective jurisdictions. The national unions exercised total control within these prescribed jurisdictions, much like the member states of the United Nations. The primary functions of the A.F. of L. were to charter national unions, to support appropriate legislation, and to resolve jurisdictional conflicts between the nationals. The federation could also request the support of the nationals for specific programs, such as the campaign for the eight-hour day. In all cases in which action by a national was required to implement a program, the federation was forced to rely on voluntary compliance. The only disciplinary measure available to it was to expel recalcitrant nationals, a solution that was neither palatable nor efficacious.

The national unions constituting the A.F. of L. were to prove both a strength and a weakness of American labor—a strength in that they brought permanence and stability to the union movement, and a weakness in that they denied a place in the house of organized labor to significant numbers of American workers. Most of the national unions were craft-type organizations, and this limited their potential for growth. The exclusive jurisdiction they enjoyed over certain trades operated to exclude unskilled and semiskilled workers from existing unions, particularly in manufacturing industries.

Although many of the early national unions were "pure" craft unions, admitting to membership only those working with specific tools or materials and having similar skills, this did not remain the dominant form of organization. By the turn of the century, most nationals had become amalgamations of several related crafts and had names such as the Brotherhood of Carpenters and Joiners. Some, like the Amalgamated Meat Cutters and Butcher Workmen, were quasi-industrial in character, admitting semiskilled as well as skilled workers. A few, such as the United Mine Workers and the Brewery Workers, were industrial unions.

Membership in *affiliated* unions grew modestly following the formation of the A.F. of L., rising from 150,000 in 1886 to 275,000 in 1892 and then stabilizing until 1897. There was some disagreement about the ability of business unions to withstand counterattacks from hostile employers. However, when Samuel Gompers at the A.F. of L. convention of 1892 posed the question, "Shall we change our methods?" he answered, to the satisfaction of the delegates, that while the trade unions had suffered some recent defeats this was not proof

> that the economic effort has been a failure, nor that the usefulness of the economic organisation is at an end. . . . [The fact that] the wage-workers of our country have maintained their organisations is the best proof of the power, influence and permanency of the trade unions. They have not been routed, they have merely retreated, and await a better opportunity to obtain the improved conditions which for a time they were deprived of.[33]

The panic and depression of 1893 demonstrated to Gompers that the union movement had come of age. In his report to the convention in that year, he noted with satisfaction that "while in every previous industrial crisis the trade unions were literally mowed down and swept out of existence, the unions now in existence have manifested, not only the powers of resistance, but of stability and permanency."[34]

DISCUSSION QUESTIONS

1. Why, if absolute union membership is growing, do union officials worry about a relative deterioration in their membership base?
2. Which of the principal variables discussed in the first section of the chapter do you believe are most significant today (this question anticipates the analysis in Chapter 13)?
3. When did collective bargaining as we presently think of it first develop in the United States?
4. Why did a politically-oriented labor movement fail to develop in the United States?
5. What is meant by the term "new unionism" as applied to the national unions which formed the American Federation of Labor?
6. Was the Knights of Labor basically a political or a union movement?
7. Do you believe that a federation such as the A.F. of L. would have developed in the absence of the threat posed by the Knights of Labor?
8. Karl Marx predicted that industrialization would lead to a revolution of the proletariat. Why did this prediction prove incorrect with respect to the United States?
9. Most of the national unions which formed the A.F. of L. were craft unions. How do you explain the absence of unions of unskilled and semiskilled workers?
10. What were the principal characteristics of "the emerging union movement" at the turn of the century?

SELECTED READINGS

The Beginnings of Unionism

Commons, John R., et al. *History of Labour in the United States*. 4 vols. New York: Macmillan, 1918, 1935. The standard early work.

Dulles, Foster Rhea. *Labor in America*. 3rd ed. New York: Crowell, 1966. A good general work.

Morris, Richard B., ed. *The U.S. Department of Labor Bicentennial History of the American Worker*. Washington, D.C.: U.S. Government Printing Office, 1976. Another good general work.

Rayback, Joseph B. *A History of American Labor, Expanded and Updated*. New York: Free Press, 1966.

Taft, Philip. *Organized Labor in American History*. New York: Harper & Row, 1964. Perhaps the best one-volume work on the subject.

The New York Times, Labor and Management. New York: Arno Press, 1973. Contains a selection of contemporary accounts from *The New York Times*.

Theories of Union Growth

Ashenfelter, Orley, and Pencavel, John H. "American Trade Union Growth: 1900–1960." In *Quarterly Journal of Economics* LXXXIII (August 1969): pp. 434–448. Quantitative data on the determinants of union growth.

Bernstein, Irving. "The Growth of American Unions, 1945–1960." In *Labor History* 2, no. 2 (Spring 1961): pp. 131–157. See also the "Comments" on Bernstein's article in *Labor History* 2, no. 3 (Fall 1961): pp. 361–380. Bernstein questions the causal role of cyclical fluctuations. In an earlier article ("The Growth of American Unions," in *The American Economic Review* XLIV, no. 3 [June 1954]) he argues that "membership is responsive to several forces and that the cycle does not predominate among them," [p. 310].

Blum, Albert A. "Why Unions Grow." In *Labor History* 9, no. 1 (Winter 1968): pp. 39–72.

Perlman, Mark. *Labor Union Theories in America.* New York: Harper & Row, 1958.

Shister, Joseph. "The Logic of Union Growth." In *Journal of Political Economy* LXI, no. 5 (October 1953): pp. 413–433.

Elements of Universality in the Labor Movement

Industrialism and Industrial Man Reconsidered. Final Report of the Inter-University Study of Labor Problems in Economic Development. Princeton, N.J.: 1975.

Kerr, Clark; Dunlop, John T.; Harbison, Frederick H.; and Myers, Charles A. *Industrialism and Industrial Man: The Problems of Labor and Management in Economic Growth.* New York: Oxford University Press, 1964.

Kerr, Clark, and Siegel, Abraham. "The Structuring of the Labor Force in Industrial Society: New Dimensions and New Questions." In *Industrial and Labor Relations Review* 8, no. 2 (January 1955): pp. 151–168.

National Unions

Ulman, Lloyd. *The Rise of the National Union.* Cambridge, Mass.: Harvard University Press, 1955. The standard reference.

Notes

1. Sidney and Beatrice Webb, *The History of Trade Unionism* (London: Longmans Green, new ed., 1920), p. 1.
2. Albert A. Blum, "Why Unions Grow," in *Labor History* 9, no. 1 (Winter 1968): pp. 47–48. Cf. Joseph Shister, "The Logic of Union Growth," in *Journal of Political Economy* LXI, no. 5 (October 1953): pp. 413–433.
3. John T. Dunlop, "The Development of Labor Organization: A Theoretical Framework," in Richard A. Lester and Joseph Shister, eds., *Insights into Labor Issues* (New York: Macmillan, 1948), p. 176.
4. David Saposs places "the first authentic organisation of a single trade and the first strike of wage-earners in the year 1786 . . . at Philadelphia." (David J. Saposs, "Colonial and Federal Beginnings," in John R. Commons et al., *History of Labour in the United States* [New York: Macmillan, 1918], I, p. 25).

5. Ibid., p. 86.
6. Ibid., p. 125.
7. Ibid., p. 156.
8. John R. Commons et al., eds., *A Documentary History of American Industrial Society* (Cleveland, Ohio: Arthur H. Clark, 1910), VI, p. 77.
9. Helen L. Sumner, "Citizenship," in Commons et al., *History of Labour in the United States,* I, p. 218.
10. John R. Commons, "Introduction," in Commons et al., *History of Labour in the United States,* I, p. 12.
11. See Henry E. Hoagland, "Humanitarianism," in Commons et al., *History of Labour in the United States,* I, pp. 485–623.
12. Ibid., p. 575.
13. Vernon H. Jensen, "Notes on the Beginnings of Collective Bargaining," in *Industrial and Labor Relations Review* 9, no. 2 (January 1956): pp. 225–234.
14. John B. Andrews, "Nationalisation," in Commons et al., *History of Labour in the United States,* II, pp. 43–45.
15. Lloyd Ulman, *The Rise of the National Union* (Cambridge, Mass.: Harvard University Press, 1955), pp. 44–45.
16. Ibid., p. 33.
17. Quoted in Andrews, "Nationalisation," p. 130.
18. See Samuel Yellen, *American Labor Struggles,* chap. I, "The Railroad Uprisings of 1877" (New York: Harcourt Brace & World, 1936).
19. Selig Perlman, "Upheaval and Reorganisation," in Commons et al., *History of Labour in the United States,* II, pp. 337–338.
20. Ibid., p. 335.
21. Ibid., p. 353, quoting the *National Labor Tribune.*
22. Ibid., p. 369.
23. Ibid., p. 423.
24. Ibid., pp. 306–307.
25. Ibid., p. 308.
26. Testimony before the Senate Committee on Education and Labor, cited in ibid., p. 309. Some of the earlier national unions, notably the National Typographical Union, had developed "pure" trade union policies, but it was not until the 1880s that "business unionism" became a generally accepted organizational pattern. (Cf. Philip Taft, *The A.F. of L. in the Time of Gompers* [New York: Harper & Brothers, 1957], pp. 2–3.)
27. Perlman, "Upheaval and Reorganisation," p. 308.
28. Cited ibid., p. 404.
29. Ibid., p. 409.
30. Ibid., p. 411.
31. The details of the Haymarket affair are drawn largely from Samuel Yellen, "Haymarket," chap. II in *American Labor Struggles,* and Henry David, *The History of the Haymarket Affair,* 2nd ed. (New York: Russell & Russell, 1958).
32. The circular is reproduced in Yellen, *American Labor Struggles,* p. 53.
33. Quoted in Perlman, "Upheaval and Reorganisation," pp. 449–500.
34. Quoted in ibid., p. 501. Cf. Ulman, *Rise of the National Union,* pp. 4 and 6.

Chapter 12
HISTORY OF UNIONISM II: THE THIRD HALF-CENTURY, HOMESTEAD STRIKE TO WORLD WAR II

We have seen how, with the formation of the American Federation of Labor, the final character and structure of the American union movement was established. Prior to 1898 however, membership in the A.F. of L. and in other unaffiliated unions grew slowly. Important elements in the business community opposed the spread of unions, and these elements were often able to rely on government support. Four developments in particular made union organizational activities and the use of such economic weapons as strikes and boycotts hazardous. First, the growth of large manufacturing firms (many of which were now corporations) meant that the unions faced adversaries financially able to withstand long strikes. Second, such firms could take effective countermeasures against union organizers. Blacklists and the use of strikebreakers were particularly effective in undermining union support. Third, the courts' interpretation of antitrust legislation as applicable to union activities made strikes and boycotts in restraint of trade subject to injunctive relief. Participants in such activities could also be sued for damages or prosecuted as criminals. Finally, public opinion was at best neutral, and often openly antagonistic, to unions.

Two classic union-management disputes illustrate the powerful forces aligned against the unions: the strike at the Homestead Mills of the Carnegie Steel Company in 1892 and the Pullman strike of 1894.

WARFARE ALONG THE MONONGAHELA

In 1892, Henry Clay Frick (the "Coke King") was in charge of negotiations for a new contract at the Homestead Mills. Frick had an antilabor reputation and had "crushed several strikes by means of the Coal and Iron Police, the Pinkerton Detective Agency, and the state militia."[1] The existing agreement with the skilled workers, represented by the Amalgamated Association of Iron and Steel Workers, was due to expire June 30, and after several months of fruitless negotiations, the company announced that if its proposed new wage scale was not accepted by June 29, the men would be dealt with only as individuals. Negotiations collapsed, on June 28 the company began to shut down, and by June 30 the entire work force had been locked out.

The 3,000 mechanics and unskilled laborers employed by the Homestead Mills decided to support the 800 members of the Iron and Steel Workers Association, and a security system was established to warn of any influx of strikebreakers or "black sheep." When the company sent a force of Pinkerton detectives to seize the mills and provide protection for strikebreakers, the result was a primitive version of modern amphibious warfare. During the night of July 5, 300 armed Pinkerton men proceeded up the Monongahela River in two barges drawn by steamboats. The barges were sighted by a strikers' picket boat the following morning, and a pitched battle ensued. It ended with the surrender of the Pinkertons, who were sent back to Pittsburgh by train. Three Pinkerton men and seven workers were killed and many wounded.

The Pennsylvania state militia established martial law in Homestead on July 12, and the company was then able to import black sheep. The union's position deteriorated further when a young anarchist, Alexander Berkman, seriously wounded Frick in his Pittsburgh office. The incident was given wide publicity, and by the middle of October it was apparent to the strikers that defeat was inevitable. The laborers and mechanics voted to return to work in November, and shortly thereafter the Homestead lodges of the Iron and Steel Workers Association allowed their members to return also. The union was eliminated from most of the steel mills in the Pittsburgh region and lost a great deal of prestige nationally as well. The dispute demonstrated that a large corporation supported by local and state authorities and willing to endure a long struggle could successfully oppose a powerful and well-organized union.

THE PULLMAN STRIKE

The usefulness of legal devices in defeating unions was demonstrated during the Pullman strike of 1894.[2] In 1893, Eugene V. Debs, a charter member of the Brotherhood of Locomotive Firemen and later associate editor of their journal, organized the American Railway Union (ARU) on an industrial base. Debs was dissatisfied with the leadership and craft consciousness of the railroad operating brotherhoods, which did not admit unskilled workers as members, and he sought to unify all the railroad workers. He was an effective leader, and within a year the ARU had 150,000 members.

The Pullman Palace Car Company owned a few miles of railroads, and its employees were eligible for membership in the new union. The company had cut wages after the depression of 1893, but rents had not been reduced on the company-owned houses in Pullman, Illinois. These actions and the authoritarian shop practices of the company helped the ARU to organize some 4,000 employees in the corporation's manufacturing facility at Pullman during the spring of 1894. The newly organized workers selected a grievance committee that met with management in early May to demand a reduction in rents, the investigation and correction of shop abuses, and the restoration of wages to their former level. Three members of the grievance committee were promptly discharged. Although these men may have been laid off as part of a normal reduction in the work force, "the employees impulsively rejected this explanation and characterized the affair as an act of bad faith,"[3] and on May 11 the plant was struck. The Pullman Company then posted a notice that the plant was closed indefinitely.

After unsuccessfully attempting to induce the company to mediate the dispute, the union announced that failure to accept mediation by June 26 would result in a boycott—the union would refuse to handle Pullman cars on any railroad for which its members worked. The company refused to negotiate, and the railroads ordered the discharge of any man who refused to switch Pullman cars. Since the other members of a train crew would refuse to work whenever a switchman was discharged, the boycott was converted into a strike.

By the end of June, Pullman travel out of Chicago was paralyzed and the strike had spread to railroads in other areas. The press was unsympathetic to the union's position. *Harper's Weekly*, for example, declared that the boycott and strike constituted "an attempt at blackmail on the largest scale," and that in "suppressing such a . . . conspiracy . . . the nation is fighting for its own existence just as truly as in suppressing the great rebellion."[4]

In July, the railroads attached mail cars to Pullman trains so that a refusal to handle them interfered with the movement of the mail. At the urging of the railroad General Managers' Association, the U.S. marshal in Chicago then requested that federal troops be sent to protect the mails. Although neither Governor John Altgeld nor the Illinois state legislature supported this request, four companies of the 15th Infantry were sent to Chicago on July 4. Violence spread, and state militias were ordered to duty in various cities throughout the nation. Meanwhile, on July 2, the Department of Justice secured an injunction restraining Debs and all members of the ARU from interfering with the movement of the mail, with interstate commerce, or with the business of 23 named railroads. This was the first important use of an injunction in a labor dispute in the United States.

On July 10, Debs was indicted for conspiracy and arrested. After his release on bail, he attempted to call a general strike in Chicago, but it was not supported by other unions. A.F. of L. affiliates and the Railroad Brotherhoods engaged in what were in effect strikebreaking activities. The strikers became discouraged and disorganized, and Debs was arrested for contempt of court. He was convicted, and eventually his conviction was upheld by the Supreme Court. When a convention of the ARU was summoned to call off the strike, only 53 delegates attended. The union had been crushed.

THE TURN-OF-THE-CENTURY HONEYMOON AND ITS AFTERMATH

Despite these and other setbacks during the early 1890s, overall union membership remained stable in poor years and grew slightly in more prosperous ones. Total union membership rose from some 400,000 in 1890 to 450,000 in 1897.* It then began to increase more rapidly, partly because of a shift in the tactics of a number of large corporations. Rather than adamantly opposing unions, these companies decided to try to "live with them." They hoped that trade agreements (contracts arrived at by collective bargaining) would eliminate strikes and work rules that restricted output and lead to industrial peace. The resulting "honeymoon" between capital and organized labor led to a quadrupling of union membership, from 450,000 in 1897 to over two million in 1904. During this period also, some 92 new national unions were chartered.

Unfortunately, the honeymoon did not last. As early as 1902, many employers, disillusioned or unimpressed with the attempt to coexist with unions, became vigorous advocates of the *open shop*. Employment in an open shop was supposedly available (open) to both union and nonunion workers on equal terms. In practice, an open shop was usually a nonunion shop. This movement assumed a national character in 1903 when D. M. Parry, president of the National Association of Manufacturers (NAM), persuaded the organization to formally oppose the recognition of unions. The NAM, which had previously been uninterested in labor matters, then "assumed the leadership in the nation-wide resistance to unionism."[5]

In October 1903, the Citizens Industrial Association was formed with Parry as Chairman. It "attacked the closed shop as being contrary to the principles of American government and institutions" and declared that " 'the time has come when the employing interests and good citizenship of the country must take immediate and effective measures to reaffirm and enforce those fundamental principles of American government guaranteeing free competitive conditions.' "[6] The open shop movement was also supported by prominent educators and clergymen.[7] Due in part to the success of this movement and in part to the defeats administered to unions by large corporations such as U.S. Steel, the upward trend in membership was checked. It remained stable at about two million from 1904 until 1910.

---

* This figure includes membership in unions not affiliated with the A.F. of L.

UNION GAINS—AND LOSSES

In a number of industries, including transportation, printing, the building trades, and coal mining, unions made substantial permanent gains in membership during the period described above. As a result, they became and remained centers of power within the A.F. of L.

The United Mine Workers of America (UMW), an early industrial union with jurisdiction over all coal mine workers, gained recognition in the bituminous coalfields in 1897, and this led to the establishment in 1898 of the *central competitive field system,* a system of regional bargaining based on " 'correct business ideas, competitive equality and . . . well recognized principles of justice.' "[8] Organizing workers in the anthracite coalfields was more difficult, but following strikes in 1900 and 1902, the mine workers there achieved what was once described as "labor's greatest tactical success." (During the 1902 strike, President George Baer of the Philadelphia and Reading Coal Company wrote a classic letter that assured the recipient that " '[t]he rights and interests of the laboring man will be protected and cared for, not by the labor agitators, but by the Christian men to whom God in His infinite wisdom, has given control of the property interests of the country.' "[9]

During the early 1900s, the building trades unions gained members steadily, particularly in the larger cities, and were able to present a united front to their employers through local *building trades councils.* A successful start was also made in organizing the garment industries. Locals were established in the ladies' garment industry by 1909, and the men's clothing union was recognized in the Chicago market in 1910. Unlike most national unions, the unions in the garment industries were organized on an industrial base.

Unions in the steel industry met a series of major defeats in the first decade of the twentieth century. After the formation of the United States Steel Corporation in 1901, the Amalgamated Association of Iron and Steel Workers faced a formidable rival. The Homestead defeat had seriously weakened the union, which at that time had only half as many members as it had in 1891. Moreover, the union leadership failed to adjust to changes within the industry. It ignored the interests of the rapidly growing proportion of less skilled and unskilled workers, and it continued to oppose or limit technological innovation despite the successful introduction of new production processes. Fearing that unless it controlled all U.S. Steel's mills it would be at a grave disadvantage (since it would be unable to prevent struck work from being done in a different plant), the union attempted to deal with the mills as a single unit. The company refused to bargain on that basis, and after prolonged negotiations a strike was called in August of 1901. Strikebreakers were imported, the union's position deteriorated, and a settlement was finally reached under which the union lost its power to represent workers in 14 mills and agreed not to seek to extend its influence.

The company continued to oppose the union, and on June 1, 1909, after posting a notice of reductions in wages, it announced that henceworth the remaining unionized mills would be open shops. Again, a strike was called, but it was unsuccessful. The Iron and Steel Workers Union was eliminated from all U.S. Steel plants, and "the . . . Corporation [became] an absolute government as far as labor was concerned."[10] U.S. Steel's antiunion stance also provided a model for other large corporations.

THE RISE AND FALL OF THE IWW

The continued failure of the American Federation of Labor and most of its affiliated unions to meet the organization needs of unskilled and semiskilled workers contributed to the rise of a radical labor organization that enjoyed a well-publicized·though brief success prior to World War I. The Industrial Workers of the World (IWW), whose members were known as Wobblies, was organized in 1905 at a Chicago convention termed the Continental Congress of the Working Class. Formed by a number of groups, including the militant Western Federation of Miners, the American Labor Union, and the Socialist Trade and Labor Alliance, the IWW was openly dualistic. It believed in the "one big union" principle and encouraged unions to secede from the "American Separation of Labor." It was committed to a program of revolutionary action and appealed particularly to certain unskilled workers in the West—lumber workers, migratory agricultural workers, construction workers, and miners. In addition, it enjoyed considerable success in organizing immigrant factory operatives in the East, where it was involved in several notable strikes, including a successful strike against the American Woolen Company in Lawrence, Massachusetts, in 1912, and an unsuccessful strike against the Paterson, New Jersey, silk mills in 1913.

The IWW was not interested in establishing permanent collective bargaining relationships, but in revolutionary action, and it failed to develop a broad appeal for American workers. It opposed World War I, and when it continued to do so after the United States' involvement, federal and state authorities moved against the organization. By the middle of the 1920s, it was moribund.

VOLUNTARISM

Throughout this period, the American Federation of Labor continued to adhere to the principle of *voluntarism,* which rejected both government involvement in labor problems and independent political activity by organized labor. Although it supported child labor laws and hours and wages legislation for female workers, the federation's leadership believed that direct economic action was a better way of advancing the interests of wage earners. In their view, legislation posed a threat to unions, making them less necessary from the workers' standpoint. Federation leaders also feared, correctly as it later turned out, that government intervention might lead to the regulation of unions and of the collective bargaining process.

In supporting the concept of a viable union movement that did not rely upon the state, Gompers became an adamant foe of the socialists. After the formation of the A.F. of L., a number of socialist leaders within the federation rejected the tenets of business unionism and tried to convert the federation into a political instrumentality. These attempts were thwarted by Gompers, McGuire, and Strasser, the conservative faction achieving a noteworthy victory at the 1894 convention. The socialists then combined with supporters of a rival candidate from the mine workers union to defeat Gompers's bid for reelection to the presidency of the A.F. of L., the only defeat he suffered within the organization until his death in 1924. When a later attempt was made to commit the federation to a socialist program, he reiterated his opposition in a much-quoted address to the 1903 convention:

> "I want to tell you Socialists, that I have studied your philosophy, read your works upon economics . . . and watched the work of your movement the world over. I have kept close watch upon your doctrines for thirty years; . . . and know what you think and what your propose. . . . I am not only at variance with your doctrines, but with your philosophy. Economically, you are unsound; socially, you are wrong; and industrially you are an impossibility."[11]

THE UNIONS DURING WORLD WAR I

During World War I, economic and political conditions favored union growth. The high level of business activity created a tight labor market, and the Wilson administration was known to be friendly to labor. The union movement did suffer some setbacks in this period—the Clayton Act, for example, which had been acclaimed the Magna Carta of American labor, failed to free labor from the threat of federal injunctions and damage suits under the Sherman Act. The environment however was one in which union organization could go forward, and total membership rose from 2.1 million (5.6 percent of the civilian labor force) in 1910 to 3 million (7.5 percent of the civilian labor force) in 1917. It reached over 5 million (12 percent of the civilian labor force) in 1920.[12]

The policies and spirit of the A.F. of L. remained basically unchanged between 1912 and 1920. The federation's leadership accepted the autonomous national union as the epitome of sound unionism, failed to devote much time or money to organizing the semiskilled and unskilled workers in manufacturing, and avoided political commitments. This helps to explain the character of the increase in union membership during this time. Growth tended to be permanent in those crafts, occupations, and industries in which a tradition of unionism existed, but temporary when workers were organized under the stimulus of government wartime policies that encouraged collective bargaining.

Before we entered the war, the government had acted to ensure an uninterrupted high level of production. A nationwide railroad strike was avoided when President Woodrow Wilson secured the passage of the Adamson Act, granting an eight-hour day to the operating brotherhoods, and in March of 1917, the President secured a pledge of support from trade union leaders. In return, they were recognized as spokesmen for all of labor and given a voice in the administration of the various boards dealing with the labor aspects of national defense. After we entered the war, a labor-management "truce" was effected under which there were to be no strikes and lockouts and management accepted the principle of collective bargaining.

The government's basic wartime labor policy was developed by the War Labor Conference Board and implemented by the National War Labor Board, created to settle disputes that threatened to interrupt production. The following principles were recognized:

1. Workers had the right to organize in trade unions and to bargain collectively through chosen representatives.
2. Employers had the right to organize in associations or groups and to bargain collectively through chosen representatives.
3. Employers should not discharge workers for membership in trade unions or for legitimate trade union activities.
4. The workers, in the exercise of their right to organize, should not use coercion to induce people to join their organizations or to induce employers to deal with them.[13]

These principles constituted the first formal general endorsement at the federal level of collective bargaining as the preferred method of resolving labor disputes.

The War Labor Board evolved a number of operational practices that were later adopted during the New Deal, including reinstatement with back pay in cases of unfair discrimination against employees, the prohibition of blacklists, recognition that peaceful striking did not prejudice reemployment, and the use of the secret ballot to determine employee representatives for the purpose of collective bargaining. Although it relied primarily on the voluntary cooperation of management and labor, the board was remarkably successful in preventing work stoppages. During its 16-month existence, it was defied in only three cases, once by a union and twice by employers.

THE IMMEDIATE POSTWAR PERIOD

After the armistice, President Wilson convened a conference of representatives of employers, organized labor, and the public to evolve principles that would serve as the basis for a national collective bargaining policy in peacetime. Most companies were anxious to end recognition of the unions with which they had been encouraged to bargain during the war, and the employer and union representatives were unable to reach an agreement. A second conference also failed to produce an agreement.

Public opinion at the time was not supportive of unionism. The Bolshevik Revolution, the wartime excesses of the IWW, the failure of the socialists to support the war effort, and the general industrial unrest that followed the armistice (including general strikes in Seattle and Winnipeg) contributed to the hostility toward unions. The Boston police strike of 1919 dramatized the presumed threat to established institutions. When city officials attempted to recruit a volunteer force to replace the strikers, President Lowell of Harvard urged his students to heed the call to duty. Gompers asked Governor Calvin Coolidge to remove the police commissioner, and the taciturn governor was catapulted to fame when he rejected the request, declaring that "there is no right to strike against the public safety by anybody, anywhere, anytime." Disclosures of graft and racketeering involving building trades and service unions in a number of cities also discredited the union movement.

THE AMERICAN PLAN

By associating trade unionism with radicalism, employers were able to gain public support for a drive against the unions. This opposition took the form of an extremely effective open shop campaign, the *American Plan,* which resembled the open shop movement of the first decade of the century. There was a conscious appeal for support on patriotic grounds; the campaign "was designed to display as its objective the return to time hallowed American principles, the inalienable right of every American to enter any trade or business he chose, to accept employment under conditions satisfactory to himself without interference from the union business agent."[14]

Ostensibly, the plan advocated the abolition of the purportedly un-American closed shop, but for many employers, the real objective was the elimination of unions from their plants. The country was soon blanketed with open shop organizations, and within a few years, unions in the printing trades, the packinghouses, the steel mills, the garment trades, the textile industry, and even such strongholds as the San Francisco building industry had fallen before the open shop campaign. The postwar depression provided an opportunity to institute wage cuts and to otherwise whittle away gains for which the unions had taken credit, and this contributed to the decline in union membership. Total membership fell from a postwar high of over 5 million to 4 million in 1922 and to 3.5 million in 1924. It is estimated that some 65 percent of the A.F. of L.'s membership losses between 1920 and 1923 occurred in unions that had expanded during the wartime labor-management truce.[15]

The antiunion campaign received an assist from the Railroad Labor Board. During the war, the government had taken over the railroads, and all the railroad unions, including the weak shop crafts, had been recognized as collective bargaining agents. This resulted in a substantial increase in their membership. At the end of the war, the railroads were returned to their owners, and the industry was regulated under the Transportation Act of 1920, which established the tripartite Railroad Labor Board, with jurisdiction over labor relations.

Following the depression of 1921, the railroads sought to cut wages, and in June of 1921, the labor board ordered wage reductions for both operating and nonoperating personnel. In March of 1922, the roads sought a further wage cut, and the wages of *nonoperating* personnel, including the shop crafts, were reduced.

The shop crafts called a strike, and the board threatened the strikers with loss of seniority unless they returned to work. The men continued to strike but got no support from the operating brotherhoods, and they returned to work on the basis of separate settlements with the individual railroads. Under some of these settlements, notably that with the Pennsylvania Railroad, outside unions were driven out of the railroad shops and 175,000 of the 400,000 workers who had struck were forced to join company unions.[16]

During the national election of 1924, the executive council of the A.F. of L. broke with its tradition of voluntarism to endorse Robert M. LaFollette, the presidential candidate of a third party, the Conference for Progressive Political Action. LaFollette carried only his home state of Wisconsin, and after the election the A.F. of L. reembraced the principle of rewarding its friends and punishing its enemies within the established two-party system.

THE RAILWAY LABOR ACT

The threat to the public welfare represented by strikes on the nation's railroads was considered intolerable, and it was evident that legislation would be passed establishing some mechanism for resolving labor disputes. Both the railroads and the rail unions wanted legislation with which they could live, and they cooperated in producing the *Railway Labor Act of 1926*. The act, which is discussed in more detail in Chapters 16 and 18, protected the right of railway employees to engage in collective bargaining and established formal procedures for resolving primary disputes (disputes over the terms of contracts). Passed during a Republican administration, the act represented the first *statutory* approval at the federal level of the principle of collective bargaining.

WELFARE CAPITALISM

During the 1920s, many employers competed with unions for the loyalty and support of their employees through employee representation plans, company unions (which are to be distinguished from independent unions confined to the employees of a single firm), and a variety of "welfare" devices, including formal benefit plans and profit sharing and bonus programs. These were part of a movement that has since been termed *welfare capitalism*. Many were bona fide human relations programs instituted by employers who recognized that an increasingly depersonalized industrial system that paid little heed to the needs of workers as human beings could not be considered completely successful. Others were simply watered-down substitutes for "outside" unionism. Simultaneously, scientific management, with its paraphernalia of time and motion studies, incentive systems, systematic upgrading, and a new—if at times obscure—vocabulary, became fashionable.

Welfare capitalism and the higher standard of living realized by most wage earners during the twenties would have made life difficult for even the most energetic union organizer, and the leadership of the A.F. of L. was far from energetic. William Green, who became president of the federation after the death of Gompers in 1924, perpetuated the fainthearted complacency that had characterized his predecessor's later years. Green urged business to accept unions as partners in production so that the unions could cooperate with management to their mutual advantage. Speaking at the Harvard Business School in 1925, he declared that " '[t]he antagonistic and hostile attitude, so characteristic of the older order in industry, must be supplanted by a friendly relationship and a sense of obligation and responsibility.' "[17] This kind of "spiritually defeated unionism" produced few new members. Company unions on the other hand continued to prosper and by 1926 had a membership of almost 1.4 million.[18]

The failure to mount a more effective organizational effort and the pro-management character of the "new concept" of unionism can be attributed partly to an ideological split in the labor movement. The Communists, under William Z. Foster, had formed the Trade Union Educational League and attempted to seize control of the union movement by "boring from within." Faced with a choice between radicalism and conservatism, the liberals within the union movement, who might otherwise have provided more vigorous leadership, supported federation policies.

During earlier periods of prosperity, wages had often failed to keep abreast of the rising cost of living, and this "wage lag" had been used as an effective argument in support of unions. There was no wage lag in the twenties; the full-time equivalent annual earnings of nonfarm workers rose steadily after 1922, while the index of consumer prices declined after 1926, primarily because of a drop in the prices of farm products.[19] Union membership, in contrast to previous experience, declined somewhat during the prosperity of the 1920s, going from 3.5 million (7.9 percent of the civilian labor force) in 1924 to 3.4 million (7 percent of the civilian labor force) in 1929.[20]

As is the case today, not everyone shared in the "new" prosperity. Shorter workweeks, higher pay, and improved benefit programs meant little to the unemployed, and unemployment was substantial for most of the decade. Estimates are that unemployment in nonagricultural industries reached at least 7.7 percent in 1924, 5.7 percent in 1925, 5.2 percent in 1926, and 6.3 percent in 1927. Seasonal and technological unemployment both increased; 1 million of the 3.3 million workers who lost their jobs between 1920 and 1929 because of technological changes remained without work.[21]

In the absence of current data, the extent of unemployment went unrecognized. The standard of living of those with jobs was rising, and an increasing variety of consumer goods and services poured from the cornucopia of American capitalism. National output, manufacturing production in particular, soared to new heights. Optimism spread throughout the business community, and speculative fever gripped the nation. Continuing prosperity was viewed not as the crest of an upward movement of business activity, but as a firm basis on which the American economy would build and progress. Herbert Hoover, in accepting the

Republican nomination for the presidency in 1928, reflected this innocent enthusiasm:

> "We in America today are nearer to the final triumph over poverty than ever before in the history of any land. . . . We have not yet reached the goal, but, given a chance to go forward with the policies of the last eight years, we shall soon, with the help of God, be in sight of the day when poverty will be banished from this nation. There is no guaranty against poverty equal to a job for every man."[22]

THE GREAT CRASH

During the initial months of his administration, Hoover's vision appeared to be correct. The big bull market in stocks soared on. It is difficult to recapture the feeling of security and confidence that prevailed in 1929. Signs of weakness in the economy were consistently ignored. A break in the stock market early in September was discounted in most circles. The *Boston News' Bureau's* "Broad Street Gossip," for example, asserted that " 'the recent break makes a firm foundation for a big bull market in the last quarter of the year.' "[23] The recovery did not materialize. On "Black Thursday," October 24, stock prices declined sharply. Worse followed on Tuesday, October 29, when, on a volume of over 16 million shares, *The New York Times* index of the average prices of 50 leading stocks dropped nearly 40 points. Security prices continued to fall, and the financial crisis was soon reflected in commodity and other markets. The *Great Depression* had arrived.

The most significant impact of the Depression on the labor force was the increase in the number of persons unemployed. Table 12.1 suggests both the magnitude and the persistence of unemployment, which peaked at 24.9 percent

Table 12.1 AVERAGE ANNUAL UNEMPLOYMENT IN THE CIVILIAN LABOR FORCE, 1929–1939

YEAR	NUMBER UNEMPLOYED (IN THOUSANDS)	PERCENTAGE OF CIVILIAN LABOR FORCE
1929	1,550	3.2
1930	4,340	8.7
1931	8,020	15.9
1932	12,060	23.6
1933	12,830	24.9
1934	11,340	21.7
1935	10,610	20.1
1936	9,030	16.9
1937	7,700	14.3
1938	10,390	19.0
1939	9,480	17.2

SOURCE: U.S. Department of Labor, Bureau of Labor Statistics, *The American Workers' Fact Book, 1960*, Table 15, p. 71.

in 1933. In contrast, only 6.8 percent of the civilian labor force were unemployed during the sharp economic downturn in 1958; 5.9 percent were unemployed during the "Nixon recession" of 1971; and 7.8 percent were unemployed when President Carter was inaugurated.

It gradually became clear that more than a chronological decade had ended. The depression into which the nation sank in the 1930s was to have a profound and lasting impact on the American people, who "found themselves living in an altered world which called for new adjustments, new ideas, new habits of thought, and a new order of values."[24] The events of the period were difficult for workers to comprehend. Having been told that the American enterprise system assured them of an ever rising standard of living and that welfare capitalism was a guarantee of economic security, they were both frustrated and disillusioned. The business community was unable to regain their confidence or support. As the Depression deepened and the number of unemployed continued to mount, dissatisfaction and disillusionment became more widespread and the demand for corrective action more intense. Politically, the response was the election of Franklin D. Roosevelt by an overwhelming majority; economically, it assumed the form of a multitude of often conflicting proposals. On the union front, the immediate result was a decline in membership, particularly in the building trades and transportation.

Few expected the Depression years to be a time of rebirth and revitalization for the union movement. However, the initial decline in membership proved far less drastic than in previous depressions. Membership soon began to stabilize and then to increase, rising from a low of slightly under 3 million members (5.8 percent of the civilian labor force) in 1933 to an estimated 8 million members (14.6 percent of the civilian labor force) in 1940.[25] Union membership continued to grow significantly both absolutely and relatively during World War II; and by 1945, it had reached 13.4 million (24.8 percent of the civilian labor force).[26]

Two disparate factors stemmed the initial decline in membership during the Depression. First, the majority of workers were organized in craft or quasi-craft unions. Such workers recognize their common interests and are more likely to remain union members when they are unemployed. Second, in many plants, unskilled and semiskilled workers organized spontaneously into industrial unions, seeing in such action their only hope of "beating the system." Thus, the Depression achieved what the craft conscious and cautious leaders of the A.F. of L. had been unwilling to attempt—the organization of many semiskilled and unskilled workers in mass production industries.

Subsequent union growth was encouraged by changes in the political environment, particularly by legislation guaranteeing workers the right to organize and to bargain collectively, and by the competition for members between the A.F. of L. and a new rival federation, the Congress of Industrial Organizations (CIO). Initially, the A.F. of L. refused to support various forms of government intervention in economic affairs. It refused at its conventions in 1930 and 1931 to support unemployment compensation legislation, and it was "officially" neutral during the 1932 election. However, as the Depression deepened and unemployment rose, the unions turned, often hesitantly, to the federal government for help. This reexamination of organized labor's basic opposition to government intervention was perhaps "the most significant long-term effect of the Great Depression upon the labor movement."[27]

Irrespective of the political philosophy of the party in power in Washington and the quality of its leadership, fundamental changes in the character of the American trade union movement were inevitable. The Great Depression "brought to a head long-run, cumulative changes in the attitudes and viewpoints of the working class in the United States."[28] However, specific responses were conditioned by contemporary events. The dramatic developments that transformed the American union movement cannot be divorced from the New Deal and the personality of its principal architect, Franklin D. Roosevelt. Although Roosevelt considered himself a friend of labor, the new administration was not initially concerned with the special problems of *organized* labor. Collective bargaining was not mentioned in the Democratic platform of 1932, and when Secretary of Labor Frances Perkins outlined her program, "a collective bargaining policy was notably absent, for [she] had little confidence in the union movement as an instrument of social advancement."[29]

SECTION 7(a) AND THE WAGNER ACT

The first significant New Deal legislation affecting union-management relations was included in the National Industrial Recovery Act (NIRA) as the price of union support for the act. This act, passed on June 16, 1933, to stimulate business and reduce unemployment, provided for industrial self-regulation through what were called *Recovery Codes.* According to section 7(a) of the act, all NIRA codes and agreements were to provide "that employees shall have the right to organize and bargain collectively through representatives of their own choosing" and "that no employee and no one seeking employment shall be required as a condition of employment to join any company union or to refrain from joining, organizing, or assisting a labor organization of his own choosing." In addition, employers subject to a code had to comply with prescribed maximum hours, minimum wages, and other conditions of employment.

The passage of the act signaled the start of one of the most significant eras in the history of American unionism. Although a major A.F. of L. organizing campaign did not develop immediately, the more dynamic nationals within the federation launched intensive membership drives under the protection presumably afforded by the act. The garment unions and the United Mine Workers, for example, made substantial gains within the year. There was also a considerable "natural" increase in union membership, often as a result of spontaneous organization at the local level in the mass production industries. Many workers joined "federal" labor unions, which were industrial-type unions attached directly to the A.F. of L. In most cases, an existing national union did not have jurisdiction over all the workers in such a local.

Many employers refused to cooperate with or to obey the boards set up to administer the labor provisions of the NIRA, and membership in company unions doubled as firms attempted to combat "outside" unionism. More important in the long run, conflict developed within the A.F. of L. over which type of union was most appropriate for workers in the mass production industries. The overt opposition of employers to the basic principles of section 7(a) was ultimately overcome by legislative and judicial action. The controversy over union structure led to a division within the house of labor that was not healed until 1955.

In 1934, Senator Robert Wagner had proposed additional legislation to curb specific employer practices that violated the spirit of section 7(a), and shortly after the Supreme Court declared the NIRA unconstitutional in 1935, Congress passed the National Labor Relations Act (NLRA) commonly known as the Wagner Act. This act expanded the rights enjoyed by workers under section 7(a) and protected unions against discriminatory practices by employers, including the establishment of company unions. Labor also benefited from a strengthening of the collective bargaining provisions of the Railway Labor Act through amendments in 1934.

Although the constitutionality of the Wagner Act was not decided until April 12, 1937, and bitter struggles between management and organized labor continued beyond that date, its passage was a recognition of the desirability of resolving industrial disputes through collective bargaining and it enabled unions to achieve recognition through elections rather than strikes or other direct economic actions. The Wagner Act was not amended until the passage of the Labor-Management Relations Act (the Taft-Hartley Act) in 1947, by which time union membership had grown to about 14.8 million (24.7 percent of the civilian labor force).[30]

THE SPLIT WITHIN THE A.F. OF L.

The struggle between the A.F. of L. and the CIO is often characterized as one between craft and industrial unionism. This is an oversimplification. There were few pure craft unions in the A.F. of L. in 1933. Many so-called craft unions admitted semiskilled and even unskilled workers as members and had become, in effect, quasi-industrial unions. In other cases, several craft unions in a given industry had amalgamated to form a single union; such unions were multicraft in nature. Even in 1933, a number of the federation's largest affiliates were industrial-type unions, and once the CIO was established, the A.F. of L. proceeded to organize additional industrial unions to compete with those affiliated with the CIO.

The initial split between the old-line A.F. of L. leadership and the more dynamic leadership of the CIO reflected (1) the failure of the A.F. of L. to aggressively organize semiskilled and unskilled workers in mass production industries and (2) the conflicts that developed when one or more established A.F. of L. unions exercised a jurisdictional claim over workers in a mass production industry who had been organized, perhaps spontaneously, on an industrial base. Thus the very foundation of the A.F. of L.'s historical basis of organization—the autonomous national union with exclusive control over the jurisdiction described in its charter—was at issue.

The more imaginative and progressive leaders in the federation, including John L. Lewis of the United Mine Workers, David Dubinsky of the International Ladies' Garment Workers, Charles P. Howard of the Typographical Workers, and Sidney Hillman of the Amalgamated Clothing Workers, urged that new national unions be established with broad jurisdiction over workers in basic manufacturing industries. These jurisdictions were to include workers already organized in local industrial-type unions. The traditionalists, wishing to maintain control over the federation and fearful of the cost and possible results of a militant organizing campaign, insisted that existing jurisdictional lines be respected. This meant that members of a federal labor union would have to be parceled out among national unions that chose to exercise jurisdiction over them and that workers who organized on an industrial base in the future would be subject to a similar cannibalization.

The issue was joined at the 1934 convention of the A.F. of L. in San Francisco. The delegates compromised on a settlement which recognized that different organizational structures were feasible and that the form or method of organization used in an actual case should be the one "best designed to rally the wage earners to the cause of organized labor, bearing in mind that in the pursuit of organization the present structure, rights and interests of affiliated National and International Unions must be followed."[31] The executive council was then instructed to issue charters to industrial unions in mass production industries. Unfortunately, this proved to be a hollow victory for the advocates of industrial unionism; the old-line leaders who controlled the executive council were reluctant to implement the directive, and the few charters that were issued were not true industrial charters. For example, the auto workers union that was chartered in August of 1935 was allowed to accept only workers directly engaged in the assembly of completed automobiles. Workers in job and contract shops and engaged in the manufacture of dies, tools, and machinery were not within the union's jurisdiction.[32]

The following year, the battle was joined again at the A.F. of L. convention in Atlantic City. Debate was heated and often vitriolic; John L. Lewis and President William Hutcheson of the Carpenters Union actually exchanged blows on the convention floor. The personal animosities that sprang up at the convention persisted for over two decades and were instrumental in frustrating later efforts to achieve unity. The advocates of industrial unionism were led by Lewis, who made a powerful appeal for industrial unionism and a united union movement. "Is it right," he asked, that because some of us are capable of forging great and powerful organizations of skilled craftsmen in this country we should lock ourselves up in our own domain? . . . Isn't it right that we should contribute something of our own strength, our own virtues, our own knowledge, our own influence toward those less fortunately situated. . . ?[33]

The minority report in favor of industrial unionism was defeated by a roll call vote, 18,024 to 10,933, and the majority report was adopted by a voice vote. However, the proponents of industrial unions were unwilling to concede defeat, and on November 9, 1935, the presidents of eight national unions formed an industrial union group within the A.F. of L., the Committee for Industrial Organization.*

The federation had no effective means of disciplining its constituent nationals, and since expelling the unions supporting the CIO would seriously weaken the federation, the committee did not believe that its actions would lead to severe retaliatory measures. It demanded full industrial charters in the steel, automobile, rubber tire, and radio industries, but the executive council of the federation refused to issue them. Instead, it called on the CIO to dissolve. When this directive was ignored, the council, to the surprise of the CIO leadership, adopted a rule enabling it to bring to trial and suspend an affiliated union guilty of fostering a dual union movement.

The eight unions originally associated, either directly or through a national officer, with the CIO and four other national unions were charged with dualism and brought to trial. Ten of these unions were found guilty and ordered to sever their connections with the CIO on or before September 5, 1936, or be suspended from the A.F. of L. The unions disregarded this ultimatum and were automatically suspended; in the spring of 1937, the unions affiliated with the CIO were also suspended from city centrals and state federations. In October, delegates to the A.F. of L. convention gave the executive council authority to revoke the charters of the suspended unions. A final attempt to resolve the differences between the two groups proved unsuccessful, and between February and May of 1938, the charters of all but one of the suspended unions were revoked. In November 1938, a new federation, the Congress of Industrial Organizations, held its constitutional convention; the division within the house of labor had been formalized. The CIO had conducted energetic organizing campaigns in 1937 and its membership grew rapidly, although it is doubtful that its total membership ever exceeded that of its older rival.[34]

LABOR'S NON-PARTISAN LEAGUE

Organized labor became more active politically during the New Deal. In 1936, the leaders of the CIO helped to form an organization called *Labor's Non-Partisan*

---

* There were only six unions in the original CIO because two of the founding presidents were not supported by their unions.

League to support the reelection of FDR. They were also active in the American Labor Party in New York State. The CIO did not, however, endorse independent (third party) political action by labor. Although the A.F. of L. refused to cooperate with the league, a number of its national unions and state federations were active in the Democratic campaign.

THE GREAT ORGANIZATIONAL DRIVES

The organizational efforts of the CIO met with phenomenal success. Under the dynamic leadership of John L. Lewis, Sidney Hillman, and Philip Murray, organizers were sent into the antiunion bastions of American industry, where they were welcomed by thousands of workers ripe for unionization. The success of the CIO galvanized the less imaginative leadership of the A.F. of L., which also began vigorous organizational drives. By 1940, the CIO, although it lost many adherents in the recession of 1937–1938, had perhaps three million members (including non-dues-paying members) in 42 national unions, while the A.F. of L. had some four million members in 105 national unions.[*]

Not surprisingly, organizational victories were not converted immediately into victories at the bargaining table. We have seen how, when the NIRA codes were in effect, many employers established company unions and resorted to a variety of discriminatory tactics to combat outside unionism. Similar opposition developed when the unions attempted to secure recognition under the NLRA. Even after the act had been declared constitutional in April of 1937, some employers, through dilatory tactics or open violations of the act, continued to thwart attempts to initiate genuine collective bargaining relationships.

Violence often accompanied organizational drives. Employer espionage was common, employer spies infiltrated union meetings and were often elected officers of local unions, and the disposition of plant security forces often resembled a military operation. The report of the LaFollette Civil Liberties Committee, which documented company practices from 1933 to 1937, noted that a certain group of firms had spent over $9 million for spies, strikebreakers, and munitions between 1933 and 1936.[35] Union organizers, members, and sympathizers also resorted to force to prevent struck plants from operating, and the *sit-down strike*, an obviously illegal device, was used to humble some of our largest corporations.

The most significant and well-publicized sit-down strike was in 1937, when General Motors workers occupied the Fisher Body plants in Flint, Michigan. The corporation obtained a court order setting a deadline for the evacuation of its plants; but Lewis, then head of the CIO, hurried to Detroit, where he was instrumental in persuading Governor Frank Murphy not to use the National Guard to

---

[*] This estimate of CIO membership, which is lower than that usually found in the literature, is based on confidential statements made by Philip Murray to the CIO executive board. (Walter Galenson, *The CIO Challenge to the A L.* Cambridge, Mass.: Harvard University Press, 1960, pp. 585–587.)

enforce the order. Under pressure from the White House, GM finally recognized the United Automobile Workers (UAW) as the bargaining agent for its members. Chrysler also signed with the UAW, after a brief sit-down strike, but Ford held out until 1941, when it was ordered to accept the union as the workers' elected representative. The sit-down strike was also used effectively by rubber workers, textile workers, and electrical workers.

The most important single victory of the new unionism, the capitulation of U.S. Steel, was achieved peacefully. The major steel companies had been determinedly antiunion since the formation of U.S. Steel in 1901, and they were a primary target of the CIO. The Steel Workers' Organizing Committee (SWOC) was formed under the capable direction of Philip Murray, one of Lewis's chief lieutenants in the United Mine Workers. After a number of company unions had been captured from within by the SWOC, it became obvious that the organizational effort was succeeding and that the question of union recognition would have to be resolved. In view of the improved business outlook and the open support of collective bargaining by the administration in Washington, the top policy makers within U.S. Steel were unwilling to risk a strike, and secret negotiations were begun between Myron C. Taylor, the firm's chairman, and Lewis. An agreement reached in March of 1937, *prior* to the Supreme Court decisions upholding the NLRA, recognized the SWOC as a bargaining agent for employees of U.S. Steel's chief subsidiary, the Carnegie-Illinois Steel Company. This agreement surprised and shocked the business community.

Most of the smaller steel companies followed the lead of "Big Steel," but a group of companies not so accurately known as "Little Steel"—Republic Steel, Youngstown Sheet and Tube, Bethlehem Steel, National Steel, Inland Steel, and American Rolling Mill—refused to recognize the SWOC. They used the complete arsenal of "union-busting" tactics, and the SWOC lost a series of bitter strikes. One incident in particular aroused widespread indignation, the 1937 *Memorial Day Massacre* at the South Chicago Works of Republic Steel. When police attempting to break up a picket line at the plant opened fire, ten workers were killed and 125 persons were injured, including 35 policemen. Little Steel abandoned its antiunion stance only when Bethlehem Steel was compelled to recognize the union following an NLRB election in 1941.

THE DEFENSE PERIOD

Meanwhile, events abroad presaged new problems for the divided labor movement. After the attack on Pearl Harbor, labor and management closed ranks in a common cause. During 1940 and 1941 however, some government labor policies were questioned by union leaders, and a number of strikes interfered with essential defense production.

The times were also changing for the CIO. John L. Lewis, who had openly opposed Roosevelt in the 1940 campaign, declaring that his reelection "would be a national evil of the first magnitude," had indicated that if Roosevelt won, he would retire as president of the CIO. He resigned at the CIO convention in November and was succeeded by his old lieutenant, Philip Murray. Lewis was unable to dominate the independent Murray, but his periodic attempts to regain a position of influence in the union movement caused problems for the two labor federations, employers, and the public.* He created several crises through his desire to demonstrate his unique leadership abilities, and he and the UMW were frequently onstage during the dramatic events of the forties.

Some had hoped that steps would be taken to unify the labor movement at the 1940 CIO convention, but Lewis ridiculed the idea, saying, " 'I have done a lot of exploring in [A.F. of L. president William Green's] mind and I give you my word there is nothing there.' "[36]

The defense period was characterized by an improvement in business conditions, a growing shortage of labor, and general labor unrest. The number of strikes increased. Some that involved Communist-dominated unions were apparently intended to disrupt defense production. The Communists were effective organizers and had risen to power in a number of major unions, including the United Automobile Workers, the United Electrical Workers, and the Mine, Mill and Smelter Workers. However, their disruptive tactics ended abruptly with the German invasion of Russia; thereafter, they became firm supporters of U.S. foreign policy and ardent advocates of uninterrupted production.**

Given the favorable economic and political climate, most unions were able to negotiate wage increases; and by early 1941, wages generally had risen by ten cents an hour or ten percent (whichever was higher). This round of increases preceded any marked rise in the cost of living. As the country became increasingly concerned about the international situation, the unions made it clear that they expected to be recognized as a full "partner in production" and to be represented on relevant emergency boards. In October 1940, FDR appointed Sidney Hillman, president of the Amalgamated Clothing Workers, to a seven-man National Defense Advisory Commission. A labor advisory committee consisting of representatives from the A.F. of L., the CIO, and the railroad brotherhoods was established to consult with Hillman, and the meetings of this committee reportedly produced the greatest degree of interunion cooperation since the establishment of the CIO.[37] Union labor was also given greater representation in the Office of Production Management, which had been established in December of 1940.

Strikes that interrupted production in several major defense industries led to the establishment of a tripartite National Defense Mediation Board in March 1941. The board consisted of three public, four employer, and four labor repre-

---

* Lewis took the United Mine Workers out of the CIO in 1942. In 1946, the union reaffiliated with the A.F. of L., only to leave it after the passage of the Taft-Hartley Act. The UMW is presently an independent union.

** By studying the position a union adopted on foreign policy issues from 1940 to 1950, it is possible to discover how closely the union followed the Communist party line, an indication of the extent to which it was subject to Communist domination.

sentatives (two from the A.F. of L. and two from the CIO). Its task was to mediate disputes and suggest voluntary arbitration, and it could also make findings of fact and recommendations for resolving a dispute. Many employers were reluctant to grant concessions that might be difficult to live with in a more competitive situation, and there was also a natural reluctance to contribute to the growth of union prestige and power. As a result, the board had to deal with bargaining impasses in a number of key industries. Nevertheless, it was quite successful. It was defied by employers in several cases and by a union in the North American Aviation strike, but these isolated instances did not undermine its position.

The demand for union shops was a thorny problem for the board until it adopted a *maintenance of membership* policy. Under this policy, employees in an organized firm were not compelled to join a union, but union members were required to continue (maintain) their membership. An escape clause that allowed union members a short period in which to resign was worked out at a later date.

The demand of the UMW for a union shop in the "captive" coal mines—mines owned and operated by some of the major consumers of coal, including steel companies and public utilities—proved a deathblow to the board. Although some 95 percent of the 53,000 workers in the captive mines belonged to the UMW, Lewis was adamant in his demand for union security. The board voted against recommending a union shop, with the CIO members dissenting. The CIO members then submitted their resignations, effectively destroying the board. The issue was eventually resolved by a three-man arbitration panel, which voted in favor of a union shop.

Public opinion, already aroused by a wave of strikes in defense industries, was inflamed by Lewis's apparent disregard of the public welfare. Restrictive labor laws were passed by various states, and on December 3, 1941, the House of Representatives passed the Smith Bill, the most extreme of the several antistrike bills that had been introduced in Congress. However, both the collapse of the National Defense Mediation Board and the Smith Bill were forgotten after the attack on Pearl Harbor, as the nation dedicated its energies to the war effort.

WORLD WAR II

The nation had probably never been as unified as it was following our entry into World War II. Organized labor pledged its full support to the government but insisted that it be represented in policy decisions and that the war not be used as a cover for unjustified attacks on unions. President Roosevelt, probably with the successful World War I experience in mind, summoned a labor-management conference that he urged to "reach unanimous agreement, as quickly as possible, on a policy under which defense production stoppages would cease for the duration of the war."[38] The conference apparently disagreed on a number of issues, but Roosevelt nevertheless announced "agreement" on the following basic points:

1. that there would be no strikes or lockouts for the period of the war;
2. that all disputes would be settled by methods that would not hamper war production; and
3. that a new National War Labor Board would be established to handle management-labor conflicts that could not be resolved by other means.[39]

The President, by executive order, established a twelve-person tripartite National War Labor Board (NWLB) on January 12, 1942; it was given statutory authority by the War Labor Disputes (Smith-Connally) Act of 1943. The board's primary concern was the settlement of "labor disputes which might interrupt work which contributes to the effective prosecution of the War." No agreement was reached on the union security issue, nor was it clear how the board was supposed to resolve the potential conflict between the settlement of wage disputes and wage stabilization. Ultimately, inflation forced the board to emphasize its role as a stabilization agency, and the settlement of disputes became to some extent a subordinate function.

The Little Steel Formula

Initially, wage problems were secondary to the union security issue (i.e., contract provisions requiring union membership and/or employer deduction of union dues). The board adopted maintenance of membership with an escape clause as a standard formula in cases in which a stronger form of union security had not been in effect. The President had hoped that wage controls would not be needed if price controls proved effective, but as prices rose, pressure mounted for a wage freeze. In April 1942, FDR presented a seven-point antiinflation program that stressed the need for wage stabilization. At that time, the board was hearing wage cases involving a number of Little Steel companies, and the criterion for wage increases that was adopted in those cases became the general standard. The board used the 15 percent increase in living costs between January 1, 1941, and May 1, 1942, as a measure of the amount by which wages could be increased to protect peacetime standards of living; this became known as the *Little Steel formula*.

At first, the formula was applied only in wage disputes; negotiated wage increases continued to create inequities in the national wage structure and to fuel inflation. Then, in September of 1942, the President requested legislation authorizing him to stabilize living costs. The *Economic Stabilization Act* was passed, directing the President to issue a general order stabilizing prices, wages, and salaries affecting the cost of living on the basis of the levels prevailing on September 15, 1942. The President conferred authority to stabilize wages on the National War Labor Board. The National Railway Labor Panel, which was supposed to conform to policies established by the board, was given jurisdiction over railroad workers.

The NWLB applied the Little Steel formula flexibly, allowing wage increases to correct "inequities." The cost of living continued to rise, and on April 8, 1943, the President issued a "hold the line" order that limited the board's discretion by confining general wage increases to the Little Steel formula unless it could be demonstrated that existing wages were substandard.[40] The board thereafter approved a variety of fringe benefit plans that let employers and unions evade an absolute freeze on payments to labor. The resulting proliferation of benefit plans had a permanent influence on the subject matter of collective bargaining. Moreover, as the number of hours worked per week increased, workers' earnings rose despite the wage freeze.

Wartime Strikes

In the spring of 1943, the United Mine Workers openly challenged the NWLB by demanding a contract that was out of line with the board's policies. They used a recent district court decision that upheld portal-to-portal pay under the Fair Labor Standards Act as the basis for their demand for additional compensation, arguing that the miners must "be in compliance with the law."* When FDR issued his "hold the line" order, Lewis, still the chief of the mine workers, was incensed and argued that by making the Little Steel formula an explicit standard for general wage increases, the government had breached the wartime no-strike agreement. Roosevelt seized the coal mines, and in June the miners struck against the government. They returned to work, struck again in October, and eventually obtained a favorable settlement. Technically, the Little Steel formula was not exceeded, since the uniform increase in wages the miners received was considered a portal-to-portal "adjustment."

An increase in the number of strikes during the first part of 1943 had generated considerable antiunion sentiment, and when the miners struck against the government, Congress passed the War Labor Disputes (Smith-Connally) Act over a presidential veto. The act gave the President power to seize any struck facility, prohibited strikes in any seized facility, required a 30-day cooling-off period in a nonseized facility before a strike could take effect, and provided for a secret strike vote. It is doubtful that the bill would have passed had it not been for the UMW's disregard for public opinion. Labor unrest increased during 1944 and 1945; workers felt that they had not received wage increases sufficient to offset the increase in living costs and were critical of the huge profits earned by many corporations during the war.

In retrospect, the impact of wartime strikes seems to have been exaggerated and the generally excellent record of the union movement given too little emphasis. From December 8, 1941, to August 14, 1945, there were 14,731 work

---

* Portal-to-portal pay included pay for nonproductive time spent on the employer's premises. The UMW had previously agreed that pay in the coal mines should start when a miner actually arrived at the point where the coal was to be mined rather than when he entered the employer's premises.

stoppages in the private, nonfarm sector. These stoppages involved some 6.7 million workers and accounted for a loss of some 36 million man-days of work, only 0.11 percent of available working time.[41] This compares with percentages of 0.32 in 1941, a postwar high of 1.43 in 1946, a postwar low of 0.12 in 1961, and an unremarkable 0.44 in 1970.[42] Nevertheless the publicity given the wartime stoppages created widespread resentment.

By the war's end, union membership had grown significantly. Although precise data are not available, it appears that between 14 and 14.5 million workers, representing about 36 percent of nonagricultural employment, were union members. The CIO unions in the mass production industries vital to the war effort had prospered, and by 1946 seven out of ten production workers in manufacturing were covered by collective bargaining agreements.[43]

The economic outlook however appeared bleak. Conversion to a peacetime economy, the provision of jobs for millions of returning servicemen, and union attempts to protect their members against cuts in take-home pay (particularly those resulting from reductions in overtime) seemed to presage a postwar depression with massive unemployment. Most industry and union leaders were eager to abolish wartime controls and return to a "free market" economy. This objective was not a harbinger of industrial peace:

> each party believed that it had suffered the most under wartime controls and that it could improve its position once the government ceased to fix the terms of the employment contract and became again only the policeman. Union members were convinced . . . that they could make up for the loss of overtime pay once freedom of action to strike and to negotiate was regained. Many employers . . . felt that unions had gained too much power and urgently needed a lesson in postwar realism. . . . In plant after plant across the country conditions were ripe for a fight. . . .[44]

DISCUSSION QUESTIONS

1. It has been noted that in labor relations, organization (by labor or management) breeds counterorganization. Do the events described in the chapter support this thesis?
2. Do you believe that federal court decisions affecting unions prior to 1935 represented an unexpectedly antiunion posture?
3. Did the principle of voluntarism prove effective? (Think of possible alternative approaches.)
4. What was responsible for the success of the *American Plan?*
5. Was Welfare Capitalism basically an antiunion movement?
6. Was the organization of the semiskilled and unskilled workers in our mass-production industries inevitable or primarily a result of the Great Depression?
7. In retrospect, can the New Deal be considered a conservative response to the events of the 1930s?
8. Was the break between the A.F. of L. and CIO a matter of principle or of personalities?
9. Was the growth of union membership during World War II predictable?

SELECTED READINGS

The Growth of Unions

Bernstein, Irving. *The Lean Years: A History of the American Worker, 1920–1933.* Boston: Houghton Mifflin, 1960. An excellent reference.

Bernstein, Irving. *Turbulent Years: A History of the American Worker, 1933–1941.* Boston: Houghton Mifflin, 1970. Like its predecessor, an excellent reference for the period covered.

Taft, Philip. *The A.F. of L. in the Time of Gompers.* New York: Harper & Brothers, 1957. A detailed account of the period.

Taft, Philip. *The A.F. of L. from the Death of Gompers to the Merger.* New York: Harper & Brothers, 1959. The definitive history of the A.F. of L. following 1924.

The Crash of 1929

Galbraith, John. *The Great Crash.* Boston: Houghton Mifflin, 1955. A lively analysis of the events of this period.

The New Deal

Bernstein, Irving. *The New Deal Collective Bargaining Policy.* Berkeley, Calif.: University of California Press, 1950. A definitive study of the events leading to the passage of the Wagner Act.

Derber, Milton, and Young, Edwin, eds. *Labor and the New Deal.* Madison, Wisc.: University of Wisconsin Press, 1957. A more comprehensive account of New Deal labor legislation.

The Formation of the CIO

Galenson, Walter. *The CIO Challenge to the AFL.* Cambridge, Mass.: Harvard University Press, 1960. See particularly chap. 1, "Background of the Struggle."

Morris, James O. *Conflict Within the AFL: A Study of Craft Versus Industrial Unionism, 1901–1938.* Ithaca, N.Y.: Cornell University Press, 1958.

Notes

1. Samuel Yellen, "The Homestead Lockout," chap. III in *American Labor Struggles* (New York: Harcourt Brace & World, 1936), p. 37. Many details of the Homestead strike are from this source.
2. For detailed accounts of this strike, see Almont Lindsey, *The Pullman Strike* (Chicago: University of Chicago Press, 1942), and Yellen, *American Labor Struggles,* chap. IV.
3. Lindsey, *The Pullman Strike,* p. 122.
4. "The Boycott of the Pullman Company," in *Harper's Weekly* XXXVIII, no. 1959 (July 7, 1894): p. 627.
5. Selig Perlman and Philip Taft, *History of Labor in the United States, 1896–1932: Labor Movements,* vol. IV in John R. Commons et al., *History of Labor in the United States* (New York: Macmillan, 1935), p. 133.

6. Ibid., p. 134.

7. Cf. ibid., p. 136.

8. Quoted in ibid., p. 27.

9. Quoted in ibid., p. 43.

10. Ibid., p. 143.

11. Quoted in ibid., p. 151.

12. Irving Bernstein, "The Growth of American Unions," in *The American Economic Review* XLIV, no. 3 (June 1954): Table I, pp. 303–304. The membership of unions affiliated with the A.F. of L. was 1,562,000 in 1910; 2,371,000 in 1917; and 4,079,000 in 1920. (W. S. Woytinsky et al., *Employment and Wages in the United States* [New York: Twentieth Century Fund, 1953], Table 53, p. 642.) These membership totals include members of nationals and internationals outside the continental United States and somewhat overestimate union membership in the United States. Woytinsky's estimates of total membership are slightly lower than Bernstein's.

13. U.S. Department of Labor, Bureau of Labor Statistics, *National War Labor Board,* Bulletin 287, p. 32.

14. Perlman and Taft, *Labor Movements,* p. 491.

15. Ibid., p. 524.

16. Ibid., p. 523.

17. Quoted in Charles A. Madison, *American Labor Leaders* (New York: Harper & Brothers, 1950), p. 112.

18. Ibid., p. 114.

19. Woytinsky et al., *Employment and Wages,* Tables 16–18, pp. 584–586.

20. Bernstein, "The Growth of American Unions," Table I, pp. 303–304.

21. These data are from a number of sources in Irving Bernstein, *The Lean Years: A History of the American Worker, 1920–1933* (Boston: Houghton Mifflin, 1960), pp. 59–61.

22. Quoted in Frederick Lewis Allen, *Only Yesterday* (New York: Harper & Brothers, 1931), p. 303.

23. Ibid., p. 324.

24. Ibid., p. 338.

25. Bernstein, "The Growth of American Unions," Table I, pp. 303–304. The 1940 figure may be somewhat high.

26. Irving Bernstein, "The Growth of American Unions, 1945–1960," in *Labor History* 2, no. 2 (Spring 1961): Table 1, p. 135.

27. Bernstein, *The Lean Years,* p. 345.

28. Joseph Shister, "The Logic of Union Growth," in *Journal of Political Economy* LXI, no. 5 (October 1953): p. 426.

29. Irving Bernstein, *The New Deal Collective Bargaining Policy* (Berkeley, Calif.: University of California Press, 1950), p. 27.

30. Bernstein, "The Growth of American Unions, 1945–1960," Table 1, p. 135.

31. American Federation of Labor, *Proceedings of the Annual Convention, 1934,* p. 41.

32. James O. Morris, *Conflict Within the AFL: A Study of Craft Versus Industrial Unionism, 1901–1938* (Ithaca, N.Y.: Cornell University Press, 1958), p. 202.

33. American Federation of Labor, *Proceedings of the Annual Convention, 1935,* pp. 541–542.

34. Cf. Walter Galenson, *The CIO Challenge to the AFL* (Cambridge, Mass.: Harvard University Press, 1960), Table 19, p. 587.

35. Foster Rhea Dulles, *Labor in America*, 3rd ed. (New York: Crowell, 1966), p. 277.

36. Cited in Galenson, *The CIO Challenge to the AFL* p. 62.

37. Joel Seidman, *American Labor from Defense to Reconversion* (Chicago: University of Chicago Press, 1953), p. 26.

38. Ibid., p. 80.

39. S. T. Williamson and Herbert Harris, *Trends in Collective Bargaining* (New York: Twentieth Century Fund, 1945), p. 165.

40. This order and the other orders and acts referred to in this section may be found in the U.S. Department of Labor's *Termination Report of the National War Labor Board*, vol. II (1948). For a historical analysis of the operations of the board, see ibid., vol. I (1947).

41. U.S. Department of Labor, Bureau of Labor Statistics, *Work Stoppages Caused by Labor-Management Disputes in 1945*, Bulletin 878 (1946), p. 6.

42. U.S. Department of Labor, Bureau of Labor Statistics, *Handbook of Labor Statistics 1975—Reference Edition*, Bulletin 1865 (1975), Table 159, pp. 390–391.

43. "Extent of Collective Bargaining and Union Recognition, 1946," in *Monthly Labor Review* 64, no. 5 (May 1947): p. 765.

44. Seidman, *American Labor from Defense to Reconversion,* pp. 209–210.

Chapter 13
HISTORY OF UNIONISM III: ORGANIZED LABOR IN POST-WORLD WAR II AMERICA

The dramatic increases in union membership during the New Deal and World War II have not been repeated in the postwar period. Initially, a divided labor movement faced a hostile public and federal and state legislatures bent on curbing "excessive" union power. Since the merger of the A.F. of L. and CIO in 1955, the united labor movement has faced a variety of challenges. The unions have been hard pressed to maintain their membership base in a number of economic sectors in which they have traditionally been strong, and they have found it difficult to penetrate unorganized sectors, particularly in the South and in rural areas. Total membership declined between 1956 and 1961 and has grown slowly since then, while relative membership has continued to decline. (A major exception is the rapid growth in the public sector.)

On the legislative front, organized labor has been subjected to a variety of regulations reflecting public dissatisfaction with the collective bargaining process and the way unions have been run. In 1947, a hostile Congress passed the *Taft-Hartley Act*. Designed to create a "better balance" in union-management relations, the act defined a number of unfair practices on the part of unions, declared some of these practices illegal, placed restrictions on certain actions by unions and union representatives, and established procedures for handling labor disputes that created national emergencies. The *Welfare and Pension Plans Disclosure Act* of 1958 attempted to prevent abuses in the operation of employee benefit plans, while the *Landrum-Griffin Act,* passed in 1959, sought to ensure that the unions operated democratically. The Landrum-Griffin Act also modified the law of collective bargaining by amending the Taft-Hartley Act.

On the economic front, unions in the postwar period have sought to protect their members against (1) inflation and (2) layoffs, which were widely attributed to automation. As a result, they have been condemned as agents of inflation and opponents of technological change. They have been generally successful in strengthening and expanding employee health and welfare programs and in increasing job security.

In some cases, companies took a "hard line" in dealing with unions. General Electric's hard line bargaining stance, termed "Boulwarism," for example, was widely copied. Many firms also fought hard against union attempts to extend their organizational frontiers. In the textile industry for example, firms such as J. P. Stevens flagrantly disregarded the law. Relations between the unions and the intellectual community also deteriorated during the postwar years. Many academics and political liberals became disenchanted with union leaders because of their disinterest in broad social reforms. In their view, organized labor had become part of the establishment.

THE RECONVERSION PERIOD

There is no easy way to convert from a war to a peacetime economy. However, the events of 1945–1946 suggest that the Truman administration added to the nation's problems by failing to develop basic criteria for a postwar labor program and by prematurely relaxing wartime controls on the economy.

In November of 1945, President Harry Truman convened a labor-management conference to discuss (1) basic policies with respect to labor-management relations and (2) machinery for settling labor disputes. Although those attending the conference accepted the principle of collective bargaining and made an earnest effort "to reach an understanding on how to make collective bargaining function better," there was no agreement on such specifics as delineating managerial prerogatives, the unionization of foremen, the need for legislation restricting union security, and the establishment of machinery for settling jurisdictional disputes.[1]

On August 16, 1945, Truman had announced that wage increases that did not result in price increases were permissible. Union leaders argued that higher wages to cover losses in take-home pay resulting from reductions in overtime could be absorbed without price increases. Government economists supported this position. So too did the President, who declared that "wage increases are . . . imperative—to cushion the shock to our workers, to sustain adequate purchasing power and to raise the national income."[2] Employers, faced with the task of converting to peacetime operations, refused to grant wage increases unless prices could also be raised. Labor discontent increased, and the number of man-days lost per month as a result of strikes skyrocketed. The National War Labor Board was disbanded, and a successor agency, the *National Wage Stabilization Board*, was established by executive order.

The new board had to approve voluntary wage or salary increases that were tied to requests for price increases, but it had no jurisdiction over disputes. Generally, wage increases were allowed if they did not exceed the average straight-time hourly rates in effect in January 1941 by more than 33 percent. This was equivalent to an increase of about 18½ cents an hour above the Little Steel formula in most basic manufacturing industries. The steel industry refused to grant such an increase unless it could raise its prices, and a major steel strike followed. It was settled only after the President had approved a price rise of $5 a ton. This was followed by an executive order that allowed price increases to compensate for "wage increases consistent with the country's new wage pattern."[3]

Overall, the conversion to peacetime production was smoother and more rapid than had been anticipated. Consumers had unusually large liquid assets and were eager to buy goods, particularly durable ones that had not been available during the war, and many firms embarked on substantial capital equipment replacement and expansion programs. The predicted depression failed to materialize, and when wartime price controls expired on June 30, 1946, a postwar inflationary spiral gained momentum. Although a substitute price control measure was passed, the powers of the Office of Price Administration were curbed and prices continued to rise. After the midterm elections, price controls (except those on rents, sugar, and rice) and all wage and salary controls were lifted. Prices rose some 15 percent between June and December of 1946, cancelling, in real terms, the wage increases of the reconversion period.

Union membership increased only slightly between 1945 and 1946, then spurted upward as the economy converted to peacetime production. By 1947, unions had 14.8 million members, representing 23.9 percent of the total labor force, or approximately one-third of the employees in nonagricultural establishments.[4]

The postwar wage disputes were in marked contrast to the bitter disputes that had characterized the concerted management effort to establish open shops after World War I. The postwar strikes tended to be prolonged tests of economic strength that tried the public's patience, but the survival of unionism was not an issue. Nevertheless, the public did not always support the unions, and union leaders made a serious strategic error in overestimating the willingness of the man in the street to endure strikes that created national emergencies or were a serious local inconvenience. A wave of strikes in the steel, meat-packing, automobile, oil, electrical manufacturing, and railroad industries, and well-publicized local strikes against utilities, transportation firms, and municipal government created a widespread demand for legislation to protect the public welfare.

Two incidents in particular aroused public resentment in 1946: a strike in the bituminous coalfields and a brief nationwide strike of railroad engineers and trainmen. The coal strike resulted in the seizure of the mines by the government. The railroad strike began on May 23 and ended two days later, after President Truman threatened to seize the roads and operate them under the protection of the military. Shortly after, a highly restrictive labor measure, the Case Bill, was passed by both houses of Congress. Although it was vetoed by the President, a number of states also enacted restrictive legislation in 1946.

THE TAFT-HARTLEY ACT

The sweeping victory of the Republicans in the 1946 election was interpreted as a popular mandate to check union abuses, and Congress passed the *Labor-Management Relations Act*, popularly known as the *Taft-Hartley Act,* over a presidential veto on June 23, 1947. This act, which will be examined in detail in Chapter 17, although designed ostensibly as an amendment to the National Labor Relations Act, went far beyond that objective; it was an omnibus bill with a host of disparate provisions. Although it was clear that restrictive legislation would be passed, union leaders persistently refused to participate in the formulation of what was certain to be a much modified national labor policy. This failure was due in part to a political miscalculation—a widespread belief that a Democratic victory in 1948 would lead to repeal of such legislation. It was also due to an unwillingness or inability on the part of union leaders to concede that the union movement was now one of the principal power blocs in the economy and that legislation was needed to prevent it from abusing its power.

Despite its restrictive and controversial character, the Taft-Hartley Act did not reverse a public policy of accepting unions and encouraging free collective bargaining. Well-established collective bargaining relationships did not appear to be significantly affected by the act, although some of its provisions probably constrained union organizational efforts, particularly in the South. Nevertheless, the passage of the act convinced the leaders of the A.F. of L. that they would have to assume a more direct role in the political sphere. The result was the establishment of *Labor's League for Political Education* in September 1947* and, ultimately, the endorsement of Adlai Stevenson for President in 1952, a notable departure from the federation's traditional policy of nonpartisanship.**

THE 1947–1950 WAGE "ROUNDS"

In 1947, new contracts that provided about 15 cents an hour were negotiated without strikes in most basic industries. These were the first of a series of voluntary annual wage increases that contributed to inflation in the postwar period.

---

* The CIO had already established a Political Action Committee (PAC) in 1943, and after its merger with the A.F. of L., the new federation formed a Committee on Political Education (COPE).

** The executive council had however endorsed Robert LaFollette in the 1924 campaign.

The negotiations in the bituminous coal industry were an unwelcome, but not unexpected, exception to the general pattern of peaceful settlements in 1947. The federal government was operating the bituminous coal mines when the United Mine Workers terminated their open-ended contract, and it secured an injunction restraining the officials of the union from continuing the contract termination notice. John L. Lewis refused to obey the court order, and both he and the union were found guilty of civil and criminal contempt. Lewis delivered an impassioned plea against "the ugly recandescence of 'government by injunction,'" but the convictions and resulting fines were upheld by the Supreme Court.

Inflation, competition for the best "wage package" between unions in key industries, and controversy over the interpretation and application of the Taft-Hartley Act contributed to a continued atmosphere of industrial unrest. There were major strikes by coal miners, East Coast maritime workers, East Coast longshoremen, meat-packers, and automobile workers in 1948, and by coal, steel, and automobile workers in 1949. In 1948, a pattern of hourly wage increases of 11 to 13 cents was established in basic manufacturing industries; in 1949, the emphasis was on initiating or improving welfare and pension plans.

Negotiations in the automobile industry in 1950 ended in the most important single agreement since the Taylor-Lewis pact in steel in 1937—the five-year General Motors contract. Underlying the agreement was a recognition of the inflationary bias in the postwar economy. In such an economy, producers want no interruptions in production and workers want assurance that they will be protected against increases in the cost of living. During the life of the five-year contract, strikes were permitted over production standards but not over wages. In return, the union was given a wage package that included an automatic quarterly adjustment tied to the Consumer Price Index of the Bureau of Labor Statistics and annual increases reflecting increased productivity.* The contract also specified a modified union shop and a liberal pension and insurance package.

There was a steady expansion in the type and number of fringe benefits in the postwar period, and this trend has continued. According to one survey, in 1978 the cost of supplemental benefits to U.S. firms was equivalent to 36.9 percent of the firms' payrolls.[5] The demand for a *guaranteed annual wage* during 1955 and 1956 reflected this trend. In 1955, the United Automobile Workers obtained supplemental unemployment benefit (SUB) payments for a maximum period of 26 weeks (extended to 39 weeks in 1958 and to 52 weeks in 1961), and the United Steel Workers obtained a full year of coverage after a strike in 1956.**

---

* The two-year GM contract negotiated in 1948 had also provided cost-of-living increases.
** These plans provided payments in addition to the benefits received from state unemployment insurance funds; the payments were related to one's length of employment, and the employer's liability was limited.

THE EXPULSION OF COMMUNIST-DOMINATED UNIONS FROM THE CIO

During the late forties, the CIO was faced with a serious internal problem. Communist party members or sympathizers had gained control of a number of CIO unions. Under a provision of the Taft-Hartley Act, officers of national unions had been required to sign an affidavit that they were not Communists. This served to spotlight Communist activity within various nationals. In addition, testimony during several investigations of subversive activity alerted the CIO to the threat these unions posed to the union movement. Despite the substantial loss in membership such action entailed, 11 Communist-dominated nationals were expelled from the CIO in 1949 and 1950. This action had a significant impact on subsequent merger negotiations with the A.F. of L. because as the larger of the two federations, the A.F. of L. had to be given the dominant role in the unified union movement. The A.F. of L. reported a total membership of over seven million in 1950; the CIO claimed some five million members, and its actual membership was probably considerably less. There were also some 2.5 million workers in unaffiliated unions. The recession of 1949–1950 reduced union membership, but the Korean crisis triggered an expansion in business activity that stimulated union growth.

THE KOREAN CRISIS

The problems that beset the economy during the Korean conflict and later during the Vietnam War are significant because such crises can develop at any time. Inflation increased rapidly following the outbreak of hostilities, and the federal government was forced to establish wage and price stabilization agencies. The gross national product rose from $285.1 billion in 1950 to $329 billion in 1951, while the Consumer Price Index (1957–1959 = 100) rose from 83.8 in 1950 to 90.5 in 1951. The Federal Reserve Board Index of Industrial Production, which had fallen to 64.7 in 1949 (1957–1959 = 100), rose to 74.9 in 1950 and to 81.3 in 1951. On January 25, 1951, the Office of Price Stabilization rolled back prices to the level of November 1950, and the following day, the Wage Stabilization Board (WSB) instituted a temporary wage freeze, which the coal miners, because of an adroit maneuver by Lewis, were able to circumvent. It became evident that a general wage increase would have to be granted, and an increase of 10 percent was approved in February.

In December 1950, representatives of the A.F. of L., the CIO, and independent unions had formed a *United Labor Policy Committee* to present labor's views on basic policy issues. The committee felt that it was not given enough say in certain policy decisions, and organized labor withdrew from all government mobilization agencies, including the Wage Stabilization Board, following the February wage increase. In the spring of 1951, a peace formula was evolved under which a new Wage Stabilization Board was appointed, the labor representatives returned to their government posts, and existing wage orders were modified to permit "productivity increases."

This new board was plagued with a series of problems, including the steel dispute of 1951–1952, in which the board recommended an increase that was twice the size the director of Defense Mobilization deemed reasonable. During the dispute, which was heavily charged with political overtones, the director of Defense Mobilization resigned and the board was dissolved. It was later reconstituted, but without authority to intervene in labor-management disputes. A brief strike in April 1952 led to the seizure of the steel mills by President Truman. The Supreme Court declared the seizure unconstitutional, and a second walkout followed. It was settled after a 12½ cent an hour increase, which set a national pattern for 1952, was granted.

Later that year, John L. Lewis came onstage, demanding that the new WSB approve the increase of $1.90 a day that he had negotiated for the bituminous coal miners. In October, when the board disallowed 40 cents of the increase, the miners walked out. Nineteen fifty-two was an election year, and the administration considered a major strike immediately before the election a potential political disaster. After a conference between Lewis and President Truman, Lewis ordered his men back to work. In December, Truman approved the $1.90 a day wage boost so that President-elect Dwight D. Eisenhower could take over in "as calm and stable an atmosphere as possible." The chairman and the four industry members of the Wage Stabilization Board promptly resigned. An interim Wage Stabilization Committee consisting of the public members of the WSB then functioned until wage controls were ended in February 1953. The recession of 1953–1954 had a dampening effect on wage demands in 1953, and increases of only 5 cents an hour were common. In 1954, a wage package of about 10 cents an hour was negotiated in many industries; 5 cents represented a direct wage increase and 5 cents was devoted to fringe benefits.

Union membership expanded rapidly during the Korean crisis, increasing from 14.3 million (22.3 percent of the labor force) in 1950 to 16.9 million (25.5 percent of the labor force) in 1953.[6]

Our experience with wage controls from 1950 to 1952 was similar in many respects to our experience with such controls during World War II and suggests that in the absence of comprehensive economic controls, there must be considerable flexibility in wage controls. It also leaves unanswered the question of whether a single board should be charged with administering wage controls *and* settling labor disputes. It is unreasonable to expect a board responsible for settling such disputes to also function effectively as a wage stabilization agency. On the other hand, the separation of these functions may lead to decisions that are unrealistic and impossible to live with.

THE A.F. OF L.-CIO MERGER

The passage of the Labor-Management Relations Act alerted labor to the grow-ing hostility toward unions, and following the Korean crisis, there was a renewed interest in unifying organized labor. There was, after all, a structural similarity between the rival federations, and the concept of industrial unions had long been acceptable to the A.F. of L. The United Labor Policy Committee had demonstrated that the A.F. of L. and the CIO could cooperate effectively at the national level, and continued cooperation would be helpful in organizing cam-paigns, in lobbying activities, and in coordinating bargaining among unions negotiating with the same employer. The personal animosities that had helped perpetuate the division within the union movement became less significant as the principal figures in the original controversy disappeared from the scene. Philip Murray, the head of the CIO, and William Green, president of the A.F. of L., both died within a fortnight in 1952, and there had been a con-siderable turnover in the leadership of national unions due to deaths and retirement.

The new president of the A.F. of L., George Meany, proved to be dynamic and progressive. He was a realist, much easier to deal with than his predecessor had been, and he was willing to "treat with the CIO leaders on a practical basis as equals, without the offensive tone of moral superiority which Green had adopted."[7] The leaders of the CIO had also become more pragmatic. In December of 1954, *The New York Times* commented that

> [r]ealism has become quite a commodity in the upper echelons of the C.I.O. No longer do Mr. [Walter] Reuther and his colleagues walk with their heads in the clouds excoriating the frailties of the mere mortals around them. The practicalities of running giant union[s] have given them a sophistication that blends a large measure of ward politics with their old idealism.[8]

Other developments helped to create an environment favorable to a merger. Prior to 1949, the CIO had included a number of Communist-led nationals, and it had belonged to the World Federation of Trade Unions (WFTU) which was controlled by Communists. By 1953, the CIO had expelled the Communist-dominated nationals and had left the WFTU to join the A.F. of L. in the Inter-national Confederation of Free Trade Unions. CIO leaders had long charged the A.F. of L. with not moving aggressively enough in dealing with discrimina-tion, graft, and corruption in its family of unions. In 1953 however, the A.F. of L. moved swiftly and dramatically to expel the racketeer-infested International Longshoremen's Association (ILA). An internal struggle for the presidency of the CIO between the heads of its largest constituent unions, Walter Reuther of the UAW and David J. McDonald of the Steelworkers Union, gave additional impetus to the merger movement. McDonald, after losing the election, indicated that he would take his union out of the CIO unless a merger was achieved.

The time was ripe for unity, and in 1953 committees from the two federa-tions met to consider the problems involved.[9] Meany insisted that an agreement not to raid other unions was a necessary preliminary to serious merger discussions. The CIO had already established an *internal disputes plan*, and the A.F. of L. established a similar plan before the formal merger. Both plans provided for arbitrators to hear and resolve questions of jurisdiction internal to each federation. In June, a no-raiding pact was negotiated which provided that a signatory union would respect the legal and contractual rights of all unions in the rival federation irrespective of its own formal grant of jurisdiction. This froze existing bargaining relationships so that merger talks could go forward. In June of 1954, the pact was signed by 65 A.F. of L. and 29 CIO unions with a combined membership of over ten million; by the end of 1954, 31 out of 32 CIO unions and 75 out of 111 A.F. of L. unions had signed.

Merger talks continued, and for a time it appeared that disputes over the jurisdictional limits of the national unions would make further negotiations fruitless. However, after recognizing that the integrity of existing unions should be preserved whenever possible, the negotiators agreed to proceed without evolving precise jurisdictional lines. This constructive action assured the ultimate success of the negotiations, and on February 9, 1955, agreement was reached on terms for a merger.

When the CIO and A.F. of L. conventions met in New York in December 1955, the merger was approved (unanimously by the A.F. of L. and by a vote of 5,712,077 to 122,002 by the CIO). The two federations formally merged at a joint convention on December 5. The new AFL-CIO had a total membership of some 15 million in what had been, previously, 32 CIO and 109 A.F. of L. national unions. For a quarter of a century, the American union movement had been divided by inflamed emotions and bitter rivalries, but these same rivalries provided a competitive spark that generated vigorous organizational activity. By 1955, industrial unionism had ceased to be a burning issue, and many of the more partisan leaders of an earlier day had been replaced by persons whose orientation was not to the bitterness of the past but to a future that promised organizational gains and a more influential political role for a reenergized union movement. Most of organized labor had come full circle since October 1935, when John L. Lewis of the Mineworkers and William Hutcheson of the Carpenters had traded punches on the A.F. of L. convention floor.

STRUCTURAL ISSUES

The A.F. of L. contributed the bulk of the membership of the new federation and was given a greater voice in its administration. Both of the top executive posts, that of president and secretary-treasurer, went to the A.F. of L., while the new director of organization came from the CIO.

A special *industrial union department* headed by Reuther, was formed to represent the interests of nationals organized on an industrial base. The Teamsters attempted to bring their entire membership into the department, but the executive council of the federation ruled that unions could only bring in that portion of their membership organized on an industrial base. The original membership of the department, which was controlled by a nucleus of 31 former CIO unions, was 7.2 million; the 35 A.F. of L. unions that joined the department accounted for 2.6 million members.

Although the constitution of the AFL-CIO provided that state and local centrals had to merge within two years, these mergers were not completed until 1961. The internal disputes settlement plans of both the A.F. of L. and the CIO were incorporated into the constitution, and the interfederation no-raiding agreement was extended for two years. During this period, a joint committee was to devise a permanent no-raiding agreement and machinery for resolving jurisdictional disputes. The joint committee was unable to devise an acceptable permanent no-raiding plan, and on February 6, 1958, the executive council decided that the impartial umpire under the existing disputes machinery should rule on charges of raiding whether or not the unions involved had signed the no-raiding pact.

Between 1955 and February 1971, there were 36 mergers involving 77 unions. Over one-third of these mergers were effected during the final three years of that period. However, "the number of mergers involving overlapping jurisdictions [fell] far short of its potential," and in a number of cases represented the reluctant route to survival for unions "faced with declining memberships in declining industries."[10] An additional 21 mergers occurred between February of 1971 and August of 1978.[11] Smaller unions, recognizing the economies of scale and the greater organizing potential of a large membership base, found it advantageous to merge with other unions in the same or related industries or occupations. Larger and stronger organizations with overlapping jurisdictions were less likely to merge formally, although such a move could be advantageous in bargaining with giant firms or conglomerates. In 1979, the Retail Clerks International Union and the Amalgamated Meat Cutters and Butcher Workmen (which was the result of a 1968 merger) merged to become the United Food and Commercial Workers, the largest union in the AFL-CIO. The new union displaced the American Federation of State, County and Municipal Employees, which had become the largest affiliate as a result of a 1978 merger with the Independent New York State Civil Service Employees Association. A number of formerly independent unions also joined the AFL-CIO, including four of the five operating brotherhoods on the railroads, which merged into the single United Transportation Union in 1969.

For most larger unions, cooperation in organizing the unorganized and in coordinating collective bargaining objectives and strategies appears more probable than formal mergers.[12] Various mutual assistance pacts have been negotiated, including a number among national unions bargaining with the same multiplant corporation. The continued growth of conglomerates bargaining with unions in different industries should encourage this trend.

Following the merger, serious jurisdictional disputes developed between the skilled building trades and metal trades unions and certain industrial unions, including the auto and steel workers. At issue was the organization of (1) workers doing maintenance-type construction work in industrial plants, (2) the increasing number of skilled technicians in automated factories, and (3) workers installing equipment on missile bases. The problem came to a head in the spring of 1961, when 30 industrial unions representing some six million workers demanded that the federation put an end to interunion warfare. In December, the biennial convention of the AFL-CIO amended its constitution to provide for the inescapable resolution of such jurisdictional disputes on a case by case basis. Complex procedures were established, with the final decision resting with the executive council. Meanwhile, a separate 11-member Missile Sites Labor Commission established by the federal government in May of 1961 had considerable success in stabilizing labor relations at various missile centers.

THE POSTMERGER UNION MOVEMENT

We shall take only a brief look at developments affecting the union movement since 1955, since these matters are discussed in greater detail in Parts Four and Five.

Malpractices and Reform

The disclosure of graft and corruption in some half-dozen national unions during hearings before several congressional investigating committees in the 1950s had shocked not only the public but the leaders of both the A.F. of L. and the CIO. An *Ethical Practices Committee* was established by the new federation to put an end to corruption, and in 1957 three unions, including the largest AFL-CIO affiliate, the International Brotherhood of Teamsters, Chauffeurs, Warehousemen and Helpers of America, were expelled for a variety of malpractices.* This action did little to offset the increasingly unfavorable climate of public opinion created by such activities, and there were continued demands for legislation compelling individual unions to clean house.

In August 1958, the *Welfare and Pension Plans Disclosure Act* required the "registration, reporting, and disclosure of employee welfare and pension benefit plans." However, federal officials felt that the act had no teeth, and it was strengthened by Public Law 87–420, approved by President John F. Kennedy on March 20, 1962.

In September 1959, the *Labor-Management Reporting and Disclosure Act* (Landrum-Griffin Act) was passed. The objectives of this act were (1) to outlaw various practices documented by congressional investigating committees, (2) to

---

* The Bakery and Confectionery Workers and the Laundry Workers were also expelled. In addition, the United Textile Workers, the Distillery Workers, and the Allied Industrial Workers were suspended for varying periods. The membership of the three expelled unions was some 1,518,000 at the date of their expulsion.

provide greater democracy within the union movement, and (3) to clarify or modify some aspects of the law of collective bargaining by amending the Taft-Hartley Act.

The attempts of the AFL-CIO to discipline national unions met with only occasional success. The Teamsters continued to expand their jurisdiction and increase their membership even after their expulsion, and the International Brotherhood of Longshoremen, which had been established by the AFL to challenge the expelled ILA, admitted defeat in 1959 and merged with the older union. This enabled the "cleansed" ILA to affiliate with the AFL-CIO on a probationary basis and to be formally readmitted in 1961. Waterfront corruption continues however: in June of 1978, a number of ILA officials were indicted in Miami on charges of conspiring to control business activities on the docks in Atlantic and Gulf Coast ports; and in January 1979, Anthony M. Scotto, the president of the union's largest local, was indicted in New York on federal racketeering charges and subsequently convicted.

Following the death of John L. Lewis in 1969, the UMW was involved in a series of scandals. Apparently Lewis, despite his image as a statesman, had been connected with questionable financial and investment practices on the part of the union. In 1972, confessions relating to the 1969 murder of a UMW insurgent leader and executive board member implicated a number of the union's local, district, and national officials. W. A. "Tony" Boyle, then president of the UMW, was later sent to prison for his role in the murder. In 1972, the 1969 election of Boyle was voided under provisions of the Landrum-Griffin Act, and he was convicted of making illegal political contributions from union funds.

Postmerger Membership Trends

Aggregate trends in union membership reflect changes in the membership of unions affiliated with the AFL-CIO, independent national unions, and the rapidly growing professional associations and public employee associations. Before 1968, such associations were not included in the biennial Department of Labor Survey of union membership, and the analysis here is limited to the number of persons in national and international unions, plus the number in local unions directly affiliated with the AFL-CIO.* Table 13.1 shows the estimated membership of these unions for the years 1958–1976. Figure 13.1 shows changes in union membership from 1930 to 1976, and Figure 13.2 shows the percentage of the total

---

* National union *plus* association membership (including members of local unions directly affiliated with the AFL-CIO but excluding Canadian members and members of single firm unions) was estimated at 22.7 million in 1976, representing 23.4 percent of the labor force and 28.5 percent of nonagricultural employment. The U.S. Department of Labor has estimated that national union and association membership in the United States totaled 22.8 million in 1978, representing 22.2 percent of the labor force and 26.6 percent of nonagricultural employment. ("Labor Union and Employee Association Membership—1978," *Press Release USDL: 79–605,* August 31, 1979, p. 1.)

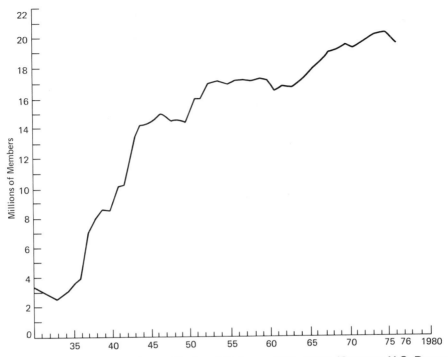

Figure 13.1   Membership in National Unions, 1930–1976[a] (Source: U.S. Department of Labor, Bureau of Labor Statistics, *Directory of National Unions and Employee Associations, 1977,* Bulletin 2044, Chart 2, p. 62.)

[a] Excludes Canadians but includes members in other areas outside the United States. Members of local unions directly affiliated with the AFL-CIO are also included. Members of single firm and local unaffiliated unions are excluded. For the years 1948–1952, midpoints of membership estimates, which were expressed as ranges, were used.

labor force and the percentage of employees in nonagricultural establishments organized in those same years. Obviously, the merger between the A.F. of L. and the CIO did not lead to the expected organizational gains. The absolute number of union members declined until 1961. The number of union members as a percentage of both the total labor force and employees in nonagricultural establishments has continued to decline.

Between 1951 and 1970, unions of government employees, service workers, workers in wholesale and retail trades, and transportation workers (employees of airlines and trucking firms) grew substantially. At the same time, unions of railroad employees, textile workers, and workers in the furniture industries showed significant declines in membership.[13] Since 1970, the American Federation of Teachers; the State, County and Municipal Employees; the American Federation of Government Employees; the Teamsters; the Retail Clerks; and the

Communications Workers have reported significant gains in membership.[14] The Service Employees union has organized low wage workers in the health services and some nonprofit sectors; under the leadership of Cesar Chavez, migrant agricultural workers have been organized by the United Farm Workers (AFL-CIO) in California; and professional athletes have unionized several major sports. However, a coordinated general effort to organize workers in Atlanta has been unsuccessful, and a major campaign to unionize the Southern textile industry has achieved few results to date.

The most impressive recent increases in membership have been in unions in the public sector. These gains are a result of the absolute growth in employment in this sector, the passage of laws in a number of states protecting the right of

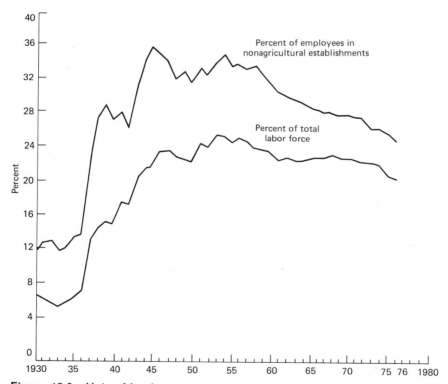

Figure 13.2   Union Members as a Percentage of the Total Labor Force and of Employees in Nonagricultural Establishments, 1930–1976[a] (Source: U.S. Department of Labor, Bureau of Labor Statistics, *Directory of National Unions and Employee Associations, 1977,* Bulletin 2044, Chart 3, p. 63.)

[a] Excludes Canadians but includes members in other areas outside the United States. Members of local unions directly affiliated with the AFL-CIO are also included. Members of single firm and local unaffiliated unions are excluded. For the years 1948–1952, midpoints of membership estimates, which were expressed as ranges, were used.

Table 13.1 MEMBERSHIP IN NATIONAL UNIONS 1958–1976[a]

YEAR	UNION MEMBERSHIP (IN THOUSANDS)	PERCENTAGE OF TOTAL LABOR FORCE	PERCENTAGE OF EMPLOYEES IN NONAGRICULTURAL ESTABLISHMENTS
1958	17,029	24.2	33.2
1959	17,117	24.1	32.1
1960	17,049	23.6	31.5
1961	16,303	22.3	30.2
1962	16,586	22.6	29.9
1963	16,524	22.2	29.2
1964	16,841	22.2	28.9
1965	17,299	22.4	28.5
1966	17,940	22.7	28.1
1967	18,367	22.7	27.9
1968	18,916	23.0	27.9
1969	19,036	22.6	27.0
1970	19,381	22.6	27.3
1971	19,211	22.1	27.0
1972	19,435	21.8	26.4
1973	19,851	21.8	25.9
1974	20,199	21.7	25.8
1975	19,553	20.6	25.3
1976	19,634	20.3	24.5
1977			
1978			
1979			
1980			

SOURCE: *U.S. Department of Labor, Bureau of Labor Statistics, Directory of National Unions and Employee Associations, 1977,* Bulletin 2044, Table 6, p. 61.
[a] Excludes Canadians, but includes members of locals directly affiliated with the AFL-CIO.

state and municipal employees to organize and bargain collectively, the issuance of executive orders by Presidents Kennedy and Nixon authorizing collective bargaining by federal employees, and vigorous organizing campaigns.

Continuing Organizational Problems

The unions have already done an effective job of organizing those workers most susceptible to organization, and unions with security arrangements in growth industries will continue to show a "natural" increase in membership. Achieving any further increases in the *percentage* of union members in the labor force is likely to prove increasingly difficult, however, for various reasons.[15] In a number of basic industries, the steel and automobile industries for example, almost all of the hourly rated production workers have already been organized; the nonunion firms that remain tend to be smaller firms that are difficult to organize; and firms in this country have been hard hit by foreign competition. Even in construction, an industry in which union membership has grown whenever employment has risen, nonunion competition now poses a serious threat to well-established unions.

In fact, it has been estimated that organization of the construction labor force may have dropped below 50 percent by the end of 1979.

The degree of unionization has always varied geographically. Workers in the North are more highly organized than those in the South, and urban workers have been easier to organize than those in rural areas. Any further expansion of union membership will require a much greater organizational effort because the prevailing mores in many target areas are, at best, not receptive to unions.

It is usually assumed that demographic and social factors presently make it more difficult for unions to increase their power base. For example, the growing importance, both relatively and absolutely, of industries with many female workers, together with the increased participation rate of women in the total labor force, is often thought to add to organizational problems, and it is true that many women workers are not firmly committed to the labor force, are disinterested in unionism, and are employed in industries that are hard to organize. In addition, many young workers, unaware of the early struggles of organized labor and the gains achieved by the union movement over the years, see little reason to join unions. Some young workers do not want to be part of a movement that they identify with the establishment; in their view, union leaders have become organization men in a corrupt society. Other unorganized workers, including professional employees, technicians, and research workers, and many white-collar workers in service industries and financial institutions, have a middle-class orientation that makes them question the need for unionization.

On the other hand, a 1977 *Quality of Employment Survey* conducted for the U.S. Department of Labor concluded that 33 percent of the nonunion respondents in the sample would vote for unionization and that

> none of the growing segments of the labor force exhibits an inherently negative view of trade unions or to the prospects of joining a union. Younger workers, women, and [more] educated workers are no less willing to join a union *when their job conditions warrant it* than their older, male, or less educated counterparts.[16]

Although it indicates a more widespread acceptance of unionization than is commonly perceived, the survey does not refute the argument that *if* our mixed enterprise system continues to provide jobs at adequate wages for most of the labor force, *if* workers are protected against the more common forms of economic insecurity by a variety of public and private security programs, and *if* unorganized firms unilaterally provide many of the economic and extraeconomic benefits presumably derived from union membership, it will be difficult for most unions to recruit, and in some cases to retain, members. This *membership crisis* will be intensified if affluence creates a general middle-class orientation that encourages workers to identify with management.

In view of these circumstances, it appears that Lane Kirkland, the new president of the AFL-CIO, should give very high priority to a major organizational campaign targeted at service industry workers, white-collar workers, women workers, and, regionally, workers in the South.

Internal Problems

The changing demographic composition of the membership of a number of national unions and the protection afforded dissidents under the Landrum-Griffin Act have created several problems for union leaders. Since the late sixties, there has been a significant rise in (1) the number of contested union elections, with a resultant turnover in old-line officers, and (2) the number of new contracts rejected by union members. This has created instability in some of the more "mature" collective bargaining relationships, including those in the steel and bituminous coal industries.

The Unions and Inflation

The persistent inflation of the past 30 years has contributed to the growing hostility toward unions. From 1946 to 1956, inflation was basically the result of excess demand; but between 1956 and 1959, wage increases greater than increases in productivity—particularly deferred wage increases built into long-term collective bargaining agreements—became a significant inflationary force. During and after the recession of 1960–1961, the upward pressure on wages lessened. The Kennedy administration followed a policy of early intervention in major collective bargaining talks to ensure that any agreements reached did not conflict with the national interest. This policy apparently met with singular success when the steel negotiations of 1962 resulted in a noninflationary wage settlement. However, the subsequent abortive attempt of U.S. Steel to raise prices and the President's violent censure of the corporation and its executives destroyed the potentially constructive impact of the settlement.

As we have pointed out previously, economists disagree about the efficacy of the wage and price guideposts of the Kennedy and Johnson administrations, but there is little doubt that the nation's military involvement in Vietnam resulted in a renewal of demand-pull inflation. From 1969 to 1971, wages and prices continued to rise in the face of increasing unemployment. Wage increases in certain highly visible industries, notably the construction industry, served as a pattern for increases throughout the economy, and the Consumer Price Index (1967 = 100) rose from 104.2 in 1968 to 121.3 in 1971. In March of 1971, President Richard M. Nixon, by executive order, established the Construction Industry Stabilization Committee to review proposed wage increases in that industry. Although the President was opposed to wage and price controls, the failure of his fiscal and monetary "game plan" to reduce inflation and the dollar crisis that resulted from the deterioration in our balance of payments position, led to an unexpected 90-day wage and price freeze on August 15, 1971. During the subsequent phase II of the President's program, which began on November 14, 1971, and ended on January 11, 1973, a tripartite Pay Board and a public Price Commission held down the rate of increase in wages and prices.

The substitution of voluntary wage and price controls (phase III) after January 11 proved a disaster. The new program lasted five months, during which time prices increased at an annual rate of 24.4 percent. A 60-day wage and price freeze was followed on August 12, 1973, by a phase IV "phase-out" of controls.

In 1974 and 1975, a recession lessened inflationary pressures. However, the Council on Wage and Price Stability was established by the Ford administration, and several *inflation summit conferences* were held. Confronted with rising prices and high unemployment, President Jimmy Carter instituted new wage-price guidelines in October 1978. The AFL-CIO opposed these voluntary guidelines, arguing that if government intervention was unavoidable compulsory controls would be more acceptable to organized labor. Double digit inflation took hold early in 1979, and corporate profits generally continued to rise. It was unrealistic to expect organized labor to conform to a 7 percent wage standard in such circumstances, and the wage guidelines were breached in a series of major collective bargaining negotiations. At the end of 1979, the CPI was rising at an annual rate of over 13 percent, which suggests that the new 7½ to 9½ percent wage guideline "range" proposed by President Carter's new Pay Advisory Committee may serve as a base rather than an upper limit for union negotiators during 1980.

Other Problems

Meanwhile, union opposition to employers' attempts to eliminate work rules and practices they considered unnecessary or inefficient led to well-publicized strikes that further antagonized the public. The steel strike of 1959 and the strikes of railroad telegraphers, newspaper composing room employees, and the East Coast dock workers all involved restrictive work rules. In February 1962, the operating brotherhoods on the railroads aroused considerable public ire when they refused to accept the recommendations of a presidential commission concerning revision of the elaborate system of work rules, work practices, and methods of compensation on the roads. The controversy was finally resolved by a special act of Congress.

A number of firms and industries tried to resolve complex problems of adjustment to changes in technology through long-range studies removed from the brinkmanship pressures of contract negotiations. In the steel, meat-packing, and West and East Coast longshore industries, for example, study committees helped unions and management respond creatively to technological change.

The rapid growth of public employee unions, which was accompanied by an increase in strikes despite the general prohibition of strikes by government employees, raised a number of critical issues, including the desirability of compulsory arbitration. During this period, too, the union movement lost the support of many liberals, who believed that organized labor, despite its support of national civil rights legislation, had not moved with vigor to eliminate discrimination at the local level and also was not sufficiently responsive to the needs of disadvantaged members of the community.

"SOCIAL UNIONISM": ORGANIZED LABOR AND THE INTELLECTUAL COMMUNITY

A small minority of national union leaders believed that the union movement had an obligation to develop a broad reform program and become an instrument for social change. Walter Reuther, president of the United Automobile Workers, was the most prominent and perhaps the most articulate advocate of the new "social unionism." His dissatisfaction with the business union philosophy of Meany and other national union leaders led in 1968 to the formation of an alliance between the UAW and the independent Teamsters' union.

The Alliance for Labor Action (ALA) was designed to organize millions of workers, to aid liberal candidates for public office, and to support a variety of social welfare programs that would help minority workers and farm workers, and, more generally, provide universal health care and low cost public housing. This strange alliance of the UAW with a union expelled from the AFL-CIO for unethical practices was in part a move of desperation; Reuther had hoped to advance his creative social philosophy after his anticipated election to the post of president of the federation, but Meany's refusal to retire at 65 frustrated that ambition. The UAW charged that the federation leadership " 'lacked the social vision and the dynamic qualities essential to fulfill the role of a creative force for constructive social change in a free society' "[17] and disaffiliated from the federation. The ALA never became an influential force. Most leaders of national unions were not interested in Reuther's social action program, and two years after his death in 1970, the new leadership of the UAW dissolved the ALA.

The lack of a broadly based union commitment to social reform among postwar union leaders has troubled liberals and social activists, and relations between organized labor and the intellectual community have deteriorated. Although the AFL-CIO remains formally neutral in regard to support of the Democratic and Republican parties, it has supported recent Democratic presidential candidates with the exception of George McGovern, and organized labor plays an active role in Democratic party politics at the national and state levels. Meany also demonstrated in several instances that the federation was no longer committed to business unionism in the traditional sense but would actively support a variety of progressive causes, including civil rights. Nevertheless, many academics and political liberals have continued to be disenchanted with what they perceive as the narrow business-union orientation of organized labor. In their view, Meany's firm support of U.S. intervention in Vietnam discredited the federation's position on social issues.

Despite the retirement of Meany and the recent turnover in the old-line leadership of a number of national unions and in the executive council of the AFL-CIO, organized labor appears unlikely to embrace in the near future the type of broad social and economic reforms envisioned by these critics. Kirkland, who was Meany's personal choice to succeed him, will probably conform to the general course that Meany set for the federation. Whether more liberal national union leaders such as William Winpisinger of the machinists (an avowed socialist but a pragmatic business unionist at the bargaining table), Jerry Wurf of the public employees, Douglas Fraser of the auto workers, and William Wynn of the food and commercial workers will generate a new spirit that will appeal to workers in unorganized sectors as well as to members of the intellectual community is unclear.

Most union members today consider themselves part of the middle class, evince little sense of responsibility toward unorganized workers, and are often critical of welfare and other government programs to provide aid to the less fortunate. They frequently oppose affirmative action and other civil rights programs that threaten established employment practices including seniority systems. Intellectuals who condemn such attitudes as reactionary and perceive organized labor as co-opted by the establishment misinterpret the traditional role of American unions. Organized labor in this country is not radically oriented. It is not a revolutionary arm of the proletariat, nor is it a cohesive mass movement in support of social change. It operates pragmatically, seeking to advance the interests of its members within the institutional framework of our existing enterprise system.

A CONCLUDING COMMENT

A quarter century after the merger of the A.F. of L. and the CIO, the expectation of significant membership gains by a union movement more responsive to the needs of the current generation of workers has not been realized.* The community appears increasingly less sympathetic to the cause of organized labor, and unions find it difficult to appeal to unorganized workers. The reasons for this loss of appeal are complex and reflect economic, social, and political changes within a nation with one of the highest material standards of living in the world.[18]

Workers unaware of the early struggles of unions cannot visualize the organized labor movement as a militant protector of the rights and interests of wage earners. Unions today obtain recognition procedurally, through the National Labor Relations Board, and employers can no longer engage in antiunion activities with impunity. Many unions enjoy a high degree of institutional security, and most labor disputes are resolved within a framework established by our law of collective bargaining. Union leaders do not generate the enthusiasm associated with popular causes; few of the rising generation were fired in the crucible of overt industrial conflict, and many leaders appear to be prototypes of our pluralistic society's "organization man."

---

* As we have pointed out before, the public sector has been an obvious exception. However, the fiscal problems facing many cities and the public resentment aroused by what are considered strikes against the public welfare may make it more difficult for public sector unions to achieve comparable gains in the future.

The growth, relatively and absolutely, of the white-collar labor force; the shortening of the workweek and the concomitant increase in leisure time; the larger number of more educated persons in the population; and the protection afforded significant portions of the labor force by private health and welfare programs and social security have contributed to the middle-class orientation of American workers.

At the same time, an increasing number of workers, particularly the younger and more educated members of the labor force, have become concerned about the quality of life in both work and nonwork environments. The inability to fulfill their personal needs and expectations in the workplace may encourage such persons to seek a more active role in structuring the "web of rule" that regulates the employment relationship and in pursuing greater autonomy as employees. Collective bargaining appears to be an appropriate instrument for achieving these objectives, but traditional business unionism may not prove responsive to such needs. This too may make it more difficult for organized labor to appeal to unorganized workers. It may also threaten organized labor's existing power base, as workers with new lifestyles replace the current generation of union members.

DISCUSSION QUESTIONS

1. What factors were responsible for (a) the passage and (b) the content of the Taft-Hartley Act?
2. Was the merger of the A.F. of L. and CIO inevitable or the result of circumstances peculiar to the 1950–1954 period?
3. Has the failure of the union movement to maintain its membership base been due to factors external or internal to the movement?
4. Why have relations between the union movement and the intellectual community deteriorated?
5. What led to the passage of the Landrum-Griffin Act? Do you believe that the act has proved successful?
6. What organizational problems presently confront the union movement?
7. Do you expect that "social unionism" will prove appealing to the "new" generation of union leaders?
8. What role did unions play in the 1980 presidential campaign?

SELECTED READINGS

The A.F. of L.-CIO Merger

Goldberg, Arthur J. *AFL-CIO: Labor United.* New York: McGraw-Hill, 1956. See particularly chaps. 1–4.

Seidman, Joel. "Efforts Toward Merger, 1935–1955." In *Industrial and Labor Relations Review* 9, no. 3 (April 1956): pp. 353–370. The same issue also contains other articles on the subject.

The Unions in the 1970s

Dunlop, John T. "Past and Future Tendencies in American Labor Organizations." In *Daedalus* (Winter 1978): pp. 79–96.

"Strategies and Problems in Union Organizing." In *Proceedings of the Thirty-First Annual Meeting, Industrial Relations Research Association, August 29–31, 1978.* Madison, Wisc.: Industrial Relations Research Association, 1979, pp. 212–249. Four papers that provide a recent overview of union organizing problems.

Notes

1. Joel Seidman, *American Labor from Defense to Reconversion* (Chicago: University of Chicago Press, 1953), pp. 223–224.
2. *The New York Times,* October 31, 1945, quoted in ibid., p. 220.
3. Seidman, *American Labor,* p. 233.
4. U.S. Department of Labor, Bureau of Labor Statistics, *Handbook of Labor Statistics, 1975—Reference Edition,* Bulletin 1865, Table 158, p. 389.
5. Chamber of Commerce of the United States, *Employee Benefits 1978* (Washington, D.C.: 1979), p. 5. The benefit payments described include compulsory social security contributions by employers.
6. U.S. Department of Labor, *Handbook of Labor Statistics, 1975,* Table 158, p. 389.
7. Joel Seidman, "Efforts Toward Merger, 1935–1955," in *Industrial and Labor Relations Review* 9, no. 3 (April 1956): p. 370.
8. *The New York Times,* December 12, 1954, p. E–7.
9. The description of merger negotiations relies heavily on Seidman, "Efforts Toward Merger, 1935–1955."
10. Lucretia M. Dewey, "Union Merger Pace Quickens," in *Monthly Labor Review* 94, no. 6 (June 1971): p. 63.
11. Charles J. Janus, "Union Mergers in the 1970s: A Look at the Results," in *Monthly Labor Review* 101, no. 10 (October 1978): p. 13.
12. Cf. John T. Dunlop, "Structural Changes in the American Labor Movement and Industrial Relations System," in *Proceedings of the Ninth Annual Meeting, Industrial Relations Research Association, 1956* (Madison, Wisc.: Industrial Relations Research Association, 1957), pp. 12–29.
13. U.S. Department of Labor, Bureau of Labor Statistics, *Directory of National Unions and Employee Associations, 1971,* Bulletin 1750, p. 73.
14. U.S. Department of Labor, Bureau of Labor Statistics, *Directory of National Unions and Employee Associations, 1975,* Bulletin 1937, pp. 60 ff, and *Directory of National Unions and Employee Associations, 1977,* Bulletin 2044, pp. 61 ff.
15. Cf. Ronald Berenbeim, "The Declining Market for Unionization," *The Conference Board Information Bulletin* no. 44 (August 1978). For a somewhat more optimistic analysis of growth trends see Irving Bernstein, "The Growth of American Unions, 1945–1960," in *Labor History* 2, no. 2 (Spring 1961): pp. 135–151.
16. Thomas A. Kochan, "How American Workers View Labor Unions," in *Monthly Labor Review* 102, no. 4 (April 1979): p. 30. Emphasis added.
17. *The New York Times,* April 11, 1969, p. 39.
18. For papers that provide a recent overview of union organizing problems, see the section "Strategies and Problems in Union Organizing," in *Proceedings of the Thirty-First Annual Meeting, Industrial Relations Research Association, August 29–31, 1978* (Madison, Wisc.: Industrial Relations Research Association, 1979), pp. 212–249.

Chapter 14
UNION STRUCTURE AND GOVERNMENT AND COLLECTIVE BARGAINING

The immediately preceding chapters described the growth and present condition of American unions. In the remaining chapters of Part Three we take a closer look at the participants in collective bargaining. In this chapter, we will describe the structure and government of American unions, how unions organize and prepare for collective bargaining, and the weapons they use to achieve their goals. In Chapter 15, we will describe how management handles employee relations and collective bargaining and the weapons it uses.

UNION STRUCTURE AND GOVERNMENT

Union and Association Membership

We have already described the growth in union and association membership in Chapter 13. According to the latest available biennial survey of the Bureau of Labor Statistics, an estimated 23.1 million U.S. workers were union or association members in 1976.* Some 19.5 million were members of the 175 national unions

* For preliminary BLS estimates of membership in 1978 see *supra,* footnote p. 297.

with headquarters in the United States (15.3 million were members of the 112 national unions affiliated with the AFL-CIO), 3.2 million were members of professional and state and municipal employee associations, 42,000 were members of locals affiliated directly with the AFL-CIO, and 332,000 were members of single firm or unaffiliated local unions.[1] Excluding members of the latter group of unions and Canadian members, 23.4 percent of the labor force and 28.3 percent of nonagricultural workers were union or association members in 1976.[2]

Union membership is concentrated in a few states; in 1976, New York, California, and Pennsylvania accounted for almost one-third of all union members, and these states plus Illinois, Ohio, and Michigan accounted for over half of the total membership. Over half of the members of employee associations were in the same six states plus New Jersey and Texas.[3]

The Structure of the Union Movement

The basic structural axis of the AFL-CIO is shown as the middle vertical line in Figure 14.1 The individual union (or association) member belongs to a local union (or chapter) that has been chartered by a national union (or association) affiliated with the federation.

Local, state, and national unions have also developed a variety of arrangements to coordinate their economic and political activities. These cooperative arrangements are represented by the supplementary axes in Figure 14.1.

In 1976, national unions ranged in size from the 17 member Siderographers union (an AFL-CIO affiliate of plate-printing artists employed in printing

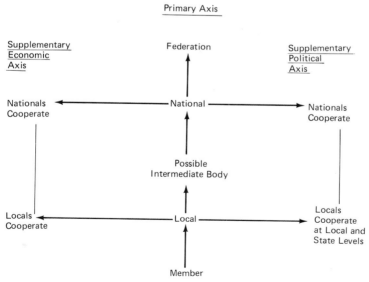

Figure 14.1   The Basic Structure of the AFL-CIO

paper money, bonds, and securities) to the 1.9 million member Teamsters (an independent union). Membership is concentrated in the larger organizations, with the 16 largest accounting for 60 percent of all members.[4] The distribution of unions and associations by number of members in 1976 is shown in Table 14.1. The national unions and employee associations reporting 100,000 or more members in 1976 are shown in Table 14.2.

In 1976, the 175 national unions in existence had 68,155 locals, and the 35 employee associations in existence had 14,939 "chapters." Over half of the locals had been chartered by 16 large unions; two-thirds of the association chapters had been chartered by the National Education Association (an independent association).[5] It is estimated that most locals probably have fewer than 300 members; probably less than 10 percent have more than 1,000 members.[6]

Union Jurisdictions

As we saw in Chapter 13, the main reason given by the A.F. of L. for its refusal to issue charters to industrial unions during the Great Depression was the need to protect the formal jurisdiction granted to existing national unions in their charters. Although the sanctity of exclusive jurisdiction was eventually violated by the dualism that resulted from the formation of the CIO, by NLRB decisions about the units from which collective bargaining representatives will be elected, and by the no-raiding pact that preceded the formation of the AFL-CIO, the protection of jurisdictional rights remains a fundamental objective of American unions. Any invasion of an established jurisdiction, or any prospective invasion of a formal jurisdiction as a result of an organizing campaign, is viewed as a threat to the preservation of job opportunities for the union's members and to the survival and growth of the union itself.

The jurisdiction of a national union has a single dimension: the occupational or industrial categories specified in its charter. There is a second dimension to the jurisdiction of local unions, namely the *geographic* area within which they are permitted to organize and bargain. Geographic jurisdictions are usually clear cut. Disputes over who should organize certain types of workers on the other hand have been among the most serious internal problems of organized labor.

Under our law of collective bargaining, the National Labor Relations Board determines the unit in which an election to select the bargaining representative is conducted. If two or more unions are trying to organize the same group of workers, the board in determining the occupational categories to be included in the bargaining (electoral) unit may indirectly determine the type of union that will represent the workers.

Types of Unions

There are five basic categories of unions: pure craft unions, amalgamated unions, quasi-industrial unions, pure industrial unions, and multiindustry unions. A

Table 14.1 THE DISTRIBUTION OF NATIONAL UNIONS AND EMPLOYEE ASSOCIATIONS BY SIZE, 1976[a]

SIZE OF ORGANIZATION	UNIONS AND ASSOCIATIONS COMBINED		UNIONS						ASSOCIATIONS			
			TOTAL		MEMBERS						MEMBERS	
	NUMBER	PERCENT OF TOTAL	NUMBER	PERCENT OF TOTAL	NUMBER (IN THOUSANDS)	PERCENT OF TOTAL	NUMBER AFL-CIO AFFILIATES	NUMBER UNAFFILIATED UNIONS	NUMBER	PERCENT OF TOTAL	NUMBER (IN THOUSANDS)	PERCENT OF TOTAL
Total[b]	210	100.0	175	100.0	21,129	100.0	112	63	35	100.0	3,028	100.0
Under 1,000 members	25	11.9	24	13.7	9	c	5	19	1	2.9	1	c
1,000 and under 5,000	39	18.6	27	15.4	71	.3	7	20	12	34.3	42	1.4
5,000 and under 10,000	11	5.2	10	5.7	71	.3	6	4	1	2.9	8	.3
10,000 and under 25,000	34	16.2	24	13.7	378	1.8	19	5	10	28.6	141	4.7
25,000 and under 50,000	30	14.3	26	14.9	884	4.2	20	6	4	11.4	114	3.8
50,000 and under 100,000	20	9.5	19	10.9	1,353	6.4	15	4	1	2.9	73	2.4
100,000 and under 200,000	20	9.5	16	9.1	2,345	11.1	14	2	4	11.4	556	18.4
200,000 and under 300,000	11	5.2	10	5.7	2,369	11.2	9	1	1	2.9	207	6.8
300,000 and under 400,000	3	1.4	3	1.7	995	4.7	3	—	—	—	—	—
400,000 and under 500,000	4	1.9	4	2.3	1,781	8.4	4	—	—	—	—	—
500,000 and under 1,000,000	9	4.3	9	5.1	6,324	29.9	9	—	—	—	—	—
1,000,000 and over	4	1.9	3	1.7	4,547	21.5	1	2	1	2.9	1,887	62.3

[a] Because of rounding, sums of individual items may not equal totals.
[b] National and international labor unions and employee associations were asked to report their average dues-paying membership for 1976. One hundred seventy-four labor unions reported a total of 21,126,000 members, and the bureau estimated on the basis of other information that membership of the one union that did not report was 3,000. Members of local unions directly affiliated with the AFL-CIO were not accounted for in the estimates. Also excluded are members of unaffiliated unions not interstate in scope. Membership figures for areas outside of the United States were compiled primarily from union reports to the bureau.
[c] Less than 0.05 percent.

SOURCE: U.S. Department of Labor, Bureau of Labor Statistics, *Directory of National Unions and Employee Associations, 1977*, Bulletin 2044, Table 8, p. 65.

Table 14.2 NATIONAL UNIONS AND EMPLOYEE ASSOCIATIONS REPORTING 100,000 OR MORE MEMBERS, 1976[a]

ORGANIZATION[b]	MEMBERS (IN THOUSANDS)	ORGANIZATION[b]	MEMBERS (IN THOUSANDS)
Unions:		Unions:—*Continued*	
Teamsters (ind.)	1,889	Railway Clerks	211
Automobile Workers (ind.)	1,358	Rubber	211
Steelworkers	1,300	Painters	195
Electrical (IBEW)	924	Retail, Wholesale	200
Machinists	917	Iron Workers	179
Carpenters	820	Oil, Chemical	177
State, County	750	Fire Fighters	174
Retail Clerks	699	Electrical (UE) (ind.)	165
Laborers	627	Sheet Metal	153
Service Employees	575	Government (NAGE) (ind.)	150
Meat Cutters	510	Transit Union	150
Clothing and Textile Workers	502	Transport Workers	150
Communications Workers	483	Boilermakers	145
Teachers	446	Bakery	135
Hotel	432	Bricklayers	135
Operating Engineers	420	Maintenance of Way	119
Ladies' Garment	365	Printing and Graphic	109
Musicians	330	Woodworkers	109
Paperworkers	300	Typographical	100
Mine Workers (ind.)	277	Associations:	
Transportation	265	National Education	1,887
Government (AFGE)	260	Civil Service (NYS)	207
Postal Workers	252	Nurses	200
Electrical (IUE)	238	Police	135
Plumbers	228	Classified School Employees	109
Letter Carriers	227	California	112

[a] Based on union and association reports to the bureau, with membership rounded to the nearest thousand. All unions not identified as (ind.) are affiliated with the AFL-CIO.
[b] For mergers and changes in affiliation since 1976, see Appendix A.
SOURCE: U.S. Department of Labor, Bureau of Labor Statistics, *Directory of National Unions and Employee Associations, 1977*, Bulletin 2044, Table 9, p. 65.

union's actual jurisdiction may be modified over time. Survival requires that unions respond to "the inward pressures created by changes in environments: in product and labor markets and in the larger community," and as these responses occur, structural modifications take place that make "pure" structural typologies less meaningful.[7]

A *pure craft union* includes workers possessing the skill of a specific craft. According to one definition, "a craft involves a high degree of manual dexterity, the exercise of considerable independent judgment in carrying out prescribed operations, responsibility for a valuable product and equipment, and extensive preliminary training which may be incorporated in a formal apprenticeship program."[8] The Major League Baseball Players Association, the Journeyman

Horseshoers, the Siderographers, and the Aeronautical Examiners are pure craft unions. Most national unions identified as craft unions are either amalgamated unions or quasi-industrial unions.

An *amalgamated union* represents skilled workers in related trades who believe that their interests can be advanced more effectively through combined action. Thus, a relatively small skilled group may affiliate with a larger organization in order to enhance its bargaining power, or a union of workers possessing a skill made obsolete by technological change may merge with a union having jurisdiction over a surviving skill. Amalgamated unions include the Actors and Artistes of America, with nine different professional "branches"; the Plate Printers,' Die Stampers' and Engravers' Union; several "craft" unions in the building trades such as the Bricklayers, Masons, and Plasterers; and the United Transportation Union, which has jurisdiction over all the operating trades on the railroads except the locomotive engineers. Many amalgamated unions no longer retain their "pure craft" character and have become quasi-industrial unions.

A *quasi-industrial union* will include workers in one or more skilled crafts plus the semiskilled and perhaps unskilled workers employed in the same sector of an industry. The inclusion of these workers helps the crafts to control apprenticeship and hence entrance into the trade; and by insulating the membership from possible nonunion competition and strikebreaking, the union also provides a more effective bargaining base. Examples include the Boilermakers, Iron Shipbuilders, Blacksmiths, Forgers, and Helpers; the Metal Polishers, Buffers, Platers, and Helpers; and a number of "craft" unions in the building trades. The work over which these unions have jurisdiction is not coterminous with the industries in which their members are employed.

A *pure industrial union* has a work jurisdiction coterminous with an industry and admits as members all workers employed in the industry. Examples include the Furniture Workers, the Glass Bottle Blowers Association, and the Grain Millers.

A *multiindustry union* has a jurisdiction that extends beyond a single industry. Most industrial unions have gradually been converted into multiindustry unions. Examples include the United Automobile, Aerospace and Agricultural Implement Workers (UAW); the Amalgamated Clothing and Textile Workers; the former Brewery, Flour, Cereal, Soft Drink and Distillery Workers, which merged with the Teamsters in 1973; the Oil, Chemical and Atomic Workers; and the United Steel Workers (USW), which has locals in basic steel, steel fabrication, and steel distribution, and in the aluminum, can, and nonferrous metal mining industries. The industries within the jurisdiction of a multiindustry national are usually related in some fashion. They may use similar technology or the same material inputs or produce for similar markets; or the firms may be integrated vertically or be part of a conglomerate. A local affiliated with a multiindustry national generally operates within a single industry.

Any analysis of the structure, organization, and operation of a union movement with such a variety of components is necessarily complex; we shall turn first to an examination of the most comprehensive structural unit, the AFL-CIO.

THE AFL-CIO

The American Federation of Labor and Congress of Industrial Organizations (AFL-CIO) is *not* a union. It is a loose association of autonomous national unions that may be compared to member states of the United Nations. National unions join the federation voluntarily and retain almost complete autonomy over their internal affairs. In addition to affiliated national unions, there are state and local *subfederations* that cooperate in political matters and *national trade and industrial departments* and *local department councils* consisting, respectively, of national unions and of local unions that coordinate their collective bargaining and political activities. The formal structure of the AFL-CIO in 1980 is shown in Figure 14.2. This formal structure is supplemented by a variety of informal arrangements.

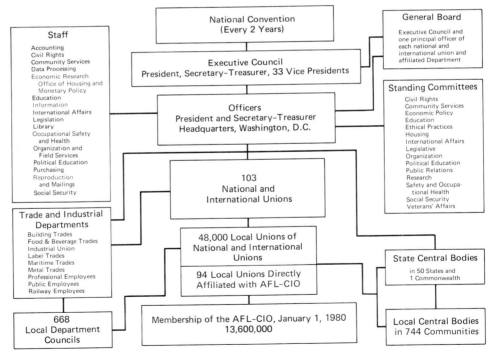

Figure 14.2 The Structural Organization of the American Federation of Labor and Congress of Industrial Organizations in 1980 (Source: American Federation of Labor and Congress of Industrial Organizations.)

Individual workers do not normally enjoy "citizenship" in the federation. However, the AFL-CIO functions as a national union for the 94 local unions directly affiliated with it. Such affiliation is usually temporary; eventually the locals are turned over to an appropriate national union (either an established one or one that has been newly chartered). In the case of locals affiliated with an organizing committee, the committee will presumably form the basis for a new autonomous national union.

The AFL-CIO is a limited sovereign power. Its formal authority over affiliated nationals is confined to four areas: the settlement of internal disputes, ethical practices, totalitarian domination, and civil rights. It can expel an affiliate, but this is a hollow threat in the case of a well-established national. Except in the case of directly affiliated local unions, the federation does not represent workers in collective bargaining, nor can it dictate the bargaining or political objectives of affiliated nationals.

The principal functions of the federation include (1) representing the interests of organized labor through lobbying and public relations; (2) supporting candidates for public office through its Committee on Political Education (COPE); (3) organizing the unorganized; (4) chartering new national unions; (5) providing research and other technical support services; (6) resolving jurisdictional disputes between affiliated unions; (7) enforcing its six ethical practices codes (a dormant activity since the passage of the Landrum-Griffin Act); (8) encouraging national unions to adopt and implement more progressive civil rights programs; and (9) representing American labor in international organizations. These functions fall into two broad categories: external activities designed to present organized labor's views to a variety of publics and internal activities.

Official federation policies are usually formulated by the biennial convention that is the supreme governing body of the organization. The executive council is the formal governing body between conventions, and the president, as chief executive officer, implements constitutional and policy provisions between meetings of the council.

The Convention

There is no formal separation of powers in the AFL-CIO, all the fundamental governing powers rest with the biennial convention. In practice, basic policies, which will be significantly influenced by a strong chief executive, are formulated and modified on an ongoing basis, and the convention may be called on to ratify policy decisions already in effect.

The number of convention delegates is based on a national's reported membership on which a per capita tax (presently 19 cents a month) has been paid with a relative decline in delegate strength as membership increases. However each delegate of a national union, organizing committee or directly affiliated local casts one vote for *each member* he or she represents. Each state and local central body and each national trade and industrial department has only one delegate and one vote. Under this arrangement, the larger national unions—particularly two groups, the building trades unions and the unions affiliated with the industrial union department—constitute the principal power blocs at the convention.

The convention functions in much the same way as a national political convention. Policy resolutions are prepared in or referred to committees whose members are appointed by the president, and the administration usually has effective control over resolutions and petitions. Most of the work of the convention is done off the floor, and a vote usually represents formal acquiescence to policies for which the necessary support has already been generated. The convention has authority to suspend and to expel affiliates.

The Administrative Framework of the Federation

OFFICERS

The chief executive officers, the *president* and the *secretary-treasurer,* are elected by the convention. The president supervises the affairs of the federation and presides at meetings of the executive council and the general board. A capable president, in control of the federation's administrative machinery, develops a strong political base and can expect a long tenure in office. Except for one term, Samuel Gompers served as president of the A.F. of L. from 1886 until his death in 1924; William Green was president from 1924 until his death in 1952; and George Meany served as president of the A.F. of L. and subsequently of the AFL-CIO from 1952 to 1979. There are 33 vice-presidents, who usually represent the very largest unions, strategic industry groups such as the building trades or public employees, a rough balance between former A.F. of L. and former CIO unions, and more recently, the interests of nonwhite and female union members.[9]

The *executive council,* composed of the two principal executive officers and the 33 vice-presidents, is the governing body of the federation between conventions. It is responsible for "the organization of unorganized industries by means most appropriate for that purpose," and keeping the federation free of corrupt and totalitarian influences. It has the authority to suspend affiliates upon a two-thirds vote and acts as an appellate tribunal in jurisdictional disputes. Its decisions are generally approved by the convention.

There is also a *general board,* consisting of the members of the executive council plus the principal officer of each affiliated national union, trade, and industrial department. Meetings of the board are called by the president or the executive council. The board functions as a visible source of approval for the policies and actions of the administration and as a sounding board for innovative policy proposals.

The constitution of the federation provides for 15 *standing committees* (for example, the legislative and political education committees) and for such other standing committees as may be necessary to carry on the activities of the federation. The Committee on Political Education is unique because it functions as an active operating arm of the federation, with its own headquarters and field staff. Under federal law, unions cannot contribute money directly to political parties or candidates, and COPE is financed through voluntary contributions. COPE's national staff concentrates on presidential campaigns and the election of United States senators and representatives. However, "the sole endorsement at the national level comes in Presidential contests and traditionally is made by the General Board [not the AFL-CIO as a whole]."[10] COPE's 50 state organizations cooperate with its national staff and endorse candidates for the U.S. Senate and House of Representatives, for governorships, for state legislatures, and for other state posts.

Federation Departments

The AFL-CIO has nine *trade and industrial departments*. Seven departments consist of national unions with related interests. There is also a *Union Label Department*, consisting of nationals that use union labels to increase the sale of union-made goods, and an *Industrial Union Department* (IUD), consisting of unions that have members organized on an industrial base and pay a per capita tax to the department on this portion of their membership.

The first group, which includes the Building and Construction Trades, the Food and Beverage Trades, the Maritime Trades, the Metal Trades, the Professional Employees, the Public Employees, and the Railway Employees departments, coordinate the legislative activities and some bargaining activities of their affiliates and attempt to resolve jurisdictional disputes between affiliates. The IUD serves as a base within the federation for industrial unions formerly affiliated with the CIO. It has encouraged coordinated bargaining by its affiliated nationals, and over 60 "committees" have participated in such bargaining. A number of *staff departments* provide research and advisory services to the federation's officers and affiliated organizations.

The *Department of Organization and Field Services* is an operational unit under the direction of the president. It has a director and a field staff who help established unions with organizing campaigns, initiate organizing drives in industries or plants with little or no previous history of organization, and help to coordinate joint bargaining efforts. The federation's role in organizational efforts has been limited because federation officials believe that the basic responsibility for organizing rests with the unions active in the various crafts and industries. However, many national unions are reluctant or unable to mount and sustain an adequate organizational effort, and the federation's present organizing "philosophy" may have to be modified if the relative decline in union membership is to be reversed.

Federation Finances

The principal source of federation income is the *per capita tax,* presently 19 cents per month, on the full paid-up membership of national unions, organizing committees, and directly affiliated local unions. The organization's General Fund income for the year ending June 30, 1979, was $27.8 million, of which $25.2 million represented per capita tax payments.[11] The financial resources of the federation are modest. The total assets of the basic General Fund on June 30, 1979, were $24.8 million, of which $19 million represented the value of the organization's national headquarters and the George Meany Labor Studies Center land and buildings.[12]

THE NATIONAL UNIONS

The national union is the dominant governing unit and, in most industries, the locus of economic power within the union movement. The national unions affiliated with the AFL-CIO are autonomous, self-governing units, and most of them exercise close control over their affiliated locals. The centralization of power in the national union reflects the characteristic emphasis of American unions on the collective bargaining process, a desire to "take wages out of competition"— that is, to have uniform wages and benefits for employees of firms producing for the same product market—and the consequent evolution of a supralocal form of organization as product and labor markets expanded.

This development had two dimensions: the assumption by the nationals of operational control over at least some aspects of collective bargaining and the formal transfer of constitutional authority to the nationals, often at a later date. The centralization of authority in the national union has tended to increase over time and is generally higher in unions (like the USW) that were organized "from the top down" than in unions (like the UAW) that grew out of grass roots movements.[13]

Craft union locals in local market industries often retain considerable control over the bargaining process, particularly in the building and construction trades. The authority of the national may be recognized by a requirement that it approve new contracts, but this is often a pro forma arrangement. In addition, some craft and industrial unions have developed structural units between national and local unions that parallel the bargaining units of the employers with whom the unions negotiate.

The Functions of National Unions

The principal functions of a national union include organizing unorganized workers, protecting its basic jurisdiction and the jurisdictions of its affiliated locals, helping locals and intermediate bodies with collective bargaining, supporting affiliates on strike by providing strike benefits and other forms of aid, supporting legislative and other programs of interest to its membership, and supporting the general programs of the AFL-CIO. If it appears that these functions can be better served through combined action with other unions, the national *may* cooperate with these unions on a formal or informal basis. The federation departments described previously are designed to encourage such cooperation. More recently, national unions have formed coalitions to bargain with firms dealing with several unions and have cooperated in organizational campaigns in certain industries and geographic areas.

National unions must respond to, and seek compromises between, the demands of different constituencies *within* their jurisdiction—differences, for example, between low seniority and high seniority workers, between blue-collar and white-collar workers, or between the bulk of their membership and highly skilled members. In the larger national unions, intermediate organizations may be set up to represent members in different industries or regions, members that work for major corporations having agreements with the union, or occupational subgroups. There are for example separate collective bargaining departments within the UAW for the aerospace industry, the General Motors Corporation, and highly skilled members.

The Finances of National Unions

National unions and their affiliated locals get money from three principal sources: initiation fees, monthly dues, and special assessments. Most of these charges seem reasonable; the higher fees and dues are usually required by unions that have obtained high wage scales or superior benefit programs for their members or both.

Since 1947, unions have been prohibited by the Taft-Hartley Act from requiring an initiation fee that the NLRB finds excessive or discriminatory. Most initiation fees appear modest relative to the wages and benefits received by the membership. Initiation fees are shared, with 50 percent commonly going to the parent national. Craft unions tend to have somewhat higher initiation fees than industrial unions. Although in most cases these higher fees, which can often be paid in installments, reflect a "service" payment by new members for gains already achieved by the union, high initiation fees have occasionally been used to restrict entry into a trade.

The primary source of income for national unions is the monthly or quarterly *per capita tax* paid by affiliated locals and financed out of the *monthly dues* received by the locals. The per capita tax is set by the national and is generally less than $6 a month.

Assessments, which may be either voluntary or compulsory, are irregular charges levied for a specific purpose and for a limited time. For example, an assessment may be used to build up a depleted strike benefit fund. Assessments must usually be approved by the national convention of the union or a membership referendum; in emergencies, they may be levied by the executive board.

National Constitutions

The constitution of each national union is its formal source of authority. In principle, the powers of a national derive from its members, and most constitutions provide for a democratic form of government based on the representation of members by delegates at national conventions. Most constitutions give the national supreme authority over affiliated locals, as well as the power to review such matters as the content of collective agreements, strike authorizations, and the administration of a local's finances. In the case of contracts negotiated by affiliates in local market industries, the right to review contracts may be limited to provisions that are supposed to conform to national policy.

Actually, the degree of democracy in a national union often falls short of that suggested by its constitution; moreover, most nationals are operated less democratically than locals. National unions generally function as political organizations rather than rule enforcement agencies, and violations of their rules by locals are often handled informally.[14] Title I of the Landrum-Griffin Act, a "Bill of Rights of Members of Labor Organizations," attempts to protect union members against arbitrary acts by union officials. A major study of the act recently concluded that "title I has been effective in guaranteeing union democracy." However, it is presently "of no help to members [who as individuals are] financially unable . . . or . . . are fearful of bringing suit [against a union]."[15]

Local unions that refuse to conform to national standards or directives or unions whose officers have been found guilty of corrupt activities may be placed in *trusteeship* or *receivership*. The national union then seizes the assets of the local and takes control of its affairs through appointed trustees or receivers. In some cases, notably those of the United Mine Workers and the Teamsters, this device has been used to stifle local opposition to the administration of the national union. Recognizing that trusteeship powers are both indispensable and open to abuse, the Landrum-Griffin Act provides standards for establishing and administering trusteeships, limiting their duration to 18 months "unless the labor organization shall show by clear and convincing proof that the continuation of the trusteeship is necessary for a purpose allowable under [the act]."[16]

National Conventions

The typical national constitution makes the annual or biennial convention the supreme governing body, the source of constitutional authority, the sole legislative body, and the ultimate court of appeal within the union. In practice, the chief elected officers of the union may effectively control its operations. The convention is a delegate body in which the locals are represented on a per capita membership basis, often modified according to some formula that reduces the relative delegate or voting strength of larger locals. Most national conventions are tightly run political forums, similar in operation to the conventions of the AFL-CIO. The administration controls the convention through appointments to key committees, and roll call votes are often the end result of off-the-floor maneuvering. Nevertheless, the convention is an important channel of communication between the national union and its members and a partial substitute for a general membership meeting.

Appeals from decisions of the president or executive board are usually heard by the convention, although the UAW and the Upholsterers have set up review boards composed of disinterested members of the public to handle such matters.[17] Under the convention appeals system, a committee hears an appeal and then reports its decision to the convention for approval. In practice, this does not seem to be a very equitable system. According to one study, having the convention review appeals merely "serves to ratify pardons granted by the union's president, to justify his political expediencies, and to confirm the dominance of the national union in most matters."[18]

National Officers

The *general executive board* or *executive council* is the highest administrative authority in a national union. It charters local unions, is responsible for running the union between conventions, is the initial appellate body at the national level, and supervises the work of union officials. The typical board consists of the principal executive officers (the president and the secretary-treasurer) and a number of vice-presidents, who are usually officers of intermediate or local subordinate organizations. In large industrial unions, the vice-presidents are often elected on a regional basis and serve as administrators of the various regions. The distribution of power between the chief executive officer and the board varies according to the formal power structure established by the constitution, the power base of key members of the board, and the personality and ability of the various officers, particularly the chief executive.

The principal officers of national unions are usually not militant idealists, but professional unionists who have risen through the ranks, are committed to the union as a career, and function as business executives. Their salaries are usually significantly higher than those of subordinate officials of the national, local officers, and working members, but in general they do not appear excessive compared with the salaries of their counterparts in business.[19] The salaries and expense accounts of the 20 highest paid union presidents in 1977 are shown in Table 14.3; salary and other payments to the 20 highest-paid business executives included in the *Forbes 1977 Survey* are shown in Table 14.4. There is no predictable relationship between the size of a union's membership and the salary of its president. The Landrum-Griffin Act provides a variety of safeguards against illegal payments to union officers but does not prohibit an individual from receiving a salary for more than one office. Some executives of national and local unions holding several offices receive salaries totaling well over $100,000 a year; in 1976, one vice-president of the Teamsters received $192,000 from six posts.[20] According to *Business Week*, "multiple jobs and salaries—and handsome benefits—are a way of

Table 14.3 SALARIES, ALLOWANCES, AND EXPENSES OF THE 20 HIGHEST PAID NATIONAL UNION PRESIDENTS, 1977

UNION	TOTAL SALARY PLUS ALLOWANCES AND EXPENSES (IF AVAILABLE)
1. Teamsters	$169,453
2. Operating Engineers	130,154
3. Hotel and Restaurant Employees	126,951
4. Seafarers	125,699
5. Retail Clerks[a]	123,000
6. Laborers	109,776
7. Railway and Airline Clerks	104,378
8. Plumbers	100,370
9. Iron Workers	100,355
10. Teachers (AFT/UFT)	98,286
11. Maritime	91,398
12. Sheet Metal Workers	90,026
13. Meat Cutters[b]	89,692
14. Painters	87,330
15. State, County and Municipal Employees	81,505
16. Service Employees	80,835
17. Electrical Workers (IBEW)	80,498
18. Longshoremen (ILA)	75,948
19. Carpenters	75,488
20. Steelworkers[a]	75,000

[a] Changed office in midyear.
[b] Chairman.
SOURCE: Based on data from "Where Tradition and Politics Rule," from the May 15, 1978 issue of *Business Week*, Tables pp. 94 and 96, by special permission, © 1978 by McGraw-Hill, Inc., New York, N.Y. 10020. All rights reserved.

life in the Teamsters. In 1976 more than 50 officials at the local and regional levels made more than $70,000."[21]

Most national officers enjoy a long tenure; as administrators, they develop a strong political base, and in the absence of a two-party system, they have a great advantage over opposition candidates. (One union, the International Typographical Union, has a formal two-party system.[22]) The Landrum-Griffin Act requires that officers of national unions be elected not less than once every five years. This and other provisions of the act have increased the possibility of effective opposition to the administration developing within a national union. Recently, the presidents of several large nationals, including the United Steel Workers, the International Union of Electrical Workers, and the United Mine Workers, were defeated after bitter election campaigns.

There are two types of *subordinate officials* in nationals: members of the headquarters staff and organizers and international representatives. These officials are usually appointed by the administration and are part of the union bureaucracy.

Handling participation by a national in the collective bargaining process is often a function of the international representatives. However, national unions are presently providing greater assistance to locals in such matters as negotiating and administering benefit plans, adjusting to technological changes, industrial engineering, and handling grievances.[23]

INTERMEDIATE ORGANIZATIONS

Three types of intermediate organizations have evolved in the union movement: (1) *subfederations* of affiliates of different national unions that support legislation and other political actions favorable to the interests of their members or carry forward public and community relations programs; (2) the units described in the preceding section, internal to and administered by individual national unions, which are designed to increase administrative efficiency, enhance the union's bargaining capability, or provide a vehicle for the representation of special interests

Table 14.4 THE TOTAL REMUNERATION OF THE 20 HIGHEST PAID CHIEF EXECUTIVES OF FIRMS IN THE 1977 *FORBES* SURVEY

COMPANY	CHIEF EXECUTIVE	SALARY & BONUS[a] ($000)	TOTAL REMUNERATION[b] ($000)
1. Fluor	J. Robert Fluor	549	1,121
2. G. D. Searle	Donald H. Rumsfeld	252	1,113
3. Warner Communications	Steven J. Ross	905	1,103[a]
4. Ford Motor	Henry Ford II	682	1,011
5. General Motors	Thomas A. Murphy	475	996
6. Int'l. Tel. & Tel.	Harold S. Geneen[c]	986	994
7. Amer. Broadcasting	Leonard H. Goldenson	750	954
8. Zenith Radio	John J. Nevin	238	904
9. Norton Simon	David J. Mahoney	800	825
10. McGraw-Edison	Edward J. Williams	301	817
11. Tandy	Charles D. Tandy	790	816
12. IBM	Frank T. Cary	333	807
13. Revlon	Michel C. Bergerac	794	797
14. Tenneco	Wilton E. Scott	496	794
15. Ryder System	Leslie O. Barnes	452	774
16. American Home Prods.	William F. Laporte	385	770
17. PepsiCo	Donald M. Kendall	510	750
18. Mobil	Rawleigh Warner, Jr.	725	745
19. Exxon	Clifton C. Garvin, Jr.	696	724
20. American Tel. & Tel.	John D. deButts	722	722

[a] Excludes amounts contingently payable in later years in accordance with long-term incentive program.
[b] Includes bonuses paid in cash or in unrestricted shares of company stock—salary, bonus, director's fees, and deferred compensation. Excludes stock options.
[c] Succeeded by Lyman C. Hamilton, Jr. 1/1/78.
SOURCE: "The Boss' Paycheck: Who Gets the Biggest," in *Forbes* 121, no. 11 (May 29, 1978): Table, p. 87.

within the national; and (3) *combinations of local unions,* which increases their effectiveness as bargaining agents.

The 50 state and one commonwealth federations, and the 744 local and city central organizations, all of which belong on the right-hand (political) axis of Figure 14.1, are the principal organizations in the first category. The expansion of public sector employment at the state and local level, the increase in union membership among public employees, and the growing number of legislative issues affecting labor have increased the potential political impact of such organizations, and state federations and city centrals will probably become even more influential in the future.[24]

The second category of intermediate organizations includes *corporate councils, industry councils,* and *occupational subdivisions* within a national that handle collective bargaining or provide services to affiliated locals and their members. These units belong on the central axis in Figure 14.1. Examples include the *corporation and industry councils* and *departments* of the UAW; the *district lodges* of the Machinists Union in the aircraft, air transport, and railroad industries; and the various *national trade divisions* of the Teamsters.

The third category of intermediate organizations, which form the left-hand (economic support) axis of Figure 14.1, has three principal subcategories: (1) in industries, with a local market, local unions affiliated with the *same national* may coordinate their bargaining efforts; (2) again, in industries with a local market, locals affiliated with *different nationals* having jurisdiction over workers in a single industry may coordinate their bargaining (and political) activities; or (3) *district* or *regional offices* of a *national union* may provide supportive services to, and less frequently handle collective bargaining for, affiliated locals.

The extent of a product market and degree of cooperation among employers usually determine whether a local or a national union is the dominant influence on an intermediate body involved in collective bargaining. Intermediate organizations that represent special occupational groups within industrial unions often enjoy considerable independent power; the Skilled Trades Department of the UAW, for example, can effectively veto proposed basic agreements.

LOCAL UNIONS

Union members usually equate unionism with their local union. Local union officials handle the day-to-day problems of contract administration; crises are discussed and voted on at meetings of the local; the members of the union administration with whom a member has direct contact are local elected or appointed officials; and the fraternal, community service, and political activities of the union in which individual members may be involved are carried forward at the local level. Locals are usually organized on (1) an *amalgamated* or *quasi-*industries, with a local market, local unions affiliated with the *same national* may in an area have been organized by an industrial union, a single local may be given jurisdiction over all such firms or over those firms producing for the same market. Such broader jurisdictions provide greater administrative efficiency and a more effective bargaining base.

Local unions have two core functions, internal administration and collective bargaining. They have evolved two distinct "governments" to carry out these functions, one to handle relations within the local union organization, and the other to handle the local's continuing relationship with employers.[25] As *union members,* workers are subject to the constitution and bylaws of their locals as administered by the elected officers of the locals; as *employees,* they are subject to the provisions of the collective bargaining agreements negotiated with their employers and policed by the unions' business agents or shop stewards.

General membership meetings presumably provide a democratic forum for determining local policies, for expressing dissent, and for disciplining members who have violated a local's constitution or bylaws. Attendance at these meetings is usually poor, with only 5 to 10 percent of a local's membership present, and the machinery of the organization is usually controlled by the officers and a small core of active members. This does not mean that the local is not a *functional democracy;* its leaders must be responsive to the needs of members to continue in office. Moreover, attendance at meetings is much higher when a discussion of a critical issue such as a contested election, a strike authorization vote, or the ratification of a contract is on the agenda. Skilled craftsmen in local market industries and members of locals in isolated communities may also find that union meetings have economic or social functions that make participation more meaningful.[26]

The degree of autonomy enjoyed by locals is a pragmatic response to (1) external factors, including the structure of product and labor markets, the quality of management in the area, and management's attitude toward unionism; and (2) internal factors, including the type and size of a local, the quality of the local's leadership, the bureaucratic structure of the national union to which it belongs, the attitudes of the members toward unionism, the degree to which members participate in the affairs of the local, and the cultural and political variables peculiar to an area. These factors interact with and are responsive to changes in the work and nonwork environments.

The quality and career commitment of a local's leadership are usually considerably below those of a national's officials, although a large local may have highly professional officers and gradually develop a bureaucratic structure resembling that of a national union. The Landrum-Griffin Act requires a local to "elect its officers not less than once every three years by secret ballot among the members in good standing."

The day-to-day administration of contracts is usually the responsibility of an elected *business agent* in nonfactory, multiemployer craft or amalgamated locals. In industrial plants, it is the responsibility of the *shop steward* or a *committee man or woman.* Business agents act as an intermediary between small employers and their labor force. An agent is a local's principal representative in negotiations, functions as an employment agent for the members of the local, protects the local's jurisdiction, polices collective agreements, and handles grievances (disputes over the interpretation of contracts) in firms that have contracts with the local. Business agents are usually the most powerful officers in locals and often hold other elective posts as well. They are full-time officials and are usually able to develop a broad base of political support that ensures their reelection.

Factory locals have no counterpart of the business agent. They are represented in a shop by one or more *stewards* who are not necessarily members of a union's bargaining team. Shop stewards are a factory worker's continuing point of contact with a union and usually represent workers in the first stage of a grievance procedure.

Collective bargaining at the local level is handled by a committee led by a chief negotiator. In craft and quasi-industrial unions, business agents are key members of negotiating teams; in industrial unions, international representatives —full-time paid officials usually appointed by a national's president to advise and assist a number of locals—may share or assume the major responsibility for collective bargaining. International "reps" often represent a union at a higher level of a grievance procedure. Shop stewards and local officers who demonstrate unusual competence and an awareness of broad policy issues are highly visible to a firm's management and are often recruited for lower level management positions.

UNION MEMBERS

The cellular unit of the American union movement is the individual union member.[27] As we have seen, local unions are the structural units with which a member identifies most closely, and the officials of a local represent the members' point of continuing contact with the organized labor movement. Typical union members consider their locals service organizations designed to help them obtain higher wages, job security, and dignified treatment at their place of employment.[28] Most are "inactives," participating only occasionally in union meetings and having no formal or informal leadership roles within the local organization. The union is not a "way of life" for such members, who usually exhibit a *dual loyalty* to both the union and their employer. During a crisis, they will rally behind their leaders in a demonstration of solidarity, but their support usually represents their perception of the local as a service organization rather than an ideological commitment to the union or to the "labor" movement.

The small proportion of active members in a typical local includes persons for whom participating in union affairs provides psychic satisfaction, persons who view a local elective office as a vehicle for upward social and economic mobility, and some members who consider the union an instrument for achieving more broadly oriented institutional reforms.

INTERNAL UNION PROBLEMS: DEMOCRACY, DISCRIMINATION, CORRUPTION AND RACKETEERING

Analyzing the organization and structure of the American union movement provides a perspective for discussing three problems that have concerned both the general public and students of organized labor: the alleged lack of democracy within unions, discriminatory practices within unions, and corruption and racketeering within the union movement.

Union Democracy

In principle, the power of a national union rests on a democratic base, and a local union meeting exemplifies a type of grass roots democracy. In practice, democracy is a latent rather than an active operational concept in most national unions, and local union meetings, while more closely approximating a democratic model, are usually controlled by the local administration.

In most national unions, the increasing centralization of power and the control of both the convention and the administrative machinery of the union by a small elite have contributed to the decline of effective opposition to the incumbent administration and to the development of a self-perpetuating bureaucracy. Such developments are not unique to labor organizations, but are a manifestation of Robert Michels's more general *Iron Law of Oligarchy*.[29] If *functional democracy* is defined as the kind of grass roots democracy represented by New England town meetings coupled with independent judicial procedures, most national unions must be considered undemocratic. However, the centralization of power and rule by an elite are not inevitably equated with an absence of *functional democracy*. Centralization of power may be essential if a union is to be responsive to the needs of its members, bargain effectively, and administer agreements "responsibly." Although the balance between these objectives and optimal internal democracy is elusive, most national unions seem reasonably responsive to their constituencies and may be considered functionally democratic.

Despite the low attendance at membership meetings, participatory democracy is more common in local unions, particularly during crises. Most local officials do not have the support of an entrenched bureaucracy, must stand for reelection more frequently than the officers of nationals, and consequently are alert to the needs and temper of their members.

Discrimination

Functional democracy becomes sullied if a union discriminates against prospective members because of their race, their sex, or some other personal characteristic. The constitutions of national unions do not contain discriminatory admissions clauses, but some locals of a limited number of national unions continue nevertheless to discriminate against members of minority groups. The most serious violations of individual rights under union security arrangements also appear to involve racial discrimination. Such discrimination usually reflects community mores and is most common in local market industries in which local unions have considerable autonomy.

The officers of the AFL-CIO and of many national unions were in the forefront of the fight for civil rights legislation, but they have often been unable or reluctant to use sanctions against local unions charged with discriminatory practices. The basic problem facing the AFL-CIO in its attempts to eliminate such practices is that short of expelling an affiliated union, it has no way of effectively disciplining it, and expulsion, while cleansing the federation, cannot ensure that the offending affiliate will mend its ways.

The protection afforded members of minority groups under the Taft-Hartley Act as it is currently interpreted by the NLRB and under the Landrum-Griffin Act and the efforts of federal agencies to compel unions to conform to the provisions of our civil rights legislation have reduced discrimination. However, minority groups are still not equally represented in some unions with a long history of discrimination. Apparently, some type of federally enforced quota system will be necessary for such unions to achieve a racially balanced membership.* In some cases, it may be necessary to admit a *disproportionately* large number of minority group members into unions or apprenticeship programs. Not unexpectedly, union members often oppose such "special opportunities" for minority groups.

Corruption and Racketeering

The waterfront investigation conducted by the New York State Crime Commission in 1952 and 1953 and the McClellan Committee's investigation into the affairs of a limited number of unions and labor-management consultants in 1958 and 1959 focused public attention on a variety of corrupt and illicit practices in certain sectors of the organized labor movement.[30] The former provided the basis for a bistate compact between New York and New Jersey regulating the longshore industry in the Port of New York; the latter provided the basis for many of the substantive provisions of the Landrum-Griffin Act.

Corruption and racketeering are not new to the union movement, but these investigations undoubtedly exaggerated their incidence and magnitude. The public tended to blame such practices solely on the union officials involved, forgetting or not realizing that corruption and racketeering are two-way streets and that employers, and in some cases local political officials, were also involved in payoffs and "sweetheart contracts."[31] According to a former district attorney of New York,

---

* Legislation to this effect is discussed below, pp. 418–422.

one of the chief obstacles in the fight to eliminate the labor racketeer is the unwillingness of employers to come forward with evidence of crime in their possession. . . . Nor is it always fear that dictates their decisions. Just as often, . . . it is satisfaction with their selfish and sometimes felonious arrangements.[32]

There is also confusion about the relationship between these practices and the alleged lack of democracy within the union movement. Undemocratic procedures may contribute to the development of such practices, but the correlation is shaky at best; some of the most autocratically run unions have been free of corruption and racketeering.

The traditional types of labor racketeering are associated with highly competitive industries producing for a local market and having either a casual or a highly mobile labor force.[33] According to one observer, "either condition may be sufficient, but when the two appear simultaneously they almost inevitably will stimulate a measure of corruption."[34] Conversely, "systematized racketeering is virtually absent in the oligopolistic industries, the railroads, aircraft production and many others."[35] Since similar market conditions have not led to corruption and racketeering in other countries, this may be a peculiarly American phenomenon. However, the limited extent of labor racketeering in the United States indicates that it is not an inevitable by-product of business unionism.

Corruption and racketeering are not unique to the union movement. On the contrary, they appear to be a pervasive phenomenon in American life:

> racketeering in labor unions appears to flow from a general slackness in American society, an emphasis upon material gain, and practices prevalent in many areas of the business community. . . . [T]he difficulties appear to lie in the ethical and social values prevailing in the business community and in society in general.[36]

These comments are not offered as an apology for corruption and racketeering in the union movement but as a reminder that the quasi-public character of unions gives organized labor a special obligation to resist the venal pressures of a materialistic society.

UNION OBJECTIVES IN COLLECTIVE BARGAINING

Unions have a variety of economic and extraeconomic objectives at the bargaining table and, on a continuing basis, during the administration of a contract. Their most important goals are:

1. increased contract benefits for their members,
2. effective contract administration, and
3. union security.

A limited number of unions also have broad social and economic goals which require that they become involved in political activity, particularly at the national level, which is external to formal collective bargaining relationships.[37]

Specific bargaining objectives (which are analyzed more thoroughly in Chapters 20–22) depend on the type of union, the immediate and long-run needs of its members as interpreted by the union leadership, external conditions at the time of negotiations, and membership and leadership expectations about future developments. Bargaining strategy and tactics are affected by the relative size and resources of a national and its affiliates, the locus of power in the national, the structure of bargaining in the industry, the issues being discussed, and *coercive comparisons* of gains achieved by other unions or within nonunion firms.

Preparing for Negotiations

Before negotiations begin, the leadership of a union must (1) evaluate the current contract, including the grievance procedure; (2) identify the principal demands of the members; (3) analyze contracts recently negotiated in the same industry or geographic area, or with other groups with which the union's performance will be compared; (4) set bargaining priorities; (5) identify the employer's probable bargaining objectives; and (6) anticipate the employer's responses to union demands. The sophistication of the union's research will depend on the complexity of the issues to be discussed, the resources available for research, and the quality of the employer's preparation for collective bargaining.

Union leaders usually base their bargaining priorities on their perception of membership needs and their estimate of what is economically feasible. In small locals in local market industries, the general membership meeting may help to formulate or approve bargaining objectives. In larger locals or in supralocal intermediate organizations, a wage committee may formulate bargaining demands that are then submitted to the members for discussion and approval.

Conducting Negotiations

In local market industries, a local bargaining committee usually conducts negotiations, although a national may have to approve basic contract provisions. In industries in which firms in different localities compete for a market, the national normally assumes a more influential role. An international representative may assist in negotiations or serve as the chief negotiator. The principal executive officers of the national may participate in key bargaining sessions with major corporations or in industrywide negotiations. Representatives from different constituencies within the union (for example, white-collar workers or highly skilled workers) may also participate in negotiations.

Collective bargaining procedures must conform to certain statutory requirements, and the terms of any agreement reached must be in accord with relevant statutes. Although some union officials prefer to negotiate without the help of a legal staff, most negotiators rely on lawyers for advice and counsel. Lawyers may serve in a purely advisory capacity or they may be members of a negotiating team.

Ratifying Contracts

Once an agreement has been reached, a contract must usually be presented to a union's membership or to a delegate group for ratification. Particular constituencies may have their own representatives within the delegate body, and these delegates may have veto power over all or part of the contract. The increasing number of younger, better educated union members has contributed to a rise in the number of contracts rejected in various industries. What happens when union leaders fail to be responsive to the needs of their membership was illustrated dramatically by the rejection of two tentative agreements in the bituminous coal industry in 1978.

The quality of preparations for negotiations and the experience, skill, and knowledgeability of the bargaining team are important determinants of the ability of a union's leadership to realize the expectations of the membership. Adequate preparation and bargaining expertise cannot ensure success at the bargaining table; the union's demands must be supported by economic muscle and a variety of weapons.

UNION WEAPONS

Collective bargaining is basically an economic power struggle between two institutions. The parameters that determine their relative bargaining strength are analyzed in Chapter 19. The weapons used to support the union's bargaining posture include strikes, picket lines, boycotts, and coalition bargaining.

Strikes

The major economic sanction available to a union is the membership's collective refusal to work. The right to strike is generally denied to public employees and has been circumscribed in the private sector when a work stoppage threatens the public welfare. Where permissible, the right to strike has an important second dimension. Union members and leaders believe that individual employees have a continuing right to their jobs (that the jobs are to an extent the worker's property), and the right to strike is assumed to involve a correlative right to return to work. A *sympathetic strike* occurs when employees not directly involved in a labor dispute walk out to demonstrate their support of other workers on strike. Such strikes often involve secondary boycotts.

The number of work stoppages, workers involved in strikes, and man-days of idleness resulting from strikes between 1927 and 1979 are shown in Table 14.5. Most of the strikes and the vast majority of idleness due to strikes during a year stem from the renegotiation of contracts. However, the *relative incidence* of strikes is higher in negotiations involving initial agreements. Although a union is formally responsible for a decision to strike, a firm's management, to avoid the

Table 14.5 WORK STOPPAGES IN THE UNITED STATES, 1927–1979[a] (workers involved and days idle in thousands)

| | WORK STOPPAGES | DURATION | | WORKERS INVOLVED | | DAYS IDLE DURING YEAR | | |
YEAR	NUMBER	MEAN[b]	MEDIAN	NUMBER	PERCENTAGE OF TOTAL EMPLOYED[c]	NUMBER	EST. TOTAL PERCENTAGE OF WORKING TIME[c]	PER WORKER INVOLVED
1927	707	26.5	c	330	1.4	26,200	d	79.5
1928	604	27.6	d	314	1.3	12,600	d	40.2
1929	921	22.6	d	289	1.2	5,350	d	18.5
1930	637	22.3	d	183	.8	3,320	d	18.1
1931	810	18.8	d	342	1.6	6,890	d	20.2
1932	841	19.6	d	324	1.8	10,500	d	32.4
1933	1,695	16.9	d	1,170	6.3	16,900	d	14.4
1934	1,856	19.5	d	1,470	7.2	19,600	d	13.4
1935	2,014	23.8	d	1,120	5.2	15,500	d	13.8
1936	2,172	23.3	d	789	3.1	13,900	d	17.6
1937	4,740	20.3	d	1,860	7.2	28,400	d	15.3
1938	2,772	23.6	d	688	2.8	9,150	d	13.3
1939	2,613	23.4	d	1,170	3.5	17,800	.21	15.2
1940	2,508	20.9	d	577	1.7	6,700	.08	11.6
1941	4,288	18.3	d	2,360	6.1	23,000	.23	9.8
1942	2,968	11.7	d	840	2.0	4,180	.04	5.0
1943	3,752	5.0	d	1,980	4.6	13,500	.10	6.8
1944	4,956	5.6	d	2,120	4.8	8,720	.07	4.1
1945	4,750	9.9	d	3,470	8.2	38,000	.31	11.0
1946	4,985	24.2	d	4,600	10.5	116,000	1.04	25.2
1947	3,693	25.6	d	2,170	4.7	34,600	.30	15.9
1948	3,419	21.8	d	1,960	4.2	34,100	.28	17.4
1949	3,606	22.5	d	3,030	6.7	50,500	.44	16.7
1950	4,843	19.2	8	2,410	5.1	38,800	.33	16.1
1951	4,737	17.4	7	2,220	4.5	22,900	.18	10.3
1952	5,117	19.6	7	3,540	7.3	59,100	.48	16.7
1953	5,091	20.3	9	2,400	4.7	28,300	.22	11.8
1954	3,468	22.5	9	1,530	3.1	22,600	.18	14.7
1955	4,320	18.5	8	2,650	5.2	28,200	.22	10.7

Year							
1956	3,825	18.9	7	1,900	3.6	33,100	.24	17.4
1957	3,673	19.2	8	1,390	2.6	16,500	.12	11.4
1958	3,694	19.7	8	2,060	3.9	23,900	.18	11.6
1959	3,708	24.6	10	1,880	3.3	69,000	.50	36.7
1960	3,333	23.4	10	1,320	2.4	19,100	.14	14.5
1961	3,367	23.7	9	1,450	2.6	16,300	.11	11.2
1962	3,614	24.6	9	1,230	2.2	18,600	.13	15.0
1963	3,362	23.0	8	941	1.1	16,100	.11	17.1
1964	3,655	22.9	8	1,640	2.7	22,900	.15	14.0
1965	3,963	25.0	9	1,550	2.5	23,300	.15	15.1
1966	4,405	22.2	9	1,960	3.0	25,400	.15	12.9
1967	4,595	22.8	9	2,870	4.3	42,100	.25	14.7
1968	5,045	24.5	10	2,649	3.8	49,018	.28	18.5
1969	5,700	22.5	10	2,481	3.5	42,869	.24	17.3
1970	5,716	25.0	11	3,305	4.7	66,414	.37	20.1
1971	5,138	27.0	11	3,280	4.5	47,589	.26	14.5
1972	5,010	24.0	8	1,714	2.3	27,066	.15	15.8
1973	5,353	24.0	9	2,251	2.9	27,948	.14	12.4
1974	6,074	27.1	14	2,778	3.5	47,991	.24	17.3
1975	5,031	26.8	11	1,746	2.2	31,237	.16	17.9
1976	5,648	28.0	11	2,420	3.0	37,859	.19	15.6
1977	5,506	29.3	14	2,040	2.4	35,822	.17	17.6
1978	4,230	33.2	17	1,623	1.9	36,922	.17	22.8
1979	4,800	d	d	1,700	d	33,000	.15	d

[a] The number of stoppages and workers relate to stoppages beginning in the year; average duration, to those ending in the year. Days of idleness include all stoppages in effect. Workers are counted more than once if they were involved in more than one stoppage during the year.

Available information for earlier periods appears in *Handbook of Labor Statistics, 1978*, BLS Bulletin 2000 (1979), Table 151. For a discussion of the procedures involved in the collection and compilation of work stoppage statistics, see BLS *Handbook of Methods*, BLS Bulletin 1910 (1976), chap. 27.

[b] Figures are simple averages; each stoppage is given equal weight regardless of its size.

[c] Agricultural and government employees are included in the total employed and total working time; private household, forestry, and fishery employees are excluded. An explanation of the measurement of idleness as a percentage of the total employed labor force and of the total time worked is found in "Total Economy" Measure of Strike Idleness," in *Monthly Labor Review*, October 1968.

[d] Not available.

SOURCE: U.S. Department of Labor, Bureau of Labor Statistics, *Analysis of Work Stoppages, 1978*, Bulletin 2066, Table 1, p. 9. 1979 data from BLS "Work Stoppages, 1979," *Press Release USDL 80–56*, January 29, 1980.

public onus of a *lockout,* may induce a union to go on strike by refusing to meet one or more of its key demands.*

In some situations, a union may take aggressive action in advance of a contract expiration date. For example, if the management or the customers of a firm try to stockpile output so that the operations of the customers will not be affected by a shutdown, a union may refuse to allow its members to work over-time, urge them to stage a work slowdown, or have them engage in what the United Mine Workers terms a *stabilizing work stoppage.*

In some industries, a high degree of mechanization or automation makes it hard for unions to put economic pressure on employers by striking. Oil refineries and telephone exchanges, for example, can be operated by a few supervisory personnel. Other industries are similarly automated. Although American union leaders have traditionally opposed the arbitration of primary disputes, in such industries voluntary arbitration may be accepted at some future date as a sub-stitute for strikes.**

Strikes involving contract negotiations (*primary disputes*) usually begin with a formal *strike vote* by a union's membership or a union policy committee. Many union constitutions require that a local strike be authorized by the officers of a national, for strike benefits to be paid.

The majority of union-management contracts prohibit strikes during the life of the agreement—that is, strikes over the interpretation of the contract (*secondary disputes*). However, *unauthorized,* or *wildcat,* work stoppages may result from jurisdictional disputes between or within unions, dissatisfaction with a specific action or decision by an employer, or dissatisfaction with the way a national's officers have represented the interests of a local or some segment of its membership. If a firm's management retains the right to act unilaterally on certain matters, a union may be given the right to strike over those matters during the life of the contract. Under the General Motors contract in the automobile industry, for example, grievances involving management-initiated changes in production standards do not go to arbitration. The UAW has the right to strike when such grievances are not resolved by other means.

Employees of the federal government and most state and local governments are forbidden to strike, and the Labor Management Relations Act, the Railway Labor Act, and laws in a number of states provide special procedures for re-solving "emergency" disputes in the private sector. Rather than assume the legal and public relations risks inherent in a work stoppage, employees in the public sector and in private enterprises that affect the public interest may resort to a *partial strike substitute* or *job action,* such as a work slowdown or a refusal to work overtime. *Demonstration picketing* involving mass meetings, parades, and

---

* The Bureau of Labor Statistics does not distinguish between strikes and lockouts in its annual analysis of work stoppages.
** The experimental negotiating agreement (ENA) in the steel industry is discussed briefly below, p. 425.

the picketing of legislative chambers and government executive offices has also been used by public employees as a strike substitute.

Other Union Weapons

For a strike to be effective, striking employees must prevent other workers from operating a facility. A union can also put pressure on an employer by *picketing* to close its supply and distribution channels. Picketing is an integral element in a union's total strike strategy. Strikers patrol points of egress to their employer's premises, or in some cases the site of mobile employment, displaying signs informing the public of the existence of and reasons for the strike, urging other employees and potential strikebreakers to honor their picket lines, and, if practicable, urging customers to cease patronizing their employer.

The term *boycott* is used somewhat loosely in the United States, but it is generally applied to an organized attempt by workers to persuade *consumers, other employers,* or *employees of other employers* to stop dealing with the employer involved in a labor dispute. The legal distinction between primary and secondary boycotts is imprecise. In theory, *primary* boycotts are directed at the customers and employees or potential employees of the *employer* with whom the union has a dispute. *Secondary* boycotts are designed to exert pressure on *other* persons to stop dealing with the employer. Primary boycotts are permitted under federal and state law, but some types of indirect or secondary boycotts have been declared not only unfair labor practices but illegal.

Secondary boycotts involve pressure on presumably innocent parties, yet the economic activities of those parties may be so closely related to the activities of the primary employer that strikers are at a considerable disadvantage if they are denied the use of billiard shot tactics, as boycotts are sometimes called. For example, construction work is usually performed by a general contractor and a number of subcontractors. If the striking employees of one subcontractor cannot enlist the support of members of unions working for other subcontractors on the same project, their bargaining strength can be materially lessened. *Voluntary* agreements with management which in effect permit such boycotts in the construction industry are permitted under a 1959 amendment to the Taft-Hartley Act.

Whipsaw, or *discriminating, strikes, common contract expiration dates,* and *coalition bargaining* have also been used by unions to increase their bargaining leverage. A union dealing with a number of firms in a highly competitive industry may try to *whipsaw* employers by moving against a single (often weaker) firm. If it can get an attractive settlement by threatening to strike that firm while permitting competitors to operate, the union will then attempt to force the other firms to comply with the terms of the initial agreement.

Having *common expiration dates* for all contracts with a multiplant firm or with all the firms under contract in an industry (the reverse of whipsaw tactics) may strengthen a union's bargaining position if the firm or industry cannot maintain partial production.

The presence of a number of national unions in different plants of a single employer, a situation that has become more common with the development of conglomerates, has encouraged *coordinated*, or *coalition*, *bargaining*. The unions feel that unless they bargain as a unit, a large, diversified employer will negotiate with the union in the weakest bargaining position first and then try to negotiate the same basic terms with the other unions representing its workers.

The effectiveness of union weapons depends on a complex of factors, including the willingness and ability of employers to withstand work stoppages; the resources available to a union to support a strike, including strike benefits, external sources of support such as welfare and unemployment insurance benefits, and the availability of other jobs; the morale and financial resources of individual union members; the climate of public opinion; and the probability of executive, judicial, or legislative intervention. If public intervention seems probable, the bargaining postures of both the union and the employer will be conditioned by the expected attitude of the intervener.

SUMMARY

This chapter has described and analyzed the structure and organization of the American union movement, union objectives and procedures in collective bargaining, and the weapons used by American unions. Several points deserve emphasis: first, diversity rather than similarity characterizes the structure of American unions; second, the AFL-CIO is not a monolithic organization with effective control of its affiliates, but a loose federation of autonomous national unions; third, although individual union members usually identify with their local union, national unions are the principal locus of power in most industries.

Unions are probably operated as democratically as other American institutions, and they are generally free of corruption and the influences of racketeers. However, the quasi-public status unions have obtained under our law of collective bargaining suggests that this is not enough, that union leaders must demonstrate a highly developed moral sense. Unions have a special obligation to avoid discriminatory practices; instances of discrimination in admission requirements, in the operation of apprenticeship programs, and in the administration of contracts represent singular failures to respond to the conscience of our time.

DISCUSSION QUESTIONS

1. Why is association membership now added to union membership in computing the number of organized workers in the United States?
2. Can you think of economic variables that might be responsible for the structural organizational axes in Figure 14.1? (This question anticipates analysis in succeeding chapters.)

3. Why may the "unit appropriate to collective bargaining" differ from the actual bargaining unit?
4. Where is the locus of power within the AFL-CIO?
5. Do you expect more unions to become multiindustrial during the next decade?
6. Do you expect that the number of national unions will increase or decrease?
7. Do the various Departments of the AFL-CIO perform similar functions?
8. Should the compensation of federation and national union officials be equivalent to that of their corporate counterparts?
9. Do you believe that American unions are "reasonably" democratic?
10. Do you agree with Taft that "racketeering in labor unions appears to flow from a general slackness in American society?"
11. How would you, as a union leader, formulate your bargaining demands for the next contract negotiation?
12. Distinguish clearly between primary and secondary disputes. Which are more likely to result in work stoppages?

SELECTED READINGS

Union Structure and Government

Barbash, Jack. *American Unions: Structure, Government, and Politics.* New York: Random House, 1967.

Barbash, Jack, ed. *Unions and Union Leadership.* New York: Harper & Brothers, 1959.

Estey, Marten. *The Unions: Structure, Development, and Management.* 2nd ed. New York: Harcourt Brace Jovanovich, 1976.

Estey, Marten; Taft, Philip; and Wagner, Martin, eds. *Regulating Union Government.* Industrial Relations Research Association Publication No. 31. New York: Harper & Row, 1964.

Ginsburg, Woodrow L. "Union Growth, Government and Structure." In *A Review of Industrial Relations Research.* Vol. I. Madison, Wisc.: Industrial Relations Research Association, 1970.

Peterson, Florence. *American Labor Unions, What They Are and How They Work.* 2nd rev. ed. New York: Harper & Row, 1963.

Strauss, George, and Warner, Malcom, eds. "Symposium: Research on Union Government." In *Industrial Relations* 16 no. 2 (May 1977). An excellent recent reference.

Taft, Philip. *The Structure and Government of Labor Unions.* Cambridge, Mass.: Harvard University Press, 1954.

The Trade Union Monograph Series, commissioned by the Trade Union Study of the Center for the Study of Democratic Institutions and published by Wiley under the general editorship of Walter Galenson, includes ten studies, each dealing with the structure and government of a major national union.

Union Finances

Hickman, Charles W. "Labor Organizations' Fees and Dues." In *Monthly Labor Review* 100 no. 5 (May 1977): pp. 19–24. A good source of more recent data.

"Symposium—Union Financial Data." In *Industrial Relations* 14 no. 2 (May 1975): pp. 131–157, a basic reference.

Local Unions

Barbash, Jack. *Labor's Grass Roots.* New York: Harper & Brothers, 1961.

Lahne, Herbert J., and Kovner, Joseph. "Local Union Structure: Formality and Reality." In *Industrial and Labor Relations Review* 9 no. 1 (October 1955): pp. 24–31.

Sayles, Leonard R., and Strauss, George. *The Local Union.* Rev. ed. New York: Harcourt Brace & World, 1967.

Union Leadership

Barbash, Jack. *Labor's Grass Roots.* Chaps. 5–8. New York: Harper & Brothers, 1961.

Seidman, Joel; London, Jack; Karsh, Bernard; and Tagliacozzo, Daisy L. *The Worker Views His Union.* Chap. 8. Chicago: University of Chicago Press, 1958.

Union Democracy

Cook, Alice H. *Union Democracy: Practice and Ideal,* particularly chap. I. Ithaca, N.Y.: Cornell University Press, 1963.

Seidman, Joel. *Democracy in the Labor Movement.* 2nd ed., chap. I. *ILR Bulletin No. 39.* Ithaca, N.Y.: NYS School of Industrial and Labor Relations, Cornell University, 1969.

Union Discrimination

Jacobsen, Julius, ed. *The Negro and the American Labor Movement.* Garden City, N.Y.: Doubleday, 1968.

Marshall, Ray. *The Negro and Organized Labor.* New York: Wiley, 1965.

"Studies of Negro Employment." Published by the Industrial Research Unit, Wharton School, University of Pennsylvania, Philadelphia, under the general direction of Herbert R. Northrup. An excellent series.

Taft, Philip. *Organized Labor in American History.* Chap. 50, "Organized Labor and the Negro." New York: Harper & Row, 1964.

Corruption and Racketeering

Barbash, Jack. *The Practice of Unionism.* Chap. XIII, "Racketeering and Unions." New York: Harper & Brothers, 1956.

Hutcheson, John. *The Imperfect Union.* New York: Dutton, 1970.

Kennedy, Robert F. *The Enemy Within.* New York: Harper & Brothers, 1960.

Petro, Sylvester. *Power Unlimited—The Corruption of Union Leadership.* New York: Ronald Press, 1959.

Taft, Philip. *Corruption and Racketeering in the Labor Movement.* 2nd ed. *ILR Bulletin No. 38.* Ithaca, N.Y.: NYS School of Industrial and Labor Relations, Cornell University, 1970. An excellent reference.

Coalition Bargaining

Chernish, William N. *Coalition Bargaining—A Study of Union Tactics and Public Policy.* Philadelphia: University of Pennsylvania Press, 1969.

Schwarz, Philip J. *Coalition Bargaining.* Key Issues Series—No. 5. Ithaca, N.Y.: NYS School of Industrial and Labor Relations, Cornell University, January 1970.

Strike Benefits

Curtin, Edward R. "National Union Strike Benefits, 1967." In *The Conference Board Record* IV (September 1967): pp. 31–35. An analysis of strike benefit programs in 113 national unions.

Notes

1. U.S. Department of Labor, Bureau of Labor Statistics, *Directory of National Unions and Employee Associations, 1977,* Bulletin 2044, Table 2, p. 59; Table 5, p. 60.
2. Ibid., Table 6, p. 61.
3. Ibid., pp. 73–74.
4. Ibid., p. 63.
5. Ibid., p. 77.
6. Florence Peterson, *American Labor Unions, What They Are and How They Work,* 2nd rev. ed. (New York: Harper & Row, 1963), p. 73.
7. John T. Dunlop, "Structural Changes in the American Labor Movement and Industrial Relations System," in *Proceedings of the Ninth Annual Meeting, Industrial Relations Research Association, 1956* (Madison, Wisc.: Industrial Relations Research Association, 1957), p. 12. This excellent article analyzes changes in union structure since the 1920s.
8. Arnold R. Weber, "Craft Representation in Industrial Unions," in *Proceedings of the Fourteenth Annual Meeting, Industrial Relations Research Association, December 1961* (Madison, Wisc.: Industrial Relations Research Association, 1962), fn. 3, p. 83.
9. Jack Barbash, ed., *American Unions: Structure, Government, and Politics* (New York: Random House, 1967), p. 103.
10. *This Is the AFL-CIO,* Publication No. 20, rev. (Washington, D.C.: AFL-CIO, November 1969), p. 9.
11. *Proceedings of the Thirteenth Constitutional Convention of the AFL-CIO, November 15–20, 1979* (Washington, D.C.: AFL-CIO, n.d.), vol II, *Report of the Executive Council,* statement no. 2, p. 8.
12. Ibid., statement no. 1, p. 6. For financial statistics for 1976 for *national* and *local* unions reporting under Labor Management Reporting and Disclosure Act see U.S. Department of Labor, Labor-Management Services Administration, *Union Financial Statistics 1976* (Washington, D.C.: U.S. Government Printing Office, 1980).
13. Cf. Jack Barbash, "Rationalization in the American Union," in Gerald G. Somers, ed., *Essays in Industrial Relations Theory* (Ames, Iowa: Iowa State University Press, 1969), p. 152.
14. U.S. Department of Labor, Bureau of Labor Statistics, *Disciplinary Power and Procedures in Union Constitutions,* Bulletin 1350, p. 1.

15. Janice R. Bellace and Alan D. Berkowitz, *The Landrum-Griffin Act: Twenty Years of Federal Protection of Union Members' Rights,* Industrial Research Unit, The Wharton School, (Philadelphia: University of Pennsylvania Press, 1979), p. 83.

16. *Title III, sec. 204.* For an analysis of the use of this device, see U.S. Department of Labor, Bureau of Labor Management Reports, *Union Trusteeships: Report of the Secretary of Labor to the Congress upon the Operation of Title III of the Labor-Management Reporting and Disclosure Act, September 1962.*

17. See Jack Steiber, Walter E. Oberer, and Michael Harrington, *Democracy and Public Review: An Analysis of the UAW Public Review Board* (Santa Barbara, Calif.: Center for the Study of Democratic Institutions, 1960).

18. Charles Craypo, "The National Union Convention as an Internal Appeal Tribunal," in *Industrial and Labor Relations Review* 22, no. 4 (July 1969): p. 506.

19. Cf. Philip Taft, *The Structure and Government of Labor Unions* (Cambridge, Mass.: Harvard University Press, 1954), p. 112.

20. *Business Week,* "Where Tradition and Politics Rule," Industrial Edition Number 2534 (May 15, 1978), p. 101. See also *The Wall Street Journal,* August 17, 1973, pp. 1, 23.

21. Ibid., p. 96.

22. See Seymour Martin Lipset, Martin A. Trow, and James S. Coleman, *Union Democracy: The Internal Politics of the International Typographical Union* (Glencoe, Ill.: Free Press, 1956).

23. Barbash, *American Unions,* p. 92.

24. Cf. Philip Taft, *Labor Politics American Style: The California State Federation of Labor* (Cambridge, Mass.: Harvard University Press, 1968), p. 249.

25. Jack Barbash, *Labor's Grass Roots* (New York: Harper & Brothers, 1961), p. 1; and Bernard Karsh, "Union Traditions and Membership Apathy," in *Proceedings of the Spring Meeting, Industrial Relations Research Association, May 1958,* in *Labor Law Journal* 9, no. 9 (September 1958): pp. 644–645.

26. Cf. William Spinrad, "Correlates of Trade Union Participation: A Summary of the Literature," in *American Sociological Review* 25 no. 2 (April 1960): pp. 237–244 and John C. Anderson, "Local Union Participation, A Re-examination," in *Industrial Relations* 18, no. 1 (Winter 1979): pp. 18–31.

27. For an overview of union members, see U.S. Department of Labor, Bureau of Labor Statistics, "Earnings and Other Characteristics of Organized Workers, May 1977," Report 556.

28. Various typologies of union members have been developed. See for example, Joel Seidman et al., *The Worker Views His Union* (Chicago: University of Chicago Press, 1958), p. 242.

29. Cf. Robert Michels, *Political Parties: A Sociological Study of the Oligarchical Tendencies of Modern Democracy,* trans. by Eden and Cedar Paul (New York: Hearst's International Library, 1915), particularly "Final Considerations," pp. 400–402.

30. The *Hearings* of the McClellan Committee—technically, the Select Committee on Improper Activities in the Labor or Management Field of the U.S. Senate—have been published in some 40 volumes. The more significant findings are included in the committee's *Interim Report* (85th Cong., 2nd sess., *Senate Report No. 1417*), its *Second Interim Report* (86th Cong., 1st sess., *Senate Report No. 621*), and its four-part *Final Report* (86th Cong., 2nd sess., *Senate Report No. 1139*).

31. Cf. Philip Taft, "The Responses of the Bakers, Longshoremen, and Teamsters to Public Exposure," in *Quarterly Journal of Economics* LXXIV, no. 3 (August 1960): pp. 411–412.
32. *The New York Times,* July 2, 1956, p. 11, quoting from a bulletin of the Commerce and Industry Association.
33. Philip Taft, *Corruption and Racketeering in the Labor Movement,* 2nd ed., *ILR Bulletin No. 38,* (Ithaca, N.Y.: NYS School of Industrial and Labor Relations, Cornell University, 1970), pp. 34–35.
34. Ibid., p. 35.
35. Ibid.
36. Ibid., p. 36.
37. Cf. Frederick H. Harbison and John R. Coleman, *Goals and Strategy in Collective Bargaining* (New York: Harper & Brothers, 1951), pp. 12–17.

Chapter 15
MANAGEMENT POLICIES AND ORGANIZATION FOR COLLECTIVE BARGAINING

Most managements would prefer not to deal with unions: they consider union participation in setting the terms of employment as an unnecessary interference with basic managerial rights. In the United States, the natural reluctance of employers to deal with labor on a collective basis was reinforced by the deeply held conviction that if the market economy was left to itself, it would provide an equitable distribution of income and assure a cooperative and harmonious relationship between labor and capital.

During the nineteenth century and early in the twentieth century, companies actively opposed efforts to organize their workers; they were generally supported in this enterprise by the nation's judiciary. Following World War I, many of the newer "professional" managers began to recognize that employee relations required the same expertise as other managerial functions. However, they continued to believe that the introduction of a union represented an undesirable interference with managerial prerogatives, that a free market economy would provide enough jobs at adequate wages for those who wanted to work, and that well-conceived employee relations programs would ensure a productive labor force. The prosperity of the period persuaded the public that these people were correct and that the nation had in fact solved its major labor problems. The depression of the early thirties shattered this complacent view of American capitalism, and despite the determined opposition of most of the business community, the encouragement of collective bargaining became public policy with the passage of the Wagner Act in 1935. Today, our law of collective bargaining requires a firm's management to bargain collectively with a certified representative of its employees, and union-management relations have become one of top management's principal concerns.

In the latter part of this chapter, we will analyze the impact of unions on management decision making, discuss management policies and strategy in regard to collective bargaining, and describe the principal weapons used by management to support its bargaining position. To provide a perspective for this analysis, we will first describe how the management function in a nonunion firm is expanded when management recognizes and responds to the human dimensions of the employment relationship. In this discussion, we will use the terms *employee relations* to refer to the relations between labor and management in the absence of unions, *union-management relations* to refer to the continuing institutional relationship between (representatives of) organized labor and management, and *personnel relations* to refer to *staff* activity (employment interviews, welfare plan administration) in support of management's direction of a labor force. Unfortunately, these terms are used loosely and at times interchangeably in many firms.

EARLY ATTITUDES TOWARD EMPLOYEE WELFARE

In economic models, a firm's management is often considered synonymous with its owners. The model makers recognize that in a corporation, the management function is legally divorced from ownership; but they assume that top management acts as a trustee or an agent of the owners and will strive to maximize profits for their benefit.[1] The *management function* includes all the activities designed to help management achieve this goal.[2] However, one cannot assume that managers will conform predictably to the postulates of economic theory: management decisions are often based on predictions relating to an uncertain future; managers vary in their innate optimism, in their willingness to innovate, in the extent to which they plan ahead, and in their sensitivity to social, cultural, and political influences. A variety of goals may modify or replace profit maximization; a firm's policy makers may seek a "reasonable" profit or a stated percentage return on sales, total capital, or stockholders' equity. Alternatively, they may focus on increasing the firm's sales volume, increasing its share of the product market, or simply perpetuating a managerial clique. However, the survival of the firm is the most basic management objective, and this requires at a minimum the profitable operation of the firm in the long run.* Managers generally believe that they

---

* In other words, the firm must cover all its costs in the long run, including relevant opportunity costs. In practice, the threat of a loss may put more pressure on management than the possibility of larger profits.

must have complete authority over all decision making within the firm to achieve this objective. There is no role for unionism in such a construct.

Prior to World War I, most managers seemed unaware that managing workers required the same energy and talent as managing other aspects of an enterprise. Interest in the human dimensions of the employment relationship developed as a by-product of the *scientific management* movement early in the twentieth century.[3] Frederick Taylor, the father of this movement, argued that better working conditions, better safety procedures, and the use of incentive systems of wage payment could lower unit labor costs.[4] His emphasis on the proper design of jobs and the development of specific job requirements stimulated interest in improving management procedures for (1) recruiting, training, and developing personnel; (2) improving working conditions; and (3) securing the cooperation of employees. Taylor thus provided the rudimentary foundation for our present employee relations and personnel functions. The distinction between the *employee relations function* and personnel administration is often blurred; the former includes all management policies and programs that directly affect employees, including the supervision of the firm's labor force by line management; *personnel administration* refers to the more limited staff activities that support management's employee relations effort.

During World War I, many firms developed formal policies and programs to attract, retain, and increase the productivity of employees. These programs, which often emphasized personnel policies rather than policies relating to the management of employees on an operational basis, were directed by "employment" or "personnel" managers. Union membership soared during the war, and after the armistice management responded to the threat posed by unions in two quite different ways: many firms, particularly those that had been organized for the first time during the war, began an all-out offensive against unionism; others set up or expanded employee welfare programs or formal personnel programs to compete with what the unions offered.

Employee representation plans (ERPs) and "company" unions were established in many firms to provide a safety valve for employee discontent and reduce the appeal of "outside" unions. Under such arrangements, representatives of a firm's employees met with management to discuss problems involving workers. This consultation did not constitute true collective bargaining, but it was a limited substitute for formal grievance procedures. ERPs helped to make many employers more cognizant of and responsive to the needs of their employees. Meanwhile, firms in general began to differentiate between the employee relations and personnel functions; the latter became a staff function supporting the total employee relations effort.

At the end of the 1920s, studies conducted by Elton Mayo and a group of associates from the Harvard Graduate School of Business Administration at the Hawthorne (Illinois) works of the Western Electric Company provided a foundation for a "human relations" approach to employee relations. Mayo and his colleagues found that the response of individual workers to managerial actions reflected the response of the work "group" with which the employee identified. This focused attention on the important role of work groups within an enterprise and suggested that in order to elicit cooperation from employees, management should first win over these groups. However, there were no unions at the Hawthorne works, and Mayo's group failed to recognize that union members could constitute an important social group within a firm.

Human relations enjoyed a considerable vogue during the 1940s and helped to improve the overall quality of employee relations (and union-management relations) programs. Many constructive features of the human relations movement have also been incorporated into current employee relations and personnel programs. Nevertheless, there are serious limitations to a simplistic "health and happiness" approach to the management of employees.

During the 1960s, the somewhat nebulous field of *organizational behavior* began to acquire greater academic legitimacy than the more traditional forms of employee relations. The character of the emerging management function that will modify or supplant employee relations in the future is not clear, but it will probably reflect ongoing research in a number of disciplines.

EMPLOYEE RELATIONS IN NONUNION FIRMS

The preceding discussion suggests the importance to management of soundly conceived employee relations and personnel programs. Many managers recognize that satisfied employees are more likely to be efficient and that consistent, equitable treatment is essential to elicit an employee's cooperation in achieving management goals. Frequently, the cost of an employee relations program is considered an investment to be amortized over the length of an employee's career with the firm.* Many managers also recognize that failing to handle employee relations successfully can create conditions favorable to unionism.

Some nonunion firms may be able to operate without formal employee relations programs, but most large firms recognize the value of such programs and employ professionals to run them. The way employee relations programs are organized varies tremendously, but a personnel program is usually the centerpiece of such efforts in nonunion firms. As we have suggested before, good employee relations cannot be achieved by a simple health and happiness approach; workers resent paternalistic treatment. Nor is the adoption of formal employee relations policies and programs enough. To secure the cooperation and loyalty of individual employees and groups of workers, employees must be made aware of such policies and programs, and they must be administered objectively and consistently *on a continuing basis.*

A company's policies regarding employee relations are based on its philosophy of employee relations, its willingness and ability to identify and support distinct

---

* Programs and policies that "tie" employees to a firm increase the rate of return on this type of investment.

employee relations and personnel functions, and the employee relations and personnel policies and programs of other firms in the same labor and product markets and the same geographic area. If a firm's management, for competitive reasons or out of a desire for prestige, wishes the firm to enjoy a reputation as a good place to work, or if it has a sense of responsibility toward its employees, it will establish a personnel program that is responsive to the needs of its employees as part of its overall employee relations effort, and it will review the operation of this program on a continuing basis.

A personnel program can create and maintain good employee relations only if

1. top management recognizes the value of the program and sets its basic goals;
2. there is adequate financial support for the program;
3. there is a competent staff organization to administer it;
4. the responsibilities of line and staff officials in connection with the program are clearly defined; and
5. a two-way communications system is set up to ensure that (a) employees are fully informed about personnel policies and procedures that affect them and (b) top management can evaluate and make revisions in the program on the basis of objective reports of how well it works.

Organizational tables for personnel departments vary greatly; in a small firm, the plant manager may handle this function, while in a major corporation a vice-president for employee relations or personnel may be supported by staff specialists, each with his or her own function. Basic employee relations and personnel policies should be established by a firm's top management with the advice and counsel of the personnel department, but the department should function primarily as a staff organization to help the line management with personnel problems.[5] The distinction between line and staff functions may not be clear, particularly in firms where the two functions are handled by a single executive. Conflicts may develop between line managers interested in "getting out" production and members of the personnel staff who are oriented toward the problems of individual workers or groups of workers. To minimize such conflicts, top management must ensure that line and staff officials understand what each is trying to accomplish and are prepared to cooperate in a common enterprise. Sometimes cooperation may be difficult to achieve, since

> each group of management specialists will tend to view the "interests of the enterprise" in terms which are compatible with the survival and the increase of its special function. That is, each group will have a trained capacity for its own function and a "trained incapacity" to see its relation to the whole.[6]

Top management must be alert to departures from established employee relations and personnel procedures. Although minor modifications in procedures may be appropriate, modifications designed to solve immediate problems may compromise the long-run objectives of the firm. Line managers have a key role in interpreting and implementing personnel policies, but they are often reluctant to assume such responsibilities. Top management must impress on subordinate line managers the nature and relative priorities of their personnel responsibilities, and line managers should not be permitted to shift those responsibilities to the personnel department.

The presence of informal work groups and the existence of unwritten shop rules modifying established procedures may make it difficult for a firm's top management to evaluate the effectiveness of the firm's employee relations and personnel programs. Communications difficulties may compound such problems. The same language may mean quite different things to employees, foremen, and managers, and as a result, management communications may fail to convey what was intended. Management must also realize that information detrimental to subordinates may be "filtered out" of upward communications, and that employees may doubt the credibility of downward communications.[7] The "distance" between the chief executive's office and workers in the shop is often great, and what management thinks is happening in the shop may not be what is really going on.

First-line supervisors have an important function in both nonunion and union firms. They represent the point of contact between management and individual employees or work groups. They deliver the verbal or written orders that represent the final distillation of top management decisions involving employees, they are responsible for initiating upward communications assessing a worker's performance or identifying potential trouble spots in the shop, and they often exercise final disciplinary authority. It is essential that first-line supervisors act in an objective and consistent fashion; authoritarian or inconsistent behavior on their part can undermine any employee relations or personnel program. Higher levels of management must support supervisors who carry out their responsibilities in accordance with established plant practices and procedures; arbitrarily overruling them will reduce their future effectiveness.

A Summary Comment

Most nonunion employers are aware of the human dimensions of the employment relationship. Particularly in larger firms, some type of employee relations function has been developed to ensure that employees are treated equitably and consistently. This function usually includes a more narrowly delimited personnel administration function, the precise style and components of which vary considerably between firms. The introduction of a union may not require a significant shift in a firm's orientation toward its employees. However, the union inevitably challenges management's control over the employment relationship, and this usually requires a major adjustment in the decision-making process within the firm. Management can no longer set the terms and conditions of employment unilaterally, and operating decisions that affect the employment relationship may be challenged via a formal grievance procedure.

THE INTRODUCTION OF A UNION

Companies threatened with a union organizing campaign can be expected to resist, and their efforts are often successful if the union fails to make a strong emotional appeal to unorganized workers. Some employers have mounted all-out offensives against unionism, engaging in unfair labor practices, publicly castigating union leaders and the institution of unionism, and attempting to enlist broad community support for their antiunion position. Such reactions however are increasingly rare; more typically, a firm will try to persuade its employees through verbal and written communications and a variety of positive actions that they do not need a union and that the presence of a union will cause a deterioration in the existing labor-management relationship.

Once a union has organized a majority of a firm's employees (or, more accurately, once it has received a majority of the votes in a union representation election), the firm is compelled by law to recognize the union as the exclusive representative of its employees and bargain with it. Although the recognition of a union is a preliminary to actual bargaining, the character of the bargaining relationship will be affected by the way in which recognition was achieved.

The success of an organizational campaign is often viewed as the result of a failure on the part of management. It is assumed that if the firm's employee relations program had been effective, its employees would not have been susceptible to the appeals of union organizers. Perhaps the greatest trauma is experienced by managers who have consciously tried to be good employers. Not realizing that a paternalistic personnel program seldom generates much commitment to a firm and that unilateral decisions are often interpreted as arbitrary, they are surprised and hurt when their "loyal" employees give their allegiance to an alien organization.

The timing of an attempt to organize a firm's employees may come as a surprise, but a company usually knows whether it is a logical organizational target, and it should be prepared to enter into a collective bargaining relationship if the organizing campaign succeeds. The experiences of other firms in the same industry or bargaining with the same union can help the company adjust to the presence of a union.

Most managements realize that American unions do not wish to assume responsibility for the operation of a firm. However, they know that the union will attempt to regulate their exercise of managerial authority in matters affecting employees, and they resist this potential infringement on their managerial prerogatives. The initial response to the introduction of a union depends on the firm's "philosophy" of management, its existing employee relations policies, the circumstances in which its employees were organized, the extent of unionization within relevant product and labor markets, management's attitude toward and evaluation of the union and its leaders, and the surrounding social and cultural climate.

In view of the overt opposition of the business community to unionism and collective bargaining during the New Deal, the ease with which most firms adapted to the presence of a union is remarkable. This adaptation was the result of several factors:

1. Within a relatively short period, employers were required by law to bargain with the union representing the majority of employees in a bargaining unit and were also deprived of their most effective antiunion weapons, the injunction and various forms of discrimination against workers on account of union activity.

2. The need to cooperate with labor in a common cause during World War II and the Korean crisis, often in accordance with government directives, accelerated the integration of unions into firms.

3. Continued advances in the social sciences since World War II led to a greater appreciation by management of the role of unions in our society and the functions of the bargaining process.[8]

The process of accommodation was aided by a general upgrading of the employee relations function as more and more top managements took a direct hand in setting the basic goals of employee relations policies and administering union-management relations and personnel programs and as the caliber of managers responsible for these programs improved.

Most managements engaged in collective bargaining today probably "accept" unions; that is, they do not actively attempt to dislodge them from their plants, and they try to adapt to the requirements of a continuing bargaining relationship. However, unions are still viewed as competitors for the loyalty of a firm's employees, and the loss of unilateral control over the employee relations function is considered an unfortunate constraint on the firm's operational flexibility. Even making a limited accommodation to the presence of a union takes time, and an effective union-management relations program can only be developed as the nature and requirements of a particular bargaining relationship become clear. Employee relations policies and programs that were appropriate in a nonunion environment but that are now obsolete cannot be modified or abandoned overnight.

MANAGEMENT POLICIES AND ORGANIZATION FOR COLLECTIVE BARGAINING

Under collective bargaining, management acquires the additional responsibility of developing and administering a *union-management relations program*, a responsibility that includes *negotiating* and *administering contracts*. The organization for collective bargaining and the descriptive title of this function vary widely. What we have called employee relations is often expanded to include union-management relations and personnel administration and called *labor relations*. Well-conceived and consistently administered personnel policies and programs are an essential part of union-management relations, and a firm's existing personnel program should not be downgraded because a union is introduced. The emphasis placed on each function will depend on previous policies and procedures, management's fundamental conception of the role of the union, and the extent to which the union tries to regulate what are considered managerial prerogatives.

Firms that have employee relations or personnel programs may have little difficulty in developing effective union-management relations programs, but firms that did not have such programs before the introduction of a union face a challenging assignment. Some may hire outside consultants to help develop appropriate policies and programs and even to represent them in negotiations. Small firms in particular may be reluctant to assign top caliber executives to union-management relations and consequently employ consultants, often lawyers, to negotiate and help administer contracts. At a minimum, a firm's management should commit the same degree of talent and energy to these functions as does a union. However, union-management relations are only one of the responsibilities of top management, and this equivalent commitment may not be made.

Management Objectives

Five broad categories of management objectives in collective bargaining have been identified:

> *first,* the preservation and strengthening of the business enterprise; *second,* the retention of effective control over the enterprise; *third,* the establishment of stable and "businesslike" relationships with the bargaining agents; *fourth,* promotion of certain broad social and economic goals; and *fifth,* advancement of personal goals and ambitions.[9]

The specific policies and procedures a firm's management considers "appropriate" to the union-management relations function, and the character of the resulting collective bargaining relationship will reflect the weight management attaches to these basic objectives. If management interprets "the retention of effective control" and "stable and businesslike" relations to mean that the union must in no way threaten the profitable operation, survival, or growth of the firm, it may be difficult to develop a constructive bargaining relationship.

The creation of a constructive relationship requires that each party recognize the need of the other to survive.[10] Union leaders, particularly in newly established bargaining relationships, are under considerable pressure to be aggressive, and management must usually make the initial overtures toward an accommodation based on mutual rather than individual survival.

The Union-Management Relations Program

A successful union-management relations program must help a firm reach its economic objectives. Six principles have helped many managements develop such programs.[11]

The first and most basic requirement is that top management assume ultimate responsibility for union-management relations. In the exercise of this responsibility, "the best goal for most firms is a stable relationship with the union on terms that permit the firm to be competitive and to adapt itself to changing conditions."[12] In some cases, management may be able to pursue a hard line in bargaining without threatening the institutional security of a union. And whether a firm genuinely accepts a union or remains openly hostile, it must recognize that

> [T]he establishment of a sound labor relations policy is a prerequisite to successful collective bargaining. This means that the management of the company should give thought to its basic philosophy of relations with employees and their representatives. . . . Whether in writing or not, this basic philosophy should be well understood as the foundation of the company's labor policy.[13]

Second, management must resist the temptation to develop expedient solutions to short-run problems. Failure to consider the long-run consequences of such "solutions" may threaten the ultimate profitability and survival of the firm.

Third, the firm's union-management relations and personnel policies must produce operational results consistent with the firm's basic economic objectives.

Fourth, management must try to make union leaders and members aware of the constraints affecting the firm's ability to improve terms and conditions of employment. In addition to product and labor market pressures, these constraints include pressures from lower level managers, customers, suppliers, the firm's board of directors, stockholders, and possibly government officials and agencies. A greater appreciation of these pressures and of management's total function may be created by (1) trying, on a continuing basis, to communicate to union leaders the character and magnitude of relevant variables, particularly the constraints imposed by competition in product markets; (2) supporting statements about the firm's inability to meet union demands with statistical or other evidence; and (3) placing an executive with a line rather than a staff background in charge of union-management relations.

Fifth, management must recognize that union-management relations have two distinct subfunctions: (1) *negotiating* the terms of contracts and (2) *administering* contracts on a daily basis. Both subfunctions are important, and a firm must develop appropriate policies and procedures relating to each one.

Sixth, in devising these policies and procedures, an employer must recognize that union-management relations have extraeconomic dimensions. The social and political structure of an employment relationship is altered by the introduction of a union, and personal tensions may develop that can vitiate well-motivated and presumably "sound" policies and procedures.

Management Weapons

Success at the bargaining table depends on management's total approach to union-management relations, including its ability to communicate economic constraints affecting its bargaining posture to union officials and members and the effectiveness with which it uses the weapons available to it. Many management weapons employed in the nineteenth century and early in the twentieth century to thwart union organizers or to weaken a union once a firm had been organized have been declared unfair or illegal. The discharge of workers for union activities, blacklists, and yellow-dog contracts are no longer accepted. In addition, the use of injunctions has been drastically curtailed since the passage of the Norris-LaGuardia Act in 1932. Some employers may intentionally use unfair labor practices to block the organization of their work force or to weaken an established union, but most managements comply with our law of collective bargaining and are prepared to deal with an authorized representative of their employees.

The fundamental economic weapon of a firm is its *ability to withstand a strike.* This is a function of such variables as the extent and degree of competition in an industry, the current financial condition of the firm, general economic conditions, the availability of substitute products, and the accuracy of the firm's estimate of the union's ability and willingness to strike for a prolonged period.

In theory, the management counterpart of a strike is a *lockout*—closing a plant to put economic pressure on a union to accept an offer or make significant bargaining concessions. In practice, lockouts are little used because they subject the employer to an economic loss it would prefer to avoid.

Before World War II, employers often tried to keep operating when their employees "hit the bricks" by hiring *strikebreakers,* or "scabs." However, a firm that has accepted the principle of collective bargaining is not disposed to jeopardize the rapport it has established with a union by using strikebreakers, and at present most union firms do not try to operate during a strike. If a firm is shut down by a strike resulting from a jurisdictional dispute or some political problem internal to a union or if it is threatened with a long strike because the union is "frozen" in an apparently untenable position, management may try to operate the struck facility. It may also try to *contract out* struck work, but it will rarely do so if it wishes to maintain a harmonious bargaining relationship with the union.

Small firms in highly competitive industries, particularly in local product or labor markets, may find that unless they join forces with other employers, the superior bargaining power of the union allows it to take the initiative in bargaining and to dominate contract negotiations. *Multiemployer bargaining* (often by associations) may be used to offset the union's superior bargaining power in such situations. Under this type of arrangement, a negotiating team represents all the firms in a *bargaining coalition,* and no firm is expected to conclude a separate agreement. Cooperating employers may agree to lock out their employees if a union strikes any one of them. A *common contract expiration date* may also be used to prevent whipsawing.

The rapid increase in construction wages late in the 1960s was responsible for an interesting development in the building and construction industry. To reduce the pressure on contractors from large corporations anxious to have new production facilities completed, top executives of some 100 major corporations formed a *Construction Users Anti-Inflation Round Table* to support contractors who resisted inflationary wage settlements and thereby moderate the rate of increase in construction costs.

Employers in several industries, including air and rail transport, have entered into cooperative arrangements to provide limited *financial assistance* (strike insurance) to struck firms. In the railroad and airline industries, unions are reluctant to engage in industrywide stoppages because they fear that the carriers or the government will obtain an injunction against the strike. However, during a partial shutdown, customers will presumably use other carriers, diverting revenues to the competitors of the firms that have been struck. Strike insurance programs were developed to reduce the resulting economic pressure on struck carriers.*

Negotiating Contracts

Contract negotiation is fundamentally a power struggle in which bargaining objectives are supported by threatening to use the weapons described in this chapter and in Chapter 14. Adequate *preparation* for contract negotiations is essential. The National Association of Manufacturers has outlined seven important preliminaries:

1. a thorough study of the present contract . . . with a view to identifying sections that require modifications;
2. a close analysis of grievances in order to discover unworkable or poor contract language, or situations that are creating problems in supervisory-employee relationships;
3. frequent conferences with line supervision for the dual purpose of improving the supervisor's knowledge of contract administration and obtaining information as to how the contract is working out in practice;
4. a review of current union agreements signed by typical and comparable companies in the community and the industry, with the same or other unions;
5. a study of labor relations reporting services and . . . employer association reports on labor relations matters for the purpose of keeping abreast of recent developments that may affect future contract negotiations;
6. the collection and analysis of economic data on issues likely to be of importance in the next negotiations;
7. the study and analysis of arbitration decisions under the current contract

---

* In the railroad industry, strike insurance helps cover the overhead (fixed) costs of roads that have been struck. The airline deregulation act of 1978 (Public Law 95–504) terminated the existing airlines mutual aid pact and required that any future pact would require the air carriers involved to submit the issues causing a strike to binding arbitration upon the request of the striking employees. It is unlikely that the carriers will enter into such an agreement.

with a view to formulating proposals for changes in the language of the contract at the next negotiations.[14]

A *pattern-setting* firm, that is, a firm whose contract serves as a model for other firms, will usually have to prepare more intensively for negotiations, while a pattern follower must cost out the provisions of a relevant key settlement to determine whether it can afford to conform to a local or an industry pattern. If the pattern appears too costly, a firm must be prepared to document its case for exceptional treatment. Setting negotiating priorities may be difficult in multi-employer and association bargaining, but management should not relinquish this responsibility to a joint negotiating team or the staff of an employer association.[15]

Competent people, including at least one executive with line experience, should be assigned to a negotiating team. The chief negotiator (preferably a line executive) should have the authority to make commitments on behalf of the management representatives within defined limits. A large firm will presumably have an adequate union-management relations staff, a small firm may have to hire an outside consultant or depend on experts from a regional or industry employer association. Because of the complexities of many contract negotiations and the need for contract language that is legally precise, a lawyer may be included on the negotiating team. However, a legalistic approach to collective bargaining makes it difficult to develop a constructive bargaining relationship, and a lawyer should not be the company's chief negotiator unless there are unusual legal problems confronting the negotiators.

A negotiating team should have definite instructions concerning bargaining priorities and the extent of its authority to make commitments. Top management should not compromise its bargaining position or the status of its negotiators by withdrawing concessions to which the negotiating team has agreed or by granting concessions that it had indicated would never be authorized.

In addition to establishing its own basic policies in regard to collective bargaining and identifying possible bargaining trade-offs, management must develop estimates of the union's demands and trade-offs and be reasonably confident that it can predict the reaction of union representatives to various proposals and counterproposals. This means that management must understand the structural organization of the union, it must have identified the locus of power within the union (which may vary according to the issue under negotiation), it must have identified relevant internal and external political constraints on the union's leaders, and it must have adequately "researched" the union's general and specific bargaining objectives.

A union is a service-rendering organization, and management must recognize the *institutional parameters*, including political imperatives, that affect the union leaders' and union negotiators' behavior. Union leaders are interested in perpetuating their unions and in maintaining or advancing their own elective or appointive status within the union hierarchy. As a result, they may sometimes act irrationally in terms of management's economic calculus. A firm should allow a union's leaders to receive appropriate credit for contract improvements; otherwise the stability of the bargaining relationship may be threatened.

Administering Contracts

The equity and consistency with which a contract is administered are important determinants of the *quality* of a bargaining relationship. Contract administration is basically a management function, but if it is not handled objectively, the union leadership may assume an aggressive role in contract implementation and interpretation. There is an unfortunate tendency, particularly in the early period of a bargaining relationship, to concentrate managerial talent and energy on contract negotiation at the expense of contract administration. This may be costly in the long run; lower level supervisors trying to meet production targets may ignore established procedures or permit informal shop rules or practices to develop, and once instituted, these practices are difficult to eliminate. As one observer points out, in bargaining between larger firms and industrial unions "the most harmful concessions have been made not in contract negotiation but through continuous concession in contract administration."[16]

Effective contract administration requires good upward communications, quick and objective assessments of the immediate and long-run implications of departures from established practices and procedures, and the rapid and accurate downward reporting of changes in contract interpretation.

The Role of First-Line Supervisors

The role of first-line supervisors is altered significantly by the introduction of a union. Their authority in the shop is circumscribed by a collective agreement, and many types of decisions are subject to review under grievance procedures. Although some supervisors, particularly those with long years of service, may find it difficult or impossible to adjust to the presence of a union, a definitive study of the impact of collective bargaining has concluded that "as a general rule, foremen make the change from opposing the union to administering the union-management contract with surprising smoothness."[17]

Changes in Established Bargaining Relationships

As management accommodates successfully to the imperatives of a collective bargaining relationship, a number of interrelated developments may occur:

1. The responsibility for union-management relations may become more centralized; contract administration however may be delegated to lower levels of management.
2. The handling of union-management relations may become more professional. Those responsible for administering the function may be better

prepared for the task, and in large firms they may have specific training in the behavioral sciences.

3. Bargaining may become less emotional and more factual.
4. Management may become more aware of the political constraints affecting union leaders and try to avoid actions that might place "responsible" union leaders in vulnerable positions in their own organizations.
5. In situations in which the union leadership is aware of the competitive pressures affecting the firm and appears willing to act responsibly, management may discover the constructive potential of a "mature" bargaining relationship.

The management of a firm should not try to "purchase" good union-management relations by adopting a conciliatory or permissive approach to collective bargaining. Such a response to the presence of a union, though perhaps effective in the short run, may commit the firm to substantive contract provisions or to contract interpretations that limit managerial flexibility and are unnecessarily costly in the long run.

SUMMARY

In this chapter, we have reviewed management policies and organizations for collective bargaining. We have noted that a competent management will develop an employee relations function in the absence of unions and will administer employee relations and personnel policies objectively and consistently. The introduction of a union is usually achieved without the overt industrial warfare of an earlier day.

Unions necessarily limit managerial prerogatives, and collective bargaining is basically an adversary relationship. It involves both contract negotiation and contract administration. The structure of the union-management relations function varies considerably from one firm to another; however, well-managed firms will devote the same expertise, resources, and energy to this function as to other management functions. Such firms will also recognize the institutional constraints affecting union negotiators.

DISCUSSION QUESTIONS

1. Why is it necessary to distinguish between employee relations, union-management relations and personnel relations? How would such functions be staffed in a small firm?
2. Why might the chief operating officer of a firm and the head of the union that has organized the firm's employees have different perspectives regarding employee welfare?
3. Distinguish between a sophisticated human relations function and a "health and happiness" approach to employee relations.
4. To what extent should management rely upon lawyers in collective bargaining?
5. If American unions do not wish to assume responsibility for the operation of firms

with which they bargain, why do managements typically resist efforts to organize their employees?

6. Is contract negotiation or contract administration a more important facet of the management collective bargaining function?

7. Why are strikes more frequent causes of work stoppages than lockouts?

8. Why should management identify the institutional parameters affecting union leaders' and union negotiators' bargaining calculus?

SELECTED READINGS

The Role of Work Groups

Landsberger, Henry A. *Hawthorne Revisited: "Management and the Worker," its Critics, and Developments in Human Relations in Industry.* Ithaca, New York: Cornell University Press, 1950.

Roethlisberger, F. J. *Management and Morale.* Cambridge, Mass.: Harvard University Press, 1946.

Roethlisberger, F. J., and Dickson, William J. *Management and the Worker.* Cambridge, Mass.: Harvard University Press, 1939. This is a basic reference on the subject.

Human Relations and Organizational Behavior Studies

Katzell, Raymond, and Yankelovich, Daniel. *Work, Productivity and Job Satisfaction.* New York: Harcourt Brace Jovanovich, 1975.

Landsberger, Henry A. "The Behavioral Sciences in Industry." In *Industrial Relations* 7 no. 1 (October 1967): pp. 1–19.

Rush, Harold M. F. *Behavioral Science: Concepts and Management Application.* New York: National Industrial Conference Board, 1969. Contains an excellent bibliography of behavioral science theory and philosophy.

Strauss, George. "Organizational Behavior and Personnel Relations." In *A Review of Industrial Relations Research.* Vol. I. Ed. by Woodrow L. Ginsburg, E. Robert Livernash, Herbert S. Parnes, and George Strauss. Madison, Wisc.: Industrial Relations Research Association, 1970.

Employee Relations in Nonunion Firms

Gardner, Burleigh B., and Moore, David G. *Human Relations in Industry.* 4th ed. Homewood, Ill.: Irwin, 1964.

Myers, Scott. *Managing Without Unions.* Reading, Mass.: Addison-Wesley, 1976.

Pigors, Paul, and Myers, Charles A. *Personnel Administration.* 8th ed. New York: McGraw-Hill, 1976.

Strauss, George, and Sayles, Leonard R. *Personnel: The Human Problems of Management.* 3rd ed. Englewood Cliffs, N.J.: Prentice Hall, 1972.

Strike Insurance Plans

Hirsch, John S., Jr. "Strike Insurance and Collective Bargaining." In *Industrial and Labor Relations Review* 22 no. 3 (April 1969): pp. 399–415.

Management Policies and Organization for Collective Bargaining

Division for Personnel Administration, National Industrial Conference Board. *Personnel Practices in Factory and Office: Manufacturing.* New York: National Industrial Conference Board, 1964.

Freeman, Audrey. *Managing Labor Relations.* New York: National Industrial Conference Board, 1979.

Janger, Allen R. *Personnel Administration: Changing Scope and Organization.* New York: National Industrial Conference Board, 1966.

Ryder, Meyer S.; Rehmus, Charles M.; and Cohen, Sanford. *Management Preparation for Collective Bargaining.* Homewood, Ill.: Dow Jones-Irwin, 1966.

Seybold, Geneva. *Employee Communication: Policy and Tools.* New York: National Industrial Conference Board, 1966.

Slichter, Sumner H.; Healy, James J.; and Livernash, E. Robert. *The Impact of Collective Bargaining on Management.* Washington, D.C.: Brookings Institution, 1960. A definitive reference.

Many monographs and handbooks dealing with these subjects are available, including various publications of the Chamber of Commerce of the United States and the National Association of Manufacturers.

Notes

1. The possibility of developing a simple functional definition of management is discussed in Neil W. Chamberlain, *The Union Challenge to Management Control* (New York: Harper & Brothers, 1948), pp. 20–26.

2. Chamberlain identifies three types of management functions—direction, administration, and execution—but notes that "except in a popular sense there is no common agreement as to what the *managerial* function is." (Ibid., p. 26.) Cf. Thomas A. Mahoney, Thomas H. Jerdee, and Stephen J. Carroll, "The Job(s) of Management," *In Industrial Relations,* Bulletin 27 (Ithaca, N.Y.: NYS School of Industrial and

3. This section draws heavily on Edwin E. Witte, *The Evolution of Managerial Ideas In Industrial Relations, Bulletin* 27 (Ithaca, N.Y.: NYS School of Industrial and Labor Relations, Cornell University, reissued March 1958).

4. Taylor's classic work was *The Principles of Scientific Management* (New York: Harper & Brothers, 1911).

5. National Industrial Conference Board, *Improving Staff and Line Relations,* Studies in Personnel Policy No. 153 (New York: National Industrial Conference Board, 1956), p. 9.

6. Reinhard Bendix, "Bureaucratization in Industry," in Arthur Kornhauser, Robert Dubin, and Arthur M. Ross, eds., *Industrial Conflict* (New York: McGraw-Hill, 1954), p. 170. See also Melville Dalton, "Conflicts Between Staff and Line Managerial Officers," in *American Sociological Review* 15 (June 1950): pp. 342–351.

7. Cf. Harold L. Wilensky, "The Failure of Intelligence: Knowledge and Policy in Government and Industry," in *Proceedings of the Nineteenth Annual Meeting, Industrial Relations Research Association, December 28–29, 1966* (Madison, Wisc.: Industrial Relations Research Association, 1967), pp. 166–167.

8. Cf. Georges Spyropoulos, "An Outline of Developments and Trends in Labour Relations," in *International Labour Review* 99, no. 3 (March 1969): pp. 323–325.

9. Frederick H. Harbison and John R. Coleman, *Goals and Strategy in Collective Bargaining* (New York: Harper & Brothers, 1951), p. 7. Cf. E. Wight Bakke, *Mutual Survival: The Goal of Unions and Management*, 2nd ed. (Hamden, Conn.: Archon Books, 1966), pp. 2–3.

10. Cf. Bakke, *Mutual Survival*, particularly p. 18.

11. Cf. Sumner H. Slichter, James J. Healy, and E. Robert Livernash, *The Impact of Collective Bargaining on Management* (Washington, D.C.: Brookings Institution, 1960), pp. 10–13. See also Audrey Freeman, *Managing Labor Relations* (New York: National Industrial Conference Board, 1979).

12. Slichter, Healy, and Livernash, *Impact of Collective Bargaining*, p. 11.

13. Subcommittee on Collective Bargaining, Industrial Relations Committee, National Association of Manufacturers, *When Management Negotiates: A Guidebook for Sound Collective Bargaining* (New York: National Association of Manufacturers, 1967), p. 7.

14. Ibid.

15. The experience of the trucking industry in this regard is instructive. Cf. Industrial Relations Department, American Trucking Associations, *Collective Bargaining in the Trucking Industry, 1962* (Washington, D.C.: American Trucking Associations, 1962).

16. E. Robert Livernash, "The Relation of Power to the Structure and Process of Collective Bargaining." Reprinted with permission from the *Journal of Law and Economics,* vol. VI. Copyright 1963 by the University of Chicago Law School, pp. 25–26.

17. Slichter, Healy, and Livernash, *Impact of Collective Bargaining*, p. 13.

Part IV
GOVERNMENT REGULATION OF COLLECTIVE BARGAINING

Chapter 16
THE REGULATORY FRAMEWORK I: HOW THE LAW OF COLLECTIVE BARGAINING EVOLVED

In a pluralistic industrial society, the government shares in formulating and implementing the web of rule that regulates the employment relationship. In Part Two, we described a variety of laws that affect this relationship directly or indirectly but are not concerned with encouraging or regulating collective bargaining. In the chapters in Part Three dealing with union history, we referred a number of times to the legislation that affected the growth of unions and the extension of collective bargaining. In this chapter and the two following chapters, we will deal more specifically with the law of collective bargaining.

Whereas earlier we were concerned with legislation affecting wage and salary workers *generally*, here we are concerned with the regulation of the continuing relationship between *organized* labor and management and with public policy as it affects that relationship. In this chapter, we will review the development of our law of collective bargaining; and discuss the Railway Labor Act, the Norris-LaGuardia Act, and the National Labor Relations (Wagner) Act. In Chapter 17, we will discuss the current federal regulatory framework provided by the Labor-Management Relations (Taft-Hartley) Act, as amended, and review briefly state legislation applicable to the private sector. In Chapter 18, we will discuss other relevant federal legislation; we will consider contemporary issues relating to labor disputes that create a national emergency, railway labor legislation, and equal employment opportunity legislation; and we will summarize federal and state laws regulating collective bargaining in the public sector.

Our collective bargaining statutes are products of an evolutionary process involving changing concepts of individual liberty and social welfare. Students interested in the details of this process can refer to the standard works in the field described in the chapter *Selected Readings*; we will limit our coverage here to the more significant antecedents of current law. Although our discussion will emphasize federal legislation, it is important to note that prior to the Depression, federal law was not controlling and that many matters are still subject to state regulation. A number of states have "Little Wagner" or "Little Taft-Hartley" acts that apply to intrastate industries, and in one area—the permissible degree of union security—states can preempt federal jurisdiction. States can also assume jurisdiction over union-management relations in firms engaged in interstate commerce when the National Labor Relations Board refuses to assert its jurisdiction, and an increasing number of states have laws regulating collective bargaining in the public sector.

The history of social legislation in this country, including the regulation of union-management relations, is largely a history of overcoming judicial opposition to any limits on certain individual rights guaranteed by the Constitution, including positive rights to life, liberty, and property. Both Congress (by the Fifth Amendment) and the states (by the Fourteenth Amendment) are forbidden to interfere with these rights without due process of law. The courts generally defined *freedom of contract* as a property right, and actions by organized groups, including unions, that interfered with the exercise of this right could be held illegal. The use of strikes, picketing, and boycotts could be restricted under this doctrine, and laws protecting individual workers or unions that interfered with freedom of contract were also suspect. Offsetting these very substantial limitations on the right of workers to organize, to bargain collectively, and to use economic weapons in pursuit of their objectives is the right of the states as custodians of police power to pass laws promoting the public welfare and the power of Congress to protect the general welfare through legislation regulating commerce between the states.

Before the early 1930s, labor relations in the United States were *controlled* by the *courts*. Initially, *under common law*, unions were held to be illegal conspiracies, but the courts, by modifying common law through the process of judicial review, permitted unions first to exist and then to use various economic weapons. Union leaders were generally opposed to government intervention in, and regulation of, collective bargaining. American workers wanted to *participate* in this process however, and denied that opportunity, they

> made two principal demands upon the law. One was for the right to form, join, and assist labor organizations and, through them, to bargain collectively with employers. The second was for the maximum freedom to use economic weapons—strikes, boy-

cotts, picketing, and other concerted activities—to spread unionization and wring concessions from employers.[1]

During the New Deal, the courts, by accepting broader definitions of the police power and interstate commerce, upheld federal and state *statutes* protecting workers' rights to organize and bargain collectively and permitted unions to use additional economic weapons to achieve their objectives. More recently, federal and state governments, recognizing the public interest aspects of collective bargaining and the public character of unions, have begun to subject the collective bargaining process and the internal affairs of unions to greater public control. A review of the evolution of our law of collective bargaining will identify the factors which contributed to these developments.

Five phases in the evolution of our public policy toward unions and collective bargaining have been identified: (1) a phase of *suppression,* essentially through judicial decision, which lasted until 1842; (2) a phase of *grudging toleration,* which lasted from 1842 until the passage of the Norris-LaGuardia Act in 1932; (3) a brief period of *benevolent toleration* from 1933 to 1935*; (4) a phase of *encouraging* union organization and the initiation of collective bargaining relationships, which lasted from 1935 to 1947; and most recently, a phase of *acceptance and encouragement* of collective bargaining within a more extensive *regulatory framework.*[2]

THE EARLY CONSPIRACY CASES

Early in the 1800s, some employers who opposed collective action by their employees turned to the courts for support, arguing that such action not only interferred with their rights as employers but also burdened the community by artificially and unnaturally raising the price of labor and the commodities it produced.

In our legal system, there are three types of remedies if a person is injured by the acts of another: prosecution of the offender as a criminal, a civil suit for damages, or the issuance of an injunction by a court of equity requiring the offender to cease and desist from further specified actions(s). Cases involving the activities of trade unions were infrequent during the first half of the nineteenth century, but those that did arise often involved the criminal prosecution of union leaders or members under the common law doctrine of conspiracy. This doctrine, first developed by the English courts, was adopted in the Philadelphia Cordwainers' Case (*Commonwealth* [Pa.] v. *Cordwainers*) in 1806.

In 1805, the journeymen cordwainers (shoemakers working on cordovan leather) of Philadelphia had presented the Society of Master Cordwainers with a

---

* The Clayton Act of 1914, the policies of the War Labor Board during World War I, and the Railway Labor Act of 1926 reflected a spirit of benevolent toleration, but these laws and policies had either limited applicability or were short-lived.

new schedule of wages to be paid for the production of various types of shoes. The masters refused to grant any increases, and the workers struck. The workers were defeated, and after the strike had ended, eight workers were indicted for combining and conspiring to raise their wages. The recorder (judge) instructed the jury in the case as follows: " 'A combination of workmen to raise their wages may be considered in a two-fold point of view: One is to benefit themselves . . . the other is to injure those who do not join their society. The Rule of law condemns both.' "[3] Not unexpectedly, the jury found the defendants guilty.

A number of other jurisdictions accepted the doctrine that the combination of workers to raise their wages was a criminal conspiracy. It was assumed that such combinations necessarily sought ends destructive of the rights of others. The effect of these early decisions, some 19 in number, was to make unions illegal. Nevertheless, union membership gradually increased, and in 1842, the right of workers to form such organizations was clearly affirmed by a Massachusetts court in the case of the *Commonwealth* [Mass.] v. *Hunt.*

In 1835, Boston shoemakers had formed a Journeymen Bootmakers' Society. The society's constitution provided that a member could not work with a non-member in a shop in which the majority of workers belonged to the society; that is, the society insisted on a closed shop. In 1840, a worker who had been expelled from the society and who worked in a closed shop refused to apply for readmission to the union; he was discharged and complained to the district attorney in Boston. The district attorney secured an indictment against seven leaders of the society, charging them with criminal conspiracy. They were tried and found guilty, and the case was appealed to the Supreme Court of Massachusetts. This court, in reversing the convictions, established the legality of trade unions by holding that the formation of a labor union was lawful and that so long as the *means used* to do it were not unlawful the doctrine of criminal conspiracy did not apply. Judges in other jurisdictions looked to the Massachusetts court for precedents, and the decision was widely copied. Although the Massachusetts case did not inter the doctrine of criminal conspiracy, it discouraged its use, and the period of suppression of unions gave way to the period of grudging toleration. The issue in the courts became whether the *purpose* of a combination (union) was lawful and whether *lawful means* were used to accomplish that purpose.

In most jurisdictions in the nineteenth century, the legitimate objectives of collective action by labor were narrowly construed. This construction reflected the training, political philosophy, and economic beliefs of the judiciary as well as the mores of the community. An important question in early cases following *Commonwealth* v. *Hunt* was whether organized workers had "just cause" for a specific action. In striking, picketing, and boycotting, workers harmed their employers, and the question of a just cause came down to whether the right of unions to take such actions was superior to the right of employers to conduct their business. Was the injury to employers "a necessary incidental in the exercise of the workers' rights?"[4] Since most courts considered the right to do business and make a profit a property right, an initial presumption was established that if a union interfered with this right by overt acts, the burden of proving that such interference was justifiable lay with the union.

A different line of reasoning in the last half of the nineteenth century accepted the legality of the motives of union members, leaving only the determination of the legality of the means they used in pursuit of their goals to the courts. The right to strike for a closed shop, the legality of secondary boycotts, the extent to which "peaceful" picketing was permitted—these and other issues were resolved differently by various state courts, and as a result, "radically different conceptions of labor policy . . . prevailed in this country around the turn of the century."[5]

The early common law cases usually involved state courts, but toward the close of the nineteenth century, federal legislation designed to preserve competition in commodity markets was declared applicable to union activity and federal courts assumed a more important role in union-management relations. Restraint of trade had been a consideration in a number of the early conspiracy cases at the state level; with the passage of the Sherman Act in 1890, restraint of trade became a statutory federal offense, and through a series of court decisions, the act was held to apply to unions. However, before considering the application of antitrust legislation to unions, we shall first review another development, the increasing use of what proved to be a highly effective weapon for employers, the *labor injunction.*

INJUNCTIONS AND THE RESTRAINT OF TRADE

Prior to the last decades of the nineteenth century, employers involved in labor disputes typically sought remedies at law *after* the commission of alleged wrongful acts; union officials or union members were charged with a *specific* illegal act or acts and then tried in court. There was however another way in which firms with a grievance could protect themselves; they could obtain an *injunction* from an equity court against an action that threatened irreparable damage to their property or property rights. As we have seen, the right to conduct a business and the expectation of a profit were considered property rights. If a union threatened to do things that would interfere with the exercise of these rights, an employer could ask for an injunction to *prevent* or stop such actions. Physical damage to buildings and acts of violence against persons were already punishable as crimes; the importance of injunctions was that they could be used to halt strikes and boycotts that had not caused, and probably would not cause, physical harm to people or property. The federal injunction against Eugene V. Debs in the Pullman Strike of 1894 was the first significant use of this device. Thereafter, injunctions were frequently used by employers to inhibit organizational activity by unions and to curb the use of various union weapons.

Under some conditions, an injunction can be of value in preventing irreparable harm to an individual, but the history of the injunction's use in labor disputes indicates that it was gravely misused. Temporary *restraining orders,* or injunctions *ad interim,* which were usually issued without notice and without a hearing, were particularly burdensome to unions, since they could be used to crush incipient organizational activity. Although a permanent injunction against such activity might not be issued after a formal hearing had been held, a union's cause could by then be damaged irretrievably.

THE SHERMAN ACT

The Sherman Act of 1890,[6] which was designed to curb monopolies in restraint of trade, did not mention labor combinations or labor disputes. Section 1 of the act made illegal

> [E]very contract, combination in the form of trust or otherwise, or conspiracy, in restraint of trade or commerce among the several States, or with foreign nations. . . .

Section 2 of the act declared that

> Every person who shall monopolize or attempt to monopolize, or combine or conspire with any other person or persons, to monopolize any part of the trade or commerce among the several States, or with foreign nations, shall be deemed guilty of a misdemeanor.

The attorney general could prosecute violators of the act as criminals or seek injunctions against illegal acts. Jurisdiction over restraint of trade cases was given to the federal courts, and injured parties could sue for triple damages. It was not clear at first whether the Sherman Act applied to labor unions and their activities, but the Supreme Court held that it did. Union activities in restraint of trade, including secondary boycotts, became vulnerable to injunctions, and the unions themselves became subject to suits for damages. As a result, the Sherman Act became an important weapon in the battle against unions.

The term *boycott* usually refers to a refusal to deal with a particular firm or the encouragement of others—either employees or customers of a firm—to stop dealing with it.* The refusal of union members to buy goods produced by *their* employer and attempts to persuade other customers not to buy from an employer *directly* involved in a labor dispute constitute *primary boycotts.* There is no simple legal definition of a secondary boycott, although all true secondary boycotts involve two employers. According to Cox,

> The element of "secondary activity" is introduced [by] a refusal to have dealings with [some] one who has dealings with the offending person. . . . The union brings pressure upon the employer with whom it has a dispute (called the "primary employer") by inducing the *employees of other employers* who deal with him (called the "secondary employers") to go on strike—or *their customers*

---

* Technically, a strike is a boycott because employees refuse to deal with their employer.

not to patronize [them]—until the secondary employers stop dealing with the primary employer. Or the union may simply induce the employees of a secondary employer to refuse to handle or work on goods—or [its] customers not to buy goods—coming from the primary employer while they perform the rest of their duties.[7]

In court cases in which a distinction has been made between primary and secondary boycotts, the former have usually been held lawful and the latter condemned.

The leading secondary boycott case under the Sherman Act arose when the hat workers' union tried to organize the Loewe hat firm in Danbury, Connecticut.[8] When the union imposed a nationwide boycott on Loewe hats, the firm suffered substantial losses. It then sued for triple damages under section 1 of the act. The suit was dismissed by a lower court, but in February 1908, the Supreme Court, holding that the Sherman Act applied to labor combinations in restraint of trade, remanded the case for trial. The union was found guilty, and damages of slightly over one-quarter of a million dollars were awarded to the Loewe firm. When the case was appealed, the Supreme Court held that the union and its individual members were jointly liable under the act, and it appeared that the members might lose their personal possessions in satisfaction of the judgment. However, the A.F. of L. arranged two "Hatters' Days" that raised some $215,000 of the final $234,000 settlement.

A second leading case developed from a boycott of the Bucks Stove and Range Company in 1907. The company, which had been placed on a "We Don't Patronize" list published in the *American Federationist*, claimed that the boycott was unlawful and secured an injunction ordering that its name be removed from the list. The injunction was not obeyed, and the officers of the A.F. of L. were fined for contempt. Although the judgment was set aside because of a legal technicality, the Supreme Court declared that such boycotts were unlawful.[9]

THE CLAYTON ACT[10]

Alerted to the danger of injunctions and of prosecution under the Sherman Act, the unions exerted political pressure to change the law. Their efforts met with apparent success when pro-union sections (6 and 20) were included in the Clayton Act of 1914. Labor leaders and many legal scholars believed that this act "curtail[ed] the power of federal courts to issue injunctions in cases involving economic conflict between labor unions and business concerns, whenever the evidence showed that the particular union had some real economic interest at stake which was adversely affected by the employment practices followed by the company in question."[11] They also believed that the act made lawful certain "self-help" activities of unions, including secondary boycotts. In 1914, Samuel Gompers hailed the Clayton Act as the Magna Carta of American labor, but his enthusiasm proved premature. In a series of decisions, the Supreme Court held that the Clayton Act had not made lawful any conduct by unions that was not lawful before the passage of the act and that unions were not immune from prosecution under the Sherman Act. The leading cases in which these interpretations were developed were the Duplex case and the Bedford Stone case.[12]

The Duplex Printing Press Company was one of four companies that manufactured printing presses for newspapers. The machinists' union, which had organized the other manufacturers, struck Duplex, and when the company refused to recognize the union, it instituted a secondary boycott of Duplex presses. The company asked for an injunction to stop the boycott, but both the federal district court and the circuit court of appeals denied the request in light of the provisions of the Clayton Act. The Supreme Court however held that although the Clayton Act states that the antitrust laws could not be used to stop labor organizations from *lawfully* pursuing their legitimate objectives, it did not legalize union activities that were illegal at the time of its passage. The Court held that secondary boycotts were unlawful and therefore not protected by the Clayton Act.

The Bedford Cut Stone case involved a nationwide boycott of Indiana limestone, instituted by the National Stone Cutters' union in an attempt to organize workers in the Indiana limestone quarries. The Bedford Company took advantage of the right of private persons to sue for injunctions under the Clayton Act and asked that the boycott be enjoined. The Supreme Court, using the same argument it used in the Duplex case, declared that the union's action was an undue and unreasonable restraint of commerce.

Meanwhile, the unions had suffered a setback on another front. In 1914, the mines of the Coronado Coal Company at Prairie Creek, Arkansas, which had been shut during a labor dispute, were opened with nonunion employees. Apparently at the urging of unionized operators, the United Mine Workers tried to organize this nonunion operation. After an outbreak of violence, an injunction was obtained ordering the UMW to stop interfering with operations at Prairie Creek. Violence continued, and the company sued for damages under the Sherman Act.

The suit first reached the Supreme Court in 1922.[13] The Court held that unincorporated unions could be sued as entities but that because mining was not an interstate business and the union had not intended to interfere with interstate commerce, there had been no violation of the Sherman Act. At a second trial, evidence was introduced that the union had intended to interfere with interstate commerce, but again the judge directed a verdict for the defendants. The company appealed; in reviewing the appeal, the Supreme Court held that substantial new evidence had demonstrated an intent to interfere with interstate commerce, and a third trial was ordered.[14] An out-of-court settlement was finally reached under which District 21 of the UMW paid $27,500 damages. This decision was significant because it established that a strike that affected a struck firm's products "entering and moving in interstate commerce" was illegal and made the union responsible for such a strike liable for damages.

THE LEGALITY OF YELLOW-DOG CONTRACTS

While the Coronado case was being argued, still another roadblock was put in the path of union organizing efforts. In 1917, the Supreme Court held that an employer could secure an injunction restraining union organizers from trying to organize workers who had agreed as part of their contract of employment not to join a labor organization.[15] Contracts containing such clauses, widely known as *yellow-dog contracts* or *documents,* were effective means of maintaining a nonunion shop. Their popularity had increased as a result of earlier court decisions that had declared a federal and a state statute prohibiting them unconstitutional.[16]

The 1917 case involved the Hitchman Coal and Coke Company of West Virginia and the United Mine Workers. The company had individual agreements with its employees that the mine was to be run on a nonunion basis and that any worker joining a union would lose his job. An organizer from the UMW began to secretly enroll employees in the union, and when this activity was discovered, the company obtained an injunction restraining the union from further organizing and ordering the employees to stop violating their contracts. In reviewing the case, the Supreme Court held that an employer was free to make nonmembership in a union a condition of employment and that an attempt to induce employees to breach such an agreement was unlawful. The effectiveness of yellow-dog contracts as an antiunion device resulted from the restrictions they imposed on the activities of union organizers.

As the decisions we have described indicate, prior to World War I (indeed until the 1930s), the law—or rather court interpretations of common and statutory law—generally favored employers: "judicial policy in essence was one of selective suppression of organized labor's activities whenever they trenched too heavily upon the interests of any other segment of society."[17] The temper of the time was such that federal and state legislatures were content to allow the courts to regulate industrial relations. Thus the "law" of collective bargaining rested on the common law and on judicial interpretations of antitrust legislation. Meanwhile, other developments testified to growing, if limited, government support for unionism and collective bargaining.

WORLD WAR I

While unions were discovering the reluctance of the judiciary to support their organizational activities, the executive and legislative branches of the federal government began to support the principle of collective bargaining. A number of reports contributed to this development: the commission appointed by President Grover Cleveland to investigate the Pullman Strike of 1894 urged employers to accept unions and recommended that yellow-dog contracts be made illegal; the reports of the Anthracite Commission and the Industrial Commission in 1902 and of the Commission on Industrial Relations in 1915 supported the principle of collective bargaining and condemned specific antiunion tactics used by employers.[18] There was growing recognition that forming a union was an appropriate way for workers to share in decisions affecting the employment relationship and that judicial intervention had been, on balance, hostile to the unions.*

Before the U.S. entry into World War I, President Woodrow Wilson appointed a tripartite *War Labor Conference Board* to recommend principles and policies to govern relations between workers and employers in essential industries. The board's report, which provided "the basis of adjudication of disputes . . . and constituted . . . a code of industrial law for the period of the war,"[19] was implemented by a tripartite *National War Labor Board* (NWLB). The rights granted to workers under the policy statement of the NWLB represented a formal endorsement of collective bargaining that foreshadowed the basic principles underlying the National Labor Relations Act of 1935. The board insisted that workers had the right to be represented for purposes of collective bargaining, and it issued orders prohibiting unfair labor practices. It did not compel an employer to recognize an "outside" union in preference to a company union however, and a substantial increase in the number of employee representation plans and company unions accompanied the wartime expansion in union membership. The wartime agreement helped to assure uninterrupted production during the war, but the formal rapport between organized labor and management dissolved after the cessation of hostilities.

THE RAILWAY LABOR ACT[20]

The prosperity of the 1920s contributed to an endorsement of the principle of collective bargaining in the Railway Labor Act of 1926. The Constitution gives Congress the power to regulate interstate carriers (such as railroads), and it began to do so with the Interstate Commerce Act of 1887. Fearful that federal intervention to prevent work stoppages on the railroads might limit their power, the railroad brotherhoods (the operating crafts), who had a very effective political lobby, insisted that Congress provide impartial machinery to help resolve such disputes. Since 1888, a series of federal laws has attempted to provide such a mechanism.

During World War I, when the government operated the railroads, unions representing both the running trades and the shop crafts gained members. After the armistice, control of the roads was returned to their owners, but they continued to be regulated under the Transportation Act of 1920. A *permanent* tripartite *Railroad Labor Board* was set up to investigate *primary disputes* (disputes over the terms of *new* contracts) and make public its findings. The act also called for *adjustment boards* to be established by agreement between the parties to collective bargaining to resolve *secondary disputes* (disputes over the interpretation of *existing contracts*). However, the nonoperating unions and the carriers were

---

* The Lloyd-LaFollette Act of 1912 (37 *Stat.* 555) allowed federal postal employees to join unions that were "not affiliated with any outside organization imposing an obligation or duty upon them to engage in any strike, . . . against the United States."

unable to agree on the establishment of such boards, and many secondary disputes went to the Railway Labor Board for settlement.

There were two fundamental weaknesses in the Transportation Act of 1920: no provision was made for enforcing board orders, and the ability of the board to resolve disputes on a continuing basis was jeopardized by specific decisions that were unsatisfactory to one or both parties. This last problem stemmed from the board's *permanence*. An unsatisfactory decision in a primary dispute by an *ad hoc board* (one appointed to handle a specific dispute) would have been less likely to impair the future usefulness of the procedures established by the act. The action of the board in a shop crafts' strike in 1922, which in effect outlawed the strike, was particularly unpalatable to the unions and made it obvious that the act was not achieving its goals.

Realizing that more extensive regulation of union-management relations on the railroads was inevitable, and not wishing to have rules and procedures developed by groups outside the industry, the unions and carriers agreed on the basic provisions of the *Railway Labor Act of 1926*. This act, passed by a Republican administration, recognized the right of railroad workers to organize and to bargain collectively, free from employer interference.

The act, which was upheld in a 1930 Supreme Court decision,[21] provided for the establishment of a *permanent* three-member Board of Mediation to help resolve *primary disputes* and for the appointment at the discretion of the President of ad hoc boards to investigate and make recommendations in primary disputes that could not be resolved by the mediation board. *Boards of adjustment* were to be created by agreement between labor and management to decide *secondary disputes*. However, the nonoperating unions and the carriers were again unable to agree on the level (intrasystem, regional, or national) at which adjustment boards should function, and boards were not established for many classes of employees. The bipartisan boards that were established were often deadlocked, and there was no provision in the law for resolving such impasses. In addition, the law failed to provide machinery for selecting employee representatives, and it did not compel a carrier to deal exclusively with the representative of the majority of a given class of workers.

The 1926 act was amended in 1934 to correct such operational defects and to protect more fully the workers' right to organize. The amendments, which were passed over the opposition of the carriers, did several things:

1. They established a bipartisan *National* Railroad Adjustment Board (NRAB) with four divisions to handle secondary disputes. Each division had jurisdiction over specific kinds of workers; management and the unions were equally represented on each board, and in the event of a tie vote, if the board members could not agree on a neutral referee, the National Mediation Board would appoint a referee.
2. Carriers who failed to comply with orders of the NRAB became subject to criminal penalties.

3. Machinery was set up to select bargaining agents who would be formally recognized by the National Mediation Board, and the "majority of any craft or class of employees" was given "the right to determine . . . the representatives of the craft or class." Ten years later, in 1944, the U.S. Supreme Court declared that these representatives had an obligation to act on behalf of *all* the workers in a bargaining unit *without discrimination*.[22]

4. The number of persons on the National Mediation Board was increased from three to five.

5. Any form of union security arrangement was declared a violation of the act. This provision was sponsored by the railroad *unions*, who feared that the establishment by the carriers of company-dominated labor organizations with a right to union security might destroy "outside" unions.

In 1936, the coverage of the act was expanded to include air transport, and in 1951, when company unions were no longer feared, the unions were given the right to negotiate a union shop (employees are required to join a union) and the checkoff (the employer deducts union dues from a worker's pay).

THE NORRIS-LAGUARDIA ACT[23]

Union demands for relief from the use of injunctions by employers were finally met following the publication of *The Labor Injunction*,[24] written by two noted liberal legal scholars, Felix Frankfurter and Nathan Greene, and the midterm congressional elections in 1930. The Norris-LaGuardia Act, passed by a Democratic House and a Republican Senate and signed by a Republican President, disallowed injunctions in labor disputes except under carefully prescribed conditions. For an injunction to be issued, it had to be shown that (1) unlawful conduct threatened or committed by a union implied substantial and irreparable damage greater to the complainant than the damage the union would suffer if its actions were prohibited, (2) a lawsuit would be of no use in the situation, and (3) local peace officers were unable or unwilling to protect the complainant. Furthermore, during a labor dispute, an injunction could not be issued by a federal court to prevent people from engaging in most of the kinds of union activities associated with such a dispute. The definition of a *labor dispute* was also broadened to include

> . . . any controversy concerning terms or conditions of employment, or concerning the association or representation of persons in negotiating, fixing, maintaining, changing, or seeking to arrange terms or conditions of employment, *regardless of whether or not the disputants [stood] in the proximate relation of employer and employee*.[25]

This provision, which made it impossible to enjoin any activities of organized labor in pursuing its own interests except in carefully defined circumstances, "really did what many had thought Congress was trying to do in . . . Section 20 of the Clayton Act."[26]

The Norris-LaGuardia Act ultimately reached far beyond the banning of injunctions in labor disputes when the Supreme Court in a series of decisions held that those activities of organized labor that were not enjoinable were, in fact, *legal*. The only apparent basic limitation on the unions' activities was that they could not join with employers to achieve an end forbidden by the country's anti-trust laws.[27] The same objective could however be pursued independently by a union. In the 1941 Hutcheson case, which involved a secondary boycott of Anheuser-Busch beer by the carpenters' union, Justice Felix Frankfurter, speaking for a majority of the Court, declared that

> [S]o long as a union acts in its self-interest and does not combine with non-labor groups, the licit and the illicit . . . are not to be distinguished by any judgment regarding the wisdom or unwisdom, the rightness or wrongness, the selfishness or unselfishness of the end of which the particular union activities are the means.[28]

Many experts believe that Congress had not intended to legalize such activities as secondary boycotts, sympathetic strikes, and other restraints of trade; in dissenting, Justice Owen J. Roberts held that the majority opinion was a "process of construction, never, as I think, heretofore indulged by this court. . . . I venture to say that no court has ever undertaken so radically to legislate where Congress has refused to do so."

The Norris-LaGuardia Act was also important in two other respects. First, it was widely copied at the state level. By 1941, some 24 states had antiinjunction laws, of which 17 were "Little Norris-LaGuardia Acts" patterned after the federal legislation. Second, the declaration of policy in the act was a clear affirmation of the need to protect workers' rights to organize and to engage in collective bargaining, and also to refrain from such activities. This policy declaration, together with the several federal reports mentioned previously, the policy statement of the World War I War Labor Conference Board, and the provisions of the Railway Labor Act show that even before Franklin D. Roosevelt took office, many features of what is often considered innovative New Deal labor legislation had either been included in federal statutes or accepted in principle.[29] Under the New Deal, a *general* public policy toward collective bargaining and the protection of the rights of organized labor was evolved. We have described the 1934 amendments to the Railway Labor Act that reflected this policy; we turn now to the legislation that encouraged the establishment of collective bargaining more generally, the Wagner Act and its precursor, Section 7(a) of the National Industrial Recovery Act.

SECTION 7(a) OF THE NATIONAL INDUSTRIAL RECOVERY ACT[30]

Two basic objectives of the Roosevelt administration were the revival of business and the reduction of unemployment. The *National Industrial Recovery Act* was an attempt to achieve these ends by having business regulate itself through *recovery codes.* The Depression had shattered the confidence of the A.F. of L.'s leaders in voluntarism. Also, the methods used by employers to prevent the organization of their workers, including the use of company unions to fight "outside" unionism, had convinced labor leaders that government support of the right to organize and bargain collectively was essential. To secure labor support for what was in essence a bill to aid industry, a labor section (7[a]) was included in the NIRA. This section required all recovery codes to provide

> (1) that employees shall have the right to organize and bargain collectively through representatives of their own choosing, and shall be free from the interference, restraint, or coercion of employers of labor, or their agents . . . ; and (2) that no employee and no one seeking employment shall be required as a condition of employment to join any company union or to refrain from joining, organizing, or assisting a labor organization of his own choosing. . . .

Section 7(a), like section 20 of the Clayton Act, was hailed as the Magna Carta of American labor, and a number of unions launched organizing campaigns in basic industries. They were met by determined opposition from employers, and it soon became evident that union rights under the NIRA were far from clear and that company unions had not been outlawed. A leading student of New Deal Labor legislation has pointed out that

> Sec. 7(a), a short and seemingly clear declaration of policy in a statute otherwise marked by complexity, lifted the lid of Pandora's box. The haste and inexperience from which it was derived were breeding grounds of ambiguity; it raised more questions than it provided answers. . . . The President, his advisers, and Congress . . . had committed themselves, probably without realizing it, to a broad policy of intervention in collective bargaining that was to lead far beyond 7(a).[31]

Section 7(a) did not provide a way of determining who was to represent employees in a specific collective bargaining situation; it did not require employers to recognize and deal with such a representative; and there was no effective means of enforcing the section (although violators could be denied the use of the Blue Eagle, the symbol of cooperation in the recovery program). The National Association of Manufacturers maintained that company unions were still legal because the act stipulated only that employees could not be *compelled* to join such a union or to refrain from joining an outside union. As a result, there was a substantial increase in the number of employee representation plans and company unions.

In August of 1933, the President created a *National Labor Board* (NLB) to settle the issues brought up by the application of section 7(a). The widespread refusal of firms to comply with the decisions of this board led to proposals for permanent labor legislation outside the framework of the NIRA. Congress however was unable to agree on appropriate legislation. Senator Robert Wagner's proposed Labor Disputes bill, for example, was opposed by both the Communist Trade Union Unity League and the National Association of Manufacturers! Convinced that some action was necessary, Roosevelt drafted and sent to Congress Public Resolution No. 44, authorizing the President to establish a board or boards with power to implement the principles in 7(a); subsequently, the first National Labor Relations Board was created by executive order.*

This board followed and further developed the administrative common law of the NLB: discriminatory antiunion practices were outlawed, a secret ballot was required in elections to choose employee representatives, and the principle of majority rule within collective bargaining units was reaffirmed. When problems arose in selecting units "appropriate to collective bargaining," the board permitted craft units to be carved out of larger units if there was a history of such a practice or the situation called for such a move. Employers were required to bargain in good faith, to make counterproposals, and to make reasonable efforts to reach agreements with the representatives of their employees. However, because the board lacked enough power to enforce its directives, Senator Wagner set out to win congressional approval for permanent legislation that would effectively proscribe the employer practices that had vitiated section 7(a).

THE NATIONAL LABOR RELATIONS (WAGNER) ACT[32]

The act finally presented by Wagner has been criticized as one-sided legislation favoring unions at the expense of management. Employees were given specific rights under the act, but no parallel rights of employers were specified and employer, not union, practices were proscribed. This is understandable: the act was designed to overcome an imbalance in union-management relations; it was a pragmatic response to the opposition of many businesses to a stated national policy.

Employers bitterly opposed the bill, and at first Roosevelt did not support it fully. He finally endorsed it in May of 1935, just before the Supreme Court declared the NIRA unconstitutional.[33] The Court's decision was a major blow to the President, and he reacted by declaring that his entire New Deal program, including the Wagner bill, must go forward. On July 5, 1935, he signed the National Labor Relations Act. Like its predecessors, it was hailed as the Magna Carta of labor; this time, the description proved accurate.

The Wagner Act was concerned with the preliminaries to collective bargaining; it protected those attempting to organize unorganized workers and those who joined labor organizations, and it ensured that once workers had been organized, their representatives would be given a seat at the bargaining table. It did not regulate the bargaining process as such or the internal affairs of labor organizations. A three-man *National Labor Relations Board* was established to administer the act. The language of specific provisions was often quite general, and the board was ultimately given considerable leeway in interpreting the act.

Although the lack of mutuality in the act was understandable in the context of the times, it should have been recognized more generally that if and

---

* The board allowed the 17 regional offices of the NLB, as well as the several industrial boards that had been created to handle problems in specific industries, to continue operations.

when unions became firmly established, the balance of power might tilt so far in their favor that the act would have to be modified. The act would also have to be amended to correct operational defects. These limitations were recognized explicitly by a number of supporters of the act; on July 21, 1935, for example, Harry Millis wrote President Roosevelt that the act was " 'not a complete labor code. In the long run it will need to be amended in the light of experience.' "[34] The act was not to be amended however until after World War II, when public resentment created by a wave of strikes in basic industries and elsewhere gave Congress a mandate to pass legislation to achieve a "proper balance" between the parties to collective bargaining.

An immediate problem was the refusal of many firms to comply with the orders of the NLRB. Many large companies believed that the act would be declared unconstitutional, and they openly violated it. As a result, the years from 1935 to 1937 witnessed some of the most violent labor disputes in U.S. history. Even after the constitutionality of the act was established by a group of decisions handed down by the Supreme Court in April of 1937, some employers continued to fight a rearguard action against our national labor policy, apparently believing that in the area of labor-management relations, they were peculiarly able to recognize a higher law.[35]

THE EFFECT OF THE ACT ON UNIONS AND MANAGEMENT

The Wagner Act was designed to protect the right of employees to organize and bargain collectively and to provide a method of selecting representatives for collective bargaining. National labor policy as reflected in the act made the following assumptions:

1. The American system of industrial relations should be based upon strong unions and free collective bargaining. . . .
2. The law should not intervene in labor disputes by restricting strikes, boycotts, or picketing in aid of unionization or collective bargaining. . . .
3. [The] substantive terms and conditions of employment [should be left] entirely to private negotiation.
4. [T]he creation and enforcement of the rights to organize and bargain collectively were the best method of achieving industrial peace without undue sacrifice of personal and economic freedom.[36]

The Basic Provisions of the Act

Section 1 of the National Labor Relations Act contained statements of congressional findings and of federal labor policy that established the act's constitutionality. The need to eliminate obstructions to the flow of commerce between the states was emphasized, and the provisions of the act were asserted to be necessary to offset forces that aggravated business depressions. According to the final paragraph of the section, it was "the policy of the United States to eliminate the causes of certain substantial obstructions to the free flow of commerce and to mitigate and eliminate these obstructions when they have occurred by encouraging the practice and procedure of collective bargaining. . . ."

Section 2 contained relevant definitions. Section 3 created the three-member board to administer the law. Sections 4, 5, and 6 described how the National Labor Relations Board was to be organized. It was to be an administrative and quasi-judicial agency: its principal administrative function was to be the determination of employee representatives in collective bargaining units; as prosecutor and judge, it was to have jurisdiction over charges of unfair labor practices against employers.

The more important substantive provisions of the act were in section 7, "Rights of Employees"; section 8, "Unfair Labor Practices"; and section 9, "Representatives and Elections." The heart of the act, section 7, set forth the *positive rights* of employees "to self-organization, to form, join, or assist labor organizations, to bargain collectively through representatives of their own choosing, and to engage in concerted activities, for the purpose of collective bargaining or other mutual aid or protection." The act did not establish any specific right to refrain from any or all of these activities. Its objective was to make collective bargaining the basis of union-management relations, not to protect individual employees from the actions of labor organizations.

Section 8 *proscribed five employer practices.* The prohibitions reflected experience under section 7(a) of the NIRA and were directed at attempts by employers to circumvent the spirit, if not the letter, of the law. The practices mentioned were *not* made *illegal* but were declared *unfair labor practices.* According to section 8 it was unfair for an employer:

1. To interfere with, restrain, or coerce employees in the exercise of the rights guaranteed in section 7.
2. To dominate or interfere with the formation or administration of any labor organization or contribute financial or other support to it. . . .
3. By discrimination in regard to hir[ing] or [the] tenure of employment or any term or condition of employment to encourage or discourage membership in any labor organization: *Provided* that nothing . . . shall preclude an employer from making an agreement with a labor organization (not established, maintained, or assisted by any action defined in this Act as an unfair labor practice) to require as a condition of employment membership therein, if [the] organization is the representative of the employees as provided in section 9(a), in the appropriate collective bargaining unit covered by [the] agreement when [it is] made.
4. To discharge or otherwise discriminate against an employee because he has filed charges or given testimony under this Act.
5. To refuse to bargain collectively with the representatives of his employees, subject to the provisions of section 9(a).

There was still a fear (reflected in paragraphs 8[2] and 8[3]) that employers might continue to try to establish company unions, and 8(3) permitted an outside (noncompany dominated) union to negotiate a union security agreement calling for a closed shop. In brief, workers were to be given every opportunity to join an outside union of their choice, and once such a union had been selected as their bargaining agent, the employer had to bargain with it. Since the phrase "to bargain collectively" was not defined, paragraph 5 of section 8 had to be interpreted by the National Labor Relations Board and the courts. Nothing in the act compelled an employer or a union representative to reach agreement on matters subject to collective bargaining.

Section 9 prescribed how bargaining representatives were to be selected. The split between the A.F. of L. and CIO had not yet developed, and the presumption was that the board would favor outside unions affiliated with the A.F. of L. rather than independent or company-dominated unions. According to section 9(a):

> [R]epresentatives designated or selected for the purposes of collective bargaining by the majority of the employees in a unit appropriate for such purposes, shall be the exclusive representatives of all the employees in such unit for the purposes of collective bargaining in respect to rates of pay, wages, hours . . . , or other conditions of employment.

Thus, the majority union was required to represent all workers in the collective bargaining unit regardless of whether they were members of that union. It was left to the board to define the phrase "other conditions of employment."

Section 9(b) gave the board the power to determine a unit "appropriate to collective bargaining"; this was interpreted to mean the *electoral* unit in which the bargaining agent was to be selected. Once it had been selected, the actual bargaining could go on at a different level.

Section 9(c) provided that if a question of representation arose, the board could hold a secret ballot election among the employees in a unit or use any other suitable method of ascertaining their choice of a bargaining agent.

The remaining provisions of the act were largely procedural. The board could not prosecute cases involving unfair labor practices on its own initiative, but only after charges had been filed. It could issue cease and desist orders or orders requiring affirmative action, but it had no statutory power to compel recipients of such orders to obey them. If one of its orders was disobeyed, it had to petition a circuit court for "the enforcement of [the] order and for appropriate temporary relief. . . ." The court, which could not question the board's findings if they were supported by facts, could enter a decree enforcing, modifying, or denying its petition. If the court order was disobeyed, the offending party could then be held in contempt of court.

To summarize: the act was concerned with the preliminaries to collective bargaining; it provided for the selection of exclusive bargaining agents and required employers to bargain with such agents; but it did not regulate the bargaining process, nor did it, except in the union security provision in section 8(3), touch on specific substantive bargaining issues.

Continuing Problems

The National Labor Relations Board faced a variety of problems of definition and interpretation in administering the National Labor Relations Act. Many provisions of the act, representing initial and tentative incursions into unchartered areas, were necessarily general. The board's problems were compounded by the internal division within organized labor; the authors of the act had not thought that the board would be called on to resolve disputes between "legitimate" outside unions. In fact, the board in defining bargaining (electoral) units often determined whether a union affiliated with the A.F. of L. or the CIO would represent employees.

The more important issues the NLRB had to decide included:

1. what specific employer practices constituted interference with *employees' rights, restraint of employees'* attempts to exercise their rights, or *coercion* of employees;
2. at whose request (an employer's or a union's) a representation election should be ordered;
3. what constituted a unit appropriate to collective bargaining;
4. what employees were covered by the act—whether for example foremen were members of management or employees within the meaning of the act;
5. what was meant by "collective bargaining";
6. what was included under "other conditions of employment"; and
7. what constituted the exercise of free speech in organizational campaigns and collective bargaining disputes—when for example did freedom of speech become coercive.

The answers to these and other questions were gradually spelled out in decisions of the board, and these decisions, subject to court review, became the basis of the modern *administrative common law* of collective bargaining.

Often, the board was unable to evolve simple and consistent operational policies. Changes in the structure of the labor movement, in the balance of power between management and organized labor, and in the membership of the board led to significant changes in policy. At first, the board tended to resolve policy disputes in favor of unions, but as the unions' membership increased and they became more firmly established, both the board and the Supreme Court began to demonstrate greater "neutrality" in borderline cases.

At the outset, statements by employers opposing unions were likely to be considered coercive; later, employers were held to be free to discuss possible disadvantages of union membership with their employees so long as there was no evidence of coercive behavior.[37] In determining units appropriate to collective bargaining, the board tended initially to favor industrial over craft unions on the ground that its function was to aid the rapid growth of collective bargaining. However, in 1937, under the *Globe doctrine,* the board held that if there was no precedent to indicate whether a craft or an industrial unit should be chosen the craft(s) involved could vote on the issue of separate representation.[38] As the personnel of the board changed, it went farther and authorized *craft severance elections* when a "true" craft sought separate representation.

Orginally, the board would order representation elections only when petitioned to do so by a union; later, employers were permitted to petition for elections when they were caught between two unions, each of which sought recognition and neither of which would request an election for fear of losing it.

Dualism in the union movement also put employers over the barrel in another situation. If after an NLRB election a firm had been ordered to deal with a union affiliated with one of the major federations, the firm was by law required to deal with the certified bargaining agent. At the same time, a union from the rival federation could picket the firm and institute a secondary boycott to compel the company to deal with it. In such cases, there was no relief from economic pressure on an employer to violate a board order. Similar problems arose in connection with other provisions in the law, which it was generally agreed would have to be modified in the light of experience.

Unfortunately, issues such as the propriety of unionizing foremen, the permissibility of various types of union security arrangements, and the use of secondary boycotts in labor disputes proved highly divisive, and it was impossible to get congressional agreement on modifications of the act for 12 years. When the National Labor Relations Act was finally "amended," the climate of public opinion was such that Congress did much more than correct technical defects in the act. Instead, it passed an omnibus bill that was not internally consistent and introduced new and sometimes disparate matters into our law of collective bargaining.

THE FIRST POST-WORLD WAR II LEGISLATION

The growing strength of unions, the confusion introduced into collective bargaining arrangements by the rivalry between the A.F. of L. and the CIO, the question of whether certain union practices that many legislators felt were contrary to the public interest (such as jurisdictional strikes and featherbedding) should be allowed, and opposition to closed shops suggested that there was a need for limited remedial legislation. In extreme cases, these issues created a climate of opinion that could be used by interests hostile to unionism and to collective bargaining.

There were antecedents to the Labor-Management Relations Act of 1947 (the Taft-Hartley Act) at both the state and federal levels. State legislatures had begun to prohibit specific union activities and practices as early as 1939, and by 1947, some 35 states had passed collective bargaining laws that were in some degree restrictive or had replaced "Little Wagner Acts" with restrictive legislation. During the ten years from 1936 to 1946 (following the passage of the National Labor Relations Act but before the 80th Congress, which passed the Taft-

Hartley Act, came in session), some 169 bills relating to national labor relations policy were introduced in Congress; many of these bills anticipated the major provisions of the Taft-Hartley Act.[39] Most of the proposed legislation reflected a basic shift in public policy—a feeling that the statutory law of collective bargaining should not be limited to encouraging union organization and regulating the preliminaries to collective bargaining.

In December of 1945, President Truman called for legislation that would enable the President to appoint *fact-finding panels* whenever a labor dispute or a threatened dispute seriously affected the national interest or interstate or foreign commerce. This statement marked "a turning point in the history of labor legislation, . . . the first time since the Wagner Act that a chief executive had favored, or called for the passage of, legislation that would affect the law of labor in this country."[40]

Two restrictive acts became effective in 1946. The Lea (Anti-Petrillo) Act banned certain featherbedding practices by the musicians union in radio broadcasting; and the Hobbs Act, aimed at stopping featherbedding by the Teamsters, ended the exemption of labor unions from prosecution under the Federal Anti-Racketeering Act. The Case bill, a more general measure, was vetoed by the President after passing both houses, but many of its restrictive provisions reappeared in the 80th Congress in the Hartley bill offered in the House and in the Taft bill offered in the Senate.

These statutes and proposals foreshadowed major changes in our federal labor law, and the election of 1946, which produced a Republican majority in both houses of Congress, was considered a popular mandate to pass restrictive legislation. The question facing the administration and the Congress was not whether a new labor law would be passed, but how comprehensive and how restrictive it would be.

SUMMARY

During the nineteenth century, organized labor confronted essentially hostile legislative and judicial systems. In the absence of laws covering their activities, unions were subject to court control, and it was not until 1842 that the right of workers to organize for the purpose of collective bargaining received judicial sanction. The objectives of unions and the means they used to achieve them continued to be subject to judicial scrutiny however, and after 1890 the Sherman Act was held to apply to organized labor. Acceptance of unions increased in the early part of the twentieth century, but except in the railroad industry, collective bargaining had no statutory support.

The Great Depression was the catalyst for the passage of legislation encouraging union organization and collective bargaining. The Wagner Act, admittedly an unbalanced statute, was passed in 1935, and it was not amended until 1947, by which time perceived excesses by organized labor had generated broad support for restrictive labor legislation.

DISCUSSION QUESTIONS

1. How did the *freedom of contract* doctrine affect early union organizational efforts?
2. In the absence of statutory regulation of collective bargaining, how is it possible to identify the period 1842–1932 as one of *governmental grudging toleration* toward unions?
3. What, in the preceding question, is the significance of the 1842 date?
4. Prior to the Great Depression, what weapons were available to employers to combat unions?
5. Why was the Clayton Act initially considered the Magna Carta of American labor?
6. Identify specific actions or legislation at the federal level supporting collective bargaining which preceded the New Deal.
7. In what sense did the NIRA give birth to the Wagner Act? What were the basic objectives of the latter act?
8. Why do you think the Communist Party opposed the Wagner Act?
9. Was the lack of "balance" in the Wagner Act predictable?
10. To what extent was the Wagner Act responsible for the "rebirth" of unions during the 1930s?

SELECTED READINGS

The Law of Collective Bargaining

Brown, Douglass V., and Myers, Charles A. "Historical Evolution." In *Public Policy and Collective Bargaining.* Ed. by Joseph Shister, Benjamin Aaron, and Clyde W. Summers. Industrial Relations Research Association Publication No. 27. New York: Harper & Row, 1962.

Gregory, Charles O. and Katz, Harold A. *Labor and the Law.* 3rd. ed. New York: Norton, 1979. An excellent general work.

Morris, Charles J., ed. in chief. "History of the National Labor Relations Act." Part I in *The Developing Labor Law.* Published for the Labor Relations Law Section of the American Bar Association. Washington, D.C.: Bureau of National Affairs, 1971. Contains good short summaries of the development of our law of collective bargaining.

The Wagner Act

Bernstein, Irving. *The New Deal Collective Bargaining Policy.* Berkeley and Los Angeles: University of California Press, 1950.

Cortner, Richard C. *The Wagner Act Cases.* Knoxville, Tenn.: University of Tennessee Press, 1964.

Fleming, R. W. "The Significance of the Wagner Act." In Derber, Milton, and Young, Edwin, eds., *Labor and the New Deal.* Madison, Wisc.: University of Wisconsin Press, 1957, pp. 121–155.

Ross, Philip. *The Government as a Source of Union Power.* Providence, R. I.: Brown University Press, 1965.

Notes

1. Archibald Cox, *Law and the National Labor Policy* (Los Angeles: Institute of Industrial Relations, University of California, 1960), p. 2.
2. The first four phases were identified by Selig Perlman in "The Principles of Collective Bargaining," in *Annals of the American Academy of Political and Social Science* 184 (March 1936): pp. 156–158. Perlman noted that an additional stage, that "of absorption or assimilation[,] comes with political dictatorship." (Ibid., p. 158.)
3. Quoted in Elias Lieberman, *Unions Before the Bar* (New York: Harper & Brothers, 1950), p. 13. This book, generally sympathetic to the union point of view, describes some two dozen famous American labor cases.
4. Harry A. Millis and Royal E. Montgomery, *Organized Labor* (New York: McGraw-Hill, 1945), p. 505.
5. Charles O. Gregory and Harold A. Katz, *Labor and the Law*. 3rd ed. (New York: Norton, 1979), p. 81.
6. *26 Stat*, 209 (1890).
7. Cox, *Law and the National Labor Policy*, p. 31. Emphasis added.
8. *Loewe* v. *Lawlor*, 208 U.S. 274 (1908).
9. *Gompers* v. *Bucks Stove and Range Co.*, 221 U.S. 418 (1911).
10. *38 Stat*, 730 (1914).
11. Gregory and Katz, *Labor and the Law*, p. 161.
12. *Duplex Printing Press Co.* v. *Deering*, 254 U.S. 443 (1921); *Bedford Cut Stone Co.* v. *Journeymen Stone Cutters' Association*, 274 U.S. 37 (1927).
13. *United Mine Workers of America* v. *Coronado Coal Co.*, 259 U.S. 344 (1922).
14. *Coronado Coal Co. et al.* v. *United Mine Workers et al.*, 268 U.S. 295 (1925).
15. *Hitchman Coal and Coke Co.* v. *Mitchell*, 245 U.S. 229 (1917).
16. *Adair* v. *United States*, 208 U.S. 161 (1908); *Coppage* v. *Kansas*, 236 U.S. 2 (1915).
17. Charles J. Morris, ed. in chief, "History of the National Labor Relations Act," Part I in *The Developing Labor Law*, published for the Labor Relations Law Section of the American Bar Association (Washington, D.C.: Bureau of National Affairs, 1971), p. 12.
18. Cf. Irving Bernstein, *The New Deal Collective Bargaining Policy* (Berkeley and Los Angeles: University of California Press, 1950), pp. 18–19.
19. U.S. Department of Labor, Bureau of Labor Statistics, *National War Labor Board*, Bulletin No. 287 (1922), p. 11.
20. *44 Stat* 577 (1926). A good basic reference is the National Mediation Board's *Railway Labor Act at Fifty: Collective Bargaining in the Railroad and Airline Industries* (Washington, D.C.: U.S. Government Printing Office, 1977).
21. *Texas and New Orleans R.R. Co.* v. *Brotherhood of Railway and Steamship Clerks*, 281 U.S. 548 (1930).
22. *Steele* v. *Louisville and Nashville Railroad Company*, 323 U.S. 192 (1944).
23. *47 Stat* 70 (1932).
24. New York: Macmillan, 1930.
25. Sec. 13(c), emphasis added.
26. Gregory and Katz, *Labor and the Law*, p. 189.

27. The leading case is *Allen Bradley* v. *Local 3, International Brotherhood of Electrical Workers,* 325 U.S. 797 (1945).
28. *United States* v. *Hutcheson,* 312 U.S. 219 (1941).
29. Cf. Bernstein, *The New Deal Collective Bargaining Policy,* chap. II, "Sources of Ideas."
30. *48 Stat,* 198 (1933).
31. Bernstein, *The New Deal Collective Bargaining Policy,* pp. 38–39.
32. *49 Stat,* 449 (1935).
33. *A.L.A. Schechter Poultry Corp.* v. *U.S.,* 295 U.S. 495 (1935).
34. Bernstein, *The New Deal Collective Bargaining Policy,* p. 149. See also Harry A. Millis and Emily Clark Brown, *From the Wagner Act to Taft-Hartley* (Chicago: University of Chicago Press, 1950), p. 267.
35. The leading decision was *N.L.R.B.* v. *Jones and Laughlin Steel Corporation,* 301 U.S. 1 (1937).
36. Cox, *Law and the National Labor Policy,* pp. 10–11. Cox also noted that "the Wagner Act was designed to raise the national wage level. . . ." (Ibid., p. 12.)
37. *N.L.R.B.* v. *Virginia Electric and Power Company,* 314 U.S. 469 (1941).
38. *Globe Machine and Stamping Co., and Metal Polishers Union Local No. 3,* 3 N.L.R.B. 294 (1937).
39. Millis and Brown, *From the Wagner Act to Taft-Hartley,* p. 333.
40. Ibid., p. 357.

Chapter 17
THE REGULATORY FRAMEWORK II: CURRENT LAW OF COLLECTIVE BARGAINING

In his State of the Union Message to the 80th Congress on January 6, 1947, President Truman recognized the need for changes in the law of collective bargaining. He "asked for action to prevent jurisdictional disputes, to prohibit secondary boycotts and 'unjustifiable objectives,' to provide for machinery to help solve disputes arising under existing collective bargaining agreements, and to create a temporary joint commission to investigate the whole field of labor-management relations."[1] On June 23, a much more comprehensive statute than he had requested, the *Labor-Management Relations Act* (LMRA, popularly known as the Taft-Hartley Act, after its sponsors in the Senate and House), was passed over the President's veto.[2] This act provides the basic regulatory framework for union-management relations in the private sector in the United States today. However, the law of collective bargaining is not static. Decisions of administrative agencies —principally the National Labor Relations Board—and of the courts "amend" the law on a continuing basis. The alterations that result reflect the changing context of collective bargaining and changes in board and court personnel.

THE BACKGROUND OF THE TAFT-HARTLEY ACT

Congress did little homework on the various problems in the field of labor-management relations before voting on the Taft-Hartley Act. No commission was appointed to develop legislation, and at no time, according to the definitive study of the act, was "any systematic, nonpolitical study or investigation authorized or undertaken by Congress before it acted on many complex and technical matters about which it had relatively little accurate information."[3]

Characterized as "the offspring, . . . of an unhappy union between the opponents of all collective bargaining and the critics of abuse of union power,"[4] the Taft-Hartley Act was designed to protect the rights and interests of individual workers, employers, and the public in the collective bargaining process and in industrial disputes. It continued to encourage collective bargaining, but this basic policy thrust was blunted by provisions protecting the individual worker's right to *refrain* from joining a union or bargaining collectively. The act also banned certain practices by labor unions. It treated unions as established institutions that should be regulated to protect the public interest and ensure a more equal balance of power between the parties to collective bargaining.

Passage of the Taft-Hartley Act changed the law of collective bargaining in five areas: it corrected "technical" defects in the Wagner Act, it protected the rights of individual employees in their relations with unions, it made up for a lack of mutuality in prior legislation, it set limits on purportedly dangerous accretions of economic and political power (including the "monopoly power"*) of well-established unions, and it dealt with the threat of Communist infiltration of the labor movement. The act had five principal parts, three of which are relevant here: Title I, which amended and superseded the National Labor Relations Act; Title II, which dealt with the conciliation of labor disputes in industries affecting commerce and with national emergencies; and Title III, which originally covered lawsuits by and against labor organizations, restrictions on payments to employee representatives, boycotts and other unlawful combinations, restrictions on political contributions, and strikes by government employees.

There have also been significant amendments to the act: in October 1951, a provision dealing with union security was eliminated; in 1959, Title VII of the Landrum-Griffin Act strengthened and expanded the bans on certain union activities in the 1947 statute; and in 1974, the jurisdiction of the NLRB was extended to include private nonprofit health care institutions.

In 1977, a *Labor Reform Act* supported by the AFL-CIO passed the House of Representatives. Had it become law, the act would have expanded the membership of the NLRB from five to seven persons, allowed panels of two members

---

* The term was used loosely in reference to the power of unions as monopolistic "sellers" of labor, multiemployer bargaining, industrywide bargaining, the principle of exclusive representation in collective bargaining, infringements on managerial prerogatives, and the more extreme types of union security.

to hear routine appeals involving unfair labor practices, expedited representation elections, provided *penalties* in addition to remedies for certain violations of the Taft-Hartley Act by *employers,* and required the NLRB to seek injunctions against discriminatory discharges during organizing campaigns. The bill was bitterly opposed by management groups and was returned to committee after a Senate filibuster in June of 1978. This was a major defeat for organized labor. We will discuss Titles I and III before discussing Title II, since the former titles are interrelated in a number of respects.

GENERAL POLICY STATEMENTS IN THE ACT

Title I of the Taft-Hartley Act is preceded by a "Short Title and Declaration of Policy" which states that it is public policy

> to protect the rights of *individual* employees in their *relations with labor organiza-tions* . . . to define and proscribe practices on the part of *labor and management* which affect commerce and are inimical to the general welfare, and to *protect the rights of the public* in connection with labor disputes affecting commerce. (Emphasis added.)

There is also a second policy statement that is essentially the policy statement of the Wagner Act expanded to include a rationale for mutuality in the law of collective bargaining.

TITLE I: AMENDING THE NATIONAL LABOR RELATIONS ACT

Title I of the Taft-Hartley Act attempts to carry out the policies described above by amending the National Labor Relations Act to clarify or modify certain provisions of the act and various NLRB and court decisions relating to those provisions. It also introduces "new" matters into the law of collective bargaining. Many provisions of Title I are verbatim or slightly modified restatements of provisions of the Wagner Act, and a number of the "new" matters are simply codifications of decisions of the NLRB and the courts.

Coverage and Procedures

Title I spells out the kinds of workers *not* subject to the jurisdiction of the NLRB. These include government employees,* employees of Federal Reserve Banks, agricultural workers,** domestic servants, persons working for their

---

* The Postal Reorganization Act of 1970 made most aspects of union-management relations in the postal service subject to the jurisdiction of the NLRB.
** The unionization of migrant farm workers in California under the leadership of Cesar Chavez led to the passage, in 1975, of a California act regulating collective bargaining by such workers in that state. Although several bills covering agricultural workers have been introduced in Congress, none has yet been passed.

parents or their spouses, independent contractors, supervisors, and persons employed by employers subject to the Railway Labor Act.

Title I also expands the membership of the NLRB from three to five persons and permits panels of three members to act on behalf of the full board. In addition, it provides for a general counsel to prosecute cases involving unfair labor practices. Critics of the board had long charged that it could not serve effectively as both prosecutor and judge, and the general counsel appointed by the President is independent of the board. The law is administered by the NLRB and the general counsel, acting through 33 regional offices and 76 other field offices. Only the general counsel can decide whether a complaint of unfair labor practices will be prosecuted. A refusal to prosecute is not subject to review, even if it frustrates board policy.

It is the board's responsibility, as it was under the Wagner Act, to (1) certify employees' representatives in units appropriate to collective bargaining and (2) hear and decide allegations of unfair labor practices. It cannot act on its own initiative but must wait until a question of representation or a charge of unfair behavior is presented to it. In fiscal 1979, it received over 41,000 allegations of unfair labor practices and more than 13,000 representation petitions.[5]

There are three steps to an *enforceable* decision in cases involving an unfair labor practice: a hearing before an *administrative law judge,* an appeal to the board, and enforcement or review proceedings in a U.S. court of appeals. Only final orders of the board are subject to court review. Board certifications of bargaining representatives are not final orders and are not usually subject to review. Its options in unfair labor practice cases are purely remedial; it cannot impose penalties or force an employer to agree to a particular contract proposal. It may however require the reinstatement of employees and the payment of lost wages and benefits, with interest.

Some 90 to 95 percent of the cases involving unfair labor practices are disposed of informally and never reach the board. Nevertheless, its backlog of cases has been high. To help end delays in selecting bargaining agents in representation cases, the board was authorized in 1959 to let its regional directors handle such cases. Despite an average of two years in getting an enforceable decision in unfair labor practice cases, Congress has refused to authorize a similar delegation of power in such cases.

Protecting Employee Rights

Section 7 remains the heart of the National Labor Relations Act as amended by Title I. The rights granted to employees there are continued, and a new clause provides that employees "shall also have the *right to refrain* from any or all of such activities except to the extent that such right may be affected by [a union security] agreement. . . ." (Emphasis added.) The right to strike is protected by sections 7 and 13. What is forbidden and permissible to employers and unions gives substance to the rights of employees under section 7. The protective umbrella over employee activities is broad, but it cannot be described precisely because it depends on how the NLRB and the courts define and interpret employer and union interference with workers' rights.

Unfair Labor Practices by Employers

Section 8 of the Wagner Act was a relatively simple section banning five unfair practices by employers. Section 8 of Title I of the Taft-Hartley Act has six principal subsections, the last two added by the Landrum-Griffin Act. Section 8 of the original National Labor Relations Act is section 8(a) of Title I. Subsections (1), (2), (4), and (5) are identical to old subsections 8(1), 8(2), 8(4), and 8(5). The ban on unfair labor practices in 8(3) is unchanged, but the proviso that allowed a union to negotiate union security agreements has been modified significantly.

Union Security: Sections 8(a)(3) and 14(b)

Section 8(a)(3) of Title I outlaws the closed shop. Initially, it made a *union shop* (one in which workers could be required to join a union on or after the thirtieth day following the beginning of their employment) a bargainable issue only after a secret ballot election had shown that a firm's employees wanted such an arrangement. Over 90 percent of the workers who voted in such elections favored a union shop, and in 1951, the requirement that an election be held was eliminated. The law now requires a referendum only when 30 percent or more of the employees in a bargaining unit file a petition indicating that they wish to withdraw their representative's authority to negotiate a union shop agreement.

The 30 days grace allowed workers in a union shop before they had to join a union turned out to be impractical in the building and construction industry, and the Landrum-Griffin Act added a subsection (8[f]) to Taft-Hartley which provided in part that membership in labor organizations in the building and construction industry could be required after only seven days of employment.*

Public disapproval of union security arrangements, particularly in rural and southern states, was responsible for another provision of Title I allowing state laws restricting such arrangements to take precedence over the federal law. According to section 14(b), "nothing in this Act shall be construed as authorizing the execution or application of agreements requiring membership in a labor organization as a condition of employment in any State or Territory in which such execution or application is prohibited by State or Territorial law." In 1980, 20 states had *right to work* laws that prohibited various types of union security arrangements.**

---

* The new section also permits employers and unions in the building and construction industry to negotiate prehire agreements—that is, to negotiate terms and conditions of employment before workers in a bargaining unit are actually hired. This provision reflects the lack of continuing employment relationships usual in the industry.

** For an analysis of the union security issue see pp. 537–548.

A union may set its own rules regarding the admission and retention of members. However, section 8(a)(3) of the Taft-Hartley Act forbids an employer to discriminate against an employee for not belonging to a labor organization if "membership was not available [to the employee] . . . on the same terms and conditions generally applicable to other members, or . . . was denied or terminated for reasons other than the failure . . . to render the periodic dues and the initiation fees uniformly required as a condition of . . . membership." In effect, this gives statutory support to an *agency shop* (in which employees must support a union financially) rather than a union shop.

A 1974 "health care" amendment to Title I provides that an employee of a health care institution who is a member of a religious group "which has historically held conscientious objections to joining or financially supporting labor organizations shall not be required to join or financially support any labor organization as a condition of employment." In lieu of initiation fees and dues, such a person may be required to pay equivalent sums to a nonreligious tax-exempt charity.

Proscribed Employer Practices

Section 8(a)(1) of Title I makes it an unfair labor practice for an employer "to interefere with, restrain, or coerce employees in the exercise of the rights guaranteed in Section 7." This *general* provision is automatically violated when an employer engages in *any* unfair labor practice. Examples of illegal conduct include threatening employees with losing their jobs or losing benefits if they join a union, threatening to close down a plant if it is unionized, questioning employees about their union activities or membership in a way that tends to stop them from joining or being active in a union, spying on union gatherings, and timing wage increases to defeat an organizing campaign.[6]

Section 8(a)(2) forbids employers to dominate or interfere with the formation or administration of a labor organization or contribute financial or other support to it. The NLRB distinguishes between "domination" and "interference." In a case of domination, it will order the union disestablished, whereas in a case of interference, it will issue a cease and desist order against the employer.

Violations of section 8(a)(3)—which forbids discharging workers or discriminating against them in some other way connected with their employment because they have been active in a union or other protected group—are the most common complaints in allegations of unfair labor practices by employers. The cessation of business operations, allegedly to avoid unionization, has raised interesting issues with regard to discriminatory discharges. The Supreme Court has ruled that an employer has an absolute right to stop doing business entirely for any reason, including an antiunion animus.[7] However, a firm does not have the right to close down part of its operations, to transfer work to another plant, or to open a new plant (a *runaway plant*) to replace a closed plant in order to avoid unionization. In such cases, the NLRB must determine whether the firm was motivated by an antiunion animus or by economics. In one leading case, the

Supreme Court held that a partial closing was an unfair labor practice if its purpose was to "chill unionism" in any of the employer's remaining plants.[8]

Strikes and lockouts are, respectively, the ultimate economic weapons of unions and employers. Unless a union engages in unfair labor practices, a strike during contract negotiations and after a contract expiration date is a protected activity. A lockout on the other hand is usually held by the NLRB to be an unfair interference by an employer in the concerted activities of its employees, and only two types of lockouts are considered permissible: (1) economically motivated lockouts that are *defensive* and not the result of an antiunion animus—for example, lockouts that enable an employer to cease operations in advance of a strike that might result in the spoilage of perishable merchandise; and (2) multi-employer lockouts used to counter whipsaw strikes.[9] However, the Supreme Court has now ruled that an *offensive,* or *bargaining, lockout* does not *necessarily* interfere with the employees' rights as protected by Taft-Hartley and is not a per se violation of the act.[10]

Section 8(a)(4) continues the protection from retaliatory actions given by the Wagner Act to employees who file charges or testify against employers.

Section 8(a)(5) makes it an unfair labor practice to refuse to bargain collectively. The phrase "to bargain collectively" is defined in section 8(d),* which must be read in conjunction with 8(a)(5), and 8(b)(3), which imposes a parallel obligation on unions. Employers are not required to agree to any particular union demand, but they must bargain in "good faith" about (1) "mandatory" bargaining subjects and (2) any nonmandatory ("permissive") subjects about which the parties have agreed to negotiate. The NLRB may be called on to decide whether an employer was engaging in "good faith" or "surface" bargaining, a decision that may rest on the board's perception of the employer's overall conduct during negotiations.

Violations of 8(a)(5) may be difficult to remedy because ordering an employer to bargain in good faith does not compensate workers for losses resulting from the employer's delay in bargaining in good faith. The NLRB will not demand that employees "receive in the form of backpay an amount equal to the increased benefits which they likely would have received through collective bargaining had the employer bargained in good faith."[11] Its refusal to do so is based in part on a Supreme Court decision that the board cannot compel an employer to agree to a specific contract provision.[12]

If an employer's actions violated both the National Labor Relations Act and a collective bargaining agreement, the NLRB usually deferred to an established grievance procedure rather than processing an unfair labor practice charge, even if an arbitration proceeding has not yet been held.[13] Such a deferral was considered to be in accord with the fundamental intent of the act to promote industrial peace and stability "by encouraging the practice and procedure of collective bargaining." However, in the *Suburban Motor Freight, Inc.* case, the

---

* See *infra,* pp. 399–400.

Board recently held that it would no longer defer to an arbitration proceeding unless the unfair labor practice issue had been presented to and considered by the arbitrator.[14] It should be noted that deferring to arbitration in cases of discrimination that may also involve violations of the Civil Rights Act does not relieve an employer or a union of responsibility under that act.[15]

In dealing with violations of the Taft-Hartley Act, the NLRB has shown a proper concern that a change of ownership should not be allowed to subvert the act, and the responsibilities and liabilities of successor firms have gradually been defined by the board and the courts.[16] The delay in handling charges of unfair labor practices and the absence of penalties for such conduct have encouraged some firms to disregard "fairness" in combating organizing campaigns. This tactic may be successful; although the firms may ultimately be held guilty of unfair labor practices, the unions' organizational efforts may be blunted. The payment of back wages to employees discharged for union activity is considered a modest price to pay for stopping an organizing campaign. The prolonged overt opposition to union organizational efforts by the J. P. Stevens Company, which led one judge to label it "the most notorious recidivist in the field of labor law," is a classic case in point.

Proscribed Union Practices

Section 8(b), which defines seven kinds of unfair practices by labor organizations or their agents, is the most significant addition to the National Labor Relations Act made by Title I. Some of the provisions in the section provide mutuality in the law of collective bargaining; others are a less easily justifiable expansion of government regulation and control. The first three subsections provide mutuality by banning unfair practices by unions in much the same way that section 8(a) bans unfair practices by employers.

According to section 8(b)(1), it is unfair for a labor organization or its agents to restrain or coerce either *employees* who are trying to exercise the rights guaranteed in section 7 or *employers* when they are selecting their representatives for collective bargaining or the adjustment of grievances. Examples of union conduct considered "unfair" under section 8(b)(1) include picketing in such numbers that nonstriking employees are physically barred from work, the use of force or acts of violence on a picket line or in connection with a strike, threats to do bodily injury to nonstriking employees, and threats that employees will lose their jobs unless they support the union.[17]

The section does not impair the right of a labor organization to make its own rules with respect to the acquisition of members. That is, it does not require unions to admit members on a nondiscriminatory basis. However, the NLRB has held that under section 9, a certified bargaining agent has an obligation to represent all members of a bargaining unit fairly and impartially. If the agent does not do so, it is "an infringement of a Section 7 right, and . . . a violation of section 8(b)(1)."[18] Thus, the NLRB attacks discrimination through unfair labor practice proceedings; the LMRA does not include specific prohibitions against discrimination in employment similar to those in the Civil Rights Act.

Section 8(b)(2) of Title I prohibits a union from causing or attempting to cause an employer (1) to commit discriminatory acts in violation of section 8(a)(3) or (2) to discriminate against an employee who was denied membership in a union or whose membership was terminated for some reason other than a failure to pay the usual initiation fees and dues. A related section, (8[b][5]), states that it is unfair for a union to require employees covered by a union shop agreement to pay, "as a condition precedent to becoming a member" a fee that the NLRB finds excessive or discriminatory. This statement is qualified by the proviso that in making such a finding, the board shall consider the practices and customs of labor organizations in the industry and the wages currently paid to the employees. In practice, the board usually accepts customary admission fees.

Section 8(b)(3) imposes on unions the same obligation to bargain in good faith that section 8(a)(3) imposes on employers.

Protecting Third Parties: Section 8(b)(4)

The provisions of section 8(b)(4) reflect a principal objective of the Taft-Hartley Act, the insulation of "innocent" third parties from union-management disputes. Among the practices it prohibits are secondary boycotts and sympathetic strikes, recognition strikes against *another* firm unless it is failing to bargain with a certified union, strikes *against* certification (employers can no longer be subjected to economic pressure to violate the law), and forcing or requiring an employer to assign work in accordance with a particular work jurisdiction unless the employer "is failing to conform to an order or certification of the Board determining the bargaining representative for employees performing such work."

The desire to insulate "neutral" employers from labor disputes not directly involving their own employees is understandable, but a broad ban on secondary activities ignores the possibility that such activities may be justifiable when there is an economic community of interest between two firms—when for example work is subcontracted to a nonunion firm that ignores established union standards.

Although the intent of Congress to outlaw secondary activity by unions seemed clear, the language in section 8(b)(4), described as "one of the most labyrinthine provisions ever included in a federal labor statute,"[19] was interpreted to permit unions to achieve otherwise unlawful objectives by (1) inducing *individuals* to engage singly in such conduct; (2) inducing persons employed by a neutral employer who (a) are not "employees" under the act (supervisors, for example) or (b) work for an organization not defined as an "employer" or "person" (a government agency, for example) to stop work; and (3) exerting pressure on a secondary *employer*, rather than its employees, *to induce it* to stop dealing with a primary employer. This last tactic sometimes resulted in *"hot cargo" clauses* in contracts, in which employers agreed to refuse to handle goods received from other employers with whom a union had a dispute. Congress attempted to close these loopholes in the Landrum-Griffin Act, which broadened and clarified the ban on secondary boycotts. Under Landrum-Griffin, the proscription against secondary activity was extended to *any individual* employed by *any person in commerce,* including employees of rail and air carriers.

Section 8(b)(4) has *two provisos*. The first makes it lawful for a person to refuse to cross a picket line at *another employer's* place of business if the employees of that firm are engaged in a bona fide strike. The second, added by Landrum-Griffin and designed to permit consumer boycotts, states that nothing in the section

> shall be construed to prohibit *publicity, other than picketing,* for the purpose of truthfully advising the public . . . that a product or products are produced by an employer with whom the labor organization has a primary dispute and are distributed by another employer, as long as such publicity does not have an effect of inducing [a secondary boycott]. (Emphasis added.)

The Supreme Court has held that under this proviso, the use of placards and the distribution of handbills (so-called *informational picketing*) are permissible under certain conditions. Picketing is always coercive, and the NLRB must decide in particular cases whether it is informational. The board and the courts have interpreted the law generously. For example, union members who are not employees of a firm may picket it to advise the public that it does not pay union wages.

In the *Tree Fruits* case in 1969, the board held that peaceful picketing of a retail store to persuade customers not to buy a *particular* struck product was allowable.[20] In a later case, the board held that picketing to urge a consumer boycott of a single product, a brand name gasoline that was the *mainstay* of a neutral establishment's business, was illegal. It now appears however to have retreated* from this position.[21]

The board has held that to enjoy protection under the law, a secondary employer must be a true neutral and not an "ally" of the primary employer in a dispute; that is, it must not be owned by the same person(s), or engaged in the same integrated operations, or performing "farmed-out" struck work. Examples of prohibited secondary activity include:

1. picketing a firm to force it to stop doing business with another firm that has refused to recognize a union;
2. asking the employees of a plumbing contractor not to work on connecting air conditioning equipment manufactured by a nonunion employer that the union is attempting to organize;

---

* In January 1980, the Supreme Court agreed to hear a case that will allow it to elaborate on the "conditions under which strikers may picket an otherwise neutral retailer that sells the product of the company being struck." (*The Wall Street Journal,* January 8, 1980, p. 4.)

3. urging employees of a building contractor not to install doors made by a manufacturer that was not unionized or that employed members of a rival union; and

4. telling an employer that its plant will be picketed if it continues to do business with an employer the union says is "unfair."[22]

Title VII of the Landrum-Griffin Act also prohibits hot cargo clauses, with two exceptions: such clauses may be negotiated with contractors and subcontractors at a common construction site and with employers involved in "an integrated process of production in the apparel and clothing industry." However, it is an unfair labor practice for a union to strike or picket a firm to enforce such a provision. The building trades unions have lobbied strenuously for permission to picket all the contractors working on a construction project. In 1975, a bill permitting such *common situs picketing* passed the Congress but was vetoed by President Gerald Ford; a similar bill was rejected by the House of Representatives in 1977.

Controlling Featherbedding: Section 8(b)(6)

According to this antifeatherbedding section, it is an unfair labor practice for a union "to cause or attempt to cause an employer to pay or deliver or agree to pay or deliver any money or other thing of value, in the nature of an exaction, for services which are not performed or not to be performed." The intent here was to outlaw work rules requiring the employment of unnecessary workers. Interpreting the language of the statute strictly, the Supreme Court has held that a union is not guilty of an unfair labor practice if its members are ready to perform the unnecessary services for which payment is demanded.

Restrictions on Picketing: Section 8(b)(7)

This section, added to Taft-Hartley by the Landrum-Griffin Act, is designed to insulate "innocent" employers and their employees from certain forms of coercion. It makes recognition and organizational picketing an unfair labor practice in three circumstances: (1) when the employer has lawfully recognized another labor organization, (2) when a valid election has been held within the preceding 12 months, and (3) when a petition for a representation election has not been filed within a reasonable period of time, defined as within 30 days from the time the picketing began. Peaceful picketing or other forms of publicity are allowed after 30 days, provided they do not "induce any individual employed by any other person in the course of his employment, not to pick up, deliver or transport any good or not to perform any services." The NLRB must determine on a case-by-case basis whether a work stoppage or a refusal to work was induced by such informational picketing.

A Comment on Section 8(b)

The basic philosophy underlying NLRB decisions in cases involving section 8(b)(4) and other parts of section 8(b) is that union activities which are not clearly forbidden are permissible as long as they are not coercive. In interpreting the section, the board has gradually assumed a more comprehensive role in regulating collective bargaining procedures, the substantive terms of collective agreements, and the weapons of industrial conflict. This trend has concerned some observers, who believe that it may erode the essentially private character of collective bargaining arrangements. Thus far, this fear seems premature; collective bargaining is still a private process, and the parties to it are generally free to determine for themselves the terms and conditions of an employment relationship.

Section 8(c): The "Free Speech" Amendment

Under the Wagner Act, employers were reluctant to make statements opposing unions for fear of being accused of unfair labor practices. The NLRB has held that in the absence of an overt threat, such statements are an unfair labor practice if they are part of a "pattern of coercion." According to section 8(c) of the LMRA,

> [t]he expressing of any views, argument, or opinion, or the dissemination thereof, whether in printed, graphic, or visual form, shall not constitute or be evidence of an unfair labor practice . . . if such expression contains no threat of reprisal or force or promise of benefit.

In deciding whether a specific expression of opinion contains a threat, the board must balance the employer's right to free speech against the possibility of interference with, restraint of, or coercion of employees in the exercise of their rights under the act. It has distinguished between unfair labor practice cases and representation cases, holding that free speech is fully protected only in the first type of case. In representation cases, conduct that destroys the "laboratory conditions" necessary for an election violates election rules even though it does not constitute an unfair labor practice.[23] It is sometimes hard to distinguish between illegal threats to close a plant if a union wins a representation election and legitimate "prophecies" of what may happen if such an event occurs. The permissibility of an employer's statements depends on the context in which they are made.[24]

The permissibility of peaceful picketing, although not an issue under the National Labor Relations Act, is related to the protection afforded free speech. Court decisions vary as to whether peaceful picketing is "free speech" and hence permissible regardless of its objectives. At present, such picketing is not equated with free speech and may be enjoined if its objective is unlawful, if it violates the expressed policy of the federal government or a state government, or if an injunction is needed to protect normal business operations.[25]

Section 8(d): The Obligation to Bargain Collectively

Before the passage of the Taft-Hartley Act, the NLRB had gradually defined the obligation of employers "to bargain collectively." Section 8(d) translated the administrative law of board decisions into statutory law and extended it to apply to unions as well. It is now

> . . . the *mutual obligation* of the employer and the representative of the employees to meet at reasonable times and confer *in good faith* with respect to wages, hours, and other terms and conditions of employment, or the negotiation of an agreement, or any question arising thereunder, and *the execution of a written contract* incorporating any agreement reached . . . but such obligation does not compel either party to agree to a proposal or require the making of a concession. (Emphasis added.)

In defining "good faith," the board has held that an employer must (1) come to the bargaining table prepared to reach an agreement, (2) make counterproposals, and (3) be prepared to supply the union with all the information in its possession necessary and relevant to the union's duty to represent the employees in the bargaining unit adequately.[26] The total conduct of the parties is the standard used to test the "quality" of negotiations. It was essentially this test that led the board to rule in 1964 that the General Electric Company's hard line bargaining approach, termed Boulwarism, constituted an unfair labor practice.

Assuming that the parties bargain in good faith until they reach an impasse, they are under no legal compulsion to agree to a particular substantive proposal; nor can the NLRB, in seeking remedy, require them to agree to a specific contract provision.

The board has distinguished between *mandatory* and *nonmandatory* bargaining subjects. A few subjects, including pay "for services which are not performed or not to be performed," a closed shop, and "hot cargo" clauses, may not be discussed. Mandatory subjects include "wages, hours, and other terms and conditions of employment." The board has gradually expanded its list of mandatory bargaining subjects. In general, any matters not normally considered managerial prerogatives are held to be appropriate bargaining issues. Subjects considered to be managerial prerogatives include

> [t]he corporate or other structure of the business, the size and personnel of the official and supervisory force, general business practices, the products to be manufactured, the location of plants, the schedules of production, [and] the methods and processes and means of manufacturing. . . .[27]

Although managerial prerogatives are not ordinarily mandatory bargaining subjects, they may become so in specific negotiations, particularly when there is a possibility that a unilateral exercise of managerial authority may have an antiunion motive. The "gray areas" include decisions about the partial termination of business operations, the relocation of plants, and the subcontracting of work.[28] The NLRB has rejected the *residual rights theory,* according to which matters not mentioned specifically in a contract may be handled at the discretion of management. This has raised the issue of whether a firm, through a general "management rights" clause, can define (or reserve) an area of unilateral control. The decision of the Supreme Court on the leading case, *American National,* holds "that an employer's insistence upon a broad management-rights clause . . . is not a *per se* violation of Section 8(a)(5) . . . and that the Board must decide in each case whether the good faith requirements . . . have been met."[29]

Section 8(d) also mandates certain procedures in contract negotiations, including 60 days' advance notice of a wish to terminate or modify a contract and notification of the Federal Mediation and Conciliation Service (and the relevant state agency) within 30 days after such notice.

Section 9: "Representatives and Elections"

The Wagner Act gave the NLRB little guidance in determining units "appropriate to" collective bargaining or in selecting bargaining representatives. The board gradually devised various rules and procedures to help it strike a balance between the goals of stability in collective bargaining relationships and self-determination for employees. Section 9 of the act, which dealt with representatives and elections, was expanded by the LMRA; new definitions were introduced and procedural requirements were clarified. A number of amendments translated controlling board and court decisions into statutory law; others sought to give more latitude or protection to individual employees, members of occupational groups, and employers.

The basic policy of *exclusive* representation according to *majority rule* spelled out in the Wagner Act is unchanged, and the NLRB continues to determine the unit appropriate to collective bargaining. Usually, the unit is established informally by stipulation. The board's discretion in determining which kinds of employees will be included in bargaining units has been limited in three respects: (1) professional employees can now vote on whether they should be included in a unit containing nonprofessionals, (2) guards cannot be included in units with other employees, and (3) the board cannot "decide that any craft unit is inappropriate . . . on the ground that a different unit has been established by a prior board determination" *unless* the craft workers vote *against* separate representation. The board has interpreted the third restriction flexibly, holding that it cannot decide against a craft unit *solely* on the basis of a prior determination. Although the law provides that "in determining whether a unit is appropriate . . . the extent to which the employees have organized shall not be controlling," the board considers historical practices in an industry in making its decisions.[30]

Under section 14(a) of the LMRA, supervisors are excluded from protection under the act, although an employer may *voluntarily* recognize and bargain with a union of supervisory employees.

According to the NLRB, the act does not require that a representative be selected by any particular procedure so long as it is clearly the choice of a majority of workers in a unit.[31] If there is some question about this, the representative is normally determined through a secret ballot election conducted by the board. If an employers' unfair labor practices disrupt an election, the board may use signed *union authorization cards* as the basis for a bargaining order.[32] Unions have urged that the law be amended to allow more general use of such cards.

There are two types of representation elections: a *consent election,* in which the parties agree that a question of representation exists and that an election should be held, and in the absence of such agreement, an *election directed by a regional director* after a formal hearing. Section 9(c) now provides that an election may be held if an *employer* files a petition "alleging that one or more individuals or labor organizations have presented to him a claim to be recognized as [a] representative." Once a bargaining agent has been designated, it must represent all workers in a unit "equally and fairly . . . without regard to their union membership or activities."[33]

To provide stability in bargaining relationships, an election cannot be held if a valid election has been held within the preceding 12 months. The board has also ruled that "a valid contract for a fixed period of 3 years or less will bar an election for the period covered by the contract," although it will approve an election among employees covered by such a contract in certain circumstances.[34] For example, a contract that discriminates among employees on the basis of race will not operate as a bar to an election.[35]

Employees can petition for an election to *decertify* their bargaining representative. When such a petition is filed—under current regulations, by at least 30 percent of the employees in a unit—the board must investigate the matter. A hearing may then be held and if necessary, an election authorized. Similar procedures are provided for deauthorizing a union shop; in this case, the 30 percent standard is included in the statute.

Rights of Economic Strikers in Representation Elections

The law recognizes two categories of strikers: *"economic" strikers,* in disputes involving conventional bargaining issues, and *"unfair labor practices" strikers,* who are protesting an alleged violation of section 8(a) by an employer. Under the Wagner Act, unfair labor practice strikers retained their status as employees, and both economic strikers and their replacements could vote in a representation election. Under Taft-Hartley, economic strikers whose positions had been filled were not eligible to vote in a representation election. It was soon apparent however that depriving economic strikers of this right could pose a serious threat to a union's position as bargaining agent, and the law was changed again by the Landrum-Griffin Act. At present, economic strikers who are not entitled to reinstatement, as well as their replacements, are eligible to vote in any election conducted within 12 months after the beginning of a strike.

Regulating Unions' Internal Affairs

Sections 9(f) and 9(g) of the Taft-Hartley Act as originally passed involved the government to a limited degree in regulating the internal affairs of unions, since a union that wanted to use the procedures of the board had to file certain statements and reports. The Landrum-Griffin Act broadened the scope of government intervention. Sections 9(f) and 9(g) of the LMRA were repealed, and the regulations in Landrum-Griffin were applied to unions regardless of whether they were covered by the National Labor Relations Act or desired access to the NLRB.

Section 9(h): The Non-Communist Affidavit

Fear of Communist domination of unions was responsible for section 9(h), which excluded a labor organization from coverage under the act unless its officers and the officers of any national or international union with which it was affiliated signed affidavits saying that they were not members of the Communist party or affiliated with it. Management officials were not required to sign similar affidavits, and section 9(h) was widely resented by unionists, particularly those who were recognized opponents of Communism.

Section 504(a) of the Landrum-Griffin Act repealed 9(h) but made it a crime for a person who was or had been a member of the Communist party to hold a *union office* "during or for five years after the termination of his membership in the Communist Party." In 1965, this provision of the Landrum-Griffin Act was declared unconstitutional.[36]

Section 10: A Statutory "No-Man's-Land"

Much of section 10, which deals with the prevention of unfair labor practices, concerns procedural matters not important here. However, the section also made significant changes in the law of collective bargaining. One change attempted to resolve a serious problem involving the jurisdiction of the NLRB. The appropriations the board got from Congress did not enable it to exercise its jurisdiction over all the cases technically covered by the act, and it refused—on an industry basis —to assume jurisdiction over firms doing less than a stipulated volume of business.

Under Taft-Hartley, the NLRB was authorized to cede power over firms in industries other than mining, manufacturing, communications, and transportation, except where they were predominantly local in character, to an appropriate state agency if a state statute covering labor-management relations was consistent with the federal law. The courts held that if the NLRB refused to assume jurisdiction over "covered" firms, a state could not assume jurisdiction unless such a cession of power had been made. None was made, and employees of small firms in certain industries and all firms engaged in certain types of operations were denied protection.

The Landrum-Griffin Act sought to eliminate this legal "no-man's-land" by permitting states or territories with comparable statutes to assume jurisdiction over small firms when the board declined to do so. However, the board cannot "decline to assert jurisdiction over any labor dispute over which it would assert jurisdiction under the standards prevailing upon August 1, 1959." Moreover, since fewer than 20 states have comprehensive laws regulating collective bargaining, a statutory no-man's-land continues to exist in many jurisdictions.[37]

Jurisdictional Disputes

Section 10 mandated significant changes in board procedures for handling certain kinds of unfair labor practice cases. Section 10(k) provides that when a labor organization or its agents have been charged with an unfair labor practice involving a jurisdictional dispute, the NLRB is to hear and determine the dispute unless, within ten days after the charge has been filed, the parties themselves settle the dispute or set up machinery for voluntarily settling it. The intent of the section was to encourage the establishment of private machinery for settling jurisdictional disputes.

Initially, the NLRB was unwilling to make a work assignment in jurisdictional disputes, but in 1961, the Supreme Court held that the board had to decide which union had a right to disputed work and "award such tasks in accordance with its decision."[38]

Reintroducing the Labor Injunction

The Wagner Act authorized the NLRB to seek a temporary injunction in *any* unfair labor practice case, and this power is continued by section 10(j) of Taft-Hartley. It is used rarely, generally in "situations where the violations are clear and flagrant and where immediate relief seems necessary."[39] In fiscal 1979, 62 injunctions were sought under section 10(j).[40]

Section 10(1) of Taft-Hartley "reintroduced" the labor injunction in several controversial situations and provided special procedures for handling the unfair labor practices *by unions* mentioned in section 8(b)(4). The Landrum-Griffin Amendments extended these procedures to union practices covered in 8(e) and 8(b)(7). When a union has been charged with an unfair labor practice under one of these subsections, "the preliminary investigation of such charges [is to] be made forthwith and given priority over all other types of cases." (Section 10(m), added by Landrum-Griffin, also provides priority handling for cases related to sections 8(a)(3) and 8(b)(2)). If there is reasonable cause to believe that the charge in such a case is true, an officer or a regional attorney of the board (*not* the board) *must* petition a U.S. district court "for appropriate injunctive relief . . . or [a] temporary restraining order." Similar procedures are *not* required in the event of unfair labor practices by *employers*, thus creating a singular lack of mutuality in an ostensibly "balanced" act. In fiscal 1979, the general counsel of the NLRB sought 182 injunctions under section 10(1).[41]

Title I in Perspective

Many provisions of Title I codified precedents embodied in board decisions or clarified issues that had not been resolved under the National Labor Relations Act or had proved disruptive in collective bargaining. Not everyone would agree that all these changes were desirable, but insofar as they dealt with specific procedural or policy issues under the act, it was proper to include them in the basic statute regulating collective bargaining. Other provisions of Title I went beyond clarification of the original act and the resolution of policy issues, introducing new matters into the law and expanding the role of government in collective bargaining. The degree of union security considered permissible was limited, and more restrictive state laws regarding union security were given precedence over the federal law. Broad prohibitions were placed on secondary activities of labor organizations, reversing a tradition of nonintervention by the government, and injunctions were reintroduced into labor disputes in a singularly unbalanced fashion. The desirability of many Title I provisions is debatable. A number of the provisions of Title II and Title III are further evidence of a disjointed expansion of national labor policy. As indicated earlier, a number of Title III provisions relate to union and management actions regulated under Title I, and we will therefore discuss the Title III provisions in the following section. A brief discussion of union liability under the Sherman Act will also precede our analysis of Title II of the LMRA.

TITLE III: A MISCELLANY

Title III of the Taft-Hartley Act contains a number of disparate subtitles. *Section 301* allows suits to be instituted in district courts when a contract between an employer and a labor organization has been violated; it also states that labor organizations shall be bound by the acts of their agents and that "in determining whether any person is acting as an 'agent' . . . the question of whether the specific acts [they] performed were actually authorized or subsequently ratified shall not be controlling." Many unions have insulated themselves against damage suits by contract provisions limiting their liability. If both parties wish to create a constructive bargaining relationship, there should be little recourse to damage suits.

In 1962, a basic conflict developed between the Norris-LaGuardia and Taft-Hartley acts as a result of the Supreme Court's decision in the *Sinclair* case.[42] The Court held that the former act prevented the issuance of an injunction under section 301 when a union violated a no-strike pledge in an agreement that required arbitration of contract disputes. In a later decision, the Court recognized the need to accommodate the two acts and permitted an injunction to be issued against a strike when the collective bargaining contract contained a mandatory grievance adjustment or an arbitration procedure.[43]

Section 302, which sought to stop corruption in the labor-management field, prohibited a variety of payments by employers to employee representatives. In 1959, section 505 of the Landrum-Griffin Act amended subsections (a), (b), and (c) of this section. Under 302(c), the checkoff of union dues (automatic deductions of dues from wages by an employer) is permitted only under specified conditions. Such a payroll deduction must be authorized in writing and is not valid for more than one year.

Section 303, which covers boycotts and "other unlawful combinations," has had a significant impact on the collective bargaining process. It reemphasizes the concern of the 80th Congress with the unfair labor practices *by unions* enumerated in section 8(b)(4) by making these practices *unlawful* and a basis for damage suits. There are practices against which the general counsel is also *required* to seek an *injunction*. There is an obvious lack of mutuality in the section, since no similar action is required in the case of employer practices.

The inclusion of *section 304*, which amended the Federal Corrupt Practices Act, reflected a belief that organized labor was becoming too powerful politically. The section prohibits contributions or expenditures by labor organizations in connection with any election involving *federal* executive or legislative offices. The law previously had prohibited such campaign contributions by corporations. Both the A.F. of L. and the CIO, and later the combined federation, responded by setting up separate organizations to solicit funds for political purposes, and the actual effect of the provision was to increase the political expenditures and activities of organized labor.

Section 305 of Taft-Hartley made it unlawful for employees of the federal government or any of its agencies to strike. This section was supplanted in 1955 by Public Law 330, which makes such a strike a federal felony.

The Sherman Act Revisited

In the 1940s, the Supreme Court had held that unions were only liable under the Sherman Act if they acted collusively with employers to restrain trade. Three more recent decisions indicate that the Court has begun to question the broad immunity of unions to prosecution under our antitrust laws. In two 1965 cases, the Court indicated that provisions of a collective bargaining agreement that affect competitive conditions in product markets are not necessarily protected by the Taft-Hartley Act and that they may be violations of the Sherman Act. In a 1975 case involving a secondary boycott in the construction industry, the Court declared that labor unions and union organizing tactics are not automatically exempt from our antitrust laws.

The 1965 *Pennington* case involved an agreement between the United Mine Workers and the Bituminous Coal Operators Association.[44] The union was charged with conspiring with the employers in the association to eliminate smaller, more marginal, operators from the industry by imposing the terms of the industry's 1950 basic wage agreement upon nonsignatory companies irrespective of their ability to pay. The union argued that the Sherman Act did not apply to the agreement, since it dealt with wage standards. Although the case was remanded for a new trial, the Supreme Court disagreed with the union's position, holding that "[o]ne group of employers may not conspire to eliminate competitors from the industry and the union is liable with the employers if it becomes a party to the conspiracy."[45]

The *Jewel Tea* case involved an agreement between a Chicago meatcutters' union and a group of food stores; it provided that meat could not be sold before 9 a.m. or after 6 p.m., even in stores in which no butchers were employed.[46] Jewel Tea sued the union and the employers' association under the Sherman Act, charging (1) that the clause represented a conspiracy between the union and those stores that did not wish to operate at night and (2) that it was designed to ban night operations by large self-service chains selling precut meats. Although the Supreme Court held that the provision was related to a legitimate bargaining objective (the regulation of hours of work), it indicated that in different circumstances, it might decide that the impact of such a provision on a product market overrode the interest of a union in protecting its members' standards of employment, that is, the impact on a labor market.

In the 1975 *Connell* case, which involved the picketing of a building contractor to force it to boycott nonunion subcontractors, the Supreme Court ruled that the picketing union was not automatically exempt from antitrust legislation and remanded the case to a lower court for trial.[47] The unsettled legal status of such union activities indicates the need for greater consistency between the language of the Sherman, Norris-LaGuardia, and Labor-Management Relations acts.

The Taft-Hartley Act did not directly address the nebulous "union monopoly" issue, although the ban on the closed shop, the proscription of secondary activities by unions, and the limitations on union contributions in federal political campaigns may be considered attempts to reduce the "monopoly power" of organized labor.

TITLE II: THE CONCILIATION OF LABOR DISPUTES IN INDUSTRIES AFFECTING COMMERCE; NATIONAL EMERGENCIES

Title II of the Labor-Management Relations Act provides for government assistance in resolving union-management disputes. The principal types of third-party intervention in the settlement of such disputes include:

1. *conciliation*: intervention designed to bring the parties into a bargaining relationship with each other. This is presently required under our basic law of collective bargaining, and the term conciliation is now used synonymously with mediation.
2. *mediation*: third-party intervention to establish a possible basis for agree-

ment when an impasse develops or appears likely to develop during negotiations. Mediation is designed to make collective bargaining work, not to supplant it. The parties to a dispute are not required to agree to terms developed by a mediator.

3. *voluntary arbitration*: the parties to a dispute may *agree* to submit a dispute to a neutral third party (an arbitrator) for settlement. They are under no compulsion to enter into such an agreement, but once they do so, they must comply with the decision of the arbitrator.

4. *fact-finding*: third parties may intervene to clarify the issues in a dispute, usually in the hope that public opinion will put pressures on the parties to reach an agreement. Fact-finding may be considered compulsory when procedures for it are established by statute or a panel is appointed by the chief executive of the relevant level of government (the President, a governor, or a mayor). The basic flaw in simple fact-finding is that no recommendations are made as to how a dispute should be settled.

5. *fact-finding with recommendations*: fact-finding that involves specific recommendations for settling a dispute. The parties to the dispute are not required to accept the recommendations, but it is assumed that public opinion, and perhaps pressure from the executive or legislative branch of the government, will encourage them to do so.

6. *seizure*: government operation of struck or shutdown facilities. The government may rely on economic pressure (fear of a loss of profits or of wage increases during the period of government control) or on public opinion to encourage a settlement, or seizure may be combined with compulsory arbitration.

7. *compulsory arbitration*: when the parties to a dispute are legally obligated to accept intervention by a third party, who will render a decision in the dispute with which they are obligated to comply. In the United States, compulsory arbitration in the private sector has been rejected as inconsistent with free collective bargaining.

8. *selection of a final offer*: a form of compulsory arbitration in which a third party chooses between the final proposals (or perhaps alternative final proposals) from the parties to a dispute.

9. *advisory arbitration*: a kind of arbitration in which the parties to a dispute are not compelled legally to conform to an award. Advisory arbitration is provided under some state laws regulating collective bargaining in public employment. The laws assume that the state cannot delegate its sovereign authority to an arbitrator.

The Taft-Hartley Act assumes that it is in the public interest (1) to resolve disputes about the terms of collective agreements through private bargaining between the parties and (2) to resolve disputes involving contract interpretation and administration through formal grievance procedures established by collective agreements. An *independent* agency, the *Federal Mediation and Con-*

ciliation Service, was established under Title II to help realize these objectives.*
In addition, the title includes injunction and fact-finding procedures that are
designed to help resolve "national emergency" disputes.

The Mediation of Labor Disputes

The primary function of the Federal Mediation and Conciliation Service is to
help settle primary labor disputes in industries affecting commerce. Under Title
I, 60 days' notice must be given of a desire to change the terms of a collective
agreement, and the service must be notified of a dispute within 30 days. Under
Title II, the service can proffer its services on its own motion or upon the request
of either party if it believes that a dispute "threatens to cause a substantial interruption of commerce." If an agreement is not reached, the director of the service
is expected to "seek to induce the parties voluntarily to seek other means of
settling the dispute . . . including submission to the employees . . . of the employer's last offer of settlement . . . in a secret ballot." The last tactic is rarely
used, since it would undoubtedly result in a firming of the union's position and a
rejection of the employer's offer.

A 1974 amendment extending coverage under the act to workers in the nonprofit health care industry provides for a 90 rather than a 60 day notice of termination of an agreement, makes disputes in that industry automatically subject to
mediation by the federal service, and provides for fact-finding with recommendations.

Title II of Taft-Hartley urges the parties to a collective agreement to establish *grievance procedures* for the adjustment of *secondary* disputes and directs
the Mediation and Conciliation Service to intervene in such disputes "only as a
last resort and in exceptional cases." The Supreme Court has recognized the
desirability of deferring to grievance arbitration. In 1960, in the "Steelworkers
Trilogy" cases, the Court described the arbitration of grievances as part of the
continuing collective bargaining process. It declared that (1) it would not consider an issue nonarbitrable in the absence of a contractual agreement by the
parties to exclude the issue from arbitration; (2) in reviewing arbitration decisions, federal courts cannot consider the merits of a dispute but only whether
the dispute comes under the terms of a contract; and (3) federal courts cannot
substitute their interpretation of a contract for that of an arbitrator. Thus the
parties to a dispute cannot resort to the courts to reverse an arbitration decision.[48]

National Emergency Disputes

The fundamental thrust of our federal law of collective bargaining has been to
provide a regulatory framework that gives the parties to collective bargaining

* This agency replaced the Conciliation Service, which had been part of the Department of
Labor and which some management officials believed was therefore unable to function
objectively.

maximum freedom to negotiate terms and conditions of employment. The government is however expected to prevent or put an end to work stoppages that pose an imminent threat to the public welfare. The Title II procedures relating to "national emergencies" are a compromise between these objectives. Although a work stoppage may be delayed or temporarily halted, there is no ultimate ban on the right to strike or to lock out employees.

Title II defines *emergency disputes* as work stoppages "affecting an entire industry or a substantial part thereof . . .[which] will, if permitted to occur or to continue, imperil the national health or safety." The title does not mention the public welfare per se, refer to disputes that affect the nation's *economic* health, or apply to local emergency disputes or disputes in the public sector, the two types of disputes that have most frequently inconvenienced the public and created what have been perceived to be public emergencies.

The emergency procedures in Title II are initiated by the President.* If the President decides that a threatened or actual work stoppage imperils the nation's health or safety, the chief executive

> *may* appoint a board of inquiry to inquire into the issues involved . . . and to make a written report [which] shall include a statement of the facts with respect to the dispute . . . but *shall not* contain any recommendations. (Emphasis added.)

After receiving this report, the President *may* direct the attorney general to petition a district court for an injunction to stop the strike or lockout.

During the period of an injunction, the parties to a dispute must try to settle their differences with the help of the Mediation and Conciliation Service. Upon the issuance of an injunction, the President reconvenes the original board of inquiry. If no settlement has been reached after 60 days, the board reports "the current position of the parties and the efforts which have been made for settlement, [including] a statement by each party of its position and a statement of the employer's last offer of settlement."

This report is made public, and within 15 days, the NLRB must determine by a secret ballot whether the employees in the dispute wish to accept the employer's last offer. Union members on strike are unlikely to repudiate their leaders, and votes taken in accordance with this provision have resulted in overwhelming rejections of employers' offers.** The results of the vote must be certified by the attorney general within five days, and action must then be taken to have the injunction discharged.

At no point during the total injunction period of 80 days are any recommendations made by an independent fact-finding agency, and the effect of voting

---

* This step was taken 35 times between 1947 and the end of 1979, most recently in the bituminous coal dispute of 1978. Strikes occurred in 30 cases. The Carter administration did *not* invoke the Taft-Hartley Act in the over-the-road trucking strike in 1979.

** In several cases in which a union agreed to terms before a vote, the union leadership may have feared that the members would accept the employer's terms. In one case, the voting was boycotted.

on the last offer is to assure union members not only that they are free to strike but also that strikes are authorized by law, a result clearly not in accord with the objectives of Title II.

When the injunction is discharged, the President must "submit to the Congress a full and comprehensive report of the proceedings . . . together with such recommendations as he may see fit to make." These recommendations will determine the ultimate action taken in a dispute. In some cases, an ad hoc board of inquiry may be appointed to recommend a settlement.

A Concluding Comment

The inclusion of national emergency disputes procedures in the LMRA is another reflection of the failure of Congress to distinguish between (1) amendments designed to clarify or modify administrative and procedural aspects of the law of collective bargaining and (2) legislation addressing "new" problems. Identifying and resolving emergency disputes involves parameters that are not relevant to most collective bargaining relationships. It would be more appropriate, and probably more effective, to deal with work stoppages creating potential or actual emergencies in a separate statute. If disputes in rail, air, and possibly highway and water transport were included in such a statute, it would introduce much needed consistency into our federal labor legislation. These matters are discussed further in Chapter 18.

THE IMPACT OF TAFT-HARTLEY ON COLLECTIVE BARGAINING

As we have noted, many provisions of the LMRA translated into statutory law board and court decisions that had already provided much of the framework of our law of collective bargaining. Other amendments expanded federal control over union-management relations by regulating concerted activities by unions and setting up a more comprehensive regulatory framework for private bargaining, including special procedures for handling national emergency disputes.

Although not internally consistent or "balanced," the act has not proved to be a "slave labor" law; nor have its disparate provisions had an adverse impact on most established bargaining relationships, particularly those between the larger and more visible employers and unions. As the chairman of the NLRB noted in 1973, "[w]e know that despite our growing case load, the truly experienced employers who have a relationship with a truly experienced labor organization very rarely see an agent of the National Labor Relations Board."[49]

The impact of the act on less well-established bargaining relationships and on the extension of union organization is less certain. The bans on specific union activities and the protection extended to employees as individuals, to employers, and to neutral third parties have given psychological support to antiunion employers. A variety of provisions, including the authorization of the states to pass restrictive right-to-work laws, have hindered organizational efforts, particularly in rural areas and in the southern states. However, other factors have probably played a more significant role in checking the relative growth of unions since World War II.

There are various ill-advised and inconsistent provisions in the act, including the preemption of federal law by state laws in section 14(b). There are also unfortunate omissions, such as the failure to require that unions admit as members all the employees in a bargaining unit. Certain provisions thwart the intent of the legislature to provide mutuality in our law of collective bargaining—for example, the declaration that specified unfair labor practices by *unions* are also *illegal,* the priority given to handling certain unfair labor practices on the part of *labor organizations,* the *mandatory injunction* procedures that also apply to them, and (prior to 1959) the non-Communist affidavit required of union officials. Finally, the act fails to provide an effective mechanism for the ultimate resolution of emergency disputes.

Our federal law of collective bargaining continues to emphasize the desirability of resolving union-management disputes privately. The role of government is confined in the main to establishing and implementing a procedural framework for private bargaining that increases its effectiveness as a means of resolving disputes, makes it more equitable, and minimizes the impact of the government on the substantive provisions of collective agreements.

Despite all this, the act expanded the role of government in the bargaining process and involved the NLRB more intimately in what are ostensibly private arrangements. Board decisions have gradually increased the number of matters subject to mandatory bargaining and limited managerial prerogatives. Recently, the board has begun to reexamine the application of antitrust legislation to certain aspects of union-management relations. Understandably, the board is responsive to the dynamic inherent in our industrial society. However, modifications of the regulatory framework should be based on clear policies determined by the Congress, and not on the predilections of the changing personnel of a quasi-judicial agency. This suggests that the administration and technical implementation of the law by the board and the general counsel should be subject to continuing congressional review.

STATE LEGISLATION

A number of states, primarily the more highly industrialized northern and western ones, have passed laws regulating union-management relations in private sector firms engaged in *intrastate commerce.* More recently, an increasing number of states have enacted legislation regulating union-management relations in the *public sector.* This public sector legislation, which is discussed in Chapter 18, is significant because it appears unlikely that the federal government will be inclined—or even permitted under the Constitution—to regulate union-management relations in the public sector as it does those in the private sector.

At present, fewer than 20 states have comprehensive statutes similar to the Wagner Act or the LMRA. Almost all the states provide mediation services, although the majority do not have a permanent full-time mediation agency. About half of the states have "Little Norris-LaGuardia Acts," some half-dozen have laws similar in some respects to the Landrum-Griffin Act, some three dozen have fair employment practices acts, about half have equal pay laws, and 20 have right-to-work laws.

This state legislation reflects community mores: most of the comprehensive laws and "Little Norris-LaGuardia Acts" are found in industrial states; no industrial state has a right-to-work statute. These conditions are not likely to change in the near future. The political climate in the states that do not have comprehensive collective bargaining laws is not hospitable to legislation that would encourage union organization and collective bargaining. The restrictions placed on unions by many state laws do not appear to have had a significant impact on established bargaining relationships. They may however have an adverse impact on union organizational campaigns.

SUMMARY

Federal collective bargaining legislation continues to encourage union organization and collective bargaining. However, since 1947, Congress has attempted to provide greater mutuality and balance in the law, on the assumption that unions, as established institutions with significant economic power, should be regulated in the public interest.

The basic framework for union-management relations in the private sector is set by the general legislation discussed in this chapter. Other laws also affect the internal affairs of unions, particular subjects and procedures of collective bargaining, and collective bargaining in the public sector. These laws are discussed in Chapter 18.

DISCUSSION QUESTIONS

1. In general, did the provisions of the Taft-Hartley Act amend the Wagner Act "in the light of experience" (under the latter Act)?
2. Did the Taft-Hartley Act provide "appropriate balance" in our law of collective bargaining?
3. How were the union security provisions of the Wagner Act altered by the 1947 amendments to the Act?
4. Distinguish between *unfair labor practices* and *illegal actions* under our current law of collective bargaining.
5. Should employees be "made whole" for prospective contract gains which were not realized because of their employer's refusal to bargain?
6. Should economic strikers be allowed to vote in a union representation election?
7. Do the Title II national emergency provisions of the Taft-Hartley Act appear to provide an effective means of resolving such disputes? (This question anticipates the analysis in the following chapter.)
8. How are charges of discrimination by employers and unions against members of minority groups handled by the NLRB?

9. Has the J. P. Stevens textile company recognized any unions and entered into bona fide collective bargaining with them since this text was written?
10. Does the state in which your college or university is located have a "Little Wagner" or "Little Taft-Hartley" Act? Does it have a right-to-work law?

SELECTED READINGS

The Law of Collective Bargaining

Aaron, Benjamin, and Meyer, Paul Seth. "Public Policy and Labor-Management Relations." In *A Review of Industrial Relations Research*. Vol. II. Industrial Relations Research Association Series. Madison, Wisc.: Industrial Relations Research Association, 1971. Unusually complete bibliographical references.

Commerce Clearing House. *(Annual) Guidebook to Labor Relations*. Chicago: Commerce Clearing House.

Cox, Archibald. *Law and the National Labor Policy*. Los Angeles: Institute of Industrial Relations, University of California, 1960.

Evans, Robert, Jr. *Public Policy Toward Labor*. New York: Harper & Row, 1965.

Goldberg, Joseph P. "The Law and Practice of Collective Bargaining." In Goldberg, Joseph P.; Ahern, Eileen; Haber, William; and Oswald, Rudolph A., eds. *Federal Policies and Worker Status Since the Thirties*. Madison, Wisc.: Industrial Relations Research Association, 1976, pp. 13–41.

Gregory, Charles O., and Katz, Harold A. *Labor and the Law*. 3rd ed. New York: Norton, 1979.

Morris, Charles J., ed. in chief. *The Developing Labor Law: The Boards, the Courts, and the National Labor Relations Act*. Published for the Labor Relations Law Section of the American Bar Association. Washington, D.C.: Bureau of National Affairs, 1971. Supplements published annually.

Ross, Philip. *The Government as a Source of Union Power*. Providence, R.I.: Brown University Press, 1965.

Shister, Joseph; Aaron, Benjamin; and Summers, Clyde W., eds. *Public Policy and Collective Bargaining*. Industrial Relations Research Association Publication No. 27. New York: Harper & Row, 1962.

Taylor, Benjamin J., and Witney, Fred. *Labor Relations Law*. 2nd ed. Englewood Cliffs, N.J.: Prentice-Hall, 1975.

Wellington, Harry H. *Labor and the Legal Process*. New Haven, Conn.: Yale University Press, 1968.

The National Labor Relations Board has also produced two excellent guides to the National Labor Relations Act, both of which are updated periodically. These are *A Guide to Basic Law and Procedures Under the National Labor Relations Act* and the *Summary of the National Labor Relations Act*. The editions referred to in this text were published, respectively, in 1978 and 1973.

Procedural and Structural Reforms

Brown, Douglass V. "The Role of the NLRB" In *The Next Twenty-Five Years of Industrial Relations*. Ed. by Gerald G. Somers. Madison, Wisc.: Industrial Relations Research Association, 1973, pp. 111–117.

Miller, Edward B., chairman NLRB. *Remarks* before the Labor Relations Law Section of the American Bar Association, Washington, D.C., August 7, 1973. *NLRB Release R–1297.*

National Labor Relations Board, Chairman's Task Force on the NLRB. *Interim Report and Recommendations for 1976* (mimeo).

National Emergency Disputes

Aaron, Benjamin. "National Emergency Disputes: Some Current Proposals." *Spring Meeting Industrial Relations Research Association 1971*. In *Labor Law Journal* 22, no. 8 (August 1971): pp. 461–474.

Aaron, Benjamin, and Meyer, Paul S. "Public Policy and Labor-Management Relations." In *A Review of Industrial Relations Research*. Vol. II. Industrial Relations Research Association Series. Madison, Wisc.: Industrial Relations Research Association, 1971, pp. 40–46.

Bernstein, Irving; Enarson, Harold L.; and Fleming, R. W., eds. *Emergency Disputes and National Policy*. Industrial Relations Research Association Series. New York: Harper & Brothers, 1955.

Cullen, Donald E. *National Emergency Strikes*. Ithaca, N.Y.: NYS School of Industrial and Labor Relations, Cornell University, October 1968.

State Legislation

Katz, Harold A., and Feldacker, Bruce S. "The Decline and Fall of State Regulation of Labor Relations." In *Labor Law Journal* 20, no. 6 (June 1969): pp. 327–345.

Killingsworth, Charles C. *State Labor Relations Acts*. Chicago: University of Chicago Press, 1948.

Northrup, Herbert R., and Bloom, Gordon F. *Government and Labor*. Chap. 9, "State Labor Relations Acts and Controls." Homewood, Ill.: Irwin, 1963.

U.S. Department of Labor. *Growth of Labor Law in the United States*. Washington, D.C.: U.S. Government Printing Office, 1967, pp. 197–205.

Notes

1. Harry A. Millis and Emily Clark Brown, *From the Wagner Act to Taft-Hartley* (Chicago: University of Chicago Press, 1950), p. 364.
2. *61 Stat*, 136 (1947).
3. Millis and Brown, *From the Wagner Act to Taft-Hartley*, p. 362.
4. Archibald Cox, *Law and the National Labor Policy* (Los Angeles: Institute of Industrial Relations, University of California, 1960), p. 15.
5. *Forty-Fourth Annual Report of the National Labor Relations Board for the Fiscal Year Ended September 30, 1979*, pp. 1–2. The board received a much smaller number of petitions regarding the deauthorization of union shops, the amendment of certifications, and the clarification of collective bargaining units.
6. National Labor Relations Board, *A Guide to Basic Law and Procedures Under the National Labor Relations Act*, 1978, p. 19.
7. The leading case is *Textile Workers* v. *Darlington Mfg. Co.*, 380 U.S. 263 (1965).
8. Ibid.

9. For a more complete discussion of lockouts, see Charles J. Morris, ed. in chief, *The Developing Labor Law: The Boards, the Courts, and the National Labor Relations Act,* chap. 20. Published for the Labor Relations Law Section of the American Bar Association (Washington, D.C.: Bureau of National Affairs, 1971).

10. The leading case is *American Ship Bldg. Co.* v. *NLRB,* 380 U.S. 300 (1965). In a companion case, the Supreme Court held that in the absence of an antiunion motivation, employers could not only lock out employees to counter a whipsaw strike plan but also continue to operate with temporary replacements. (*NLRB* v. *Brown Food Store,* 380 U.S. 278 [1965].)

11. Elliott Bredhoff, "The Scope of 'Good Faith Bargaining' and Adequacy of Remedies," in *Proceedings of the Twenty-Sixth Annual Meeting, Industrial Relations Research Association, December 28–29, 1973,* p. 115.

12. *H. K. Porter Co.* v. *NLRB,* 397 U.S. 99 (1970).

13. Leading cases include *Spielberg Mfg. Co.,* 112 NLRB 1080 (1955), and *Collyer Insulated Wire,* 192 NLRB 837 (1971).

14. National Labor Relations Board, Division of Information, *Weekly Summary of NLRB Cases,* W–1686, January 7–11, 1980, p. 4.

15. See Jay S. Siegal, "Deferral to Arbitration Awards in Title VII Actions," in *Labor Law Journal* 25, no. 7 (July 1974): p. 398. Reprinted from *Labor Law Forum* (March 1974). The leading case is *Alexander* v. *Gardner-Denver Co.,* 415 U.S. 36 (1974).

16. Leading cases include *John Wiley & Sons* v. *Livingstone,* 376 U.S. 543 (1964); *NLRB* v. *Burns International Security Service, Inc.,* 406 U.S. 272 (1972); and *Golden Gate Bottling Co.* v. *NLRB,* 414 U.S. 168 (1973).

17. *A Guide to Basic Law and Procedures,* p. 31.

18. Morris, *The Developing Labor Law,* p. 734. The leading case is *Miranda Fuel Co.,* 140 NLRB 181 (1962). For an analysis of this obligation, see Jean T. McKelvey, ed., *The Duty of Fair Representation* (Ithaca, N.Y.: NYS School of Industrial and Labor Relations, Cornell University, 1977).

19. Benjamin Aaron, "The Labor-Management Reporting and Disclosure Act of 1959," reprinted from *Harvard Law Review* 73 no. 5 and no. 6 (March and April 1960): p. 1113.

20. *N.L.R.B.* v. *Fruit and Vegetable Packers, Local 760, (Tree Fruits Labor Relations Committee, Inc.),* 377 U.S. 58 (1964).

21. *NLRB Finds Secondary Boycott in Brand-Name Gasoline Picketing, NLRB Release R–1342,* June 21, 1974, p. 1. Affirmed by the Supreme Court on appeal, *NLRB* v. *Steelworkers Local 14055,* 429 U.S. 807 (1976). The NLRB effectively voided the 1974 ruling when it refused to reconsider the case in accordance with the Court's instructions because the local union had been disbanded. (*The Wall Street Journal,* May 3, 1977, p. 3.)

22. *A Guide to Basic Law and Procedures,* p. 38.

23. Cf. Morris, *The Developing Labor Law,* pp. 72–77. The leading cases are *General Shoe Corp.,* 77 NLRB 124 (1948), and *Dal-Tex Optical Co.,* 137 NLRB 274 (1962). Leading cases involving misstatements of fact prior to an election include *Hollywood Ceramics Co.,* 140 NLRB 221 (1962); *Shopping Kart Food Market, Inc.,* 228 NLRB 1311 (1977); and *General Knit of California, Inc.,* 239 NLRB 101 (1978).

24. Ibid., p. 75.

25. Benjamin J. Taylor and Fred Witney, *Labor Relations Law,* 2nd ed. (Englewood Cliffs, N.J.: Prentice-Hall, 1975), chap. 18. The leading recent case is *Hudgens* v. *NLRB,* 424 U.S. 507 (1976).

26. Cf. Morris, *The Developing Labor Law,* chap. 11, "The Duty to Bargain in Good Faith."

27. Commerce Clearing House, *1977 Guidebook to Labor Relations,* (Chicago: Commerce Clearing House, 1977), p. 285.

28. See for example, *Fibreboard Paper Products Corp.* v. *NLRB,* 379 U.S. 203 (1964).

29. Morris, discussing *NLRB* v. *American Nat'l Ins. Co.,* 343 U.S. 395 (1952), in *The Developing Labor Law,* p. 409.

30. The leading case establishing criteria for cases involving craft severance is *Mallinkrodt Chemical Works,* 162 NLRB 387 (1966). Cf. Morris, *The Developing Labor Law,* pp. 228–229.

31. *A Guide to Basic Law and Procedures,* p. 10.

32. *NLRB* v. *Gissel Packing Co.,* 395 U.S. 575 (1969).

33. *A Guide to Basic Law and Procedures,* p. 10.

34. Ibid., p. 14. Cf. Morris, *The Developing Labor Law,* pp. 167–180.

35. *Pioneer Bus Co.,* 140 NLRB 54 (1962).

36. *United States* v. *Archie Brown,* 381 U.S. 437 (1965).

37. Current jurisdictional standards are summarized in the most recent revisions of *A Guide to Basic Law and Procedures Under the National Labor Relations Act* and the *Summary of the National Labor Relations Act,* also published by the NLRB and updated periodically.

38. *NLRB* v. *Radio and Television Broadcast Engineers Local 1212, International Brotherhood of Electrical Workers,* 364 U.S. 573 (1961).

39. Morris, *The Developing Labor Law,* pp. 845–846.

40. *Forty-Fourth Annual Report of the National Labor Relations Board, 1979,* Table 20, p. 315.

41. Ibid.

42. *Sinclair Refining Co.* v. *Atkinson,* 370 U.S. 195 (1962).

43. *Boys Market Inc.,* v. *Retail Clerks, Local 770,* 398 U.S. 235 (1970).

44. *United Mine Workers* v. *Pennington,* 381 U.S. 657 (1965).

45. Ibid., pp. 665–666.

46. *Local 189, Amalgamated Meat Cutters* v. *Jewel Tea Co.,* 381 U.S. 676 (1965).

47. *Connell Construction Co.* v. *Plumbers Local 100,* 421 U.S. 616 (1975).

48. *United Steelworkers of America* v. *Warrior and Gulf Navigation Co.,* 363 U.S. 574 (1960); *United Steelworkers of America* v. *American Manufacturing Co.,* 363 U.S. 564 (1960); *United Steelworkers of America* v. *Enterprise Wheel and Car Corp.,* 363 U.S. 593 (1960). For a discussion of these cases, see Max S. Wortman, Jr., Craig E. Overton, and Carl E. Block, "Arbitration, Enforcement and Individual Rights," in *Labor Law Journal* 25, no. 2 (February 1974): pp. 77–79.

49. Edward B. Miller, "Deferral to Arbitration—Temperance or Abstinence," speech before the Georgia Bar Association, Atlanta, May 4, 1973 (*NLRB Release R–1285*), p. 14.

Chapter 18
THE REGULATORY FRAMEWORK III: MORE FEDERAL LEGISLATION, CONTINUING PUBLIC POLICY ISSUES, AND PUBLIC SECTOR LEGISLATION

In Chapter 17, we examined the basic federal statute regulating collective bargaining in the private sector. In this chapter, we will consider (1) other federal legislation that affects bargaining in the private sector; (2) possible changes in the law of collective bargaining as it relates to national emergency disputes, work stoppages in rail and air transport, and equal employment opportunities; and (3) federal and state regulation of union-management relations in the public sector.

ADDITIONAL FEDERAL LEGISLATION AFFECTING UNION-MANAGEMENT RELATIONS

Four laws that do not deal with collective bargaining procedures per se have a significant impact either on those procedures or on the content of collective agreements. These laws are (1) the *Labor-Management Reporting and Disclosure Act of 1959, as Amended* (the Landrum-Griffin Act); (2) the *Welfare and Pension Plans Disclosure Act of 1958, as Amended* (the Teller Act); (3) the *Employment Retirement Income Security Act of 1974* (ERISA, or the Pension Reform Act); and (4) the *Occupational Safety and Health Act of 1970* (OSHAct). These acts involve the government more intimately in the regulation of unions, in on-going collective bargaining relationships, and in the content of collective agree-ments and welfare and pension plans. They are further evidence of Congress's view that union-management relations should be regulated in the public interest.

The Labor-Management Reporting and Disclosure Act of 1959[1]

Except for the elimination of the union shop authorization poll in 1951, no major amendment was made to the Labor-Management Relations Act between 1947 and 1959. There was a consensus that "technical" defects in the act should be remedied, but Congress was unable to agree on new legislation. By 1958, Con-gress was also concerned about two additional problems: the lack of democratic procedures in a number of unions, and corruption and collusion both within the union movement and between management and union officials and consultants.

In 1959, Congress addressed both the amendment of the Labor-Management Relations Act and these additional problems in the *Labor-Management Reporting and Disclosure Act* (the Landrum-Griffin Act). The Title VII amendments to Taft-Hartley were discussed in Chapter 17; Titles I–VI of the Landrum-Griffin Act deal with the elimination of undemocratic and corrupt practices from union-management relations. Unlike the Wagner Act and the Labor-Management Relations Act, these titles apply to labor organizations regardless of whether they seek certification from the NLRB. They apply also to unions and employers covered by the Railway Labor Act, but not to the government as an employer.[*] The Landrum-Griffin Act involves the government in the internal affairs of unions in several ways: by regulating various internal operations of labor organiza-tions and certain industrial relations activities of employers and labor relations consultants, by defining new federal crimes, and by requiring unions and man-agements to file various reports and make specified information available to individual union members and employees.

Supporters of the Landrum-Griffin Act assumed that union members were willing to exercise the responsibilities of membership in a democratic organiza-tion and that, given the chance, they would put an end to many of the abuses that had been the focus of the McClellan investigation. Unfortunately, most union members have little interest in day-to-day union operations. Protecting their rights to be active in union affairs through legislation may fail to create a desire for democracy among an apathetic membership and have little effect on the existing power structure.

TITLE I

This "Bill of Rights of Members of Labor Organizations" gives all members of a labor organization equal rights and privileges within the organization. It entitles

[*] The government and any corporations wholly owned by the government are specifically excluded from coverage as employers by section 3(e).

them to freedom of speech and assembly, within reasonable limits, and forbids an increase in initiation fees, dues, or assessments without a vote. It protects the right of union members to sue the organization, safeguards members from improper disciplinary actions, and requires unions to give any employee affected by a collective bargaining agreement a copy of the agreement on request. However, Title I does *not* clearly guarantee the right of every worker in a bargaining unit to join the union representing the unit. Had such a provision been included, the act would probably not have been passed.

Unlike other sections of the Landrum-Griffin Act, which are enforced by the Secretary of Labor, the "Bill of Rights" can only be enforced through a civil suit brought by someone whose rights have allegedly been infringed. This has limited the number of complaints under Title I.*

TITLE II

Title II contains requirements for reporting by labor organizations, officers and employees of labor organizations, and employers. It calls for various reports to the Secretary of Labor designed to give union members adequate information about the operations of their bargaining representatives. These reports replace those required under the LMRA. Title II also repeals the requirement that union officials sign a non-Communist affidavit and requires employers to report payments to labor organizations, union officials, and labor relations consultants. These reports are public documents, and the Secretary of Labor may publish any information they contain.

TITLE III

This section of the Landrum-Griffin Act is designed to prevent national unions from assuming unwarranted control over the affairs of local affiliates through *trusteeships*. Although presumably set up to provide financial help to insolvent organizations or to "cleanse" a local of irresponsible or corrupt influences, trusteeships have sometimes served as the mechanism by which a national union assumed control over a dissident local. They have also been a source of revenue for national unions or individual trustees. However, Title III recognizes the need for trusteeships in certain circumstances. A trusteeship can

> be established and administered by a labor organization . . . for the purpose of correcting corruption or financial malpractice, assuring the performance of collective bargaining agreements or other duties of a bargaining representative, restoring democratic procedures, or otherwise carrying out the legitimate objects of [the] labor organization.

A trusteeship set up for such purposes is valid for 18 months. At the end of that time, it becomes invalid unless the union can present "clear and convincing proof" that its continuation is necessary.

---

* The Title VII amendments to the LMRA make the NLRB responsible for enforcing the provisions of that title.

TITLE IV

This title requires union officials to stand for election by secret ballot within stated periods. It also entitles any union member in good standing to run for a union office, to vote, and to support candidates without being interfered with in any way. A union's leadership cannot legally penalize members for such activities or seek reprisals of any kind.

Title IV requires that officers of national or international unions be elected at least once every five years, officers of intermediate bodies (such as joint councils or general committees) once every four years, and officers of local unions once every three years. It protects opposition candidates by requiring unions to comply with reasonable requests to distribute campaign literature at a candidate's expense and to treat all candidates equally in calculating the cost of such distributions. If despite these safeguards, internal procedures prove inadequate "for the removal of an elected officer guilty of serious misconduct," the Secretary of Labor may begin removal proceedings.

TITLE V

Title V defines the *fiduciary responsibility* of union officials, prohibits certain persons from holding elective offices in unions, and amends section 302 of the LMRA to make additional types of payments by employers or employer associations illegal. It gives individual union members the right to sue union officers who have allegedly violated their fiduciary responsibilities if the organization involved refuses to take appropriate action. Officers of labor organizations must be bonded.

Section 504 initially made it unlawful for persons who were or had been members of the Communist party or who had been convicted of stated crimes to serve (1) as union officers or employees except in an exclusively clerical or custodial capacity or (2) as labor relations consultants or as officers or employees, except in an exclusively clerical or custodial capacity, of employer associations engaged in collective bargaining. The sanctions relating to Communist party members were ruled unconstitutional by the Supreme Court in 1965.[2]

Subsections 302(a), (b), and (c) of the LMRA are amended by section 505, which in effect prohibits payments to "industrial relations consultants" who engage in such practices as negotiating "sweetheart" contracts, buying "strike insurance" from union officials, and advising clients on how to avert the unionization of their employees. It also forbids payments by the operator or owner of a motor vehicle of "a fee or charge for the unloading, or in connection with the unloading, of the cargo of such vehicle" except lawful payments to employees for their services. This last provision was intended to prevent such payments to members or officers of certain locals of the Teamsters' Union.

TITLE VI

Title VI contains a number of miscellaneous provisions. The more significant of these:

1. empower the Secretary of Labor to investigate possible violations of the act (but not violations of Title I or amendments made by the act to other statutes);
2. make extortionate picketing for "the personal profit or enrichment of any individual," unlawful;
3. state that the act does not impair the ability of a state to enact and enforce its own general criminal laws;
4. make it unlawful for a union to discipline any of its members "for exercising any right to which [they are] entitled under the provisions of [the] Act"; and
5. make it unlawful to use force or violence to interfere with union members attempting to exercise any of the rights to which they are entitled under the act.

A SUMMARY COMMENT

Since the passage of the Landrum-Griffin Act, the ethical climate of union-management relations has improved, the interests of individual union members have received more protection, and opposition candidates have been able to oust the presidents of a number of major national unions, including the Steelworkers, the United Mine Workers, and the Electrical Workers. However, legal sanctions to help create and maintain an institutional environment conducive to grass roots democracy can only provide the *potential* for greater membership participation in union affairs. If those who belong to an organization do not take an interest in the way it is run, one cannot legislate such an interest. In this connection, a recent study of the act concluded that

> further regulation of the internal affairs of unions, will, most likely, produce only diminishing returns in eradicating stubborn areas of union abuse while, at the same time, reducing the democracy inherent in a self-regulating voluntary organization.[3]

The Welfare and Pension Plans Disclosure Act of 1958, as Amended[4]

The rudimentary regulation of health, welfare, and pension funds under section 302 of the LMRA did not eliminate the irresponsible and corrupt practices that accompanied the mushroomlike growth of some of these funds. The Welfare and Pension Plans Disclosure Act of 1958 attempted to ensure the proper administration of these funds by regulating their operations. However, the law did not give the government enough power to investigate qualifying plans, to enforce the disclosure of wrongdoing, or to take remedial action. The provisions of the Landrum-Griffin Act that established the fiduciary responsibility of union officials and amended section 302 of the LMRA were likewise of only modest help.

The Welfare and Pension Plans Disclosure Act was amended in 1962 to give the Secretary of Labor power to investigate reported violations of the act and to enforce it more effectively. Administrators, officers, and employees of welfare and pension plans who handle funds must now be bonded, and detailed operating records must be maintained "on the matters of which disclosure is required." In addition, stealing or embezzling from an employee benefit plan, making false statements or concealing facts in relation to documents required by the 1958 act, and offering, accepting, or soliciting "any fee, kickback, commission, gift, loan, money or [other] thing of value" to influence the operations of an employee benefit plan are now statutory federal crimes. The responsibility for supervising the operation of the act lies with the Office of Labor-Management and Welfare-Pension Reports in the Department of Labor.

The Employment Retirement Income Security Act of 1974 (ERISA)[5]

ERISA established standards for private pension plans that must be *incorporated into* new and existing plans. It is designed to provide *portability* and *vesting* in such plans and to ensure that workers with a specified number of years of service will receive benefits even if a firm ceases operations.* The act tries through favorable tax provisions to expand retirement benefits for employees in small firms without formal pension plans. Under the act,

1. an existing or newly established plan must include all employees with at least one year of service who are 25 years of age;
2. a pension plan must conform to one of three alternative schemes for vesting benefits;
3. plans must meet funding standards designed to ensure that they are actuarially sound;
4. a public corporation insures workers against a loss of benefits of up to $750 a month in the event a firm terminates operations with insufficient assets in its pension fund; and
5. tax deductions may be taken against current earnings for contributions made to pension plans by (a) self-employed persons and (b) persons not covered by private or government pension plans.

ERISA, in combination with earlier legislation, provides needed safeguards for private pension plans and helps to ensure that workers' expectations of receiving benefits under such plans will be realized.

The Occupational Safety and Health Act of 1970 (OSHAct)[6]

The basic provisions of the Occupational Safety and Health Act of 1970 were examined in Chapter 8. The act does not directly regulate collective bargaining

---

* *Portability* refers to a transfer of pension credits to the pension plan of a new employer; *vesting* refers to the right of an employee who leaves a firm before reaching retirement age to receive pension benefits after reaching a certain age if he or she has worked a specified number of years for the firm. The act has a very limited impact on portability.

procedures, but it has far-reaching implications for union-management relations. It authorizes extensive intervention in a firm's operations by federal regulatory authorities to ensure that appropriate safety and health standards are established and observed, and it identifies specific employee and union rights relating to safe and healthful conditions of work.

Since occupational health and safety are intimately related to physical working conditions, they are mandatory bargaining subjects. Employees have never been required to continue working under conditions that endanger their safety or health, and section 502 of the Taft-Hartley Act provides, in part, that refusing to work under abnormally dangerous conditions is not to be considered a strike. However, before the passage of the 1970 act, occupational safety and health were not high priority items in most negotiations, and bargaining demands related to these matters were often traded for economic concessions. Today, this scenario has changed; occupational health and safety have become major issues in many negotiations, and the right to refuse to work under unusually dangerous conditions has assumed unexpected significance.

The OSHAct gives employees the right to participate in the establishment and review of safety standards. An "authorized representative" of a firm's employees may accompany federal officials inspecting working conditions, and no employee may be discharged or discriminated against for exercising rights protected by the act. To date, the act has had a more limited impact than anticipated. However, as Nicholas Ashford points out in *Crisis in the Workplace,* "collective bargaining has the potential to go far beyond the mandates of the OSHAct, by obligating employers to interact closely with workers and not merely comply with government standards."[7]

CONTINUING PUBLIC POLICY PROBLEMS

The next three sections discuss possible changes in our federal law of collective bargaining as it relates to national emergency disputes, the resolution of union-management disputes in rail and air transport, and equal employment opportunity. The first two problems are related and reflect a fundamental conflict between the freedom to engage in strikes and lockouts, which is generally considered essential if disputes are to be resolved by private bargaining, and the need to restrict that freedom to prevent or end work stoppages that threaten the public welfare. This conflict poses a dilemma for lawmakers: "under what conditions can the rights of the public to continued production be said to override the rights of the parties to shut down production?"[8]

National Emergency Disputes

Labor-management disputes that pose an *imminent* threat to public health or safety and disputes in major industries that might, if they continued, have a serious impact on the national economy will not be tolerated.* There is however a continuing debate over the types of statutory procedures that should be available to deal with such disputes. Those at one extreme argue that the existence of such procedures would encourage their use and undermine the collective bargaining process, that strikes or lockouts should not be forbidden except in rare 'true" emergencies, and that the President or Congress should intervene only on an ad hoc basis. Those at the other extreme believe a ban on work stoppages that create national emergencies should be combined with statutory procedures, including compulsory arbitration, for settling critical disputes.

Opponents of intervention perceive "free" collective bargaining (or more properly, the kind of collective bargaining that occurs with our existing regulatory framework) as essentially a power struggle whose outcome depends on the kinds of economic pressure each side can bring to bear on the other. Thus they see strikes and lockouts as instruments for *resolving* disputes. They agree that the right to strike is not absolute, but they do not consider limitations on that right to be, as a rule, in the public interest.** Those who favor statutory procedures for intervention argue that strikes in a number of industries in the private sector and strikes by public employees may harm or inconvenience the public *before* they have any significant effect on the bargaining position of negotiators.

EXISTING LEGISLATION
A variety of existing laws deal with "emergency" disputes. Certain sections of Title II of the Taft-Hartley Act apply to work stoppages in firms engaged in interstate commerce (except those in the rail and air transport industries) that "imperil the national health or safety." The Railway Labor Act applies to disputes in rail and air transport, and all levels of government generally prohibit strikes by public employees. However, an increasing number of states permit strikes by designated categories of public employees in certain circumstances.

DESIGNING NEW LEGISLATION
Legislation to reduce the incidence and duration of national emergency disputes in the private sector should (1) identify "critical" industries in which a work stoppage *may* create a national emergency; (2) set up procedures through which the federal government can help resolve potential emergency disputes through collective bargaining; (3) set up procedures for preventing or ending *specific* work stoppages posing an *imminent* threat to the public welfare; and (4) take into account the long-run interests of both the parties to collective bargaining

---

* The general analysis and many of the conclusions in this section apply to emergency disputes at the local and state levels.

** The extent to which the right to strike is protected by the Constitution is unsettled. Apparently, workers do not have an unqualified right to strike, but a lawful strike in the private sector is generally protected. A strike may be unlawful if it is called for an unlawful purpose or carried out in an unlawful manner.

and the public. Requiring the parties to a dispute to accept the recommendations of a fact-finding panel or to agree to compulsory arbitration may put an end to a work stoppage, but if the "solution" to the dispute does not remove its underlying causes, it may hinder rather than encourage the development of a more constructive bargaining relationship.

It is unlikely that any definition of a national emergency dispute will be operationally useful in all circumstances. Given an open-ended statutory definition of situations likely to create emergencies, however, it should be possible to identify industries, groups of firms, and in some cases single firms whose output is critical enough to warrant a special effort to resolve disputes without work stoppages. Mediators can be assigned to critical industries on a continuing basis, and organizations likely to be involved in emergency disputes can be encouraged to create standing committees to analyze bargaining issues, to begin talks well in advance of contract expiration dates, and to take advantage of whatever government assistance is available. It should also be possible to develop statutory guidelines for intervening in *particular* union-management disputes that pose an imminent threat to the public welfare.

Since some bargaining impasses cannot be prevented, it may be necessary to resort occasionally to *voluntary arbitration*. Until recently, this method of resolving disputes was anathema to supporters of free collective bargaining, but it is beginning to receive wider support. One potential benefit of an arbitration plan is a possible revitalization of the bargaining process because of the negotiators' disinclination to allow outside parties to resolve complex issues.

Experience in the basic steel industry, a somewhat special case, supports this theory. Following World War II, the stockpiling of domestic steel prior to the expiration of contracts had created exaggerated "swings" in employment, and consumers of steel had turned to foreign sources of supply during strikes. To avoid a work stoppage during the 1974 contract negotiations, management and union officials worked out an *Experimental Negotiating Agreement* (ENA) in 1973. The ENA stipulated that the 1974 contract talks must begin well in advance of the August 1 renewal date and that unresolved primary issues would be submitted to an impartial arbitration panel if an agreement was not reached by April 15. Agreement was reached on a three-year contract without resorting to arbitration, and similar provisions for resolving disputes were included in the new contract. In 1977, a contract was again negotiated prior to the ENA deadline. Despite the depressed state of the steel industry the 1980 negotiations were also completed without a work stoppage.

INTERVENING IN SPECIFIC DISPUTES

In peacetime, *national* emergencies are generally created by work stoppages that affect the country's economy or its defense posture rather than the physical health or safety of the population. The circumstances in which an imminent threat to the public welfare may develop cannot always be defined in advance.

The political aspects of a work stoppage must also be considered. If the public *believes* an emergency exists, elected officials will be under pressure to end it even if the danger to the public welfare is remote.

Work stoppages rarely create an immediate threat to the public welfare, and they may be tolerated for a considerable period. An absolute ban on them would be both unnecessary and unwise, since "even in a *critical* industry a strike of moderate duration is not too heavy a price to pay for the preservation of our system of free determination of wages and conditions of employment."[9] There are other reasons for rejecting such a ban. It would alter the economic calculus that is the basis for the private resolution of disputes; it would force negotiators to change their bargaining strategy and tactics; and rather than leading to the resolution of disputes through collective bargaining, it might encourage the use of whatever alternative statutory procedures were provided for the ultimate resolution of such disputes.

It would not be wise to require government intervention in labor disputes at some specified stage of the bargaining process. Instead, the President could be directed to intervene, following whatever emergency procedures are established, when national or international considerations, including the state of the economy, indicate that there is a serious, imminent threat to the national welfare. Alternatively, a statute could mandate the appointment by the President of an ad hoc board to decide if intervention is needed. The present language of Title II of the LMRA would have to be modified only slightly to allow such action.

Once it has been determined that a threatened or actual work stoppage is an emergency, the law should require that production be sustained or resumed for a stipulated period, preferably 60 or 90 days. During this period, the President should have the option of using one or more statutory procedures to end the dispute or of refraining from further intervention if there is a possibility that the dispute may be resolved with the help of government mediators. This "arsenal of weapons" approach, adopted initially and most prominently in the Slichter Act in Massachusetts, has two principal strengths: (1) it leaves the parties to a dispute uncertain about which option the President will choose, and (2) the President can take whichever course of action appears most likely to lead to a constructive resolution of the dispute. Of course, given the political constraints in a particular situation and the "style" of the chief executive, the option selected may be predictable.

The options allowed by law might include (1) a decision not to intervene, at least immediately; (2) the appointment of a fact-finding panel to make recommendations; (3) a recommendation that the parties voluntarily agree to binding arbitration; (4) the partial operation of an essential industry while mediation continues; (5) a decision, subject to the approval of Congress, to resolve a dispute through compulsory arbitration, perhaps by the selection of the last offer; or (6) settlement of the dispute through ad hoc legislation. The last option is always available and may be exercised when other courses of actions have failed.

If the general thrust of our analysis is correct, a drastic overhaul of existing provisions for dealing with national emergency disputes is not necessary. If a major revision of the Railway Labor Act is undertaken, broader restructuring of federal legislation dealing with national emergency disputes should also be considered. Title II of the LMRA could be revised, or a separate statute applicable to all emergency disputes could be devised.

Some experts believe that procedures for resolving emergency disputes should not be prescribed by a statute. They argue that in a "true" national emergency, which occurs rarely, it should be the responsibility of the President to recommend to Congress a way of settling the dispute on an ad hoc basis.

The Railway Labor Act[10]

In Chapter 16, we noted that Congress, using its power to regulate interstate commerce, passed a succession of laws designed to prevent work stoppages on the railroads. The essentiality of rail and, later, air transport has made these industries exceptions to the general presumption that the private and social costs of intervention to avert or end work stoppages in the private sector outweigh the benefits.

Union-management relations in rail and air transport are presently subject to the disputes resolution procedures of the Railway Labor Act of 1926, as amended. This act provides for the resolution of disputes involving contract negotiations (so-called "major" or "interest" issues) in rail and air transport through mediation by the National Mediation Board, and if mediation proves unsuccessful, for (1) the voluntary submission of unresolved issues to arbitration or (2) for fact-finding by ad hoc emergency boards empowered to make recommendations. In the case of rail transport, it also provides for the compulsory arbitration, by panels of the permanent 34-member National Railroad Adjustment Board, of secondary (so-called "minor") disputes that have not been resolved by established grievance procedures. The 1936 *Air Carrier Amendments* to the Railway Labor Act authorized the establishment of a *National Air Transport Board* to resolve secondary disputes in air transport, but the appointment of such a board has not yet been necessary.

The Railway Labor Act does not ban work stoppages in primary disputes, nor does it require that unresolved primary disputes be submitted to arbitration. However, it was assumed at the time the law was passed that most primary disputes would be settled with the assistance of the National Mediation Board and that less tractable disputes would be submitted to arbitration. In rare instances in which it might be necessary to appoint an emergency board, both parties were expected to feel a moral obligation to accept the recommendations of the board.

Prior to World War II, the Railway Labor Act was considered a model law. Between 1926 and 1941, only 17 emergency boards were appointed and there were only two minor strikes. The act has continued to function effectively in resolving "routine" primary disputes; between 1950 and 1969, "nearly 98 per cent of docketed mediation cases [were] resolved without resort to an emergency board."[11] However, since 1941, when President Roosevelt intervened to avert a nationwide strike by the standard railroad unions scheduled for December 7, the act has functioned with considerably less success in critical wage and work rules disputes. There were 17 major strikes (idling 10,000 or more workers) in the rail industry between 1950 and 1969, 12 of which occurred after 1960.[12] Between 1955 and 1969, only 32 of 404 cases that were not settled by mediators, withdrawn, or dismissed, were submitted to arbitrators, and since World War II, railroad unions have generally rejected "adverse" recommendations of emergency boards.[13]

On the other hand, the act functioned more satisfactorily in the early 1970s[14] and on balance seems to have been more of a success than a failure during the first 50 years of its existence.[15] It is not clear whether the act will be as effective in preventing strikes in the 1980s, but it appears that despite the relative decline in the importance of railroads, particularly as passenger carriers, the public will not tolerate a regional or national work stoppage. Consequently, when the procedures dictated by the act do not produce a contract settlement, ad hoc intervention by the President or Congress can be anticipated. In some dozen disputes since the end of World War II, the President has used his "good offices" to bring about an agreement. In several cases, legislation was passed to resolve specific disputes, and on two occasions, President Truman seized the railroads. Intervention in primary disputes became more necessary as bargaining relations in the rail industry deteriorated. Relations between management and the unions worsened as the industry declined in importance and as the unions attempted to preserve work for their members in the face of technological innovations that decreased the roads' need for manpower. Increased competition from the airlines and the trucking industry also made management unsympathetic to any union proposal that raised operating costs.

The reluctance of the parties to bargain seriously before an emergency board was appointed also reduced the effectiveness of private negotiations. A board was almost automatically appointed if there was a bargaining impasse, and the parties were reluctant to make concessions that might serve as a basis for less advantageous recommendations. The length of mediation procedures under the act also discouraged bargaining. There is no time limit on mediation—between 1950 and 1969, the average duration of mediation activities was 184 days, and the longest mediation procedure took 1,118 calendar days. Although emergency boards are supposed to submit a report within 30 days, the average duration of emergency board hearings was 63 days, and the longest hearing took 1,154 days.[16]

A variety of proposals have been advanced to provide more effective procedures for resolving disputes, among them (1) a major revision of the Railway Labor Act, (2) extension of the Title II procedures of the Taft-Hartley Act to rail and air transport and the revision of those procedures along the lines suggested in the preceding section, and (3) the development of a statute applicable to all national emergency disputes, including those disputes in rail and air transport.

Even if no substantive changes were made in the Railway Labor Act, existing procedures could be made more effective by avoiding protracted mediation and extended emergency board hearings. The appointment of emergency boards should not be considered inevitable, and both union and management representatives should be encouraged to bargain seriously well in advance of contract expiration dates. More sensitive issues should be discussed during the life of a contract and not left till the last minute. If more viable bargaining relationships are not developed in the rail industry in the near future, the pressure for some form of compulsory arbitration of primary disputes may become more intense.

Equal Employment Opportunity

In Chapter 9, we examined one of the nation's most critical domestic issues, the persistence of overt and institutional discrimination in employment. In Chapter 17, we noted that the National Labor Relations Board has attacked various types of discrimination in employment as unfair labor practices. We shall now examine the relationship between equal employment opportunity legislation and the law of collective bargaining.

A number of laws prohibit discriminatory employment practices: Title VII of the Civil Rights Act of 1964 prohibits discrimination by employers, unions, employment agencies, and joint apprenticeship committees with respect to compensation and the terms, conditions, or privileges of employment; the 1963 Equal Pay Act Amendments to the Fair Labor Standards Act require employers to pay equal wages to men and women performing equal work under similar working conditions; the Age Discrimination in Employment Act of 1967, as amended in 1978, prohibits discrimination on the basis of age against persons between 40 and 70; and Executive Order 11246, as amended by Executive Order 11375, prohibits discrimination by federal contractors and subcontractors or on federally assisted construction projects; and the Rehabilitation Act of 1973 prohibits discrimination against persons with physical or mental disabilities by employers holding federal contracts of over $2,500.

The Taft-Hartley, Landrum-Griffin, and Railway Labor acts do not address the problem of discrimination in employment directly, and none of the antidiscrimination laws we have just mentioned amends the federal statutes regulating collective bargaining. As a result, inconsistencies may develop in the administration and interpretation of collective bargaining and equal employment opportunity legislation; what is considered "fair" or "equitable" under some acts may be illegal under the Civil Rights Act. For example, under the Taft-Hartley Act, a union is apparently free to have discriminatory membership requirements so long as it represents all workers in a bargaining unit "fairly" on a nondiscriminatory basis; under Title VII of the Civil Rights Act, it is "unlawful . . . for a labor organization . . . to exclude or to expel from its membership, or otherwise to discriminate against, any individual because of his race, color, religion, sex, or national origin."

The failure of Congress to include a Title VII-type ban on discriminatory practices in the Taft-Hartley and Landrum-Griffin acts reflected a consensus that the law of collective bargaining should not regulate the substantive content of union-management agreements and an awareness of political considerations that made it impossible to include civil rights provisions in either act at the time of its passage. By 1964, the political climate had changed, and it was possible to pass legislation banning a variety of discriminatory practices. The result was the Civil Rights Act.

Under Title VII of that act, the recruitment, hiring, training, compensation, transfer, promotion, and dismissal of employees and other rules, procedures, and contract provisions relating to employment must be nondiscriminatory, that is, they must be "blind" as to race, color, religion, sex, or national origin. Standards that appear to be neutral on the suface are not necessarily acceptable; in a leading case, the Supreme Court held that Title VII "proscribes not only overt discrimination but also practices that are fair in form, but discriminatory in operation."[17]

If an employer or a union is charged with unlawful discrimination against an individual, the Equal Employment Opportunity Commission (EEOC) will attempt to mediate the dispute. If no settlement is reached, it may, under a 1972 amendment, initiate a civil action in a U.S. district court to do something about the discriminatory practice. According to the EEOC, "[w]here discriminatory employment provisions or customs exist, both the union and employer are jointly and severally liable" and "a union has the affirmative responsibility, . . . to bargain with the employer to remedy unlawful employment discrimination."[18]

This kind of relief had not been available under the Taft-Hartley Act; the basic thrust of NLRB decisions had been that "discrimination, standing alone, is not inherently destructive of employees' rights under Section 7 of the [National Labor Relations Act]."[19] The NLRB has attacked discriminatory practices by a union by finding that the union was not representing all workers in the bargaining unit "fairly" and was therefore guilty of an unfair labor practice. For a time, it would also disqualify a union as bargaining agent if it engaged in discriminatory practices or was unwilling to take positive action to correct past discriminatory practices, but it has recently discontinued this practice.[20] The board has also held that the elimination of discrimination is a mandatory subject of bargaining.

The machinery for remedying discriminatory acts under Title VII of the Civil Rights Act is independent of remedial procedures available under a collective agreement or state law. A worker or group of workers can seek redress under Title VII *after* using grievance procedures if the *final* decision of the arbitrator goes against them.[21]

There is a distinction between remedying discriminatory practices under Title VII and requiring positive action under Executive Order 11246, as amended by Executive Order 11375. These orders require the Office of Federal Contract Compliance in the Department of Labor to try to ensure that employers who have federal contracts not only do not discriminate but also take appropriate "affirmative action" to correct imbalances in their labor force. This may involve setting *quantitative goals, not quotas*, specifying that certain percentages of a firm's labor force, particular occupational classifications, or various levels of supervisory personnel should be drawn from designated minority groups.

In 1979, the Supreme Court ruled that although the Civil Rights Act did not *require* preferential treatment of minorities to remedy past discrimination, it did not prohibit such treatment. The Court therefore ruled that employers could *voluntarily* agree to affirmative action programs giving special preference to black workers to eliminate "manifest racial imbalance" in traditionally white-only job classifications. Note that this decision permits the correction of racial imbalances that were created *prior* to the passage of the act in 1964.[22]

Initially, many people feared that equal employment opportunity legislation would require drastic changes in traditional employment practices. Major changes have occurred in some cases, but on the whole, the EEOC and the courts have emphasized the elimination of specific practices that have a discriminatory impact rather than the banning of certain kinds of employment practices per se. For example, nondiscriminatory job-related educational requirements and testing procedures may be used to determine whether job applicants are qualified for employment. However, educational requirements and objective preemployment tests that are not job related will be ruled illegal. The Supreme Court has held that in evaluating such practices, "[t]he touchstone is business necessity. If an employment practice which operates to exclude Negroes cannot be shown to be related to job performance, the practice is prohibited."[23] If there is statistical evidence of discrimination in hiring, an employer must prove that its recruitment and hiring practices are fair.

Seniority provisions have been scrutinized closely by the EEOC. Although EEOC determinations and court decisions involving the "neutrality" of seniority systems have not been completely consistent, it appears that segregated seniority lists and lines of progression will be challenged, and if they are found to be discriminatory, they will be ordered replaced by a plantwide seniority system.[24]

The courts have generally supported EEOC attempts to liberalize seniority provisions relating to transfers and promotions, but they have been less supportive of attempts to modify dismissal procedures resulting from "valid" seniority systems. Changes in a "last hired, first fired" standard might require *preferential* treatment for minorities that would deprive employees with long years of service of their basic rights under a collective agreement. The Supreme Court has ruled that layoff procedures set up under a bona fide seniority system that was established before the passage of the Civil Rights Act and was not discriminatory *in intent* will be allowed to stand even if their effect is discriminatory.[25] Title VII provides no relief for employees locked into inferior positions as a result of such long-standing seniority systems, but employees who have been discriminated against since the Civil Rights Act became effective are entitled to various forms of redress, including retroactive seniority.[26] As noted earlier, employers may *voluntarily* agree to affirmative action programs to correct racial imbalances in their labor force.

A SUMMARY COMMENT

As a result of equal employment opportunity legislation, a variety of substantive bargaining issues and related contract provisions that were once considered matters for private determination by the parties to collective bargaining may now be scrutinized by the government. The Taft-Hartley, Landrum-Griffin, and Railway Labor acts should be amended to reflect this change in policy and provide parallel bans on discrimination. Such action will help to eliminate *overt* discrimination, even if it fails to reduce the more pervasive forms of *institutionalized* discrimination.

THE LAW OF COLLECTIVE BARGAINING IN PUBLIC EMPLOYMENT

Both employment and union and association membership in the public sector have experienced rapid growth since World War II. Between 1945 and 1976, when total nonagricultural employment increased by almost 100 percent, from 40.4 to 79.4 million, government civilian employment increased more than 150 percent, from 5.9 to almost 15 million.[27] Federal civilian employment decreased slightly, from 2.8 to 2.7 million; the number of state and local government employees increased from 3.1 to 12.2 million.[28] During the 20 years from 1956 to 1976, when the proportion of employees organized in unions in nonagricultural establishments dropped from a third to less than a quarter, the number of government workers who belonged to unions had increased from 12.6 to 20.1 percent (in 1976, 39.2 percent were members of unions and employee associations).[29] The 1960s were termed "the decade of the public employee." By 1970, 35 years after the passage of the Wagner Act, the percentage of public workers organized exceeded the percentage of workers organized in the private sector. Yet prior to 1959, there was no legislation requiring any government unit to bargain with organizations representing its employees, and today only half of the states have *comprehensive* statutes *mandating* such bargaining.

The Time Lag in the Public Sector

There were independent associations of public employees and some limited activity by unions representing such workers during the nineteenth century and early in the twentieth century, but these employee organizations generally relied on lobbying to improve wages and working conditions. New Deal legislation supporting collective bargaining was limited to the private sector. The disinterest in establishing a similar regulatory framework for public employees reflected a number of factors:

1. the belief that a sovereign government could not delegate or share its authority and was therefore prohibited from negotiating with representatives of its employees.
2. the belief that public employees did not have the right to strike and that political pressure would be more effective than collective bargaining in advancing their interests. Many public employee organizations formally disavowed strikes.
3. the fact that the basic conditions of public employment were established by federal, state, or local legislatures and could be modified in response to political pressure from employee organizations.
4. the development of civil service systems whose structured personnel practices and merit systems presumably assured objectivity in hiring and promotion.
5. the fact that before World War II, public employees enjoyed a degree of job security and a variety of fringe benefits not available to most workers in the private sector. In addition, their wages were often tied to wages for comparable work in the private sector.

The relative deterioration in the position of public workers following World War II was attributed to the gains private sector workers had secured through collective bargaining. At the same time, a number of established unions that were faced with a decline in membership recognized the organizational potential of the rapidly expanding public sector. The competitive threat posed by these unions induced many associations of public employees, including the National Education Association, to try to establish collective bargaining relationships and to assume a more aggressive bargaining posture.

Organizations of public employees usually found it difficult to establish effective bargaining relationships, and although the courts had held that the right of all workers to form and join unions was protected by the First and Fourteenth amendments, public employees, in the absence of supportive legislation, continued to be denied the opportunity to bargain collectively. The first state act giving bargaining rights to public employees was passed in 1959, a quarter of a century after the passage of the Wagner Act. By 1977, 33 states had passed legislation mandating some type of collective "negotiations" for some or all state or local government employees, "four had authorized bargaining by statute for certain groups under restrictive circumstances and one had extended the right by executive order."[30] Similar rights have been extended to federal employees, initially by a series of executive orders and finally by statute as part of the Civil Service Reform Act of 1978.[31] The first such order, in 1962, not only encouraged the organization of employees and collective bargaining at the federal level but gave impetus to the passage of state legislation and the organization of public employees at the state and local levels.

Differences Between the Private and Public Sectors

It is not unreasonable to assume that a process which works well in the private sector may also function effectively in the public sector, and most union officials, as well as many students of union-management relations, believe that the regulatory framework developed for the private sector needs only minor changes to be usable in the public sector. This assumption ignores a number of differences between the sectors, including dissimilar economic constraints and significant political parameters affecting public employment.

Private and public enterprises do not employ an identical economic calculus. A private firm's chief goal is presumably to maximize its profits, given the constraints of the marketplace; a public employer, while necessarily concerned with raising tax revenues to cover expenditures, provides many services for which users are not charged. Services are often provided at a loss, and the government as a whole is not required to operate at a profit. Moreover, many government services are considered essential and would be demanded even if their cost increased substantially.

This is not to argue that economic constraints are inoperative in the public sector; recent events have shown the chilling impact of the "fiscal crunch" facing many municipal and state governments on collective bargaining. In the absence of such crises, a public employer is less subject to the economic discipline characteristic of much of the private sector. The political implications rather than the economic cost of employee demands often dominate the public employer's bargaining calculus, and a strike or a threat to strike has essentially political dimensions.

There are other significant differences:
1. Authority and responsibility are usually more widely diffused in the public sector, and the public management negotiator often lacks authority to conclude an agreement.
2. The frequent turnover of elected officials and their understandable attempts to protect their political base may result in agreements that underestimate or ignore the long-run costs of contract provisions.
3. If unions of public employees are unable to achieve their objectives at the bargaining table, they may use their political muscle to make an "end run" around the public manager or chief executive and lobby for additional concessions from their employer, typically a legislative body. The possibility of such *double-deck bargaining* is enhanced if the legislature is reluctant to delegate decision-making authority to its management negotiators.

4. The scope of bargaining may be limited in the public sector because certain matters are mandated by statute or by civil service regulations.
5. At the other extreme, collective bargaining in the public sector may involve basic policy issues such as class size or length of class period, matters that would be considered managerial prerogatives in the private sector.[32]
6. Determining units appropriate for collective bargaining can be more difficult in the public sector.
7. Finally, the common prohibition against work stoppages by public employees has created a need for acceptable alternatives to strikes to resolve intractable labor-management disputes.

Strikes by Public Employees

The question of whether private sector bargaining procedures are workable in the public sector often reduces to the question of whether public employees can be allowed to strike. Some argue that a ban on strikes undermines the bargaining process by contravening the economic calculus that determines the negotiators' bargaining postures. Actually, this view is simplistic: a different bargaining calculus is operative in the public sector; moreover, bargaining has been effective in jurisdictions in which strikes are forbidden, and alternatives to the strike have been developed in the private sector for situations in which a work stoppage threatens the public welfare.

Prohibitions against strikes by public employees are usually based on one or more of three premises: (1) that the government as a sovereign agent is not required to negotiate with its employees; (2) that public services are by definition essential and that an interruption in such services is automatically a threat to the public welfare; and (3) that when individuals enter public employment, they assume an obligation to provide uninterrupted services. The first and third premises are of secondary importance. If certain public services are not essential and if the workers providing those services have complied with statutory procedures for resolving a bargaining impasse, it would appear appropriate and constitutionally permissible to permit such workers to strike. If essentiality is the criterion in determining whether a ban on work stoppages is appropriate, two questions arise: (1) is it possible to define "essentiality" objectively and in advance and (2) is the public status of an employer a criterion of one category of essential services?

A variety of public services, including garbage collection, security patrols, the provision of utilities, and mass transportation, are provided by *private* firms in many areas. On the other hand, a work stoppage by park attendants, public library workers, or clerical workers in town offices is not an imminent threat to public health or safety. In these circumstances, some experts have argued that the essentiality of a service or a product—not the status of an employer—should determine whether work stoppages are permissible.[33]

Other experts reject the possibility of making such distinctions, arguing for example that the "trouble with allowing the right to strike only in 'nonessential' government services is that the definition of essentiality is extremely difficult and rests primarily on philosophical rather than factual considerations."[34] The public's response to actual work stoppages is often perceptual rather than philosophical. If the public *believes* that an emergency exists, irresistible pressure will be put on elected officials to settle the dispute.

The debate is academic in many respects. Public workers have struck despite statutory bans on strikes, and the most effective stoppages have been by workers supplying essential services. Public employees providing nonessential services may find strikes counterproductive; their pay stops, but the government agency they work for does not usually lose any revenue and there may be little pressure to restore nonessential services. Most jurisdictions continue to ban strikes by public employees, although some dozen states let certain categories of state or local employees strike under certain conditions—for example, if a public employer rejects the recommendations of a fact-finding panel or an advisory arbitration award.

If strikes are prohibited, legal alternatives to a strike must be provided. State laws that authorize comprehensive bargaining by public employees often encourage voluntary arbitration of contract disputes, and 19 states had mandated some form of binding arbitration by the end of 1977.[35] Compulsory arbitration is usually limited to disputes involving specified essential services: typically, police and fire protection. Nevertheless, it represents a considerable departure from the traditional position that the state cannot delegate to a third person the authority to resolve a dispute. Procedures for the conduct of collective bargaining and for the resolution of disputes are increasingly being related to the budget-making process to ensure that money will be available to meet the terms of collective agreements, fact finder's recommendations, or arbitration awards.

Regulating Labor-Management Relations in the Federal Sector

Before 1962, federal employees had the right to join labor organizations that did not strike, and under the Lloyd-LaFollette Act of 1912, postal employees were permitted to lobby individually or collectively. This right was informally extended to other federal employees as well. However, Congress did not *require* that organizations of federal employees be recognized as collective bargaining agents, and federal employees were specifically excluded from coverage under the National Labor Relations Act and the Labor-Management Relations Act.* Most unions and professional associations of federal employees engaged primarily

---

* The LMRA also banned strikes by federal employees. In 1955, Public Law 330 made the act of striking or of asserting that federal employees had the right to strike a felony.

in lobbying, but there were instances of collective bargaining with the Department of the Interior, the Government Printing Office, and the Tennessee Valley Authority.

In 1961, President Kennedy appointed a task force to study labor relations in the federal sector. The report of that task force led to the issuance in January 1962 of an executive order (10988) encouraging the organization of federal service employees. This order was supplemented by two presidential directives in May of 1963. The first established "Standards of Conduct for Employee Organizations" similar to those established for the private sector by the Landrum-Griffin Act; the second established a "Code of Fair Labor Practices" containing provisions similar to the Taft-Hartley Act.

Although these presidential directives were similar in many respects to the legislation regulating collective bargaining in the private sector, there were significant differences. The central, "bread and butter" issues in private negotiations—wages, hours, benefits, and many basic working conditions—are in the case of federal employees established by Congress and not subject to negotiation. Collective agreements also had to include a strong management rights clause that removed additional subjects from negotiation; and since a separate agency was not established to administer the presidential orders, "management" conducted the elections to determine employee representatives and was responsible for administering the Code of Fair Labor Practices. Finally, two types of recognition were allowed in addition to exclusive recognition: *formal* recognition of organizations that did not qualify for exclusive recognition if at least 10 percent of the employees in a unit belonged, and *informal* recognition of organizations which enabled them to "present to appropriate officials [their] views on matters of concern to its members."

In 1967, President Johnson appointed a panel to review Executive Order 10988 and to recommend changes. Although never released officially,* the report of the panel was the basis for many of the recommendations of an informal study group appointed by President Nixon, recommendations that led to Executive Order 11491 in October 1969.

This order replaced Executive Order 10988, the Standards of Conduct, and the Code of Fair Labor Practices. It established a three-member *Federal Labor Relations Panel* and a *Federal Services Impasses Panel*, strengthened the regulatory system established under Executive Order 10988, and generally provided greater parallelism with the procedures, practices, and terminology of labor-management relations in the private sector. It did not expand the scope of public sector bargaining significantly.[36] However, representatives of federal employees were given an advisory role in determining wages under the Federal Pay Comparability Act of 1970, which authorized the establishment of a five-member *Federal Employee Pay Council*. In August of 1971, President Nixon modified Executive Order 11491 by Executive Order 11616, which required that grievance

* A draft of the report was included in the *1968 Annual Report* of the Department of Labor.

procedures for resolving secondary disputes be included in labor-management agreements.

Under the Postal Reorganization Act of 1970, which converted the postal service into a public corporation, postal employees are subject to the representation and unfair labor practices provisions of the Taft-Hartley Act rather than the procedures established under Executive Order 11491.[37] Postal employees are allowed to bargain over wages, hours, and working conditions, but they cannot seek to make union membership compulsory and they cannot strike. Unresolved contract issues must be submitted to arbitration.

Most organizations of federal employees would prefer to be subject to statutory regulation approximating that provided in the private sector, but prior to 1978, Congress was reluctant to pass such legislation, feeling that existing procedures were working reasonably well. With the exception of widely publicized postal strikes and "job actions" by air controllers, there have been few work stoppages by federal employees. There were, for example, only two strikes by federal employees in 1974, none in 1975, one in 1976, and two in 1977. As a quid pro quo for federal employee and AFL-CIO support of the 1978 Civil Service Reform Act, statutory authority for the federal labor relations program was included in that act. Although the provisions dealing with union-management relations did little to broaden the scope of collective bargaining in federal employment,* three agencies were established to administer the government's personnel management function:

1. an *Office of Personnel Management*, in overall charge of the function;
2. a *Federal Labor Relations Authority*, to administer the provisions of the act dealing with union organization and representation and collective bargaining;
3. a *Merit Systems Protection Board*, to hear appeals and grievances with respect to employees who are not represented by unions.

For the present however, the "law" of collective bargaining remains more restrictive in the federal sector than in the private sector or under some of the more comprehensive laws covering state and local public employees.

Regulating Labor-Management Relations in State and Local Governments

As we noted earlier, in the nineteenth century and early in the twentieth century, organizations of employees in the public sector were usually independent associations that engaged in lobbying rather than collective bargaining and recognized that they did not have the right to strike. In some jurisdictions, unions had

---

* According to the management rights section (7106), "nothing in this chapter shall affect the authority of any management official . . . to hire, assign, direct, lay off, and retain employees in [an] agency, or to suspend, remove, reduce in grade or pay, or take other disciplinary action."

organized certain kinds of employees, usually skilled blue-collar workers. However, the American Federation of State, County and Municipal Employees, the first national union for such workers and presently the second largest affiliate of the AFL-CIO, was only chartered in 1936.

Although some de facto collective bargaining was done by associations and unions, the first law mandating bargaining with representatives of state and local public employees was passed in Wisconsin in 1959. The bulk of state legislation regulating collective bargaining by public employees was passed during the decade following the issuance in 1962 of Executive Order 10988 for federal employees. By 1972, 21 states had laws mandating collective bargaining or "discussions" of labor-management issues with all or most municipal and state employees; 15 states, including some of the preceding 21, had separate statutes for teachers; 10 had laws covering firemen or policemen; and other states had laws with more limited objectives.[38] According to the latest Bureau of Labor Statistics survey, as of May, 1979, 38 states and the District of Columbia had statutes or executive orders that provided a legal framework for collective bargaining for some or all of their employees; 23 states and the District of Columbia had comprehensive statutes, 11 states had comprehensive legislation limited to specific groups of employees, and 4 states granted some or all public employees limited bargaining rights.[39]

The considerable increase in the number of *formal* collective bargaining relationships is in part a product of the conversion of independent associations of state and municipal employees, including professional workers, into labor organizations with a more traditional trade union orientation. Many of the associations, whose total membership exceeds *union* membership in state and local employment, are now seeking to be certified as representatives for collective bargaining.

State Legislation

The provisions of state public employee relations laws vary tremendously, and we will not attempt to summarize them here. We shall however make some general observations relating the principal characteristics of these laws to our earlier discussion of the special dimensions of labor-management relations in the public sector.

Basic decisions must be made as to the coverage of such statutes. Should state and local government employees be covered by a single statute, or should the two categories be treated separately? Should all employees in a jurisdiction be covered by the same statute, or should some (members of the police or fire departments or teachers) be covered by separate legislation? A choice must be made between requiring management and employees to "meet and confer" or mandating collective bargaining. A comprehensive statute should protect the right to join labor organizations and to bargain collectively; establish the rights and responsibilities of, and proscribe certain unfair labor practices by, the parties to collective bargaining; assign responsibility for administering the law to an appropriate agency; indicate clearly if the right to strike is proscribed generally or selectively; and provide some alternatives to a strike for resolving intractable disputes.[40]

There is no *federal* legislation regulating collective bargaining in the *nonfederal* public sector. Many existing state laws are more comprehensive than the provisions of the Civil Service Reform Act regulating labor-management relations in federal employment and tend to approximate the preemptive federal legislation regulating collective bargaining in the private sector. Despite pressure from unions and some academics for a federal statute providing "model" minimum standards for regulating labor-management relations in the public sector at the state and local levels, the passage of such legislation appears unlikely for both practical and constitutional reasons.

Some experts believe that legislation cannot be developed that would be appropriate for all jurisdictions. The former chairman of the U.S. Civil Service Commission, for example, concluded that

> the role of bargaining in the public service . . . is not an issue which is susceptible to uniform treatment across the country even in jurisdictions of like form and purpose. . . . The unique characteristics of each community and each jurisdiction are such that case-by-case study and action are required. . . .[41]

In 1974, when the coverage of the Fair Labor Standards Act was extended to state and local government employees, it was believed that this might serve as a precedent for a federal law regulating collective bargaining in the nonfederal public sector.[42] However, the wage and hour amendments were struck down by the Supreme Court on the ground that they did not represent an appropriate extension of congressional power under the commerce clause of the Constitution.[43] The present Court would probably rule similarly in regard to federal regulation of labor-management relations in the nonfederal public sector.[44]

The possibility that more states will pass comprehensive legislation regulating labor-management relations in state and municipal employment has been diminished by growing public and legislative concern over disruptive strikes by such employees and by what has been perceived as irresponsible bargaining demands by the representatives of some of these workers. As for the future, the bargaining confrontations that can be anticipated between municipal unions and employers in financially hard-pressed cities will probably create political environments increasingly hostile to more comprehensive supportive legislation.[45]

SUMMARY

This chapter supplemented the discussion of the general law of collective bargaining in Chapter 17 with a review of other components of the federal regulatory framework, including the Landrum-Griffin Act, the Welfare and Pension Plans Disclosure Act, the Employment Retirement Income Security Act, and the

Occupational Safety and Health Act. It also analyzed three important problem areas in our public policy relating to collective bargaining: the resolution of national emergency disputes, the resolution of union-management disputes in rail and air transport, and the need for equal employment opportunity. Finally, it reviewed the extension of collective bargaining to the public sector and discussed the differences between private and public sector bargaining.

This analysis of the development and present structure of our law of collective bargaining provides an essential framework for the description and analysis of collective bargaining in the chapters that follow.

DISCUSSION QUESTIONS

1. To what extent do the several acts discussed in the first section of the chapter actually impact upon the collective bargaining process?
2. Do you believe that it was logical to include amendments to the Taft-Hartley Act in Title VII of the Landrum-Griffin Act?
3. In your opinion, what constitutes a true national emergency dispute?
4. What are the presumed advantages and disadvantages of the "arsenal of weapons" approach to the resolution of emergency disputes?
5. Do you believe that uniform procedures should be provided for the settlement of all national emergency disputes including those in rail and air transport?
6. Should the Taft-Hartley Act be amended to eliminate inconsistencies with the Civil Rights Act?
7. How have existing seniority systems been affected by Equal Employment Opportunity legislation?
8. What law (or laws) regulates collective bargaining by public employees in the state in which your college or university is located?
9. To what extent is the regulatory framework for private sector bargaining transferable to the public sector?
10. Should public employees have the right to strike? Do any public employees have this right under the law(s) discussed in your answer to question 8?

SELECTED READINGS

The LMRA in Operation

A summary of the first ten years of operation of the LMRA is given in several articles in "The Taft-Hartley Act After Ten Years—A Symposium," *Industrial and Labor Relations Review* 11, no. 3 (April 1958). This "Symposium" and the text of the LMRA were later reprinted as a separate volume.

The Landrum-Griffin Act

Aaron, Benjamin. "The Labor-Management Reporting and Disclosure Act of 1959." Reprinted from *Harvard Law Review* 73, nos. 5 and 6 (March and April 1960). A good early reference.

Bellace, Janice R., and Berkowitz, Alan D. *The Landrum-Griffin Act: Twenty Years of Federal Protection of Union Members' Rights.* Industrial Research Unit, The Wharton School. Philadelphia: University of Pennsylvania, 1979. A basic reference.

OSHAct

Ashford, Nicholas Asrounes. *Crisis in the Workplace: Occupational Disease and Injury, a Report to the Ford Foundation.* Cambridge, Mass.: MIT Press, 1976.

National Emergency Disputes

Aaron, Benjamin. "Collective Bargaining Where Strikes Are Not Tolerated," in Richard L. Rowan, ed., *Collective Bargaining: Survival in the 70's?* Report No. 5, Labor Relations and Public Policy Series. Industrial Research Unit, Department of Industry, The Wharton School. Philadelphia: University of Pennsylvania Press, 1972, pp. 129–153.

Aaron, Benjamin. "National Emergency Disputes: Some Current Proposals." *Proceedings of the Spring Meeting, Industrial Relations Research Association 1971,* in *Labor Law Journal* 22, no. 8 (August 1971): pp. 461–474.

American Enterprise Institute. *Legislative Analysis. Proposals on Emergency Disputes in Transportation.* Washington, D.C.: American Enterprise Institute, June 8, 1971.

The articles in the special section "Exploring Alternatives to the Strike." In *Monthly Labor Review* 96, no. 9 (September 1973): pp. 33–66.

Equal Employment Opportunity

Lopatka, Kenneth T. "Developing Concepts in Title VII Law" and other articles in *Equal Rights and Industrial Relations.* Ed. by Leonard J. Hausman, Orley Ashenfelter, Bayard Rustin, Richard F. Schubert, and Donald Slaiman. Madison, Wisc.: Industrial Relations Research Association, 1977.

Rail and Air Transport

Burgoon, Beatrice M. "The Railway Industry." *Proceedings of the Spring Meeting, Industrial Relations Research Association 1974.* In *Labor Law Journal* 21, no. 8 (August 1970): pp. 491–498.

Eggert, Gerald G. *Railroad Labor Disputes—The Beginnings of Federal Strike Policy.* Ann Arbor, Mich.: University of Michigan Press, 1967.

Kaufman, Jacob J. *Collective Bargaining in the Railroad Industry.* New York: Kings Crown Press, 1954.

"Labor Relations in Transportation." Five articles in *Industrial and Labor Relations Review* 25, no. 1 (October 1971): pp. 3–94.

Lecht, Leonard A. *Experience Under Railway Labor Legislation.* New York: Columbia University Press, 1955.

National Mediation Board. *The Railway Labor Act at Fifty: Collective Bargaining in the Railroad and Airline Industries.* Washington, D.C.: National Mediation Board, 1976.

U.S. Department of Labor, Bureau of Labor Statistics. *Airline Experience Under the Railway Labor Act,* Bulletin 1683; *Handling of Rail Disputes Under the Railway Labor Act, 1950–69,* Bulletin 1753.

Union-Management Relations in the Public Sector

Aaron, Benjamin; Grodin, Joseph R.; and Stern, James L., eds. *Public-Sector Bargaining.* Industrial Relations Research Association Series. Washington, D.C.: Bureau of National Affairs, 1979. The best recent reference.

American Assembly. *Collective Bargaining in American Government.* Report of the Fortieth American Assembly, Columbia University, October 28–31, 1971.

Hildebrand, George H. "The Public Sector." In *Frontiers of Collective Bargaining.* Ed. by John T. Dunlop and Neil W. Chamberlain. New York: Harper & Row, 1967, pp. 125–154.

Jascourt, Hugh D., ed., *Government Labor Relations: Trends and Information for the Future, Vol. I, 1975 to 1978.* Oak Park, Ill.: Moore Publishing Co. and the Public Employment Relations Research Institute, 1979.

Moskow, Michael H.; Loewenberg, Joseph; and Koziara, Edward Clifford. *Collective Bargaining in Public Employment.* Chap. II, pp. 19–79. New York: Random House, 1970.

National Governors' Conference 1967 Executive Committee. *Report of Task Force on State and Local Government Labor Relations.* Chicago: Public Personnel Association, 1967.

Rehmus, Charles M. "Labour Relations in the Public Sector in the United States." In *International Labour Review* 109, no. 3 (March 1974): pp. 199–216.

Roberts, Harold S. *Labor-Management Relations in the Public Service.* Honolulu: University of Hawaii Press, 1970.

Stanley, David T., with the assistance of Carole L. Cooper. *Managing Local Government Under Union Pressure.* Washington, D.C.: Brookings Institution, 1972.

Stieber, Jack. *Public Employee Unionism: Structure, Growth, Policy.* Washington, D.C.: Brookings Institution, 1973.

Taylor, George W. "Collective Bargaining in the Public Sector." In *The Next Twenty-Five Years of Industrial Relations.* Ed. by Gerald G. Somers. Madison, Wisc.: Industrial Relations Research Association, 1973, pp. 27–35.

Twentieth Century Fund Task Force on Labor Disputes in Public Employment. *Pickets at City Hall.* New York: Twentieth Century Fund, 1970.

Wellington, Harry H., and Winter, Ralph K., Jr. *The Unions and the Cities.* Washington, D.C.: Brookings Institution, 1971.

Zagoria, Sam, ed. *Public Workers and Public Unions.* Published for the American Assembly, Columbia University. Englewood Cliffs, N.J.: Prentice-Hall, 1972.

Notes

1. *73 Stat,* 519 (1959).
2. *United States* v. *Archie Brown,* 381 U.S. 437 (1965). The criminal prohibition continues for five years after such conviction or termination of imprisonment.

3. Janice R. Bellace and Alan D. Berkowitz, *The Landrum-Griffin Act: Twenty Years of Federal Protection of Union Members' Rights,* Industrial Research Unit, The Wharton School (Philadelphia: University of Pennsylvania, 1979), p. 317.

4. *72 Stat,* 997 (1958); *76 Stat,* 35 (1962).

5. *88 Stat,* 829 (1974).

6. *84 Stat,* 1590 (1970).

7. Nicholas Asrounes Ashford, *Crisis in the Workplace: Occupational Disease and Injury, a Report to the Ford Foundation* (Cambridge, Mass.: MIT Press, 1976), p. 495.

8. George H. Hildebrand, "An Economic Definition of the National Emergency Dispute," in Irving Bernstein, Harold L. Enarson, and R. W. Fleming, eds., *Emergency Disputes and National Policy,* Industrial Relations Research Association Publication 15 (New York: Harper & Brothers, 1955), p. 4.

9. David L. Cole, "Focus on Bargaining: The Evolving Techniques," in *The American Federationist* 81, no. 5 (May 1974): p. 17. Emphasis added.

10. *44 Stat,* 577 (1926).

11. U.S. Department of Labor, Bureau of Labor Statistics, *Handling of Rail Disputes Under the Railway Labor Act, 1950–69,* Bulletin 1753, p. 1.

12. Ibid., p. 40.

13. Ibid., pp. 33–34.

14. Donald E. Cullen, "Emergency Boards Under the Railway Labor Act," chap. VI in National Mediation Board, *The Railway Labor Act at Fifty: Collective Bargaining in the Railroad Industry,* 1976, pp. 176–183.

15. Charles M. Rehmus, "The First Fifty Years—And Then?" chap. IX in *National Mediation Board, The Railway Labor Act at Fifty,* p. 259.

16. BLS, *Handling of Rail Disputes,* pp. 30–31.

17. *Griggs v. Duke Power Co.,* 401 U.S. 424 (1971), p. 431.

18. William H. Brown III, "Can Collective Bargaining Survive Without Protecting the Rights of Minorities and Women?" in Richard L. Rowan, ed., *Collective Bargaining: Survival in the 70's?,* Report No. 5, Labor Relations and Public Policy Series. Industrial Research Unit, Department of Industry, The Wharton School (Philadelphia: University of Pennsylvania Press, 1972), p. 311.

19. Kurt L. Hanslowe, Laurence J. Cohen, and Evan J. Spelfogel, eds., *The Developing Labor Law: The Boards, The Courts, and the National Labor Relations Act. 1973 Supplement.* Published for the Labor Relations Law Section of the American Bar Association (Washington, D.C.: Bureau of National Affairs, 1974), p. 5.

20. *Forty-Second Annual Report of the National Labor Relations Board for the Fiscal Year Ended September 30, 1977,* p. 25.

21. Cf. Sanford Cohen and Christian Eaby, "The Gardner-Denver Decision and Labor Arbitration," in *Labor Law Journal* 27, no. 1 (January 1976): pp. 18–23.

22. *Steelworkers v. Weber,* Supreme Court Nos. 78–432, 78–435 and 78–436 (June 27, 1979).

23. *Griggs v. Duke Power Co.,* p. 431.

24. A leading case is *Local 189, United Papermakers and Paperworkers, AFL-CIO v. United States,* 416 F. 2d 980, *cert. denied,* 397 U.S. 919 (1970).

25. *Teamsters v. U.S.,* 431 U.S. 324 (1977).

26. "Equal Employment Opportunity," unsigned note in *Labor Law Journal* 28, no. 8 (August 1977): p. 552.

27. U.S. Department of Labor, Bureau of Labor Statistics, *Handbook of Labor Statistics 1978*, Bulletin 2000, Table 42, p. 134. Data from employer payrolls rather than *Current Population Survey*.

28. Ibid.

29. John F. Burton, Jr., "The Extent of Collective Bargaining in the Public Sector," chap. 1 in Benjamin Aaron, Joseph R. Grodin, and James L. Stern, eds., *Public-Sector Bargaining*, Industrial Relations Research Association Series (Washington, D.C.: Bureau of National Affairs, 1979), Table 1, p. 3, based on Bureau of Labor Statistics data.

30. B. V. M. Schneider, "Public-Sector Labor Legislation—An Evolutionary Analysis," chap. 6 in Aaron, Grodin, and Stern, eds., *Public-Sector Bargaining*, pp. 192–193.

31. *92 Stat*, 1111 (1978).

32. Cf. Arvid Anderson, "Public Collective Bargaining and Social Change," in *Report of: Section of Labor-Relations Law, American Bar Association* (Chicago: American Bar Association, 1969), p. 239.

33. Cf. John F. Burton, Jr., "Can Public Employees Be Given the Right to Strike?" *Spring Meeting Industrial Relations Research Association 1970* in *Labor Law Journal* 21, no. 8 (August 1970): pp. 474–475.

34. Benjamin Aaron, "Collective Bargaining Where Strikes Are Not Tolerated," in Rowan, ed., *Collective Bargaining*, p. 148.

35. Kevin J. Corcoran and Diane Kutell, "Binding Arbitration Laws for State and Municipal Workers," in *Monthly Labor Review* 101, no. 10 (October 1978): p. 36.

36. Cf. J. Joseph Loewenberg, "Development of the Federal Labor-Management Relations Program: Executive Order 10988 and Executive Order 11491," in *Labor Law Journal* 21, no. 2 (February 1970): pp. 73–78.

37. Frederick C. Cohen, "Labor Features of the Postal Reorganization Act," in *Labor Law Journal* 22, no. 1 (January 1971): pp. 44–50.

38. Lee C. Shaw, "The Development of State and Federal Laws," in Sam Zagoria, ed., *Public Workers and Public Unions*, published for the American Assembly, Columbia University (Englewood Cliffs, N.J.: Prentice-Hall, 1972), pp. 26–27. For details of this legislation, see Harold S. Roberts, *Labor-Management Relations in the Public Service* (Honolulu: University of Hawaii Press, 1970), pp. 192–301; U.S. Department of Labor, Labor-Management Services Administration, *Summary of Public Sector Labor Relations Policies*, 1976.

39. U.S. Department of Labor, Labor-Management Services Administration, *Summary of Public Sector Labor Relations Policies: Statutes, Attorney Generals' Opinions and Selected Court Decisions* (Washington, D.C.: U.S. Government Printing Office, 1979), p. v.

40. For other views concerning basic provisions that should be included in such legislation, see Charles M. Rehmus, "Labour Relations in the Public Sector in the United States," in *International Labour Review* 109, no. 3 (March 1974): p. 206; and Benjamin Aaron, "Reflections on Public Sector Collective Bargaining," *Spring Meeting Industrial Relations Research Association 1976*, in *Labor Law Journal* 27, no. 8 (August 1976): p. 458.

41. John W. Macy, Jr., "The Role of Bargaining in the Public Service," in Zagoria, ed., *Public Workers and Public Unions*, p. 6.

42. See for example, Hugh D. Jascourt, "Public Sector Labor Relations in 1974," in *Labor Law Journal* 26, no. 5 (May 1975): p. 312.

43. *National League of Cities et al.* v. *Usery,* and *State of California* v. *Usery,* 426 U.S. 833 (1976).

44. Cf. Charles Redenius, "Public Employees: A Survey of Some Critical Problems on the Frontier of Collective Bargaining," in *Labor Law Journal* 27, no. 9 (September 1976): p. 598.

45. Cf. Aaron, "Reflections on Public Sector Collective Bargaining."

Part V
UNION-MANAGEMENT RELATIONS

Chapter 19
THE COLLECTIVE BARGAINING PROCESS

We have analyzed union and management approaches to collective bargaining, and we have described the regulatory framework of collective bargaining. In Part Five, the concluding section of the book, we will describe and analyze the collective bargaining process, the content of collective agreements, and the economic and extraeconomic impact of unions. In this chapter we will describe the collective bargaining process, develop two simple bargaining models, and describe the family of bargaining structures in the United States.

Collective bargaining is the basic mechanism through which American unions advance the interests of their members.* A "good" contract will provide workers with both economic and less easily quantifiable extraeconomic benefits without threatening the continued operation of a firm. For most managers and union leaders, collective bargaining represents an effective and essentially conservative method of resolving conflicts within our existing institutional framework. Although bargaining is done within a regulatory framework, the substantive terms of collective agreements or contracts are not generally subject to government

* Legislation proposed or supported by unions has also helped to advance the interests of their members.

control.* The vast majority of union-management agreements are negotiated without work stoppages. However, since the news media emphasize occasional breakdowns in the bargaining process, the public tends to exaggerate the incidence of overt union-management conflicts.

Critics have charged that accommodations reached by collective bargaining may ignore the public interest. Restrictive work rules, strikes by public employees, "emergency" strikes in the private sector that are perceived as endangering the public welfare, the belief that unions exacerbate inflation by their demands, and the lack of commitment on the part of some unions to civil rights programs have contributed to this negative assessment. The majority of union and management officials probably believe that it is neither their function nor their responsibility to consider the possible public welfare implications of either the bargaining process or the substantive terms of private agreements. They may however find it necessary to address such implications in public statements about contract settlements, and in some highly "visible" bargaining relationships the possibility of government intervention may be a significant bargaining constraint.** The impact of collective bargaining extends beyond matters that may be negotiated privately (as, for example, when cost-of-living adjustments affect the rate of inflation), and this broader impact is relevant in any assessment of the role of unions in our society. We cannot attempt such an assessment yet. We shall do so after we have examined the operational procedures and framework of collective bargaining in some detail.

We have already seen how unions and managements approach collective bargaining and how their actions are constrained by the current regulatory framework. In this chapter, we will discuss the nature of the bargaining process, examine two bargaining models, and describe the principal types of bargaining structures in the American economy. We will analyze substantive contract provisions in Chapters 20–22.

THE NATURE OF THE BARGAINING PROCESS

In Part One, we noted that the development of an acceptable framework within which the web of rules linking workers, management, and work processes can evolve and be modified through time is an imperative of all forms of industrialization. In the absence of unions, such rules may be developed informally in the workplace, more formally by management or the state acting unilaterally, or through some type of combined or pluralistic arrangement. The analysis in Parts One, Two and Three indicated that in the United States market forces did not compel employers to devise employee relations and personnel policies and programs that would satisfy the total economic and extra-

---

* Certain substantive matters are regulated or prohibited. For example, closed shops and hot cargo agreements are prohibited, and the permissible types of union security may be further restricted by state law.
** Bargaining in the public sector is of course inevitably intertwined with the political process.

economic needs of workers. Nor does it seem probable that in the absence of unions, most managements, concerned primarily with the technological and economic constraints affecting operating decisions, would voluntarily devote as much time or energy to the human relations aspects of production.

Collective bargaining compels managers to recognize and adapt to the human resource implications of decision making within the firm. The bargaining process, which is based upon a power relationship, helps to produce an accommodation between representatives of organized labor and management by providing a form of employee participation in the managerial decision-making process in matters relating to the workers' welfare. The representative nature of this form of participatory democracy derives from the need for collective action for such participation to be effective. Union members participate indirectly in two types of decisions: (1) decisions about the substantive contract provisions that will govern the employment relationship for a specified period (called *primary* or *interest issues*) and (2) decisions about the administration (interpretation and application) of those "constitutional" provisions during the life of the agreement (called *secondary issues*).

In addition, some unions engage in a continuing dialogue with management about intractable or complex problems that can be dealt with more effectively when the pressures involved in contract negotiation are not a factor. Disemployment resulting from automation, problems relating to the removal of a plant to a different location, the (re)training of employees because of changes in job requirements, the introduction of more flexible working hours, and improvements in the quality of life in the work environment are some of the topics that have been subjected to continuing study. However, the negotiation and administration of contracts remain the chief subjects of collective bargaining in the United States.

Contract negotiations are conducted periodically and are generally reported in the popular media. Disputes involving contract administration, which are usually resolved informally or through formal grievance procedures, receive little publicity. Continuing dialogues over issues like those mentioned above have received considerable publicity, but the potential scope of this kind of bargaining is unclear.

The *continuous nature* of the bargaining process deserves emphasis. The way a contract is administered on a daily basis affects the security of individual workers, of union leaders, and of the union as an institution. The success with which a contract is implemented from day to day determines the spirit in which future negotiations are approached and, ultimately, the character of an ongoing bargaining relationship.

Effective contract negotiation is also a continuing process: both unions and management must decide their respective demands and lines of resistance in advance of a contract expiration date. Certain technical matters may be settled beforehand, perhaps with expert help, and supplemental agreements covering complex or highly technical matters may be negotiated after the basic contract has been drawn up. Particular provisions may also be modified at a later date.

The development of bargaining demands, bargaining priorities, and a bargaining strategy may require *intra*organizational bargaining among the constituencies of the negotiators.[1] In corporationwide or multiemployer bargaining, differences in the needs and priorities of union members in local plants or individual firms may lead to substantial modifications of master contract provisions.

The Legal Framework of Bargaining

Since the passage of the Wagner Act in 1935, the selection of a representative for the purpose of collective bargaining—a precondition for starting a bargaining relationship—has usually been accomplished through a representation election conducted by the National Labor Relations Board, and recognition of a union is rarely a *bargaining* issue. A union that is the designated bargaining agent for a "unit appropriate" for collective bargaining (that is, the employee unit in which the representation election is held) becomes the exclusive bargaining agent for all the workers in the unit and is charged with representing them without discrimination. In a nonunion plant, an employer may "bargain" with workers under an employee representation plan or bargain voluntarily with a minority union. In discussing collective bargaining generally however, we will assume that the parties involved are an employer or an employer association and an "outside" majority union that is the exclusive bargaining agent for all the workers in a bargaining unit.

Unions and employers are obligated to bargain in good faith about wages, hours, and other terms and conditions of employment, and to incorporate the terms of their agreement in a written contract. As we saw in Chapter 17, the NLRB, subject to court review, determines what is meant by "good faith" and "other terms and conditions of employment." The board has gradually expanded the matters subject to bargaining and recently has required that matters not mentioned in a contract and not specifically excluded from a grievance procedure are subject to arbitration during the life of a contract. Companies dislike such "open-ended" contracts, and many employers have tried to limit the matters subject to such action during the life of a contract.

Collective Bargaining: An Art or a Science?

Collective bargaining is often described as an art. Many issues cannot be resolved by a formula, and "nonobjective" factors, including institutional considerations, the personalities and psychological needs of the negotiators, and conscious attempts to manipulate the attitudes of various groups, may impart emotional overtones to the bargaining process. Nevertheless, the participants do have more or less clearly defined objectives; bargaining is usually done within a framework of identifiable economic, political, and social constraints; and many bargaining issues are dispassionately studied and reviewed. The fact that collective bargaining is generally considered to be charged with drama is a result of the publicity accompanying the negotiation of major agreements and those bargaining situations in which overt conflicts have developed, situations in which the dramatic dimensions of the bargaining process are understandably magnified.

Criticism of the bargaining process often centers on the "Kabuki routine" of union-management negotiations—the unrealistically large initial demands by the unions and the miserly counterproposals by employers inevitably faced with prospective losses or a decline in profits; the attempts to discredit the demands, logic, and integrity of the other side; the lack of progress during early negotiations, which may persist to the final hours of a contract; the apparently final stalemates over one or more basic issues; and the urgent round-the-clock bargaining that precedes last-minute settlements. Finally, with catastrophe averted, the antagonists emerge from a smoke-filled room to face the TV cameras and inform the public that free collective bargaining in the American tradition has produced a reasonable settlement, one that reflects the balanced interests of workers, shareholders, and the public, and one that foreshadows a period of industrial peace. Each group then acknowledges its respect and admiration for its adversary and pledges cooperation in "getting back to work."

Although extreme examples of ritualistic bargaining behavior are less common today, the role playing that is part of the bargaining process is understandable in light of the institutional framework of most bargaining relationships. It may even have constructive and therapeutic functions, since

1. the union leadership, in formulating demands and making concessions, must try to reach a compromise between conflicting membership interests. Such a compromise is often more feasible "under pressure."
2. participation by individual union members, even at a remove, in a "struggle" with their employer provides a release of tensions and frustrations.
3. union members are often more willing to "live with" a hard-earned contract than one that was obtained easily.

As the parties gain experience, a more stable or mature bargaining relationship tends to evolve. In such situations, the theatrical overtones of negotiations may be designed to convince various publics (the firm's stockholders, the business community, local union officials, the union's constituency, or potential government interveners) that a negotiator was not outmaneuvered or that contract terms which might be considered inimical to the public interest either were not, or that they were the necessary price of industrial peace.

Constructive Developments in Bargaining

The publicity given the more dramatic union-management conflicts has obscured a number of developments that have dampened the hostile overtones of many bargaining relationships. For example:

1. Unions now are able to obtain recognition through the ballot box, and the bitterness and personal animosities that often colored the early stages of bargaining relationships in the past do not develop or are attenuated.

2. Most managements have concluded that in view of the legal encouragement given collective bargaining, some sharing of managerial prerogatives with organized labor is unavoidable. In addition, an increasing number of firms recognize that a successful human relations approach to labor-management problems requires some changes in the more traditional process of managerial decision making. By encouraging the "acceptance" of unions, these developments have increased the possibility of a peaceful resolution of bargaining issues.

3. Managers are more aware of the institutional and political pressures on union leaders and are willing to provide some degree of union security in order to have a "responsible" union leadership.

4. An increasing number of substantive contract provisions are "frozen" for long periods and do not have to be renegotiated each time a contract expires. Once a pension or welfare plan has been negotiated, its basic contours usually remain fixed.

5. Because of their complexity, benefit plans and systems of wage payment may have to be studied in advance by specialists, and arguments about their structure are more likely to be resolved by objective evidence. A computer analysis of hundreds of contracts by the Industrial Union Department of the AFL-CIO, for example, has provided valuable supporting data for national and local unions in their negotiations.

6. "Package" agreements and long-term contracts have encouraged more flexibility in bargaining. Variations in the components of a package and the duration of an agreement create a larger number of potential "trade-offs," and union leaders can negotiate contracts broadly similar to basic pattern-setting settlements while still giving their constituents "something different."[2]

7. A sustained high level of economic activity has made many employers more optimistic about long-run economic prospects, and this, together with the more general availability of objective economic data, has narrowed the differences between the economic projections of management and union leaders.

8. The increased willingness of management and union negotiators to use the services of third parties in mediating primary disputes and arbitrating secondary disputes has helped to reduce overt conflict. Allowing a third party to suggest a settlement is often a way of saving face when bargaining positions have hardened.

9. Finally, the establishment of either ad hoc or permanent committees to analyze complex bargaining issues has removed many highly technical and potentially explosive issues from the crisis atmosphere that often accompanies contract negotiations.

To summarize: *collective bargaining* as practiced in the United States is a conservative process. Its objective is to *reach agreement* on the rules and terms of a *continuing employment and institutional relationship* for a specified period, rules that include some method of peacefully resolving differences over the interpretation and application of the substantive provisions of a contract. In the vast majority of cases, the weapons of overt union-management warfare are kept in reserve, to be displayed for an occasional dramatic effect or, more importantly, to remind one's adversary of the cost of failing to reach an agreement.

BARGAINING POWER

Collective bargaining is an exercise of power. The power of each negotiator is an unquantifiable compound of factors relevant to a *given* bargaining relationship, in particular (1) the product and labor market constraints that determine the level at which negotiations occur and whether the agreement will follow a pattern set elsewhere, and (2) the willingness of each side to initiate or endure a work stoppage. Professor E. Robert Livernash has emphasized that basically

> power in collective bargaining is [a function of] the relative willingness and ability to strike or take a strike, however complex the variables may be which determine relative willingness and ability. . . .
>
> There is, however, no very satisfactory theory of power by which one can assess the relative willingness and ability of unions and managements to strike and to take a strike. Nor can the economic consequences of power be clearly separated from market forces.[3]

The union is usually the aggressor in negotiations, giving notice of its desire to discuss the terms of a new contract and presenting a list of demands. Management usually *responds* to union demands, that is, it develops counterproposals; although recently, an increasing number of financially hard-pressed managements, particularly in the public sector, have demanded "give-back" or "take-away" items in return for bargaining concessions. Thus, unions of municipal employees have been asked to have their members assume the employer's share of contributions to pension funds, to exclude overtime earnings from the base used to compute pension benefits, to give up a variety of payments for time not worked, and to increase productivity in various ways. In the construction industry, nonunion competition has forced union contractors to demand that restrictive work rules be changed and that lower wage rates be negotiated for certain types of work, such as the construction of single family homes.

In Chapter 5, we noted that employers and union leaders and members often use different criteria in developing their demands: an employer may think in terms of hourly earnings including overtime; the union leadership, in terms of the standard hourly rate; the membership, in terms of take-home pay. Preliminary discussions or continuing study groups can help to ensure that the negotiators are talking about the same thing. Agreement on the data relevant to a negotiation and on the way the data are to be used will also reduce the likelihood of disagreement. (The U.S. Department of Labor's recent monograph, *The Use of Economic Data in Collective Bargaining*, may be helpful in this regard.[4])

The initial union "shopping" or "grocery" list is usually long. Some of the union's bargaining demands—and management's counterproposals—will be absolutes; some will be dropped or modified in return for an acceptable quid pro quo. Some "throwaway" items are a form of "bargaining camouflage," while other "political" demands, advanced to satisfy pressure from a negotiator's constituency, will be withdrawn "reluctantly" as negotiations proceed. During negotiations, weaknesses are concealed and strengths exaggerated; realistic minimal objectives and "new" operational "trade-offs" may become visible only as the bargaining proceeds, particularly when a strike deadline approaches.[5] To bargain effectively, negotiators must continually estimate the relative strength of each side. They must also estimate their opponents' estimate of the balance of power. Bargaining priorities and strategies are necessarily interdependent and are subject to modification on the basis of developments during negotiations. By raising their opponent's estimate of the cost of a work stoppage, skilled negotiators can in effect "create" additional bargaining power.

One of the basic initial objectives of a negotiating team is to discover the "true" bargaining priorities of their opponent, particularly those demands the opponent believes must be met to avoid a work stoppage. Until these demands have been identified, the parties will be reluctant to bargain over important substantive issues. Experienced negotiators try not to reveal their true preferences prematurely because this might permit their opponents to make unexpected gains. Under these conditions, collective bargaining requires a "large" initial demand, since

> initial demands must permit what is frequently termed "room for bargaining," and this the large demand does. Such demands set up a context in which information can be gained during the course of negotiation to elect a firm strategy.[6]

The bargaining process helps to identify the "sticking points" of the negotiators, that is, the maximum concessions that can be obtained or the minimum concessions that must be made to avoid a work stoppage. If a negotiating team is committed to one or more demands that it is unwilling to alter, it should be flexible concerning other issues. It should be understood that until the entire contract has been "wrapped up," any agreement on specific substantive issues is only tentative.

A new contract is expected to represent a net gain for union members. If one or more existing contract provisions are modified unfavorably, it is usually assumed that this fact will be offset by improvements elsewhere in the contract. If a firm faces an economic crisis or if the economy is depressed, a union may find it difficult to obtain other than token concessions, and in extreme cases it may be forced to agree to "give-backs" to preserve job opportunities. In such situations, the ritual of negotiations and minor contract modifications may help union leaders to "save face."

BARGAINING MODELS

Economists have tried to develop various collective bargaining models capable of generating reliable predictions. The *Hicksian model,* which relates an acceptable wage to the length of the potential work stoppage required to reach an agreement, and the *bilateral monopoly model* are frequently used by theoretical economists to show how wages are determined under collective bargaining.[7] The preceding discussion suggests why these and other attempts to develop predictive models have not been entirely successful. Bargaining involves individual and institutional economic, political, and social goals, many of which are difficult if not impossible to quantify. Each bargaining relationship and each negotiation is to some degree unique, and this complicates the problem of developing a theory that can be generally applied. Even if the statistical data relevant to a specific negotiation can be identified, a determinate *ex ante* solution will elude the theorist, since the negotiators' valuations and bargaining objectives will be modified during the bargaining process by their *changing estimates* of the opponents' possible actions.[8] Moreover, the fact that the bargaining process is also used to satisfy the personal (psychological) needs of the negotiators can lead to apparently "irrational" actions.[9]

Game theory has been applied to a variety of situations involving the resolution of conflicts, including industrial relations. It will probably provide a foundation for operationally useful union-management bargaining models at some future date, though it has yet to produce a generally accepted model. Walton and McKersie for example, use the theory to help explain distributive bargaining and integrative bargaining, two of the four "systems of activity," that they believe illuminate conflict resolution in union-management negotiations.[*10]

Despite the absence of a generally acceptable bargaining model, two simple models are available that provide an adequate framework for analyzing union-management negotiations at the introductory level and suggest, within limits, the possible outcome of such negotiations. These are the *range theory* described briefly in Chapter 5 and Professor Neil Chamberlain's analysis, which incorporates his concept of bargaining power.[11] The weapons available to unions and management described in earlier chapters provide the coercive underpinnings for these models.

---

* *Distributive bargaining* refers to activities used to attain one party's objectives when they conflict with the objectives of one's opponent; *integrative bargaining* refers to situations in which a solution can benefit both parties or where one party's gains are not offset by equal losses by one's opponent. The other processes are attitudinal structuring and intraorganizational bargaining.

Bargaining in the Public Sector

As we saw in Chapter 18, there are important differences between bargaining in the private and public sectors—different economic constraints on the negotiators, prohibitions or restrictions on strikes by public employees, the fragmentation of bargaining units in the public sector, a lack of authority on the part of negotiators for public entities to make commitments, and political overtones to negotiations in the public sector.

Political rather than economic constraints may be more persuasive in the public sector, and power relationships may depart significantly from those in conventional private sector bargaining models. Thus, public sector negotiators would have to make considerable modifications in the bargaining calculus in each of the models described below.

A Simple Range Theory of Bargaining

The range theory we shall describe here assumes that the union leadership wishes to (1) perpetuate the union as an institution, which usually requires that the firm or firms it is dealing with continue to operate at a profit, and (2) secure certain essential improvements in its contract. It also assumes that management wants a "stable relationship with the union on terms that permit the firm to be competitive and to adapt to changing conditions."[12]

Let us assume that the union leadership has formulated a set of goals that it would like to obtain and that it believes it could conceivably obtain; these will be *maximum* objectives. It will also have another set of objectives that it believes it must obtain; these will be its *minimal* objectives. Management meanwhile will have formulated a *minimal package* of concessions it believes it must make to maintain an adequate supply of workers and another package containing the *maximum concessions* it believes it can grant and still operate at a profit. The demands of each negotiating group may also reflect pressures from their own side and their personal goals.

The union and employer minima (the lower limits on what they will accept or offer) will be based on conditions in relevant product and labor markets, applicable legal minimum wage provisions, benefit schedules under unemployment compensation, and various institutional considerations, including *coercive comparisons* (contract gains negotiated elsewhere that are used as bench marks in bargaining). Comparisons may be made with settlements reached by other firms in the same industry or labor market or by other unions that are viewed as rivals in terms of leadership of the union movement or for prestige. The minima will also take into account the estimated costs of failing to reach a settlement, that is, the cost of a work stoppage.

If the employer's maximum offer (which is unknown to the union) is equal to or greater than the union's minimum demands (which are unknown to the employer), a contract can theoretically be negotiated without a work stoppage.

If there is a gap between the employer's maximum offer and the union's minimum demand, an agreement cannot be reached unless as a result of bargaining a change is made in one or both bargaining packages. The possible family of demands and concessions can be visualized as falling along a continuum extending above the "cost" of the present contract, or in the case of an initial contract, above the existing employment costs. "Hourly labor" cost estimates based on a total package of demands and concessions are a useful measuring rod in negotiations.

The range theory may be represented by a diagram, as in Figure 19.1. If there is an overlap between the employer's maximum offer and the union's minimum demands, there is a *bargaining range* within which a contract can be reached. If there is no overlap (if Umin is greater than Emax), there will be a work stoppage unless the bargaining process, by shifting one or both of these limits, creates an overlap.

Even if a bargaining range exists, there is no guarantee that a work stoppage will be avoided. The negotiators for each side are unaware of the exact location of their adversary's "sticking points" (the union's minimum and the employer's maximum), and they may erroneously conclude that the two do not overlap. A deterioration in union-management relations during the bargaining process may also make compromise difficult and create a deadlock. In such situations, the bargaining process is not functioning effectively—an agreement is not being reached although a settlement is theoretically possible.

The range theory does not predict where, within a range of potential settlements, a final settlement will fall. The bargaining power and skill of each negotiating team and the impact of the negotiations on their expectations and tactics will shape the terms of the contract. Probably, the more competition

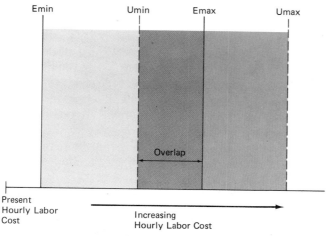

Figure 19.1 A Simple Range Theory Model

there is in product or labor markets (other things being equal), the narrower the range of indeterminateness will be. The bargaining range will also be smaller when industry contracts follow a pattern.

The range theory has both descriptive and predictive value; institutional as well as economic variables can be incorporated into the model, and it can be made responsive to what are often crucial short-run bargaining pressures. Whether it should be considered a determinative theory because it reveals a potential bargaining range or indeterminative because the precise cost of the final settlement and of the trade-offs made to achieve it cannot be predicted is largely a matter of semantics. In either case, the theory reflects the basic forces affecting most collective bargaining relationships.

Chamberlain's Bargaining Power Theory

Chamberlain has developed a theory of bargaining power based on the ability of negotiators to induce their adversaries to agree to their terms. In terms of a simple economic calculus, each party will compare the (estimated) cost of disagreeing to the (estimated) cost of agreeing to the opponent's terms to find out if an agreement is possible. If the cost of agreeing for one or both sides is equal to or less than the cost of disagreeing (that is, if the ratio of the cost of disagreement to the cost of agreement is equal to or greater than 1), the parties should be able to reach a mutually satisfactory agreement. If the cost of disagreeing is less to both parties than the cost of agreeing, they will not agree, and unless a third party intervenes in the negotiations, there will be a work stoppage.

During negotiations, a settlement becomes more likely as the cost of agreeing to the other side's terms is lowered or the cost of disagreeing is raised. If a union grants a concession that makes it less costly for an employer to agree to its terms, or conversely, if it succeeds in convincing the employer that a strike is probable (thereby raising the cost of rejecting its demands), the likelihood of reaching a settlement increases. As a contract expiration date approaches and the possibility of a strike or lockout becomes more likely, each party's estimate of the cost of disagreement tends to rise, improving the prospect for a settlement.[13]

Again, a work stoppage may occur despite the fact that a settlement is presumably possible (i.e., despite the fact that for at least one side, the cost of disagreeing exceeds the cost of agreeing). The stoppage may be due to a miscalculation or to a hardening of positions. Two types of miscalculations are possible: the union may underestimate what it will cost the employer to agree to the union's terms or overestimate the cost of rejecting them, and the employer may underestimate the cost to the union of agreeing to the company's offer or overestimate the cost of refusing it.

Both this bargaining theory and the range theory emphasize the modifications in bargaining goals and lines of resistance that occur during negotiations, and both recognize that a work stoppage may occur when agreement is possible, due to miscalculation or misunderstanding. If this occurs, and a negotiator's public posture or relevant institutional constraints make a retreat from a stated position impracticable, mediation can be of great value by shifting the onus for modifying a bargaining stance to an outsider.

WORK STOPPAGES AND COLLECTIVE BARGAINING

Strikes and lockouts are the ultimate sanctions available, respectively, to unions and employers. Lockouts are relatively infrequent in the United States because employer intransigence in negotiations is likely to induce a strike. As a result, criticisms of work stoppages have usually been directed at strikes. A strike or a lockout is popularly considered the result of an inability to resolve differences by bargaining. In practice, the cost of not reaching an agreement is a basic ingredient in the negotiators' bargaining calculus, and the possibility of a work stoppage is an essential element of our system of collective bargaining. In a sense, "the few strikes that take place are . . . the cost of the strike option which produces settlements in the large mass of negotiations."[14] The avoidance of overt conflict is not always to be equated with a "sound" bargaining relationship; by making unnecessary concessions or tolerating uneconomic work practices, a firm's management may pay too high a price for industrial peace.

An occasional work stoppage may even have a therapeutic value. If the negotiators have never experienced a strike or a lockout, or if the impact of such an experience has been dimmed by the passage of time, management and union estimates of the cost of a work stoppage may depart substantially from reality. In such circumstances, a strike or lockout may produce a more constructive approach to future negotiations by revealing or reemphasizing the economic constraints on bargaining demands, strategies, and tactics.[15]

The right to strike or lock out employees is not absolute in a free society. However, these rights should be circumscribed only when their exercise would pose a clear threat to the public welfare. It is better to risk a strike in borderline cases than to attempt a restructuring of basic labor laws that might destroy a bargaining calculus proven effective in the great majority of cases.

RATIFYING AGREEMENTS

Once negotiations have been successfully concluded, the actions of the negotiators must usually be ratified before a contract becomes effective. In most cases, top management has already approved the actions of its representatives, and they are authorized, within limits, to commit the firm to an agreement. Union negotiators usually lack such authority, and a contract proposal must generally be submitted to the membership or a representative body of members for ratification.[16] The vast majority of agreements are ratified without significant opposition.

During the 1960s there was an increase in the number and proportion of contract rejections. Dissent was encouraged by a number of factors, including attempts by local union leaders and members to offset the increasing centralization of collective bargaining in the hands of national leaders, failures to resolve problems involving local plant work rules and working conditions, the encouragement given union members to act autonomously by the Landrum-Griffin Act, and an increase in the number of younger union members who disagreed with the bargaining priorities of their leaders. However, a study of contract rejections in Louisville, Kentucky, between July 1966 and November 1969 showed "that the traditional concern of the union member about economic factors [was] the primary causal element in the rejection of tentative settlements."[17] This continues to be the case. Recent contract rejections have reflected membership dissatisfaction with provisions that did not offer enough protection against inflation or, in cases where the introduction of new technology or the closing of certain plants was an issue, with provisions dealing with termination allowances and pension plans.

SUPPLEMENTAL AGREEMENTS

After the terms of a basic contract have been ratified, it may be necessary to negotiate supplemental agreements covering welfare plans, incentive methods of wage payment, or local work rules and working conditions.[18] The varying priorities of different groups of members often influence the terms of these supplemental agreements. However, the practice of negotiating local supplements after a basic contract has been worked out may pose a serious problem: should workers be permitted to strike over local issues? The possibility that they will do so enhances the bargaining power of local unions, and if such strikes are permitted, they may encourage management and national union leaders to try to solve local problems before bargaining on national issues.[19]

THE CONTENT OF COLLECTIVE AGREEMENTS

Under our law of collective bargaining, negotiators are not required to reach an agreement on any issue, but once an agreement has been reached, it must be put in writing. The basic agreement plus supplemental agreements and significant contract interpretations under the grievance procedure make up the substantive portion of the web of privately negotiated rules that govern the employment relationship. The contents of the over 190,000 contracts in effect in the United States defy description. However, there are broad similarities among most contracts, and identical provisions are often found in contracts covering a single firm or industry, or the members of a particular union or group of unions in a given industry or dealing with the same employers. The contracts of craft unions are usually less detailed and less comprehensive than those of industrial unions.[20] Collective agreements in the United States typically cover the following topics:[21]

1. *recognition of the union* as the exclusive bargaining agent for the workers in the unit appropriate to collective bargaining.
2. *the duration of the agreement* and the giving of *advance notice* if a change in terms is desired.
3. *union security arrangements.* These provisions generally require that workers join the union, that dues be checked off, and that basic union rights be protected. An increasing number of contracts also specify that employees must be admitted to membership in the union without discrimination.
4. *managerial rights* or prerogatives. Contracts may also contain waiver clauses in which the union agrees not to bargain about "new" items during the life of the contract. These can be considered *management security* provisions.
5. *wages and hours,* including, in some cases, procedures for establishing and regulating incentive systems of wage payment. Rate structures and incentive systems are often complex and may be covered by supplemental agreements.
6. *payments for time paid for but not worked,* including vacation and holiday pay.
7. *individual security.* In addition to seniority provisions, there may be other protective provisions relating to such matters as promotions, layoffs (furloughs), discharges, transfers, and military leave. There may also be clauses protecting employees from the effect of technological change.
8. *a formal grievance procedure* that protects individual employee's rights under the contract by establishing rules for resolving questions about its day-to-day administration. Grievance procedures often produce a type of "continuous" collective bargaining; they provide a way of "bending" the terms of a master contract to meet the requirements of a local bargaining relationship, and they establish procedures for making essential modifications in substantive provisions during the life of the contract.
9. *working conditions,* including local departures from practices specified in a master contract.

Contracts with craft unions may also contain provisions relating to *apprenticeship training* and a description of the *union's jurisdiction,* including a definition of *work claimed.* A variety of employee *welfare plans* may be set up to assure individual workers of security while they are employed, when they are furloughed, and when they retire. Such plans are often complex, and they may not be subject to major annual revision. Detailed provisions of these plans may be included in separately negotiated supplemental agreements rather than a general contract.

Table 19.1 shows the principal matters covered in the current (1979) three year contract between the United Auto Workers and the General Motors Cor-

Table 19.1 TOPICS LISTED IN PRINCIPAL CONTRACT HEADINGS IN THE GENERAL CONTRACT BETWEEN THE GENERAL MOTORS CORPORATION AND THE UAW

Recognition, including union security, the checkoff of dues, and a management rights clause
Representation
Grievance procedure
Seniority
Disciplinary layoffs and discharges
Production standards
Call-in pay
Working hours
Wage payment plans
Union bulletin boards
Establishment of new plants
Wages
Leaves of absence
Strikes, stoppages, and lockouts
Skilled trades and apprenticeships
Vacation pay allowances
Holiday pay
General provisions
Pension plan, insurance program, the supplemental unemployment benefit plan and employee stock ownership plan. (This is a general reference provision noting that agreements covering these four subjects are supplements to the general contract.)
Waiver
Plus: Appendices and various interpretations of specific contract clauses.
Statements, and letters included for information

SOURCE: Based on the *Agreement Between General Motors Corporation and the UAW, September 14, 1979.*

poration. The increasing variety of contract provisions and the often intricate relationships between specific provisions resulting from package settlements have made the negotiating process more complex. However, as we have noted before, the increase in the number of potential trade-offs may also make it easier to reach a settlement.

COLLECTIVE BARGAINING STRUCTURES IN THE UNITED STATES

The concept of a *bargaining structure* is used to show, basically, "who bargains with whom over what." In analyzing the broad spectrum of bargaining relationships, it is helpful to note:

1. *the active participants in the bargaining process,* who may vary with the issues under negotiation.
2. *the size and scope of the bargaining unit,* which normally reflects the nature and extent of relevant product and labor markets. As a rule, craft

unions are more likely to be sensitive to labor market parameters and industrial unions to product market parameters.

3. *the locus of power in a given bargaining relationship,* the distribution of decision-making power *within* each bargaining group, and the influence of the government on decision making in cases where government representatives try to influence the negotiators, either informally or through established procedures.[22]

4. *the substantive issues* in a negotiation.

5. possible *interrelationships between bargaining units* in the same firm, locality, industry, region, or industrial sector. There is a distinction between (1) *structured* formal and informal bargaining relationships and (2) *coercive comparisons* that may affect negotiations.

Despite the wide variety of bargaining relationships in the United States, the major types of bargaining structures are fairly easy to identify.[23]

Bargaining Units

To analyze a bargaining structure, we must identify the units on whose behalf bargaining is carried on. The concept of a single bargaining unit is often an oversimplification; in actuality, "a given bargaining structure [may be] comprised of a *multiplicity of units* tied together in a complicated network of relationships by social, legal, administrative, and economic factors."[24]

The legal "unit appropriate to collective bargaining" is an *electoral* unit; bargaining may be conducted at the same level, at a higher level, or, less frequently, at a lower level. A union selected by workers in separate plant elections may bargain with the corporation owning all the plants or with an association of several employers. Conversely, even though a union has been selected as a bargaining agent in a corporationwide election, certain substantive issues may be negotiated at the plant level. Unions bargaining with the same employer or with a group of employers in the same industry may cooperate informally or conduct formal joint negotiations.

In determining an "appropriate unit," the National Labor Relations Board tries to select one that has "a coherent and recognizable community of interest" and is "capable of carrying on successful bargaining."[25] Once an appropriate unit has been identified by the NLRB, the *electoral* unit tends to remain fixed even if different units are later identified in the same industry because of changes in the industry's structure, the content of jobs, or technology.[26] Craft severance elections are an exception; recent NLRB decisions have made it easier for "traditional" crafts to petition for severance from a larger electoral unit. This possibility has made industrial unions more responsive to the needs of craft groups within established bargaining structures.

Unions often prefer to bargain with all employers competing in the same product market. This lets them "take wages out of competition" and helps ensure that no firm has a competitive advantage because of submarginal employment standards. (Uniform wage rates may not guarantee such a situation, of course, if differences in productivity create differences in unit labor costs.) When a powerful union bargains with several small (marginal) firms, some of them may be presented contracts on a take-it-or-leave-it basis. They are then under pressure to combine to increase their own countervailing power.

On the employer side, a bargaining unit may be a single plant, a single employer with more than one plant, an informal or formal group of employers in a single industry, or, infrequently, a local or regional group of employers from different industries. Single industry multiemployer units may be further subdivided geographically (into local, regional, or national units) and economically (according to the extent of their product market coverage).

Analyzing a bargaining structure in terms of specific bargaining issues is more complex. A corporationwide or unionwide "package" may be negotiated, but the allocation of increased labor costs to wage increases and improvements in fringe benefits may vary between different plants of a given firm or between different firms dealing with the same union. On the other hand, locals of the same union (or perhaps of several national unions) may bargain independently on most contract items but negotiate uniform welfare benefits. (Some building trades unions, for example, negotiate areawide welfare plans.)

Public policy toward bargaining structures has been "permissive." Once recognized, "[a] union may develop a coordinated bargaining structure, combining [electoral] units in whatever way seems most advantageous for its bargaining strategy," while employers "have been permitted a wide measure of discretion in their response to patterns of labor organization."[27]

Areas of Impact of Contract Negotiations

There may be a distinction between the *formal area of coverage* of a contract and its *effective area of impact*. The provisions of an agreement may be copied by other firms with which the union deals, by nonunion firms competing in the same product or labor market, or by other firms for whom the contract, for other reasons, provides a pattern. In the basic steel industry, recent contracts covering production and maintenance workers have been negotiated with eight to eleven major producers, although separate contracts have been signed by each firm, and the provisions of these contracts have served as a pattern for contracts negotiated with other basic steel producers, other steel producers, and firms in other industries with which the union bargains. They thus have a unionwide area of impact. In the automobile industry, the major producers prefer to negotiate individually with the UAW, although their contracts traditionally conform to the pattern established by an initial settlement with one of the "Big Three."

The *geographical* coverage of a negotiation must not be confused with the proportion of a *product market* it covers. A multiemployer contract covering all or most of the employers in a local market industry is an industrywide agreement in terms of its economic impact; a national agreement covering the employees of only one of several major corporations producing for a national market is not industrywide in its impact. If all the firms producing for a national market conform to a pattern established by a basic contract, the area of impact is both national and industrywide. Many employers producing for national markets believe that national union officials have a better grasp of industry problems than local leaders and are less likely to press for "irrational" demands that might jeopardize the competitive position of the firms with which they negotiate.

Types of Bargaining Structures

The family of bargaining structures in this country is shown in Figure 19.2. Multinational alignments of both union and management negotiators are possible, although to date, there have been no significant multinational contract negotiations involving American firms or unions. Within a given firm, industry, or union, structural alignments may vary with the substantive issues under negotiation, and any structural type may set a pattern that expands the area of direct impact of the negotiations.

Accurate data on the extent of these types of bargaining structure are not available, but a majority of the more than 190,000 collective agreements in the United States seem to be negotiated with single employers. According to a BLS survey, some 58 percent of 1,536 major agreements (agreements covering more than 1,000 workers) in effect in 1978 were with single employers.[28] Slightly over 27 percent of the contracts, covering nearly 15.5 percent of the workers, were single plant agreements; 30.5 percent, covering 38.6 percent of the workers, were multiplant single employer agreements; the remaining 42 percent, covering 46 percent of the workers, were multiemployer agreements.[29] Despite the large number of multiemployer agreements, there are few truly industrywide agree-

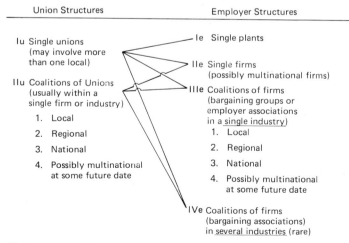

Figure 19.2   The Family of Bargaining Structures in the United States

ments in the United States—that is, few agreements that have as signatories all the employers producing for the same market. In some cases, resistance to formal *industrywide* bargaining is apparently based on a belief that it might invite an antitrust action or that the shutdown of an essential industry would inevitably lead to governmental intervention.

Multiemployer bargaining usually involves relatively small companies. It is more frequent outside the manufacturing sector and in local market industries. In 1978, only 130 of 648 multiemployer agreements noted by the BLS involved manufacturing concerns.[30] Single employer multiplant or corporationwide bargaining is more frequent in manufacturing and among larger firms producing for national markets.

Unions and managements try to develop the type of bargaining structure most likely to maximize their bargaining power. A formal multiemployer bargaining agreement is usually initiated by a union. However, in highly competitive (typically, local market) industries with many small firms, employers may try to bargain as a group to stabilize labor costs and prevent whipsawing.

As a product market expands, a union is likely to try to expand the negotiating unit to maintain a rough correspondence between the two. The development of local, then regional (conference), and finally national agreements in the over-the-road trucking industry is one example of such a response to changes in the structure of a service industry.[31] The large firms in concentrated (oligopolistic) industries are usually reluctant to enter into formal joint bargaining arrangements, although they may be willing to conform to the pattern set by a key negotiation. Sometimes external forces may encourage multiemployer bargaining. During World War II, for example, the National War Labor Board asked for joint presentations from the steel companies in the "Little Steel Case." This was the first instance of *formal* industrywide negotiations in the steel industry, although the steel companies had generally conformed to wage and benefit patterns set by U.S. Steel.

Types of Multiemployer Bargaining

Multiemployer bargaining, by either a formal employers' association or an informal bargaining alliance, takes on various forms. There are three basic types of *formal, national* multiemployer bargaining:

1. Bargaining over a single contract covering all or most of the firms in an industry with a national market. This is rare, but it occurs, for example, in the wallpaper industry and the interregional over-the-road trucking industry. Before the development of strip mining in the West, the bargaining between the United Mine Workers and the Bituminous Coal Operators Association covered a significant portion of the firms in the bituminous coal industry.
2. Bargaining that is national but not industrywide. This occurs when a

significant portion of the firms in an industry do not participate in bargaining over the master contract. Depending on how many firms follow the pattern set by the master contract, this kind of bargaining may come to resemble bargaining over a single contract. It occurs today in the basic steel, bituminous coal, men's clothing, and glass container industries.

3. National bargaining by certain firms or groups of firms within a limited industrial sector or for certain types of operations within an industry. In the building and construction industry, "national" agreements have been negotiated between national unions and large contractors who operate nationwide or worldwide.

In addition to these formal types of multiemployer negotiations, there is probably considerable informal discussion of pattern-setting contracts by firms in an industry even when negotiations are only companywide, and considerable cooperation may occur. This is probably the case, for example, in the rubber tire, automobile, meat-packing, and nonferrous metal mining industries.

Multiemployer bargaining systems have developed at the regional and local level in a variety of more highly competitive industries including the longshore, trucking, building and construction, and hotel and restaurant industries.

Some observers have charged that because multiemployer bargaining expands the area of possible work stoppages, it poses a threat to the public welfare. It has also been criticized as increasing the monopoly power of unions and of unions and employers who may cooperate in reaching settlements that are not in the public interest. Other disadvantages that have been pointed out include the tendency of high level negotiations to disregard local problems; the loss of democracy inherent in the centralization of bargaining in the hands of a small group of professional negotiators; and possible distortions in local wage patterns when agreements are reached that do not take into account the economic environment of particular bargaining relationships.[32]

Although these charges contain elements of truth, they overlook a number of factors which suggest that the adverse impact of this type of bargaining is exaggerated and that in some cases attempts to limit bargaining to a single employer may be more detrimental to the public interest. The prohibition of multiemployer bargaining in highly competitive local market industries, for example, might enable a strong union to select a particularly vulnerable initial target and then impose the costly resulting package on the other firms in the industry. Rapid increases in construction workers' wages in the early 1970s, for example, were blamed in part on the failure of employers to maintain a united front in negotiations with various building trade unions. In short, atomistic bargaining may not be practicable for many small employers, and a ban on multiemployer bargaining may complicate bargaining procedures in a way costly to individual firms. A House subcommittee investigating the impact of multiemployer bargaining in 1964 reported that an overwhelming majority of labor and management witnesses believed its advantages outweigh its disadvantages.[33]

Bargaining structures are responsive to changes in the economic environment. A recent example is the development of coalition bargaining by unions to neutralize the bargaining power of a large diversified firm negotiating with a number of national unions. Not unexpectedly, most corporations have resisted the efforts of unions to bargain as a group or to have representatives of other unions sit in on negotiations. Nevertheless, coordinated bargaining by unions appears likely to become more common, particularly in negotiations with conglomerate firms. This may encourage an eventual merger of national unions bargaining with the same firms.

BARGAINING RELATIONSHIPS

Collective bargaining relationships may be classified according to their basic *character* as well as their structure. The character of a specific bargaining relationship reflects its history; each party's view of the functions of unionism and collective bargaining (which may be related to the bargaining approach, strategy, and tactics of the other side); and relevant economic, social, political, and cultural parameters. Although each bargaining relationship is unique, the vast majority fall into one of five categories:[34]

1. *Hostile.* A relationship is hostile when an employer does not accept a union, when it consciously recognizes the legal necessity of entering into a collective bargaining relationship but actively opposes unionism and collective bargaining. Usually, management's opposition to the union takes only the forms permitted by law, but it nevertheless involves the union in a continuing struggle to survive as an institution.

2. *Armed truce.* An armed truce exists when a firm's management, although it may not genuinely "accept" the union, is resigned to the fact that it must bargain, and the bargaining relationship becomes more orderly and stable.

3. *Harmonious.* A working harmony can develop between a firm and a union when the firm's management genuinely accepts the union, and the union recognizes

   that [the] attainment of its objectives is dependent in large measure on the continued prosperity and well-being of the company with which it bargains. . . . [H]owever, each side recognizes that the other can and will use force to achieve its objectives if necessary. Strikes, though rare, are by no means eliminated . . . working harmony is based as much upon hard-boiled realism as it is on mutual confidence and trust.[35]

   When such a relationship exists, it is possible to respond creatively to labor problems. General Motors and the UAW, for example, have used traditional bargaining procedures in a flexible and creative way.[36]

4. *Cooperative.* Cooperation between unions and management is relatively rare. A cooperative rather than an adversary relationship "usually de-

velops out of some kind of economic crisis and is limited to small companies which bargain with small local unions."[37] However, in mature bargaining relationships, the negotiators may recognize that collective bargaining is a process that may be used to create "additional values or mutual benefits . . . [and that] over the long run, [a] considerable joint gain can be produced by the attitudes of trust and confidence which exist among employees, union officials, and management."[38]

5. *Collusive.* Some unions and managements may cooperate in illegal or at least unconventional activities at the expense of customers of the firm, competitors, or the suppliers of labor or materials or even the union membership. Restrictive apprenticeship programs, and limitations on the number of competitors in an industry or region through licensing or other arrangements and sweetheart contracts are possible results of such collusion.

"Constructive" Relationships

It is unrealistic to expect that an adversary relationship based on economic power will usually develop into a cooperative (type 4) relationship. The vast majority of bargaining relationships fall into categories 2 and 3, and "working harmony" is the most that can be expected in most bargaining relationships under present conditions.

Experience after World War II indicates that in many cases, firms that accept unions but that also maintain a hard line bargaining posture can develop a satisfactory long-run relationship with a union. The relationship between General Motors and the UAW is an example of a "militantly constructive" relationship in which management has avoided "giveaways":

> General Motors . . . saw clearly from the start the importance of both good agreements and good administration of agreements. General Motors saw that the rise of unions threatened the freedom of management to run the plants and that this freedom would be gradually nibbled away unless the company was willing, if necessary, to take long and expensive strikes to protect it. Hence, top management made it clear to subordinate management and to the union that the company was prepared at any time to take strikes over certain rights or procedures that top management regarded as essential to efficient operations.[39]

General Motors' approach may be contrasted with that of firms which tolerated an erosion of management control over production standards and shop practices during World War II and the immediate postwar period in the mistaken belief that they were creating "constructive" bargaining relationships. When economic conditions deteriorated, these firms found that their permissive actions had placed them at a competitive disadvantage. In some cases, the adoption of a more aggressive bargaining approach enabled companies to regain the authority they had relinquished; in other cases, firms were forced to "buy out" uneconomic practices, and some firms were never able to regain their former competitive position.

Boulwarism

The most widely publicized attempt by a firm's management to assume the initiative in collective bargaining has been termed *Boulwarism* after Lemuel R. Boulware, who introduced his concept of *job marketing* while working for the General Electric Corporation in 1947.[40] Boulware urged GE's management to develop a carefully researched and competently administered union-management relations program, supported by a variety of communications techniques, that would enable the company to "take the lead at the bargaining table by making an offer at the appropriate time that [would become] the essential basis for [a] final settlement."[41] His intention was to provide contract improvements that appeared reasonable and proper in terms of the company's competitive position; the " 'balanced best interests' of all 'contributor-claimants' to the business—that is, employees, customers, shareholders, vendors, and neighbors, or public, along with government";[42] relevant coercive comparisons; and general economic conditions.

It is probably true that "the public image of Boulwarism [was] a lot 'tougher' than the careful approach of the high caliber negotiators who handle[d] General Electric's employee relations."[43] There were, moreover, certain factors that helped to assure its success for a limited period. General Electric is a diversified and decentralized corporation with a large number of plants that are not interdependent, and it can continue to operate if only a few plants are struck. It bargains with several unions, the largest of which (the International Union of Electrical Workers [IUE]) was plagued with internal discord for a long time, and it was willing to devote enough resources to what was, in fact, a highly sophisticated approach to union-management relations. However, the replacement of the president of the IUE, coalition bargaining by the unions negotiating with GE, a Supreme Court decision finding the corporation guilty of unfair labor practices in its implementation of Boulwarism, and a change in top management led General Electric to adopt a more conventional bargaining posture beginning in its 1973 negotiations.

SUMMARY

In this chapter, we described the collective bargaining process, discussed two simple bargaining models, described the contents of typical union-management contracts, and analyzed the kinds of bargaining structures found in the United States.

According to federal labor law, collective bargaining is the preferred method of adjusting and compromising the conflicting interests of workers and management. The presence of a union necessarily limits managerial prerogatives, and this method of resolving conflicts usually requires a readjustment of the managerial decision-making process in matters affecting the employment relationship. The bargaining process is essentially based upon a power relationship; nevertheless, the outcome of negotiations is based increasingly on fact and reason rather than on emotion and force. The aim of collective bargaining is agreement; the parties to it all have a stake in the continuity of the firm. Most of the weapons of overt labor-management conflict are held in reserve. They provide support for the negotiators' positions, but they are used much less frequently than is commonly believed.

Bargaining structures are a response to the economic and institutional environments peculiar to particular bargaining relationships and have an essential variability.

During World War II and the immediate postwar period, American management was usually able to accommodate successfully to the requirements of collective bargaining. More recently, a trend toward a harder line in bargaining has been observed. This trend is essentially a reaction to loose practices, particularly in the administration of contracts, which developed under more permissive economic conditions. Firms such as General Motors that did not lose control over the administration of contracts have not been forced to "buy out" uneconomic practices, and despite their tough bargaining postures, they have often been able to develop a constructive long-run approach to union-management relations. In these firms, collective bargaining continues to reflect a power relationship based on conflicting institutional needs and objectives; however, both parties recognize that their *mutual survival* is necessary to the success of the firm, the maintenance of job opportunities for union members, and the survival of the union.

DISCUSSION QUESTIONS

1. Is collective bargaining actually a conservative method of conflict resolution?
2. To what extent does the federal government regulate the substantive content of collective agreements?
3. What is meant by the *Kabuki routine* in collective bargaining? Do you consider it a rational process?
4. Distinguish clearly between the two basic types of decisions governing the employment relationship that result from collective bargaining.
5. What is meant by *effective* contract administration?
6. Why must union leaders *mediate* among their constituency?
7. Do continuing study committees represent a bona fide type of collective bargaining?
8. Why, under the range theory, might there be a work stoppage when an overlap exists?
9. What is meant by the term "taking wages out of competition?"
10. Do you believe that critics are correct in asserting that collective bargaining ignores the public interest?

11. What do you consider the most important determinant(s) of bargaining structure?
12. Do you expect that in general more constructive bargaining relationships will develop during the 1980s?

SELECTED READINGS

The Bargaining Process

Beal, Edwin F.; Wickersham, Edward D.; and Kienast, Philip. *The Practice of Collective Bargaining.* 5th ed. Homewood, Ill.: Irwin, 1976.

Chamberlain, Neil W., and Kuhn, James W. *Collective Bargaining.* 2nd ed. New York: McGraw-Hill, 1965.

Cullen, Donald E. *Negotiating Labor-Management Contracts.* Bulletin 56. Ithaca, N.Y.: NYS School of Industrial and Labor Relations, Cornell University Press, 1965.

Davey, Harold W. *Contemporary Collective Bargaining.* 3rd ed. Englewood Cliffs, N.J.: Prentice-Hall, 1972.

Slichter, Sumner H.; Healy, James J.; and Livernash, E. Robert. *The Impact of Collective Bargaining on Management.* Chap. 30, "Negotiation of Union-Management Contracts." Washington, D.C.: Brookings Institution, 1960.

Stevens, Carl M. *Strategy and Collective Bargaining Negotiation.* New York: McGraw-Hill, 1963.

Walton, Richard E., and McKersie, Robert B. *A Behavioral Theory of Labor Negotiations.* New York: McGraw-Hill, 1965.

Bargaining Models

Bishop, Robert L. "Game-Theoretic Analyses of Bargaining." In *Quarterly Journal of Economics* LXXVII, no. 4 (November 1963): pp. 559–602.

Coddington, Alan. *Theories of the Bargaining Process.* Chicago: Aldine, 1968.

Flanders, Allan. "Bargaining Theory: The Classical Model Reconsidered." Chap. 1 in *Industrial Relations: Contemporary Issues.* Ed. by B. C. Roberts. Published for the International Industrial Relations Association. New York: St. Martin's Press, 1968. An imaginative reappraisal of more traditional bargaining theory.

Gerd, Korman, and Klapper, Michael. "Game Theory's Wartime Connections and the Study of Industrial Conflict." In *Industrial and Labor Relations Review* 32, no. 1 (October 1978): pp. 24–39. A review of the introduction of game theory into the study of labor relations.

The Structure of Collective Bargaining

Kelly, Matthew A. "Adaptations in the Structure of Bargaining." In *Proceedings of the Nineteenth Annual Meeting, Industrial Relations Research Association, 1966.* Madison, Wisc.: Industrial Relations Research Association, 1967, pp. 290–302.

Livernash, E. Robert. "New Developments in Bargaining Structure." In *Trade Union Government and Collective Bargaining: Some Critical Issues.* Ed. by Joel Seidman. New York: Praeger, 1970, pp. 241–259.

Livernash, E. Robert. "The Relation of Power to the Structure and Process of Collective Bargaining." In *Journal of Law and Economics* VI (October 1963): pp. 10–40.

Rehmus, Charles M. "Multi-employer Bargaining." Institute of Labor and Industrial Relations, University of Michigan-Wayne State University, Reprint Series 36 (from *Current History* [August 1965]).

Weber, Arnold R. "Stability and Change in the Structure of Collective Bargaining." In *Challenges to Collective Bargaining*. Ed. by Lloyd Ulman. Published for the American Assembly, Columbia University. Englewood Cliffs, N.J.: Prentice-Hall, 1967, pp. 13–36.

Weber, Arnold R., ed. *The Structure of Collective Bargaining*. New York: Free Press, 1961.

Bargaining Experiences

Northrup, Herbert R., and Rowan, Richard L. *Multinational Collective Bargaining Attempts*. Industrial Research Unit, The Wharton School. Philadelphia: University of Pennsylvania, 1979.

Somers, Gerald G., ed. *Collective Bargaining: Contemporary American Experience*. Industrial Relations Research Association Series. Madison, Wisc.: Industrial Relations Research Association, 1980. Analyzes collective bargaining in ten industries.

Notes

1. For an analysis of this process, see Richard E. Walton and Robert B. McKersie, *A Behavioral Theory of Labor Negotiations* (New York: McGraw-Hill, 1965), chaps. VIII and IX.
2. Cf. Benson Soffer, "On Union Rivalries and the Minimum Differentiation of Wage Patterns," in *Review of Economics and Statistics* XLI, no. 1 (February 1959): pp. 53–60.
3. E. Robert Livernash, "The Relation of Power to the Structure and Process of Collective Bargaining," reprinted with permission from the *Journal of Law and Economics*, Vol. VI. Copyright 1963 by the University of Chicago Law School, pp. 18 and 39.
4. U.S. Department of Labor, Labor-Management Services Administration, *The Use of Economic Data in Collective Bargaining*, a report by Marvin Friedman of Ruttenberg, Friedman, Kilgallon, Gutchess & Associates (Washington, D.C.: U.S. Government Printing Office, 1978).
5. A working classification of negotiating tactics was developed by Professor Carl M. Stevens in his *Strategy and Collective Bargaining Negotiation* (New York: McGraw-Hill, 1963), p. 57.
6. Ibid., p. 33.
7. See John R. Hicks, *The Theory of Wages*, 2nd ed. (New York: St. Martin's Press, 1963), pp. 140ff. Most intermediate texts in microtheory discuss bilateral monopoly. For an analysis of the feasibility of developing a general model, see Joseph Shister, "Collective Bargaining," chap. II in Neil W. Chamberlain, Frank C. Pierson, and Theresa Wolfson, eds., *A Decade of Industrial Relations Research, 1946–1956,*

Industrial Relations Research Association Publication No. 19 (New York: Harper & Brothers, 1958), pp. 50–56. See also John G. Cross, *The Economics of Bargaining* (New York: Basic Books, 1969).

8. Cf. Bevars Dupre Mabry, "The Pure Theory of Bargaining," in *Industrial and Labor Relations Review* 18, no. 4 (July 1965): p. 486.

9. For a discussion of such psychological needs, see William H. Knowles, "Non-economic Factors in Collective Bargaining," in *Power in Industrial Relations: Its Use and Abuse, Proceedings of the Spring Meeting, Industrial Relations Research Association, May 2–3, 1958,* reprinted from *Labor Law Journal* (September 1958): pp. 698–704. Professor J. Pen has suggested that "[w]hat we need is a rational theory of possibly irrational processes." (J. Pen, trans. by T. S. Preston, *The Wage Rate Under Collective Bargaining* [Cambridge, Mass.: Harvard University Press, 1959]), p. xiii.

10. Cited in note 1 above.

11. Cf. Neil W. Chamberlain, *A General Theory of Economic Process* (New York: Harper & Brothers, 1955), pp. 80–85.

12. Sumner H. Slichter, James J. Healy, and E. Robert Livernash, *The Impact of Collective Bargaining on Management,* (Washington, D.C.: Brookings Institution, 1960), p. 11.

13. A bargaining model based on the work of Neil Chamberlain is developed by Allan M. Cartter in his *Theory of Wages and Employment* (Homewood, Ill.: Irwin, 1959), pp. 116–133.

14. Livernash, "The Relation of Power," p. 33. Cf. *Collective Bargaining: A Report by the President's Advisory Committee on Labor-Management Policy* (May 1, 1962), p. 1, and Committee for Economic Development, Independent Study Group, *The Public Interest in National Labor Policy* (New York: Committee for Economic Development, 1961), pp. 86 and 90. According to a noted mediator, Theodore Kheel, "the 'prospect' of a cessation of work is the most effective strike deterrent ever devised." ("Letter to the Editor," *The New York Times,* September 4, 1967, p. 20).

15. Slichter, Healy, and Livernash, *Impact of Collective Bargaining,* p. 945. Cf. Lowell Laporte, *Labor Relations, Unions, and Strikes, Managing the Moderate-sized Company,* Report No. 6 (New York: National Industrial Conference Board, 1968), pp. 13–15.

16. For a discussion of union ratification procedures, see Clyde W. Summers, "Ratification of Agreements," in John T. Dunlop and Neil W. Chamberlain, eds., *Frontiers of Collective Bargaining* (New York: Harper & Row, 1967), pp. 75–102, and Herbert J. Lahne, "Union Contract Ratification Procedures," in *Monthly Labor Review* 91, no. 5 (May 1968): pp. 7–10.

17. Charles A. Odewahn and Joseph Krislov, "Contract Rejections: Testing the Explanatory Hypotheses," in *Industrial Relations* 12, no. 3 (October 1973): p. 296.

18. Cf. E. Robert Livernash, "Special and Local Negotiations," in Dunlop and Chamberlain, *Frontiers of Collective Bargaining,* pp. 27–49.

19. Ibid., p. 47.

20. Margaret K. Chandler, "Craft Bargaining," in Dunlop and Chamberlain, *Frontiers of Collective Bargaining,* pp. 57–58.

21. Cf. *Basic Patterns in Union Contracts,* 9th ed. (Washington, D.C.: Bureau of National Affairs, May 1979).

22. Arnold R. Weber, ed., *The Structure of Collective Bargaining* (New York: Free Press, 1961), p. xv.

23. Cf. Matthew A. Kelly, p. 290; E. Robert Livernash, "New Developments in Bargaining Structure," in Joel Seidman, ed., *Trade Union Government and Collective Bargaining: Some Critical Issues* (New York: Praeger, 1970), pp. 241–243; and Arnold R. Weber's summary description in "Stability and Change in the Structure of Collective Bargaining," in Lloyd Ulman, ed., *Challenges to Collective Bargaining* (Englewood Cliffs, N.J.: Prentice-Hall. Published for the American Assembly, Columbia University, 1967), pp. 14–15.

24. Weber, "Stability and Change," p. 14. Emphasis in original.

25. John H. Fanning, member NLRB, "Representation Law: A Responsive Approach to the Exercise of Employer Rights," Address to Pacific Coast Labor Law Conference, University of Washington School of Law and the Labor Law Section of the Seattle-King County Bar Association, Seattle, April 18, 1969 (*NLRB Release R–1139*), p. 9.

26. Cf. John H. Fanning, member, NLRB, "The Taft-Hartley Act—Twenty Years After," Address to the New York University Institute of Labor Relations, Twentieth Annual Conference on Labor, New York, April 17, 1967 (*NLRB Release R–1076*), pp. 9–10.

27. Douglass V. Brown and George P. Shultz, "Public Policy and the Structure of Collective Bargaining," in Weber, ed., *The Structure of Collective Bargaining*, p. 315.

28. U.S. Department of Labor, Bureau of Labor Statistics, *Characteristics of Major Collective Bargaining Agreements, January 1, 1978,* Bulletin 2065, Table 1.8, p. 12.

29. Ibid.

30. Ibid.

31. See Ralph C. James and Estelle Dinerstein James, *Hoffa and the Teamsters: A Study of Union Power,* chap. 8, "The Teamster Presidency and National Bargaining" (New York: Van Nostrand, 1965). The various national agreements in the building and construction industry were also responses to expansion in the geographic area within which effective product market competition had developed. For a discussion of the basic types of area agreements in this industry, see John T. Dunlop, "The Industrial Relations System in Construction," in Weber, ed., *The Structure of Collective Bargaining*, pp. 267–270.

32. Charles M. Rehmus, "Multi-employer Bargaining," Institute of Labor and Industrial Relations, University of Michigan-Wayne State University, Reprint Series 36 (from *Current History*, August 1965), pp. 95–96.

33. 88th Cong., 2d sess., General Subcommittee on Labor, House Committee on Education and Labor, *Report: Multiemployer Association Bargaining and Its Impact on the Collective Bargaining Process, December 1964* (December 1965), p. 1.

34. A number of scholars have established similar classification systems. Our analysis draws most heavily from Frederick H. Harbison and John R. Coleman, *Goals and Strategy in Collective Bargaining* (New York: Harper & Brothers, 1951). Their analysis was based on studies of mass production industries.

35. Ibid., p. 54.

36. James J. Healy, ed., *Creative Collective Bargaining: Meeting Today's Challenges to Union-Management Relations* (Englewood Cliffs, N.J.: Prentice-Hall, 1965), p. 75.

37. Harbison and Coleman, *Goals and Strategy in Collective Bargaining*, p. 89.

38. Walton and McKersie, *A Behavioral Theory of Labor Negotiations*, p. 23.

39. Slichter, Healy, and Livernash, *Impact of Collective Bargaining*, pp. 11–12. See also Healy, ed., *Creative Collective Bargaining*, pp. 60–69.

40. A generally sympathetic account of Boulware's policies is presented in Herbert R. Northrup, *Boulwarism* (Ann Arbor, Mich.: Bureau of Industrial Relations, Graduate School of Business Administration, University of Michigan, 1964). See also Lemuel R. Boulware, *The Truth About Boulwarism* (Washington, D.C.: Bureau of National Affairs, 1969).

41. Northrup, *Boulwarism*, p. 161.

42. Ibid., p. 30.

43. Ibid., p. 156.

Chapter 20
COLLECTIVE AGREEMENTS I: EMPLOYEE COMPENSATION AND HOURS OF WORK

We have seen that collective bargaining is a continuing institutional relationship that involves negotiation and administration of contracts. This, and the following two chapters, discuss the basic provisions of collective agreements that establish the terms and conditions of employment and regulate the employment relationship. In this chapter, we will discuss contract provisions relating to the form and amount of employee compensation and hours of work, and consider some theoretical aspects of wage determination under collective bargaining. In Chapter 21, we will discuss individual job security and work rules, and in Chapter 22, we will discuss union and management security provisions.

There is no prototype union contract. The provisions of a particular contract depend on a complex of factors, including the bargaining structure of the industry, the extent of nonunion competition, current and prospective economic conditions facing the firm and the industry, whether the firm is a pattern setter or pattern follower, and a variety of institutional considerations. All contracts however must deal in some way with the basic bargaining issues which will be discussed.

As we have noted, the parties to collective bargaining assume somewhat different roles during the negotiation and administration of contracts. The union usually initiates bargaining over the *terms* of a contract through a contract termination notice or, in a newly organized firm, through notice that it wishes to enter into negotiations. The employer, who is responsible for the *administration* of the contract, makes the day-to-day decisions about the direction of the work force. Many of these management decisions may be challenged under a grievance procedure; others may be reserved to management. Both "administrative" matters and managerial prerogatives protected by a contract may become negotiable upon the expiration of a contract. The specific matters deemed "appropriate to collective bargaining" may ultimately be defined by the National Labor Relations Board.

DETERMINING EMPLOYEE COMPENSATION UNDER COLLECTIVE BARGAINING

Wages are identified in the Labor-Management Relations Act as one of the matters appropriate to collective bargaining. Union-management discussions usually touch on the general wage level of the firm, the structure of wages within the firm, and the types of supplemental compensation to be included in a wage package. Although the impact of unions on absolute and relative wage levels is controversial, most labor economists agree that unions have had a significant impact on the procedures and practices that determine employee compensation and on the forms of compensation workers receive.

Components of Employee Compensation

Most contract provisions involve direct or indirect costs for employers. Many of these costs are related to some form of current or deferred *compensation* to *employees,* but others, such as the cost of safety equipment, lunch and shower rooms, and on-the-job training programs required by a contract, have no direct effect on employee paychecks.

Employee compensation includes (1) *direct wage* and *salary* payments plus (2) various *supplemental,* or *fringe* benefit, payments—such as payments for time not worked, contributions to pension or insurance plans, and supplemental unemployment compensation. Supplemental compensation is often based on an individual's status as an employee rather than the number of hours worked or the skill with which work is done. All employees, for example, usually enjoy the same medical insurance coverage.

Determining and Administering Wages Bilaterally

The most obvious impact of collective bargaining on wages has been to remove them from the unilateral control of employers. As we noted in Chapter 15, it is incorrect to assume that when there are no unions, companies fail to develop wage policies or that wages in nonunion firms are unstructured. Most employers have some type of wage policy, try to develop a consistent internal wage structure, and consciously relate that structure to the external labor market. Under collective bargaining however, wage policies and structures are jointly determined.

Both the general level of wages in a plant or firm and the internal wage structure must be related to the external labor market. Although union and management representatives may not use such terms, the *wage contours* relevant to the employer's operations must be identified and *key wage rates* within the firm related to specific contours.* If a firm with several plants is producing for a national market, the negotiators must decide whether to establish uniform rates for particular occupations or job categories or to relate plant wage structures to local labor markets.

Union and employer negotiators may have different standards of reference. An employer is concerned about the relative labor costs of firms competing in the same product market; union leaders may be more interested in standardizing wages in relevant labor markets or in firms bargaining with the same union.

Wage policies are also based on institutional imperatives; for example, the union leadership's need to match gains won by other unions and the employer's willingness to pay higher wages rather than grant some type of union security.

Rationalizing the Structure and Administration of Wages

The presence of a union will usually compel an employer who lacks a wage policy or has only a loosely formulated policy to establish a rational policy. It will force an employer who had adopted such a definite wage policy unilaterally to review, defend, and perhaps reformulate that policy. Negotiating the first contracts may be difficult, particularly if bitterness engendered during an organizing campaign persists or the negotiators are unable to agree on the "facts" relevant to the wage issues being discussed.

The Basic Wage Bargain

Once a continuing bargaining relationship has been established, the parties usually try to negotiate a "responsible" wage policy, one that is fair to the firm's employees and also takes into account the need of both the firm and the union to survive as institutions. Although union and management negotiators often have different ideas about what is "fair," economic constraints are key determinants of wage policies, and it should be possible to develop bench marks for negotiations. Ideally, subcommittees will accomplish this before formal negotiations start.

Wage criteria are usually identified more precisely when the wage package is negotiated. The most common criteria include the productivity of labor per man-hour, the cost of living, the firm's ability to pay a certain wage rate, and wages in other firms (1) in the same local or regional labor market, (2) in the

---

* See *supra*, pp. 121–123.

same industry, or (3) bargaining with the same union. Theoretical supports for a negotiator's bargaining posture and government statutes and policies must also be included in the negotiators' bargaining calculus. Arguments in favor of particular wage demands may be addressed to one or more of the following audiences: the union membership, the employer, the public, and the government.

Wage criteria are used selectively and opportunistically and are buttressed by arguments based on "fairness" and "equity." During inflationary periods, union leaders argue that wages must be increased to offset increases in the cost of living, but when living costs fall, they are unwilling to accept wage reductions —it then becomes necessary to maintain consumer purchasing power. Employers will reject the argument that high profits indicate an ability to grant substantial wage increases but will plead their inability to meet union demands when profits decline.

Union negotiators do not seek simply to maximize wages. Rather, they try to achieve a *combination* of objectives for the union as an organization and for its members. The members who have the most effect on the negotiators' decision-making calculus may vary "depending upon (a) the formal bargaining unit, (b) the degree of unionization of the wage earners, (c) membership restrictions, and (d) [the] locus of political power within a trade union concerning wage rates."[1]

The *functional distribution of income,* that is, labor's relative share of the national income, has not been a dominant concern of most union negotiators in the United States. However, the political objectives of organized labor may involve reducing inequalities in income.[2]

The Internal Wage Structure

The negotiation of basic wage packages is the most highly publicized aspect of collective bargaining. However, an *internal wage structure* must also be established and administered on a continuing basis. Under collective bargaining, earnings within job classifications are equalized or become more uniform.

An employer who bargains with a union is likely to adopt some method of "scientific" wage determination. In many cases, each job in a plant is described, assigned a weight, and then priced on the basis of some objective standard. This *job evaluation* procedure helps to eliminate subjective elements from the process of wage determination and wage administration and to reduce the number of wage grievances during the life of a contract.

The *administration of a job evaluation plan,* although presumably objective, often creates internal problems for union leaders, who are subject to pressures from members who feel that individual or group equities have been ignored. The mediation of such complaints is a continuing process *within* many unions. Job evaluation plans are not usually included in contracts. A BLS survey of 1536 contracts covering 1,000 or more workers in effect on January 1, 1978, found that only 239 contained formal job evaluation systems. Of these 239 contracts, 210 were with manufacturing concerns.[3]

The development of the industry wage structure in basic steel is an outstanding example of wage simplification and standardization. A 1944 decision by the War Labor Board allowed the parties to collective bargaining to mutually determine "equitable" wage relationships, and the resulting "Cooperative Wage Study" reduced thousands of different wage rates to 30 basic wage classifications. This was done with a "minimum disruption of the historical wage structure existing in the industry."[4] Uniform wage scales, with the exception of a southern differential since eliminated, were first established in the plants of the United States Steel Corporation. The system was then extended to other major producers.

Wage standardization may be impractical in companies with many product lines in which internal wage structures are related to a variety of wage contours. It may also be impractical when the membership of a union is employed in a number of industries or local labor markets. In such cases, a *craft union* will usually emphasize *wage standardization,* at least within local labor markets, whereas an *industrial union* may accept *wage differentials* reflecting competitive conditions in product markets. This may create problems for an industrial union whose membership includes highly skilled employees, since their wage demands may reflect a local, occupational wage contour rather than an industrial wage contour. Recent demands by skilled workers in the automobile, rubber, railroad, and aircraft industries for special wage increases are cases in point.

The Impact of Unions on Wage Administration

The union's role in wage administration is often underemphasized. This is due to the union leadership's reluctance to participate in wage administration on a continuing basis. It prefers to let management make the initial decisions about rating new jobs, rerating altered jobs, or pricing new items in incentive systems. However, it normally reserves the right to challenge such decisions under established grievance procedures. If a contract allows a union to participate in rating new or modified jobs, the employer is usually protected against a work stoppage during the life of the contract if the parties cannot agree on a new rate. Such disagreements are often resolved through arbitration.

Unions are generally opposed to any reduction in an individual's rate of pay. Despite changes in the content of a job, the members of *skilled craft unions* expect to receive the standard rate for all work performed, and the unions agree to wage reductions only in unusual circumstances—for example, if the growth of nonunion firms threatens the continuation of union operations or a major technological change eliminates the need for skilled workers.

A change in production processes or the content of a job poses a different problem for the leaders of an *industrial* union. They are interested in protecting their members' employment opportunities and earnings levels, not in preserving work requiring a particular skill, and they may not insist that an existing wage rate be applied to a new or altered job classified as paying a lower rate. In such cases, presently employed workers may be paid their old rate or a stated percentage of that rate on the new or altered job or on a lower-rated job to which they are transferred. For example, the 1977 basic steel contract provided a guarantee of 90 percent of their present pay to workers *transferred* to lower paying jobs. Wage rates that apply to *individual* workers rather than to a particular job are called *red circle, red letter,* or *personal rates.*

To summarize: the presence of a union removes wage determination and administration from the unilateral control of an employer, makes the basic components of a firm's wage structure subject to negotiation, and makes the day-to-day administration of that structure subject to review by the union, which may use an established grievance procedure to correct inequities. Although wages are usually determined more systematically in a union firm and the resulting wage structure is usually more rational, there is no prototypal union wage structure. A firm's internal wage structure will reflect the nature of its production processes, the skills required of its employees, the geographic extent of its labor and product markets, and various institutional parameters. In the following sections, we will review selected aspects of wage determination and administration under collective bargaining.

Methods of Wage Payment

Under collective bargaining, methods of paying wages are negotiable. As we have noted, unions try to "take wages out of competition," usually by getting the same hourly rate for all workers in a particular job classification. This equalizes earnings, but it will not result in equal unit labor costs if individual productivity varies. Unions tend to oppose incentive systems that tie compensation to productivity. Union leaders, and many union members, believe that output standards under such systems will be based on the production of pace-setters, reducing the take-home pay of other workers or exposing them to health and safety risks as they strive to maintain previous income levels.[5]

Unions do not invariably oppose such systems, however; a union may accept a straight piecework system or some other "equitable" incentive system that was in operation before the unionization of a firm's labor force, or it may agree to the introduction of such a system if it will prevent a significant reduction in the number of job opportunities for union members. The United Steel Workers accepted various long-established incentive systems, the International Ladies' Garment Workers' Union accepted piece rates as a means of taking wages out of competition, and the Amalgamated Clothing Workers helped to establish a system of *uniform labor costs* based on garment grades. Under this system, the number of workers performing a given operation (making a vest, for example) and individual employee earnings may vary between shops, but *labor costs* for producing a given grade of garment are uniform.

Union attitudes toward incentive systems may also change. Under the United Mine Workers' "theory of competitive equality," miners of bituminous coal were paid different tonnage rates so that mines with poorer veins of coal and mines located farther from coal consumers could compete with more fortunately situated mines. When the mechanization of mining and the use of more efficient means of transporting coal made such differences less significant, the union established uniform day rates.

Most contracts provide for compensation on an hourly basis. According to a 1976 BLS study of 1,711 major collective bargaining agreements* covering some 7.6 million workers, 1,504 contracts covering over 5.5 million workers had one or more jobs for which workers were paid on an hourly basis. Only 467 contracts allowed some form of incentive pay.[6]

Periodic Wage Increases

In a nonunion firm, wages will presumably reflect conditions in relevant labor and product markets. Wages may decline during an economic downturn and increase when labor markets tighten. Under collective bargaining, wages may be renegotiated upon the expiration of the contract, and this has led to periodic increases in wage rates. Except in unusual circumstances—for example, when jobs may be lost because of competition from foreign manufacturers, substitute products, or nonunion firms—union members expect annual wage increases and union leaders try to get them. Key negotiations assume great importance because of the likelihood of coercive comparisons and a general spillover effect.

Following World War II, employers began to negotiate *long-term contracts* in an effort to achieve more stable operations. These contracts provided both automatic increases in wages, and perhaps fringe benefits, on an annual basis and cost-of-living adjustments (COLAs) tied to increases in the Consumer Price Index. These automatic increases in wages and benefits, coupled with the reluctance of unions to negotiate wage reductions, have made wages flexible upward but inflexible downward. This in turn has created a *ratchet effect* that has contributed to the persistent inflation of recent years.

Interpersonal Differentials and Personnel Practices

There are significant differences between the rational wage structures developed by firms in the absence of unions and the more formal arrangements developed under collective bargaining. In the absence of unions, management is likely to emphasize the relationship between individual productivity and unit labor costs, and pay ranges may be established within which individual rates are determined on a merit basis. Unions deemphasize individual differences in efficiency, at least within an occupation or a labor grade. This may lead to the establishment of single rates rather than rate ranges or to a rapid automatic progression to the maximum wage within a rate range, so that the maximum rate becomes the

---

* Contracts covering 1,000 or more workers, but not railroad, airline, or government employees.

expected rate.[7] According to a BLS survey, 616 of the 1,711 major agreements in effect on January 1, 1976, provided for a wage progression. An analysis of 586 of these agreements showed that 436 provided automatic progressions, only 52 had merit ranges, and 76 had a combination of the two.[8]

Unions try to enforce a standardization or simplification of wage rates for several reasons: standard rates help to take wages out of competition, are easy to explain and defend to the membership, appear to conform to worker concepts of equity, and make it easier to process complaints about wages. Uniform wage rates do pose problems for management, since, as we have noted, uniform wages do not produce uniform unit labor costs. To counteract the resulting tendency toward a higher wage cost per unit of output (sometimes termed a lower "efficiency" wage), firms may tighten their hiring practices and continually review their production methods. If rate ranges are established, a firm must develop objective standards for determining levels of compensation within a range. Although such decisions may not be negotiable, unions will try to reserve the right to challenge them.

The Wage Package

During 1967 contract negotiations with the major automobile producers, the UAW, in addition to a sizable wage increase, demanded a variety of benefits designed to provide its blue-collar members with the psychological advantages and status of white-collar workers, but "with greater financial guarantees."[9] According to the union, hourly rated workers were considered "expendable," whereas the more privileged salaried workers were considered part of the firm's overhead, that is, their salaries were considered "part of the continuous costs of doing business." The UAW therefore proposed

> That the blue collar worker be put on a salary ending the hourly system of pay. That he be guaranteed a full month's pay if he is off the job during any part of the month because of layoff or illness or for personal reasons. . . . That a combination of company money and state unemployment benefits be used to guarantee most of a worker's income for a year in case of layoffs.

Although these objectives were not realized, they suggest the type of "new" issues relating to the total security of union members which may be brought to the bargaining table.

Before World War II, fringe benefits were usually limited to white-collar workers. The small proportion of blue-collar workers who were covered by private benefit programs were employed in the main by larger corporations in stable industries that had developed such programs as part of the welfare capitalism movement of the 1920s. Today, conditions are much different; unions no longer confine their demands to a given rate per unit of time or output. Instead, they may ask for "total job security," arguing that employers (and the government) owe workers more than simply an adequate wage.

The increase in supplementary forms of compensation, basically a product of collective bargaining, has been the most significant change in employee compensation since World War II:

> In 1929 employer expenditures for legally required and private insurance and welfare programs in the private economy amounted to 1.4 percent of total compensation. . . . in 1970 employer expenditures for supplementary benefits (including Social Security) amounted to about 24 percent of compensation for manufacturing production workers. . . .[10]

The components of total compensation for all *nonoffice* workers in the private nonagricultural sector in 1976 are shown in Table 20.1. Pay for working time represented 77.4 percent of the workers' total compensation.*

The cost of supplementary benefits, which represents a direct labor cost, varies widely. According to one study,

> fringe expenditures are relatively greater in unionized establishments than in non-union plants; expenditures increase with increases in average hourly earnings and with the size of the plant; expenditures are larger in metropolitan areas than nonmetropolitan areas and larger in the north than in the south and west.[11]

The negotiation of a private benefit program and continuing improvements in the program may be politically valuable to union leaders in situations in which it is difficult to secure significant wage increases. Some fringe benefits may not increase *current* unit labor costs, yet they represent an identifiable bargaining gain. Changes in the total benefit package also give union leaders an opportunity to respond to specific needs of different constituencies within the union.

Pattern Following

In the absence of unions, firms will usually respond in a similar way to competitive pressures in tight labor markets. Conscious pattern following, which is related to the postwar phenomenon of identifiable "rounds" of wage increases, generally appears to be a by-product of coercive comparisons that are made in a union environment. However, pattern following is not limited to the union sector. *Nonunion* firms may follow wage patterns because they need to match the going market rate to recruit and retain competent employees, because they want to treat their employees equitably, or because they want to forestall the unionization of their employees.

In a few cases, when the major firms in an industry are not unionized, a pattern may be set by nonunion firms. The textile industry is a case in point. In some years, major southern producers, responding to labor market pressures and gains by workers in unionized industries, have unilaterally improved wage scales

---

* Supplementary benefit payments in 1978 for a sample of 858 firms were described in Chapter 5, pp. 85–86.

Table 20.1 NONOFFICE EMPLOYEE COMPENSATION IN THE PRIVATE NONAGRICULTURAL ECONOMY, 1976*

COMPENSATION PRACTICE	ALL INDUSTRIES			MANUFACTURING			NONMANUFACTURING		
	PERCENT OF COMPEN-SATION	DOLLARS PER HOUR ALL HOURS	DOLLARS PER HOUR WORK HOURS	PERCENT OF COMPEN-SATION	DOLLARS PER HOUR ALL HOURS	DOLLARS PER HOUR WORK HOURS	PERCENT OF COMPEN-SATION	DOLLARS PER HOUR ALL HOURS	DOLLARS PER HOUR WORK HOURS
Total compensation	100.0	$6.08	$6.54	100.0	$6.38	$6.98	100.0	$5.84	$6.20
Pay for working time	77.4	$4.71	$5.06	75.2	$4.80	$5.25	79.4	$4.63	$4.92
Straight-time pay	74.6	4.54	4.88	71.7	4.57	5.00	77.2	4.51	4.79
Premium pay	2.8	.17	.18	3.5	.22	.24	2.2	.13	.14
Overtime weekend, and holiday work	2.4	.15	.16	2.9	.19	.20	2.0	.11	.12
Shift differentials	.4	.02	.03	.6	.04	.04	.2	.01	.01
Pay for leave time (except sick leave)	5.7	.35	.38	6.8	.43	.47	4.8	.28	.30
Vacations	3.1	.19	.21	3.8	.24	.27	2.6	.15	.16
Holidays	2.1	.13	.14	2.6	.17	.16	1.7	.10	.10
Civic and personal leave	0.1	.01	.01	.2	.01	.01	.1	.01	.01
Employer payments to vacation and holiday funds	0.3	.02	.02	.1	.01	.01	.5	.03	.03
Employer expenditures for retirement programs	8.3	.50	.54	8.5	.54	.60	8.0	.47	.50
Social security	4.6	.28	.30	4.5	.28	.31	4.7	.27	.29
Private pension plans	3.7	.22	.24	4.1	.26	.28	3.3	.20	.21
Employer expenditures for health benefit programs[2]	6.6	.40	.43	7.4	.47	.51	5.9	.34	.37
Life, accident, and health insurance	4.4	.27	.29	5.3	.34	.37	3.6	.21	.22
Sick leave	.6	.04	.04	.6	.04	.04	.7	.04	.04
Worker's compensation	1.5	.09	.10	1.5	.09	.10	1.6	.09	.10

Employer expenditures for unemployment benefit programs								
Unemployment insurance	1.5	.09	.10	1.6	.10	.11	1.4	.08	.08
Severance pay	1.3	.08	.08	1.3	.08	.09	1.3	.07	.08
Severance pay funds and supplemental unemployment benefit funds	.1	.01	.01	.2	.01	.01	(1)	(1)	(1)
	.1	(1)	(1)	.1	(1)	(1)	.1	(1)	(1)
Nonproduction bonuses	.4	.03	.03	.5	.03	.03	.4	.02	.01
Savings and thrift plans	.1	(1)	(1)	.1	(1)	(1)	.1	(1)	.02
									(1)
Wages and salaries (gross payroll)[3]	84.0	5.11	5.49	83.1	5.30	5.80	84.8	4.95	5.26
Supplementals to wages and salaries[4]	16.0	.97	1.05	16.9	1.08	1.18	15.2	.89	.94

* Nonoffice workers in manufacturing are equivalent to production workers.

[1] Less than 0.05 percent, or $0.005.

[2] Includes other health benefit programs, principally State temporary disability insurance, not presented separately.

[3] Includes all direct payments to workers. They consist of pay for time worked, pay for vacations, holidays, sick leave, and civic and personal leave; severance pay; and nonproduction bonuses.

[4] Includes all employer expenditures for compensation other than for wages and salaries. They consist of expenditures for retirement programs (including direct pay to pensioners under pay-as-you-go private pension plans); expenditures for health benefit programs (except sick leave); expenditures for unemployment benefit programs (except severance pay); payments to vacation and holiday funds; and payments to savings and thrift plans.

[5] Nonoffice workers in manufacturing are equivalent to production workers.

[6] Relates to establishments employing 20 or more workers.

NOTE: Because of rounding, sums of individual items may not equal totals.

SOURCE: U.S. Department of Labor, Bureau of Labor Statistics, *Handbook of Labor Statistics 1978*, Bulletin 2000, Table 113, p. 393.

and supplements, setting patterns that have been followed in the unionized northern sector of the industry.

Otto Eckstein and Thomas A. Wilson have analyzed the interdependence of wage settlements under collective bargaining in a number of heavy industries.[12] The industries they have studied "are high wage industries, have strong industrial unions, typically consist of large corporations that possess considerable market power, and are geographically centered in the Midwestern industrial heartland." They are interdependent for three reasons:

> First, because of the considerable input-output connections among them, they tend to prosper together. . . . Second, because of the geographical concentration and perhaps because of some general similarity in the kinds of mechanical skills required, the industries constitute at least a weakly linked labor market. . . . Third, typically a wage pattern is known to exist in these industries. While no one industry is always the leader in establishing this pattern, autos and steel probably play more of a leadership role than the others. But whoever initiates the pattern, it has a very considerable influence on all subsequent settlements in the group.

There are also *political* relationships among the unions dealing with the firms:

> Some unions are bargaining agents in several industries. Geographic proximity, including proximity of some large plants, makes the members of different unions aware of each others' settlements, and puts pressure on their leaders to achieve as good a settlement as the rest of the group.

Although similar patterns of interdependence were not found in other industries, considerable spillovers from the key group were observed. The study concludes that wages in interdependent industries are determined in wage rounds and that "once the pattern for a round is set in early key bargains, the movements of wages in the remaining months or years are largely determined until the next round is settled."

Pattern following does not always result in the standardization of wages between firms. On the contrary, conforming to pattern increases may freeze traditional wage differentials. Moreover, smaller (often marginal) firms and firms on the periphery of a basic industry (such as the small parts suppliers in the automobile industry) or firms facing unusually severe competition may be permitted to deviate from a pattern. Unions in the United States may be characterized generally as "leveling wages up" while permitting some deviations below a pattern in cases of demonstrated hardship. On several occasions, the United Automobile Workers negotiated contracts with the financially hard pressed American Motors Corporation that were less costly than agreements negotiated with the Big Three. In 1980, the union negotiated a contract with Chrysler that provided improvements below those negotiated with General Motors and Ford, and the Rubber Workers have agreed to lower wage rates for the nontire operations of major tire producers. In the public sector, the efforts of public employee unions to continue to negotiate wage increases that parallel those in the private sector may cause serious union-management confrontations as financially pressed cities and towns are unable to finance wage increases matching those in the private sector.

Annual Increases Under Long-Term Contracts

Once negotiated, the *basic structure* and *relative level* of plant or firm wage rates are frozen for the life of a contract. To some, this has been evidence that unions have had a moderating influence on wage increases during the postwar era. This may have been true for a short time, but hardly since the advent of "cost-of-living" raises and deferred "annual improvements" in long-term contracts. The major purpose of these provisions is to make such contracts, which presumably assure the employer of uninterrupted production, acceptable to unions.

In 1980, 80 percent of the workers included in a BLS study of major collective bargaining agreements (agreements covering 1,000 or more workers) in the private nonfarm sector had three-year contracts. According to data available on some 8.3 million of the 9.4 million workers in these major collective bargaining units, at least 4.9 million workers were scheduled to receive deferred wage rate increases averaging 5.1 percent, or 45.0 cents an hour, in 1980.[13] Many of these workers were also among the 5.5 million workers whose wages were subject to scheduled cost-of-living reviews.

Deferred increases, based originally on anticipated increases in productivity but which now also reflect inflation, were designed to increase workers' real incomes. Escalator clauses involving cost-of-living adjustments, or COLAs, are intended to prevent real incomes from falling as prices rise. The first widely publicized cost-of-living escalator combined with an annual improvement factor was in the UAW 1948 contract with General Motors.

Although only 40 percent of the major contracts had cost-of-living clauses in 1980, the wages of almost 59 percent of the workers covered by such contracts were protected by COLAs. The most common COLA provides an increase of one cent per hour in wages for every 0.3-point movement in the Consumer Price Index.* This means that more highly paid workers receive proportionately lower increases as the CPI rises. COLAs may be made quarterly, semiannually, and annually. The longer the period between adjustments, the less effective a COLA is, and unions are now negotiating more frequent adjustments. Some contracts limit, or "cap," the absolute adjustment that may be made during the life of the contract, some are open ended, and others guarantee a minimum increase even if the contract formula requires a lesser amount.

COLAs are not a primary bargaining demand during noninflationary periods, and at such times, unions may agree to drop them to obtain other contract improvements. Unions periodically attempt to incorporate cost-of-living increases into base rates. If the American economy continues to exhibit an inflationary bias, the number of cost-of-living escalator provisions will probably increase, caps will

---

* Nearly 80 percent of the contracts specified use of the national all-cities CPI index.

be raised or eliminated, and most of the resulting wage increases will ultimately be folded into the permanent wage structure.

Summary

Collective bargaining typically produces a more coherent internal wage structure and more uniformity in the wage structures of firms in the same bargaining contour or affected by the same or similar coercive comparisons. However, it is hard to generalize about the objectives of unions and employers in wage negotiations, since they often react differently to product and labor market constraints. Employers are interested in the direct and indirect labor costs associated with various contract provisions and would prefer some link between wages and productivity. Depending on the type of members they have, unions may be interested in obtaining equal treatment for (1) workers in firms producing for the same market, (2) workers in the same labor market whose employers may or may not compete in the same product markets, (3) workers within the union's jurisdiction, which may not coincide with product or labor markets. The most general union objective is to bring the wages of workers doing similar work up to the same level in order to "take them out of competition." However, union leaders are not unaware of the possible adverse impact of wage increases on employment, and they may agree to give up prior, or negotiate more modest, gains if hard times descend on a firm or an industry.

The pressure for uniformity is less strong with respect to the various non-wage provisions of collective agreements. Thus a national union may have more control over wage rates than over working rules; differences in welfare plans may be permitted among firms within the jurisdiction of a given national union; and certain employers may be allowed more latitude in enforcing individual or group production standards.

MODELS OF WAGE DETERMINATION
UNDER COLLECTIVE BARGAINING

In the preceding sections, we analyzed the impact of unions on the way wages are set, the rate at which they are increased, and the growth of fringe benefits. In this section, we will consider certain theoretical implications of wage determination under collective bargaining. As we have noted before, economists often use wage rates as a proxy for the various forms of employee compensation in a bargaining package. We will follow this convention, recognizing that the analysis of changes in wage rates and of wage structures is much more complex than the discussion here suggests.

Unions have a variety of interrelated economic and political goals, and it is unreasonable to assume that union leaders seek simply to maximize wages. However, the union leadership is probably interested in (1) higher wages for the services of its current membership, (2) some assurance of job opportunities for workers presently employed or recently furloughed, and (3) the survival of the union. The relative weights assigned to these objectives depend on variables relevant to particular negotiations. During a recession, most American unions will probably try to protect existing wage standards, even if this results in some additional unemployment. Their actions are based on three assumptions: that some unemployment will develop even if wages are lowered, that it is harder to bring wages back to a higher level once they are reduced than it is to regain employment opportunities, and that since we as a nation are committed to a high level of employment, any unemployment that develops will be temporary.

In the more usual case, unions are interested in raising the wages of their members. The impact of union actions in pursuit of this objective can be demonstrated graphically. The supply and demand curves for an occupation in a particular industry are represented by the lines SS and DD in Figure 20.1. In the absence of a union, they will yield an equilibrium wage of W, and E workers will be employed. If a union is introduced into the industry, it may try to raise wages by (1) negotiating a higher wage rate or (2) limiting the supply of labor by restricting entry into the union or into the occupation, perhaps through licensing requirements.

Generally, a union will establish a higher wage rate, W′, through collective bargaining. In this case, if the supply of labor and the demand for it remain unchanged, employment will fall from E to E′₁, and E′₁ E′₂ workers will be unable to find jobs in union firms. If the union has organized all the firms in the industry, the workers who would like to find jobs in the industry at a wage of W′ but cannot do so will look for work elsewhere, increasing the supply of labor available to, and decreasing the wage rate in, other industries. This will produce a misallocation of resources. In the union firms, wages will be higher, employment

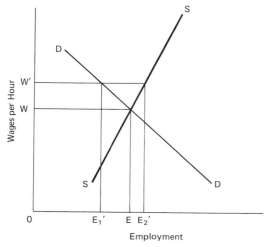

Figure 20.1   How Wage Increases Affect Employment: A Static Model

will be lower, and product prices will presumably be higher; in other industries, market wages will be lower and additional resources will be used to produce goods that are less valuable to consumers. (A similar situation may occur if workers belonging to one union obtain higher wages than workers belonging to other unions.)

If the union has not organized *all* the firms in the industry, the lower wages in the nonunion sector will give producers there a competitive advantage that may decrease job opportunities in the union sector. During the late 1970s for example, the increase in union wage scales in the construction industry encouraged the growth of open shops.

A union, particularly a craft union, may also try to increase wages by reducing the supply of labor. In Figure 20.2, assume that SS represents the existing supply of qualified skilled workers. Given an industry demand, DD, these workers will be employed at a wage of W. If as a result of restricting entry into the trade, the supply of workers is limited to OS', these workers will be employed at a new equilibrium wage of W'. Again, a higher wage may be obtained at the expense of nonunion workers or members of other unions. The union must either have all competing firms under contract or ensure that workers denied membership are unable to qualify for jobs elsewhere, perhaps because of licensing requirements, if this differential wage advantage is to be maintained.

Negotiated Wage Increases

Both of the routes to higher wages described above have been used by American unions, but negotiated wage increases have been most common. This does not mean that the absolute level of employment has in fact decreased in the union

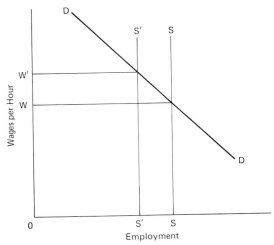

Figure 20.2   How Restricting Entry into a Craft Affects Wages

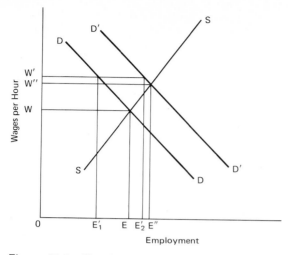

Figure 20.3   How Wages Affect Employment Under Unionism: A Dynamic Model

sector or that the absolute level of wages has decreased in the nonunion sector as a result of collective bargaining. In an economy with a high secular growth rate, the more likely results are a reduction in the rate of growth of employment in the union sector and in the rate of increase in wages in the nonunion sector. The static analysis above did not predict these results because it failed to account for changes in variables over time.

We can however develop a new dynamic model of the relationship between wages and employment. Suppose, as in Figure 20.3, that a union has again negotiated a wage increase from W to W'. In a static model, employment would decline from E to E'_1. Suppose however that the derived demand for workers in the industry increases from DD to $D'D'$. Union firms will then employ E'_2, workers at the union rate, a larger number than either E'_1 or E. If the industry was not unionized, the shift in demand would have produced a new equilibrium wage of W'' and employment would have reached a still higher level, E''. Again, wages are higher and employment is lower under collective bargaining. In our dynamic model, the impact of the union has been concealed by the "veil of time"; the union has apparently succeeded in raising wages without decreasing the number of jobs.

If it appears that a wage increase will markedly *reduce* job opportunities for *presently employed* members, union leaders can be expected to soften their wage demands. The United Mine Workers union under the leadership of John L. Lewis was an outstanding exception to this rule, consistently pressing for higher wages in the face of declining employment opportunities. The union defended its action on the ground that a substitution of capital for labor was inevitable in the coal industry, that a more moderate wage policy would not produce a significantly larger number of jobs, and that increased mechanization, by increasing productivity, would enable the industry to meet competition from other fuels. According to Lewis, the union decided that it was " 'better to have a half million men working in the industry at good wages, high standards of living, than to have a million men working in the industry in poverty and degradation.' "[14]

In Chapter 6, we described a case in which it was theoretically possible for a union to raise wages and employment simultaneously; this was the case of a monopsonistic labor market.* Although such a case is of theoretical interest, a high degree of monopsony power is probably uncommon, and even where unions do obtain significant wage gains through the exercise of countervailing power, the gains appear to be one time occurrences. This helps to explain why some unions have a relatively greater impact on wages early in a bargaining relationship.

Reductions in the Supply of Labor

Significant reductions in the supply of labor as a result of restrictions on entering an occupation have been rare in the United States. The most notable examples of the imposition of such restrictions by unions have been in the building trades at the local level. However, a government licensing system designed to prevent unqualified persons from practicing a trade or profession may also limit the supply of labor. Barbering, plumbing, operation of a taxicab, and the practice of medicine are examples of occupations that require a license.

Legislation that has limited the supply of labor has undoubtedly helped to raise the *general level* of wages in the United States. This legislation, which has been supported by the union movement, includes legislation making school attendance compulsory through a certain age, legislation limiting the number of hours that may be worked before high overtime rates must be paid, social security legislation that encourages retirement from the labor force, and laws restricting immigration. Contract provisions reducing working time and encouraging retirement have also limited the supply of labor.

Raising the Marginal Revenue Productivity of Union Labor

Unions may raise the marginal revenue productivity of their members by helping to increase the efficiency of individual workers and helping to stimulate demand for a product. Such cooperative endeavors are usually the result of adversity, as when union firms are losing business to nonunion competitors or the demand for an industry's product is declining. Union labels on consumer goods are designed to encourage the purchase of goods made by union workers, and unions have occasionally helped to finance advertising campaigns designed to increase the demand for their employers' products.

---

* See *supra*, p. 112.

A different type of "cooperation" is involved in union support of restrictive practices by employers that result in higher prices. Union leaders try to maximize their members' welfare, and if monopolistic practices in product markets will help them do this, they can be expected to cooperate with employers at the expense of consumers. If the demand for a product is inelastic and competitors can be excluded from a market, unions and management may cooperate to restrict competition and share in the resulting "monopoly profits."

A Concluding Comment

This brief theoretical analysis suggests that union negotiators will favor a monopolistic rather than a competitive environment. However, we cannot evaluate the impact of collective bargaining on the basis of this analysis; we do not know how labor and product markets would function in the absence of unions. Union and management negotiators may serve as transmission belts for imperfectly competitive market forces, and the independent economic impact of collective bargaining may be less than an abstract analysis suggests. Moreover, the extra-economic benefits of unions may well outweigh the presumed adverse impact of collective bargaining on the allocation of resources. We shall return to these matters in Chapter 23.

HOURS OF WORK

Provisions regarding hours of work and time paid for but not worked are the second basic component of collective agreements. Earlier in the chapter, we noted that one way in which unions have raised wages is by limiting the supply of labor. Contract provisions and federal and state legislation restricting hours of work have helped achieve this result.

During the late nineteenth and early twentieth centuries, some craft unions in local market industries and a few early industrial-type unions were able to negotiate reductions in the number of hours worked by their members but general reductions in the scheduled workday and workweek were the result of legislation or were initiated by employers and financed, in effect, by increased productivity.

During the 1920s, employers often introduced an 8-hour day and a 5½ day week for white-collar workers and, to a more limited degree, production workers in major manufacturing concerns. During the 1930s, the NIRA codes and the Fair Labor Standards Act made a 40-hour week the norm. Since then, reductions in work schedules and additional time off with pay have usually been initiated by unions with nonunion workers also benefiting. Two more recent ideas, the 4-day, 40-hour week and flexible workdays (or *flexi-time*), have reflected *management's* interest in improving productivity by developing "new patterns" of working time; unions are more interested in reducing than in redistributing the hours of work. Although a 4-day, 32-hour workweek without a reduction in pay is a long-run union objective, unions have so far settled for reducing working hours by negotiating more paid holidays and more vacation time.

Some unions may negotiate a shorter workweek during recessions, and the AFL-CIO has supported a proposal to amend the Fair Labor Standards Act to make a 7-hour workday and 35-hour workweek with double time for overtime standard. The unions' support is based on the assumption that a shorter workweek will create more jobs rather than on considerations of health, safety, or a need for additional leisure. Whether further *legal* limits on the standard workweek can be justified by welfare considerations is debatable.

Hours Provisions in Collective Agreements

Under collective bargaining, hours standards and work schedules are jointly determined by unions and management. Employee preferences help to determine what constitutes "excessive" hours of work and whether increases in productivity will be used to increase wages and benefits or give workers more paid and unpaid leisure. The resulting reductions in scheduled working hours and increases in payments for time not worked represent contributions to employee welfare that in some cases have greatly altered the lifestyles of union members. In many instances, collective bargaining has been the vehicle through which blue-collar workers have obtained benefits that were granted unilaterally to professional, office, and technical workers.

A collective agreement (1) defines normal or scheduled or standard hours of work (that is, the number of hours per day and per week an employee may be required to work without getting overtime pay); it (2) defines departures from normal work schedules and requires overtime pay for work done during such periods, both to discourage such scheduling and compensate workers for giving up time off the job; and it (3) prescribes the conditions under which workers will receive pay for time not worked.[15]

Specific contract provisions define regular work schedules, limit the number of hours employees can be asked to work, guarantee workers additional (compensatory) pay for working less desirable shifts (*shift premiums*) or pay for "nonproductive" time spent at a place of employment (rest periods, washup time), identify paid holidays, and specify the length of paid vacations.

The employer's freedom to schedule work is limited both directly and indirectly by a collective agreement. It is limited directly by provisions defining the regular workday and workweek, specifying starting and quitting times, instituting shift differentials, limiting compulsory overtime (this was recently a critical issue in negotiations in the automobile industry), and requiring penalty pay for irregular work scheduling, including call-in pay for reporting when work is not available. It is limited indirectly by clauses enforcing local work practices, continuing past practices, counting idle time as work time, and liberalizing vacation and seniority practices.

Reducing the Hours Increases the Pay

Under collective bargaining, reductions in the workday or workweek are integrally related to compensatory wage increases. Except in unusual circumstances, it is expected that a reduction in hours will be accompanied by a proportionate increase in hourly rates. As the workday becomes shorter, it becomes increasingly difficult to "recover" such wage increases through increases in productivity. The feasibility of shortening the workday also varies widely. Multishift firms and firms whose operations are continuous may find that a workday of less than eight hours is not only costly but also poses serious technical problems.

The cost of pay for time not worked and other supplementary pay received by workers by virtue of their employment may make overtime less costly than hiring additional employees when a firm is faced with a temporary increase in demand. The cost of hiring and laying off temporary workers may also encourage employers to schedule overtime. The preference of many employees for overtime rather than additional leisure is another factor in its popularity.

Once an eight-hour day and a five-day week have been established, further reductions in hours, particularly for production workers, are likely to involve an increase in the number of paid holidays or the length of paid vacations rather than a reduction in standard work schedules. Employers favor such provisions because additional time off with pay seldom has as great an impact on scheduling and operating costs as a general reduction in hours.

Developments Since World War II

Although the length of the scheduled workday and workweek have generally remained stable since World War II, unions have been instrumental in increasing the amount of paid time away from work on an annual basis. They have also negotiated a variety of other benefits related to work schedules that have spilled over to nonunion jobs. Any list of specific developments would have to include the following gains:

1. The number of paid holidays has been increased to nine or more in most major contracts. Before World War II, few production workers received holiday pay. The National War Labor Board ruled that six paid holidays were acceptable under the wartime wage stabilization policy, and following the war, most organized workers received this many days. By the late 1960s, 60 percent of the major collective bargaining agreements with holiday provisions provided eight or more holidays with pay.[16]
2. Some holidays may be *floating* holidays, used to create three-day weekends. Others may be local holidays. The 1979 agreement between the

UAW and General Motors, for example, provides that "one holiday of greater local importance which must be designated in advance by mutual agreement locally in writing" could be substituted for Memorial Day.

3. The percentage of workers covered by agreements providing paid vacations has increased. During World War II, the NWLB approved one week of paid vacation after one year of employment and two weeks after five years, and by the end of 1944, some 85 percent of all union workers were covered by vacation plans. By 1952, nine out of ten workers were covered. Since then, the proportion has remained constant.[17]

4. The service requirements for vacation periods have been reduced and the length of vacations has been increased. A Bureau of Labor Statistics study of benefit provisions in major contracts during the four years ending in 1966 found that

> 3 of the 4 years, the most common change in vacation provisions consisted of reducing the period of service required for 4 weeks of vacation or raising the maximum vacation to 4 weeks or both. [The] next most frequent [change] was a reduction in [the period of] service required for 3 weeks of vacation.[18]

5. In some firms, the length of vacations of employees with many years of service has been increased prior to their retirement to help them "phase out" of the labor force.

6. In several industries, including the basic steel industry, the aluminum industry, and the can manufacturing industry, "sabbaticals" may be taken by qualifying employees. In basic steel, the top half of the seniority roster is entitled to a 13-week sabbatical and junior employees can take an additional three-week vacation, every fifth year. However, the union's expectation that prolonged vacations will increase job opportunities for younger workers is apparently unfounded.

7. Many contracts have required call-in pay for four hours.

8. Premium rates have been granted for working a sixth or seventh day. Premium pay for Sunday work, and to a lesser extent for Saturday work, has become more common in industries with continuous production processes.

9. "Short workweek" pay (partial compensation for unworked hours in a standard workweek) has been negotiated in a few industries, including the automobile and steel industries. It is designed in part to encourage better production planning.

10. Finally, the amount of overtime has sometimes been regulated to spread work at premium rates among the membership. Some contracts also put an absolute limit on the amount of overtime that may be scheduled. For example, the basic contract between the International Ladies Garment Workers' Union and the dress manufacturers limits overtime to the first five days of the week and to not more than one hour per day in an

attempt to provide more stable employment in what is a highly competitive industry.

Basic Current Provisions

According to a BLS survey of 1,536 major collective bargaining agreements, as of January 1, 1978, some 89 percent specified a weekly schedule of hours of work, and 84 percent of these contracts specified a 5-day, 40-hour week.[19] Only 145 contracts provided for a scheduled workweek of less than 40 hours. Ninety-one percent of the contracts provided for premium pay on weekends; 91 percent provided for vacations with pay, and 80 percent of this 91 percent increased vacation periods according to an employee's length of service. A maximum vacation of 5 to 5½ weeks was provided in 541 (48 percent) of the contracts specifying maximum paid vacations. Paid holidays were provided in 84 percent, and 80 percent of this 84 percent provided nine or more holidays a year. The modal number of holidays, ten, was provided in 28 percent of these contracts.

Some employers find it hard to accept the fact that these benefits are now expected and that management may get little credit for including them in agreements. The AFL-CIO has emphasized that holidays and vacations "are recognized as essential rights of the workers, provided by union contract and earned just as wages are earned."[20]

Recent Initiatives

In recent years, unions have concentrated on reducing the number of hours worked annually rather than the number of hours worked daily or weekly. There are indications however that the desire of many union members for larger blocks of leisure on a continuing basis may ultimately encourage union leaders to seek shorter workdays and workweeks. A small but increasing number of nonunion firms have adopted a *ten-hour workday and a four-day workweek.* However, premium overtime rates are not paid after eight hours of work, and unions have been reluctant to adopt this work format. According to another BLS study of major collective bargaining agreements,

> [d]espite the publicity surrounding the 4-day, 40-hour week, particularly among smaller companies, only a handful of the major agreements made any reference to it. No agreement provided a 4-day, 40-hour week for all regular full-time employees.[21]

Unions have not been interested in negotiating an eight-hour day in combination with a four-day workweek since it is doubtful that they could maintain their members' current level of take-home pay given a 20 percent reduction in scheduled working time. Thus, the prediction that a 32-hour workweek will become common by 1990 in unionized industries seems premature. However, in

1976, apparently as an initial move toward a 32 hour workweek, the UAW negotiated five more (optional "personal") holidays for 1977 and an additional seven for 1978. In 1979 the union obtained an increase to 26 personal holidays over a three-year contract period.

Interest in improving the quality of work life has encouraged some firms to adopt various types of "*flexi-time*," giving workers some degree of freedom to choose which hours they will work within a "lengthened" workday. Flexi-time usually requires that all employees be at work during a basic time *band* (for example, from 10 a.m. to 3 p.m. with a half-hour or hour-long lunch period), but permits them to schedule the remainder of their workday to suit themselves as long as they work during other standard time bands (for example, 7 a.m. to 10 a.m. and 3 p.m. to 6 p.m.). Such arrangements have proved popular among white-collar workers in urban areas, where they have relieved commuting pressures. According to a 1978 American Management Association survey, the use of flexi-time had doubled since 1974, and 6 percent of all employees were on flexi-time.[22] Thus far, flexi-time has not surfaced as a serious bargaining issue. However, unions in industries with production processes that are not continuous may be receptive to it.

Future Developments

For new patterns of working time to be generally adopted, we will need both a high level of employment and continued economic growth. Otherwise, higher or stable incomes with greater leisure will not be realistic bargaining alternatives. Under less favorable economic conditions, union leaders can be expected to renew their demands for a reduction in the length of the *standard* workday (with proportionate increases in pay) to increase job opportunities. This will conflict with the desire of many employed union members to earn more money by working overtime and the general disinclination of employers to raise hourly rates simply to prevent a drop in take-home pay.

Despite a renewed interest in shorter workweeks, additional reductions in hours under collective agreements will probably be instituted gradually and, at least in the near future, will continue to take the form of additional paid holidays and longer vacations. Holidays will continue to be incorporated into three-day weekends, the number of local holidays will probably increase, and personal holidays (for example, a worker's birthday) may be allowed. Further reductions in service requirements for vacations and longer vacations for employees with high seniority can also be expected.

The phasing out of workers approaching retirement by gradually extending their vacations is a promising innovation. Earlier retirement on a voluntary basis may be made more attractive and more practical by private and public pension programs. This would reduce hours of work on a lifetime basis and presumably increase individual welfare.

Any decision concerning "the" optimal length of a workday, a workweek, or a working lifetime cannot be made solely on the basis of an economic calculus. However, it is not clear that employee preferenees concerning the trade-off between work and leisure will be given greater consideration in collective bargaining. Instead, innovations such as a four-day workweek and flexi-time are more likely to be adopted by nonunion firms. Should these innovations become more popular, differences in the preferences of union leaders and individual members may continue to delay their introduction in the union sector.

SUMMARY

In this chapter, the first of three chapters on basic contract provisions, we reviewed provisions relating to the amount and form of employee compensation. We discussed how the wage provisions of a contract are administered, presented a brief theoretical analysis of the impact of collective bargaining on the wage-employment relationship, and discussed the regulation of hours of work and payments for time not worked.

We did not analyze the impact of collective bargaining on various types of wage differentials, the functional distribution of income, money wage rates, real wages, or the price level. We shall analyze both the economic impact and the extraeconomic dimensions of collective bargaining in Chapter 23.

DISCUSSION QUESTIONS

1. What basic types of wage decisions must be made by management?
2. What types of *institutional imperatives* affect wage determination under collective bargaining?
3. Why does the presence of a union usually result in greater rationalization of (1) a firm's wage structure and (2) wage administration?
4. Should all employees be paid a salary?
5. What factors are responsible for the increasing interdependence of wage settlements under collective bargaining?
6. Why have some unions obtained relatively greater wage increases during the initial stages of a bargaining relationship?
7. How is the employer's freedom to schedule work limited under a collective agreement?
8. Do you believe that unions in general will press for further reductions in daily and/ or weekly hours of work in the coming decade?

SELECTED READINGS

Wage Administration

Dunn, J. D., and Rachel, Frank M. *Wage and Salary Administration: Total Compensation Systems.* New York: McGraw-Hill, 1971.

Pattern Following

Alexander, Kenneth. "Market Practices and Collective Bargaining in Automotive Parts." In *Journal of Political Economy* LXIX, no. 1 (February 1961): pp. 15–29.

Hildebrand, George H. "External Influences and the Determination of the Internal Wage Structure." In *Internal Wage Structure*. Ed. by J. L. Meij. Amsterdam: North-Holland Publishing Company, 1963.

Levinson, Harold M. "Pattern Bargaining: A Case Study of the Automobile Workers." In *Quarterly Journal of Economics* LXXIV (May 1960): pp. 296–317.

Seltzer, George. "Pattern Bargaining and the United Steelworkers." In *Journal of Political Economy* LIX (August 1951): pp. 319–331.

Hours of Work

Hedges, Janice Neipert. "Flexible Schedules: Problems and Issues." In *Monthly Labor Review* 100, no. 2 (February 1977): pp. 62–65.

Hedges, Janice Neipert. "New Patterns for Working Time." In *Monthly Labor Review* 96, no. 2 (February 1973): pp. 3–8.

Levitan, Sar A., and Belous, Richard S. *Shorter Hours, Shorter Weeks: Spreading the Work to Reduce Unemployment*. Baltimore, Md.: Johns Hopkins University Press, 1977. A concise recent reference.

Poor, Riva, ed. *4 Days 40 Hours and Other Forms of the Rearranged Workweek* (New York: New American Library, 1973).

Notes

1. John T. Dunlop, *Wage Determination Under Trade Unions* (New York: Augustus M. Kelley, Inc., 1950), p. 44.
2. Cf. George H. Hildebrand, "The Economic Effects of Unionism," in Neil W. Chamberlain, Frank C. Pierson, and Theresa Wolfson, eds., *A Decade of Industrial Relations Research, 1946–1956*, Industrial Relations Research Association Publication 19 (New York: Harper & Brothers, 1958), p. 135.
3. U.S. Department of Labor, Bureau of Labor Statistics, *Characteristics of Major Collective Bargaining Agreements, January 1, 1978*, Bulletin 2065, Table 3.1, p. 32.
4. Sumner H. Slichter, James J. Healy, and E. Robert Livernash, *The Impact of Collective Bargaining on Management* (Washington, D.C.: Brookings Institution, 1960), p. 566. The definitive study is Jack W. Stieber's *The Steel Industry Wage Structure: A Study of the Joint Union-Management Job Evaluation Program in the Basic Steel Industry* (Cambridge, Mass.: Harvard University Press, 1957).
5. For an analysis of union opposition to piecework systems, see Sumner H. Slichter, *Union Policies and Industrial Management* (Washington, D.C.: Brookings Institution, 1941), pp. 296–305.
6. U.S. Department of Labor, Bureau of Labor Statistics, *Major Collective Bargaining Agreements: Wage Administration Provisions*, Bulletin 1425–17, pp. 2–3. See also *Major Collective Bargaining Agreements: Wage-Incentive, Production-Standard, and Time Study Provisions*, Bulletin 1425–18, which analyzes 1,438 agreements, of which 442 had some type of incentive system.
7. Cf. Slichter, Healy, and Livernash, *Impact of Collective Bargaining*, pp. 602ff.

8. BLS, *Major Collective Bargaining Agreements: Wage Administration Provisions,* p. 7.

9. *The New York Times,* July 13, 1967, p. 26.

10. U.S. Department of Labor, Bureau of Labor Statistics, George Ruben, "Major Collective Bargaining Developments—A Quarter-Century Review," *Current Wage Developments,* 26, no. 2 (February 1974) p. 47, with original sources cited on p. 54.

11. Harland Fox, "Comparing the Cost of Fringe Benefits," in *The Conference Board Record* IV, no. 5 (May 1967): p. 35. Based on Chamber of Commerce and Bureau of Labor Statistics data.

12. Otto Eckstein and Thomas A. Wilson, "The Determination of Money Wages in American Industry," in *Quarterly Journal of Economics* LXXVI, no. 3 (August 1962): pp. 379–414. For a criticism of their position, see Timothy W. McGuire and Leonard A. Rapping, "The Determination of Money Wages in American Industry: Comment," in *Quarterly Journal of Economics* LXXXI, no. 4 (November 1967): pp. 684–689. Eckstein and Wilson replied to this comment in the same issue, on pp. 690–694. Quotations are from "The Determination of Money Wages," pp. 384, 385, and 387.

13. Edward Wasilewski, "Scheduled Wage Increases and Escalator Provisions in 1980," in *Monthly Labor Review* 103, no. 1 (January 1980): pp. 9–13.

14. Justin McCarthy, *A Brief History of the United Mine Workers of America* (Washington, D.C.: United Mine Workers Journal, n.d.), p. 7.

15. Our discussion draws on Slichter, Healy, and Livernash, *Impact of Collective Bargaining,* pp. 223–238.

16. BLS, "Major Collective Bargaining Developments," p. 49 and U.S. Department of Labor, Bureau of Labor Statistics, *Major Collective Bargaining Agreements: Paid Vacation and Holiday Provisions,* Bulletin 1425–9, p. 58.

17. BLS, "Major Collective Bargaining Developments," pp. 49–50, *Major Collective Bargaining Agreements: Paid Vacation and Holiday Provisions,* pp. 4–5.

18. Douglas K. Fridrich and Michael E. Sparrough, "Benefit Provisions in Major Agreements," in *Monthly Labor Review* 91, no. 6 (June 1968): p. 41.

19. These data and the data immediately following are based on various tables in *Characteristics of Major Collective Bargaining Agreements, January 1, 1978,* Part IV, "Hours, Overtime, and Premium Pay," and Part V, "Paid and Unpaid Leave."

20. Rudolph Oswald, "The Growth of Longer Vacations," *American Federationist,* 74, no. 11 (November 1967), p. 19.

21. U.S. Department of Labor, Bureau of Labor Statistics, *Major Collective Bargaining Agreements: Hours, Overtime and Weekend Work,* Bulletin 1425–15, p. 5.

22. *The Wall Street Journal,* April 11, 1978, p. 1.

Chapter 21
COLLECTIVE AGREEMENTS II: INDIVIDUAL SECURITY

In addition to contract provisions relating to the amount, type, and method of remuneration and the scheduling of work, unions negotiate a variety of formal work rules and practices that regulate the employment relationship. Union leaders see labor as a unique factor of production, and they try to protect their members' equity in particular skills and jobs, to ensure that their members are treated "fairly" and humanely, to guarantee them satisfactory working conditions, and to insulate them against the risks and costs associated with change in a dynamic economy.

Collective agreements regulate two types of managerial decisions: (1) decisions about *personnel* matters, such as which individuals are assigned to particular jobs, and (2) decisions about the methods, organization, and pace of *production* that have a discernible impact on employees.* Employees also develop *informal* work rules and practices. The equitable administration of the resulting work rules and their modification over time in response to the changing needs of the firm and its employees are critical components of the collective bargaining relationship.

---

* See, for example, some of the principal headings in the General Motors contract, listed in Table 19.1, p. 464.

Work rules are important to union members as *individuals*; they regulate job assignments, help to determine how individual compensation is related to the internal wage structure of the firm, and constitute a mechanism by which union leaders can respond to the extraeconomic needs of members. The ability of a union's leadership to respond to such needs will affect the political security of the officers and, ultimately, the security of the union as an institution.

WORK RULES AND INDUSTRIAL JURISPRUDENCE

We have noted that even in the absence of unions, well-managed firms find it necessary and helpful to develop rules governing the employment relationship, to administer these rules equitably and consistently, and to set up two-way communication systems to help "manage" change. Work rules are established by informal agreement in nonunion firms, and in both union and nonunion establishments, a variety of shop practices become accepted procedures with the passage of time. However, there is no guarantee that unilaterally instituted and applied rules and practices will take into account employees' concepts of equity and consistency, and it is a principal function of unions to see that they do.

The regulation of the employment relationship has two dimensions: the negotiation of rules governing that relationship during the life of a contract and the establishment of a process of judicial review to ensure that the contract is administered equitably. The rights and responsibilities established by collective agreements may be termed a "system of *industrial jurisprudence*."[1] In the United States, in contrast to many industrial nations, this system has been evolved *privately* by the parties to collective bargaining, not by the government. The protection it affords workers is probably the most significant achievement of our system of collective bargaining.

The importance of particular work rules and practices varies according to the interests and needs of individual employees and work groups, and contract provisions often represent compromises between constituencies within a union. Thus, work rules may be incorporated in a master agreement with a proviso that they be subject to modification at the local level, or they may be included in agreements that supplement the master contract. Neglecting local work rules and practices in negotiations covering several plants or with several employers may cause contract rejections and local strikes.

The Impact of Work Rules

To employers, work rules are infringements on managerial prerogatives that may lessen the efficiency of the plant or firm. Obviously, work rules may have such an effect. However, absent work rules, an increase in economic efficiency may involve individual or social costs. In a highly competitive product market, submarginal employers may remain "competitive" by enforcing unreasonable and socially costly work standards; in a world of imperfectly competitive markets, there is no guarantee that without unions we would be more likely to achieve a "socially optimal" allocation of resources. As one observer emphasizes, "opinions as to what is reasonable are bound to differ, but failure to apply a rule of reason [to work practices] would be to accept the employers' requirements, no matter how harsh and extreme, as the proper standard."[2]

Collective bargaining provides a mechanism by which some of the human costs of change that might otherwise become social costs may be shifted to the firms generating them. In such cases, the relevant question is not whether a union work rule has a social cost but whether there is another way of protecting workers that would have a lower *net* social cost. We shall discuss these matters in more detail in Chapter 23.

Types of Work Rules

The substantive work rules established by collective agreements and the rules established informally in shops fall into five categories: (1) rules that establish a procedure for reviewing management actions—typically, a grievance procedure; (2) rules that regularize and perhaps restrict access to job opportunities; (3) rules that ensure a safe and pleasant work environment; (4) rules that regulate and in some cases restrict employees' productive efforts; and (5) rules that protect workers adversely affected by technological or organizational innovations.

REVIEWING MANAGEMENT ACTIONS: GRIEVANCE PROCEDURES

Unions generally recognize that for a firm to operate efficiently, management must have the authority to make decisions about matters covered in a contract during the life of a contract, but they insist that this authority be subject to challenge. The rules establishing a procedure for formally reviewing management decisions give the system of industrial jurisprudence its judicial component. Usually, disputes about contract *rights* are reviewed under a grievance procedure. An essential element of most of these procedures is a voluntary agreement to submit grievances that the parties have been unable to resolve by themselves to a third party for settlement.

The arbitration of grievances, which is basically an American device, was not common before World War II. However, the National War Labor Board in an effort to reduce work stoppages often ordered the inclusion of grievance arbitration procedures in contracts, and the postwar Labor-Management Conference called by President Truman in 1945 agreed that it was desirable that "the parties . . . provide by mutual agreement for the final determination of any unsettled grievances or disputes involving the interpretation or application of the agreement by an impartial chairman, umpire, arbitrator, or board."[3] According to a 1978 Bureau of Labor Statistics study of 1536 major collective bargaining agreements (those covering 1,000 or more workers), 1473, or 96 percent included both grievance and arbitration provisions.[4]

The Typical Grievance Procedure

Most grievance procedures have a similar structure. A typical procedure has three or four *steps* that enable an employee to institute and process a grievance at successively higher administrative levels with a final authority—usually an impartial arbitrator—having power to make a binding decision if the union and employer representatives cannot resolve the dispute. A four-step grievance procedure in an industrial plant might operate as follows:

1. An employee who believes that a contract violation has occurred—for example, that a new or modified job has been improperly rated—will discuss the grievance informally with the union shop steward. The steward may discuss the matter informally with the first-line supervisor before "accepting the grievance." If the steward believes that the grievance is justified, or perhaps if he is under political pressure to do something for the workers he represents, he will begin formal proceedings by presenting the grievance in writing to a supervisor.

2. If the issue is not resolved by the supervisor's answer, the steward or the chief steward will then discuss the grievance with the plant superintendent or a representative of the industrial relations staff. Most grievances are resolved at this point. However, in nonroutine cases, the grievance may be taken a step higher.

3. At this point, the grievance might be handled by the local union president or the regional representative of a national union and the plant superintendent or, perhaps in a firm with several plants, the corporate director of union-management relations.

4. If the grievance is still not resolved, the matter will go to arbitration. A neutral arbitrator will hear evidence and then make a formal decision. Arbitrators usually serve on an ad hoc basis, although permanent "umpires" are retained by some large firms and industry associations.

To be effective, a grievance procedure must prescribe in advance the specific steps to be followed, time limits must be put on each step to ensure that grievances are either settled promptly or referred to a higher authority, and there must be some way of finally resolving a dispute. Only a small minority of grievances go to arbitration; most are settled after one or two steps, often informally and without putting anything in writing. Grievances that have a significant impact on the security of workers' jobs or incomes, that involve fundamental policy issues, or that union leaders believe to be politically important tend to be resolved at higher levels.

The Grievance Procedure in Operation

Operationally, a grievance procedure will reflect the "character" of a union-management relationship. It may be viewed legalistically or as a constructive way of resolving problems. The parties' "philosophy" about the procedure, particularly during the initial period of a bargaining relationship, is likely to have a significant impact on the quality of the relationship. Used constructively, a grievance procedure can be a way of modifying or expanding a contract in response to economic or institutional changes; it can also provide a way of "bending" the terms of a master contract to meet the particular requirements of a local bargaining relationship. When it is used in this way, a grievance procedure helps create a less authoritarian work environment.

Conversely, a grievance procedure may be used as an instrument of conflict: to frustrate change, to alter the intended effect of a specific provision of a collective agreement, or to achieve during the life of a contract an objective that could not be achieved during negotiations. If a firm's management has identified certain areas in which it wishes to prevent further union penetration of its prerogatives, it may try to exclude disputes in such areas from the grievance procedure or perhaps from arbitration. Union members may be permitted to strike over such "excluded" issues during the life of a contract.

The knowledge that management actions under a contract can be challenged and that an employer must be prepared to demonstrate to a third party that its actions were justified tends to produce better management. This is because (1) more careful consideration is given to the implications of substantive contract provisions during negotiations; (2) more attention is paid to the clarity of contract language; (3) more effort is made to train foremen and other lower level managers to handle various aspects of the union-management relations function; and (4) contracts are administered more thoughtfully and consistently.

In addition to providing a peaceful way of resolving disputes, a grievance procedure may (1) create potentially constructive channels of communication between individual employees, union representatives, and an employer; (2) provide union and employer participants with valuable training in contract administration and interpretation and help them to understand the logic of adversary positions; (3) provide a therapeutic outlet for worker unrest; and (4) in cases in which union leaders, for political reasons, feel it necessary to support a grievance that may be unjustified, provide a valuable face-saving device. The existence of a mechanism for challenging management actions also moderates employee resistance to change. Finally, the demonstrated value of objective third-party solutions to grievances involving critical issues has led to the use of ad hoc and permanent committees of outside experts to study complex *interest* issues outside the crisis atmosphere created by contract deadlines.

RULES REGULARIZING AND LIMITING ACCESS TO JOB OPPORTUNITIES

Employers and unions generally accept the principle that an employee acquires increasing equity in a job over time. The nature of this equity will depend on the level of skill required of workers in a firm or industry, the continuity of employment normal in the firm or industry, and whether job opportunities in the firm or industry are expanding or contracting. Craft unions are interested in preserving and regulating access to *particular jobs* requiring the *specific skills* of their members. Industrial-type unions are more likely to be concerned with maintaining *employment opportunities* for their members at the same or at a higher wage level. If employment within firms is intermittent, unions may try to regulate the supply of labor on an industry basis or to negotiate hiring hall or work-sharing provisions that ensure an equitable distribution of work among their members. A firm's internal labor market is less structured under such conditions.

A craft union will try to protect its members' job equity by controlling entrance into a trade or the hiring process and by negotiating work rules that provide employment and income security for the membership while protecting the union's jurisdiction. Entry level jobs in firms organized by industrial unions are typically for unskilled or semiskilled workers, and industrial unions are usually unable to negotiate or enforce rules that would give their members priority in obtaining an *initial* job with a firm. However, the unions do try to negotiate work assignment, layoff, discharge, and recall procedures that apply to workers already employed by the firm or laid off. These procedures give the unions some control of the firm's internal labor market, so that the external labor market has a direct effect on wage and employment decisions only at "ports of entry" into the firm.

Controlling entry into a trade and access to employment opportunities (and thereby restricting the supply of labor available to a firm or a group of firms) presumably increases the bargaining power of a union and improves the relative economic position of its members. However, the ability of individual unions to reduce, or limit increases in, the supply of labor is more limited than an abstract analysis might suggest. A union is rarely able to control the total supply of labor in a given market and completely insulate its members from nonunion competition.

Apprenticeship Training

A craft union may be able to control entry into a trade through compulsory apprenticeship training programs or statutory licensing requirements. Only a minority of unions have formal apprenticeship programs. Most skilled workers, even in trades with such programs, acquire proficiency in their craft through other channels—through informal on-the-job training, through jobs as helpers, through vocational education, or through military service. It is not practical to try to exclude such persons from membership in a union or from jobs in firms organized by the union. A nonunion labor pool is usually a threat to union standards, and a policy of *inclusion* is preferable to one of *exclusion* if the union wants to retain control of the work within its jurisdiction. Exceptions may occur if the nonunion labor does not represent such a threat.

If a union has organized the employees of all the competitors in a relevant product market and has de facto closed shops in all firms under contract, closing the union's membership book to persons who have not completed formal apprenticeship training will exclude them from employment. This has occurred only in a few skilled trades in local market industries such as building and construction.

Regulations affecting the operation of an apprenticeship system may be included in a collective agreement. The duration of apprenticeships, the number of hours of classroom instruction required, and the wages of apprentices are prescribed. The number of apprentices may be controlled by (1) limiting the number per shop, building site, or employer; (2) fixing the ratio of apprentices to skilled workers; (3) requiring an unduly long period of apprenticeship; or (4) requiring employers to pay apprentices more than they are worth.

Employers, rather than unions, are usually responsible for a failure to employ the maximum number of apprentices authorized by collective agreements. This is because they are reluctant to assume the cost of training skilled workers who may later look elsewhere for jobs. Employers are more willing to train people in particular facets of a firm's operation. If the skills they learn are not transferable (are specific rather than general), this tends to "tie" workers to the firm.

In many cases apprenticeship training has not been adequately correlated with future job opportunities. Few apprentices may be taken on during recessions, so that there is a shortage of qualified workers when economic conditions improve.

Training and Retraining

Although industrial unions do not usually try to control entry into jobs, they do negotiate work rules, including seniority provisions, that limit an employer's freedom to discharge employees and encourage promotion from within. These unions also seek a voice in the administration of training and retraining programs designed to prepare employees for new jobs or for existing jobs requiring different skills. A 1960s Bureau of Labor Statistics study of major collective bargaining agreements showed that 19 percent had formal training provisions and that 32 percent of the workers in the study were affected by them.[5] These programs were concentrated in six industries in which there had been continued technological change and in the larger firms, particularly those negotiating with three unions—the Steelworkers, the UAW, and the Brotherhood of Electrical Workers. The need for mid-career training, particularly for workers adversely affected by technological change and for women reentering the labor force after raising families, will undoubtedly increase the number and scope of such contract provisions.

Minority Group Employment

Federal pressure to increase employment opportunities for minority groups and women may increase the number of on-the-job training programs if the workers who are hired lack the basic mathematical, mechanical, and verbal skills required for higher level jobs within industrial plants. The admission of minority workers and women to formal apprenticeship programs has become a sensitive issue, particularly in some highly skilled building trades. There are two dimensions to the problem: (1) the need to ensure that members of minority groups and women are not discriminated against when they seek to enter such programs and (2) the need to provide a disproportionate number of minority group workers and women with training and employment opportunities to compensate for past discrimination. The federal government, through the Office of Federal Contract Compliance, has encouraged the establishment of *affirmative action plans* to increase the percentage of minority group and women workers in large firms and in the building trades in various cities.

Licensing Laws

Certain workers, most frequently barbers, plumbers, stationary engineers, electricians, and taxi drivers, must be licensed to practice their trade, presumably to protect the public's health and safety. Licensing examinations are usually set by boards composed of union or employer representatives, and these boards may try to control the rate of entry into a trade in a state or local labor market. In some cases, licensing requirements may be used to exclude minority group workers or women from jobs. This kind of discrimination is not limited to the skilled trades; professional groups have also misused licensing statutes to attain similar objectives.

Union Control Over Hiring

Unions may try to regulate hiring in two situations: (1) a skilled craft may try to restrict hiring to members of the union and (2) unions in industries in which employment is intermittent may try to limit employment opportunities to union members and to distribute such opportunities equitably.

CLOSED SHOPS
These hire only union members and are a traditional way of limiting access to job opportunities.* It should be noted that closed shops, which have been outlawed by the Taft-Hartley Act, do not reduce the supply of labor unless unions also close their membership books.

HIRING HALLS
An employer may be required to use an external agency such as a union or jointly run hiring hall as a source of employees. Where there is a hiring hall or work referral system, the union agrees to supply workers to employers upon request. Typically, those who have been waiting longest for work are called first. Such an arrangement approximates the rehiring procedures under a seniority system.

* Various types of union security arrangements are described in Chapter 22.

Hiring halls and similar devices are usually confined to the more highly skilled trades, particularly those in which employment is intermittent, and to a few unions whose members are employed on an intermittent or casual basis. In such employments, particularly in local market industries in which the typical employer is a small firm, a hiring hall may improve the organization and operation of labor markets. According to a BLS study,

> such an arrangement allows employers to fill their labor needs quickly and efficiently from a single source. For these workers, there is the advantage of a single clearing house for the jobs. . . .[6]

If the number of workers in the labor pool is not restricted relative to demand, the improvement in the allocative process can be considered a net benefit to society. The longshore industry in the port of New York is a case in point. Before the institution of formal hiring procedures, the labor pool in the industry was excessive. The surplus of labor supported corrupt and illicit hiring arrangements, often involving criminal elements. Today, hiring in the port is controlled by a bistate commission that has reduced the number of longshoremen, checkers, clerks, and miscellaneous workers through a process of "decasualization" and helped the International Longshoremen's Association negotiate an annual wage guarantee.

If a union has the sole authority to refer workers to employers, the employers will try to retain the right to reject applicants and to discharge new hires whose work during a probationary period is unsatisfactory. Otherwise, a work referral system may protect submarginal employees and raise labor costs unnecessarily.

RESTRICTIONS ON HIRING IN CONTRACTS WITH INDUSTRIAL UNIONS

In addition to occasional hiring hall requirements, there are two types of provisions in an industrial union's contract that may limit the employer's freedom to hire whomever it wishes. The first type concerns seniority provisions that, in effect, require promotion from within. These tend to limit hiring to entry level jobs or to certain highly specialized trades for which there is no internal promotional ladder. The second type concerns provisions which require that workers furloughed for economic reasons be recalled in an order that is the reverse of the order in which they were laid off. These provisions, which regularize *re*hiring, insulate workers, once they are hired, from external labor market pressures. They also help to perpetuate a dual labor market.

Rules Against Subcontracting

Firms may subcontract production or maintenance processes to reduce their costs. Thus, automobile manufacturers may subcontract the fabrication of tools, dies or jigs, and basic steel producers depend on building and construction trades to overhaul and periodically rebuild furnaces and other production facilities. Unions usually accept established subcontracting practices but maintain that once their members have acquired control of a job, they can prohibit subcontracting or at least require that proposed subcontracting arrangements be negotiated. The Supreme Court has ruled that subcontracting work previously done by members of a bargaining unit is a matter "appropriate for collective bargaining" under the National Labor Relations Act.

Unions have recently tried to acquire more control over subcontracting, particularly in firms and industries in which employment is declining, and more generally in periods of high unemployment. The 1977 basic steel agreement provided for a major review of contracting out by a tripartite commission of high level representatives of the companies and the union and one impartial member. The commission will apparently deliver a divided report. Although the union had indicated that the resolution of disputes over contracting out would be a top priority during its 1980 negotiations little was accomplished due to the complexity of the issue.[7]

Promotions, Layoffs, and Disciplinary Discharges

In addition to regulating entry into employment, unions try to establish rules that will (1) preserve their members' "earned equities" in employment, (2) let a union control access to "better" employment opportunities within a plant or firm, and (3) protect their members from arbitrary disciplinary actions, particularly arbitrary discharge. Unions believe that in the absence of such provisions, employers may not recognize relative equities and may ignore the human implications of their decisions. Employers generally view the right to promote, lay off, and discipline workers as nonnegotiable managerial prerogatives, particularly in the early stages of a bargaining relationship. However, the critical importance of these procedures usually leads to their regulation under a collective agreement. Many nonunion firms have also found it helpful to formulate objective policies and procedures for handling promotions, layoffs, and less frequently, disciplinary discharges.

Rules that establish disciplinary procedures try to protect workers against arbitrary action on an *individual basis*; rules regulating promotions and temporary and permanent nondisciplinary layoffs try to establish priorities *among employee claimants* to job opportunities. The latter rules protect presently employed workers or workers awaiting recall by insulating them from external labor market pressures. Seniority is the generally accepted standard for ordering such priorities.

SENIORITY

The seniority principle, which assumes that a worker's "equity" in employment increases with his or her length of service, is considered a reasonable basis for ranking employment rights by workers, managers, and union leaders. This principle, used originally as an objective means of determining the order in which employees should be laid off and recalled, is also used (1) to ration scarce employment opportunities and determine which workers will have access to "better" jobs within a firm (*competitive status* seniority); and (2) to determine an employee's eligibility for various benefits and the amount of those benefits (*benefit* seniority).[8] Seniority may also be considered in assessing penalties for disciplinary infractions.

Length of service is measurable, and in the judgment of most unions and many managements it is an objective basis for ordering layoffs and recalls. Management is less willing to base decisions on seniority in other situations involving workers. Unions support seniority systems because their objectivity reduces conflicts between various interest groups within a union. However, at least one study suggests that many employees do not favor the seniority principle and "would prefer rules that stress evaluation of [their] qualification[s] and performance rather than . . . [their] length of service."[9]

Administering Seniority Systems

BENEFIT SENIORITY

Benefit seniority, which applies to such items as pensions, vacations, and eligibility for bonuses and profit-sharing plans, is usually plantwide or corporation-wide. The type and level of specified benefits are tied to an employee's length of service with a firm, or perhaps with several firms in industries in which workers are not continuously employed by a single firm. The administration of benefit seniority is generally straightforward and involves few problems.

COMPETITIVE STATUS SENIORITY

Rules regarding this type of seniority are often complex. The seniority unit and the weight given to length of service in determining an employee's relative status may vary according to the type of action in which seniority is a consideration. For example, the *seniority unit*, that is, the unit of employment in which the employee's relative status is determined, may be narrower for promotions than for layoffs, or seniority may be given less weight in temporary transfers than in permanent ones. The occupational mix of a firm's employees, the way production is organized, the employee turnover rate, the opportunity for upward mobility within the firm, and the extent to which management insists that factors other than seniority be considered in various situations shape the way the principle of competitive status seniority is defined and applied. *Superseniority* with respect to layoffs and recalls may be given to certain categories of employees, to specified employees considered essential to the efficient operation of the firm, or to designated union officials.

Groups of employees will try to structure the seniority system so that it will work to their advantage. Thus, skilled workers may press for narrow seniority units for promotion, thereby restricting the number of candidates for higher paying jobs, and for wide units for layoffs, so that they can displace, or "bump," workers in other departments or divisions of the firm.

Seniority provisions pose sensitive problems in the area of civil rights: should workers excluded from employment, training, or promotional opportunities as the result of past discriminatory practices be given some type of *seniority credit*? No union is likely to accept a system of seniority credits that discriminates against workers who have "earned" their seniority. However, recent court decisions have held that workers assigned to segregated units within a plant may now bid for jobs in other units on the basis of their plantwide, rather than unit, seniority. Thus, major steel producers have been forced to eliminate dual seniority systems at southern mills that had excluded black workers from white seniority "ladders." Persons discriminated against after the passage of the Civil Rights Act of 1964 are entitled to seniority from the date of the discrimination. Note that unintentional discrimination after 1964 which results from a neutral and bona fide seniority system is not grounds for disturbing an existing seniority system. However, in 1979 the Supreme Court held that private employers could *voluntarily* agree with a union to give special preference to black workers to eliminate a "manifest racial imbalance" in jobs traditionally filled by whites.[10]

Layoffs and Discharges

Protection against being arbitrarily discharged is one of the most basic components of job security. There are four types of discharges: (1) discharges for not doing a satisfactory job; (2) temporary discharges (layoffs or furloughs) for economic reasons; (3) permanent discharges for economic reasons; and (4) disciplinary discharges. Unions try to negotiate rules that (1) protect a worker's equity in employment once he or she has completed a probationary period; (2) establish objective standards for reductions in a work force when it must be cut for economic reasons including technological change; and (3) ensure that individual discharges are not arbitrary.

Most employers would like to retain unilateral authority to discharge inefficient workers. In industries where employment is intermittent and employers use a union hiring hall, they often have the right to reject any worker sent to them; but where employment is continuous, unions have made it hard for management to get rid of a worker once he or she has completed a probationary period of employment. The burden of proof of unsatisfactory performance is on the employer when an employee is discharged, and unless the employer is reasonably certain of its ability to defend its actions in arbitration proceedings, no action may be taken. Employers must also prove that there is just cause for the disciplinary dismissal.

Seniority is the most widely accepted criterion for establishing priorities among workers when layoffs are necessary for economic reasons and when workers are recalled. Some agreements provide for sharing whatever work remains (or, more accurately, sharing unemployment) among all the members of a seniority unit before layoffs are made for economic reasons. Some 25 percent of the 1,845 agreements analyzed in one BLS study had work-sharing provisions, most of them effective until the average workweek reached a minimum of 32 hours a week. In addition, 7.3 percent of the agreements restricted overtime during slow or layoff periods; nearly one in five agreements restricted subcontracting that would result in layoffs or subcontracting when employees had already been laid off; and more than a third restricted the hiring of new employees during slack periods or when workers had been laid off.[11] When the workweek had been reduced to the contractual minimum, layoffs could begin, usually in reverse order of seniority.

Workers in the steel, automobile, rubber, and glass industries are now covered by *supplemental unemployment benefit plans* under which a furloughed worker may receive as much as 95 percent of his or her weekly take-home pay. In some cases, this has led to the adoption of a principle of *juniority* in making temporary reductions in a work force. Junior employees continue to work while senior employees are furloughed without losing seniority and without a significant reduction in their income.

Multiplant firms in declining industries, firms that are transferring operations to new locations, and firms that are merging may negotiate *transfer provisions* that protect the employment opportunities of senior workers. They may also be given the option of continuing to work for the firm or receiving *severance pay* based on the number of years they have been with the company. Although transferred workers may not have the same relative status at a new location or within a merged firm, the expansion of the seniority unit gives them more job security. The 1977 basic steel agreement, negotiated when a shutdown of major facilities was imminent, gave workers 41 years of age or older with 20 years of service the right to two full years of supplemental unemployment benefits and then, if they were eligible, a rule of 65 pension (based on a combination of age and service), plus a pension supplement until they began to receive social security benefits.

Promotions

Jobs within a firm vary in pay, in status, in the opportunity they provide for advancement, and in their general desirability, and the concept of earned equity in employment also applies to access to "better" jobs. The selection of employees for promotions and transfers was long considered an essential managerial prerogative. Nevertheless, when workers eligible for promotions were of roughly equal ability, many employers promoted them on the basis of seniority.

Unions try to guarantee access to "better" employment opportunities according to objective criteria, and eligibility and selection for promotions and transfers in union firms is based increasingly on seniority. This represents a significant departure from procedures in those nonunion plants in which management decides whether to fill vacancies from within and in which advancement may be based on favoritism or discrimination.

Promotions are seldom based *solely* on seniority; skill and ability are also considered. There are two types of skill and ability standards: under the first, a senior employee will be promoted if he or she meets the *minimum qualifications* for a job; under the second, a senior employee will be given preference only if the workers who "bid" for a job are *equally qualified*. Both rules tend to favor senior employees because in the first situation, an employer must be prepared to convince an arbitrator that a senior employee who was not promoted could not have done the job, and in the second situation, the firm must be able to show that a junior employee given preference over a senior employee is not only more able but clearly superior to ("head and shoulders above") the senior employee.

The institution of seniority systems in industrial plants usually results in promotion from within unless an employer is prepared to show that no one currently on the payroll is qualified for an opening. Generally, newcomers are hired only for entry level jobs or for jobs requiring special skills. One result has been improvements in hiring, training, and prepromotional procedures to provide a pool of promotable employees. Employers have also tried to define and measure qualifications other than seniority more carefully.

The Impact of Seniority Rules

Seniority has been criticized on three grounds: (1) it lowers worker mobility by "tying" employees with long service records to the firm; (2) it decreases output by reducing the likelihood that workers will be dismissed for not meeting management-imposed production standards; and (3) it reduces the motivation of more able junior employees, whose opportunities for advancement are restricted, to excel at their jobs.

A seniority system probably does reduce the mobility of employees who have worked for a firm for several years, but it is not a significant factor in the employment decisions of the younger workers, who are the most mobile element in our labor force. Protecting workers who have been with an employer for a long time from being discharged may lower efficiency; on the other hand, objective standards for establishing a worker's competitive status and eligibility for benefits may improve morale and increase worker productivity. A seniority system may also encourage a firm's management to improve its employee selection and training procedures to minimize the adverse impact of the system on employee productivity.

Disciplinary Discharges

The system of industrial jurisprudence protects individual employees from arbitrary disciplinary actions. Union leaders maintain however that collective bargaining does not "eliminate" discipline. They acknowledge that management is responsible for the efficient operation of a firm and do not question its right to suspend, discharge, or otherwise discipline a worker "for cause." However, they insist on joint determination of disciplinary procedures, particularly those involving disciplinary discharges. Disciplinary rules and procedures must be clear, they must be made known to employees in advance, and they must be implemented equitably and consistently.

Serious disciplinary cases usually involve subjective considerations, and the circumstances of each case must be taken into account. Penalties must also be consistent with the culture of a particular work environment. Contracts recognize a need for flexibility in two ways: (1) there are no lists of actions for which employees may be *automatically* disciplined, except for violations of certain critical rules (smoking in a munitions plant or assaulting a supervisor); and (2) *specific* penalties are not prescribed for most offenses.[12]

Unions are understandably reluctant to have a hand in disciplining workers. This is considered a management function in which union involvement could be politically dangerous. In disciplinary cases, the burden of proof of misconduct is generally on the employer. Management must be prepared to establish both the factual basis for a disciplinary action and the reasonableness of the penalty imposed. In discharge cases, union leaders may feel compelled by institutional pressures to prosecute grievances that obviously lack merit.

THE WORK ENVIRONMENT

Unions want employers to provide a safe work environment, and most agreements have provisions relating to occupational safety and health. Recently, concern over the "quality" of work life has begun to stimulate interest in providing more satisfactory "total" work environments. Increasing numbers of employers and union leaders recognize that work satisfies psychological as well as economic needs. A work environment that provides little psychological satisfaction is frustrating for individual workers, decreases the quality and quantity of output, and may ultimately lead to social and political unrest. Most employers consider that providing safe and pleasant working conditions is "good" business because (1) it cuts down the cost associated with accidents and on-the-job illness, including premiums for various types of private and public insurance, and (2) workers whose morale is high tend to be more efficient.

Safety and Health

The safety and health provisions negotiated by unions may be based on state and federal legislation, recognized hazards in particular kinds of work, and, less frequently, a desire to restrict output or protect existing jobs. Contract limitations in the longshore industry on the weight to be carried in a single sling, limitations on output under incentive systems of wage payment, and "full crew" laws in the railroad industry have all been defended as safety measures, although one of their primary objectives is to maintain jobs for union members.

In the 1970s, greater emphasis was placed on contract provisions relating to occupational safety and health. The Occupational Safety and Health Act of 1970, which provided more rigorous and complex safety standards and procedures and permitted the presence of union representatives during OSHAct inspections of production facilities was instrumental in moving such contract provisions toward center stage. As we noted in Chapter 18, occupational safety and health have become major issues in many negotiations, and the right of workers acting in good faith to quit work under abnormally dangerous conditions has assumed greater significance.

The establishment and implementation of safety and health standards that comply with OSHAct are often intimately related to a firm's operating procedures and to other bargaining issues and contract provisions. Safety considerations may be key determinants of the way technological changes are made and of the rules governing the operation of new or modified equipment.

The Quality of Work Life

The changing demographic structure of the labor force and the national emphasis on environmental issues and the quality of life have led to considerable scholarly interest in the quality of work life in America. There is continuing debate as to whether economic objectives are still of paramount importance to employees or have been supplanted by other goals that reflect a widespread dissatisfaction with the quality of the life on the job.

To date, neither union leaders nor union members have shown great interest in this debate. The UAW was an early exception; it instituted a program to improve the quality of work life at one plant in Bolivar, Tennessee, in 1973, and during 1973 contract negotiations with General Motors, the union and the firm agreed to set up a joint committee to improve the quality of work life. However, Douglas Fraser, president of the UAW once commented that the "best way to 'humanize' the work place is to get away from it," and the union has also sought to negotiate more paid time away from work.[13]

Many companies have tried to make life more satisfying for their employees through job enrichment programs (making individual jobs more varied and challenging), by giving employees a voice in decision making, by following a policy of management by objectives (in which subordinates help shape the objectives and then are evaluated on the basis of their success in reaching them), by sponsoring sensitivity training and encounter groups, and by productivity bargaining (which through joint committees attempts to ensure that employees receive a proper share of the savings resulting from changes in work rules designed to increase productivity).[14] However, most union leaders would probably agree with William Winpisinger, the president of the Machinists Union, that "the way to enrich the job is to enrich the paycheck." Unions also fear that management may use job enrichment programs as a cloak for speedups. Union leaders will become more interested in such programs when their members force such a response. Programs providing more flexible working hours appear to be a likely initial area for joint union-management efforts to improve the quality of work life.

REGULATING PRODUCTIVE EFFORT

Rules regulating employees' productive efforts are not unique to union firms. In the absence of a union, management will develop formal rules to direct the work force, particularly in larger establishments. Informal rules and practices limiting output or otherwise regulating production may also be enforced informally by a firm's employees. Most informal rules reflect a consensus that certain production norms and procedures are "reasonable" and necessary if job opportunities and earnings are to be maintained in the face of management attempts to increase output and reduce manpower requirements. Collective bargaining enables unions to participate in formulating and administering rules regulating the quality of work, the speed of assembly lines, manning requirements, and the introduction of new equipment.

Most managements see union work rules as curtailing their freedom of action in ways that increase, or prevent them from decreasing, their costs. Critics of unions often exaggerate the extent and cost of work rules. Apparently restrictive rules may not be enforced rigorously. For example, in many areas, work rules in the building trades are not enforced on single family residential construction projects or perhaps on residential construction more generally, and restrictive rules may not be enforced on commercial or industrial construction projects in areas where there is significant nonunion competition. Moreover, the job protection afforded workers by a union contract may make them more willing to accept and adjust to innovation. Nevertheless, it is clear that some work rules unnecessarily restrict output or otherwise interfere with efficient operations. These are often termed "*make-work*" rules.

Saving and Making Work

The term *make-work* misrepresents the *original* justification for many restrictive rules. It suggests that at some time, a conscious effort was made to *create additional* jobs in the face of opposition from an efficiency conscious employer. This happens rarely; most so-called *make-work* rules were never intended to *make* work, but simply to *save* work or jobs threatened by a change in technology or the organization of production. They were designed to protect *employed* members of the labor force.* Once negotiated however, such rules do not only save work for the present generation of employees, they may also create job opportunities for succeeding generations of workers. *Save-work* rules are thus

---

* Racketeering unions may however force employers to hire *additional,* unneeded, workers.

transformed into *make-work* rules. In addition, work rules and practices that were not restrictive when they were originally instituted may become so as the technology and organization of production change or if employers permit loose production standards to develop. However, the "red letter" rates negotiated by industrial unions to protect the wages of individual workers affected by technological or organizational change are not perpetuated.

The acceptance and perpetuation of a restrictive work rule is presumably based on conscious trade-offs. The union has given up something in return, often a more substantial wage increase, so that the cost to the employer of accepting or continuing the rule is presumably less than the cost of refusing to adopt it or eliminating it. With the passage of time, the cost of eliminating a restrictive rule tends to rise; whatever the original justification for the rule, the workers protected by it tend to assume that they have a right to do the job as it has always been done and to strenuously resist change.

Effective contract administration requires that management review formal and informal work rules and practices on a continuing basis and modify or eliminate those that cannot be justified. A major change in technology, the introduction of a new product line, or the opening of a new production facility may enable management to initiate a comprehensive review of existing work rules. Study committees established well in advance of such events may help unions and management develop equitable procedures for modifying existing work rules.

Although most save-work rules are informal, established practices will be recognized by arbitrators, and contracts may codify accepted shop practices. National contracts may require a firm's management to recognize local work rules and working conditions. For example, the longstanding section 2B of the basic agreement between the U.S. Steel Corporation and the United Steelworkers states in part that

> the term "local working conditions" . . . means specific practices or customs which reflect detailed application of the subject matter within the scope of wages, hours of work, or other conditions of employment and *includes local agreements, written or oral* on such matters. It is recognized that it is impracticable to set forth in this Agreement all of these working conditions, which are of a local nature only. (Emphasis added.)

An abortive attempt by management to eliminate this provision so as to have more flexibility in organizing production led to a lengthy strike in 1959.

Reasons for "Make-Work"

According to Slichter, Healy, and Livernash, whose study of the impact of collective bargaining on management has been a classic in the field for 20 years,

> [f]our principal conditions stimulate the interest of unions in make-work practices: (1) shrinking employment in an industry . . . ; (2) intermittent employment; (3) union success in negotiating unusually high rates of pay and attractive conditions

of work; and (4) conditions that enable a substantial portion of the union's membership to benefit from make-work practices.[15]

A *craft union* negotiates restrictive work rules because a reduction in the number of jobs or in the skills required to do the work within its jurisdiction threatens not only the incomes and job security of the membership but the jurisdiction and institutional security of the union itself. An *industrial union* is less likely to negotiate such rules because technological and organizational innovations may not threaten the total number of job opportunities within the union's jurisdiction. However, industrial unions may enforce output limitations on non-machine-paced operations to prevent a reduction in manpower requirements or incentive pay. Not unexpectedly, such rules have been concentrated in a limited number of industries: local transportation, building and construction, entertainment, the longshore industry, and the operating (running) trades on the railroads.

Types of Restrictive Work Rules

Slichter, Healy, and Livernash[16] identify 11 kinds of work rules that deliberately limit the output of certain groups of employees to increase the number of jobs:

1. Limits on the size of loads that may be handled—for example, the weight of sling loads in the longshore industry or the number of bricks per hod or pallet.
2. Restrictions on the duties of workers in given occupations. Teamsters' locals, for example, may prohibit drivers from unloading trucks.
3. Requirements that work be done twice. For example, the old "bogus" rule of the International Typographical Union requiring that when local advertisements were run in more than one newspaper, the copy be reset, read, and corrected. In practice, the work was often never done but "given up" for some other contractual gain.[17]
4. Requirements that unnecessary work be done, for example, that three coats of plaster be used in residential construction.
5. Limits on the number of machines a worker may operate or tend—for example, the number of looms that may be handled by weavers in the textile industry.
6. Requirements that work crews—longshore gangs, stage crews, flight crews, and train crews for example—be unnecessarily large. Perhaps the best known of such rules was the requirement that a fireman be employed on trains with diesel engines. The elimination of this rule in freight service involved prolonged negotiations and a series of interventions by the federal government that culminated in legislation establishing an arbitration board.
7. Prohibitions on the use of modern equipment or tools—for example, prohibitions by painters on the use of spray guns in construction.

8. Rules requiring less efficient methods of work—for example, prohibitions on the off-site fabrication of piping and fixtures in the plumbing trades.
9. Requirements that employees have excessive relief time—for example, unnecessary rest or cleanup periods or long coffee breaks.
10. Rules requiring unneeded standby crews—for example, local standby bands when traveling bands perform or standby musicians when mechanical music is used.
11. Rules enforcing loose production standards or limiting a worker's speed or daily output. Traditional output standards may be maintained despite technological changes that increase a worker's productivity.

The term *featherbedding* is often used interchangeably with "make-work," but it is also used in a more limited sense to refer to rules that require the employment of a specified number of unnecessary workers, usually members of a given craft. Requiring the presence of standby musicians for a show or a fourth person (the "featherbird") in the cockpit of commercial jets is considered featherbedding, whereas limiting daily output or doing work in a manner made obsolete by a technological change is "making work"

Management's Responsibility for "Save-Work" Rules

Many widely publicized save-work rules were accepted by management because of short-run considerations. The railroads agreed to employ firemen on diesel locomotives because they did not anticipate the decline in steam power. In February of 1937, when the firemen negotiated the National Diesel Agreement, Class I railroads had 43,624 steam locomotives and only 218 diesels; in 1959, when the carriers started trying seriously to eliminate "unnecessary" firemen, the railroad industry had 28,163 diesels and only 754 steam locomotives.[18]

Broadway producers acknowledge that rules requiring the employment of unnecessary stagehands and musicians were accepted initially to meet production deadlines and realize short-run profits. In 1959, American Airlines agreed to have four crew members—three pilots and a flight engineer—on the flight deck of the first jet aircraft, which had been designed for a crew of three, to obtain a competitive advantage over other airlines, which would not have jets operational for another six months. The fourth crew member, "the featherbird," was eliminated only after a series of lengthy disputes involving a number of airlines.[19]

In the construction industry, in which a strike by a single craft will shut down an entire project, a contractor is likely to accept a work rule that adds little to its total costs. A series of such concessions may saddle the industry with a costly superstructure of restrictive rules.

Once work rules are adopted, it is difficult to eliminate them. However, there are recent examples of the elimination of well-entrenched rules. In 1960, the Pacific Maritime Association "bought out" a number of restrictive rules in the

West Coast longshore industry. The association agreed to pay $5 million a year for 5½ years into a fund to be administered jointly with the International Longshoremen's and Warehousemen's Union. The money would be used to provide a wage guarantee for younger workers and retirement benefits for older men. One feature of the agreement was a provision that machines were to be used where possible to lighten work. By 1966, the net gain to the industry from the elimination of work rules and increased mechanization had reached an estimated $120 million.[20]

A number of financially hard-pressed municipalities are trying to either "buy back" or compel unions to modify work rules that lower the productivity of its workers. The cities' demands include one rather than two officers in police cars, larger sanitation trucks, and fewer or shorter coffee breaks. In New York City, members of the police force agreed to "give back" a day off following a blood donation.

Unions in the construction industry have been compelled to eliminate or revise a variety of contract provisions in an effort to prevent a further loss of work to nonunion firms. In May 1978, the National Constructor's Association, a group whose members include the largest unionized contractors and design constructors, and eight national building trades unions negotiated an agreement covering 11 southeastern states that

> included . . . a variety of management rights and work rule clauses generally associated with efficiency and productivity. For example, strikes, standby crews, featherbedding and organized coffee breaks and rest periods are banned; overtime won't be worked except in unusual circumstances; there won't be any limits on production or on the use of tools or equipment; and stewards will be working journeymen.[21]

A Summary Comment

Formal restrictive work rules are less numerous than is generally assumed. Well-managed enterprises have been able to avoid or to eliminate save-work rules or practices. The more restrictive and costly work rules and practices are found (1) in poorly managed firms, (2) in certain highly competitive local market industries, (3) in declining industries, and (4) in contracts negotiated by craft as opposed to industrial unions. The cost of restrictive rules and practices cannot be estimated with any confidence, but the greatest cost probably results from informal shop practices enforced by both unorganized and organized workers.[22] This cost involves some combination of lower wages for employees, lower profits for employers, higher prices for the consumer, and a reduction in the rate of economic growth.

On the other hand, work rules force management to recognize a union member's equity in employment and help to offset the social cost of technological and organizational change. It is often hard to determine on the basis of cost-benefit analysis whether a particular rule is a constructive solution to the conflict between management's pursuit of efficiency and the union member's pursuit of job and income security or an "unreasonable" restriction on productivity. Save-work rules are probably not a socially optimal way of protecting workers from change in the long run.

REGULATING TECHNOLOGICAL CHANGE

In an earlier chapter, we noted that technological change has probably not reduced the total number of job opportunities in the economy but that it has modified or eliminated employment opportunities in specific occupations, industries, and geographic areas. American unions generally accept the inevitability of technological innovation. However, the broadly diffused benefits of technological change are not usually part of the calculus that determines a union's reaction to a *specific* change. The union is concerned about the impact of the change on the short-run employment and income prospects of its membership rather than the long-run impact on employment in society at large.

In the 1950s and early 1960s, automation focused interest on technological unemployment and stimulated a number of unions and managements to try new ways of cushioning the impact of technological change. To date, the effect of automation has not been dissimilar to that of the more traditional types of technological change. However, some experts believe that the number of workers displaced by computer-controlled production techniques will be much greater in the 1980s.

Changes in production processes and techniques and in the organization of production are initiated by management and do not usually constitute a major threat to the job or income security of union members. Many changes are not bargainable issues; others may be challenged, often under a grievance procedure, if they involve modifications of wage or work standards. Changes that pose a major threat to worker security will be met with resistance, and collective bargaining provides a way of articulating this resistance. Often it results in contract provisions that force management to assume some of the social costs of change. A number of the restrictive work rules we have described are the result of unions' attempts to obstruct or control technological change. However, such rules usually try to *regulate* rather than prohibit change.

Unions faced with a technological change try to (1) protect the jobs of the largest possible number of presently employed union members, (2) ensure compensation for disemployed or downgraded workers, and (3) ensure their own survival as institutions.

Union Policies Toward Technological Change

Five principal types of union policies toward technological change have been identified: willing acceptance, opposition, competition, encouragement, and adjustment.[23]

Willing acceptance is the most common policy. The employer makes a change that the union accepts because it has no significant impact on skill requirements or the number of employment opportunities within the firm. Increases in productivity resulting from the change are expected to be shared with the employees, and the size of their share is usually a matter for collective bargaining.

Opposition occurs in only a small proportion of cases. The initial refusal of longshoremen to handle containers is one example. Instead of bluntly refusing to accept a change, some unions may oppose the introduction of new ways of doing things indirectly—for example, by requiring that an unnecessary number of workers be employed. A policy of opposition cannot succeed unless the union can also prevent the use of new techniques or equipment in other firms. In the long run, there is little likelihood a union will be able to prevent technological change by opposing it—though it may delay its introduction for a limited period.[24]

Sometimes a union will try to maintain control of work done by its members by making an older process of production more *competitive,* possibly by allowing a reduction in wages. This competitive approach may be successful for a short time, but again, the union cannot expect to prevent the introduction of a new device or process permanently.

A union may adopt a policy of *encouragement* of technological change when it is trying to help a firm or industry remain competitive. Unions may also encourage innovations when profit-sharing plans are in effect or employees are paid under an incentive system. However, management must be alert to prevent the development of loose production standards that may be costly to eliminate.

A policy of *adjustment* represents an attempt by a union to control the introduction or use of new equipment, processes, or materials. It may refer to new work and pay standards that accompany routine changes, or to conscious efforts by unions "to deal with extraordinary opportunities or special problems presented by technological changes."[25] The latter category includes many "creative" responses to technological change.

Management negotiators should evaluate both the short- and long-run costs and benefits of different "creative" policy options. Not "costing out" a response may saddle an industry with an unexpectedly large financial burden. For example, underestimates of increases in productivity from the use of container ships caused employers in the port of New York to underestimate the cost of the guaranteed income and fringe benefit payments that they had agreed to make when they bought out the International Longshoreman's Association rule book. This was one factor that placed the port at a competitive disadvantage during the 1970s.[26]

The Determinants of Policy

Contract provisions relating to technological change are usually tailored to the needs of particular bargaining relationships. They are affected by the organization of production within a firm and the relative bargaining power of the union and management. According to Slichter, Healy, and Livernash, four conditions determine what kind of policy will be adopted:[27]

1. *The nature of the union.* A craft union threatened by a technological change may try to *obstruct* or *prevent* it. An industrial union, which will still have jurisdiction over employees working on a new process, will probably try to *regulate* the change.

2. *The economic condition of the industry, enterprise, or occupation.* If an employer faces a serious competitive threat, a union may encourage innovation to preserve job opportunities. If a firm or an industry is expanding, a union is more likely to favor a policy of adjustment because the resulting reduction in the demand for labor may be relative rather than absolute.

   The reaction of unions in declining industries is less certain. A union may follow a policy of competition in an effort to reduce costs and save jobs. On the other hand, if a decline in employment opportunities seems inevitable, the union may adopt a policy of obstruction to preserve job opportunities for as long as possible. Craft unions in declining industries may be forced to accept changes they would resist under more favorable conditions.

3. *The nature of the technological change.* According to Slichter, Healy, and Livernash,

   This is the most important determinant. . . . Three factors are of utmost importance to the unions: (1) the effect of the change on the number of jobs on the process or in the bargaining unit; (2) the effect on the *degree* of skill and responsibility of the employees; and (3) the effect on the *kind* of skill or other qualifications required to do the work.[28]

   These three factors determine the number of employees within the firm who will remain within a union's jurisdiction.

4. *The state of development of the technological change and of the union's policy toward it.* Competition from nonunion plants or substitute products may force unions to stop opposing a change and try to adjust to it.

Contract provisions supporting these different strategies will reflect the parameters of specific bargaining relationships. An "adjustment strategy" in an industrial corporation with several plants may include job and income protection for the most senior employees; interplant and interarea transfer rights, with relocation allowances for less senior employees; and severance allowances for discharged workers, including those who decline transfers.[29] The threat to job and income security posed by the more massive types of innovation has led a number of unions to shift from a strategy of *job protection* to one of *income protection,* with the stress on monetary compensation for workers discharged as a result of technological change. In such situations, the gains from innovation are shared on a *long-run* basis only with those workers who keep their jobs.

Well-managed firms recognize that most major technological innovations involve considerable lead time and that the right kind of advance planning can minimize the impact of various changes on the company's labor force. The establishment of a joint union-management Human Relations Committee in the steel industry, the continuing study of the labor problems resulting from the relocation of plants in the meat-packing industry under the Armour Plan, and the tripartite committee set up at Kaiser Steel to evolve a long-range plan for sharing the fruits of progress between employees, stockholders, and the public are evidence of a growing awareness of the value of union-management cooperation in cushioning the impact of technological change.[30]

Some union leaders have suggested reducing the workweek without reducing workers' weekly paychecks to offset the disemployment effects of automation. This kind of work-sharing policy may be of some help in a transitional period when an innovation destroys employment opportunities, but a reduction in hours cannot by itself provide *long-run* job security in a firm or industry.

SUMMARY

A recurrent theme in this chapter has been the role of the union as an institutional mechanism that lets employees challenge management's decision-making authority, makes the jobs of individual workers more secure, and assures employees of more consistent and equitable treatment. The work rules negotiated by unions constitute a legislative framework for the system of industrial jurisprudence—typically including a grievance procedure—that regulates the employment relationship. In the majority of bargaining relationships, unions put no direct restrictions on managerial initiative, but they reserve the right to challenge specific management actions. This has made management more alert to the effect of their decisions on employees.

Work rules are found in nonunion as well as union firms. Moreover, informal rules and practices are more numerous, and probably more costly, than the formal rules popularly identified with unionism. Work rules tend to acquire legitimacy with the passage of time and to become increasingly costly to eliminate. Good managers avoid making expedient compromises that ignore the long-run impact of ostensibly reasonable rules. They are also alert to the need to modify work rules as technological, organizational, or market conditions change. Rules that require the employment of unnecessary workers are most likely in a limited number of industries in which unions have considerable bargaining leverage and in which technological change, fluctuations in demand, or the intermittent nature of employment relationships make job security a particularly serious issue.

DISCUSSION QUESTIONS

1. Do you consider the economic or extraeconomic aspects of collective bargaining to be of greater importance to the average union member?

2. Do local and national union officials have similar perspectives regarding work rules?
3. Is union participation in the formulation of the "web of rule" desirable in private enterprises?
4. Do union or management officials tend to place greater emphasis on contract administration?
5. Are any managerial or academic personnel at your college or university organized? If so, what kind of grievance procedure has been established? If they are not organized, how are grievances handled?
6. Why do craft unions and industrial unions usually adopt somewhat different rules regulating access to job opportunities within a firm?
7. Why has the subcontracting of work by industrial firms become a more sensitive bargaining issue?
8. Should management have unilateral authority to discharge inefficient workers?
9. What, conceptually, is the difference between *make-work* and *save-work*?
10. Why have restrictive work rules become such an important bargaining issue in the public sector?

SELECTED READINGS

Grievance Procedures

Kuhn, James W. "The Grievance Process." In *Frontiers of Collective Bargaining*. Ed. by John T. Dunlop and Neil W. Chamberlain, pp. 252–270. New York: Harper & Row, 1967.

Slichter, Sumner H.; Healy, James J.; and Livernash, E. Robert. *The Impact of Collective Bargaining on Management*. Chaps. 23–26. Washington, D.C.: Brookings Institution, 1960. This is a definitive work, a revision of Slichter's *Union Policies and Industrial Management,* published in 1941.

Apprenticeship Training

Employment and Training Report of the President. Published annually by the U.S. Government Printing Office. A good source of current data.

Slichter, Sumner H.; Healy, James J.; and Livernash, E. Robert. *The Impact of Collective Bargaining on Management*. Chap. 4, "Union Policies in Training and Apprenticeship." Washington, D.C.: Brookings Institution, 1960.

Work Referral Systems

Slichter, Sumner H.; Healy, James J.; and Livernash, E. Robert. *The Impact of Collective Bargaining on Management*. Chap. 3, "The Control of Hiring." Washington, D.C.: Brookings Institution, 1960.

U.S. Department of Labor, Labor-Management Services Administration, Office of Labor-Management Policy Development. *Exclusive Work Referral Systems in the Building Trades,* July 1970.

Layoffs and Discharges

Slichter, Sumner H.; Healy, James J.; and Livernash, E. Robert. *The Impact of Collective Bargaining on Management*. Chap. 6, "Work-Sharing and Layoff Systems," and chap. 21, "Disciplinary Policies and Procedures." Washington, D.C.: Brookings Institution, 1960.

Tillery, Winston L. "Layoff and Recall Provisions in Major Agreements." In *Monthly Labor Review* 94, no. 7 (July 1971): pp. 41–46.

U.S. Department of Labor, Bureau of Labor Statistics. *Major Collective Bargaining Agreements: Layoff, Recall, and Worksharing Procedures.* Bulletin 1425–13.

Transfer Provisions

U.S. Department of Labor, Bureau of Labor Statistics. *Major Collective Bargaining Agreements: Severance Pay and Layoff Benefit Plans.* Bulletin 1425–2.

U.S. Department of Labor, Bureau of Labor Statistics. *Major Collective Bargaining Agreements: Seniority in Promotion and Transfer Provisions.* Bulletin 1425–11.

Promotions

Slichter, Sumner H.; Healy, James J.; and Livernash, E. Robert. *The Impact of Collective Bargaining on Management.* Chap. 7, "Promotion Policies and Procedures." Washington, D.C.: Brookings Institution, 1960.

U.S. Department of Labor. *Major Collective Bargaining Agreements: Seniority in Promotion and Transfer Provisions.* Bulletin 1425–11.

Disciplinary Discharges

Slichter, Sumner H.; Healy, James J.; and Livernash, E. Robert. *The Impact of Collective Bargaining on Management.* Chap. 21, "Disciplinary Policies and Procedures." Washington, D.C.: Brookings Institution, 1960.

Occupational Safety and Health

U.S. Department of Labor, Bureau of Labor Statistics. *Major Collective Bargaining Agreements: Safety and Health Provisions.* Bulletin 1425–16.

The Quality of Work Life

Barbash, Jack. *Job Satisfaction Attitudes Surveys.* Paris: Organization for Economic Co-operation and Development, 1976.

Bok, Derek C., and Dunlop, John T. *Labor and the American Community,* pp. 351–360. New York: Simon & Schuster, 1970.

Levitan, Sar A., and Johnston, William B. *Work Is Here to Stay, Alas.* Salt Lake City, Utah: Olympus Publishing Co., 1973.

O'Toole, James, ed. *Work and the Quality of Life: Resource Papers for "Work in America."* Cambridge, Mass.: MIT Press, 1974.

Rosow, Jerome M., ed. *The Worker and the Job: Coping with Change.* Published for the American Assembly, Columbia University. Englewood Cliffs, N.J.: Prentice-Hall, 1974.

Work in America, Report of a Special Task Force to the Secretary of Health, Education, and Welfare. Cambridge, Mass.: MIT Press, 1973.

Restrictions on Productivity

Bok, Derek C., and Dunlop, John T. *Labor and the American Community.* Chap. 9, "The Impact of Collective Bargaining on Productivity." New York: Simon & Schuster, 1970.

Leiter, Robert D. *Featherbedding and Job Security.* New York: Twayne, 1964.

Mathewson, Stanley B. *Restriction of Output Among Unorganized Workers.* New York: Viking Press, 1931.

Northrup, Herbert R.; Storholm, Gordon R.; and Abodeely, Paul A. *Restrictive Labor Practices in the Supermarket Industry.* Philadelphia: University of Pennsylvania Press, 1967.

Roethlisberger, F. J., and Dickson, William J. *Management and the Worker.* Cambridge, Mass.: Harvard University Press, 1946.

Slichter, Sumner H. *Union Policies and Industrial Management.* Chap. VI, "Make-Work Rules and Policies." Washington, D.C.: Brookings Institution, 1941.

Slichter, Sumner H.; Healy, James J.; and Livernash, E. Robert. *The Impact of Collective Bargaining on Management.* Chap. 11, "Make-Work Rules and Policies." Washington, D.C.: Brookings Institution, 1960.

Weinstein, Paul A., ed. *Featherbedding and Technological Change.* Lexington, Mass.: Heath, 1965.

Responses to Technological Change

American Federation of Labor and Congress of Industrial Organizations. *Labor Looks at Automation.* Washington, D.C.: AFL-CIO, December 1966.

Aronson, Robert L. *Jobs, Wages, Changing Technology.* Ithaca, N.Y.: NYS School of Industrial and Labor Relations, Cornell University, Bulletin 55, July 1965.

Mesthene, Emmanuel G. *Technological Change: Its Impact on Man and Society.* Cambridge, Mass.: Harvard University Press, 1970.

Slichter, Sumner H. *Union Policies and Industrial Management.* Chaps. VII–IX. Washington, D.C.: Brookings Institution, 1941.

Slichter, Sumner H.; Healy, James J.; and Livernash, E. Robert. *The Impact of Collective Bargaining on Management.* Chap. 12, "Union Policies Toward Technological Change." Washington, D.C.: Brookings Institution, 1960.

Somers, Gerald G.; Cushman, Edward L.; and Weinberg, Nat, eds. *Adjusting to Technological Change.* Industrial Relations Research Association Publication Number 29. New York: Harper & Row, 1963.

Notes

1. Sumner H. Slichter, *Union Policies and Industrial Management* (Washington, D.C.: Brookings Institution, 1941), p. 1.
2. Ibid., pp. 165–166.
3. *Monthly Labor Review* 62, no. 1 (January 1946): p. 42.
4. U.S. Department of Labor, Bureau of Labor Statistics, *Characteristics of Major Collective Bargaining Agreements, January 1, 1978*, Bulletin 2065, Table 8.1, p. 105. See also the same bureau's *Major Collective Bargaining Agreements: Grievance Procedures,* Bulletin 1425–1.

5. U.S. Department of Labor, Bureau of Labor Statistics, *Major Collective Bargaining Agreements: Training and Retraining Provisions,* Bulletin 1425–7, p. 2. This 1969 study examined 1,823 agreements, each covering 1,000 workers or more.

6. U.S. Department of Labor, Labor-Management Services Administration, Office of Labor-Management Policy Development, *Exclusive Work Referral Systems in the Building Trades,* July 1970, p. 3.

7. *The Wall Street Journal,* November 12, 1979, p. 2, December 10, 1979, p. 14, and April 16, 1980, p. 5.

8. Sumner H. Slichter, James J. Healy, and E. Robert Livernash, *The Impact of Collective Bargaining on Management* (Washington, D.C.: Brookings Institution, 1960), p. 106.

9. Philip Selznick and Howard Vollmer, "Rule of Law in Industry: Seniority Rights," in *Industrial Relations* 1, no. 3 (May 1962): p. 116.

10. *Steelworkers* v. *Weber,* Supreme Court Nos. 78–432, 78–435, 78–436, June 27, 1979.

11. Winston L. Tillery, "Layoff and Recall Provisions in Major Agreements," in *Monthly Labor Review* 94 no. 7 (July 1971): pp. 44–45.

12. Slichter, Healy, and Livernash, *Impact of Collective Bargaining,* pp. 628–629.

13. *The Wall Street Journal,* January 26, 1977, p. 24.

14. See Richard E. Walton, "Innovative Restructuring of Work," in Jerome M. Rosow, ed., *The Worker and the Job.* Published for the American Assembly, Columbia University, (Englewood Cliffs, N.J.: Prentice-Hall, 1974), pp. 148–149. See also Irving Bluestone, "Creating a new world of work," in *International Labour Review* 115, no. 1 (January–February 1977): pp. 1–10, and Gerald Somers, chairman, editorial board, *Collective Bargaining and Productivity* (Madison, Wisc.: Industrial Relations Research Association, 1975).

15. Slichter, Healy, and Livernash, *Impact of Collective Bargaining,* p. 335.

16. Ibid., pp. 317–332.

17. See Paul Jacobs, *Dead Horse and the Featherbird* (Santa Barbara, Calif.: Center for the Study of Democratic Institutions, 1962).

18. Robert D. Leiter, *Featherbedding and Job Security* (New York: Twayne, 1964), pp. 77–78.

19. Jacobs, *Dead Horse and the Featherbird,* pp. 40–56.

20. See Max D. Kossoris, "Working Rules in West Coast Longshoring," in *Monthly Labor Review* 84, no. 1 (January 1961): pp. 1–10 and "1966 West Coast Longshore Negotiations," in *Monthly Labor Review* 89, no. 10 (October 1966): pp. 1067–1069.

21. "NCA and Labor Wrap Up New Kind of Labor Pact," in *Engineering News-Record* 200, no. 21 (May 25, 1978): p. 9.

22. Benjamin Aaron, "Governmental Restraints on Featherbedding," in Paul A. Weinstein, ed., *Featherbedding and Technological Change* (Lexington, Mass.: Heath, 1965), p. 105. (Reprinted from *Stanford Law Review* V 1953.)

23. Cf. Slichter, Healy, and Livernash, *Impact of Collective Bargaining,* pp. 344–362.

24. Ibid., p. 371.

25. Ibid., p. 361.

26. *The New York Times,* August 18, 1971, pp. 33 and 41.

27. *Impact of Collective Bargaining,* pp. 345–348.

28. Ibid., pp. 346–347.

29. Cf. Jack Barbash, "The Impact of Technology on Labor-Management Relations," in Gerald G. Somers, Edward L. Cushman, and Nat Weinberg, eds., *Adjusting to Technological Change.* Industrial Relations Research Association Publication 29 (New York: Harper & Row, 1963), pp. 46ff.

30. See Robert L. Aronson, *Jobs, Wages, & Changing Technology* (Ithaca, N.Y.: NYS School of Industrial and Labor Relations, Cornell University, July 1965), pp. 51–61; James J. Healy, ed., *Creative Collective Bargaining: Meeting Today's Challenges to Labor-Management Relations* (Englewood Cliffs, N.J.: Prentice-Hall, 1965); Charles C. Killingsworth, "Cooperative Approaches to Problems of Technological Change," in Somers et al., eds., *Adjusting to Technological Change,* pp. 61–94; and James L. Stern, "Collective Bargaining Trends and Patterns," in *A Review of Industrial Relations Research,* vol. II (Madison, Wisc.: Industrial Relations Research Association, 1971), pp. 128–132.

Chapter 22
COLLECTIVE AGREEMENTS III: INSTITUTIONAL SECURITY

We have seen that through the collective bargaining process workers are able to participate in establishing the terms and conditions of employment and in administering and interpreting substantive contract provisions. Most of the provisions of collective agreements relate to and affect employees as individuals. Collective bargaining is also an *institutional* relationship, and collective agreements usually contain provisions providing varying degrees of institutional security for the contracting parties. These provisions affect the power structure of a bargaining relationship and, indirectly, the security of employees covered by the agreement.

The importance of institutional security to a union is clear. Unless the union can maintain its membership base and generate adequate revenues, its effectiveness as a bargaining agent will be diminished or even destroyed. The emphasis on, and the high incidence of, formal union security provisions is unique to the United States. Most union leaders believe that employers are basically hostile to unionism and that American workers, who are less class conscious and less politically committed than many of their foreign counterparts, are often reluctant to join and support unions. In these circumstances, achieving some type of contractual security has become a fundamental bargaining objective.

Contract provisions that protect the employment opportunities of a union's members also enhance the security of the union and union leadership. Some of these provisions may give the union control over entry into a trade or over hiring; others may outline work rules that protect the membership from disemployment or a dilution of skills caused by technological changes. Such provisions, which are of particular importance in highly skilled trades and industries where employment is intermittent, were discussed in Chapter 21.

Unions necessarily limit the unilateral exercise of managerial authority, and managements naturally try to restrict the scope of collective bargaining. They may do so by negotiating contract provisions that (1) establish a *broad base* of managerial authority or (2) identify *specific management functions* that will not be shared with the union. Provisions of this kind may be considered *management security provisions*. However, managers are probably less interested than union leaders in formal security provisions. Many firms believe that hard bargaining and effective contract administration are more effective ways of preventing unions from infringing on managerial prerogatives.

Following World War II, it was often assumed that as the adversary character of collective bargaining relationships was muted by the passage of time, there would be less controversy over such provisions. Many students of labor-management relations thought that institutional security would not be a critical issue in "mature" bargaining relationships. Management, they reasoned, would recognize that a secure union would be able to adopt a more constructive approach to the negotiation and interpretation of contracts and this, in turn, would diminish the need for strong management rights provisions. However, the difficulties many unions have encountered in extending, and in some cases protecting, their organizational base, and management's recent efforts to obtain more control over the direction of the work force and more freedom to make changes in production techniques have reemphasized the importance of such provisions. Union and management security may well be critical bargaining issues in the 1980s, particularly in firms threatened by nonunion or foreign competition and in newly established plants of multiplant firms under contract with a union.

In this chapter, we will (1) describe the various types of union security arrangements negotiated in the United States, (2) analyze present legislation regulating such arrangements, (3) discuss the "right-to-work" controversy, (4) describe the types of provisions management has negotiated in an attempt to limit the scope of collective bargaining, and (5) consider the current and prospective significance of such management rights provisions.

UNION SECURITY PROVISIONS

American union leaders are more interested than their foreign counterparts in providing union security through formal contractual provisions. They are convinced that unions in this country face a struggle for survival as a result of several factors:

1. The hostility of employers toward unionism.
2. The lack of class consciousness in the labor force and a correlative lack of identification with unionism. Although relatively few workers seem opposed to union membership on principle, it is hard to recruit and retain members and to develop stable sources of revenue. High employee turnover rates may accentuate these problems.
3. The need to protect a union's status as bargaining agent against competition from other labor organizations. This was an important consideration during the period of rival unionism that followed the split between the A.F. of L. and the CIO.
4. The (relative) decline in employment in traditionally highly organized industries, occupations, and geographic areas.
5. The current emphasis of management on the need for increased productivity to meet nonunion and foreign competition, which has encouraged open shops. In the construction industry, for example, *merit shops* employing union and nonunion workers have replaced union shops in some areas.

Types of Union Security Arrangements

Formal union security provisions vary in terms of the degree of compulsion they exert on the employees of a firm to become union members. Some contracts simply recognize a union as a bargaining agent, others call for a union shop. The most basic type of union security, *recognition as a bargaining agent*, is based on federal law, which states that workers have the *right to organize* into unions of their own choosing, that an employer *must bargain collectively* with the representative selected by a majority of the employees in a unit appropriate to collective bargaining, and that this bargaining representative shall be the *exclusive bargaining agent* for all the workers in the unit. Other types of union security arrangements are agreed on by the parties to collective bargaining. They include provisions indicating an employer's approval of union membership, a requirement that union members stay members for the life of a contract, agency shops, modified union shops, union shops, preferential hiring, and closed shops.

The type of union security arrangement that is negotiated depends on the legal status of these various arrangements; the occupations of the workers covered by an agreement; the stability of employment within a firm and an industry; customary practices in an area, occupation, or industry; the relative bargaining power of the union; and in some cases, the employer's philosophy regarding union security arrangements.

APPROVAL OF MEMBERSHIP

A firm may agree to indicate its support of the principle of unionism to new employees and encourage them to join the union. The impact of such encouragement will depend on the spirit in which it is given and the cohesiveness of the work force.

MAINTENANCE OF MEMBERSHIP

Sometimes employees are not required to join a union, but an employee who is or becomes a member must maintain his or her membership for the life of the contract. Such an arrangement usually has an *escape clause* that permits a member to resign from the union during a specified period, typically during the 15 days prior to a contract expiration date. Few workers exercise this option; once they join a union, they are usually willing to remain members, although they may be reluctant to support the union financially or to be active in its affairs.

AGENCY SHOPS

Employees in an agency shop are not required to become union members, but they must pay a *service fee,* usually equal to the customary union dues and fees, to the bargaining agent. This type of arrangement occurs (1) when an employer accepts unionism and collective bargaining and acknowledges that members of a bargaining unit have an obligation to support the union financially but also believes that they should not be forced to join a union against their will and (2) in some states where union shops have been prohibited by law. However, a majority of the states that ban union shops also ban agency shops.

UNION SHOPS

Under a union shop provision, an employer is free to hire workers who are not union members, but they must join the union within a specified period, usually 30 or 60 days after they start a job. This is the most common type of union security arrangement in the United States, as well as the most extreme type permitted by federal law.

MODIFIED UNION SHOPS

A union shop arrangement may be modified to protect workers who are in a bargaining unit at the time the union shop is negotiated but do not wish to join the union. When General Motors first agreed to a union shop in 1950, for example, workers already in the UAW were required to continue their membership and new employees were required to join the union, but employees then on the payroll who were not union members were not required to join. Exceptions may also be made for workers whose moral or religious convictions prevent them from joining labor organizations.

PREFERENTIAL HIRING

Sometimes a contract requires that an employer give preference to union members in hiring. The impact of such a provision depends on the relationship between the demand for additional workers and the extent to which the union has organized the potential supply of labor. If there are more union members than there are job opportunities, a preferential hiring arrangement is equivalent to a closed shop. Preferential hiring is often combined with a *union hiring hall* arrangement under which the union functions as an employment agency. Such arrangements are common in casual and intermittent employments. Under the Taft-Hartley Act, union hiring halls cannot discriminate against nonmembers.

CLOSED SHOPS

An employer's freedom to hire whomever it wishes may be restricted by a requirement that *prospective* employees belong to a union. Before the passage of the Taft-Hartley Act, this form of union security arrangement was common in *highly skilled trades,* such as building and construction and printing, and in industries where employment was *casual and intermittent,* as in the longshore and maritime industries, where the unions operated hiring halls. If a union does not restrict the number of members it accepts relative to the number of jobs that exist and admits qualified workers as members on a nondiscriminatory basis, a closed shop in combination with a hiring hall can provide employers with a reliable source of qualified workers while distributing job opportunities more equitably among applicants.

The majority of *industrial unions* have not tried to obtain a closed shop. Most of their members are not highly skilled, and they cannot control entry into most occupations within their jurisdiction.

A CLOSED SHOP AND CLOSED UNION

Under this kind of arrangement, a union with a closed shop refuses to admit applicants to membership, thereby depriving them of job opportunities in firms under contract with the union. In theory, a union interested in making employment more regular in an industry where it is normally casual or intermittent could use this kind of arrangement to "balance" the number of qualified workers and the number of jobs. However, such an arrangement can easily be abused; it can be used to limit the supply of labor and increase the wages of favored insiders.

If an increase in the demand for workers will probably be temporary, union officials may admit workers as members on a temporary basis. Persons who agree to pay the union a weekly, monthly, or single fixed fee are given *permit cards* allowing them to work in a closed shop for a stipulated period. In casual and intermittent employments, a permit card system may function like a seniority system. However, refusing to open a union's membership books when there has been a permanent increase in the demand for labor may simply be a means of providing the union, or its local officers, with a source of "additional" revenue on a continuing basis.

CHECKOFFS

Financial security is a basic component of institutional security, and unions generally try to supplement the kind of arrangements we have just described with a *checkoff provision* under which an employer agrees to deduct union dues and fees from employee paychecks and to remit the funds to the union. In some cases, this may be the only type of union security provided by the contract.

When a checkoff arrangement is *voluntary,* each employee must authorize the deduction of dues and fees from his or her check; when the arrangement is *compulsory* this is not necessary. Checkoff arrangements are a convenient way of ensuring relatively stable revenues for a union, and they enhance its bargaining power. In New York State, the penalty of revocation of checkoff arrangements is one of the principal means of discouraging strikes by public employees.

Legislation Affecting Union Security

The Wagner Act left the determination of union security arrangements to the parties to collective bargaining.* A closed shop or some less coercive union security arrangement was acceptable as long as it was negotiated with a bona fide labor organization representing the employees in a bargaining unit. As we noted in Chapter 17, the Taft-Hartley Act, a 1951 amendment to that act, and the Landrum-Griffin Act, made a number of changes in the law relating to union security.

Closed shops were prohibited by the Taft-Hartley Act, which specified in effect that the union shop was the most restrictive union security arrangement permitted. The minimum waiting period before union membership can be made compulsory is 30 days after entering employment, except in the building and construction industry, where, thanks to a 1959 amendment recognizing the brevity of employment in many of the building trades, it is seven days.

An unusual provision, section 14(b), allows more restrictive state legislation to govern union security arrangements in interstate as well as intrastate commerce. In 1979, right-to-work statutes were in effect in 20 states, none of which were primarily industrial states.

The desirability of banning closed as opposed to union shops is debatable. Industrial unions are usually satisfied with union shop arrangements, and craft unions usually admit qualified persons as members because they realize that, except in local market industries in which all the major employers have contracts with the union, excluding qualified persons from membership creates a pool of nonunion labor that represents a competitive threat to union members.

If a union admits all qualified workers as members, the distinction between a closed shop and a union shop appears to be one of degree rather than substance. People who reject closed shops but accept union shops apparently believe that the abuses of individual rights possible under the former arrangement outweigh any advantages it may have. Opposition to union shops, which is at the heart of the right-to-work controversy, reflects a more fundamental controversy over the acceptability of union security arrangements.

The Taft-Hartley Act originally stated that a union shop could not be bargained over until it had been approved by the workers in a bargaining unit in a special secret ballot election. This provision reflected the belief that autocratic

---

* The Railway Labor Act originally outlawed union security provisions but was amended in 1951 to permit union shop agreements.

union leaders often imposed union security arrangements on workers who were opposed to compulsory union membership. Between August 22, 1947, and October 22, 1951, the National Labor Relations Board conducted 46,119 union shop authorization polls. Over 91 percent of those voting and 77.5 percent of those eligible to vote favored a union shop, and it was approved in 97.1 percent of the polls.[1] These results persuaded Congress that such elections represented an unnecessary expenditure of federal funds, and they were discontinued in 1951.

Union shop arrangements may also be rescinded by secret ballot elections. Deauthorization polls are mandatory when they are sought by 30 percent or more of the employees in a bargaining unit. Although they are infrequent, they are a potentially valuable form of protection for workers who are dissatisfied with a union's policies or leadership. In fiscal 1979, labor organizations lost the right to negotiate union shop agreements in 69 percent of the 134 deauthorization polls the NLRB conducted.[2]

As we noted in Chapter 17, the Taft-Hartley Act does not outlaw discriminatory membership requirements. However, an *agency shop* rather than a *union shop* is the most coercive type of union security permitted when workers have been denied admission to a union or have had their membership revoked for reasons other than a failure to pay the customary union dues and fees. Actually, the protection afforded such nonmembers may be more apparent than real. A "cooperative" employer can find other reasons for discharging workers whose presence may jeopardize a harmonious union-management relationship; and by ostracizing nonmembers, union members may make working in a shop untenable for them.

Compulsory dues checkoffs, which have been criticized as an undemocratic way of collecting "tribute" from union members, were outlawed by the Taft-Hartley Act. According to section 302, an employer must receive a *voluntary* written assignment of dues to the union from an employee. Such an assignment cannot be irrevocable for longer than a year or beyond the termination date of the current contract, whichever occurs first. A compulsory checkoff appears reasonable when an employer has agreed to some form of compulsory membership arrangement, and this provision apparently was included in the Taft-Hartley Act in an attempt to weaken the financial base of unions and thereby reduce their bargaining power.

The Impact of Taft-Hartley

The union security provisions of the Taft-Hartley Act have had less impact than either their supporters or their critics anticipated. Union security provisions are still common, and the union shop has become the principal contractual form of union security in the United States. According to a BLS survey of 1,536 major collective bargaining agreements (each covering 1,000 or more workers) in effect on or after January 1, 1978, 89 percent of the 7 million workers surveyed were covered by union security provisions, and 61 percent by some type of union shop arrangement.[3] Unions with established bargaining relationships were not seriously affected by the ban on compulsory checkoffs, and in many situations in which a closed shop was traditional, it was not eliminated but driven underground.

The results of the union shop authorization polls conducted after the passage of the Taft-Hartley Act convinced many observers that workers who are union members are not, on principle, opposed to union security arrangements.[4] Moreover, the recent trend toward open shops in some industries threatened by nonunion and foreign competition often reflects management attempts to acquire more flexibility in the organization of production rather than a philosophical commitment to open shops. In such situations, unions may be forced to modify restrictive work rules or agree to other "give-backs" to keep a union shop.

The fact that workers cannot be discharged or refused employment because of nonmembership in a labor organization, even under a union shop agreement, if they are willing to pay the union the customary dues and fees has probably helped to eliminate discriminatory admissions practices by unions. At present, various undemocratic and discriminatory procedures and practices within unions can presumably be challenged under the Landrum-Griffin Act and the Civil Rights Act. It is doubtful that forbidding union shops would significantly advance the interests of minority group employees, particularly in geographic areas or industries in which discrimination has been customary.

The impact of section 14(b) on union membership has been largely prospective. In general, union membership has not declined in states having right-to-work laws, but unions have found it harder to attract new members in the absence of union security arrangements. This fact poses a considerable threat to unions in industries in which employers may shift their operations to right-to-work states, particularly states in the Sunbelt. In the fall of 1978, General Motors agreed to give "preferential consideration" to UAW members employed by GM if they sought jobs at new GM plants in the South. The union believed that this would make it easier to organize such plants.

Congress and most state legislatures have been reluctant to make union membership mandatory for government workers. As government employers gain experience in collective bargaining, union security arrangements will undoubtedly become more common in the public sector. However, nonindustrial states and states with right-to-work laws are unlikely to authorize such arrangements for public employees.

Attempts to repeal right-to-work provisions, a symbol of restrictive labor legislation, have led to greater political involvement on the part of organized labor. Although efforts to repeal such legislation have been unsuccessful, unions have been able to prevent the passage of right-to-work legislation in additional states outside the South. However, future campaigns in support of right-to-work laws may prove more successful.

Despite the increasingly hard line approach of some managements to collective bargaining, the suggestion that the federal government should ban union shops is unlikely to receive broad support. On the other hand, organized labor will probably be unable to generate enough support to repeal section 14(b) of the Taft-Hartley Act.

The Right-to-Work Controversy

The debate over the right-to-work reflects a fundamental disagreement concerning the acceptability of union security arrangements in a free society. There are two basic issues: (1) whether the degree of union security should be determined by the government or by private parties through collective bargaining and (2) whether the states rather than the federal government should regulate union security.

Two preliminary observations are in order. First, the term *right to work* is a misnomer; the question is not whether a worker has an inalienable right to a specific job, but whether an employee otherwise acceptable to an employer should be denied or discharged from a job because of a refusal to join or financially support a union or because he or she has been excluded from membership in a union. Second, the debate has been unnecessarily complicated by emotional rhetoric.

Arguments For and Against the Right-to-Work

The arguments concerning right-to-work legislation are a compound of moralistic philosophy, appeals to democratic principle, and explicit and implicit assessments of the impact of union security arrangements on bargaining power. The points at issue include whether a worker in a free society should be compelled to join a private organization, whether all workers in a bargaining unit have an obligation to pay for the services performed by their bargaining agent, whether an open shop is a practicable alternative to a union shop, the violations of democratic procedures possible in an institutionally secure union with an entrenched leadership, and the relationship between union security and union "responsibility." Basically, power, rather than philosophical, considerations underlie the debate. Many opponents of union shops believe that relieving a union of much of the burden of maintaining its organizational strength and providing it with a stable source of revenue would have the "unfortunate" result of increasing the union's bargaining power, while in the unions' view,

> the real aim of these "right-to-work" laws is to undermine trade unions. Behind the high-sounding false slogan is an anti-labor purpose—to destroy or to weaken free American trade unions. . . .[5]

COMPULSORY UNION MEMBERSHIP

Proponents of right to work argue that arrangements making union membership compulsory violate the basic democratic principle that no citizen should be compelled to join a private organization. According to the Chamber of Commerce of the United States, "THE ISSUE IS ONLY THIS: Should any American be forced, under penalty of loss of livelihood, to join and support a particular private organization, whether it be a union, church, civic club, or any other group?"[6]

Supporters of union shops point out that a union must, by law, represent all the workers in a bargaining unit without discrimination. They argue that the analogy between unions and other voluntary organizations is false; they believe that "the non-paying non-member who enjoys the benefits of trade unionism is like a member of the community who refuses to pay taxes . . . , and refuses to vote in the community's elections."[7] However, the implication that exclusive representation is an unwanted burden on unions is specious; they demand this right. The argument that collective bargaining has important social benefits and that all the workers in a unit have a responsibility to support such a constructive process is more persuasive.

"FREE RIDERS"

Perhaps the most effective case against right-to-work legislation is based on the argument that no member of a bargaining unit should be a free rider. Unions claim (1) that it is unreasonable, if not immoral, for workers to refuse to pay a service fee to support an organization that is required by law to represent them; (2) that without union security arrangements, unions would have to continually divert resources to recruiting and retaining members; and (3) that given the principle of exclusive representation, the bargaining services provided by a union are in a sense collective goods whose cost of production should be shared by their consumers.[8] This last argument is somewhat different from essentially moralistic attacks on "free riders."

Opponents of right-to-work legislation point out that in the limited number of cases in which religious convictions make it impossible for a person to join or contribute to the support of a union, acceptable alternatives can be devised. For example, a sum equivalent to the usual union dues and fees may be paid to a designated charity. This position appears reasonable; however, the acceptability of such alternatives should not be left to the discretion of the parties to collective bargaining but specified by law.

Supporters of "the right to work" reject these arguments, primarily on moral grounds. They emphasize that unions demand the status of exclusive representatives and that it is immoral to require a member of a free society to become a captive passenger.

THE HOSTILE OPEN SHOP

Advocates of union security believe that most so-called open shops, that is, most firms in which employment is presumably open to union members and non-members alike, are actually hostile to unionism. They therefore see a prohibition on union shops as a continuing threat to established unions and a barrier to the organization of additional workers. Supporters of right-to-work legislation often insist that they believe in, and support, the right to organize and bargain collectively, but they maintain that once these rights are protected by law, there is no need for formal union security provisions. They argue that a "true" open shop is a viable alternative to the union shop.

INTERNAL DEMOCRACY

Supporters of right-to-work legislation argue that a union's internal operations are often autocratic. They believe that workers who object to a union's policies or procedures should be able to withdraw from the union or refuse to join it without being penalized. They argue that unions dependent on voluntary support are more responsive to the needs of their members.

Supporters of the union shop believe that these arguments exaggerate the potential dangers of compulsory membership. They point out (1) that there are already statutes regulating the internal affairs of unions and that it is not necessary to ban union shops to ensure that unions operate democratically; (2) that under the Taft-Hartley Act, loss of membership in a union results in a loss of employment only if a worker refuses to pay a sum equivalent to customary dues and fees; and (3) that union leaders who show little concern for the needs of the membership will not stay in office long.

Assuming that one is not opposed to unions and collective bargaining, one's evaluation of these arguments will depend on the relative weight attached to (1) the superior effectiveness and possibly greater constructive potential of the bargaining agent in a union as opposed to an open shop and (2) the possibility that despite the protection afforded them by the Taft-Hartley, Landrum-Griffin, and Civil Rights acts, the rights of individual union members may be violated.

REASONABLE AND RESPONSIBLE UNIONS

Finally, there is disagreement over the impact of union security on the "character" of bargaining relationships. Critics of union shops contend that the leaders of a secure union may be insensitive to their members needs and give them less weight than their own goals.

Supporters of union shops argue that unless a union is secure, its leaders may be forced to respond to frivolous or highly personal demands for action, that this will lead to irresponsible bargaining positions and more frequent challenges of management decisions during the life of a contract, and that leaders of a union that is institutionally secure can act more reasonably and responsibly.

Objective observers have concluded that union security may contribute to the development of a more constructive bargaining relationship. According to the late Sumner Slichter,

> An assured status for the union is not a guarantee of successful union-employer relations but it is a prerequisite. . . . The employer is likely to have more freedom in shops where the status of the union is established than in one where its position is more or less precarious.[9]

However, a *formal* union security arrangement is not a prerequisite for the development of a constructive bargaining relationship; what is required is genuine acceptance of the union by management. This is consistent with our previous observation that considerations of relative power underlie the right-to-work debate. Union opposition to right-to-work laws is based on the belief that employers who have not accepted unionism will use such legislation to weaken existing unions and to prevent unions from organizing more workers. The fact that right-to-work laws have been passed in states in which the general climate of opinion is often hostile to unions indicates that such fears are not unfounded.

The Impact of Right-to-Work Legislation

Apparently, unions that are least in need of the protection afforded by formal union security provisions have the least trouble negotiating them, whereas relatively weak unions may find it impossible to get management to agree to a formal union security arrangement. This suggests that the impact of right-to-work legislation on *existing* collective bargaining relationships is small; however, it cannot be quantified. In states in which such legislation has been adopted, employers and unions with well-established bargaining relationships did not seem to consider the prohibition of formal union security provisions a critical matter. As early as 1957, *Fortune* magazine concluded that such laws had had "singularly little effect" on labor relations, perhaps because few states had any effective enforcement apparatus.[10] A subsequent study of the impact of the Texas right-to-work statute found that it had little effect on union-management relations and that

> "Right-to-Work" proposals are of much less importance than either side to the controversy has been willing to admit. The issue is a symbolic one. What is at stake is the political power and public support of management and of unionism.[11]

Other observers have suggested that the amount of money and effort that has gone into supporting and opposing such legislation shows that it is of more than symbolic importance. According to Kuhn, right-to-work laws "strike at the unions' main resource, dues," and could, by opening up existing union shops, "bring about a drop in union membership . . . of from 6 to 15%."[12] He believes that such laws "have a decided and substantial effect upon union strength and bargaining, but . . . cannot prove it."[13]

The impact of right-to-work laws is therefore largely prospective. They may (1) reduce the rate of growth of union membership as employment expands; (2) accentuate a decline in membership resulting from changes in the composition of the labor force; (3) accentuate a decline in membership resulting from decreases in employment in firms, industries, and areas in which employers (and possibly employees) are not receptive to unionism; or (4) prevent unions from maintaining their membership base when presently organized firms transfer operations to such areas.

Union Security: Summary and Conclusions

The most basic question relating to union security is who should rule on the desirability of a union shop—the parties to collective bargaining or the state. Those who believe that effective, responsible unions are an essential component of our pluralistic industrial society tend to favor the removal of this issue from the political arena; those who accept unions but believe that union security arrangements pose a substantial threat to individual rights and those who are hostile to unionism are more likely to accept limits on the freedom of private parties to negotiate such arrangements.

This last position involves a subsidiary issue: should limits on the right to negotiate a union shop be imposed by the federal government or by the states? Ceding such authority to the states, while probably politically expedient, is illogical in view of the scope of federal legislation regarding collective bargaining.

On balance, secure unions are more likely to make the compromises so necessary between private interest groups in a pluralistic society. Given the protection afforded union members and prospective members by the Taft-Hartley, Landrum-Griffin, and Civil Rights acts, the potential contribution of the union shop to the development of stable and responsible collective bargaining relationships probably outweighs its possible adverse effects. In these circumstances, union security arrangements should really be determined by private parties through the collective bargaining process.

MANAGEMENT SECURITY

Collective bargaining gives unions a voice in many matters once under the unilateral control of management.* However, most firms will resist such "encroachments" on their "rights" to the best of their ability. They will seek to retain as much control as possible over their operations and resist any attempt by a union to introduce "uneconomic" methods of production. Most managements also have an understandable desire to maintain their own power and status.

A firm's management may try to protect its prerogatives through contract provisions that prevent or limit union participation in management decisions. This provides a measure of institutional security for the firm and personal security for the management team. If the owners of the company are represented by professional managers, the managers may preserve their own status and power at the expense of the owners' objectives. Management security is however ultimately dependent on the continued operation of the firm.

Unlike union security provisions, which try to *establish* or *increase* the institutional security of labor organizations, management security provisions try to

---

* Management's right to make unilateral decisions has also been circumscribed by social legislation, including minimum wage, maximum hours, child labor, safety, equal employment opportunity, and social security laws.

prevent the *erosion* of managerial authority or to *regain* managerial prerogatives given up in previous contracts or lost as a result of the way former contracts were administered.

Initially, managerial opposition to unionism was based on the belief that a firm's management had an inalienable right to direct its operations on a unilateral basis. Under common law, owners of private property or their representatives were presumed to have lawful control of the use of such property. Managerial control over a firm's labor force derived from this right, and any attempt by workers to share in this function was considered undesirable, unnecessary, and unlawful.[14] Collective bargaining represented a direct challenge to this position, and by protecting the right to organize and bargain collectively, the federal government sanctioned this form of worker participation in management. However, the limits to such participation were not defined, and management has generally continued to resist union efforts to increase the number of matters subject to joint control.

Following World War II, the management members of the Committee on Management's Right to Manage at President Truman's Labor-Management Conference declared that

> [m]anagement has functions that must not and cannot be compromised in the public interest. If labor disputes are to be minimized . . . , labor must agree that certain specific functions and responsibilities of management are not subject to collective bargaining.[15]

Union leaders are unwilling to identify specific functions as permanent managerial prerogatives because they believe that any management decision has some impact on employee welfare and that changing conditions may make it necessary for them to try to regulate matters that they are presently willing to leave to the discretion of management. Thus the union representatives at the conference mentioned above concluded that

> it would be extremely unwise to build a fence around the rights and responsibilities of management on the one hand and the unions on the other. . . . We cannot have one sharply delimited area designated as management prerogatives and another equally sharply defined area of union prerogatives. . . .[16]

Management Rights Provisions

There are two basic types of management rights provisions: those that *enumerate specific* management rights and those that assert such rights more *generally*. In a study of 1,773 major agreements, each covering 1000 or more workers, in effect during 1963 and 1964, the Bureau of Labor Statistics found that 860 contained a formal management rights clause, that is, a provision stating "the functions reserved in whole or in part to the employer."[17] (A 1978 study found that 931 of 1,536 major collective bargaining agreements had management rights provisions.[18]) The earlier study emphasized that such clauses cannot be studied in isolation, that "virtually the entire series of [BLS] studies of [collective bargaining provisions] touches upon some aspect or abridgement of management rights. . . ."[19] The management rights clauses noted covered 3.5 million workers, 47 percent of the 7.5 million workers covered by contracts included in the study. Manufacturing industries accounted for three-fourths of the agreements containing a formal rights provision; 70 percent of the single employer agreements, but less than 14 percent of the multiemployer unit agreements had such provisions.

Managerial rights were listed in 713 contracts and referred to generally in 147. Many contracts referred to rights "in broad but discernible areas," and the frequency with which a *general* right was cited

> apparently reflected the importance of the issue in the collective bargaining framework. Thus, control of production was referred to in 82 . . . provisions, direction of the work force in 80, and management of the business in 57.[20]

The following are examples of *general provisions* regarding managerial rights:

1. The management of the Plant and the direction of the working forces, . . . are the exclusive function of the company [Ingersoll-Rand Co. and the International Union of Electrical, Radio and Machine Workers].
2. . . . the company shall continue to have the right to take any action it deems appropriate in the management of the business in accordance with its judgment [Western Electric Co., Inc. and the Communications Workers of America].[21]

Provisions enumerating managerial rights varied from simple clauses to lengthy statements including illustrations of the particular rights reserved to management. Three broad issues were emphasized in the 713 agreements studied containing enumerated rights: the direction of the work force (in 679 agreements); control of production (in 409 agreements); and the conduct of business (in 248 agreements).[22] Most provisions were prefaced by a statement of management's general rights.

Approximately one-third of the 860 managements rights provisions analyzed included "a savings clause reserving for the employer all those rights not specifically abridged or affected by the provisions in the collective bargaining agreement."[23] Over 90 percent of the agreements had provisions that "in effect restricted the management prerogative to matters not preempted by an agreement provision."[24]

In earlier chapters, we noted that the General Motors Corporation has accepted unions and collective bargaining but has been careful to prevent erosion of its decision-making authority. The basic management rights clause in a succession of GM–UAW agreements provides that

> the right to hire; promote; discharge or discipline for cause; and to maintain discipline and efficiency of employees, is the sole responsibility of the Corporation except that Union members shall not be discriminated against as such. In addition,

the products to be manufactured, the location of plants, the schedules of production, the methods, processes and means of manufacturing are exclusively the responsibility of the Corporation.

Formal management rights provisions cannot substitute for "good" management. They may allow management to control specific functions, but they cannot ensure the kind of managerial performance that will assure the survival of the firm. Challenged by unions, many firms will not try to negotiate restrictive *formal* management rights provisions, but they will assume a tougher bargaining posture. Many companies believe that hard bargaining and perceptive contract administration are the most effective defense against union penetration of management functions. Some variants of "creative" collective bargaining, including advance consultation and bargaining on a continuing basis, may enable a firm's management to involve unions in management decisions without formally relinquishing control over them.

A management security provision does not represent a *permanent* understanding about the scope of union penetration of a management function. As the Bureau of Labor Statistics study cited earlier emphasized, such a clause

> does not define those issues which are bargainable or nonbargainable as a matter of law [but] summarizes the understanding of the parties on particular issues for the term of the agreement, and it may be modified in later negotiations, as the parties see fit. [Moreover a] management rights clause by itself is not an accurate guide as to the areas in which the employer can act unilaterally and those in which his actions are abridged by the terms of the agreement. For this, one must consider the agreement in its entirety. [It] is probably of greatest significance in disputes over issues on which the contract is otherwise silent.[25]

Current and Prospective Significance of Management Rights

The relative importance of the management rights issue depends on the quality of, and conditions peculiar to, specific collective bargaining relationships, as well as on the general state of the economy. Management is particularly sensitive to challenges to its authority during the initial phases of a collective bargaining relationship and, more generally, when it is under pressure to increase efficiency and reduce costs. A firm that has just embarked on a bargaining relationship may adopt a *defensive* strategy with respect to management rights, while a firm under pressure to increase efficiency may pursue an *offensive strategy*. Competent managers recognize that once control of specific management functions is lost, it is difficult to regain, and they try to protect managerial rights and responsibilities on a continuing basis.

A number of developments have heightened interest in management rights provisions since the 1940s. After the Korean War, early in the 1960s, and during the stagflation of the 1970s, many companies trying to compete with nonunion firms and foreign producers found it hard to regain ground given up under more favorable economic conditions. Limits on the firms' ability to change production methods and techniques were particularly irritating and costly, causing many of them to take a more aggressive bargaining stance and seek more control over all facets of the management function. Many companies also became more alert to the long-run implications of what may appear initially to be relatively minor limitations on managerial prerogatives.

After World War II, various decisions by the NLRB and the federal courts increased the number of matters "appropriate to collective bargaining" and subject to arbitration under grievance procedures. Companies are particularly concerned about the refusal of the courts to accept the theory of *residual management rights,* according to which management presumably retains all those prerogatives that have not been specifically limited by a contract. In a leading decision involving the arbitrability of a contracting-out dispute in the steel industry, the Supreme Court held that the phrase

> "strictly a function of management" must be interpreted as referring only to that over which the contract gives management complete control and unfettered discretion. . . .
>
> A specific collective bargaining agreement may exclude contracting out from the grievance procedure. Or a written collateral agreement may make clear that contracting out was not a matter for arbitration. . . . Here, however, there is no such provision. . . . In the absence of any express provision excluding a particular grievance from arbitration, . . . only the most forceful evidence of a purpose to exclude the claim from arbitration can prevail. . . .[26]

As a result of such decisions, a new type of management rights provision has been included in some contracts to protect companies, and to a lesser degree unions, from "new" demands during the life of a contract. According to such a "waiver" provision in recent GM–UAW contracts,

> the parties acknowledge that during the negotiations which resulted in this Agreement, each had the unlimited right and opportunity to make demands and proposals with respect to any subject or matter not removed by law from the area of collective bargaining. . . . Therefore, the Corporation and the Union, for the life of this agreement, each voluntarily and unqualifiedly waives the right, and each agrees that the other shall not be obligated, to bargain collectively with respect to any subject or matter referred to, or covered in this Agreement, or with respect to any subject or matter not specifically referred to or covered in this Agreement, even though such subject or matter may not have been within the knowledge or contemplation of either or both of the parties at the time that they negotiated or signed this Agreement.

The organization of workers in new industrial sectors and geographic areas will also generate more interest in management rights provisions. The increased unionization of government employees has already resulted in controversies over managerial authority. Issues considered appropriate to collective bargaining in the federal sector were restricted by Executive Order 10988 of 1962, which authorized bargaining by federal employees, and Title VII of the Civil Service Reform Act of 1978, which provided statutory authority for collective bargaining in federal employment. Strong management rights provisions have been included in many agreements negotiated in the federal service. At the local and state levels, many public employers, caught in a fiscal crunch and under pressure from a conservative backlash, are trying to take the initiative in determining manpower requirements and productivity standards. In the private sector, the prospective unionization of white-collar employees, particularly professionals, will generate a variety of new bargaining issues, and many existing managerial prerogatives may be questioned.

Increasing affluence will generate new and possibly unexpected bargaining demands. For example, unions concerned with such broad social objectives as the creation of more favorable physical and social environments may demand that management consider proposals in areas that are not traditionally the concern of collective bargaining. Management can be expected to resist these pressures, and new types of management rights provisions may be developed to meet highly selective management needs. It seems likely that management rights provisions will assume greater *operational* and *symbolic* importance in the 1980s.

Unlike many of their foreign counterparts, most American union leaders continue to reject any theory of "shared power" with respect to the *overall direction* of the firm and to agree that functions not directly related to the employment relationship can be performed most efficiently by management. In 1976, the executive assistant to AFL-CIO President Meany noted that the movement overseas to give workers a voice in such overall decisions "offer[s] little to American unions" and that the AFL-CIO "[does] not want to blur . . . the distinctions between the respective roles of management and labor in the plant."[27] However, the UAW, which has a "social unionism" orientation that is unusual in the United States, recently moved in that direction. As part of an agreement to help the financially hard-pressed Chrysler Corporation, the union accepted contract provisions for Chrysler workers in early 1980 that were inferior to those in the 1979 General Motors and Ford contracts, and the corporation agreed to nominate Douglas Fraser, president of the UAW, for election to its board of directors.

Nevertheless, the interest of American union leaders and union members in various forms of direct participation in management, including worker representation on corporate boards, appears to have been exaggerated, and perhaps distorted, by social activists and sympathetic academics from a variety of disciplines.[28] For example, the widely publicized strike at General Motors' Lordstown, Ohio, plant in 1972, sparked by a speedup of a Vega assembly line, was due more to traditional worker opposition to speedups than to the demands of a younger and more highly educated labor force for a greater share in management decisions.

However, if management fails to respond to any "new" work-related needs of such workers, unions will inevitably try to penetrate more deeply into the management decision-making process and management security will become a more contentious bargaining issue.

A Concluding Note

Although collective bargaining has reduced the employer's freedom to make unilateral decisions, American unions have shown little interest in sharing management functions that are not directly related to union-management relations. However, they have been reluctant to specify the matters reserved to management because they recognize that at some future date, it may be necessary to expand the scope of collective bargaining.

Formal management security provisions represent an attempt to prevent the erosion of, or to regain, management's decision-making authority. However, negotiating a formal management rights provision is not enough; an apparently strong provision may be emasculated by other contract provisions or by loose contract administration. A strong management determined to prevent any erosion of its "essential" authority and willing to take a strike over the issue may consider management rights provisions not only unnecessary but undesirable—undesirable because an explicit list of management rights may lessen management's residual powers.

In the past, the impact of formal management security provisions has been largely symbolic. The inclusion of such provisions in a collective agreement indicated that a firm, as a matter of principle, was opposed to sharing management functions with the bargaining representative of its employees. A number of factors, including recent court decisions requiring the arbitration via grievance procedures of matters not expressly excluded from arbitration by a contract, suggest that in the final decades of the twentieth century, many employers will have to reevaluate the extent to which union infringement of managerial prerogatives has restricted their ability to respond to challenges, particularly problems associated with technological change.

The precise form of attempts to keep or regain control of specific management functions will depend on the basic character of a given collective bargaining relationship, including the degree to which management has genuinely accepted the union or unions with which it deals. The inclusion of union representatives on continuing or ad hoc study committees may help the unions articulate the human relations implications of significant innovations within a firm without directly threatening the formal decision-making process.

In some quarters, the erosion of managerial authority is considered a threat to the American enterprise system. Unions have not however tried to supplant or destroy management. The ability of American unions to participate in management through the collective bargaining process helps to explain organized labor's disinterest in a variety of alternatives that have been adopted in other nations and that have been widely publicized in this country. These alternatives include direct worker participation in basic production decisions, the installation of worker representatives on boards of directors, and radical political action. Compared to such action, collective bargaining is an essentially conservative response to the work-related human problems of our society.

SUMMARY

Collective bargaining is an institutional relationship in which the continuity of the union and of the firm are essential bargaining objectives. To help assure such continuity, unions and management may negotiate union security and management security provisions. The former attempt to *provide* or *increase* institutional security for the union; the latter try to *retain* or *regain* managerial control over what are perceived as essential managerial prerogatives.

Some observers have suggested that institutional security is not a serious problem in mature bargaining relationships. However, the relative—and in some cases, the absolute—decline in union membership and the operational flexibility that many managements require in order to respond to competitive pressures have reemphasized the importance of union and management security provisions.

DISCUSSION QUESTIONS

1. Should management consciously provide a union with (greater) institutional security?
2. What is the most extreme type of union security that should be permitted by law?
3. Why have the union security provisions of the Taft-Hartley Act had less impact than many persons anticipated?
4. Why is section 14(b) considered inconsistent with our basic federal law of collective bargaining?
5. Do you agree that no member of a bargaining unit should be a "free rider"?
6. Why did the issue of managerial prerogatives assume greater importance during the 1970s?
7. Can you identify specific management functions that should not be subject to collective bargaining?
8. Why is it considered more difficult for a management to regain than to defend managerial prerogatives?
9. Since the election of Douglas Fraser, President of the UAW, to the board of directors of the Chrysler Corporation, have additional unions sought such directorships?

SELECTED READINGS

Union Security

Golden, Clinton, and Ruttenberg, Harold J. *The Dynamics of Industrial Democracy.* Chap. VII. New York: Harper & Brothers, 1942.

Millis, Harry A., and Montgomery, Royal E. *Organized Labor,* pp. 470–485. New York: McGraw-Hill, 1945.

Northrup, Herbert R., and Bloom, Gordon F. *Government and Labor.* Chap. 8. Homewood, Ill.: Irwin, 1963.

Slichter, Sumner H. *Union Policies and Industrial Management,* pp. 53–90. Washington, D.C.: Brookings Institution, 1941.

Slichter, Sumner H.; Healy, James J.; and Livernash, E. Robert. *The Impact of Collective Bargaining on Management.* Chap. 3. Washington, D.C.: Brookings Institution, 1960.

Sultan, Paul E. "The Union Security Issue." In *Public Policy and Collective Bargaining.* Ed. by Joseph Shister, Benjamin Aaron, and Clyde W. Summers. Industrial Relations Research Association Publication No. 27. New York: Harper & Row, 1962.

Right-to-Work Laws

American Federation of Labor and Congress of Industrial Organizations, *Union Security: The Case Against the "Right-to-Work" Laws.* Washington, D.C., 1958.

Gallaway, Lowell E. "The Economics of the Right-to-Work Controversy." In *Southern Economic Journal* XXXII, no. 3 (January 1966): pp. 310–316. An analysis of the impact of union security on the allocation of labor.

Harrison, William T. *The Truth About Right-to-Work Laws.* Washington, D.C.: National Right to Work Committee, 1959.

"The Right to Work." *Proceedings of the Academy of Political Science* XXVI, no. 1 (May 1954).

Much of the literature on this subject represents partisan points of view.

Management Security

Chamberlain, Neil W. *The Union Challenge to Management Control,* New York: Harper & Brothers, 1948. An early, definitive work on the nature and extent of managerial prerogatives.

Cullen, Donald E., and Greenbaum, Marcia L. *Management Rights and Collective Bargaining: Can Both Survive?* ILR Bulletin No. 58. Ithaca, N.Y.: NYS School of Industrial and Labor Relations, Cornell University, 1966.

Notes

1. *Sixteenth Annual Report of the National Labor Relations Board for the Fiscal Year Ended June 30, 1951,* p. 54.
2. *Forty-Fourth Annual Report of the National Labor Relations Board for the Fiscal Year Ended September 30, 1979,* p. 18.
3. U.S. Department of Labor, Bureau of Labor Statistics, *Characteristics of Major Collective Bargaining Agreements, January 1, 1978,* Bulletin 2065, Table 2.1, p. 16. See also Bureau of National Affairs, *Basic Patterns of Union Contracts, May 1979,* 9th ed., Washington, D.C., pp. 84–87.
4. For dissenting views, see Sanford Cohen, "Union Shop Polls: A Solution to the Right-to-Work Issue," in *Industrial and Labor Relations Review* 12, no. 2 (January 1959): pp. 253–254; and James W. Kuhn, "Right-to-Work Laws—Symbol or Substance?" in *Industrial and Labor Relations Review* 14, no. 4 (July 1961): pp. 589–591.

5. AFL-CIO, *Facts vs. Propaganda: The Truth About "Right to Work" Laws,* Publication No. 46 (Washington, D.C., December 1957), p. 1.

6. *The Case for Voluntary Unionism* (Washington, D.C.: Chamber of Commerce of the United States, n.d.), p. 3.

7. AFL-CIO Department of Research, "Union Security: The 'Right-to-Work' Controversy," in *Labor's Economic Review* 1, no. 1 (January 1956): p. 6.

8. Cf. Allan G. Pulsipher, "The Union Shop: A Legitimate Form of Coercion in a Free-Market Economy," in *Industrial and Labor Relations Review* 19, no. 4 (July 1966): p. 531; and Derek C. Bok and John T. Dunlop, *Labor and the American Community* (New York: Simon & Schuster, 1970), pp. 99–100.

9. *Union Policies and Industrial Management* (Washington, D.C.: Brookings Institution, 1941), p. 95. Cf. Douglas McGreger, "The Influence of Attitudes and Policies," in Clinton S. Golden and Virginia D. Parker, eds., *Causes of Industrial Peace Under Collective Bargaining* (New York: Harper & Brothers, 1955), p. 31.

10. "Labor," *Fortune,* September 1957, p. 236.

11. Frederic Meyers, *"Right to Work" in Practice* (New York: Fund for the Republic, 1959), p. 45. Cf. Keith Lumsden and Craig Peterson, "The Effect of Right-to-Work Laws on Unionization in the United States," in *Journal of Political Economy* 83, no. 6 (December 1975): pp. 1247–1248; and Fred Witney, "The Indiana Right-to-Work Law," in *Industrial and Labor Relations Review* 11, no. 4 (July 1958): pp. 515–517.

12. Kuhn, "Right-to-Work Laws," pp. 588 and 592.

13. Ibid., p. 594. Cf. John M. Glasgow, "That Right-to-Work Controversy Again?" in *Labor Law Journal* 18, no. 2 (February 1967): pp. 112–115.

14. Cf. Stanley Young, "The Question of Managerial Prerogatives," in *Industrial and Labor Relations Review* 16, no. 2 (January 1963): pp. 240–253.

15. U.S. Department of Labor, Division of Labor Standards. *The President's National Labor-Management Conference; Summary and Committee Reports November 5–30, 1945,* Bulletin 77, pp. 56–57.

16. Ibid., p. 6.

17. U.S. Department of Labor, Bureau of Labor Statistics, *Management Rights and Union-Management Cooperation,* Bulletin 1425–5, pp. 1 and 5.

18. *Characteristics of Major Collective Bargaining Agreements, January 1, 1978,* Table 2.4, p. 21. See also Bureau of National Affairs, *Basic Patterns of Union Contracts, May 1979,* pp. 62–65.

19. *Management Rights and Union-Management Cooperation,* p. 3.

20. Ibid., p. 6.

21. Ibid.

22. Ibid., p. 9.

23. Ibid., p. 16.

24. Ibid., p. 19.

25. Ibid., p. 1.

26. *United Steelworkers of America* v. *Warrior & Gulf Navigation Co.,* 363 U.S. 574 (1960), pp. 584–585. For a discussion of this decision, see Charles C. Killingsworth, "Management Rights Revisited," Research Reprint Series No. 113, School of Labor and Industrial Relations, Michigan State University, reprinted from Gerald G. Somers, ed., *Arbitration and Social Change: Proceedings of the Twenty-*

Second Annual Meeting of the National Academy of Arbitrators, January 29–31, 1969 (Washington, D.C.: Bureau of National Affairs); and G. Allan Dash, Jr., "The Arbitration of Subcontracting Disputes," in *Industrial and Labor Relations Review* 16, no. 2 (January 1963): pp. 208–215. Cf. also Wallace B. Nelson, "Through a Looking Glass Darkly: *Fibreboard* Five Years Later," in *Labor Law Journal* 21, no. 12 (December 1970): pp. 755–760.

27. *The Wall Street Journal,* July 27, 1976, p. 1.

28. Cf. Douglas M. Soutar, "Co-Determination, Industrial Democracy, and the Role of Management," in *Proceedings of the Twenty-Sixth Annual Meeting, Industrial Relations Research Association, December 28–29, 1973* (Madison, Wisc., 1974), pp. 1–7.

Chapter 23
THE IMPACT OF
COLLECTIVE BARGAINING

In earlier chapters in Parts Three and Five, we have described the collective bargaining process, analyzed contract provisions regulating the terms and conditions of employment, and considered certain operational and procedural effects of the continuing institutional relationship between unions and management. We found that unions try to "take wages out of competition" and that they may reenforce imperfections in product markets when this maximizes a somewhat ambiguous membership welfare function. We also concluded that collective bargaining has had a significant impact on both the form in which employee compensation is received and the timing of increases in compensation. Finally, we showed how the limits placed on managerial action by collective bargaining plus other intangible benefits can be of equal, if not greater, importance to individual union members than the more direct economic benefits obtained at the bargaining table.

In this chapter, we will analyze the economic impact of collective bargaining in greater detail. We will discuss how contract provisions and informal work rules that touch on certain extraeconomic dimensions of the employment relationship affect both employees as individuals and the economy at large. Although it is conventional to talk about *the impact of unions,* we prefer to discuss *the impact of collective bargaining,* a distinction that recognizes the institutional dimensions of the continuing relationship between organized labor and management.

Economists are particularly interested in certain aspects of *collective* bargaining: whether unions have succeeded in creating "favorable" union wage differentials, that is, whether they have raised their members' wages above those of comparable nonunion workers or above the levels that would theoretically exist in the absence of unions; whether unions have had a discernible effect on other types of wage differentials; and whether collective bargaining has had an impact on the functional distribution of income, on money wages, on real wages, and on the general level of prices. The economic theory relevant to this analysis was developed in Chapters 5, 6, and 20, so it may be helpful to review those chapters before proceeding.

Analytical Difficulties

It is hard to estimate the *independent* impact of collective bargaining on relative wages and economic aggregates. In the social sciences, it is not usually possible to compare *what is* with *what might have been* through controlled laboratory experiments, and the difference between the two must be estimated from data that reflect the complex interaction of variables under dynamic conditions. The "veil of time" complicates the analysis by obscuring the interrelationships between variables. It is also hard to evaluate the extraeconomic dimensions of collective bargaining, which often involve intangible, unquantifiable considerations. Analysis is further complicated because the *alternative institutional arrangements* that would presumably exist in the absence of unions have not been identified. A perfectly competitive model is not a realistic alternative to existing labor markets, and most labor economists believe that the impact of unions should be evaluated relative to conditions in imperfect markets in the absence of unions. However, Professor Robert Macdonald has properly questioned this "realistic" procedure. He argues that neither a perfectly competitive market nor an imperfect nonunion (or "natural") market are, in fact, *functional alternatives* to a union model. In his view, unionism performs "indispensable functions . . . in legitimizing and stabilizing the present system," which would be significantly different in the absence of unions.[1] Thus,

> to answer the question "What would in fact have happened in the absence of unionism?" . . . requires . . . the use of a comparative market model that is a functional substitute for the unionized market. . . .
>
> [T]his demands no less than the construction of an alternative system wherein unionism is replaced by a social structure which will fulfill the functions performed by unionism.[2]

Analyzing the impact of collective bargaining is at best a hazardous exercise in which only tentative conclusions may be drawn.

The Character of the "Evidence"

Since we have no functional alternative, we must rely on conventional studies of the economic impact of collective bargaining for data. There are limitations to such studies. For example, studies of the relative wage effect of collective bargaining (of how collective bargaining raises the wages of union members relative to nonunion workers) have attempted to measure this impact in two ways. In cross section analysis, the wages of union members are compared with the wages of nonunion workers at a point in time. In historical or time series analysis, the wages of workers represented by unions are compared over time with the wages of nonunion workers.* However, factors other than the degree of union organization may be responsible for the apparent wage impact developed by such studies. Many studies fail to control for such variables as the degree of concentration in an industry, the location of plants, and the quality of the labor force and its demographic characteristics.

The possible spillover effects of collective bargaining into the nonunion sector is another complication. Some unorganized firms may copy or improve on the terms of union agreements to forestall the unionization of their employees. This *threat effect* conceals the impact of collective bargaining on money wages and wage differentials. Other nonunion firms may voluntarily match union gains on grounds of equity; or in a tight labor market, they may have to match or exceed union wage scales to recruit and retain qualified workers.

On the other hand, if an increase in wages in union firms results in layoffs, a consequent increase in the supply of labor, and a lower equilibrium wage in the nonunion sector of an industry, the relative impact of the increase will be greater than it seems measured relative to a theoretical market equilibrium wage. That is, collective bargaining will result in a higher wage in the union sector and a lower wage in the nonunion sector.

On balance, the economic impact of collective bargaining is probably less than the public and some economists assume. Two factors help explain why this impact is often assumed to be more substantial: (1) union leaders, anxious to demonstrate the effectiveness of their organizations, are eager to take credit for all the improvements in wages and working conditions provided under collective agreements, although some improvements would probably have occurred anyway; and (2) critics and opponents of unions, anxious to prove that collective bargaining has created an imbalance of economic power and a consequent misallocation of resources, are eager to accept and publicize any evidence which suggests that unions have had a substantial economic impact.

The Impact of Unions on Legislation

Unions have supported a variety of laws that have had an impact on the labor market and to a lesser degree on product markets. For example, they have

---

* These studies may concentrate on a single industry or analyze a number of industries with varying degrees of unionization.

favored various laws that have in one way or another reduced the supply of labor. Such laws may have a significant impact on *money* and *real* wage levels.

THE MICROECONOMIC IMPACTS OF COLLECTIVE BARGAINING

In this section, we will consider the impact of collective bargaining on the determination of wages within the firm. We will also examine how it affects wage differentials between firms, geographic areas, occupations, and industries, and between union and nonunion labor. In the following section, we will investigate the impact of collective bargaining within a macroeconomic framework. In the third section, we will consider some theoretical implications of contract provisions involving extraeconomic dimensions of the employment relationship.

The Impact on Wages at the Plant Level

Unions try to establish standard rates for occupational categories within a firm, within plants of the same firm in the same geographic area, and within all the plants of a firm producing for a national market. As a result, collective bargaining usually has a significant impact on a firm's *internal wage structure*. Three forces tend to make the wage structure more rational and reduce interpersonal wage differentials: (1) a desire on the part of both unions and management to evolve a uniform, rational, and internally consistent wage structure and to administer it fairly and consistently;* (2) the need to pay the going rate in a labor market to obtain an adequate supply of labor; and (3) pressures to conform to wage (bargaining) contours defined by economic and institutional considerations. When employees are paid uniform wage rates—or when variations in wages are limited to defined ranges—employers usually find it hard to compensate workers on the basis of individual efficiency. In an effort to raise worker productivity to the level demanded by the wage structure established under collective bargaining, employers may tighten personnel selection and administration procedures or engage in "productivity" bargaining in which they attempt to secure modification of restrictive work rules or other "give backs" to offset increases in wages.

Interfirm Differentials

Theoretically, workers in the same labor market in the same occupation should, if they are of equal ability, be paid the same (equilibrium) wage rate. However, most studies indicate that in the absence of unions, workers in different firms are likely to be paid different wage rates.** Frequently, interplant differ-

* A similar pressure often exists in large firms in the absence of unions.
** See *supra*, p. 118.

entials reflect "substantial variation in the wage-paying ability of various firms, combined with [a] refusal of the more profitable firms to maximize profits by paying as low wages as they could pay."[3]

The union goal of equal pay for equal work, which is designed to take wages out of competition, suggests that collective bargaining will have a leveling effect on wages, and this has occurred. Differentials between firms in the same product market that bargain with industrial unions and between firms that hire in the same labor market and bargain with skilled craft unions have typically been reduced or eliminated.

Paying workers the same hourly or weekly rate does not mean that competitors have equal unit labor costs. Thus, wage equalization may result in (1) a tightening of work rules and practices in less efficient firms, (2) the elimination of submarginal firms and an increase in employment in the remaining firms or (3) variations in the total compensation package. Unions may allow smaller firms or firms with special problems to pay lower wages or otherwise modify a wage package so that they can remain competitive.

The leveling effect of collective bargaining on wages is much less pronounced when firms produce for different markets and when an industry has different wage contours. These conditions usually generate interindustry wage differentials.

Geographic Differentials

The emphasis unions place on standard wage rates suggests that most unions would prefer to eliminate geographic differences in the wages of members in the same occupational category. The area of product market competition, the area covered by a contract, and the extent of nonunion competition will determine whether the reduction or elimination of such differences is a primary bargaining objective. Industrial unions are more likely to pursue such an objective because the firms with which they bargain often have national markets. Skilled craft unions which bargain with firms that have local or regional markets are less interested in reducing geographic differences in wages.

Although unions will normally press for a reduction in geographic differentials in wages, in some local market industries such as building and construction, in which unions have been more successful in organizing in areas in which firms pay higher wages, such differences may have widened. Geographic wage differentials have also persisted when union firms face significant nonunion competition in certain areas.

The independent influence of collective bargaining on geographic differences in wages has been less marked than its effect on intrafirm and interfirm differences. However, collective bargaining has reenforced the historical narrowing of geographic differences in wages in response to basic market forces.

Occupational Differentials

Although unions generally wish to reduce or eliminate interpersonal, interfirm, and geographic wage differentials, they often feel differently about occupational wage differentials. The types of workers that fall within a union's jurisdiction usually determine its policy in this regard. A craft union is generally interested in maintaining the relative advantage its members have in terms of wages over less skilled operatives. An industrial union on the other hand may negotiate uniform across-the-board wage increases that reduce relative differences in earnings although *absolute* differences are unchanged.

Economic constraints may counterbalance such institutional goals. However, in the United States—at least until recently—market forces have generally reduced occupational differences in wages, and collective bargaining has reenforced this trend. In manufacturing, for example, the relative advantage in terms of wages of skilled over unskilled factory workers was reduced by about one-half between 1907 and 1947.[4] It appears that this trend has resulted from a relative increase in the number of skilled and semiskilled operatives and the desire of less skilled and unskilled workers to avoid low status jobs. Both factors increased the supply of skilled labor and decreased the supply of unskilled workers relative to the demand for them.

Skilled workers were the first to organize in the United States, and this led initially to a widening of occupational differences in wages. When semiskilled and unskilled workers joined unions, this trend was reversed. The rapid growth of industrial unions in the 1930s and the negotiation of flat across-the-board wage increases during World War II and the early postwar period further reduced relative differences in the wage rates paid in different occupations.

After World War II, skilled union members initially accepted wage increases that widened or maintained the *absolute* differences between their wages and those of semiskilled and unskilled workers, though they often reduced the relative difference in their wages. However, since the late 1950s, many unions have negotiated uniform *percentage increases* rather than uniform absolute increases. During the 1960s, craft unions in a number of industries, including building and construction, the airlines, and the railroads, used their bargaining leverage to negotiate above average percentage increases, while skilled workers in a number of industrial unions, including the United Automobile Workers and the United Steelworkers, demanded superior wage settlements to help restore previous percentage differentials between their wages and those of less skilled workers.

Interindustry Differentials

Unions are less likely to have a clear policy concerning interindustry wage differentials, since economic conditions vary from one industry to another.

A "favorable" interindustry differential usually develops in response to market forces, often the demand by new or expanding industries for skilled labor in short supply. Once such a differential has been established, union leaders will be under pressure to preserve it irrespective of changes in the economic environment. Pattern following may also perpetuate existing absolute or relative differentials.

THE UNION AS A COUNTERVAILING POWER

There are parallels between the development of occupational and interindustry wage differentials in the United States. Unions have tended to be established initially in strategic occupations and profitable industries in which high wages were already being paid or in which the creation of countervailing power would help unions attain their wage objectives. As a result, unions were often able to negotiate, and for varying periods to maintain, favorable wage differentials. A one-time increase in relative wages may reflect (1) the ability of a union to end "exploitation" or, more accurately, the payment of a wage lower than the marginal revenue product in labor markets in which employers previously enjoyed monopsony power, or (2) a "shock effect" that compels firms not maximizing their profits to operate more efficiently.

Whether such differentials persist depends on the ability of the union to insulate its members from the potential leveling effect of competitive forces in product and labor markets. In highly concentrated industries, that is, industries in which a few firms account for a high percentage of total sales, unions may be able to continue to share in pure profits. However, it cannot be assumed that collective bargaining is responsible for high wages in such industries; union leaders may simply have taken credit for wage increases that were "in the cards." According to some observers, "large, oligopolistic, and progressive firms seem in any event to follow a high-wage policy," so that "[u]nionism has only an incremental, and probably a minor, effect on the outcome."[5]

Some economists have suggested that favorable wage differentials have a greater effect on the degree of unionization than vice versa; that is, high wages encourage workers to join unions and are not the result of a high degree of unionization.[6] Other economists dispute this view. Daniel J. B. Mitchell, for example, maintains that the higher wages of union workers "cannot be due to a contemporary tendency of higher-paid workers to 'purchase' union services . . . [but] rather to the tendency of unions to raise wages."[7]

Lawrence Kahn has concluded that in addition to having a *direct* effect on wages when the quality of labor and all other factors influencing wages are held constant, unions have an *indirect* effect on an industry's relative wage level:

> The indirect effects result from the fact that union wage increases induce firms to substitute capital and skilled labor for unskilled labor; hiring standards rise and thus wages are raised again. The wage increases also raise the degree of unionism in the industry, which then raises wages again.[8]

Kahn surmises that this widening of wage differentials has increased segmentation in the labor market.

INTERINDUSTRY DIFFERENTIALS AND UNEMPLOYMENT

In periods of high unemployment, workers in industries that are not highly organized may be less able to resist wage reductions or, more recently in a period of stagflation, to obtain increases comparable to those obtained in more highly organized industries. As a result, union workers in "protected" industries may enjoy increasingly favorable wage differentials.

In labor intensive industries, this is likely to stimulate nonunion competition, which may have an adverse impact on job opportunities in the union sector. The recent growth of the nonunion sector of the construction industry, for example, has had a chilling impact on the rate of increase of wages of union construction workers in many localities. Foreign competition in such labor intensive industries as the manufacture of electronic equipment and garments has moderated the rate of increase in wages and eliminated job opportunities in those industries.

Industry Studies

The bulk of the studies trying to measure what is conventionally called the independent influence of unionism have been concerned with two basic types of comparisons: (1) either they have tried to compare the relative effects of unions in specific industries on wages or (2) they have tried to measure or estimate the impact of unionism on the average wage of union as compared to the average wage of nonunion labor. As we have indicated before, it is more appropriate to consider that both types of studies measure the impact of *collective bargaining*.

Relative Wage Effects by Industry—the Empirical Evidence

By carefully reviewing earlier studies and making additional computations designed to yield comparable data, H. Gregg Lewis developed estimates *by industry* of the relative effect of unionism on wages in the United States from 1919 to 1958. According to Lewis, the majority of workers studied

> were employed in industries whose average relative wages ha[d] been raised or lowered by unionism by not more than about 4 per cent. But [the] data also suggest that the distribution of the relative wage effects . . . is somewhat positively skewed, with effects in some industries as large as 20 percent or even larger. . . .
>
> [T]he list of industries in which the [relative wage] effects were large . . . includes bituminous coal mining, some of the skilled building trades in some cities in which the trades were highly unionized, possibly barbering in some cities, and doubtfully, commercial air transportation, local transit, and ocean shipping.[9]

A colleague of Lewis's, Professor Albert Rees, "put together the available industry studies, the relevant economic theory, and data on wage movements to make informed guesses" about other cases in which unions have had a larger than average or less than average effect on relative wages.[10] According to Rees, leading candidates [for larger than average effects] would be the skilled craft unions in railroads, entertainment, and the printing trades; the teamsters; and the steelworkers. A list of candidates for additional unions with less-than-average relative wage effects would include the unions of ladies' garment workers, textile workers, shoe workers, and white-collar government workers.[11]

The increase in unionization among white-collar (and other) government employees was often associated with above average wage increases in the 1960s and early 1970s. However, several studies have suggested that more recently the impact of collective bargaining on wages within the public sector has paralleled that within the private sector.[12]

Rees has identified two general types of situations during periods of stable prices and high employment in which unions have had no measurable effect on earnings in given industries: (1) situations where unions have failed to organize a majority of the firms producing for a national market and (2) situations in which unions, despite a high degree of organization, are operating in industries in which the demand for the final product has been declining.[13]

There appear to be no simple rules for identifying industries in which unions can be expected to have a significant effect on wages. According to Lewis, "[a] high extent of unionization . . . is not sufficient for a large positive effect . . . on relative wages."[14] Nor are the "high wage" industries of Lewis and Rees necessarily the more profitable and more highly concentrated industries. The building trades and trucking, for example, are usually considered competitive industries.

The significant link between the product market and the rate of change of wages in different industries may be the ease with which new firms outside the union's jurisdictional control can enter the industry. Thus, higher wages may reflect the restrictions on entry that are common in concentrated industries. On the other hand, there are situations in which despite free entry into an industry as a whole geographic or spatial limitations enable unions such as the teamsters to protect wage standards against pressures from nonunion or runaway shops. The observed correlation between the strength of unions, the degree of concentration, and the rate of increases in wages in an industry may be the result of relying on data from manufacturing industries in which concentration ratios tend to be high.[15]

SUMMARY

This analysis supports the tentative conclusion that interindustry differentials have been determined in the main by market forces and that the influence of unions on industry wage levels is probably more moderate than both critics and supporters of unionism tend to assume.* In view of the importance of key bargains in the union sector and the possible spillover effects of collective bargaining in the nonunion sector, relative interindustry differentials may narrow. However, if we

---

* In a number of instances, *occupational* differentials secured by skilled workers have been improperly identified as interindustry differentials.

cannot maintain a high level of employment, interindustry differentials can be expected to widen as unions in highly organized industries successfully resist reductions in the rate of increase of wages or become better able to negotiate wage increases during inflationary periods in which unemployment remains high.

The Difference in the Average Wage Level of Union and Nonunion Workers

In addition to studying the impact of unionism on wages at the industry level, Lewis developed estimates of the overall impact of unionism on the average wage of union labor relative to the average wage of nonunion workers. He found that this impact varied markedly over time, that it "was greatest near the bottom of the Great Depression and was least during the periods of unusually rapid inflation and low unemployment following both world wars."[16] He concluded that:

1. unionism probably has not produced a difference of more than 25 percent in the wages of union and nonunion workers since 1920, except possibly in 1921 and 1922 and from about 1930 to about 1935;
2. since the late 1930s, unionism has not produced a difference in the average wage of union as opposed to nonunion labor of more than 20 percent;
3. the relative impact of unionism on wages from about 1945 to about 1949 was unusually small, yielding a wage differential for union and nonunion labor of perhaps 5 percent or less;
4. except during and near periods of wartime and postwar inflation, unionism was responsible for a "normal" difference of at least 10 percent in the wages of organized and unorganized workers;
5. there was a significant increase in the impact of unionism on relative wages as the rate of inflation fell from 1945–1948 to 1957–1958; and
6. in 1957 and 1958, both recession years, the rate of inflation was still large enough to prevent unions from raising the wages of unionized workers above those of nonunion workers by more than 10 to 15 percent.[17]

In the most recent period Lewis studied, the 1950s, "the average wage of union workers was about 7 to 11 per cent higher relative to the average wage of all workers . . . than it would have been in the absence of unionism," and "the average wage of nonunion workers was about 3 to 4 per cent lower relative to the average wage of all workers."[18]

More recent studies of the effects of collective bargaining on wages, studies that have used different data and more sophisticated methods, generally support Lewis's analysis, although they suggest that union-nonunion differentials may be somewhat higher than he estimated.[19] Paul Ryscavage, for example, using multiple regression analysis employing five sets of independent variables (union membership, age, school years completed, occupation, and geographic region), estimated that the effects of unions on wages was about 12 percent for all workers and that "the usual hourly earnings of organized craftsmen were . . . about 20 to 25 percent more . . . than the earnings of workers who had similar characteristics, but were not members of unions."[20]

In 1977 Rees summarized the results of recent studies and concluded that

> The strongest American unions seem to be able to raise the wages of their members by more than 30 per cent. . . . Recent estimates from cross-section [studies] of individuals suggest an effect of 15 to 20 per cent for operatives and laborers, and less than 10 per cent for craftsmen. . . .
>
> My own best guess of the average effects of all American unions on the wages of their members in recent years would lie somewhere between 15 and 20 per cent . . . a somewhat higher range than I would have guessed a decade ago. [However,] the difference is more the result of the availability of new data than of a belief that union power has been increasing.[21]

Summary: Collective Bargaining and Wage Differentials

In general, collective bargaining seems to have raised the wages of union members relative to nonunion workers, at least at certain times and in certain circumstances, but in the long run the impact of unions on wages has probably been less than is popularly assumed. Market forces appear to have been responsible for many of the long-run trends in relative wages and unions have often been able to take advantage of such forces. The extent to which a union has organized the firms producing for a particular market and the type of market that exists for a firm's products are key determinants of a union's ability to create and/or maintain wage differentials through collective bargaining.

THE MACROECONOMIC IMPACTS OF COLLECTIVE BARGAINING

We turn now to the impact of collective bargaining from a macroanalytical standpoint. Since studies of how collective bargaining affects the functional distribution of income (labor's share of the national income), the level of money wages, the level of real wages, the price level, and the trade-off between inflation and unemployment have often been inconclusive, our analysis here can only be tentative. We can however identify a number of probable macroeconomic impacts of collective bargaining.

Unions and the Functional Distribution of Income

Union leaders and some supporters of unionism and collective bargaining frequently assert that an alteration in the functional distribution of income in favor of labor (that is, an increase in labor's relative share of the national income) is a primary objective of union organization. This is probably not a conscious goal of most union members, who, because of sustained economic growth, have shared in increases in the nation's real income. Most union leaders moreover are business unionists. Despite their public pronouncements, they are more interested in the welfare of *their own members* than that of the labor force as a whole. Up to now, this nonradical stance has also been pragmatic. If declines in the rate of increase of productivity limit future increases in real wages or if inflation offsets increases in money wages, the redistribution of income on a functional basis may become a significant bargaining issue.

As we noted in Chapter 5, labor's share of the national income has increased over the long run,* though it remained relatively stable in the 1970s. Much of the long-run increase is a statistical phenomenon reflecting (1) the relative decline in agricultural output and in the number of independent proprietorships, which decreases the proportion of nonwage income in the national income; (2) the continuing relative increase in importance of labor intensive service industries; and (3) the relative increase in the size of the government sector, which by definition generates only wage income. The magnitude of the rise in labor's share of the national income is much reduced in studies that compensate for such changes.

Rees concluded that studies making such adjustments leave "a remainder that shows no particular relation to union power,"[22] while Clark Kerr found no evidence that trade unionism in the United States *through collective bargaining* had had a significant impact on labor's share of the national income. According to Kerr,

> only through quite deep penetration into economic decision-making, either directly or indirectly through government, can unionism raise labor's share more than temporarily; . . . unionism must approach the problem of distributive shares directly and consciously if it is to attain the goal of a higher relative share for labor.[23]

A more recent analysis concluded that only 2.46 percentage points of a 10.48 percentage point increase in the average employee compensation share of the national income between 1920–1929 and 1960–1969 was attributable to collective bargaining.[24]

Other writers have suggested that although collective bargaining may not have *raised* labor's share of the national income, it may have prevented a long-run *decline*. This seems unlikely. However, since the amount of capital employed in the American economy has increased relative to the supply of labor it is conceivable that in the absence of unions real wages would have increased but that labor's relative share of the national income could have decreased. It should be noted that there is a clear consensus that unions have influenced the way in

* See Table 5.6, p. 93.

which increases in real wages have been realized (through an increase in money wages rather than a decrease in prices).

Collective bargaining may have been responsible for some redistribution of income *within* the labor force, not only from nonunion to union workers but within the union sector. Unions have been most successful in organizing workers in primary as opposed to secondary labor markets, and any redistribution of income within the labor force has probably favored workers in primary markets, especially where imperfections in product and labor markets have enabled workers represented by unions to share in pure profits.

Although collective bargaining does not seem to have significantly altered the functional distribution of income, American unions may have had a less direct impact on labor's relative claim to the national product. Unions have supported tax policies, minimum wage legislation, and social insurance and welfare plans that have reduced inequalities in income. If a disproportionate share of public and private security benefits go to union members, there will be some further redistribution of income within the labor force in favor of union members. Union support of monetary and fiscal policies designed to maintain full employment has probably increased the total compensation paid to American workers, but the impact on the relative share of each factor of production in the national income is uncertain.

Further encroachment by labor on the profit component of national income may reduce the marginal efficiency of capital. This could reduce the volume of investment relative to the growth in national income and thus the rate of increase of productivity. Union members may not benefit from such a relative increase in labor's share of the national income if their *real* income (in absolute terms) is less than it would have been had the volume of investment in the country been higher.

Money Wages

Earlier in the chapter, we concluded that unions may be able to help the workers they represent obtain higher wages than nonunion workers. A further question, related to the possible impact of unionism on changes in the price level, is whether collective bargaining has contributed to a more rapid rise in the overall level of *money* wages. American experience since World War II suggests that collective bargaining has increased the rate of increase in money wages, primarily by preventing wage cuts or by negotiating wage increases during economic downturns. The ability of unions to negotiate such increases, which probably spill over into some nonunion sectors, has been strengthened by the absence of any significant downward pressure on prices in many industries.

However, Robert J. Flanagan, on the basis of a study of union and nonunion wage rates in manufacturing between 1959 and 1975, has questioned the importance of the spillover effect in recent years. According to Flanagan, "union wages in manufacturing do not appear to have influenced wage increases in non-union manufacturing," probably because of the "absence of a discernible threat effect . . . during a period in which private-sector organizing has not been very extensive or successful."[25]

Following World War II, collective bargaining may have retarded the rate of increase in money wages in tight labor markets due to the relatively modest annual wage increases provided under long-term contracts. The income protection presently provided by cost-of-living escalators makes this less likely in the future. However, the second- and third-year increases called for by such contracts continue to reflect the economic outlook at the time a contract is negotiated. This tends to make negotiated increases less responsive to actual changes in the economic environment during the life of the contract, creating what has been termed *wage inertia*.

The conclusion that collective bargaining has been responsible for some part of the increase in the level of money wages cannot be quantified. In many instances, increases in the money wages of union members, for which union leaders are eager to assume credit, represent responses to basic market forces and would probably have occurred in the absence of unions.

In view of our commitment to full employment, the political and institutional pressures on union leaders to produce annual wage gains, and the prevalence of administered pricing in product markets, it is understandable that increases in real wages have come from, and no doubt will continue to come from, increases in wage rates rather than reductions in prices. It is also probable that, except in unusual circumstances, union leaders will not only oppose any reduction in wages during an economic downturn but try to negotiate increases that not only compensate workers for past reductions in real income caused by inflation but also reflect current inflationary expectations.

In short, *in the long run,* collective bargaining has probably added somewhat to the rate of increase in money wages, and the unions have helped to ensure that increases in real incomes have been achieved through increases in the level of money wages rather than a decrease in prices.

Real Wages

The historical rise in real wages is primarily the result of increasing productivity rather than an increase in labor's share of the national income. Although studies of the impact of collective bargaining on real wages have been inconclusive, it is clear that union members who enjoy a favorable money wage differential will enjoy a corresponding real wage differential. This does not mean that unions have necessarily raised the real wages of their members above the level they would have reached in the absence of unions. It is possible that under collective bargaining, the rate of growth in national output has been reduced, and consequently the rate of increase in real wages.

Unions affect real wages in four principal ways:

1. If through collective bargaining or by supporting particular laws they limit the supply of labor, average real wages may rise although the potential national product is reduced.*
2. If by enforcing restrictive work rules or opposing technological change unions retard or prevent improvements in productivity per man-hour, the overall rate of increase in real wages will be slower.
3. Union policies may directly or indirectly influence the level of investment, and this, depending on the impact it has on aggregate employment and income, may have either a positive or a negative impact on the real income of employed workers.
4. Unions may constitute an independent force responsible for price increases, and these increases may partially offset or negate increases in money wages.

THE IMPACT ON LABOR SUPPLY

Through collective bargaining and support of various legislative measures, unions have helped to reduce the number of man-hours of labor available (which is another way of saying that they have reduced the supply of labor), and as a result, our *potential* national product is smaller. Our per capita national product has not *fallen*, but the *rate of increase* has been *reduced*. If increase in the national product were the sole criterion of social welfare, unions would be open to criticism on this score; but as we have observed repeatedly, other important considerations are involved in an overall evaluation of unionism. A reduction in the standard workday or workweek for example provides more time for a variety of activities that may make life more satisfying for workers and their families.

THE IMPACT ON PRODUCTIVITY

Reports in the popular media often stress the restrictive nature of union work rules, and it is generally assumed that unions have had an adverse impact on productivity. The analysis in Chapter 21 suggested that in the economy as a whole, this effect has been modest. Restrictive work rules and union attempts to control or oppose technological change have probably contributed to some unquantifiable reduction in the *rate of increase* in productivity, but this has not resulted in an absolute decline in the average real wage.

Unions generally try to control rather than oppose technological change, and "the general thrust of modern unionism has favored innovation" as a relatively painless way of extracting wage gains.[26] Moreover, the greater job security under collective bargaining and the resulting improvement in worker morale has undoubtedly increased productivity in some firms.

The net impact of collective bargaining on the *overall level of investment* is speculative. A static model of its effects suggests that higher money wages

---

* This assumes that reductions in working hours will not result in an increase in productivity per man-hour that offsets the loss of output resulting from the reduction in hours.

unmatched by increases in productivity encourage the substitution of capital for labor and increase the nonlabor share of real income. However, such a model fails to reflect how such variables as autonomous technological innovations; changing propensities to consume, save, and invest; various monetary and fiscal initiatives; and consumer and investor expectations may affect the relative price of capital goods, the rate of return on investment, the quality of labor required on new equipment, and the rate of economic growth.

As we pointed out in discussing the impact of unions on the functional distribution of income, a general wage increase initiated under collective bargaining might have a negative impact on investor expectations, causing a relative decrease in investment and a reduction in the rate of increase in, or in the absolute level of, national output. However, the increase in money wages since World War II does not appear to have had an adverse impact on the inducement to invest. A general climate of business optimism has been sustained by a national commitment to full employment and economic growth. Indeed, despite management claims that wage increases will reduce profits and impair investment incentives, union policies that contribute to a modest rate of inflation may help to create a favorable atmosphere for investment. However, wage increases that exceed productivity increases during a period of stagflation may discourage investment, contribute to a persistently high level of unemployment, and decrease the average worker's *real* take-home pay and disposable income, particularly when workers' marginal personal incomes are taxed at a higher rate.

Unions and Inflation

In Chapter 7, we discussed the dilemma caused by the presumed trade-off between unemployment and inflation, one of the most critical problems facing the nation. We noted the differences between demand-pull and cost-push inflation and described the attempts of successive administrations to attain a noninflationary level of full employment. We will now focus more narrowly on the possible inflationary impact of negotiated wage increases.

It is generally recognized that collective bargaining can contribute to inflation (1) by ensuring that wages rise (though perhaps not immediately, due to contracts that run for a number of years) when the price level rises or (2) by causing firms to raise their prices to cover increases in employee compensation packages. The former may be considered a response to demand-pull, the latter to cost-push, forces. In Chapter 7, we questioned the value of making such a distinction, noting that cost-push inflation will only occur if increases in wages or prices are supported or "validated" by a high level of aggregate demand. This suggests that union support of government measures to maintain a high level of employment may be more responsible for the inflationary bias in the economy than negotiated wage increases per se. However, this conclusion is necessarily speculative.

A demand-pull model appears to explain the immediate post–World War II and much of the Korean and Vietnam War inflation. Cost-push elements—primarily an upward pressure on prices due to (1) wage increases not matched by increases in productivity per man-hour and (2) administered price increases—seem to have been important from 1955 to the mid-1960s. During the 1970s, a continued high level of aggregate demand—supported by "built-in" expectations of periodic price and wage increases; the generous wage increases negotiated in certain highly visible sectors, notably construction; and the worldwide increases in the prices of farm products and oil—resulted in continuing and often accelerated price increases during periods when the unemployment rate, by traditional standards, was high. However, the independent causal role of negotiated wage increases in continuing inflation is unclear. Seemingly, some degree of inflation was inevitable during the postwar period given (1) the downward rigidity in wages in both organized and many nonunion firms, (2) a similar downward rigidity in administered prices, and (3) our commitment to full employment. Once this inflationary bias was recognized, price and wage increases became inputs in a complex feedback mechanism that helped to fulfill the inflationary expectations that had been generated.

Most economists agree that collective bargaining can serve as a transmission belt for inflationary forces, but they disagree about its role in generating inflation. Three basic theoretical positions regarding this role may be identified:

1. Union pressure for wage increases that exceed increases in productivity will lead either to an undesirable degree of inflation or to increased unemployment. If we will not tolerate inflation, we will have to accept a high level of unemployment.
2. Unions contribute to an inflationary bias within the economy, but this is not necessarily undesirable.
3. Inflation results from an increase in the supply of money. Union wage demands cannot be considered a basic cause of inflation, although they may transmit inflationary forces.

The assumptions underlying the first position were stated effectively by Professor Gottfried Haberler as long ago as 1951:

(1) There is under any given set of circumstances a certain limit beyond which the money-wage level cannot be pushed without either a rise in prices or the appearance of unemployment. (2) Our society will not tolerate an indefinite rise in prices. Sooner or later, steps will be taken through monetary or fiscal policy, or indirect control, to counteract further price rises. (3) Labor unions are not satisfied with wage increases on this side of the critical limit; they tend to push beyond it.[27]

The late Professor Sumner Slichter was a leading exponent of the second position, arguing that unions impart an inflationary bias to the economy but that a modest rate of inflation is not dangerous.[28] Many economists still believe that a *modest, nonaccelerating* rate of inflation helps to provide a favorable climate for economic growth.

Other economists have been even more sanguine about the inflationary impact of union wage demands. Milton Friedman has argued that because economic variables *appear* to operate through unions, unions have erroneously been regarded "as causes of changes rather than as intermediaries." In his view, "unions are simply thermometers registering the heat rather than furnaces producing the heat."[29] This position would probably be rejected by the majority of economists, who feel that long-term contracts that provide increases in money wages that exceed increases in productivity put an upward pressure on prices. The fact that such increases must be validated by the monetary authorities does not mean that the collective bargaining process did not *initiate* the upward movement in prices.

The first position, and possibly the second, appears, however, to overemphasize the role of collective bargaining in causing inflation. Today, wages tend to be inflexible downward in both nonunion and organized firms, and it is wrong to assume that the contribution of wage inflexibility to inflation is related uniquely to collective bargaining. In fact, recent evidence has suggested "that the responsiveness of wages to overall changes in economic conditions is significantly greater in nonunion than in unionized labor markets," and that "new inflationary pressures show up much more gradually in union than in nonunion wages."[30]

In reality, much of this current debate may be misdirected since the inflationary bias in the economy is primarily a result of an understandable commitment to full employment. Policy decisions relating to the trade-off between inflation and unemployment have been seriously constrained because, contrary to Professor Haberler's assumption, increases in prices have been more acceptable politically than an increase in, or a failure to decrease, the rate of unemployment. The resulting tilt toward price inflation has been reenforced by (1) the imperfect market structure and markup pricing in highly visible basic manufacturing industries; (2) the prevalence of local market contracts in such industries as building and construction, the service trades, and local government, which has made it difficult to implement national wage-price policies; and (3) various institutional aspects of our system of collective bargaining, including the pressure of coercive comparisons. During the decade of the 1980s, increases in the price of oil and the failure of productivity to increase in many industries may make it even more difficult to reduce the rate of inflation.

In such an environment, collective bargaining reenforces inflationary pressures, since negotiated wage settlements reflect the expectation of employers and unions that inflation will continue.

On the other hand, the country's monetary authorities may be less willing to validate increases in money wages that exceed economywide increases in productivity as national priorities change. The acceleration in the rate of inflation since 1978, a reflection in part of a decline in the economywide rate of increase in productivity, is apparently creating at least a partial consensus that inflation must be controlled even if it means an increase in the unemployment rate in the short run.

THE GUIDEPOST EXPERIENCE

Under the guidepost formula introduced by the Kennedy administration, prices, on the average, were to remain stable, and money and real wages were to increase in accordance with long-term average annual increases in productivity.* If increases in productivity in an industry exceeded the national average, prices were to be reduced. Not unexpectedly, the average increase in productivity incorporated in a succession of guidepost formulae became a *minimum* bargaining goal. Union leaders were under pressure to exceed the minimum, particularly in two types of situations: (1) when the annual increase in productivity in an industry exceeded the national standard and (2) when the economic environment in local market industries such as construction favored wage increases and the administration was unable to moderate such increases by putting pressure on a limited number of influential industry and union leaders.

The resulting price increases complicated efforts to hold down wages because union leaders then tried to negotiate additional increases in money wages to compensate for the erosion in the real value of their members' take-home pay. Meanwhile, structural changes in the economy, including changes in the composition of the labor force, contributed to an unacceptably high rate of unemployment. These factors, in combination with a balance-of-payments crisis in the summer of 1971, impelled a Republican administration to institute formal price and wage controls. *The Nixon administration's stabilization program* was reasonably effective for perhaps a year and a half, but as output increased, the controls on prices and wages contributed to a misallocation of resources and continuing shortages in some product and labor markets.

Following the termination of Phase IV of Nixon's program of controls in April of 1974, the nation experienced continuing inflation, and in October of 1978, the *Carter administration* established new "standards" or guidelines to limit the rate of increase in prices and wages. Although the Carter guidelines may have moderated the rate of increase in prices and wages somewhat, double-digit inflation has continued, reaching an annual rate of 12.7 percent in September of 1980. Since the productivity of the economy as a whole is not increasing at its previous average long-term rate, *real* wages may remain stable or even decline in the near future. This will put more pressure on union leaders to negotiate wage increases.

If we accept the inevitability of an upward tilt in the price level, a *modest nonaccelerating* rate of increase in the general price level, not overall price stability, may be the most acceptable and realistic national policy objective. Economists disagree on whether an appropriate guidepost formula, implemented by "jawboning" in highly visible bargaining relationships, would be helpful in attaining such a goal.

If guideposts are to be even moderately effective, they should not be formu-

* See *supra,* p. 145.

lated unilaterally by officials in Washington. The administration should involve organized labor, management, and representative public interest organizations in the deliberations leading to the formulation of both general guidepost policies and more specific operational standards and ensure that such policies and standards reflect a consensus of these groups.

Developing such a consensus will not be easy; there are no simple criteria for determining a workable trade-off between competing national policy objectives. Moreover, any theoretical model of "appropriate" wage-price behavior will have to be modified in the light of reality, and wage-price policies will have to be flexible over time. Given continued double-digit inflation, failure to develop a flexible incomes policy based on such a consensus will probably generate increasing pressures for formal wage-price controls.

A Summary Note

The impact of collective bargaining on economic aggregates is often exaggerated. Collective bargaining does not seem to have increased labor's share of national income relative to that of property owners, although it may have redistributed income to some extent within the labor force. It has probably contributed to an increase in the level of money wages, but union leaders have taken credit for increases that in many cases would have occurred in the absence of unions. Union members who earn higher money wages than other workers also earn higher real wages, but their real wages may be somewhat less than they would have been without collective bargaining. It is doubtful that collective bargaining has been a *significant independent* inflationary force. It has however contributed to the recent persistent inflation, and it is partly responsible for the upward wage momentum in the economy.

THE IMPACT OF UNION WORK RULES

The discussion of union work rules in Chapter 21 suggested that they are generally less restrictive than is commonly thought and that the system of industrial jurisprudence established through collective bargaining has significant extraeconomic benefits. These extraeconomic benefits, together with the opportunity the system gives workers to participate through elected representatives or perhaps as union officials in the negotiation and interpretation of rules governing the employment relationship, must be considered positive contributions in terms of individual employees.

Not surprisingly, it is hard to estimate the overall *economic impact* of work rules. If, following orthodox theory, one assumes that factors of production have been combined in an optimal fashion and that workers are producing with reasonable efficiency, a work rule that interferes with the allocation of resources will increase unit costs and result in a lower level of employment, although not necessarily in disemployment if the demand for output is increasing.

In Chapter 21, we noted that although negotiated work rules undoubtedly result in some misallocation of resources and loss of economic "efficiency," there is no guarantee that in the absence of unions we would be more likely to achieve "socially optimal" resource allocation. The relevant question is not whether a union work rule generates social costs but whether an alternative is available that would afford similar protection at a lower net social cost.

This question involves two subsidiary questions: (1) what is the impact of work rules on the enterprise and its employees and (2) what is the overall impact of such rules? Neither question can be answered definitively.

It is probable that union work rules increase the operating costs of an enterprise to some extent. It is also probable that this increase is less than most people assume. Many firms subject to the discipline of collective bargaining handle employee relations more efficiently and humanely, with consequent improvements in productivity and employee morale. According to Theodore Kheel, "a company that is unionized almost always becomes more efficient as a result."[31] And according to Slichter, Healy, and Livernash, whose study of the impact of collective bargaining we have mentioned before, "[t]he challenge that unions presented to management has, if viewed broadly, created superior and better-balanced management."[32]

Moreover, bargaining trade-offs may offset some of the costs associated with specific work rules. In the case of negotiated work rules, and initially in the case of many informal work rules and practices, the employer usually receives some quid pro quo.[33] On the other hand, if a firm does not review work rules and practices periodically, its operations may become less efficient in the long run. The transformation of "save work" rules into "make work" rules is a case in point.

Analyzing the economywide impact of work rules is also difficult. Even if one assumes that union work rules are a net burden to employers, one cannot conclude that they are necessarily a net burden to the community. This would be true only if the social costs that might otherwise be incurred, such as the cost of supporting disemployed or superannuated workers and their dependents, were less than the costs to employers. The presumed improvement in the quality of life of workers protected by union work rules and practices has broad implications. In terms of cost-benefit analysis, many such rules and practices undoubtedly increase the economic and emotional well-being of individual workers and groups of workers. Consider, for example, the positive externalities that are often associated with work rules establishing health and safety standards or requiring that seniority be considered in layoffs and promotions.

The Impact on Technological Change

The diverse conditions under which technological changes are introduced and the variety of policies unions and management may adopt make it hard to estimate the overall impact of union policies toward technological change. As a rule, unions do not oppose technological change. However, in many cases unions have forced management to *share the benefits* of innovation with employees, and they have undoubtedly succeeded in shifting some of the *costs of change* from employees to the owners or customers of firms. Under collective bargaining, the rate of introduction of innovations may decrease, bringing a consequent reduction in the rate of growth of the national product.

Unions do not necessarily increase the *net social cost* of technological change. As in the case of work rules more generally, the reduction in potential output they cause may be offset by reductions in the costs which society might otherwise be forced to assume and by intangible benefits deriving from the greater job security enjoyed by most workers represented by unions.

The Impact on Working Conditions—Health and Safety Standards

Unions are often able to achieve socially desirable objectives through their ability to negotiate *common* contract provisions, for example, uniform health and safety standards. In highly competitive local market industries, employers alert to the human dimensions of the employment relationship may be reluctant to initiate improvements in working conditions that might put them at a competitive disadvantage. Unions, by negotiating uniform improvements with competing employers, can establish socially desirable standards. Employers may be able to shift the cost of such improvements to employees through a lower rate of increase in wages or to consumers through higher prices. Again, it cannot be determined whether the resulting social benefit is greater than the associated direct and indirect costs.

A similar approach can be used in evaluating standards resulting from legislation supported by unions. If improvements in safety or health standards do not yield offsetting improvements in efficiency, cost-benefit analysis may suggest—although it may not prove—that the imposition of social costs on the employer is desirable and that the state, by mandating common standards, may in some cases achieve a net social gain.

Seniority

It is often assumed that substituting length of service for merit as a basis for promotions and layoffs under a seniority system decreases a firm's operating efficiency. However, a seniority system does not necessarily replace an objective system of layoffs and promotions based on ability. It may replace a system in which management decisions affecting human resources are based on favoritism or discrimination. In such cases, the protection and sense of equitable treatment afforded workers by a seniority system provide intangible personal benefits that increase morale and may well offset the potentially adverse impact of the system on worker productivity.

The discharge of an older worker or a marginal worker who finds it difficult or impossible to get another job may involve a substantial cost to society.

Consequently, the potential loss of output resulting from the retention or promotion of less productive employees under a seniority system may not represent a net social cost. Moreover, the psychological security seniority gives employees with longer records of service may increase their lifetime output, thus producing an actual social benefit.

The Impact on Minority Employment

The record is more questionable regarding the impact of union work rules on the employment and promotional opportunities of members of minority groups. Organized labor as a whole has supported the elimination of discriminatory work rules. However, apprenticeship and seniority systems in some localities, skilled trades, and industries continue to discriminate against minorities. Title VII of the Civil Rights Act has helped to eliminate unfair practices, but a critical issue still confronts the community: how to reduce the continuing discrimination that is the inevitable by-product of past practices.

Union members who have acquired an "earned equity" in employment naturally resent and resist programs which dilute that equity in attempting to compensate other individuals for past discrimination. This resistance is likely to create sensitive and perhaps intractable problems within local unions when such individuals assume their "rightful place" on seniority ladders or when they are given jobs, admitted into apprenticeship programs, or granted union membership in firms, industries, or geographic areas in which discrimination had been prevalent.

Summary: The Impact of Work Rules

The system of industrial jurisprudence has undoubtedly been responsible for some increase in employment costs, for some misallocation of resources, for the perpetuation of restrictive work rules and practices, and for a resulting unquantifiable reduction in the national product. The greater individual and group security this system has provided compensates to some extent for these "costs."

Unions have exercised varying degrees of control over the introduction of new technology, and this has probably retarded economic growth to some extent. In the absence of less costly alternatives, the unions' behavior may not have been inappropriate. However, it is essential that union leaders understand, and that their members be persuaded, that increased productivity has been the historical route to higher real incomes and that work rules and practices must be reviewed periodically so that unnecessarily restrictive rules can be modified or eliminated.

Most privately negotiated procedures for handling the human problems associated with large-scale technological innovations and shifts in product demand protect employees who *continue* to work. Thus, the direct benefits of unionism are not realized by many people who are most in need of the type of protection afforded by collective bargaining. This reemphasizes the need for more adequate and more generally available employment services, training and re-training programs and allowances, and relocation assistance for disemployed workers and entrants into the labor force.

A CONCLUDING NOTE

Our analysis of the *independent economic* impact of collective bargaining suggests that it is less significant than is generally assumed. However, it is hard to measure this impact, and we cannot assume that in the absence of unions any demonstrated or hypothetical impact of collective bargaining would be eliminated. Some functional alternative would almost certainly take the place of unions and collective bargaining, but we cannot say what form this alternative would take. Consequently, estimates of the impact of collective bargaining on wage-employment relationships are somewhat speculative.

There is evidence that wage dispersion has decreased under collective bargaining, that personal and occupational (and to a lesser extent, regional and interindustry) differentials have been reduced, that money wages are higher and employment is lower in some union subsectors, and that money wages are lower and employment is higher in some nonunion subsectors.

Unions may also be responsible for a higher overall level of money wages, not because wages rise more rapidly under collective bargaining during periods of prosperity (the reverse may be true under long-term contracts), but because unions are better able to resist *reductions in the rate of increase* in wages during economic downturns.

Whether collective bargaining has had an adverse impact on the real wages of employed union members is debatable. Formal and informal union work rules have probably reduced the rate of increase in national output. However, this impact may have been offset to some extent by (1) a more rapid substitution of capital for labor in organized firms and (2) possible increases in individual productivity due to the improved morale resulting from the greater job and income security enjoyed by workers who are represented by unions.

Collective bargaining has contributed to various developments in labor (and product) markets that have helped to generate and sustain inflation in recent years. A succession of national administrations have helped to "validate" the annual increases in money wages that are expected under our system of collective bargaining and that most labor economists believe spill over into nonunion employments.

Although the evidence relating to the economic impact of collective bargaining is inconclusive, the extraeconomic benefits of collective bargaining are clear. The greater dignity and status afforded workers and the improvements made in work environments as a result of collective agreements are strong arguments in favor of collective bargaining. Organized labor's support of legislation favorable to union members and to labor more generally must also be considered an important positive element in an evaluation of unionism.

DISCUSSION QUESTIONS

1. How does the average person usually judge the impact of collective bargaining?
2. Can you think of a possible functional alternative to unions and collective bargaining in the United States?
3. How does one distinguish between the *impact of unions* and the *impact of collective bargaining?*
4. What problems arise in attempting to estimate the *independent* impact of collective bargaining?
5. How may the "veil of time" conceal the actual impact of collective bargaining upon the wage-employment relationship?
6. Does the presence of a union or the structure of the industry appear to be more responsible for wage differentials?
7. Do you believe that union officials will place more emphasis upon the functional distribution of income during the 1980s?
8. Have there been any clearly discernible results of the Carter Administration's wage-price standards (guidelines)?
9. Do unions, on balance, appear to add to "built-in" inflationary pressures?
10. Do you believe that unions in general have contributed to a more "socially optimal" allocation of resources?

SELECTED READINGS

The Impact of Collective Bargaining on Relative Wages

The basic reference remains H. Gregg Lewis, *Unionism and Relative Wages in the United States: An Empirical Inquiry* (Chicago: University of Chicago Press, 1963). More recent studies are summarized in George E. Johnson, "Economic Analysis of Trade Unionism," in *American Economic Review* LXV (May 1975): pp. 23–28, Mitchell, Daniel J. B., *Unions, Wages, and Inflation* (Washington, D.C.: Brookings Institution, 1980), Chap. 3, "The Union Wage Effect," and Parsley, C. J., "Labor Union Effects on Wage Gains: A Survey of Recent Literature," *Journal of Economic Literature* XVIII, no. 1 (March 1980): pp. 1–31. Three articles are included in the section "Unions and Wages," in *Industrial and Labor Relations Review* 31, no. 2 (January 1978): pp. 183–216. Good summaries of studies covering public employment are included in David Lewin, "Public Sector Labor Relations," in *Labor History* 18, no. 1 (Winter 1977): pp. 133–144; and Daniel J. B. Mitchell, "The Impact of Collective Bargaining on Compensation in the Public Sector," in Benjamin Aaron, Joseph R. Grodin and James L. Stern, eds., *Public-Sector Bargaining*, Industrial Relations Research Association Series (Washington, D.C.: Bureau of National Affairs, 1979), pp. 118–149.

Post-World War II Inflation Theory

Bronfenbrenner, Martin, and Holzman, Franklyn D. "Survey of Inflation Theory." In *American Economic Review* LIII, no. 4 (September 1963): pp. 593–661. An excellent article, with an extensive bibliography.

Clark, John M. *The Wage-Price Problem.* Committee for Economic Growth Without Inflation, American Bankers Association, 1960.

Estey, Marten S. *Wages, Wage Policy and Inflation, 1962–1971.* Washington, D.C.: American Enterprise Institute, December 1971.

Frisch, Helmut. "Inflation Theory 1963–1975: A 'Second Generation' Survey." In *Journal of Economic Literature* XV, no. 4 (December 1977): pp. 1289–1317. Another excellent article with an extensive bibliography.

Gordon, R. A. "Wages, Prices, and Unemployment, 1900–1970." In *Industrial Relations* 14, no. 3 (October 1975): pp. 273–301.

Mitchell, Daniel J. B. *Unions, Wages, and Inflation.* Washington, D.C.: Brookings Institution, 1980.

Okun, Arthur M., and Perry, George L., eds. *Curing Chronic Inflation.* Washington, D.C.: Brookings Institution, 1978.

Rousseas, Stephen W., ed. *Inflation: Its Causes, Consequences and Control—A Symposium.* Wilton, Conn.: Calvin K. Kazanjian Economics Foundation, 1968.

Materials on this subject are also cited in Chapter 7. Various monographs of the American Enterprise Institute and articles in the *Brookings Papers on Economic Activity* may also be of interest.

Wage-Price Policy

Bowen, William G. *The Wage-Price Issue: A Theoretical Analysis.* Princeton, N.J.: Princeton University Press, 1960.

Goodwin, Craufurd D., ed. *Exhortation & Controls: The Search for a Wage-Price Policy, 1945–1971.* Washington, D.C.: Brookings Institution, 1975.

Meany, George; Blough, Roger M.; and Jacoby, Neil H. *Government Wage-Price Guideposts in the American Economy.* Charles C. Moskowitz Lectures, School of Commerce, New York University, 1967.

Mills, Daniel Quinn. *Government, Labor, and Inflation: Wage Stabilization in the United States.* Chicago: University of Chicago Press, 1975.

Sheahan, John. *The Wage-Price Guideposts.* Washington, D.C.: Brookings Institution, 1967.

Shultz, George P., and Aliber, Robert Z., eds. *Guidelines, Informal Controls, and the Market Place.* Chicago: University of Chicago Press, 1966.

Shultz, George P., and Dam, Kenneth W. "Reflections on Wage and Price Controls." In *Industrial and Labor Relations Review* 30, no. 2 (January 1977): pp. 139–151.

Weber, Arnold R. *In Pursuit of Price Stability—the Wage-Price Freeze of 1971.* Washington, D.C.: Brookings Institution, 1973.

Notes

1. Robert M. Macdonald, "An Evaluation of the Economic Analysis of Unionism," reprinted with permission from the *Industrial and Labor Relations Review* 19, no. 3 (April 1966): p. 345. © 1966 by Cornell University. All rights reserved.
2. Ibid., pp. 341 and 343.
3. Lloyd G. Reynolds and Cynthia H. Taft, *The Evolution of Wage Structure* (New Haven, Conn.: Yale University Press, 1956), p. 175.

4. Harry Ober, "Occupational Wage Differentials, 1907–1947," in *Monthly Labor Review* 67, no. 2 (August 1948): pp. 127–134.

5. Reynolds and Taft, *The Evolution of Wage Structure,* p. 339.

6. C. J. Parsley, "Labor Union Effects on Wage Gains: A Survey of Recent Literature," *Journal of Economic Literature* XVIII, no. 1 (March 1980): p. 18.

7. *Unions, wages, and inflation.* (Washington, D.C.: Brookings Institution, 1980), p. 111.

8. Lawrence M. Kahn, "Unionism and Relative Wages: Direct and Indirect Effects," in *Industrial and Labor Relations Review* 32, no. 4 (July 1979): pp. 530–531.

9. H. Gregg Lewis, *Unionism and Relative Wages in the United States: An Empirical Inquiry* (© 1963 by The University of Chicago. All rights reserved. Published 1963), p. 282.

10. Albert Rees, "The Effects of Unions on Resource Allocation," in *Journal of Law and Economics* VI (October 1963): p. 73.

11. Ibid., pp. 73–74.

12. See for example Daniel J. B. Mitchell, "The Impact of Collective Bargaining on Compensation in the Public Sector," in Benjamin Aaron, Joseph R. Grodin, and James L. Stern, eds., *Public-Sector Bargaining.* Industrial Relations Research Association Series (Washington, D.C.: Bureau of National Affairs, 1979), pp. 129–141.

13. Albert Rees, *The Economics of Trade Unions* 2nd. rev. ed. (Chicago: University of Chicago Press, 1977), p. 74.

14. Lewis, *Unionism and Relative Wages,* p. 282.

15. Harold M. Levinson, *Determining Forces in Collective Wage Bargaining* (New York: Wiley, 1966), pp. 265–267.

16. Lewis, *Unionism and Relative Wages,* p. 5.

17. Ibid., pp. 188–193.

18. Ibid., p. 5.

19. Cf. George E. Johnson, "Economic Analysis of Trade Unionism," in *American Economic Review* LXV (May 1975): pp. 24–25, Mitchell, *Unions, Wages and Inflation,* chap. 3, "The Union Wage Effect," and Parsley, "Labor Union Effects on Wage Gains."

20. Paul M. Ryscavage, "Measuring Union-Nonunion Earnings Differences," in *Monthly Labor Review* 97, no. 12 (December 1974): pp. 3 and 5.

21. Rees, *The Economics of Trade Unions,* pp. 73–74.

22. Ibid., p. 89.

23. Clark Kerr, "Trade-Unionism and Distributive Shares," in *American Economic Review* XLIV, no. 2 (May 1954): pp. 283–284.

24. F. Ray Marshall, Allan G. King, and Vernon M. Briggs, Jr., *Labor Economics: Wages, Employment, and Trade Unionism,* 4th ed., (Homewood, Ill.: Irwin, 1980), pp. 377–378.

25. Robert J. Flanagan, "Wage Interdependence in Unionized Labor Markets," in *Brookings Papers on Economic Activity* 3 (1976): p. 658. Cf. Marvin H. Kosters, "Wage Standards and Interdependence of Wages in the Labor Market," in William Fellner, proj. dir., *Contemporary Economic Problems 1979* (Washington, D.C.: American Enterprise Institute, 1979), pp. 251–252. For a contrary view see Mitchell, *Unions, Wages, and Inflation,* p. 174.

26. George H. Hildebrand, "The Economic Effects of Unionism," in Neil W. Chamber-

lain, Frank C: Pierson, and Theresa Wolfson, eds., *A Decade of Industrial Relations Research, 1946–1956,* Industrial Relations Research Association Publication 19 (New York: Harper & Brothers, 1958), p. 134.

27. Gottfried Haberler, "Wage Policy, Employment, and Economic Stability," in David McCord Wright, ed., *The Impact of the Union* (New York: Harcourt Brace & World, 1951), p. 39.

28. Sumner H. Slichter, "Labor Costs and Prices," in *Wages Prices Profits and Productivity* (New York: American Assembly, Columbia University, June 1959), p. 168. For an earlier statement of his position, see "Do the Wage-Fixing Arrangements in the American Labor Market Have an Inflationary Bias?" in *American Economic Review* XLIV, no. 2 (May 1954): pp. 322–346.

29. Milton Friedman, "Some Comments on the Significance of Labor Unions for Economic Policy," in Wright, ed., *The Impact of the Union,* p. 222.

30. *Economic Report of the President, Transmitted to the Congress January 1979, Together with the Annual Report of the Council of Economic Advisers,* pp. 62 and 63.

31. Theodore W. Kheel, "The Changing Patterns of Collective Bargaining in the United States," in Jack Stieber, ed., *Employment Problems of Automation and Advanced Technology: An International Perspective* (New York: St. Martin's Press, 1966), p. 384.

32. Sumner H. Slichter, James J. Healy, and E. Robert Livernash, *The Impact of Collective Bargaining on Management* (Washington, D.C.: Brookings Institution, 1960), p. 951.

33. Gerald G. Somers, Edward L. Cushman, and Nat Weinberg, eds., "Conclusions," in *Adjusting to Technological Change,* Industrial Relations Research Association Publication Number 29 (New York: Harper & Row, 1963), p. 211.

Chapter 24
CONCLUSION:
THE AMERICAN UNION
MOVEMENT—PROGRESS,
PROBLEMS, AND
PROSPECTS

In this final chapter, we will assess the present condition of the union movement; review the principal features of collective bargaining in the United States; summarize the impact of unions and collective bargaining on workers, employers, and the economy; consider the extraeconomic dimensions of union membership and the collective bargaining process; and, recognizing the speculative nature of such an undertaking, identify the more significant continuing and prospective problems facing the union movement.

THE UNION MOVEMENT IN 1980

Before World War II, the expansion of union organization was often accompanied by overt labor-management conflicts. Today, with the right to organize and bargain collectively established by law, the legitimacy and permanence of the union as an institution have been recognized by most elements within the business community, and membership in labor organizations is expanded through representation elections rather than picket lines and strikes. This transition was the result not only of the protection afforded unions under law but also of the favorable economic climate during World War II; the policies of the War Labor Board, which helped to stablize emergent collective bargaining relationships; and the continued economic expansion of the postwar era.

Although union membership in the United States increased from 14.3 million in 1945 to 20.2 million in 1978,* the percentage of employees in nonagricultural establishments who were union members declined significantly during the same period. Whether the failure of U.S. unions to maintain the relative strength of their membership base should be considered a crisis or merely an organizational pause before a period of renewed growth remains to be seen.

The degree of union membership varies in different industries, occupations, and geographic locations, and between the two sexes. Workers in durable goods industries, in construction, in transportation, and in the public sector are highly organized, whereas those in wholesale and retail trades, finance and insurance, personal service industries, and agriculture are not. Blue-collar workers in durable goods industries are highly organized, but white-collar workers in those industries are not. Except for teachers, few professionals are highly organized. Workers in cities are usually more highly organized than workers in less populated areas in the same geographic region, and union membership is relatively low in the South. Membership is also low among female workers, who are often employed in industries and occupations that are not highly organized.

Projections of future labor requirements indicate that the greatest increase in job opportunities will be in occupations, industries, and geographic areas in which union organization is presently weak. Worker and community attitudes and improved employee relations programs in many firms in these unorganized sectors will make it hard to mount effective organizing campaigns. High levels of structural unemployment among certain demographic subsets, the underemployment of more highly educated workers in the 25–44 age bracket (the Vietnam generation), and concern over the quality of work life may increase feelings of alienation within the labor force. However, it is not clear whether this will encourage workers to join unions or reject them as establishment institutions interested in perpetuating the status quo.

For the unions to make any general organizational gains, there may first have to be an infusion of vitality, enthusiasm, and greater idealism into the union movement. The unions will also have to develop leaders qualified to deal with the varied (and often highly technical) bargaining issues of a postindustrial economy. Whether the recent turnover in the top leadership of the AFL-CIO and a number of its affiliates will provide the impetus for such developments is unclear. However, the apparent determination of Meany's successor, Lane Kirkland, to support broadly based organizing efforts; his invitation to independent nationals, including the UAW and the Teamsters, to reaffiliate with the federation; his decision to appoint more women and minority group representatives to key positions within the federation; and his role in negotiating the 1979 "national accord"

---

* Union and association membership in the United States totaled 22.8 million in 1978.

with the Carter administration suggest that during the 1980s, a new generation of leaders may respond creatively to the challenges and opportunities that confront organized labor.

CHARACTERISTIC FEATURES OF UNION-MANAGEMENT RELATIONS IN THE UNITED STATES

Union-management relations involve management's continuing institutional relationship with the organization or organizations representing its employees. Our system of collective bargaining gives workers, through their union representatives, a role in formulating and implementing the rules and regulations affecting the employment relationship. Much of the "web of rule" that relates workers to one another and to the production process is provided by collective agreements and by the interpretation of contractual provisions during the life of an agreement under a grievance procedure. The *variety* of *continuing* union-management relationships deserves emphasis and helps to explain why a general theory that can explain the present character of, and predict future developments in, particular bargaining relationships has yet to be developed.

Unions are a response to the employment-related human problems of an industrial civilization. The extraeconomic dimensions of these problems and the union response are significant; neglect of this aspect of union membership and of the collective bargaining process has introduced an unconscious bias into some otherwise objective studies of the impact of unions. Any evaluation of unionism should recognize that the involvement, even indirectly, of individual workers in decisions relating to their conditions of employment helps to offset the sense of alienation that may accompany industrialization.[1]

Although some firms continue to neglect these problems, a majority of the present generation of managers recognize the existence of extraeconomic employee needs and try to develop policies and programs to structure the employment relationship in a way that helps to satisfy those needs. However, in the absence of unions, management may not make the same qualitative and quantitative commitment to the employee relations function that it makes to other functions.

The impact of unions on management is twofold: management can no longer establish conditions of employment unilaterally, since it must bargain with union representatives over the terms of the basic labor contract; and many of management's day-to-day operational decisions may be challenged under a grievance procedure. The popular notion that collective bargaining is an intermittent process concerned almost entirely with the negotiation of contracts is incorrect; collective bargaining is, or should be a *continuing process* based on a realization that day-to-day questions about the interpretation of contracts are often of far more importance to individual employees, and in some cases to the ultimate security of a union, than more highly publicized contract negotiations.

Collective bargaining is an institutional relationship, and institutional security is a basic objective of both parties. Unions want some form of contractual provisions requiring the workers they represent to be union members and pay dues on a regular basis. Many firms insist on some type of management rights clause to protect managerial prerogatives. It is impossible to make a permanent decision about which matters should be considered solely the responsibility of management. As a practical matter, the National Labor Relations Board may ultimately decide whether a given issue is subject to negotiation. Not unexpectedly, the number of matters considered by the board to be "appropriate to collective bargaining" has gradually increased. Its decisions are of course subject to judicial review.

Reducing Overt Industrial Conflict

As a bargaining relationship "matures," the incidence of overt industrial conflict is reduced and a constructive relationship may develop. Differences are more likely to be resolved without work stoppages when the parties recognize their mutual interest in solving problems, appreciate the factors that affect the other party's bargaining posture, feel institutionally secure, are able to agree on the "facts" relevant to a particular dispute, are willing to analyze contentious issues rationally rather than emotionally, and are free from internal political constraints that might prevent a reasonable compromise. Even constructive bargaining relationships retain their basically adversary character, however, and remain in part conflict situations.

The fact that the vast majority of collective agreements are negotiated without work stoppages reflects the realities of the marketplace, not the absence of elements of conflict. Collective bargaining relationships are based on power. Peace obtains when labor and management recognize their mutual interest in the survival of the firm, and in a particular negotiation, when at least one party is convinced that the cost of a settlement is less than the cost of not reaching an agreement. This "cost" often involves extraeconomic considerations that cannot be quantified. The important point is that such differences may be resolved peacefully through the medium of collective bargaining. It is a conservative (nonradical) way of resolving disputes between conflicting, yet at the same time cooperating, forces.

Union and management officials have become increasingly concerned about the pressures and heated controversy that often accompany contract negotiations. Three devices have helped moderate these pressures: (1) long-term contracts that provide periodic increases in wages and other benefits have reduced the frequency of contract negotiations; (2) in a few companies and industries in which complex problems have been hard to resolve during a brief period of negotiation, standing committees have been set up to study and try to resolve such problems on a continuing basis; (3) in major or key negotiations, preventive ("early bird") mediation has helped to establish a factual foundation for bargaining and resolve contentious issues in an atmosphere free from the brinkmanship that develops as contract deadlines approach. More recently, it has been suggested that major bargaining issues that cannot be resolved through negotiations be submitted to third-party arbitration, particularly in those industries, including government, in which a work stoppage would seriously inconvenience the public or have an adverse impact on the national economy. The experimental negotiating agreement in the basic steel industry is a major step forward in the voluntary arbitration of interest disputes in the private sector, and an increasing number of states provide for the arbitration of interest disputes for designated categories of public employees.

Union Democracy vs. Responsibility

Membership participation in establishing the web of rule affecting an employment relationship is usually indirect at best. This is one facet of the broader issue of responsibility versus democracy in the conduct of union affairs. Effective union leadership is often autocratic, and greater internal democracy might encourage union actions or demands that management or the public would consider irresponsible. Although an "appropriate" balance between democracy and responsibility depends on parameters relevant to particular bargaining relationships, two general observations are in order: (1) it is unrealistic to expect that responsibility can be assured by operating a union in the manner of a New England town meeting; and (2) legislation designed to make unions more democratic may eliminate specific abuses but it cannot by itself create a functional internal democracy.

A related issue is the possible conflict or lack of coincidence between individual workers' preferences and the collective demands presented by the workers' representatives. In the 1970s, there was an increase in the number of contracts rejected by militant union members. In some cases, this represented an attempt to check the increasing centralization of control in national unions; in others, it reflected the dissatisfaction of younger members with the failure of their representatives to give more weight to the quality of the work environment in setting bargaining priorities. The greater degree of protection afforded individual union members by the Landrum-Griffin Act has encouraged the development of such internal opposition.

A company that has a stable and mature relationship with a union is usually alert to the political imperatives affecting the union's bargaining posture. It will generally agree to some form of union security, and contract negotiations may be conducted in a way calculated to enhance the prestige of union officials. A firm that refuses to provide some degree of institutional security for a union and treats union leaders in a way that makes it hard for them to maintain their political base may have to deal with an increasing amount of "frivolous" bargaining demands and "irresponsible" union behavior.

Political Involvement

In addition to the economic and extraeconomic gains it has achieved at the bargaining table, the American union movement has helped workers obtain significant benefits through state and federal legislation. Many laws supported by unions have benefited nonunion as well as union workers, and some have had a broad welfare orientation. Many union leaders recognize that today continued improvements in workers' living standards are not exclusively within the control of the employer but are also dependent upon the realization of certain basic national economic objectives.

Concern about the definition and pursuit of these objectives will encourage greater political involvement on the part of organized labor. However, the formation of an American labor party is unlikely; the American union movement continues to accept the institutional framework of our mixed enterprise system, and unions will continue to function within the context of the present two-party system. There is little to suggest that the business union character of organized labor will change in the near future, although a younger and more diverse membership with new lifestyles may ultimately force unions to make a greater commitment to programs associated with a more broadly oriented "social unionism."

Management has become increasingly active politically. The failure of Congress to pass legislation authorizing common situs picketing in the building and construction industry and the successful Senate filibuster against amending the National Labor Relations Act, a major legislative priority of the AFL-CIO in 1978, were largely the result of well-coordinated lobbying by employer and industry associations.

The Law of Collective Bargaining

The character of federal legislation regulating unions and union-management relations has changed significantly since 1935. Unions are now considered quasi-public institutions, properly subject, along with union-management relations, to public control. The Wagner Act of 1935 was designed to promote union organization by guaranteeing workers certain rights and proscribing certain employer practices. Once unions became firmly established, the desirability of more "balanced" legislation became obvious. However, no comprehensive and objective study of our law of collective bargaining was undertaken before the passage of the Labor Management Relations Act of 1947 (the Taft-Hartley Act), an omnibus bill that led to greater government involvement in union-management relations.

During the following decade, the public and the Congress became concerned over the lack of democratic procedures within unions and with certain widely publicized instances of corruption and malfeasance on the part of elected and appointed union officials. The Landrum-Griffin Act of 1959 provided a bill of rights for individual union members, set standards for the conduct of union operations, and also included technical amendments to correct purported definitional and operational defects in the Taft-Hartley Act. More recently, civil rights, occupational safety and health, and pension reform legislation have begun to involve the government in certain substantive aspects of collective bargaining.

There are a number of basic inconsistencies between the federal laws regulating union-management relations. A congressional review of this legislation, including provisions for the resolution of emergency disputes, is overdue. However, greater consistency should not be achieved through greater government involvement. The tendency to try to solve intractable problems relating to collective bargaining through legislation is unfortunate and should be resisted. As Professor Richard Lester has pointed out, "government regulation in the labor field has few logical stopping points; control over one aspect of union affairs or union-management relations is prone to expand to others."[2]

THE ECONOMIC IMPACT OF COLLECTIVE BARGAINING

Unionism does not represent an institutional interference with what would otherwise be a perfectly competitive market, and it is unrealistic to measure the impact of unionism and collective bargaining in terms of such an abstract model. Most studies of the economic impact of unions have relied on comparisons of imperfectly competitive union and nonunion employment relationships. These studies have yielded results that are approximate at best; isolating the impact of unions has proved particularly troublesome due to the spillover of union gains into nonunion employment relationships. There is another serious problem involved in using an imperfect nonunion model for comparative purposes: ideally, the impact of unions should be measured relative to the conditions that would obtain in the absence of unions, but an imperfectly competitive model without unions is not a "functional alternative" to our present mixed enterprise system.[*]

Employers are not the ultimate economic constraint on unions. Employers are the significant link between product markets and unions, and their resistance to union demands is usually based on their estimate of the current and future strength of relevant labor and product market parameters, particularly the demand for their output. Employers also act as transmission belts for local extra-economic pressures, including community and class beliefs and prejudices.

The results of negotiations in certain key firms and industries are often used as bench marks by other firms, industries, and unions affected by the same or similar economic or institutional considerations. The spillover of these pattern-setting results into both union and nonunion firms is an important aspect of contemporary collective bargaining. However, several recent studies have suggested that today, the spillover into nonunion employment relationships may be less significant than economists have assumed.

The most general conclusions supported by our analysis are (1) that union

[*] See *supra*, p. 560.

leaders are not calculating monopolists committed to maximizing one or more clearly defined objectives and (2) that the overall economic impact of unions is probably less than is commonly assumed. We have also noted that unions, at times in collusion with employers, may reenforce imperfections in product markets in order to obtain higher wages for their members. In this section, we will review a number of significant conclusions from our economic analysis of collective bargaining.

The Maximization Objective

Economists usually assume that union leaders are interested in maximizing some specific economic objective or combination of objectives, most commonly "wages" or the "employment opportunities" of their membership. This assumption, while appropriate in a simple theoretical model of the labor market, fails to illuminate the bargaining calculus of most unions. There is no simple union "wage" or "employment" objective. The union members, particular subsets of members, or prospective members to be considered in formulating bargaining demands must be identified, and any conflicting goals of these groups must be reconciled before a bargaining position is developed.

Most unions are interested, at a minimum, in maintaining the existing job opportunities of presently employed (and perhaps recently furloughed) members without a reduction in money wages, and beyond this, in increasing the money wages of employed members. Only when these goals have been achieved, do unions usually evince interest in expanding the total number of job opportunities available. A union will generally sacrifice other elements of a package settlement rather than accept a reduction in wages or an increase smaller than that secured by its "competitors." In short, the most basic union objectives reflect (1) a political need to avoid any deterioration in present employment conditions and (2) the political necessity of continually improving employment conditions.

Coercive comparisons involving unions that may be more favorably situated in terms of market constraints may put severe pressure on union leaders. Other significant variables include the extent and intensity of existing or potential nonunion competition in a product market, the degree of employer resistance to specific union demands that is anticipated, and the constraints resulting from existing or potential governmental intervention in the bargaining process. The relative importance of these variables depends on the parameters peculiar to a bargaining relationship and the sophistication of the union leadership.

The potential impact of a proposed wage increase on employment usually becomes a paramount consideration only in bargaining situations in which an increase in, or a failure to decrease, labor costs will result in an immediate reduction in employment or, in extreme cases, in a shutdown of the firm. Under such adverse conditions, union leaders may permit wage differentials to develop or persist between firms in the same labor or product market. Such concessions are particularly likely to be granted to smaller firms in an industry or to firms with a peripheral relationship to the bulk of the firms organized by a union. Even in these cases, a union, in cooperation with management, will usually try to reduce unit labor costs by increasing worker productivity before accepting a reduction in wages.

Kennedy's wage-price guideposts, Nixon's wage-price "phases," and the more recent standards of the Carter administration all subjected union and management negotiators to additional constraints. Various kinds and degrees of pressure have been used to secure the "cooperation" of the parties to collective bargaining in avoiding inflationary settlements, particularly in highly visible, pattern-setting negotiations.

Finally, the importance of extraeconomic objectives must be emphasized. Changes in disciplinary procedures, improvements in grievance systems, more time for personal breaks, improvements in the quality of the work environment, more flexible working hours, or preretirement counselling for older members may be, or become, bargaining priorities. A theoretician may correctly "trade-off" wages against the "cost" of other union objectives but may fail to consider the important extraeconomic considerations that affect bargaining demands.

Money Wages

There is disagreement as to the extent to which unions have succeeded in raising the money wages of their members relative to the wages of nonunion workers. However, careful studies suggest that under favorable conditions, for example, if a craft union has organized competing firms in a local labor market, unions may be able to obtain a relative wage advantage of from 15 to 20 percent. This result, which is highly variable, may be attained at the expense of other organized, as well as unorganized, workers.

Within firms, in local labor markets, and to a lesser degree within given industries, unions have generally helped to standardize wage rates and rationalize the wage structure. The typical union wants to "take wages out of competition," and an internally consistent wage structure is easier to explain to the membership and more capable of commanding broad support.

Unions have had a significant impact on the *form* of wage gains. Their emphasis on total worker security has led to a variety of private benefit programs. The cost of such programs is considered a labor cost, and an expansion of benefits is viewed as an alternative to an increase in money wage rates.

Unions have contributed to the increasing downward rigidity in wages that has characterized the economy since World War II. They have also had a significant influence on the "timing" of wage increases. Long-term contracts are more common, and they include scheduled increases in wages as well as periodic adjustments related to changes in the cost of living.

The employment impact of the higher *money* wages that have presumably resulted from collective bargaining is uncertain and may reflect factors other than the cost of labor for individual firms. For example, by increasing aggregate demand, higher money wages may raise the marginal efficiency of investment so that total job opportunities ultimately increase.

The *inflationary impact* of unions is much debated. It appears that postwar inflation cannot be attributed primarily to union pressure for increased money wages. During the 1950s and the Vietnam War, inflation was basically the result of "demand-pull" rather than "cost-push" forces. However, during certain periods, unions appear to have had an independent inflationary impact; the highly visible rise of construction wages during the late 1960s had a considerable spillover impact at a time when increases in productivity were moderate. In addition, the downward rigidity of wages, automatic wage increases in long-term contracts, and upward wage adjustments based on increases in the cost of living have contributed to the recent sustained inflation.

Real Wages

The impact of unions on the real wage level seems to have been minor. Increases in real wages have been dependent on increases in productivity, and to a lesser extent, on shifts in the distribution of income within the economy as a whole. Some unions have undoubtedly succeeded in appropriating some portion of employers' "monopoly" profits for their members; others, by reenforcing imperfections in product markets, may have helped firms to capture larger pure profits in which the union membership subsequently shared. Since such wage gains are achieved at the expense of other union as well as nonunion workers, one cannot conclude that the union sector as a whole has benefited from such practices.

Unions have probably been responsible for some acceleration in the rate of substitution of capital for labor. By increasing the productivity of *employed* workers, this "investment impact" has helped raise their real wages. If monetary and fiscal policies maintain a high level of employment, the total real wage bill may be higher than it would have been in the absence of such wage-induced investment. Nonunion workers presumably share in such increases in the real national product.

The Supply of Labor

Some unions have succeeded in raising money wages, and probably real wages, by restricting the supply of labor. Union security provisions and restrictions on entry into an occupation are often said to have this effect, but such a result is not common. A number of other developments that have been encouraged by organized labor have had a more significant impact on the supply of labor. These include the increase in the number of years young people must attend school, compulsory retirement, restrictions on immigration, licensing laws in certain skilled trades, and the reduction in the length of the workday, the workweek and the work year. Nonunion workers as well as union members have benefited from such developments.

Craft unions may have restrictive membership qualifications, but in most cases, a qualified person can secure admittance to a union. A policy of *inclusion* is considered a better way to remove the potential threat to union standards posed by the availability of qualified nonunion workers than a policy of exclusion. In local labor markets, a de facto closed shop combined with restrictive membership qualifications may limit the supply of labor, but such cases are increasingly rare. Industrial unions are usually satisfied with a union shop and are willing to admit all applicants to membership.

Unions have been an important force in reducing working hours both through collective bargaining and through their support of federal and state maximum hours legislation. Recent attempts to reduce working hours even further to combat unemployment have not been supported by most economists. Increased leisure may be desirable on other grounds, but it seems unwise to try to lower unemployment by spreading available job opportunities more thinly.

The Demand for Labor

By preventing wage cuts, unions may help to sustain aggregate demand. In addition, individual unions may try to support or increase the demand for products in particular markets in various ways. Excluding nonunion firms from product markets may raise the demand for the products of a particular firm or group of firms; and in some local market industries, skilled craft unions, in combination— or apparent collusion—with their employers, have succeeded in excluding prospective competitors.

Some monopolistic practices that are illegal if they are undertaken in combination with employers are not illegal when a union acts alone. Antitrust legislation is generally an ill-suited remedy for problems in the field of industrial relations, but it would be an appropriate way of prohibiting actions by unions that would be illegal if they were performed in concert with an employer.

Work Rules

Union work rules are often criticized for having had an adverse impact upon productivity and costs, with a consequent reduction in output and employment. Such criticism is probably exaggerated. Most unions, for example, do not oppose but accept technological innovations. However, the wide publicity given a limited number of "classic" restrictive practices has given the union movement as a whole an undeserved reputation for bitterly opposing all forms of industrial progress.

With rare exceptions, management initiates changes in production methods and techniques. Such changes may threaten the employees' vested interest in existing job opportunities or in jobs requiring a particular skill. To protect their interests, unions may try to regulate or obstruct technological changes through a variety of work rules. Work rules are also used to restrict management's control of other aspects of the employment relationship. Such rules, which may be formal or informal, are also found in nonunion establishments. They are hard to categorize because many of them are unique to particular collective agreements or establishments.

Many firms recognize the constructive impact of work rules that protect a skilled worker's equity in a given job or an unskilled or semiskilled worker's equity in an employment opportunity. These firms are usually willing to discuss the timing of specific innovations and the best way of introducing them. A variety of special programs and procedures have been developed by firms and unions to minimize the human problems related to technological change and allow employees to share in the resulting increases in productivity.

Work rules designed to protect workers during a transitional period when new methods or systems are being introduced should not, of course, be continued indefinitely. Many work rules on the railroads and in the building trades that were originally devised to "save work" for currently employed workers became part of a superstructure of "make-work" rules that protected the jobs of succeeding generations of workers. The need to protect the job rights of workers affected by innovation does not give unions a license to insist on the use of outmoded production processes or the hiring of unneeded workers for an indefinite period.

Often, the cost and employment impact of work rules are obscured by the "veil of time." A given rule may *retard the rate of increase* in employment rather than cause an *absolute reduction* in the level of employment, and it may moderate rather than prevent a potential reduction in costs. In such cases, the "cost" of the rule is indeterminate.

On balance, union-initiated work rules probably have a negative rather than a neutral or positive impact on the productivity of individual workers. However, many of these rules are desirable in terms of a cost-benefit calculus which recognizes that they shift some of the social costs of innovation to the private sector.

Unions are more conscious of the possible adverse effect of work rules on employment during periods of reduced economic activity, and at such times, they may agree to modify or ignore violations of contract standards. Concessions may also be made to individual firms that are only marginally profitable or firms that face nonunion competition, as long as these concessions do not put other union members out of work. During the 1980s, the "hard line" bargaining stance of firms under pressure from nonunion and foreign competition will compel some unions to moderate their opposition to employer efforts to increase worker productivity and/or support efforts to protect firms from foreign competition.

Union contracts tend to make seniority rather than merit a basis for promotions, layoffs, and reemployment. The assumption is made that if workers are kept on after a trial period their performance is satisfactory and that length of service is a more objective criterion than merit. Although it is not clear whether the greater job security of employees with long service records increases or decreases average productivity, seniority does tend to have extraeconomic benefits.

During the 1970s, requirements that layoffs be inversely related to seniority frustrated a number of efforts to provide stable employment opportunities for minority groups under affirmative action programs. Changes in discriminatory seniority systems to enable minority workers to assume their "rightful place" on seniority ladders will undoubtedly cause sensitive and serious problems in many bargaining relationships.

Rules providing job security have probably reduced the mobility of labor. Unless a firm has permanently ceased operations, long-time employees who have been furloughed anticipate reemployment on a favored basis and are reluctant to seek other permanent employment.

SUMMARY

Although the overall economic impact of work rules cannot be quantified, they probably do diminish the national product, particularly in the short run. Contract provisions that help to regularize employment relationships and moderate the initial impact of technological changes are an appropriate way of recognizing a worker's equity in employment. They also force the private sector to assume some of the social costs of innovation. However, a firm's management should be alert to the potentially adverse long-run impact of restrictive practices designed to solve transitional problems; restrictive work rules are often negotiated by managers who do not consider their long-run implications.

EXTRAECONOMIC DIMENSIONS OF UNIONISM

It is hard to isolate and impossible to quantify the extraeconomic dimensions of unionism. For example, achieving an economic objective such as job security provides workers—and by extension their families—with a sense of personal well-being and contributes to their ability to enjoy a fuller and emotionally more secure and stable life. Such extraeconomic benefits are probably more significant than the economic consequences of union organization and collective bargaining. The protection of workers from arbitrary discharge is perhaps the most important achievement of organized labor; assuring them of dignified treatment at their place of employment is probably next in importance. More recently, unions have obtained a variety of supplemental benefits for hourly rated workers, benefits that in most firms had previously been available only to salaried workers. The elimination of such distinctions between salaried and hourly rated workers has had the incidental result of contributing to social and political stability.

Participating in the institutional life of a union can help members fulfill personal needs. Service as a union official, for example, provides a form of upward social mobility. The failure of unions to encourage workers to be more active in union affairs has deprived many members of a potentially rewarding experience.

Unions have also had a constructive influence on human relations through their impact on management policies and their support of social legislation. The unions' emphasis on an employee's need for dignified treatment and status has convinced nonunion as well as union employers of the value of personnel or industrial relations programs that attempt to meet the various job-connected needs of their labor force. In the case of nonunion firms, such programs may be developed to counter union organizational efforts.*

Organized labor's continued political commitment has provided workers with effective representation in the political sphere. Unions have supported a broad spectrum of federal and state laws that have, directly or indirectly, enabled American workers to enjoy a fuller life. Free public education, the prohibition of child labor, hours and wages legislation, a variety of social security programs, and, more recently, equal employment opportunity laws and other civil rights legislation, and occupational safety and health legislation have been supported by organized labor. Unions have also supported fiscal and monetary policies that encourage sustained economic growth and a high level of employment. This indirect participation in the political process has contributed to political and social stability.

SUMMARY

Unions and collective bargaining have probably had some negative impact on productivity and the allocation of resources and have contributed to the inflationary bias in the economy. However, in a society that aspires to more than material achievement, unionism and collective bargaining clearly deserve support on the basis of the extraeconomic benefits they have directly or indirectly helped to provide.

CONTINUING PROBLEMS IN THE AMERICAN UNION MOVEMENT

Some of the most significant continuing and prospective problems relating to the union movement and collective bargaining involve the general condition of the movement, its perhaps overly narrow business union orientation, the middle-class consciousness of many union members, the persistence of corruption within a small number of unions, and the absence of dynamic leadership at the national level. It is unclear whether such a movement will be able to appeal to unorganized sectors of the labor force or whether the distance between union members and (1) the growing number of white-collar and white-coverall workers and (2) the "underclass" of workers in secondary labor markets will widen. Declining productivity and a slowdown in the rate of economic growth may make it harder to increase real wages by the conventional method of increasing the national

---

* Sophisticated employee relations programs should not be confused with paternalism, which may meet with a negative response from employees.

product. This could increase organized labor's interest in the redistribution of income and create a movement with greater appeal to unorganized workers, particularly those with lower incomes. However, there is no indication as we enter the 1980s that organized labor is prepared to embrace any radical political alternative. As one study recently emphasized, "[t]here has never been a time since the foundation of the American labor movement when the influence of the Left was at a lower ebb."[3]

Other complex problems confront organized labor as we enter the eighties: how to reverse the current relative decline in union membership; how to prevent the loss of work to nonunion or foreign firms, if indeed it can be prevented; a related issue, how to counteract the increasingly hard line adopted by firms under pressure to improve employee productivity; how to develop more creative forms of collective bargaining; how to improve procedures for negotiating and administering contracts; and how much stress to put on the quality of the work environment and the quality of workers' lives in general.

There are also many unanswered questions about the American union movement: whether union leaders will demonstrate sufficient vigor in eliminating discriminatory membership and employment practices; whether unions will negotiate more "responsibly" in the public interest, and consider, for example, such things as the inflationary impact of wage settlements and the inconveniences caused by so-called emergency strikes; and whether a movement that is committed to business unionism and accepts the existing institutional framework can adapt to an economic environment in which there may be little growth in real per capita income.

The popular demand that unions negotiate more responsibly underscores a dilemma confronting unions, management, and public authorities: to what extent should the parties to collective bargaining consider the public interest in contract negotiation and administration?

There are also a variety of problems relating to the law of collective bargaining. Obvious technical defects in this legislation, including inconsistencies between statutes, need to be corrected and the desirability of further regulating welfare funds and of extending antitrust laws to cover certain union practices need to be investigated. Collective bargaining has provided a stabilizing influence in a democratic society, and any further regulation of union-management relations should be undertaken cautiously. Hastily devised legislation directed at what may be local or limited problems, perhaps of a transient nature, could weaken or destroy essential elements of our collective bargaining system.

A CONCLUDING NOTE

Some scholars of a liberal persuasion are disenchanted by what they perceive as a loss of idealism on the part of union leaders and by the tendency of both union members and their leaders to adopt middle-class standards. Union leaders are considered part of the establishment, unable or unwilling to respond creatively and with a sense of moral purpose to the problems of wage and salary workers, particularly those who are members of minority groups. Many labor economists are now concentrating on the problems of developing economies; others have become intellectual participants in the war on poverty. The recent interest in workers' feelings of alienation—the "Blue- (and White-) Collar Blues"—has been stimulated primarily by industrial psychologists and industrial sociologists rather than labor economists. During the 1960s and 1970s, student activists lost interest in unions as a cause and became interested in the civil rights movement, in antiwar protests, in poverty, in urban problems, in saving the environment.

The decrease in professional and student concern over the role of unions in the economy and the problems relating to union-management relations is both ill timed and unfortunate. Despite the relative decline in its membership base, organized labor remains an influential economic and political force, and its responses to the problems and challenges of the next decades will have a critical impact on our economy and polity. Union-management relations are important not only to the workers covered by union contracts but to other workers whose wages, fringe benefits, and conditions of work reflect the gains achieved by unions at the bargaining table. The position of the leadership of the AFL-CIO and various national unions concerning the implementation of civil rights and equal opportunity legislation will be a critical element in determining whether some of the potentially most explosive domestic issues of the 1980s will be defused. These facts, and other matters discussed in Parts Three, Four, and Five, suggest that union-management relations will continue to be an exciting and rewarding area of study and specialization, an area that should not be neglected by those interested in improving the quality of life in our society.

The failure of employers to meet the material and extraeconomic needs of wage earners as the nation industrialized created conditions favorable to unions; a similar failure to meet the needs of today's unorganized workers could lead to a renascence of trade unionism. Such a development is far from inevitable; union leaders must first acquire the vision and technical competence to infuse the union movement with a new sense of purpose.

American unions have given their members the opportunity to participate in decisions affecting employment relationships. They have also given many workers a greater sense of personal identity and status. To date however, there is little evidence that the union movement is prepared to make a significant commitment to developing the kind of society that is qualitatively and spiritually more reward-ing than our present materialistic civilization. The turning outward from business unionism to a broader social unionism by such union leaders as Douglas Fraser and the late Walter Reuther of the Auto Workers, William Winpisinger of the Machinists and the late Joseph Beirne of the Communications Workers, does suggest that at the national level, it may be possible to begin to develop a union movement responsive not only to the more immediate job-connected needs of workers but to broad societal needs. However, given the middle-class consciousness of many union members, it may be difficult to generate a broadly based commitment to even a modest version of social unionism.

This problem is not unique to the union movement. Shortly before his death, Professor Sumner Slichter, one of the most perceptive and respected students of American labor, observed that

> The greatest need of the trade-union movement is part of a broader need of American society as a whole—the need for objectives and ideals capable of enabling men to lead significant and satisfying lives. . . . [M]en strive vigorously and successfully for more production without knowing, asking, or indeed caring what the more production is for. We lack significant social purposes. Trade unions also suffer from [a] lack of adequate goals. . . .
>
> Now success has put business unionism in the position where merely being practical prevents it from having adequate social objectives. Hence, unionism needs to transform itself—to escape the results of success by embracing new goals, by becoming a champion of new and better social and economic institutions than we now possess and by becoming an instrument for achieving these new and better institutions.[4]

If organized labor is to respond successfully to this challenge, it cannot be content with past successes but must redefine its objectives, taking into account the realities of the present and the possibilities of the future.

DISCUSSION QUESTIONS

1. Do you believe that unemployment or inflation constitutes the greatest threat to the well-being of American workers at the present time? Do you think that union leaders would agree?
2. Is it possible to characterize the existing American union movement as a basically conservative force?
3. In what ways is the union movement likely to change during the 1980s?
4. How since this book was written, has the leadership of the AFL-CIO responded to the demands that members of minority groups and females be given greater leadership responsibilities within the federation?
5. Are the faculty of your college or university likely to organize for purpose of collective bargaining? If already organized, what causal factors can be identified?
6. Try to recall your views on the nature and impact of unions and collective bargaining prior to taking the course in which this text was assigned: Has the analysis in course altered those views?

Notes

1. Cf. Michael Harrington and Paul Jacobs, eds., "Summary," in *Labor in a Free Society* (Berkeley, Calif.: University of California Press, 1960), p. 182.
2. Richard A. Lester, *As Unions Mature* (Princeton, N.J.: Princeton University Press, 1958), p. 153.

3. Walter Galenson and Robert S. Smith, "The United States," chap. 1 in John T. Dunlop and Walter Galenson, eds., *Labor in the Twentieth Century* (New York: Academic Press, 1978), p. 84.

4. Sumner H. Slichter, "The Position of Trade Unions in the American Economy," in Harrington and Jacobs, eds., *Labor in a Free Society,* pp. 43–44.

INDEX OF NAMES

INDEX OF SUBJECTS